Machine Learning in Nanoelectronics

Scrivener Publishing
100 Cummings Center, Suite 541J
Beverly, MA 01915-6106

Publishers at Scrivener
Martin Scrivener (martin@scrivenerpublishing.com)
Phillip Carmical (pcarmical@scrivenerpublishing.com)

Machine Learning in Nanoelectronics

Devices, Circuits and Systems

Edited by

Ashish Maurya
Mandeep Singh
and
Balwinder Raj

Scrivener Publishing

WILEY

This edition first published 2026 by John Wiley & Sons, Inc., 111 River Street, Hoboken, NJ 07030, USA and Scrivener Publishing LLC, 100 Cummings Center, Suite 541J, Beverly, MA 01915, USA

For more information about Scrivener publications please visit www.scrivenerpublishing.com.

Wiley Global Headquarters
111 River Street, Hoboken, NJ 07030, USA

For details of our global editorial offices, customer services, and more information about Wiley products visit us at www.wiley.com.

The manufacturer's authorized representative according to the EU General Product Safety Regulation is Wiley-VCH GmbH, Boschstr. 12, 69469 Weinheim, Germany, e-mail: Product_Safety@wiley.com.

Library of Congress Cataloging-in-Publication Data

ISBN 9781394336173

Cover image: Generated with AI using Adobe Firefly
Cover design by Russell Richardson

Set in size of 11pt and Minion Pro by Manila Typesetting Company, Makati, Philippines

Printed in the USA

10 9 8 7 6 5 4 3 2 1

Contents

Preface

Researchers in nanoscience and nanoelectronics are experimenting with various tools to tackle challenges in many fields. Nanoscience and nanoelectronics not only advance machine learning (ML), but they also lay the groundwork for neuromorphic computing hardware to broaden ML algorithm implementation. Studies have been conducted on the application of machine learning to accelerate the discovery of new materials, including the use of ML to guide experimental design through the use of active learning, and the nanoscience of memristive devices to realize hardware customized for ML.

This book is a collection of possibilities of using ML in nanoelectronics and more effectively in the semiconductor devices and based circuits. Large data sets that sample widely from the range of parameters of the target problem are necessary for many applications, for effective and confident usage of machine learning. Standardizing data format and meta-data norms to facilitate cross-study comparisons is a crucial step towards drastically expanding the amount of data accessible to researchers. Since it is unknown which of the many structural or compositional descriptors are most beneficial for a particular feature, meta-data is essential for nanomaterials research. Even if there are many practical obstacles to be solved, standardisation of this kind could result in a "nanomaterials genome" that could serve as a catalyst for a variety of research projects. Because simulation allows for complete control over the initial conditions and often yields faster results than experiments, it is a popular method for producing training data for machine learning algorithms. This book has 13 chapters, each of which is summarized below.

Chapter 1: The field of nanoelectronics, characterized by devices and systems operating at nanometer scales, faces significant challenges as it continues to evolve. Quantum effects, material variability, scaling constraints, and the growing complexity of device design and production procedures are some of these difficulties. More creative ways are required because traditional procedures frequently fail to adequately handle these problems. With its potent capabilities for pattern identification, predictive modeling, and process optimization, machine learning (ML) has become a game-changing technology in this regard. This chapter delves into the integration of ML in nanoelectronics, highlighting its applications in various domains such as nanoscale device simulation, process optimization, and defect detection. The use of ML-driven surrogate models for quantum simulations, reinforcement learning for real-time parameter tuning, and predictive maintenance techniques are thoroughly examined. Case studies, such as the application of ML in the design of Nanowire Tunnel Field-Effect Transistors (TFETs), illustrate how ML accelerates design space exploration, mitigates process variations, and enhances device performance. Additionally, this chapter explores the potential of ML to revolutionize the semiconductor industry by enabling high-throughput experimentation, advancing quantum and neuromorphic computing, and supporting green manufacturing practices. There is also discussion of potential future directions, such as the creation of hybrid models, transfer learning for new materials, and autonomous systems for experimental study. Researchers and engineers can get beyond current obstacles by incorporating machine learning (ML) into nanoelectronics, which will spur innovation and guarantee the continuous development of this crucial technological field.

Chapter 2: In this era when the world is facing problems related to computing in many fields, machine learning and quantum computing offer promising progress in many fields. The enormous amount of data being generated and the developments in technology may make it difficult for the probabilistic and optimization-based classical machine learning (ML) algorithms to handle real-world challenges. This chapter focuses on machine learning to explore the opportunities in quantum. Quantum machine learning (QML), which focuses on the intersection of machine learning and quantum computing, is rapidly promoting advancement of data processing. The chapter is divided into sections that cover the different aspects of the topic. The discussion starts with an understanding of quantum data. That section is focused on difficulties linked to gathering and analyzing the quantum data. The conversation is initially led by several machine-learning models and quality algorithms of QML, which provide computation with novel ideas. The foundation of QML is the quantum computing ideas of entanglement and superposition, which are perfectly suited to addressing ML issues in the future. Advances in algorithms and growing processing capacity have made machine learning techniques useful tools for finding patterns in data. It is the creative solution for dealing with quantum challenges. The chapter also focuses on real-life case studies like drug development and many more. These case studies focused on the machine learning effect in data analysis. The discussion about the latest framework is also included for future development. The last sections include the challenges and advantages of possibilities in the quantum realm. The conclusion section shows the expectation that if quantum and machine learning are used together, many areas will benefit.

Chapter 3: The logical designs of individual and remedial platforms, as well as the investigation of their relationship, are exceedingly delicate due to substantial intratumor and interpatient heterogeneity. By utilizing pattern analysis and bracket algorithms for improved individual and remedial delicacy, the integration of AI techniques can close this gap. AI's ability to optimize material packets in accordance with predicted relationships with the target medication, natural fluids, susceptible systems, vasculature, and cell membranes—all of which affect restorative efficacy—benefits nanomedicine design as well. Next, abiotic generalizations in AI are discussed, along with the benefits and promise of combining nanotechnology with AI to create the ultimate cancer treatment in the future. One promising area for transforming the early detection and surgical treatment of stomach tumors is nanotechnology. Drug inefficacy and high rates of recurrence from surgical and pharmaceutical therapy are the main factors affecting curative efficacy in GIC patients. Nanotechnology is an emerging and cutting-edge field of research due to its unique optical properties, excellent biocompatibility, surface effects, and small-size effects, making it ideal for cancer detection and treatment. Given the drawbacks of GIC MRI and endoscopy as well as the difficulty of gastric surgery, nanotechnology has shown promise in the early detection and timely treatment of stomach disorders. Nanoparticles target tumor cells directly, permitting their identification and elimination. Additionally, it can be designed to deliver particular payloads, such as medications or contrast chemicals, to increase the precision and efficacy of cancer therapy. This work used XGBoost and RNN-CNN as a classification approach, utilizing the boosting methodology of machine learning to capture nonlinear interactions between a large number of input variables and outputs.

Chapter 4: Modern medical diagnostics rely heavily on brain signal monitoring and analysis for the identification and treatment of neurological illnesses including epilepsy, Parkinson's disease, and sleep disturbances. Accurate capture of brain electrical impulses is crucial for technologies like electroencephalography (EEG) and brain-computer interfaces (BCIs).

High power consumption, noise sensitivity, and the need for scalable and durable electrode designs are some of the major obstacles that these systems must overcome. A technology that has recently gained popularity in communication systems, multiplexing, offers the potential to address these issues. Improved data handling, lower power consumption, and uncompromised signal integrity are all benefits of multiplexing, which combines several signals for concurrent processing and transmission. The use of dense electrode arrays is made possible without adding complexity to the system, and multiplexing significantly enhances energy efficiency when applied to the capture of brain signals. Multiplexing brain signals to accomplish low-power, robust electrode sensing in medical diagnostic systems is the topic of this research. Brain signal capture, multiplexing concepts, and their incorporation into new sensing technologies are all covered. Multiplexing has the ability to transform medical diagnostics by tackling these difficulties and making them more efficient, accurate, and accessible. A multiplexer is a device used in electronics that conducts multiplexing; it passes one analog or digital input signal, chosen from a variety of input signals, into a single line. This study presents the design of a 90nm CMOS 4:1 multiplexer with low power consumption using n-Pass Time Division Techniques. This research compares and simulates a few important multiplexer factors, including area, transistor count, and power dissipation. The measured area is 4.35μm^2 and no DRC violation. We shall specify Vdd as the constant power supply in static CMOS logic. Because energy recovery does not occur as it does in the case of static CMOS logic, the whole amount of energy is wasted across the resistor, resulting in very little energy being held by the capacitor.

Chapter 5: The rapid advancement in artificial intelligence (AI), particularly in convolutional neural networks (CNNs) for machine vision tasks, has been significantly propelled by the increasing availability of large-scale data generated by edge devices that monitor our daily activities. However, CNNs are inherently memory- and compute-intensive, posing significant challenges to their deployment on conventional hardware architectures. This mismatch results in inefficiencies in power consumption, latency, and overall performance, which hinder the scalability and real-time applicability of such systems. While traditional hardware solutions, including application-specific integrated circuits (ASICs), field-programmable gate arrays (FPGAs), and graphic processing units (GPUs), have demonstrated their potential in accelerating CNN-based computations, their adoption is often limited by high development costs, extended design and validation times, elevated power requirements, and constrained throughput.

To address these limitations, a variety of deep learning hardware architectures and optimization algorithms have been proposed over recent years. These innovations aim to address critical concerns, including energy efficiency, computational speed, and the adaptability of hardware to evolving AI models. Furthermore, the emergence of techniques such as model compression has significantly contributed to optimizing the deployment of CNNs on resource-constrained devices, enabling them to perform complex computations while minimizing resource utilization. This chapter provides a comprehensive review of the progress made in the design and implementation of CNN accelerators and associated computing hardware. It systematically examines the unique features, benefits, and trade-offs of key hardware platforms, including ASICs, FPGAs, CPUs, and GPUs, in the context of CNN applications. Additionally, the chapter explores recent advancements in architectural and algorithmic optimization techniques, such as model compression and sparsity exploitation, which aim to enhance the efficiency of CNNs. The challenges currently faced in developing scalable, power-efficient, and high-performance AI systems are discussed, along with future directions to address these issues. This holistic analysis serves as a valuable resource for researchers and practitioners striving to bridge the gap between state-of-the-art AI algorithms and their practical implementation.

Chapter 6: Flexible energy storage technologies, such as flexible batteries and supercapacitors, have advanced as a result of the growing demand for wearable, flexible, and sustainable electronics. Flexible displays, wearable technology, and next-generation portable electronics all depend on these devices because they can bend, stretch, and fold without losing their functionality. It has been seen how flexible devices have changed over time, how their structures have changed to store energy, and the essential components that give them flexibility and durability—such as carbon-based nanofibers and conductive polymers. Modern applications require mechanical resilience and energy storage capacity, which are optimized by a variety of structures such as fiber, island bridges, and interdigital designs. Issues like low energy density, expensive production, and environmental impact are discussed, highlighting the necessity for more innovation. The development of flexible energy storage devices ensures the improvement energy efficiency and facilitates the shift to a resilient, flexible, and sustainable energy ecosystem.

Chapter 7: Modern artificial intelligence (AI) systems are powered by extremely efficient, specialized hardware that was made possible by the convergence of AI and Very Large-Scale Integration (VLSI) architecture.

The necessity for specialized hardware that can satisfy the demanding requirements of AI algorithms has become more and more important as AI continues to expand in complexity and scale. VLSI design for AI applications, where digital systems are customized to maximize computing performance, energy efficiency, and scalability, has seen a rise in attention as a result. At its most basic level, AI is a technology that enables computers to perform tasks that humans would perform, learn from past experiences, and adapt to new inputs. AI is being used in many industries, including finance and medical. Artificial intelligence has existed for a while. It was initially theoretically and mathematically investigated, after which it was created and put into software. Since AI is implemented in software and makes use of the current CPU, GPU, and memory system, the AI structure itself does not require hardware architecture. But as the application of AI expanded, it became crucial to implement AI using a neural processing unit as a stand-in for an AI-dedicated process, in addition to CPU and GPU.

Chapter 8: Energy consumption has been a matter of concern for the implementation of Complementary Metal Oxide Semiconductor (CMOS) based circuits due to the high density of integrated devices. Research work has continued worldwide to design the energy-efficient circuits for biomedical and space applications that have limited conventional energy. The low-power requirement is becoming a challenge at device, circuit and system architecture level. The conventional CMOS circuit styles are limited by the constant power supply voltage; its significant portion is consumed as thermal energy in resistive circuit elements. Novel device concepts and novel circuit approaches have been investigated for low energy consumption. Adiabatic logic is a circuit level approach that has made it possible to realize the ultra low power computing applications without reducing the supply voltage and node capacitances. A new single phase adiabatic or energy recovery logic and its energy performance with technology scaling have been carried out. Fair comparative study among the proposed logic, existing single-phase adiabatic logic and static CMOS logic at different technology nodes has been done. For this purpose, the 4-stage inverter chains of the proposed Single Phase Adiabatic Logic, Source Coupled Adiabatic Logic, Clocked Adiabatic Logic and Static CMOS Logic circuits were simulated at 180 nm, 90 nm and 45 nm technology nodes, and results show that the energy recovery or adiabatic logic can be used for nanoscale ultra low power application. In the last few years, multi-phase and single-phase energy recovery logics have been suggested but single-phase energy recovery logic circuits are more attractive for their reasonable speed in ultra low power integrated circuit design. Motivation behind this research work is to explore the energy efficiency and functionality of new single-phase energy recovery logic with progressive scaling.

Chapter 9: This chapter presents a modified bridge-coupled fed fractal array antenna for multiband applications using high-frequency laminate materials. The proposed antennas have a resonance frequency range of 24-40 GHz with ground-defected structure (DGS) design with 36×36 mm^2 dimensions with roger substrate, respectively. The central bridge coupled feed feeding technique is integrated with a circular congruent ring pattern ring and a bridge-coupled feed line connected to each element antenna. This integration significantly enhances antenna performance, manifesting in superior radiation properties, increased gain, enhanced directivity, and resonating behavior concerning each element, and exhibits multi-beam patterns for mm-wave 5G: V2X telemetry and IOT applications requirements, respectively.

Chapter 10: The low-speed, low-complexity, small-signal, high-voltage topologies of analog Complementary Metal Oxide Semiconductor (CMOS) circuits have given way to high-speed, high-complexity, low-voltage "mixed-signal" systems with significant amounts of digital circuitry throughout the last forty years. While device scaling has increased transistor's raw speed, non-idealities in architecture and packaging, as well as undesired interaction between various integrated circuit components, are rapidly restricting these systems' speed and precision. Today's layout and packaging have a significant impact on analog circuit design. While designing analog and mixed-signal circuits, layout-dependent effects (LDEs) invariably result in performance reductions at low technology nodes. The three main LDE sources—the well proximity effect (WPE), length of diffusion (LOD), and oxide-to-oxide spacing effect (OSE)—substantially influence transistor threshold voltage and carrier mobility. Due to LDEs pre- and post-layout simulations are different. There are some layout matching techniques to reduce these effects. To minimize the impact of these effects, techniques like common centroid matching are employed. By symmetrically arranging transistors and other components in the layout, the effects of these non-idealities are balanced, leading to more accurate and reliable circuit performance. Thus, while layout and packaging have become increasingly important in modern analog and mixed-signal design, careful consideration of layout techniques such as common centroid matching is essential to achieving optimal performance.

Chapter 11: Digital signal processing is everywhere in the world of communication. COVID-19 hit the world in a storm, so our technology helps us communicate and reduces the distance between us and the world. We are trying to improvise the communication with signal processing. Digital signal processing is a ubiquitous module used in a communication system. In today's digital era, digital processing is a necessary part. The performance of digital signal processing ICs drives the world now. All signals present in the universe are in analog format. The complexity of processing the analog signal is challenging. So we change the analog signal into digital format as ones and zeros and do all the processing. The analysis and study of FIR (Finite Impulse Response) filtering play a crucial role in the development of efficient DSP (Digital Signal Processing) processors, as it directly impacts their performance and optimization. A well-designed and thoroughly documented manuscript on FIR filters, covering both theoretical and practical aspects, is readily available. This chapter provides an in-depth explanation of FIR filters, detailing the design methodologies and offering a comprehensive comparison of various hardware architectures. This chapter also examines and reports on various multiplier and adder circuits that enhance the performance of an MAC-based FIR filter. Such comparisons highlight the trade-offs between performance, resource utilization, and efficiency in different FIR filter implementations, making it an essential resource for understanding and improving DSP systems. ADSP-21062 (Analog Devices), TMS320C6000 (Texas Instruments), XC2000/XE166 (Infineon), etc., are some of the available DSP IC in the market. Xilinx and Altera (now part of Intel) give the FPGA DSP IC.

Chapter 12: The development of dedicated deep learning (DL) accelerators and neuromorphic processors has opened up new possibilities for implementing neural network algorithms in the healthcare and biomedical applications. These specialized hardware systems present unmatched opportunities to improve the effectiveness and usefulness of DL algorithms in medical contexts, including image enhancement, disease diagnosis, and treatment monitoring. Although DL has progressed rapidly in terms of network complexity, effectiveness, and training efficiency, the evolution of specialized hardware tailored for DL algorithms lags behind. Innovative advancements in algorithms and architectures are essential to fulfill the demanding standards of efficient and affordable healthcare devices. Implementing these algorithms at the edge level is imperative to safeguard data privacy, particularly in critical medical applications. By processing data locally on specialized devices, edge computing reduces the risk of sensitive medical information being exposed to external servers, ensuring compliance with privacy regulations and enhancing patient trust. Edge computing not only minimizes the risks of data breaches but also supports applications where low-latency responses are essential, such as in wearable health monitors or portable diagnostic tools. In this study, we evaluate the numerous technological advances in DL approaches used on medical images for classification, recognition, and enhancement, both at the algorithmic and hardware levels that have been reported to address a variety of healthcare problems. Finally, we present our analysis and discuss our views on the benefits, drawbacks, and opportunities that different algorithms and neuromorphic processors bring to the biomedical and healthcare domains. This analysis signifies the importance of a synergistic evolution of algorithms and hardware to revolutionize modern healthcare.

Chapter 13: The Internet of Things (IoT) has drastically changed the idea of smart homes by connecting various devices, gadgets and systems to improve convenience, efficiency, and security of the house. In smart homes, IoT consists of a network of devices like sensors, appliances, and controllers that communicate via the internet. This connectivity allows homeowners to remotely monitor, control, and automate several aspects of their living space, ultimately enhancing their quality of life and managing the energy use more effectively. The key uses of IoT in smart homes include smart lighting, thermostats, security systems, and appliances. Smart lighting and thermostats adjust to user preferences and environmental factors, helping to optimize energy consumption and lower the expenses. IoT-enabled security systems—like smart cameras, motion sensors, and smart locks—offer real-time monitoring and notifications for improving safety and providing peace of mind.

1

Introduction to Machine Learning in Nanoelectronics

Bandi Srinivasa Rao, Rangana Bhanu Meher Srinivas, Kenguva Sai Chandar Rao, Mandeep Singh*, Anil Kumar Yadav, Balwinder Raj and Tarun Chaudhary

Department of Electronics and Communication Engineering, Dr. B. R. Ambedkar National Institute of Technology Jalandhar, Punjab, India

Abstract

The field of nanoelectronics, characterized by devices and systems operating at nanometer scales, faces significant challenges as it continues to evolve. Quantum effects, material variability, scaling constraints, and the growing complexity of device design and production procedures are some of these difficulties. More creative ways are required because traditional procedures frequently fail to adequately handle these problems. With its potent capabilities for pattern identification, predictive modeling, and process optimization, machine learning (ML) has become a game-changing technology in this regard.

This chapter delves into the integration of ML in nanoelectronics, highlighting its applications in various domains such as nanoscale device simulation, process optimization, and defect detection. The use of ML-driven surrogate models for quantum simulations, reinforcement learning for real-time parameter tuning, and predictive maintenance techniques is thoroughly examined. Case studies, such as the application of ML in the design of Nanowire Tunnel Field-Effect Transistors (TFETs), illustrate how ML accelerates design space exploration, mitigates process variations, and enhances device performance.

Additionally, this chapter explores the potential of ML to revolutionize the semiconductor industry by enabling high-throughput experimentation, advancing quantum and neuromorphic computing, and supporting green manufacturing practices. There is also discussion of potential future directions, such as the creation of hybrid models, transfer learning for new materials, and autonomous systems for experimental study. Researchers and engineers can get beyond

**Corresponding author*: mandeep.moni.singh@gmail.com

Ashish Maurya, Mandeep Singh and Balwinder Raj (eds.) Machine Learning in Nanoelectronics: Devices, Circuits and Systems, (1–42) © 2026 Scrivener Publishing LLC

current obstacles by incorporating machine learning (ML) into nanoelectronics, which will spur innovation and guarantee the continuous development of this crucial technological field.

Keywords: Machine learning, nanoelectronics devices, TFETs, neuromorphic computing, physical scaling

1.1 Introduction

1.1.1 The Need for Advanced Modeling in Nanoelectronics

Because of the particular difficulties and complexities that occur at the nanoscale, advanced modeling is crucial in nanoelectronics. Conventional modeling methods are insufficient when electronic components get smaller [1–5]. In this field, advanced modeling is essential for the following main reasons.

The Effects of Quantum
Quantum mechanical effects become important at the nanoscale. This makes it necessary to employ quantum models in order to precisely forecast how electrons will behave. Tunneling and energy level quantization are examples of processes that are not captured by classical models, which require continuous charge distribution and behavior. To account for these effects, sophisticated models like tight-binding models or density functional theory (DFT) are employed [6–10].

Increased Complexity
The interactions between gadgets become more complex as they get smaller. For instance, it is necessary to take into account the connection between various physical phenomena (mechanical, thermal, and electrical). Accurate simulations of these interactions frequently call for multiphysics modeling techniques. This aids in comprehending how various factors impact thermal management, performance, and dependability [11–18].

Properties of the Material
Materials at the nanoscale frequently have characteristics that are very different from those of their bulk counterparts. Materials may, for example, possess special optical qualities, changed band gaps, or increased electrical conductivity. Researchers can forecast these characteristics and customize

materials for certain nano electronic applications, such as semiconductors, insulators, or superconductors, thanks to advanced modeling.

Scaling of Devices

Conventional scaling rules, such as Moore's Law, might not apply as device dimensions get closer to atomic scales. To investigate the limits of scaling, particularly the consequences of short-channel effects, which can result in higher leakage currents and less gate control over the channel, sophisticated modeling techniques are required. These models aid in the creation of innovative device architectures that maintain their functionality at smaller sizes [19–27].

Methods of Fabrication

Lithography, etching, and deposition are a few of the intricate procedures frequently used in the creation of nanoscale electronics. These fabrication processes can be simulated using advanced modeling to forecast results, optimize parameters, and reduce flaws. This capacity for prediction is essential to guaranteeing excellent production performance and output [28–36].

Predicting Performance and Reliability

Reliability problems including electromigration, bias temperature instability, and hot carrier effects worsen with device size. More robust designs are produced by using sophisticated modeling tools to comprehend these reliability issues and forecast device performance under varied circumstances.

New Concepts for Devices

To evaluate the viability and performance of new device concepts, such as quantum dots, nanowires, and topological insulators, sophisticated modeling is needed. These novel architectures may provide better performance characteristics than conventional devices, but assessing their behavior generally necessitates the use of complex modeling tools [37–44].

Device Integration

There are extra difficulties when integrating several nanoscale devices into bigger systems (like circuits or networks). In order to build effective and scalable nano electronic circuits, advanced modeling makes it easier to simulate complete systems while taking device interactions into account.

1.1.2 Scope of Machine Learning Applications in Semiconductors

In the semiconductor sector, machine learning (ML) is becoming more and more significant, improving several phases like design, manufacturing, and testing. Machine learning speeds up the creation of effective semiconductors by optimizing circuit layouts and device modeling in design. Through predictive maintenance, it enhances quality control and process optimization during manufacturing, resulting in increased yields and decreased downtime. ML also helps with automated testing and failure analysis, which makes it possible to find flaws more quickly. It is an essential tool for innovation and efficiency in semiconductor technology since it also improves supply chain management and makes the discovery of novel materials easier. The next generation of electronic systems is being driven by the expanding potential applications of machine learning as the discipline develops [45–53].

1.2 Evolution of Nanoelectronics: From Macroscale to Nanoscale

1.2.1 Moore's Law, Transistor Scaling Challenges

Moore's Law:

- Moore's Law refers to Moore's perception that the number of transistors on a microchip doubles every two years.
- We consider Moore's Law for Scaling of ICs for:
  1. Better performance (higher speed)
  2. Lower power consumption
  3. More transistors for the same manufacturing cost. (More features for the same price.)
- Moore's Law is really about reducing cost per function [54–62].
- Device Scaling will slow down, but cost per function can continue to decrease indefinitely.
- The following Figure 1.1 shows the plot of MOS transistors in a microprocessor versus the introduction of dates. Here, the curve shows the count of transistors doubles for every two years according to Moore's Law.

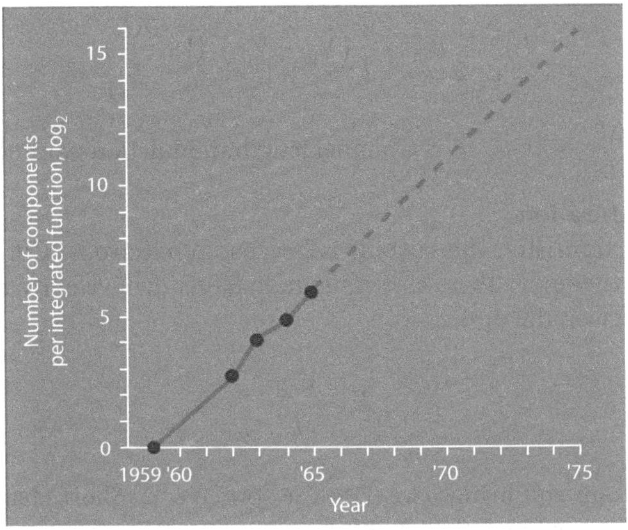

Figure 1.1 Transistor count vs. year in which microchip was introduced [25].

This phenomenon originates from advances in semiconductor technology, allowing for reducing the length of the device to $(L \rightarrow \frac{L}{\sqrt{2}})$ and area of the device to $(A \rightarrow \frac{A}{2})$ for each technology generation, allowing for making smaller transistors and making more densely packed transistors on integrated circuits.

Transistor Scaling Challenges:
In order to reduce power utilization, gaining higher speed/performance and reduction in size, we started scaling the transistor. As MOS transistor scale down in size, several physical limitations/issues need to be considered:
Issues: Short Channel Effects, Power Density, Switching Delay, Reliability
Short Channel Effects: 1. Channel Length Modulation, 2. Velocity Saturation, 3. Drain-Induced Barrier Lowering, 4. Subthreshold Leakage, and 5. Substrate and Gate Leakage [63–70].

Channel Length Modulation
Its effects are severe when the drain voltage (v_D) is very large. It affects the saturation current.

$I_D = \frac{1}{2} u_n C_{ox} \frac{\omega}{L} (V_{GS} - v_{TH})^2$ (Long channel drain saturation current equation) [26].

$$L \rightarrow (L - \Delta L)$$

$$I_D = \frac{1}{2}\mu_n c_{ox}\frac{w}{l}\left(V_{gs} - V_{th}\right)^2 (1 + \frac{\Delta L}{L})$$

Where $\frac{\Delta L}{L} \rightarrow \lambda v_{DS}$, λ is Channel length modulation parameter [23].

Velocity Saturation

In N-MOS transistor, the current is because of electrons. Current flows from drain to source. These electrons attain larger drift velocity, if we apply larger voltage on the drain end.

$$E = \frac{V_{DS}}{L}$$

As the drain end brings closer to the source end (Short channel) V_{DD} also started dropping with technology.

The effect of lowering the current is called velocity saturation [23].

$$I_D = \mu_n C_{ox}\frac{w}{l}V_{DSAT}\left((V_{GS} - V_{TH}) - \frac{V_{DSAT}}{2}\right) \rightarrow (V_{DSAT} < V_{GS} - V_T)$$
$$\rightarrow \textit{Velocity Saturation condition}$$

Drain-Induced Barrier Lowering

For a short channel MOS, there is a dependence of V_{DS} with threshold voltage. For smaller V_{DS} say $V_{DS} = 0.1V_{DD}$, the threshold voltage $V_{TH} = V_{TLIN}$. For larger V_{DS} say $V_{DS} = V_{DD}$, the threshold voltage $V_{TH} = V_{TSAT.}$ In short channel devices, these two threshold voltages are two different numbers and that is called Drain-Induced Barrier Lowering.

$$\text{The DIBL coefficient} = \frac{V_{TLIN} - V_{TSAT}}{V_{DD}, - 0.1V_{DD}} = \eta$$

Sub-Threshold Leakage

In short channel MOS devices, as drain brings closer to the source end, it is like a bipolar junction transistor. Therefore, we have some current flowing through between drain and source; when gate voltage is below V_T the current flows [71–78]. Basically, we wanted the current to be zero up to some point and then it starts going up. What we wanted was an abrupt switch-like behaviour. Because of this non-ideality, we are not able to achieve it [79–86].

Now we define a particular term that will quantize the idea that we have described; it is called subthreshold slope.

Substrate Leakage and Gate Leakage

Substrate leakage: Using the body, to adjust the threshold voltage is a valid technique and later we might try to connect this body to V_{DD} and unless the threshold voltage V_T will come down. it is not possible. The substrate leakage will kill you in this case. Gate Leakage: As the channel length decreases, if we go beyond 45nm, 22nm and so on, gate oxide becomes so small. Due to this small thickness of gate oxide, the gate current will no longer as zero. There is a mechanism called Quantum Mechanical Tunnelling which makes current to flow from gate to substrate. It is also one of the non-ideality which we need to focus on to prevent [87–94].

Reliability Issues

While transistor downscaling has improved digital circuit design, it presents difficulties for analog circuits with a large dynamic range. Time-dependent dielectric breakdown (TDDB) and hot-carrier injection (HCI) set a limit on the maximum supply voltage (V_{DDMAX}). Although longer devices can reduce HCI stress, foundry data on greater excess overdrive voltages (VddEOD) for longer devices is lacking. In analog circuits with more uniform waveforms, VddEOD can surpass V_{DDMAX} by several hundred millivolts, potentially improving dynamic signal range, even though it usually matches V_{DDMAX} for rectangular waveforms in digital circuits. To control high gate-source voltages, careful circuit design is essential, particularly while the circuit is in standby mode. Furthermore, channel hot carrier injection caused by high source-to-bulk voltages can drastically shorten HCI lifetime, which raises reliability issues as the number [95–97].

1.2.2 Physical Scaling Limits in Nanoscale Devices

The distinct behaviors of materials and events at incredibly small scales, usually in the region of nanometres, give rise to physical constraints in nanoscale devices. Quantum effects like superposition and tunneling become important at this size, changing the motion and interaction of electrons inside the device. Increased leakage currents and decreased energy efficiency are two consequences that may make it difficult to maintain performance. Figure 1.2 shows new device structures: (a) SOI MOSFET, (b) DG MOSFET and (c) Fin FET (d) schematic of carrier scattering due to channel thickness fluctuation in new device structures. Figure 1.3 presents schematic structure and equivalent circuit of a SET.

The physical scaling limits, focusing on quantum transport and atomistic effects in nanoscale devices. Key points include:

Device Scaling: In order to control short-channel effects, novel device topologies such as silicon-on-insulator (SOI), double-gate (DG), and FinFETs are being introduced as MOSFET channel diameters decrease. However, problems like surface roughness (SR) scattering, which impairs performance because of quantum phenomena, arise when scaling to nanoscale scales.
Quantum Effects: In thin channels, electron-phonon interactions and quantum confinement play a bigger role and impact carrier transport. III-V semiconductors, such as InGaAs, for instance, have high electron mobility but suffer from source-drain (SD) direct tunneling, which causes smaller devices to leak more current.
Ballistic Transport: It is anticipated that ballistic transport, in which carriers move with less scattering, may improve device performance. However, its efficacy in sub-10nm channels is limited by SR scattering, and to fully reap its benefits, gate oxide interface enhancements are required [98–103].
Nanowire FETs: To comprehend electron-phonon interactions in ultra-small devices such as nanowire FETs (NWFETs), atomistic simulations are essential. Although Ge and Si NWs exhibit comparable behavior below 2 nm,

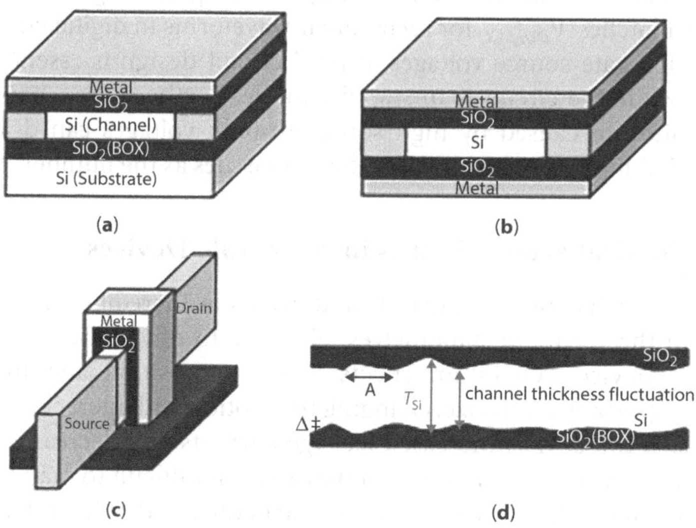

Figure 1.2 New device structures: (a) SOI MOSFET, (b) DG MOSFET and (c) Fin FET (d) schematic of carrier scattering due to channel thickness fluctuation in new device structures [18].

indicating possible universal mobility in these materials, the study emphasizes that electron mobility declines with decreasing cross-sectional diameters [104–109].

1.2.3 Various Nanoscale Device Technologies

When traditional CMOS technology reaches its physical constraints, new nanoscale devices could emerge as viable substitutes. The main points are as follows:

- Despite its great success in shrinking transistors, conventional CMOS technology is approaching its basic constraints.
- Researchers are exploring emerging nanoscale technologies to create new devices with higher density and speed.
- These new technologies include:
  - Carbon nanotubes (CNTs): Graphite sheets rolled into cylinders. Because of their metallic or semiconducting qualities, CNTs may find application in logic circuits, memory devices, and transistors. Controlling whether CNTs are metallic or semiconducting during production is one of the present difficulties, though.
  - Silicon nanowires: During synthesis, these structures are easier to manipulate than CNTs. Nanowires can be used in complicated circuits and logic gates, as well as diodes and transistors.
  - Single-electron transistors (SETs): These gadgets use quantum phenomena to regulate the passage of electrons one at a time. Although single-electron transistors (SETs) have extremely low power consumption, their speed and scalability are constrained.
  - Resonant tunneling diodes (RTDs): very quick devices having nonlinear properties that make them suitable for multivalued logic applications and high-speed circuits.
  - Quantum-dot cellular automata (QCA): a completely different kind of computing that represents binary information using electron positions rather than voltage levels.
  - Molecular electronic devices: Devices like switches and transistors are constructed from single molecules. The instability of molecules at higher temperatures persists despite benefits in terms of size and cost.

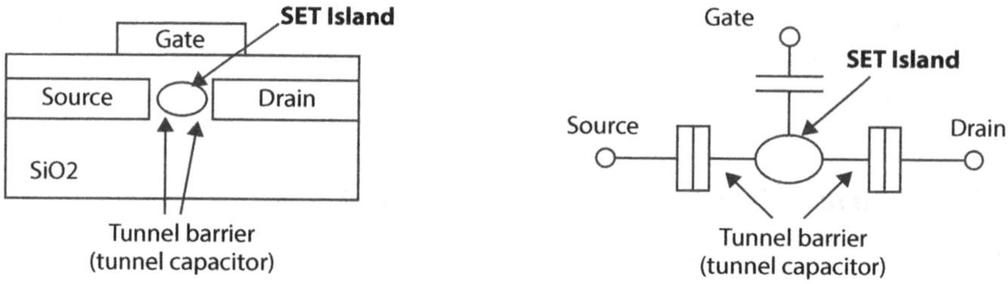

Figure 1.3 Schematic structure and equivalent circuit of a SET [17].

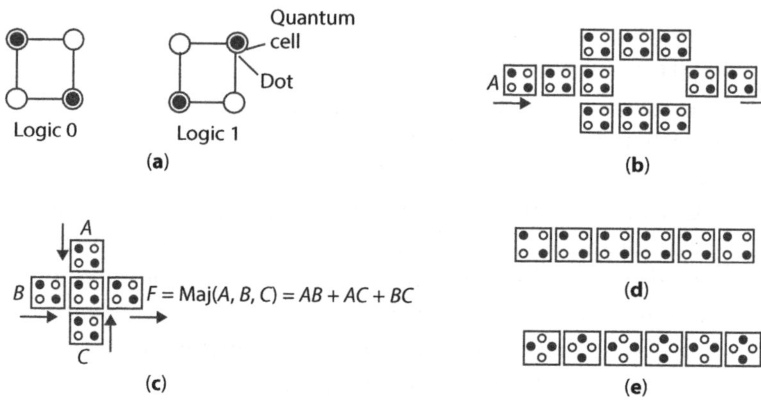

Figure 1.4 Quantum-dot cellular automata: QCA cell (a), inverter (b), majority voter (c), binary wire (d), and inverter chain [19].

- Nanoscale crossbars: A possible platform for creating large-scale nano electronic circuits is provided by crossbar structures made of nanowires or carbon nanotubes (CNTs), which are used to create programmable switches and memory cells [110–114].

- Advantages of these nanoscale devices include potentially higher density, speed, and lower power consumption.
- Challenges include:
  - Difficulty in controlling the properties of some materials during manufacturing (e.g., random metallic/semiconducting nature of CNTs)
  - Lack of established manufacturing processes for large-scale integration
  - Need for new design approaches due to the different physics at the nanoscale. Figure 1.4 gives quantum-dot

cellular automata: QCA cell (a), inverter (b), majority voter (c), binary wire (d), and inverter chain.

1.2.4 Machine Learning's Role in Overcoming Scaling Barriers

In order to overcome the scaling obstacles that different technologies encounter, especially in the design and production of semiconductors, machine learning (ML) is essential. Traditional design and production methods face many difficulties when devices get smaller to nanoscale dimensions, such as greater complexity and unpredictability. Large volumes of data produced throughout the design and production stages can be analyzed by ML algorithms, which can spot connections and patterns that humans would miss. Engineers can foresee problems, refine designs, and expedite fabrication processes with this data-driven approach, which eventually improves performance and reliability while cutting expenses and time.

Machine learning techniques are being employed more and more in the field of circuit design to automate layout and parameter optimization. Designers can quickly find configurations that satisfy demanding performance criteria and explore a wider design space by utilizing neural networks and reinforcement learning. These techniques can also be modified to accommodate new materials and structures as semiconductor technology advances. As a result, despite overcoming the inherent constraints of reducing device dimensions, ML not only speeds up the design process but also improves the ability to reach required performance metrics [115–117].

Additionally, machine learning helps with manufacturing equipment monitoring and predictive maintenance. Machine learning algorithms can predict possible faults or inefficiencies by studying operational data from machines. This allows for preemptive interventions that reduce downtime and increase yield rates. In high-stakes settings like semiconductor fabs, where even small flaws can result in significant financial losses, this predictive capacity is very important. The semiconductor sector can keep pushing the limits of scaling by utilizing machine learning, guaranteeing the economical creation of ever-more-advanced and effective products.

1.3 Machine Learning in Nanoscale Device Simulation

The fast advancement of nanoscale gadgets requires precise, proficient, and versatile reenactment procedures. Customary methodologies are many times computationally costly and restricted by the intricacy of quantum impacts. ML offers better approaches to speed up recreations, advance gadgets, and work on the exactness of existing models. This segment investigates conventional recreation procedures, the job of ML in substitute demonstrating, and how these techniques are coordinated to upgrade nanoelectronics research.

1.3.1 Traditional Simulation Techniques

The recreation of nanoscale gadgets is fundamental for the plan and advancement of electronic parts that capability at tiny aspects. Conventional reenactment strategies intend to demonstrate actual peculiarities, anticipate gadget execution, and investigate new materials at the nano-level. Be that as it may, as gadgets psychologist to nuclear scales, these reproductions experience difficulties connected with computational expense and the intricacy of quantum ways of behaving. The following is a definite outline of the center procedures utilized in nanoscale gadget recreation

The quick advancement of nanoscale gadgets requires exact, effective, and adaptable recreation methods. Conventional methodologies are in many cases computationally costly and restricted by the intricacy of quantum impacts. AI (ML) offers better approaches to speed up recreations, enhance gadgets, and work on the exactness of existing models. This segment investigates customary reenactment strategies, the job of ML in proxy demonstrating, and how these techniques are coordinated to upgrade nanoelectronics research.

1.3.1.1 Drift-Diffusion Model (DDM)

One of the oldest and most popular techniques for simulating semiconductor devices is the drift-diffusion model. It cxplains how charge carriers, including electrons and holes, move when subjected to concentration gradients and electric fields. In order to track the movement of carriers through drift (field-driven motion) and diffusion (random movement), this model solves continuity equations and Poisson's equation to account for the electric field.

Although this method is effective for conventional bulk semiconductors, it has trouble capturing quantum effects that take place in nanoscale devices, such as interference and tunnelling. Drift diffusion models' prediction ability reduces as component sizes, such as transistors, approach the nanometre range.

- Use Case: CMOS transistors and field-effect transistors (FETs).
- Limitations: Inadequate for quantum-dominated behaviours; assumptions of continuum charge distribution become less valid at nanoscale.

The Drift-Diffusion (DD) model is one of the earliest and most widely used methods for semiconductor device simulations. It models the movement of charge carriers (electrons and holes) in response to electric fields (drift) and concentration gradients (diffusion).

Key Features:

- Poisson's Equation: Determines the electrostatic potential in the device.

$$\nabla(\in \nabla\varnothing) = -q(p - n + N_D^+ - N_A^-)$$

- Carrier Current Equations: Express the carrier flux in terms of drift and diffusion:

$$J_n = qnu_nE + qD_n\nabla n$$
$$J_p = qpu_pE - qD_p\nabla p$$

Here, μ and D are mobility and diffusion coefficients, respectively [1].

Limitations: In nanoscale devices, the DD model struggles with accuracy due to the presence of quasi-ballistic transport, quantum confinement effects, and scattering phenomena.

1.3.1.2 Monte Carlo (MC) Simulations

Monte Carlo simulations use statistical methods to model the behaviour of individual carriers in semiconductor devices. Carriers are treated as particles, and their trajectories are tracked through successive scattering events with phonons, impurities, or other carriers. The stochastic nature of MC simulations makes them suitable for handling non-equilibrium conditions, such as those found in ultra-scaled devices.

Although this method offers precise information on velocity distribution, carrier mobility, and hot-electron effects, it is computationally costly, particularly when used on intricate three-dimensional systems.

Its application is therefore restricted to situations where time is sacrificed for great precision.

- Use Case: High-field transport studies in nanotransistors.
- Limitations: Time-intensive and requires significant computational resources for large systems.

MC vs. DD Model:

- MC Method: Accurately models carrier dynamics in quasi-ballistic and high-field regions, but is computationally intensive.
- DD Model: Efficient for large-scale simulations but requires parameter calibration to account for quasi-ballistic effects.
- Parameter Calibration for DD Models:
- MC simulations can generate detailed carrier velocity and density profiles, which are used to calibrate DD model parameters for increased accuracy. This calibration involves:
    - Adjusting the saturation velocity parameter to capture velocity overshoot effects in high drain bias conditions.
    - Optimizing the mobility model parameters to match injection velocity at the source-channel interface.

Hybrid Models: Combining DD with MC Simulations
To strike a balance between accuracy and computational efficiency, researchers often use hybrid models. These combine the strengths of DD and MC approaches:

- Initial DD Simulations: Used to simulate large-scale behavior.
- MC Calibration: Refines DD parameters, capturing velocity overshoot and ballistic transport effects that DD alone cannot model.

Example: In quasi-ballistic transport regions (common in sub-10 nm devices), the DD model is parameter-tuned using MC simulation data, providing accurate results with less computational overhead.

Multi-Sub band Ensemble Monte Carlo (MSB-EMC). The MSB-EMC method combines Monte Carlo simulations with quantum corrections, enabling more efficient modeling of carrier transport in 3D devices like FinFETs and nanowires. MSB-EMC solves the Boltzmann Transport Equation (BTE) to predict carrier dynamics under external fields.

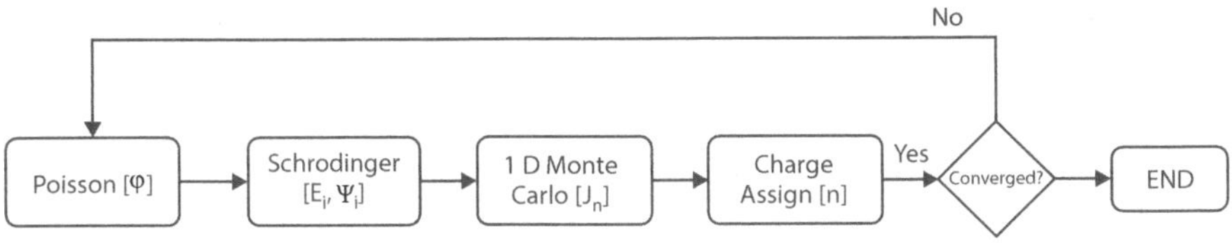

Figure 1.5 Simulation procedure describing the 3DMSB-EMC approach adopted in this work [11].

Figure 1.5 shows simulation procedure describing the 3DMSB-EMC approach adopted in this work.

- Quantum Corrections: The Schrödinger-Poisson equation is used to account for quantum confinement effects, while the Monte Carlo method models electron scattering.
- Application: MSB-EMC is effective in predicting device performance at the sub-20 nm scale, where classical drift-diffusion models fail. It offers a balance between computational efficiency and accuracy, making it suitable for design optimization of 3D FinFETs.

ML can be used to train surrogate models based on MSB-EMC outputs, speeding up parameter sweeps and improving design space exploration.

1.3.1.3 Non-Equilibrium Green's Function (NEGF) Method

One effective technique for mimicking quantum transport in devices is the NEGF method. It offers a thorough framework for simulating electron-phonon interactions, phase coherence, and quantum tunnelling. The technique is especially useful for simulating devices when traditional models are inadequate, such as quantum dots, nanowires, and ultra-thin transistors. By estimating the likelihood that electrons will pass through potential barriers, NEGF provides information about the current-voltage characteristics of nanoscale devices.

However, NEGF is only useful for very small or simple models because it requires a lot of computing power to solve many matrices for big device topologies.

- Use Case: Quantum transport modeling in nanowires and quantum dots.
- Limitations: High computational overhead makes it impractical for large-scale devices.

The NEGF formalism models quantum transport in nanoscale devices, such as FinFETs or nanowires, where phase coherence and tunneling effects dominate. NEGF is particularly effective for capturing non-equilibrium phenomena, including current flow under bias voltages.

- Application in Quantum Transport: NEGF evaluates how electrons move through confined channels by modeling both ballistic transport and scattering effects. In devices operating at the quantum limit, such as graphene nanoribbons, NEGF models charge flow through potential barriers.
- Challenges: While NEGF offers high accuracy, it is computationally demanding, especially for large systems. It is commonly used in conjunction with Poisson solvers to maintain self-consistency between electrical potential and carrier distributions.

ML techniques are now used to approximate NEGF results, allowing faster simulations by building surrogate models based on previously computed data.

1.3.1.4 Molecular Dynamics (MD)

Molecular dynamics simulations track the movement of individual atoms and molecules over time based on Newton's laws of motion. This method is used to explore the structural, mechanical, and thermal properties of materials at the nanoscale. MD simulations are effective for studying how materials behave under external stress or temperature changes, such as the thermal conductivity of graphene or nanocomposites.

However, MD lacks the ability to accurately capture quantum effects, which limits its use in electronic simulations. It is more suited for applications that involve the physical or thermal behaviour of nanoscale structures.

- Use Case: Analysing the thermal properties of nanomaterials.
- Limitations: Cannot incorporate quantum mechanical behaviour directly.

MD simulations track the motion of atoms and molecules in a system based on classical mechanics, offering insights into thermal properties, structural stability, and material interactions over time.

- Applications: MD is used to study thin-film growth, thermal conductivity, and vibration-induced effects in nanoscale devices. It helps evaluate how stress, temperature, and mechanical strain affect device performance.
- Challenges: Although MD is effective at modeling atomic-level interactions, it cannot directly account for quantum mechanical effects, limiting its use in highly quantum-confined systems. Hybrid MD-DFT approaches are sometimes employed to bridge this gap.

1.3.1.5 Quantum Mechanical Models: Density Functional Theory (DFT) and Tight-Binding (TB) Models

For precise nanoscale electronic property prediction, quantum mechanical simulations such as Density Functional Theory (DFT) and Tight-Binding (TB) models are crucial. While TB approximates similar calculations for bigger systems, DFT is utilised to determine the electronic structure and energy states of materials. The creation of new nanoelectronic devices is guided by these models, which are essential for material discovery and band structure research.

Although DFT yields accurate findings, its computing demands restrict its use to unit cells or tiny systems. TB models are helpful for extended systems since they allow for larger-scale simulations, despite their lower accuracy.

- Use Case: Predicting material properties and band structures in 2D materials like graphene.
- Limitations: DFT is computationally expensive; TB sacrifices some accuracy for scalability.

DFT is a quantum mechanical simulation technique used to calculate the electronic structure of nanoscale materials by approximating the ground-state energy as a function of electron density. It provides insight into energy levels, band structures, and quantum behavior critical for nanoscale device design.

- Advantages: DFT allows *ab-initio* calculations that do not require experimental data. It can accurately predict material properties, such as conductivity, energy bands, and effective masses of carriers (electrons and holes).

- Limitations: Although highly accurate, DFT scales poorly with system size and is computationally expensive, limiting its use for large-scale device simulations. Hybrid methods, such as combining DFT with molecular dynamics, are used to model interactions over longer timescales.

DFT plays a key role in materials discovery for nanoelectronics, such as identifying suitable channel materials for field-effect transistors (FETs), where quantum effects become significant.

The tight-binding model provides a semi-empirical solution to quantum mechanical problems by approximating the Hamiltonian matrix. It simplifies simulations by focusing on interactions between neighboring atoms rather than solving the full quantum problem.

- Applications: TB models are widely used to study graphene, carbon nanotubes, and nanoribbons. They provide efficient ways to explore how atomic-level changes affect electronic properties.
- Limitations: Although TB models are computationally cheaper than DFT or NEGF, their accuracy depends on the quality of fitted parameters and is limited to certain materials and conditions.

1.3.2 Surrogate Modeling for Device Behaviour

ML enables the development of surrogate models that approximate the behaviour of nanoscale devices without the need for expensive simulations. These models learn from traditional simulation data and experimental results, offering fast and accurate predictions.

1.3.2.1 Acceleration of Quantum Simulations

Because ML-based surrogate models can learn intricate correlations between input parameters and material properties, they can take the role of DFT and NEGF calculations. This significantly cuts down on the amount of time needed for transport simulations and band structure calculations. Due to their high processing costs, quantum simulations like DFT and NEGF are not feasible for extensive parameter sweeps. By learning from a small number of high-fidelity simulations and forecasting behaviour over uncharted territories, surrogate models offer a quicker substitute.

ML models, including Gaussian Processes (GPs) and Artificial Neural Networks (ANNs), are used to approximate the outputs of quantum simulations with high accuracy. This approach enables researchers to:

- Explore new material properties without running full-scale DFT simulations.
- Conduct design optimization faster by predicting outcomes based on limited input data.

1.3.2.2 Design Space Exploration and Optimization

Without the need for laborious simulations, machine learning (ML) approaches like reinforcement learning (RL) dynamically adjust device parameters, enhancing the performance of quantum dot systems and multi-terminal transistors. It is computationally costly to investigate the huge design space of nanoscale devices. Because fewer simulations are needed to assess various setups, surrogate models enable effective exploration.

Reinforcement learning (RL) has been particularly useful in finding optimal transistor designs by iteratively updating model parameters based on feedback from simulations.

1.3.2.3 Handling Variability and Defects

By learning from experimental datasets, machine learning models can improve simulation accuracy and resilience by accounting for device variability and flaws. Early defect detection and device-to-device variability can be accommodated using machine learning models built on experimental datasets. By spotting any weak places before fabrication starts, this increases the designs' resilience. Knowledge from earlier projects can be effectively applied to new designs thanks to transfer learning, which enables these models to adjust to new devices and materials with little retraining.

1.3.2.4 Transfer Learning for New Materials and Devices

The need for retraining can be decreased by applying machine learning models that have been trained on one set of devices to different materials or architectures. For instance, models created for devices based on graphene can be easily modified to fit carbon nanotubes.

A model that has been trained on one job can be refined to perform well on a related task using little additional data thanks to the potent technique known as transfer learning. It is especially helpful in nanoelectronics when creating novel materials or device designs.

- Mechanism: A neural network trained on DFT or TB simulation data for one set of materials can be adapted to predict properties for similar but unexplored materials with minimal additional training.
- Applications in Device Design: Transfer learning enables faster exploration of novel transistors and 2D-material-based devices, accelerating the search for optimal configurations without requiring full quantum simulations for every material or structure.

For emerging materials like molybdenum disulfide (MoS_2) or carbon nanotubes, transfer learning can leverage existing models from graphene-based studies, saving computational effort while maintaining high accuracy.

1.3.2.5 Real-Time Parameter Tuning

For *in situ* optimisation, traditional simulations are too sluggish. In order to efficiently accomplish desired behaviour in quantum systems, RL algorithms allow for real-time adjustment of control parameters. It takes a lot of time and work to adjust parameters in conventional simulations. Through on-the-fly prediction of ideal parameter settings, surrogate models allow for real-time adjustment. By continuously learning from experimental data, RL algorithms can adjust to shifting circumstances and quickly reach optimal device performance.

- Use Case: Adaptive RL systems continuously optimize plasma parameters during deposition processes, ensuring uniform material properties and improving production yield.

By augmenting conventional approaches with surrogate models and dynamic optimisation techniques, machine learning is revolutionising the simulation and design of nanoscale devices. While ML-based models increase computational efficiency and scalability, DFT, NEGF, and MSB-EMC are still crucial tools for comprehending basic physics. The creation of next-generation nanoelectronics can be accelerated by integrating machine learning (ML), which enables researchers to manage variability, optimise devices in real time, and explore bigger design spaces.

1.4 Process Optimization in Semiconductor Manufacturing

Deposition, etching, quality control, and physical layout design are only a few of the many complex processes involved in semiconductor manufacturing. Controlling yield and variability gets more difficult as device sizes go closer to the nanoscale. The dynamic issues brought forth by the intricate interdependence of parameters, drift in equipment behaviour, and material variability are difficult for traditional optimisation techniques to anticipate and handle. In order to address these issues, semiconductor manufacturing is being revolutionised by machine learning (ML) and data analytics through defect detection, self-healing systems, and real-time process control. The management of yield and variability, real-time control made possible by machine learning, and reliability through predictive maintenance and sophisticated fault-detection techniques are all covered in this section.

1.4.1 Variability and Yield in Nanoscale Manufacturing

In nanoscale manufacturing, maintaining yield—the percentage of functional devices—is critical for economic viability. However, variability arises at multiple levels.

Process Variability

Strict tolerances are required for semiconductor manufacturing procedures like lithography, etching, and deposition. However, a number of variables, such as temperatures, plasma densities, and gas flow rates, can change with time. The material composition, stress levels, and film thickness are all impacted by this process parameter drift. For example, slight changes in RF power and gas composition can have a substantial impact on the results of plasma-enhanced atomic layer deposition (PEALD), resulting in variations in film deposition across wafers. Because they introduce flaws or necessitate revision at later phases of production, these inconsistencies lower yield.

Here, machine learning methods are very helpful since they enable the system to continuously analyse sensor data and identify drifts early. In order to minimise deviations, predictive models minimise them by adjusting parameters in real time based on historical process patterns.

Tool-Based Variability

The accuracy of equipment such as chemical deposition chambers, plasma reactors, and lithography systems is crucial to the precision of semiconductor manufacture. Variability in manufacturing results is introduced by environmental conditions, ageing tools, and inaccurate sensors. For instance, electrode wear in RF plasma systems used in etching procedures might change capacitance and result in an uneven dispersion of plasma.

Predictive maintenance models that track the condition of equipment are used to manage tool-based variability. By examining tool behaviour and anticipating component failures before they interfere with production, graph-based machine learning models are able to detect fault patterns. This guarantees consistent tool performance and minimises downtime.

Material Variability

The composition, thickness, and stress levels of materials used in nanoscale devices, such as metal gates, thin films, and dielectric layers, might differ from wafer to wafer. Microscopic contamination, irregular gas fluxes, or poor deposition are common causes of material property variability. Device performance can be impacted by electrical fluctuations caused by even minor differences in stress or film thickness.

Film profiles from several production runs are analysed by ML-based models to handle material variability. The models forecast the ideal process parameters to guarantee uniform deposition and reduce stress fluctuations. For instance, ML can improve the quality and dependability of films across wafers by regulating plasma flow rates and deposition temperatures.

Conventional yield prediction methods do not account for combinatorial complexity and instead rely on experimental data. In this case, predictive insights are provided by ML models combined with graph traversal methods. ML finds hotspots and clusters of yield-detractor patterns in the physical configuration of devices using graph-based representations. By revealing hidden bottlenecks and allowing for targeted layout or process configuration changes, this improves the Design-Technology Co-Optimization (DTCO) process.

1.4.2 Real-Time Process Control with ML

Real-time process control is essential to semiconductor manufacturing in order to achieve performance metrics and preserve yield uniformity across production lines. Predictive capabilities offered by ML assist manufacturers in dynamically optimising parameters, cutting down on the amount of time needed to modify equipment settings and increasing production efficiency.

ML for Parameter Tuning

Machine learning (ML) approaches are crucial for parameter tweaking during semiconductor manufacturing because they dynamically optimise input variables such as gas flow rates, RF power, pressure, and electrode capacitance. Traditional methods rely on manual adjustments and trial-and-error processes, which are time-consuming and prone to human error. However, automated optimisation is made possible by machine learning (ML), which enables real-time learning and feedback.

Fine-Tuning Plasma Profiles and Capacitance Control

To guarantee even material distribution, plasma etching and deposition procedures need exact control over RF power, electrode capacitance, and gas flow rates. Defects like uneven film thickness or over-etched areas might be introduced by slight variations. By dynamically modifying the plasma profile and managing the capacitance of the central and outer electrodes, machine learning models were able to determine the ideal process parameters that guaranteed uniform film deposition in a PEALD research for TiO_2 films. When compared to hand tuning, our method reduced non-uniformity by 50%.

To further improve control, ML also helps engineers forecast how etching profiles would be affected by plasma conditions under different gas compositions. This guarantees optimal device performance by enabling the system to retain consistent profiles even in fluctuating settings.

Carbon Etching Profiles and Gas Flow Adjustments

The carbon etching process is sensitive to oxygen (O_2) flow rates, with minor changes impacting the final film thickness. In plasma systems, ML models pinpoint the O_2 flow rate as a crucial variable, adjusting it to regulate the thickness profile's take-off position. By maintaining constant thickness in the edge regions, the optimised profiles outperform traditional techniques in terms of precision.

Real-time modifications to electrode capacitances and plasma flow rates produced etch patterns that closely matched the required parameters, according to a study that used graph-based machine learning algorithms. The entire process was streamlined by the ML models, which found correlations and patterns that were not readily apparent through manual observation.

1.4.3 Case Study: Graph-Based Yield Prediction in IC Manufacturing

Graph traversal methods are used to find troublesome patterns in physical layouts and anticipate yield detractors. Algorithms for graph searches augmented by machine learning break down patterns into their most basic elements, group important problems, and extrapolate to find additional possible problem areas.

These techniques guarantee that design parameters are directly translated to real-time insights regarding process irregularities. ML improves yield and eliminates the need for laborious silicon test vehicles by facilitating smooth communication between design teams and process engineers in DTCO workflows.

1.4.4 Reliability, Fault Detection and Self-Heating Systems

Reliability is essential in nanoscale manufacturing, where a small defect or process variation can compromise entire production batches. ML models help monitor equipment behaviour and detect early signs of failures, facilitating preventive maintenance. Several methodologies enhance fault

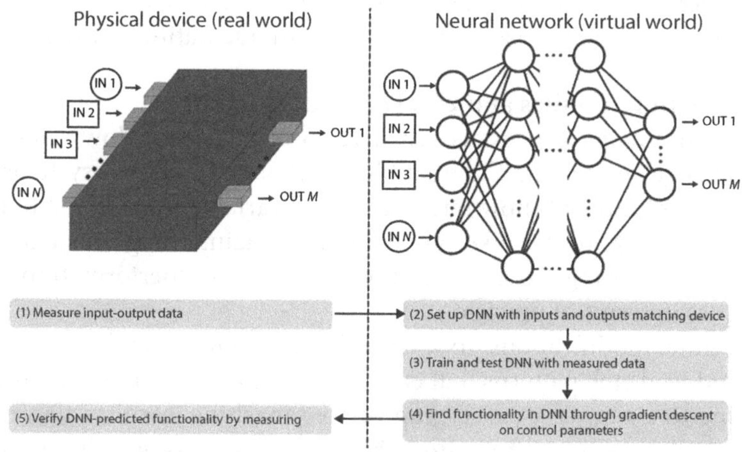

Figure 1.6 Steps for realizing functionality in a nanoelectronic device with a DNN model. (1) Input-output data are measured from the device. (2) A DNN with matching input-output terminals is set up. (3) The DNN is trained on this data and tested with unseen data. (4) Gradient descent is applied to control parameters to achieve the desired functionality. (5) Predicted control voltages are then verified on the physical device. Circles and squares indicate control and data inputs, respectively; circles in the DNN represent neurons and activation functions [16].

detection and overall process reliability. Figure 1.6 gives steps for realizing functionality in a nanoelectronic device with a DNN model.

Predictive Maintenance
ML is used in predictive maintenance to assess past equipment data and forecast probable problems. For example, GAN-based models use simulated baselines and real-time sensor data to identify anomalies.

Fault Detection Algorithms
The Support Vector Machine (SVM) algorithm, enhanced with optimization techniques such as the Horse Optimization Algorithm, has proven effective in classifying and predicting faults in plasma processes and deposition systems.

Self-Healing Systems
Reinforcement learning (RL) is used by self-healing systems to modify process conditions on their own. Without human assistance, the system automatically adjusts parameters to return to ideal settings whenever a departure from the intended specifications is identified.

1.5 Case Study: Machine Learning in Nanowire Tunnel FET Design

Nanowire Tunnel Field-Effect Transistors (TFETs) represent a cutting-edge technology in the realm of semiconductor devices, offering remarkable advantages in terms of power efficiency and scalability. As technology nodes continue to shrink, the integration of machine learning (ML) into the design and fabrication process of nanowire TFETs has shown immense potential. This case study explores the utilisation of ML for design space exploration, predictive modeling, and process variation mitigation in the context of nanowire TFETs.

1.5.1 Device Structure

A TFET's device architecture typically consists of two highly doped source and channel locations located at the far margins of the channel, as well as a channel material, which is typically a semiconductor such as silicon or germanium. A thin protective layer, such as aluminium oxide or hafnium oxide, surrounds the channel and balances the current flowing through it, forming the TFET's entrance. At the connection point, the source and channel districts make a pnp or npn intersection and are in contact with the channel material.

The main components of a nanowire TFET device are a semiconductor nanowire, which serves as the semiconductor's channel, and two heavily doped source and channel locations located at the ends of the nanowire, as seen in Figure 1.7. A thin protective layer that envelops the nanowire and balances the burrowing current through the channel shapes the TFET's door. Given its high electron mobility and low power consumption, this design may prove to be a viable option for low-power electronic devices in the future. For Si NW-TFET arrays to incorporate the basic scaling

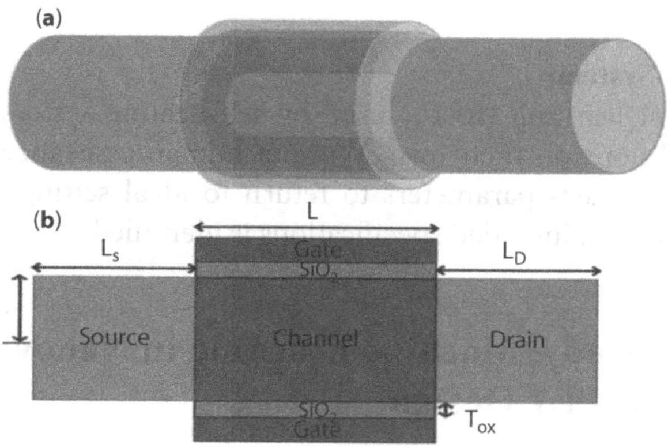

Figure 1.7 (a) Gives 3D schematic structure of Nanowire TFET, (b) shows parameters for the Nanowire TFET [21].

Table 1.1 Parameters for the Nanowire TFET.

S. no.	Parameters	Values
1	Channel Length	5nm – 15nm
2	Channel Thickness	0.65 nm
3	Oxide Thickness	3nm
4	Dielectric constant	25
5	Drain Voltage	0.5V
6	Source Doping	10^{20} cm^{-3}
7	Drain Doping	10^{20} cm^{-3}

advantages of NWs, top-down development is optimal. Parameters used for simulation is given in Table 1.1.

1.5.2 Machine Learning Approach

In the context of TFETs, machine learning (ML) approaches entail using ML algorithms and techniques to forecast device characteristics, optimise TFET design, and enhance performance. Figure 1.8 displays a thorough flowchart of the machine-learning method implementation. Accurate models that accurately depict the intricate behaviour of TFETs can be created using machine learning algorithms. These models facilitate the simulation of device functionality under various conditions, thereby aiding the iterative design enhancement process.

By identifying patterns in simulation data or real-world measurements, machine learning techniques, such as ANNs, can effectively forecast the behavior of TFETs.

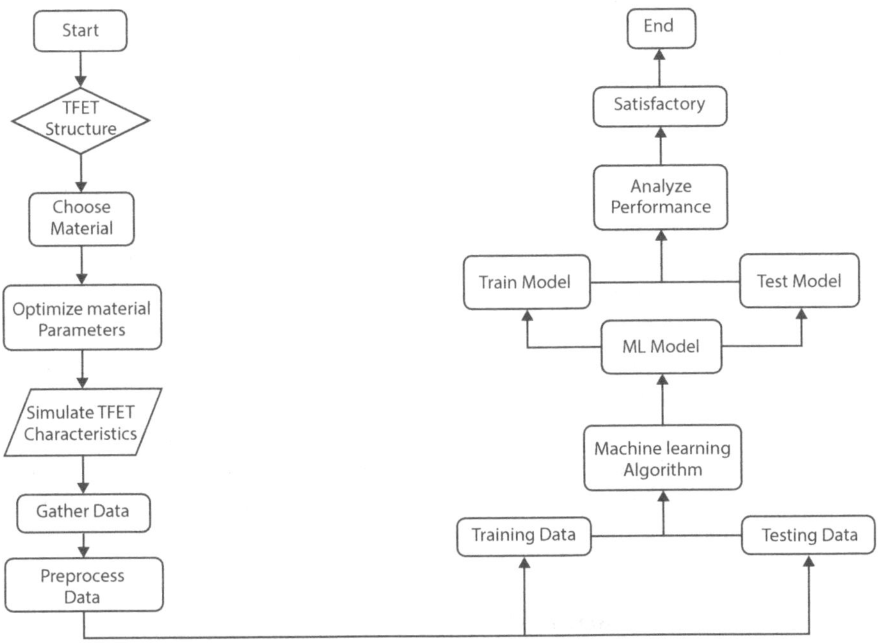

Figure 1.8 A comprehensive flow chart for machine learning algorithm [20].

1.5.3 Design Space Exploration

Objective: Efficiently explore the design space to identify optimal configurations that maximise device performance.
Methodology: Machine learning algorithms, such as genetic algorithms and Bayesian optimization, can significantly enhance the exploration of the vast design space of nanowire TFETs. By training ML models on a dataset of design parameters (e.g., gate length, oxide thickness, doping concentrations) and their corresponding performance metrics, engineers can quickly identify optimal configurations without exhaustive simulations.
Example: A neural network can be trained to predict key performance metrics like threshold voltage and on-current based on the physical dimensions and material properties of the TFETs. This predictive capability allows for rapid iteration and optimization of the device design.
Results: Using ML-driven design space exploration, the development cycle of nanowire TFETs can be accelerated, leading to the identification of high-performance designs in a fraction of the time required by traditional methods.

1.5.4 Predictive Modeling

Objective: Develop accurate predictive models to forecast device performance based on input parameters.
Methodology: Predictive modeling involves training machine learning models on a comprehensive dataset of nanowire TFET characteristics. Techniques such as neural networks, support vector machines, and random forests can be employed to create models that predict electrical characteristics (e.g., on-current, off-current, subthreshold swing) based on device geometry and material properties.
Example: A neural network model can be trained on experimental data to predict the electrical behaviour of TFETs under varying conditions. This model can then be used to simulate the performance of new designs, reducing the reliance on computationally intensive simulations.
Results: The use of predictive modeling enables rapid prototyping and iterative improvement of nanowire TFET designs, leading to more efficient development cycles and reduced time-to-market.

1.5.5 Process Variation Mitigation

Objective: mitigate the impact of process variations on device performance through data-driven insights.

Methodology: Process variations, such as fluctuations in doping concentrations and layer thicknesses, can lead to inconsistencies in device performance. Machine learning can analyse data from multiple fabrication runs to identify patterns that influence device yield and performance. Techniques like support vector regression and ensemble methods can be used to model the impact of process variations and suggest adjustments to the fabrication process.
Example: By training a support vector regression model on data from various fabrication runs, engineers can predict the yield and performance of TFETs under different process conditions. This information can be used to fine-tune the manufacturing process, minimizing the impact of variations and improving yield.
Results: The application of ML in process variation mitigation leads to more reliable and robust nanowire TFETs, ensuring that the manufactured devices meet performance specifications consistently.

1.6 Future Directions and Challenges

- **Autonomous Nanoelectronics Design**: In the future, machine learning could enable automated design systems that create nanoelectronic devices with minimal human intervention. These systems could explore a vast design space, simulate numerous configurations, and optimize designs at a scale and speed far beyond human capabilities.
- **Quantum and Neuromorphic Computing**: Quantum computing and neuromorphic computing are emerging fields within nanoelectronics. ML can assist in the design and optimization of quantum circuits and neuromorphic architectures, where traditional methods struggle due to the complex behaviors of quantum bits (qubits) or neuron-like components.
- **Integration with Artificial Intelligence (AI) Hardware**: As the demand for specialized AI hardware grows, nanoelectronics is expected to play a crucial role in developing AI-optimized processors. ML algorithms can be instrumental in designing hardware accelerators optimized for tasks like deep learning and data analytics, pushing AI computation to its physical limits.
- **High-Throughput Experimentation**: ML enables high-throughput experimentation, where thousands of potential

materials or device configurations are tested simultaneously. By analyzing results in real-time, ML models can guide experiments toward more promising avenues, significantly speeding up R&D in nanoelectronics.

- **Green Nanoelectronics**: Machine learning can support the development of environmentally friendly nanoelectronics by optimizing manufacturing processes to reduce waste and energy consumption. By predicting materials or methods that have a lower environmental impact, ML can drive the industry towards more sustainable practices.
- **Development of Hybrid Models**: One promising direction is the development of hybrid models that combine machine learning with traditional physics-based methods. By incorporating physical laws and domain knowledge into ML models, researchers can improve the accuracy, interpretability, and generalizability of predictions. Hybrid models can help bridge the gap between data-driven approaches and physics-informed constraints, particularly for complex nanoscale phenomena.
- **Data Augmentation and Transfer Learning**: Techniques such as data augmentation, where synthetic data is generated to increase the size and diversity of datasets, and transfer learning, which applies knowledge from one domain to another, are valuable in nanoelectronics. These methods can make it feasible to develop robust ML models even with limited data. Transfer learning, in particular, allows models to generalize across different types of nanoelectronic materials or devices, broadening their applicability.
- **Explainable AI (XAI) for Nanoelectronics**: Developing interpretable and explainable ML models, often referred to as explainable AI (XAI), is a critical direction for increasing trust in ML applications within nanoelectronics. XAI techniques enable researchers to understand the factors influencing an ML model's predictions, ensuring that ML outputs align with physical intuition and domain knowledge. This approach is essential for building confidence in ML-driven predictions, especially in safety-critical nanoelectronic applications.
- **Efficient Computational Frameworks**: Research into more efficient computational frameworks and algorithms is needed to reduce the computational costs associated

with training and deploying ML models in nanoelectronics. Techniques like federated learning, distributed computing, and optimized ML architectures can significantly lower the resource requirements for training models, making ML more accessible to researchers with limited computational power.

- **Integration with Quantum Computing**: Quantum computing offers a future avenue for advancing ML applications in nanoelectronics, especially as quantum processors become more powerful. Quantum ML algorithms have the potential to handle large, complex datasets and perform simulations far beyond classical computing's capabilities. Quantum-enhanced ML could provide the power to address data-intensive tasks in nanoelectronics, such as complex material discovery and device optimization.
- **Autonomous Experimental Systems**: The concept of "autonomous labs," where ML-driven robots conduct experiments, analyze results, and adjust experimental conditions in real-time, could transform nanoelectronics research. Such systems would accelerate material discovery, device prototyping, and optimization by enabling faster and more efficient experiments. Autonomous labs could reduce the human effort and time required for R&D, speeding up innovation in nanoelectronics.

1.7 Conclusion

Nanoelectronics, the field managing electronic parts and frameworks at the nanometer scale, has seen exceptional progressions because of the persistent scaling down of gadgets and the developing interest for elite execution hardware. Notwithstanding, as parts psychologist to nuclear levels, customary plan and improvement techniques battle to deal with the rising intricacy and actual limits. This is where Machine Learning assumes a groundbreaking part.

Machine learning, a subset of artificial intelligence (AI), a subset of man-made consciousness, offers progressed computational models fit for recognizing designs, anticipating results, and streamlining processes in view of immense datasets. By utilizing calculations that improve with experience, ML upgrades different phases of nanoelectronics like gadget configuration, assembling, and execution investigation. It can likewise help us in advancing materials, further developing creation processes, and anticipating gadget ways of behaving in manners that were beforehand exceptionally complicated and tedious, and some that are impossible through traditional strategies.

Coordinating Machine learning into nanoelectronics further develops productivity and accuracy as well as speeding up advancement in cutting-edge gadgets, for example, quantum spots, semiconductors, and nanoscale sensors. This combination of ML with nanotechnology vows to drive the fate of gadgets toward new outskirts through registering, information examination, and the utilization of ML calculations.

Summary

This chapter highlights how machine learning has revolutionized nanoelectronics, especially in overcoming the drawbacks of conventional design and manufacturing techniques. ML improves the effectiveness, scalability, and dependability of nanoelectronic devices by facilitating accurate simulations, process optimization, and defect reduction. Future directions that promise to better integrate machine learning into all phases of nanoelectronics research and development are also covered in the chapter, including hybrid modeling, transfer learning, and autonomous systems. These developments are expected to push the industry toward high-performance, more sustainable technology, with important ramifications for AI hardware, quantum computing, and other areas.

References

1. Shen, L., Di, S., Yin, L., Liu, X., Du, G., Parameter calibration of drift-diffusion model in quasi-ballisitc transport region with Monte Carlo method. *2017 Silicon Nanoelectronics Workshop (SNW)*, Kyoto, Japan, pp. 73–74, 2017, doi: 10.23919/SNW.2017.8242303.
2. Singh, M., Chaudhary, T., Raj, B., Design of Si and Ge Nanowire FET for Low Power Application. *J. Silicon*, Springer, 15, 1491–1497, 2023.
3. Singh, M., Chaudhary, T., Raj, B., Drain Current and Transconductance Analysis of GaN GAA Nanowire FET with High K Dielectric. *ECS J. Sci. Technol.*, 12, 15, 6070–6077, 2023.
4. Ansari, F., Chaudhary, T., Sunkaria, R.K., Singh, M., Raj, B., Comparative Analysis of Nanowire Tunnel Field Effect Transistor for Low Power Application. *J. Silicon*, 14, 12075–12084, 2022, SCI, IF=3.2.

5. Faizan, A., Mandeep, S., Tarun, C., Faizan, R.B.S., Comparative Analysis of Nanowire Tunnel Field Effect Transistor for Low Power Application. *J. Silicon*, 14, 12075–12084, 2022.
6. Thakur, Y., Khosla, M., Raj, B., Performance-Driven OFET Design for Advanced Hydrogen Gas Sensing Applications. *Analog Integr. Circ. Signal Process.*, 123, 58, Springer, April 2025.
7. Mandeep, S., Tarun, C., Balwinder, R., Drain Current and Transconductance Analysis of GaN GAA Nanowire FET with High K Dielectric. *ECS J. Solid State Sci. Technol.*, 12, 113007, 2023.
8. Mandeep, S., Tarun, C., Balwinder, R., Design and Simulation Analysis of Silicon Germanium Nanowire FET for Low Power Applications. *J. Silicon*, 15, 1491–1497, 2023.
9. Wright, T., Tse, B., Nsiye, E., Azinord, T., Medina, D., Mondesire, S., Probabilistic Modeling and Machine Learning for Preventative Maintenance Prediction in Semiconductor Manufacturing. *2024 35th Annual SEMI Advanced Semiconductor Manufacturing Conference (ASMC)*, Albany, NY, USA, pp. 1–6, 2024, doi: 10.1109/ASMC61125.2024.10545532.
10. Moldovan, D., Anghel, I., Cioara, T., Salomie, I., Machine Learning in Manufacturing: Processes Classification Using Support Vector Machine and Horse Optimization Algorithm. *2020 19th RoEduNet Conference: Networking in Education and Research (RoEduNet)*, Bucharest, Romania, pp. 1–6, 2020, doi: 10.1109/RoEduNet51892.2020.9324855.
11. Sampedro, C., *et al.*, 3D multi-subband ensemble Monte Carlo simulator of FinFETs and nanowire transistors. *2014 International Conference on Simulation of Semiconductor Processes and Devices (SISPAD)*, Yokohama, Japan, pp. 21–24, 2014, doi: 10.1109/SISPAD.2014.6931553.
12. Bruzzone, S., Iannaccone, G., Marzari, N., Fiori, G., An Open-Source Multiscale Framework for the Simulation of Nanoscale Devices. *IEEE Trans. Electron Devices*, 61, 1, 48–53, Jan. 2014, doi: 10.1109/TED.2013.2291909.
13. G, S.A., Meher Srinavas R, B., K, N., R, J., CNN Based Curved Path Detection and Obstacle Avoidance for Autonomous Rover. *2023 IEEE International Conference on Power Electronics, Smart Grid, and Renewable Energy (PESGRE)*, Trivandrum, India, pp. 1–7, 2023, doi: 10.1109/PESGRE58662.2023.10404782.
14. Huang, J., Momenzadeh, M., Lombardi, F., An Overview of Nanoscale Devices and Circuits. *IEEE Des. Test Comput.*, 24, 4, 304–311, July-Aug. 2007, doi: 10.1109/MDT.2007.121.
15. Moriya, T., Machine Learning Approaches Optimizing Semiconductor Manufacturing Processes. *2021 5th IEEE Electron Devices Technology & Manufacturing Conference (EDTM)*, Chengdu, China, pp. 1–3, 2021, doi: 10.1109/EDTM50988.2021.9420955.
16. Ruiz Euler, H.C., Boon, M.N., Wildeboer, J.T., *et al.*, A deep-learning approach to realizing functionality in nanoelectronic devices. *Nat. Nanotechnol.*, 15, 992–998, 2020, https://doi.org/10.1038/s41565-020-00779-y.

17. Takahashi, Y., Ono, Y., Fujiwara, A., Inokawa, H., Silicon single-electron devices and their applications. *Proceedings. 7th International Conference on Solid-State and Integrated Circuits Technology, 2004*, Beijing, China, vol. 1, pp. 624–629, 2004, doi: 10.1109/ICSICT.2004.1435083.
18. Tsuchiya, H., Understanding carrier transport in the ultimate physical scaling limit of MOSFETs. *2014 IEEE International Meeting for Future of Electron Devices, Kansai (IMFEDK)*, Kyoto, Japan, pp. 1–2, 2014, doi: 10.1109/IMFEDK.2014.6867045.
19. Saini, M.K., Khosla, M., Raj, B., Exploring Emerging Materials for Memristor Fabrication: A Review of Recent Progress, *ECS J. Solid State Sci. Technol.*, 13, 115004, Dec 2024.
20. Saravanan, M., Parthasarathy, E., Ajayan, J., Rahi, S.B., Device Simulation Based Machine Learning Technique for III V TFET. *2024 International Conference on Recent Advances in Electrical, Electronics, Ubiquitous Communication, and Computational Intelligence (RAEEUCCI)*, Chennai, India, pp. 1–6, 2024, doi: 10.1109/RAEEUCCI61380.2024.10547980.
21. Rohith, S., Naik, S.S., Ingalagi, P.M., Katti, S., Vimala, P., Analysis of Transfer Characteristics for Nanowire Tunnel FET. *2023 IEEE International Conference on Electronics, Computing and Communication Technologies (CONECCT)*, Bangalore, India, pp. 1–4, 2023, doi: 10.1109/CONECCT57959.2023.10234755.
22. Gatermann, C. and Sommer, R., Teaching the MOSFET: A Circuit Designer's View. *2022 18th International Conference on Synthesis, Modeling, Analysis and Simulation Methods and Applications to Circuit Design (SMACD)*, Villasimius, Italy, pp. 1–4, 2022, doi: 10.1109/SMACD55068.2022.9816264.
23. Pearce, C.W. and Yaney, D.S., Short-channel effects in MOSFET's. *IEEE Electron Device Lett.*, 6, 7, 326–328, July 1985, doi: 10.1109/EDL.1985.26143.
24. Rakús, M., Stopjaková, V., Nagy, L., Arbet, D., Analysis of MOSFET model for low-voltage applications. *2016 International Conference on Emerging eLearning Technologies and Applications (ICETA)*, Stary Smokovec, Slovakia, pp. 303–308, 2016, doi: 10.1109/ICETA.2016.7802076.
25. Schaller, R.R., Moore's law: past, present and future. *IEEE Spectr.*, 34, 6, 52–59, June 1997, doi: 10.1109/6.591665.
26. Duvvury, C., A guide to short-channel effects in MOSFETs. *IEEE Circuits Devices Mag.*, 2, 6, 6–10, Nov. 1986, doi: 10.1109/MCD.1986.6311897.
27. Bhardwaj, A., Kumar, P., Raj, B., Anand, S., Design and Performance Optimization of doping-less Vertical Nanowire TFET using Gate Stack Technique. *J. Electron. Mater. (JEMS)*, Springer, 41, 7, 4005–4013, 2022.
28. Singh, J. and Raj, B., Tunnel Current Model of Asymmetric MIM Structure Levying Various Image Forces to Analyze the Characteristics of Filamentary Memristor. *Appl. Phys. A*, Springer, 125, 3, 203.1–203, 11 Feb 2019.
29. Goyal, C., Singh Ubhi, J., Raj, B., Low Leakage Zero Ground Noise Nanoscale Full Adder using Source Biasing Technique. *J. Nanoelectron. Optoelectron.*, American Scientific Publishers, 14, 360–370, March 2019.

30. Singh, G., Sarin, R.K., Raj, B., A Novel Robust Exclusive-OR Function Implementation in QCA Nanotechnology with Energy Dissipation Analysis. *J. Comput. Electron.*, Springer, 15, 2, 455–465, June 2016.
31. Wadhwa, G., Kamboj, P., Raj, B., Design optimisation of junctionless TFET biosensor for high sensitivity. *Adv. Nat. Sci.: Nanosci. Nanotechnol.*, 10, 045001, 7, 2019.
32. Bansal, P. and Raj, B., Memristor Modeling and Analysis for Linear Dopant Drift Kinetics. *J. Nanoeng. Nanomanuf.*, American Scientific Publishers, 6, 1–7, 2016.
33. Ashima, Vaithiyanathan, D., Raj, B., Performance Analysis of Charge Plasma Induced Graded Channel Si Nanotube. *J. Eng. Res. (JER)*, EMSME Special Issue, 146–154, Aug 2021.
34. Tomar, A.S., Magraiya, V.K., Raj, B., Scaling of Access and Data Transistor for High Performance DRAM Cell Design. *Quantum Matter*, 2, 412–416, Oct. 2013.
35. Jain, N. and Raj, B., Parasitic Capacitance and Resistance Model Development and Optimization of Raised Source/Drain SOI FinFET Structure for Analog Circuit Applications. *J. Nanoelectron. Optoelectron.*, ASP, USA, 13, 531–539, April 2018.
36. Singh, S., Vishvakarma, S.K., Raj, B., Analytical Modeling of Split-Gate Junction-Less Transistor for a Biosensor Application. *Sens. Bio-Sens.*, Elsevier, 18, 31–36, April 2018.
37. Gopal, M. and Raj, B., Low Power 8T SRAM Cell Design for High Stability Video Applications. *ITSI Trans. Electr. Electron. Eng.*, 1, 5, 91–97, 2013.
38. Raj, B., Mitra, J., Bihani, D.K., V, R., Saxena, A.K., Dasgupta, S., Analysis of Noise Margin, Power and Process Variation for 32 nm FinFET Based 6T SRAM Cell. *J. Comput. (JCP)*, Academy Publisher, Finland, 5, 6, 1–8, 2010.
39. Sharma, D., Mehra, R., Raj, B., Comparative Analysis of Photovoltaic Technologies for High Efficiency Solar Cell Design. *Superlattices Microstruct.*, Elsevier, 153, 106861, May 2021.
40. Kaur, P., Buttar, A.S., Raj, B., A comprehensive Analysis of Nanoscale Transistor Based Biosensor: A Review. *Indian J. Pure Appl. Phys.*, 59, 304–318, April 2021.
41. Yadav, D., Raj, B., Raj, B., Design and Simulation of Low Power Microcontroller for IoT Applications. *J. Sens. Lett.*, ASP, 18, 401–409, May 2020.
42. Singh, S. and Raj, B., A 2-D Analytical Surface Potential and Drain Current Modeling of Double-Gate Vertical T-Shaped Tunnel FET. *J. Comput. Electron.*, Springer, 19, 1154–1163, April 2020.
43. Singh, J. and Raj, B., An Accurate and Generic Window Function for Non-Linear Memristor Model. *J. Comput. Electron.*, Springer, 18, 2, 640–647, June 2019.
44. Kaur, M., Gupta, N., Kumar, S., Raj, B., Singh, A.K., Comparative RF and Crosstalk Analysis of Carbon Based Nano Interconnects. *IET Circuits Devices Syst.*, 15, 6, 493–503, Feb 2021.

45. Kandasamy, N., Ahmad, F., Ajitha, D., Raj, B., Telagam, N., Quantum Dot Cellular Automata based Scan Flip Flop and Boundary Scan Register. *IETE J. Res.*, 66, 535–548, 2020.
46. Singh, J. and Raj, B., Design and Investigation of 7T2M NVSARM with Enhanced Stability and Temperature Impact on Store/Restore Energy. *IEEE Trans. Very Large Scale Integr. Syst.*, 27, 6, 1322–1328, June 2019.
47. Bhardwaj, A.K., Gupta, S., Raj, B., Singh, A., Impact of Double Gate Geometry on the Performance of Carbon Nanotube Field Effect Transistor Structures for Low Power Digital Design. *Comput. Theor. Nanosci.*, ASP, 16, 1813–1820, 2019.
48. Jain, N. and Raj, B., Thermal Stability Analysis and Performance Exploration of Asymmetrical Dual-k underlap Spacer (ADKUS) SOI FinFET for Security and Privacy Applications. *Indian J. Pure Appl. Phys. (IJPAP)*, 57, 352–360, May 2019.
49. Jain, N. and Raj, B., Dual-k Spacer Region Variation at the Drain Side of Asymmetric SOI FinFET Structure: Performance Analysis towards the Analog/RF Design Applications. *J. Nanoelectron. Optoelectron.*, American Scientific Publishers, 14, 349–359, March 2019.
50. Singh, J., Sharma, S., Raj, B., Mamta Khosla Analysis of barrier layer thickness on performance of In1-xGaxAs based Gate Stack Cylindrical Gate Nanowire MOSFET. *J. Nanoelectron. Optoelectron.*, ASP, 13, 1473–1477, Oct 2018.
51. Jain, N. and Raj, B., Analysis and Performance Exploration of High-k SOI FinFETs Over the Conventional Low-k SOI FinFET toward Analog/RF Design. *J. Semicond. (JoS)*, IOP Science, 39, 12, 124002-1-7, Dec 2018.
52. Goyal, C., Ubhi, J.S., Raj, B., A reliable leakage reduction technique for approximate full adder with reduced ground bounce noise. *J. Math. Probl. Eng.*, Hindawi, 2018, 3501041, 16, 15 Oct 2018.
53. Anuradha, Singh, J., Raj, B., Khosla, M., Design and Performance Analysis of Nano-Scale Memristor-Based Nonvolatile SRAM. *J. Sens. Lett.*, American Scientific Publishers, 16, 798–805, Oct 2018.
54. Wadhwa, G. and Raj, B., Parametric Variation Analysis of Charge-Plasma-Based Dielectric Modulated JLTFET for Biosensor Application. *IEEE Sens. J.*, 18, 15, 6070–6077, August 1 2018, (SCI).
55. Singh, J. and Raj, B., Comparative Analysis of Memristor Models for Memories Design. *J. Semicond.*, IoP, 39, 7, 074006-1-12, July 2018.
56. Yadav, D., Chouhan, S.S., Vishvakarma, S.K., Raj, B., Application Specific Microcontroller Design for IoT based WSN. *Sens. Lett.*, ASP, 16, 374–385, May 2018.
57. Singh, G., Sarin, R.K., Raj, B., Fault-Tolerant Design and Analysis of Quantum-Dot Cellular Automata Based Circuits. *IEEE/IET Circuits Devices Syst.*, 12, 638–64, 2018.
58. Singh, J. and Raj, B., Modeling of Mean Barrier Height Levying Various Image Forces of Metal Insulator Metal Structure to Enhance the Performance

of Conductive Filament Based Memristor Model. *IEEE Nanotechnol.*, 17, 2, 268–267, March 2018.
59. Jain, A., Sharma, S., Raj, B., Analysis of Triple Metal Surrounding Gate (TM-SG) III-V Nanowire MOSFET for Photosensing Application. *Opto-Electron. J.*, Elsevier, 26, 2, 141–148, May 2018.
60. Jain, A., Sharma, S., Raj, B., Design and Analysis of High Sensitivity Photosensor Using Cylindrical Surrounding Gate MOSFET For Low Power Sensor Applications. *Eng. Sci. Technol. Int. J.*, Elsevier's, 19, 4, 1864–1870, December 2016.
61. Saiphani Kumar, G., Singh, A., Raj, B., Design and Analysis of Gate All Around CNTFET Based SRAM Cell Design. *J. Comput. Electron.*, Springer, 17, 1, 138–145, March 2018.
62. pal Singh, G., Sohi, B.S., Raj, B., Material Properties Analysis of Graphene Base Transistor (GBT) for VLSI Analog Circuits. *Indian J. Pure Appl. Phys. (IJPAP)*, 55, 896–902, Dec 2017.
63. Kumar, S. and Raj, B., Estimation of Stability and Performance Metric for Inward Access Transistor Based 6T SRAM Cell Design Using n-type/p-type DMDG-GDOV TFET. *IEEE VLSI Circuits Syst. Lett.*, 3, 2, 25–39, June 2017.
64. Sharma, S., Kumar, A., Pattanaik, M., Raj, B., Forward Body Biased Multimode Multi-Threshold CMOS Technique for Ground Bounce Noise Reduction in Static CMOS Adders. *Int. J. Inf. Electron. Eng.*, 3, 3, 567–572, 2013.
65. Singh, H., Kumar, P., Raj, B., Performance Analysis of Majority Gate SET Based 1-bit Full Adder. *Int. J. Comput. Commun. Eng. (IJCCE)*, IACSIT Press Singapore, ISSN: 2010-3743, 2, 4, 2013.
66. Bhardwaj, A.K., Gupta, S., Raj, B., Investigation of Parameters for Schottky Barrier (SB) Height for Schottky Barrier Based Carbon Nanotube Field Effect Transistor Device. *J. Nanoelectron. Optoelectron.*, ASP, 15, 783–791, July 2020.
67. Bansal, P. and Raj, B., Memristor: A Versatile Nonlinear Model for Dopant Drift and Boundary Issues. *JCTN*, American Scientific Publishers, 14, 5, 2319–2325, May 2017.
68. Jain, N. and Raj, B., An Analog and Digital Design Perspective Comprehensive Approach on Fin-FET (Fin-Field Effect transistor) Technology - A Review. *Rev. Adv. Sci. Eng. (RASE)*, ASP, 5, 1–14, 2016.
69. Raj, B., Saxena, A.K., Dasgupta, S., Analytical Modeling for the Estimation of Leakage Current and Subthreshold Swing Factor of Nanoscale Double Gate FinFET Device. *Microelectron. Int.*, UK, 26, 53–63, 2009.
70. Soniya, Singh, S., Wadhwa, G., Raj, B., An Analytical Modeling for Dual Source Vertical Tunnel Field Effect Transistor. *Int. J. Recent Technol. Eng. (IJRTE)*, 8, 2, 603–608, July 2019.
71. Singh, S. and Raj, B., Design and analysis of hetrojunction Vertical T-Shaped Tunnel Field Effect Transistor. *J. Electron. Mater.*, Springer, 48, 10, 6253–6260, October 2019.

72. Goyal, C., Ubhi, J.S., Raj, B., A Low Leakage CNTFET based Inexact Full Adder for Low Power Image Processing Applications. *Int. J. Circuit Theory Appl.*, Wiley, 47, 9, 1446–1458, September 2019.
73. Raj, B., Saxena, A.K., Dasgupta, S., A Compact Drain Current and Threshold Voltage Quantum Mechanical Analytical Modeling for FinFETs. *J. Nanoelectron. Optoelectron. (JNO)*, USA, 3, 2, 163–170, 2008.
74. Wadhwa, G. and Raj, B., An Analytical Modeling of Charge Plasma Based Tunnel Field Effect Transistor with Impacts of Gate underlap Region. *Superlattices Microstruct.*, Elsevier, 142, 106512, June 2020.
75. Singh, S. and Raj, B., Modeling and Simulation Analysis of SiGe Hetrojunction Double GateVertical t-Shaped Tunnel FET. *Superlattices Microstruct.*, Elsevier, 142, 106496, June 2020.
76. Jain, N. and Raj, B., Device and Circuit Co-Design Perspective Comprehensive Approach on FinFET Technology - A Review. *J. Electron Devices*, 23, 1, 1890–1901, 2016.
77. Kumar, S. and Raj, B., Analysis of I_{ON} and Ambipolar Current for Dual-Material Gate-Drain Overlapped DG-TFET. *J. Nanoelectron. Optoelectron.*, American Scientific Publishers, USA, 11, 323–333, June 2016.
78. Anjum, N., Bali, T., Raj, B., Design and Simulation of Handwritten Multiscript Character Recognition. *Int. J. Adv. Res. Comput. Commun. Eng.*, 2, 7, 2544–2549, July 2013.
79. Singh, K. and Raj, B., Performance and analysis of temperature dependent Multi-Walled Carbon Nanotubes as Global Interconnects at Different Technology Nodes. *J. Comput. Electron.*, Springer, 14, 2, 469–476, June 2015.
80. Kumar, S. and Raj, B., Compact channel potential analytical modeling of DG-TFET based on evanescent–mode approach. *J. Comput. Electron.*, Springer, 14, 2, 820–827, July 2015.
81. Singh, K. and Raj, B., Temperature Dependent Modeling and Performance Evaluation of Multi-Walled CNT and Single-Walled CNT as Global Interconnects. *J. Electron. Mater.*, Springer, 44, 12, 4825–4835, Dec 2015.
82. Sharma, V.K., Pattanaik, M., Raj, B., INDEP approach for leakage reduction in nanoscale CMOS circuits. *Int. J. Electron.*, Taylor & Francis, 102, 2, 200–215, 2014.
83. Singh, K. and Raj, B., Influence of Temperature on MWCNT Bundle, SWCNT Bundle and Copper Interconnects for Nanoscaled Technology Nodes. *J. Mater. Sci.: Mater. Electron.*, Springer, 26, 8, 6134–6142, 2015.
84. Anjum, N., Bali, T., Raj, B., Design and Simulation of Handwritten Gurumukhi and Devanagri Numerical Recognition. *Int. J. Comput. Appl.*, Foundation of Computer Science, New York, USA, 73, 12, 16–21, 2013.
85. Khandelwal, S., Gupta, V., Raj, B., Gupta, R.D., Process Variability Aware Low Leakage Reliable Nano Scale DG-FinFET SRAM Cell Design Technique. *J. Nanoelectron. Optoelectron.*, 10, 6, 810–817, December 2015.

86. Sharma, V.K., Pattanaik, M., Raj, B., ONOFIC Approach: Low Power High Speed Nanoscale VLSI Circuits Design. *Int. J. Electron.*, Taylor & Francis, 101, 1, 61–73, 2014.
87. Khandelwal, S., Raj, B., Gupta, R.D., FinFET based 6T SRAM Cell Design: Analysis of Performance Metric, Process Variation and Temperature Effect. *J. Comput. Theor. Nanosci.*, ASP, USA, 12, 2500–2506, 2015.
88. Singh, S., Yadav, S., Rahul, J., Srivastava, A., Raj, B., Impact of HfO_2 in Graded Channel Dual Insulator Double Gate MOSFET. *J. Comput. Theor. Nanosci.*, American Scientific Publishers, 12, 6, 950–953, April 2015.
89. Sharma, V.K., Pattanaik, M., Raj, B., PVT variations aware low leakage INDEP approach for nanoscale CMOS Circuits. *Microelectron. Reliab.*, Elsevier, 54, 90–99, 2014.
90. Raj, B., Saxena, A.K., Dasgupta, S., Quantum Mechanical Analytical Modeling of Nanoscale DG FinFET: Evaluation of Potential, Threshold Voltage and Source/Drain Resistance. *Elsevier's J. Mater. Sci. Semicond. Process.*, Elsevier, 16, 4, 1131–1137, 2013.
91. Gopal, M., Prasad, S.S.D., Raj, B., 8T SRAM Cell Design for Dynamic and Leakage Power Reduction. *Int. J. Comput. Appl.*, Foundation of Computer Science, New York, USA, 71, 9, 43–48, June 2013.
92. Pattanaik, M., Raj, B., Sharma, S., Kumar, A., Diode Based Trimode Multi-Threshold CMOS Technique for Ground Bounce Noise Reduction in Static CMOS Adders. *Adv. Mater. Res.*, Trans Tech Publications, Switzerland, 548, 885–889, 2012.
93. Raj, B., Saxena, A.K., Dasgupta, S., Nanoscale FinFET Based SRAM Cell Design: Analysis of Performance metric, Process variation, Underlapped FinFET and Temperature effect. *IEEE Circuits Syst. Mag.*, 11, 2, 38–50, 2011.
94. Sharma, V.K., Pattanaik, M., Raj, B., Leakage Current ONOFIC Approach for Deep Submicron VLSI Circuit Design. *Int. J. Electr. Comput. Electron. Commun. Eng.*, World Academy of Sciences, Engineering and Technology, 7, 4, 239–244, 2013.
95. Kaur, P., Gill, S.S., Raj, B., Comparative Analysis of OFETs Materials and Devices for Sensor Applications. *J. Silicon*, Springer, 14, 4463–4471, 2022.
96. Sharma, S.K., Kumar, P., Raj, B., Raj, B., $In_{1-x}Ga_xAs$ Double Metal Gate-Stacking Cylindrical Nanowire MOSFET for Highly Sensitive Photo Detector. *J. Silicon*, Springer, 14, 3535–3541, 2022.
97. Raj, B., Saxena, A.K., Dasgupta, S., Analytical Modeling of Quasi Planar Nanoscale Double Gate FinFET with Source/Drain Resistance and Field Dependent Carrier Mobility: A quantum mechanical study. *J. Comput. (JCP)*, Academy Publisher, Finland, 4, 9, 1–8, 2009.
98. Bhushan, S., Khandelwal, S., Raj, B., Analyzing Different Mode FinFET based Memory Cell at Different Power Supply for Leakage Reduction. *Seventh International Conference on Bio-Inspired Computing: Theories and Application (BIC-TA 2012)*, Advances in Intelligent Systems and Computing, vol. 202, pp. 89–100, 2012.

99. Singh, J. and Raj, B., Temperature Dependent Analytical Modeling and Simulations of Nanoscale Memristor. *Eng. Sci. Technol. Int. J.*, Elsevier's, 21, 862–868, Oct 2018.
100. Singh, S., Bala, S., Raj, B., Raj, B., Improved Sensitivity of Dielectric Modulated Junctionless Transistor for Nanoscale Biosensor Design. *Sens. Lett.*, ASP, 18, 328–333, April 2020.
101. Kumar, V., Vishvakarma, S.K., Raj, B., Design and Performance Analysis of ASIC for IoT Applications. *Sens. Lett.*, ASP, 18, 31–38, Jan 2020.
102. Jaiswal, A., Sarin, R.K., Raj, B., Sukhija, S., A Novel Circular Slotted Microstrip-Fed Patch Antenna with Three Triangle Shape Defected Ground Structure for Multiband Applications. *Adv. Electromagn. (AEM)*, 7, 3, 56–63, Aug 2018.
103. Wadhwa, G. and Raj, B., Label Free Detection of Biomolecules using Charge-Plasma-Based Gate Underlap Dielectric Modulated Junctionless TFET. *J. Electron. Mater. (JEMS)*, Springer, 47, 8, 4683–4693, August 2018.
104. Singh, G., Sarin, R.K., Raj, B., Design and Performance Analysis of a New Efficient Coplanar Quantum-Dot Cellular Automata Adder. *Indian J. Pure Appl. Phys. (IJPAP)*, 55, 97–103, February 2017.
105. Kaur, P., Pandey, V., Raj, B., Comparative Study of Efficient Design, Control and Monitoring of Solar Power using IoT. *Sens. Lett.*, ASP, 18, 419–426, May 2020.
106. Bhardwaj, A.K., Gupta, S., Raj, B., Development & Analysis of Compact Model for Double Gate Schottky Barrier CNTFET. *J. Nanoelectron. Optoelectron.*, ASP, 15, 1199–1208, Aug 2020.
107. Wadhwa, G., Kamboj, P., Singh, J., Raj, B., Design and Investigation of Junctionless DGTFET for Biological Molecule Recognition. *Trans. Electr. Electron. Mater.*, Springer, 22, 282–289, 2021.
108. Verma, S.K., Singh, S., Wadhwa, G., Raj, B., Detection of Biomolecules using Charge-Plasma Based Gate Underlap Dielectric Modulated Dopingless TFET. *Trans. Electr. Electron. Mater. (TEEM)*, Springer, 21, 528–535, June 2020.
109. Jain, N. and Raj, B., Impact of underlap spacer region variation on Electrostatic and analog/RF performance of symmetrical high-k SOI FinFET at 20 nm channel length. *J. Semicond. (JoS)*, IOP Science, 38, 12, 122002, Dec 2017.
110. Singh, S. and Raj, B., Analytical Modeling and Simulation analysis of T-shaped III-V heterojunction Vertical T-FET. *Superlattices Microstruct.*, Elsevier, 147, 106717, Nov 2020.
111. Singh, G., Sarin, R.K., Raj, B., Design and Analysis of Area Efficient QCA Based Reversible Logic Gates. *J. Microprocess. Microsys.*, Elsevier, 52, 59–68, May 2017.
112. Singh, S. and Raj, B., Parametric variation analysis on hetero-junction vertical t-shape TFET for supressing ambipolar conduction. *Indian J. Pure Appl. Phys.*, 58, 478–485, June 2020.

113. Soniya, Singh, S., Wadhwa, G., Raj, B., Design and Analysis of Dual Source Vertical Tunnel Field Effect Transistor for High Performance. *Trans. Electr. Electron. Mater.*, Springer, 21, 74–82, Oct 2019.
114. Kaur, M., Gupta, N., Kumar, S., Raj, B., Singh, A.K., RF Performance Analysis of Intercalated Graphene Nanoribbon Based Global Level Interconnects. *J. Comput. Electron.*, Springer, 19, 1002–1013, June 2020.
115. Wadhwa, G. and Raj, B., Design and Performance Analysis of Junctionless TFET Biosensor for High Sensitivity. *IEEE Nanotechnol.*, 18, 567–574, 2019.
116. Singh, J. and Raj, B., Enhanced Nonlinear Memristor Model Encapsulating Stochastic Dopant Drift. *J. Nanoelectron. Optoelectron.*, ASP, 14, 958-963, 2019.
117. Kumar, M., Chaudhary, T., Raj, B., Design and Comparative Analysis of Ferroelectric Nanowire with Dielectric HfO_2 and $Al_2O_3$for Low Power Applications. *J. Electron. Mater.*, Springer, 53, 6785–6791, 2024.

2

Machine Learning to Explore Opportunities in Quantum

Jyoti Khandelwal

Department of Computer Science & Engineering, Amity University Rajasthan, Jaipur, India

Abstract

In this era where the world is facing problems related to computing in many fields, machine learning and quantum computing offer promising progress in many fields. The enormous amount of data being generated and the developments in technology may make it difficult for the probabilistic and optimization-based classical machine learning (ML) algorithms to handle real-world challenges. This chapter focuses on machine learning to explore the opportunities in quantum. The Quantum machine learning, which focuses on the intersection of machine learning and quantum computing, is rapidly promoting advancement of data processing. The chapter dives into different sections to cover the different aspects related to the topic. In the beginning, the discussion starts with an understanding of quantum data. The section focuses on difficulties linked to gathering and analyzing the quantum data. The conversation is initially led by several machine-learning models and quality algorithms of quantum machine learning (QML), which provide computation with novel ideas. The foundation of QML is the quantum computing ideas of entanglement and superposition, which are perfectly suited to addressing ML issues in the future. Advances in algorithms and growing processing capacity have made machine learning techniques useful tools for finding patterns in data. It is the creative solution for dealing with quantum challenges. The chapter also focuses on real-life case studies like drug development and many more. These case studies focus on the machine learning effect in data analysis. The discussion about the latest framework is also included for future development. The last sections include the challenges and advantages of possibilities in the quantum realm. The conclusion section shows the expectation that if quantum and machine learning are used together, many areas will benefit.

Email: jyoti.khandelwal19@gmail.com

Ashish Maurya, Mandeep Singh and Balwinder Raj (eds.) Machine Learning in Nanoelectronics: Devices, Circuits and Systems, (43–66) © 2026 Scrivener Publishing LLC

Keywords: Data analysis, frameworks, machine learning, quantum

2.1 Introduction to Quantum Opportunities

To solve the problem faster quantum computing uses advance correlation of computer science, physics, and mathematics. The three advance filed correlation make quantum computing different from classical computers [1, 2]. Not only in software the quantum computing is quickly showing improvement in hardware development also. The effect of superposition and inference make quantum computing more logical and reliable. They make the process faster and quicker for specific problem which is not possible in classical computers [3]; possible applications could include managing investment portfolios in the financial sector or modeling chemical processes, engaging responsibilities well over the current conditions in even the most advanced supercomputers available. Certain areas where quantum computers can offer a significant increase in speed are machine learning (ML), optimization, and modeling physical systems.

It was organic that quantum computation should blend avant-garde interests with another important domain. ML attained massive interest and real-life implementation in the twenty-first century, where both fields profit from each other. ML fundamentally teaches a computer to learn from data, not about direct coding [4]. In the broadest terms, machine learning is technology that allows computers to learn and adapt without direct programming; they are also divided into three general categories, as shown in Figure 2.1.

Recent literature reviews underscore that classical ML models have found wide-ranging entry points into quantum computation [5, 6], other than quantum error correction, quantum communication, quantum cryptography, and translating quantum algorithms to current hardware. While also considering quantum equivalents of the incorporation of quantum principles in their operation is rapid growth of the search area. Additionally, hybrid algorithms that combine quantum and classical computing in the near future have been created to imitate the operating mechanism of ML algorithms to a certain extent. They searched for a global optimum for the cost function but aimed to achieve that *via* the application of quantum computers. The authors gave a comprehensive review of some recent advancements in quantum machine learning in [7–9], and [10].

Figure 2.2 shows the importance of exploring opportunities in quantum through machine learning; let's discuss them one by one. Speed is one of the primary advantages of quantum computing in machine learning.

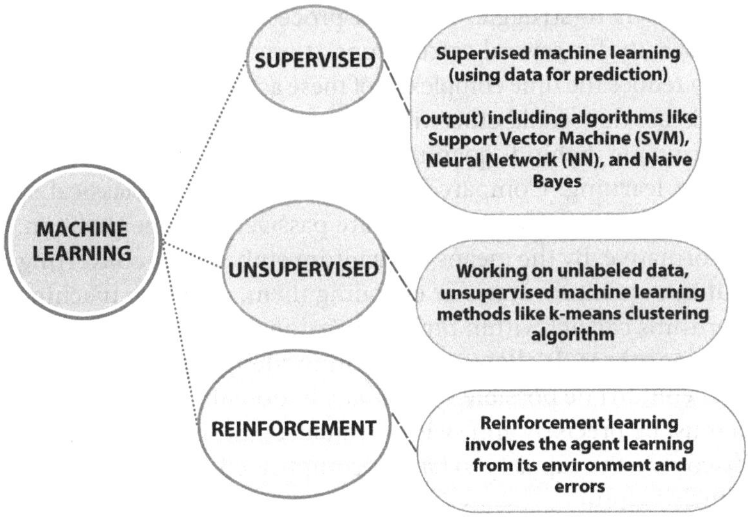

Figure 2.1 Machine learning (ML) and its types.

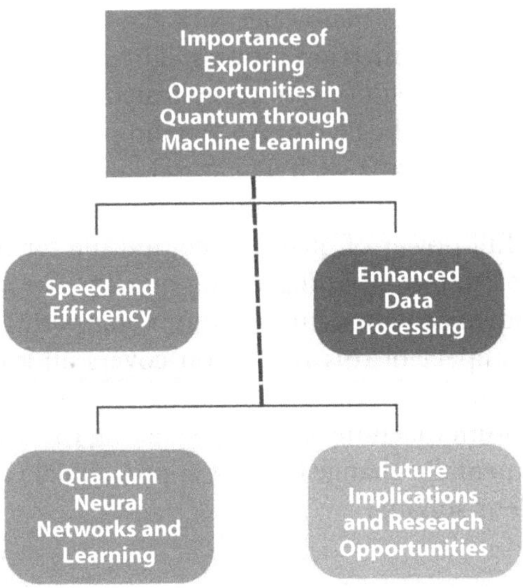

Figure 2.2 Importance of exploring opportunities in quantum through machine learning.

Quantum algorithms, such as the Quantum Principal Component Analysis (QPCA) and Quantum Support Vector Machines (QSVM), have been proven to outperform classical algorithms especially with big data. The limitations of classical hardware typically cause traditional machine learning models to struggle with data processing and optimization. Due to their capacity for several calculations at once, quantum computers can drastically reduce the time complexity of these activities, providing a means of resolving issues that would otherwise be unsolvable for classical systems [11].

The principle behind quantum computing increases the efficiency of machine learning. Compared to classical bits either classical states or quantum level of information qubits are passively in superposition, hence more informative. By the means of quantum embedding, converting classical input into quantum states or encoding them, quantum machine learning algorithms can act within high-dimensional environments rather than classical algorithms. It allows the system to identify patterns and correlations that couldn't be possible within bits. In domains where large volumes of data must be precisely and swiftly evaluated, like genomics, finance, and drug discovery, the capacity to handle complicated, high-dimensional data is extremely helpful.

Without machine learning incorporation inside the quantum computing the learning speed of Quantum Neural Networks (QNNs) will not increase. The combination increases the prediction accuracy of the QNNs. The optimization of neural network can be managed by the quantum algorithms. The optimization process lightens the computing burden and enables the processing of more complicated models. These advancements are very helpful in the field of AI, enabling quicker and more precise decision-making in domains such as natural language processing, image identification, and autonomous systems.

Currently the full power of quantum computing for machine learning has not not explored, but it is progressing quickly. The classical machine learning model advancement using quantum computing is a rich field of exploration. The impact of this revolution covers all kinds of industries ranging from healthcare to cybersecurity. Early learners and researchers benefit from quantum machine learning by taking the lead in innovations that could fundamentally change how we approach data analytics, optimization, and problem-solving.

2.2 Understanding Quantum Data

Quantum data is that which abides through the laws of quantum mechanics *via* the processed by and stored in quantum bits or qubits. Various ways can be applied to represent quantum data: through quantum states, quantum registers, and circuits. The classical data format is almost in binary form-switched on or off, 0s or 1s, but the property of superposition for quantum data refers to existing in more than one state at once: the property is found to break down into quantum data into a much wider field of information. Moreover, quantum data can show entanglement, which is the ability of one qubit's state to be correlated with another's state over large distances. Quantum teleportation and cryptography can entangle quantum data due to this characteristic. Techniques for encoding quantum data are essential for converting classical data into quantum states. These advanced methods cover a range of approaches, each with particular advantages and applications, such as quantum autoencoders, quantum convolutional neural networks, basis encoding, angle encoding, amplitude encoding, and quantum autoencoders. Quantum computation is mainly used to perform computations and secure communication faster than classical computers. These methods also work well in the fields of quantum machine learning, quantum cryptography, and quantum computing itself [12].

Superposition and entanglement are the two main characteristics of quantum information that set it apart from classical information. A small explanation is shown in Figure 2.3.

According to Figure 2.3, in superposition "A qubit is represented by a single circle that has two numbers inside of it, 0 and 1, indicating that the qubit can be in both states simultaneously" [13], and entanglement is "A linked state in which two circles, each representing a qubit, are connected by a line and a change in one affects the other".

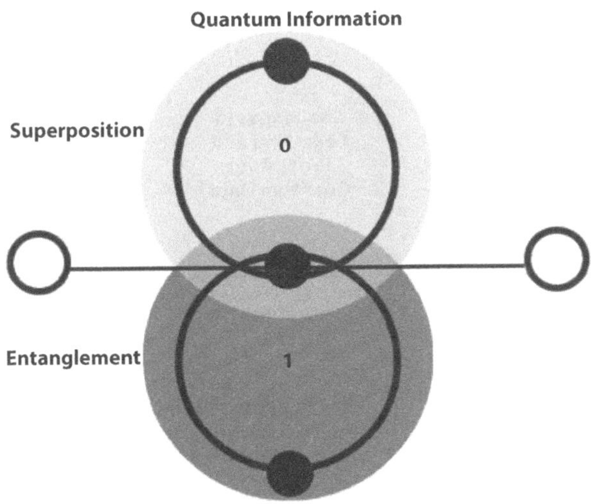

Figure 2.3 Characteristics of quantum information (superposition, entanglement).

Particles like electrons and photons can exist in more than one state at once according to quantum mechanics. The event occurrence a quantum system can concurrently inhabit multiple states is referred to as superposition. A quantum bit, or qubit, has the capacity to exist in any quantum superposition of the classical states of 0 and 1. This characteristic indicates that, in contrast to a classical bit, a qubit can convey a greater amount of information.

When two or more quantum particles become entangled, a phenomenon occurs in which the states of these particles are interconnected, irrespective of the distance separating them. Upon gauging one qubit, the state of the other qubit is immediately determined, as entangled qubits exchange information in this manner. This characteristic is fundamental to the capabilities of quantum computing and facilitates quantum communication protocols, such as quantum.

Because there is very little technology available to collect quantum data, these data are important. A few of the major obstacles are shown in Figure 2.4. Because quantum states (qubits) are brittle, the quantum

Figure 2.4 Challenges in collecting and processing quantum data.

data is extremely susceptible to outside noise. Small variations or disruptions can result in decoherence, which can lead to mistakes or a loss of data integrity. A similar factor that also affects the collection of quantum data is the absence of infrastructure for quantum data. The systems required to gather, store, and handle quantum data are less developed than those used in classical computing, which increases the likelihood of mistakes and inefficiencies in the data pipeline. Compared to classical bits, storing quantum bits is much more difficult. Quantum computing generates enormous volumes of data, necessitating additional processing and specialized algorithms. The main issue with modern technology is data security, since it can be challenging to store data securely due to a lack of qualified personne.

2.3 Machine Learning Techniques for Quantum Applications

The examination and categorization of extensive sets of vectors within multidimensional spaces is a prevalent activity in machine learning (ML). The integration of ML with "big data" denotes a considerable trend on-site, which necessitates a substantial volume and complexity of data. A burgeoning area that merges machine learning with quantum computing is referred to as quantum machine learning, or QML. The core concept of QML is to utilize the intrinsic benefits of quantum computing, including superposition, entanglement, and quantum parallelism, to enhance the effectiveness of conventional machine learning methods [14].

Machine learning models are available in a variety of forms, each appropriate for a particular kind of task. Neural networks are extremely adaptable and potent models that draw inspiration from the architecture of the human brain. Deep learning applications, natural language processing, and image recognition are some of the tasks in which they excel. Decision trees are straightforward but powerful models that are useful for regression and classification applications. They function by dividing the data into subsets according to feature values. Although they offer transparent decision-making processes, they may overfit complex datasets. Other noteworthy models are k-nearest neighbors (k-NN), a straightforward algorithm for classification and regression based on the distance between data points, and support vector machines (SVMs), which maximize the margin between data points and are useful in classification tasks. An ensemble of decision trees called random forests improves generalization and decreases overfitting to give robustness. The fundamental models for binary classification and continuous prediction tasks, respectively, are logistic regression and linear regression, which are frequently utilized for intelligible and effective learning in smaller datasets.

The restricted amount of qubits accessible and the high degree of noise encountered when employing them are two of the main issues that QC encounters. Nonetheless, it is anticipated that the soon-to-be-available Noisy Intermediate-Scale Quantum (NISQ) computers will be able to carry out calculations that demonstrate the intrinsic powers of quantum computers. The number of available qubits and fault tolerance for quantum computers still need to increase. To enhance the efficiency of rethinking conventional approaches, the quantum computing advantage or special qualities are utilized. These advantages are superposition, quantum parallelism, and entanglement; they are very effective when classical algorithms are adapted for quantum settings.

Numerous traditional algorithms, including those for data analysis, machine learning, and optimization, have been modified to take advantage of quantum efficiency and speedups. An overview of applicable machine learning models is presented below.

i. Quantum Neural Networks (QNNs)

Quantum neural networks are computational neural network models that are based on concepts from quantum mechanics. The quantum equivalents of classical neural networks are quantum neural networks, which substitute qubits and quantum gates for classical neurons and weights. They may speed up complex calculations by utilizing two quantum properties: entanglement and superposition. The feed-forward architecture is used in most quantum neural networks. This structure takes input from one layer of qubits and sends it to another layer of qubits, just like their classical counterparts. This layer's qubits evaluate the data and send the findings to the layer below. The final layer of qubits is where the journey finally ends [15]. One of the foundational equations representing the structure of a QNN can be formulated as follows:

$$|\psi_{out}\rangle = U_{out}(U_L \cdots U_2 U_1 |\psi_{in}\rangle) \tag{2.1}$$

Quantum state is represented by Ψ_{in}, this is input data state it is encoded into qubits. Unitary transformations (quantum gates) represent by $U_L \cdots U_2 U_1$. U_{out} is the final quantum operation applied before the output measurement, and ψ_{out} is the resulting quantum state after passing through the QNN.

ii. Quantum Support Vector Machines (QSVMs)

Two distinct aspects of the classical method are the focus of the Quantum Support Vector Machine (QSVM). The goal of gate-based computation is to find a useful kernel for the high-dimensional Hilbert space by taking advantage of quantum properties. Conversely, the annealing model concentrates on optimization subsequent to the kernel matrix computation. These two elements of the Support Vector Machine model are distinct yet work well together. When used appropriately, the combination of these methods offers benefits over the classical approach as well as individual methods. A classical support vector machine's fundamental formula is:

$$f(x) = sign(\sum_{i=1}^{n} \alpha_i y_i K(x_i, x) + b)) \tag{2.2}$$

Where, x is the input data point to be classified, x_i are the support vectors, α_i are the Lagrange multipliers obtained during training, y_i are the labels of the support vectors (+1 or −1), $K(x_i, x)$ is the kernel function, which maps the input into a higher-dimensional space, and b is the bias term.

iii. Quantum k-Means Clustering

Using quantum scaling and parallelism Quantum chemistry clustering algorithms take advantage of quantum computation to complete clustering faster and with less frequency [16]. While the objective of quantum k-means clustering is still to minimize intra-cluster variance, quantum computing is employed to expedite distance calculations and assignments. The assignment step's optimization and the distances' computation are where the main differences lie. In particular, quantum k-Means makes use of quantum amplitude amplification and quantum distance estimation. Using a quantum distance estimator, the distance calculation for allocating points to clusters in the quantum version of the algorithm can be carried out as follows:

$$|| x_j - \mu_i || = \sqrt{\langle\phi(x_j) | \phi(x_j)\rangle + \langle\phi(\mu_i) | \phi(\mu_i)\rangle - 2\langle\phi(x_j) | \phi(\mu_i)\rangle} \tag{2.3}$$

$\phi(x_j)$ and $\phi(\mu_i)$ are the quantum state representations of the data point x_j, and the cluster centroid μ_i, respectively. $\langle\phi(x_j)|\phi(x_j)\rangle$ is the norm of the quantum state representing x_j. $\langle\phi(x_j)|\phi(\mu_i)\rangle$ is the inner product between the quantum states corresponding to the data point x_j and the centroid μ_i. Applications include pattern recognition, customer segmentation, and data clustering.

iv. Quantum Principal Component Analysis (QPCA)

Principal component analysis has a quantum counterpart called QPCA, which is used to reduce the dimensionality of quantum data while maintaining important features [17]. Quantum algorithms, which more effectively analyze quantum states, are used for this. Positive semi-definite Hermitian matrices can be analyzed using principal component analysis (PCA), which divides numbers into eigenvectors corresponding to the largest eigenvalues. A common method for analyzing the covariance matrix of sampled vectors is principal component analysis. In classical PCA, the goal is to solve the following eigenvalue problem for the covariance matrix C:

$$C_{vi} = \lambda i_{vi} \tag{2.4}$$

Where:

$C = \frac{1}{n}\sum_{i=1}^{n} x_i x_i^T$ is the covariance matrix of the data. x_i are the data points, v_i are the eigenvectors (principal components), and λ_i are the eigenvalues that represent the variance explained by each principal component.

The covariance matrix in QPCA is represented as a quantum density matrix ρ, from which the eigenvalues and eigenvectors are extracted using quantum algorithms. The definition of the quantum density matrix QD ρ is:

$$\rho = \frac{1}{n}\sum_{i=1}^{n} |\Psi_i\rangle \langle\Psi_i| \tag{2.5}$$

Where, |ψ_i⟩ are quantum states representing the data points x_i. The covariance matrix C is replaced by the quantum density matrix ρ.

Quantum principal component analysis, or QPCA, on quantum datasets is commonly used to extract features. Noise reduction and dimensionality reduction reduce computational complexity and make it possible to identify important features. QPCA's quantum advantage is one of its main advantages. It greatly speeds up the process of identifying key components of large data sets. Under certain circumstances, QPCA offers exponential performance improvements over classical PCA due to quantum-improved performance. This makes it ideal for processing high-dimensional data and complex quantum states.

v. Quantum Boltzmann Machines (QBMs)

Quantum version of the classical Boltzmann machine Quantum Boltzmann machines are widely used in unsupervised learning, using concepts such as superposition and entanglement. Quantum Boltzmann machines (QBM) fuse quantum computation with statistical mechanics to improve neural network optimization [18]. Compared to classical models, QBM provides exponential speed by navigating large solution spaces simultaneously, so it works well in distribution modeling and data generation. Understanding quantum mechanics and the application of Boltzmann distribution analysis is essential to understanding QBM in quantum computing. Computational power increases with the power of qubits. Adopting QBM could lead to revolutionary developments in various industries.

For tasks like data generation or probability distribution learning, QBMs can be implemented using quantum annealing (used by machines like D-Wave) or quantum gates. For classical Boltzmann machines, the system is described by an energy function:

$$E(v,h) = -v^T\, Wh - b^T v - c^T h \tag{2.6}$$

Where, v represent visible layer, h represent hidden layer and W, b, c are the weights and biases. The energy function for a quantum Boltzmann machine includes the Hamiltonian H, which describes the system's total energy:

$$H = H_{visible} + H_{hidden} + H_{interactions} \tag{2.7}$$

The quantum "states" of the exposed and hidden layers, as well as their interactions, are described in each section. QBMs also incorporate superposition and entanglement to power through complex problems faster.

The Boltzmann distribution then provides the probability distribution over the states:

$$P(v,h) = \frac{e^{-E(v,h)}}{Z} \tag{2.8}$$

Z is the partition function, which normalizes the distribution. In other words, QBMs use quantum magic to help solve problems that classical methods might find difficult.

Applications of quantum Boltzmann machines (QBM) include modeling probability distributions, data creation and optimization problems. By facilitating the optimization of large and complex systems to be more effective, and accelerating convergence to the optimal state compared with classical methods, they provide a quantum advantage.

vi. Quantum Reinforcement Learning (QRL)

In quantum learning with reinforcement there are two types of interaction processes in the same interaction-based learning process: classical and quantum. Interaction between classical objects primarily comprises interactions between the interaction process between classical intelligence and quantitative intelligence, as well as the interaction process between classical intelligence and the quantitative task environment; this comprises the classical interaction. The interaction between the quantumized intelligent body and the classical task environment complements the classical interaction. Quantum states and quantum feedback mechanisms are used in quantum reinforcement learning to accelerate learning processes. Interacting with a quantum environment helps the agent learn. The update rule for quantum reinforcement learning based on classical Q-learning:

$$Q(s,a) \leftarrow Q(s,a) + \alpha\,[r + \gamma\ amax\, Q(s',a) - Q(s,a)] \tag{2.9}$$

Where, $Q(s,a)$ is the Q-value (expected utility) of taking action a in state s, α is the learning rate, r is the reward received, γ is the discount factor for future rewards, s$'$ is the next state, and $max_a Q(s',a)$ is the maximum Q-value over all possible actions in state s'.

This formula is extended in Quantum Reinforcement Learning with the use of quantum states and operators. Quantum superpositions of states can be utilized to express Q-values, and quantum circuits can be employed for both reward computation and Q-value updating. Applications for

Quantum Reinforcement Learning (QRL) can be found in robotics, optimization tasks, and game AI (like AlphaGo). It provides a quantum advantage by using quantum superposition and entanglement to improve decision-making and problem-solving skills. It may result in faster learning and more efficient exploration of the operating space.

vii. Quantum Variational Algorithms

Because of the extremely high computational cost, applications like simulating complex quantum systems or solving large-scale linear algebra problems are very difficult for classical computers. While fault-tolerant quantum computers are unlikely to be accessible anytime soon, quantum computers offer a potential solution. Existing quantum devices suffer from severe limitations, such as low qubit counts and noise processes that reduce circuit depth. A promising approach to overcome these limitations is variational quantum algorithms (VQAs), which train a parameterized quantum circuit using a classical optimizer. Virtual quantum advantages (VQAs) seem to be the best hope for gaining quantum advantage, and they have now been proposed for almost all applications that researchers have imagined for quantum computers. However, there are still issues, such as the trainability, accuracy, and effectiveness of VQAs. This is the hybrid quantum-classical algorithm in which the best solutions are found by a classical optimizer modifying the quantum circuit parameters. By using quantum circuits that are parameterized by classical variables, quantum variational algorithms, or QVAs, fuse quantum computation and classical optimization techniques. The main idea is to prepare a quantum state, measure the result, and use classical algorithms to optimize a cost function using a parameterized quantum circuit. Equation (2.10) shows the essential equation for Quantum Variational Algorithms, where the general objective is to **minimize** a cost function $C(\theta)$, where θ represents the parameters of the quantum circuit.

$$C(\theta) = \langle \Psi\ (\theta)|H|\Psi(\theta)\rangle \tag{2.10}$$

Where, $|\psi(\theta)\rangle$ is the parameterized quantum state, prepared by applying a sequence of quantum gates depending on the classical parameters θ, H is the problem's Hamiltonian (which represents the cost or energy to minimize), and $\langle\psi(\theta)|H|\psi(\theta)\rangle$ is the **expectation value** of the Hamiltonian [19], representing the cost function value for a given set of parameters θ.

The traditional optimization loop minimizes $C(\theta)$ by modifying the parameters θ. The iterations of this hybrid quantum-classical approach are as follows:

a. **Quantum Phase:** A quantum computer prepares the state $|\psi(\theta)\rangle|$ using a parameterized circuit and measures the Hamiltonian H.
b. **Classical Phase:** A classical optimizer updates the parameters θ to reduce the cost function $C(\theta)$.

Applications for Quantum Variational Algorithms (QVAs) include combinatorial optimization, quantum chemistry, and machine learning tasks like classification and clustering. By utilizing quantum computation to explore solution spaces more quickly and effectively, they may be able to solve complex optimization problems more effectively than classical algorithms, giving them a quantum advantage.

viii. Quantum-Enhanced Generative Models

To enhance tasks like data generation, learning complex distributions, and modeling, quantum-enhanced generative models integrate quantum computing with classical generative models. Compared to classical approaches, these models can more effectively explore more complex probability distributions by utilizing quantum concepts like superposition and entanglement.

For unsupervised machine learning, generative modeling with samples taken from the probability distribution is a potent method. Probability distributions exhibiting quantum correlations, which are challenging to represent with classical models, can be generated by quantum mechanical systems. In the quantum domain, generative models such as autoencoders and generative adversarial networks (GANs) are being investigated. These models' quantum iterations, such as quantum GANs and autoencoders, can use quantum properties to produce new data points and data distributions. The probability distribution $P(x)$ generated by the quantum-enhanced model can be represented as:

$$P(x) = |\langle x | \psi(\theta)\rangle|^2 \tag{2.11}$$

Where $|\psi(\theta)\rangle$ a quantum state is parameterized by classical variables θ, $|x\rangle$ is a basis state representing a classical data point, $\langle x | \psi(\theta)\rangle$ is the amplitude of the quantum state for the data point x, and $|\langle x|\psi(\theta)\rangle|^2$ gives the probability of generating the data point x.

In order to minimize a cost function (such as a loss function that measures the difference between the generated distribution and the target distribution), the model is trained by varying the parameters θ. The aim is:

$$\theta min\ D(Pdata(x)\,||\,P\theta(x)) \tag{2.12}$$

Where $Pdata(x)$ is the target data distribution, Pθ(x) is the quantum-enhanced model's distribution, D(·||·) represents a distance or divergence metric (e.g., Kullback-Leibler divergence) between the distributions.

Applications for quantum-enhanced generative models include anomaly detection, data augmentation, and image generation. By leveraging quantum-enhanced learning capabilities to efficiently model complex distributions and produce more realistic data samples compared to classical methods, they offer a quantum advantage in the handling of high-dimensional data.

2.4 Case Studies and Applications

i. Real-World Applications of Machine Learning in Quantum Computing

There are many examples; those are proofs that the practical application of a combination of machine learning and quantum computing has a trending approach. Quantum algorithms, such as the Quantum Approximate Optimization Algorithm (QAOA), is one of the main areas where machine learning techniques can be used in solving quantum optimization problems. In this approach, quantum superposition and entanglement explore the large solution spaces more efficiently as compared to the classical algorithms. The optimization is applied in many areas like operations research, logistics, and finance. In this area, the combination of quantum computing and machine learning outperforms conventional approaches in terms of amount of time and result accuracy.

Drug discovery is the interesting field where researchers are frequently using QML and ML. By using the feature of quantum computing, we can comprehend drug behaviors and interactions with unprecedented accuracy and simulate molecular interaction at a quantum level. The improved efficiency accelerated the identification of potential drug candidates, ultimately leading to more effective treatments.

The special capabilities of quantum computing in quantum-enhanced data analysis are the most advanced and most famous field. The advancement of quantum computing helps quantum parallelism; quantum machine learning algorithms can perform better in terms of regression, classification, and clustering as compared to classical computers. In this process, the data is analyzed in many factors, and better insights are forecast from complicated data, which helps industries like marketing, healthcare, and finance.

The discussed applications show that machine learning and quantum computing combinations have a great effect on opening up new possibilities for creative solutions across a range of industries.

ii. Success Stories from Industry and Academia

The combination of machine learning and quantum computing have created many remarkable success stories in recent years, not only in academia also in the growing industries. These achievements demonstrate how quantum technologies have the potential to revolutionize a number of industries.

a. **IBM and Quantum Optimization:** The IBM quantum platform was constructed to provide the expertise of a quantum processor for a range of optimization problems. The focus of the IBM quantum platform is to make substantial advancements in the field of quantum optimization. To cover all the required areas like logistics, finance, and supply chain, IBM collaborates with different companies so that optimization can be possible in every field. The best example to showcase the quantum computing impact in production and cost cutting is illustrated by IBM collaboration with the auto sector. As an outcome, an optimized schedule of production is generated.
b. **Google's Quantum Chemistry Research:** In the area of materials science and drug discovery, Google's Quantum AI lab has demonstrated the promise of quantum computing. This is achieved by molecular system simulation using quantum computing. To understand the contribution of hydrogen molecule (H2), quantum simulation is one example that they used to show that quantum computers could accurately

simulate chemical reactions more than classical computers. After this experiment, many doors are open for efficient drug discovery procedures. The process involves facilitating the quantum modeling of intricate biological processes.

c. **Rigetti Computing and Quantum Machine Learning:** Rigetti Computing is focused on machine learning application development using quantum algorithms. To explore the quantum machine learning techniques, a forest platform is introduced for the researchers. Many academic institutes collaborate with Rigetti Computing to implement and test their quantum algorithms to achieve good results in fields like clustering and classification and the feasibility of quantum enhanced learning in practical scenarios using demonstration.
d. **D-Wave's Quantum Annealing for Optimization:** D-Wave is another system that invented the technology of quantum annealing to resolve the optimization issues. The focus of D-Wave systems is to work with Google and NASA. These companies used quantum systems to resolve the practical problems. The application of D-waves can be seen in optimizing the traffic flow in urban environments and also for solving the logistical issues using quantum solutions in urban settings.
e. **University of Waterloo and Quantum Drug Discovery:** In the drug discovery field, pharmaceutical companies and the University of Waterloo's Institute for Quantum Computing (IQC) collaborate to conduct research in this field. The work is focused on applying quantum simulations to forecast the behavior and interactions of molecules. The quantum computing greatly speeds up the drug development process under this process. The commencement of this collaboration makes it clear that academic research promotion shows the great impact in the healthcare industry.

The success stories show the effect of machine learning and quantum computing in a variety of domains. The advance technologies can result in effective solutions and important breakthroughs in both business and academia.

2.5 Tools and Frameworks for Implementation

i. Overview of Quantum Computing Platforms

The IBM Quantum Platform, previously known as IBM Quantum Experience, is a web-based platform that provides both the general public and premium users with access to IBM's cloud-based quantum computing services [20]. This platform features an interactive textbook, a collection of tutorials on quantum computation, and a selection of IBM's prototype quantum processors. As of February 2021, six out of more than twenty devices available on the platform are accessible to the general public. Users can utilize this service to conduct experiments, execute algorithms, and engage with tutorials and simulations that explore the potential applications of quantum computing. Superconducting transmon qubits, located within dilution refrigerators at IBM Research's Thomas J. Watson Research Center, serve as the fundamental components of the company's quantum processors. Users interact with a quantum processor through the quantum circuit model of computation. The Quantum Composer facilitates the graphical design of circuits, whereas the Quantum Lab's Jupyter notebooks enable the programmatic development of circuits. Qiskit is employed to construct these circuits, which can subsequently be compiled into OpenQASM for implementation on real quantum systems.

The initial team to showcase capabilities beyond classical computation was Google Quantum AI in 2019, when they published findings from an experiment on random circuit sampling that could not be feasibly replicated on a classical computer. In 2023, this team achieved a significant milestone by being the first globally to report on scalable quantum error correction, demonstrating through experimental evidence that increasing the number of qubits can effectively reduce errors. Achieving these two milestones is crucial for the advancement of a large-scale error-corrected quantum computer. To support this collaboration, we are providing access to these state-of-the-art quantum processors—featuring up to 72 superconducting qubits and error rates of 0.001 and 0.003 for 1-qubit and 2-qubit gates, respectively, operating simultaneously—to researchers at the University of Chicago and the University of Tokyo.

ii. Popular Libraries and Frameworks for QML

Qiskit is an open-source software development kit (SDK) designed for interaction with quantum computers at various levels, including circuit, pulse, and algorithmic. It provides a suite of tools for creating and altering quantum programs, which can subsequently be executed on simulators on personal computers or on prototype quantum devices available through the IBM Quantum Platform. This SDK is compatible with any quantum hardware that follows the circuit model for universal quantum computation, currently supporting superconducting qubits and trapped ions. Qiskit was developed by IBM Research to enhance software development for the IBM Quantum Experience, a cloud-based quantum computing service. Outside sponsors also contribute, usually from educational institutions. Python is the major programming language used in Qiskit. Although work on the JavaScript and Swift versions has stopped, they were originally investigated. Alternatively, MicroQiskit is a small re-implementation of basic functionalities that can be easily ported to other platforms. The components of Qiskit cooperate to allow quantum computing. Regardless of experience level or area of interest, the main objective of Qiskit is to create a software stack that makes using quantum computers simpler for everyone. Users may create experiments and applications with Qiskit, and they can run them on actual quantum computers or conventional simulators. With Qiskit, one may create quantum software at both the OpenQASM machine code level and abstract levels that are appropriate for end users who are not familiar with quantum computing. The following elements give this feature.

TensorFlow Quantum (TFQ), a quantum machine learning package allows for the rapid development of hybrid quantum classical ML models. Researchers studying quantum algorithms and applications within TensorFlow can take advantage of Google's quantum computing framework. The focus of TensorFlow Quantum is on quant modeling. Hybrid classical tum and quantum information with a high-performance quantum circuit simulator it combines Cirq-generated logic and quantum computing techniques. It also provides classical quantum processing that is compatible with today's TensorFlow APIs.

iii. Step-by-Step Guide to Building a Simple QML Model

Building and testing the structured model follows a series of stages that are necessary to comprehend quantum machine learning (QML). Here is a straightforward example of utilizing QML to solve the binary classification problem. The quantum bureau network (QNN) in the example structure uses the PennyLane package to train and assess the model using a fictitious dataset.

The example shows how typical machine learning concepts, like data preparation and optimization, can be integrated with quantum computing concepts to construct a QML model. Quantum circuits, quantum layers, employing classical optimizers to minimize a loss function, and assessing the model's performance on a binary classification problem are the main areas of attention. Figure 2.5 provides a step-by-step tutorial for creating a basic QML model for a binary classification scenario.

Figure 2.5 shows the process of using PennyLane to develop a basic quantum machine learning (QML) model with the goal of addressing binary classification challenges. The initial phase of modeling is setting up the desired environment, which includes Python, PennyLane, and other dependencies. Once the environment is set up, the libraries required for quantum computing and data manipulation, including scikit-learn, NumPy, and PennyLane, are imported. Next, a quantum circuit is designed using qubits to transform classical data into is a quantum state which are then processed through changeable layers with customizable parameters. The dataset is normalized and divided into training and testing subsets with the help of scikit-learn. A quantum neural network (QNN) model is established to perform the classification task. It uses a quantum circuit with adjustable weights. The model is trained using a classical optimizer such as Adam to minimize the loss function over multiple epochs. After the training process, the performance and accuracy of the model on unseen data will be evaluated [21]. Decision boundaries can be displayed to show how the QML model classifies data into specific categories. This example combines the principles of quantum computing with classical optimization. It provides a basic overview of how to integrate quantum circuits into machine learning applications.

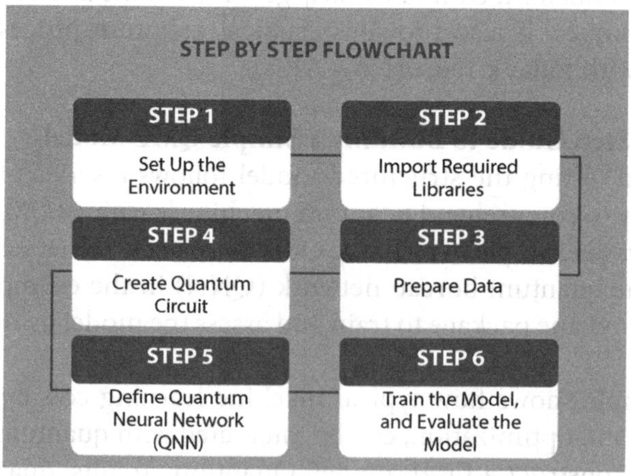

Figure 2.5 Steps to build a quantum machine learning (QML) model.

2.6 Challenges and Opportunities in QML

To build a QML model there are some prior needs to integrate, like the choice of parameterized model, loss function, and classical optimizer. The implementation of QML comes with several technical challenges due to the current state of quantum technology and the complexity of the quantum-classical models [22]. Some primary challenges are quantum noise, error correction, vanishing gradients, parameter initialization, data representation, scaling, qubit cout, short coherence times, communication latency, optimization, overfitting, lack of large quantum datasets, algorithm development, benchmarking, quantum circuit depth, gate fidelity, development tools, hardware specificity, scalability, practicality, and gradient-based training. In conclusion, even though QML has a lot of potential to solve issues that are unsolvable for classical systems, a number of technical issues still need to be resolved, from scalability and real-world applicability to hardware constraints and algorithmic complexity.

There are many challenges still, but QML presents significant opportunities across various domains. Here are some of the key opportunities in QML: quantum speedup for machine learning, it solves complex optimization problems, enhances feature space representation, improves neural network models, provides new machine learning architectures, works for applications like drug discovery and material sciences, enhances security and cryptography, better handling of high-dimensional data, speeding up reinforcement learning, artificial intelligence in quantum simulations, quantum data generation, innovation in cloud-based quantum computing, reducing resource consumption, and expanding research in quantum AI.

2.7 Conclusion

Quantum computing uses the features of quantum mechanics, including entanglement, superposition, and interference, to process information. Thus, machine learning (ML) and quantum computing are combined to improve on traditional algorithms. The foundation of data mining, the intricate process of gleaning valuable information from massive amounts of data, is learning models. A machine learning model should be able to generalize much beyond a small training set. Convexity criteria or heuristics limit our ability to control computing time on classical computers. We can achieve greater generalization efficiency because quantum computers do not encounter these problems in optimization problems.

Because classic computers are better at everything else, different formats are therefore likely to win. This chapter highlights the enormous potential of quantum machine learning (QML) and its potential to revolutionize classical machine learning. The first topic is quantum information and how it can be used to solve problems that are beyond the scope of classical thinking. Quantum Neural Networks (QNN), Quantum Support Vector Machines (QSVM), Quantum k-Means Clustering, Quantum Principal Component Analysis (QPCA) and Quantum Boltzmann Machines (QBM) are among the machine learning approaches for quantum applications examined. In addition, generative models Quantum-enhanced and quantum reinforcement learning (QRL) have also been highlighted as potential areas of innovation. This chapter presents case studies that demonstrate successful applications of QML in academia and business. It also provides an overview of quantum platforms and libraries. It covers key frameworks and tools and provides step-by-step instructions for building a basic QML model. Although QML faces hardware limitations and algorithmic complexity, many of them were able to overcome these limitations and make progress in various fields. There are also good prospects.

References

1. Dange, B.J., Gaikwad, K.M., Khodke, H.E., Gore, S., Gunjal, S.N., Kadam, K., Karmode, S., Machine learning for quantum computing bridging the gap between AI and quantum algorithms. *Int. J. Intell. Syst. Appl. Eng.*, 12, 21s, 600–605, 2024.
2. Valavanidis, A., Quantum computing: A revolutionary computing capability to sift through huge numbers of possibilities and extract potential solutions to complex problems, Jan. 2024, https://www.researchgate.net/publication/377416159_Quantum_Computing_A_revolutionary_computing_capability_to_sift_through_huge_numbers_of_possibilities_and_extract_potential_solutions_to_complex_problems.
3. Casati, G. and Benenti, G., Quantum computation and chaos, in: *Encyclopedia of Condensed Matter Physics*, F. Bassani, G.L. Liedl, P. Wyder (Eds.), pp. 9–17, Elsevier, Oxford, 2005.
4. Bhoumik, D., Sur-Kolay, S., Kumar, L.K.J., Iyengar, S.S., Synergy of machine learning with quantum computing and communication, *arXiv preprint arXiv:2310.03434*, Oct. 2023.
5. Ciliberto, C., Herbster, M., Ialongo, A.D., Pontil, M., Rocchetto, A., Severini, S., Wossnig, L., Quantum machine learning: A classical perspective. *Proc. R. Soc. A*, 474, 20170551, 2018.

6. Krizhevsky, A., Sutskever, I., Hinton, G.E., Imagenet classification with deep convolutional neural networks, in: *Advances in Neural Information Processing Systems*, F. Pereira, C.J.C. Burges, L. Bottou, K.Q. Weinberger (Eds.), pp. 1097–1105, Curran Associates, Inc., Red Hook, NY, 2012.
7. Houssein, E.H. and Abohashima, Z., Machine learning in the quantum realm: The state-of-the-art, challenges, and future vision. *Expert Syst. Appl.*, 116512, 2022.
8. Zeguendry, A., Jarir, Z., Quafafou, M., Quantum machine learning: A review and case studies. *Entropy*, 25, 2, 287, 2023.
9. Cerezo, M. and Verdon, G., Challenges and opportunities in quantum machine learning. *Nat. Comput. Sci.*, 2, 9, 567–576, 2022.
10. García, D.P. and Cruz-Benito, J., Systematic literature review: Quantum machine learning and its applications, *arXiv preprint arXiv:2201.04093*, 2022.
11. Biamonte, J., Wittek, P., Pancotti, N., Rebentrost, P., Wiebe, N., Lloyd, S., Quantum machine learning. *Nature*, 549, 7671, 195–202, 2017.
12. Rath, M. and Date, H., Quantum data encoding: A comparative analysis of classical-to-quantum mapping techniques and their impact on machine learning accuracy, *arXiv preprint arXiv:2311.10375*, 2023.
13. Liu, D., Principles and characteristics of quantum computing. *J. Phys. Conf. Ser., 2014*, 012012, The 10th International Conference on Engineering Mathematics and Physics, Barcelona, Spain, July 1-4, 2021.
14. Ramezani, S.B., Sommers, A., Manchukonda, H.K., Rahimi, S., Amirlatifi, A., Machine learning algorithms in quantum computing: A survey. *2020 International Joint Conference on Neural Networks (IJCNN)*, Glasgow, UK, pp. 1–8, 2020.
15. Beer, K., Bondarenko, D., Farrelly, T., Osborne, T.J., Salzmann, R., Scheiermann, D., Wolf, R., Training deep quantum neural networks. *Nat. Commun.*, 11, 1, 808, Feb. 2020.
16. Karthikeyan, S., Akila, M., Sumathi, D., Poongodi, T., *Quantum Machine Learning: A Modern Approach*, 1st ed., Chapman and Hall/CRC, 2024, [Online]. Available: https://doi.org/10.1201/9781003429654.
17. Bhattacharyya, S., Pan, I., Mani, A., De, S., Behrman, E., Chakraborti, S., *Quantum Machine Learning*, vol. 6, De Gruyter Frontiers in Computational Intelligence, De Gruyter, 2020, [Online]. Available: https://doi.org/10.1515/9783110670707.
18. Khang, A. and Rath, K.C. (Eds.), *The Quantum Evolution: Application of AI and Robotics in the Future of Quantum Technology*, 1st ed., CRC Press, 2024, [Online]. Available: https://doi.org/10.1201/9781032642079.
19. Au-Yeung, R., Camino, B., Rathore, O., Kendon, V., Quantum algorithms for scientific computing, arXiv, 2024, [Online]. Available: https://arxiv.org/abs/2312.14904.
20. AbuGhanem, M., IBM Quantum Computers: Evolution, Performance, and Future Directions, arXiv, 2024, [Online]. Available: https://arxiv.org/abs/2410.00916.

21. Ishaq, M.M., Haq, I.U., Gamal, A., Decentralized quantum machine learning: distributed quantum computing for enhanced learning, in: *Quantum Machine Learning: Quantum Algorithms and Neural Networks*, P. Raj, H.H. Song, D.-N. Le, N. Vyas (Eds.), pp. 149–170, De Gruyter, Berlin, Boston, 2024, [Online]. Available: https://doi.org/10.1515/9783111342276-008.
22. Barreto, A.G., Fanchini, F.F., Papa, J.P., de Albuquerque, V.H.C., Why consider quantum instead of classical pattern recognition techniques? *Appl. Soft Comput.*, 165, 112096, 2024, [Online]. Available: https://doi.org/10.1016/j.asoc.2024.112096.

3

Machine Learning (ML) and Nanotechnology to Heal Cancer: A Review

Anshu Srivastava[1*] and Shakun Srivastava[2]

[1]*Applied Science and Humanities Department, Kanpur Institute of Technology, Kanpur, India*
[2]*Mechanical Engineering Department, Pranveer Singh Institute of Technology, Kanpur, India*

Abstract
The logical designs of individual and remedial platforms, as well as the investigation of their relationship, are exceedingly delicate due to substantial intratumor and interpatient heterogeneity. By utilizing pattern analysis and bracket algorithms for improved individual and remedial delicacy, the integration of AI techniques can close this gap. AI's ability to optimize material packets in accordance with predicted relationships with the target medication, natural fluids, susceptible systems, vasculature, and cell membranes—all of which affect restorative efficacy—benefits nanomedicine design as well. Next, abiotic generalizations in AI are discussed, along with the benefits and promise of combining nanotechnology with AI to create the ultimate cancer treatment in the future.

One promising area for transforming the early detection and surgical treatment of stomach tumors is nanotechnology. Drug inefficacy and high rates of recurrence from surgical and pharmaceutical therapy are the main factors affecting curative efficacy in GIC patients. Nanotechnology is an emerging and cutting-edge field of research due to its unique optical properties, excellent biocompatibility, surface effects, and small-size effects, making it ideal for cancer detection and treatment. Given the drawbacks of GIC MRI and endoscopy as well as the difficulty of gastric surgery, nanotechnology has shown promise in the early detection and timely treatment of stomach disorders. Nanoparticles target tumor cells directly, permitting their identification and elimination. Additionally, it can be designed to deliver particular payloads, such as medications or contrast chemicals, to increase the precision and efficacy of cancer therapy.

**Corresponding author*: as@kit.ac.in

Ashish Maurya, Mandeep Singh and Balwinder Raj (eds.) Machine Learning in Nanoelectronics: Devices, Circuits and Systems, (67–88) © 2026 Scrivener Publishing LLC

This work used XGBoost and RNN-CNN as a classification approach, utilizing the boosting methodology of machine learning to capture nonlinear interactions between a large number of input variables and outputs. The research sample consisted of 348 patients—199 men and 149 women. The mean age of the patients was 50.34 ± 13.04, and their mean ± SD was 50.35 ± 13.03. High-risk actions ($P = 0.072$), time of diagnosis the age ($P = 0.033$), obscure metastases ($P = 0.0039$), and tumor period ($P = 0.0135$) were all statistically significantly correlated with GC patient survival. When examining stomach photos, the AUC was 93.54%, Accuracy was 93.54%, F1-score was 93.57%, Precision was 93.65%, and Recall was 93.87%. Combining cutting-edge machine learning methods with nanotechnology has the potential to improve stomach cancer diagnosis and therapy, opening up new possibilities for precision medicine and improving patient outcomes. Recent years have witnessed tremendous progress in cancer treatment, and combining machine learning with nanotechnology has emerged as a promising new strategy to enhance treatment results. This study investigates how platforms based on nanotechnology and machine learning might work together to improve cancer treatment. Additionally, a conceptual framework for enhanced photothermal therapy combining data mining and gold nanoparticles (AuNPs) is proposed in the paper. Combining cutting-edge machine learning methods with nanotechnology has the potential to improve stomach cancer diagnosis and therapy, opening up new possibilities for precision medicine and improving patient outcomes. Recent years have witnessed tremendous progress in cancer treatment, and combining machine learning with nanotechnology has emerged as a promising new strategy to enhance treatment results.

This study investigates how platforms based on nanotechnology and machine learning might work together to improve cancer treatment. Additionally, a conceptual framework for enhanced photothermal therapy combining data mining and gold nanoparticles (AuNPs) is proposed in the paper. Additionally, this approach helps to close the gap between clinical applications and scientific research. Predictive modeling for treatment responses, improved drug delivery efficiency, early detection techniques, and individualized treatment approaches are just a few benefits of combining machine learning and nanotechnology to improve cancer treatments. This study examines the latest developments, difficulties, and potential paths in utilizing machine learning and nanotechnology to enhance cancer treatment and enhance patient outcomes. Additionally, this approach helps to close the gap between clinical applications and scientific research. Predictive modeling for treatment responses, improved drug delivery efficiency, early detection techniques, and individualized treatment approaches are just a few benefits of combining machine learning and nanotechnology to improve cancer treatments. This study focuses on the latest developments and difficulties. It explores possible avenues for improving cancer treatment and patient end result through the application of nanotechnology and machine learning.

***Keywords*:** Cancer therapy, machine learning, nanotechnology

3.1 Introduction

Over the last few years advances in machine learning (ML) and nanotechnology was utilized in a wide range of sectors and businesses, leading to improvements in human lives. This is especially important for the healthcare industry, one of the sectors with quickest growth with the most advanced transformations [1–7].

Computational learning and nanotechnology have collaborated to prevent the spread of viruses such as COVID-19. Predictive and prognostic cancer has been treated by machine learning recently. The reason this latter approach is so exciting is that it falls under the growing umbrella of personalized and predictive medicine. In order to compile this study, we thoroughly examined the many machine learning approaches in use, the types of data being merged and how well these techniques work to detect and diagnose cancer [8–15]. Numerous trends emerge, including an increased dependence on protein biomarkers and microarray data, a strong preference for applications related to prostate and breast cancer, and a significant reliance on "older" technologies like artificial neural network (ANNs) in place of machine learning techniques that are more accessible or modern. A case-specific complaint profile is assembled using individual nonmaterials, and it is also used, using a suite of remedial nanotechnologies, to improve the outcome of treatment [16–24].

3.2 Predictive Modelling and Machine Learning's Application in Cancer Diagnostics

Personalized medicine, treatment planning, and cancer detection depend heavily on machine learning algorithms, data analysis, and predictive modelling. They make the following contributions to each of these areas.

3.2.1 Diagnosis of Cancer

It is possible to utilize machine learning techniques to evaluate medical imaging data, such as CT, MRI, and mammograms, in order to find any abnormalities or patterns that would point to the existence of malignancy [25–32]. These algorithms are trained on large datasets to find subtle characteristics that human observers would miss, leading to earlier and more accurate diagnoses. The integration of different patient data, including medical history, genetic data, and biomarker profiles, is made possible by

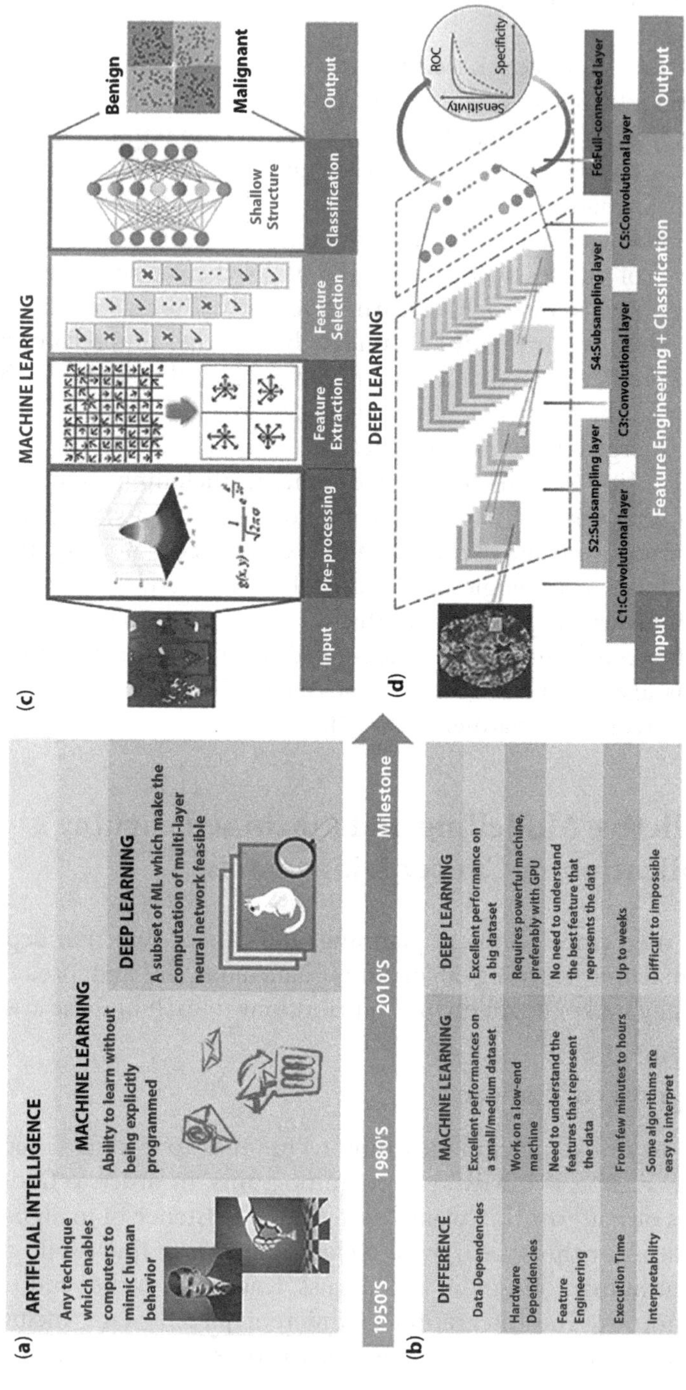

Figure 3.1 (a) The concept of the AI, ML and DL; (b) difference between machine learning and deep learning timescale of measure break through; (c) schematic model of workflow of ML; (d) schematic model of workflow of DL. Notes: Reprinted from *Cancer Letters*, 471, Huang S, Yang J, Fong S, Zhao Q., Artificial intelligence in cancer diagnosis and prognosis: Opportunities and challenges 61–71, Copyright (2020), with permission from Elsevier.

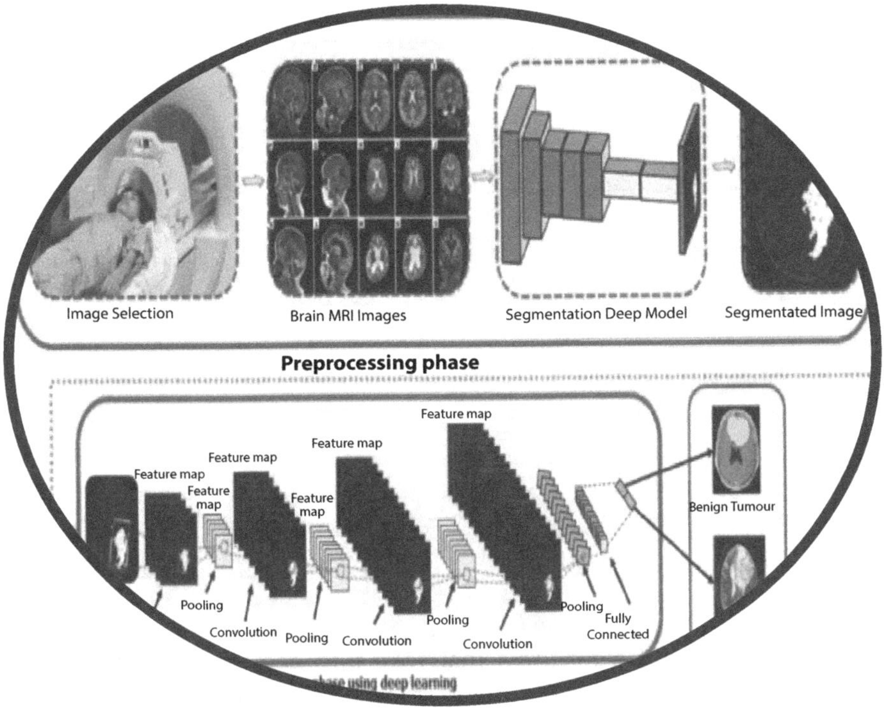

Figure 3.2 Training phase using deep learning.

data analytic tools. Algorithms can assist in the diagnosis of particular cancer types and subtypes by analyzing these databases and finding correlations and patterns [33–38].

3.2.2 Treatment Planning

A great deal of data must be gathered before cancer care and therapies can be planned and scheduled. To determine the optimal course of treatment, this information is frequently required to be shared with other professionals, patients, and caregivers. Care can be tailored to a patient's circumstances once a treatment plan has been determined [39–45]. It is sometimes a pretty complex procedure. To find patterns and correlations, machine learning algorithms examine vast amounts of patient information, such as genetic profiles, medical histories, and results of therapy. Algorithms that include this data can prescribe treatments based on possible adverse effects and response probability.

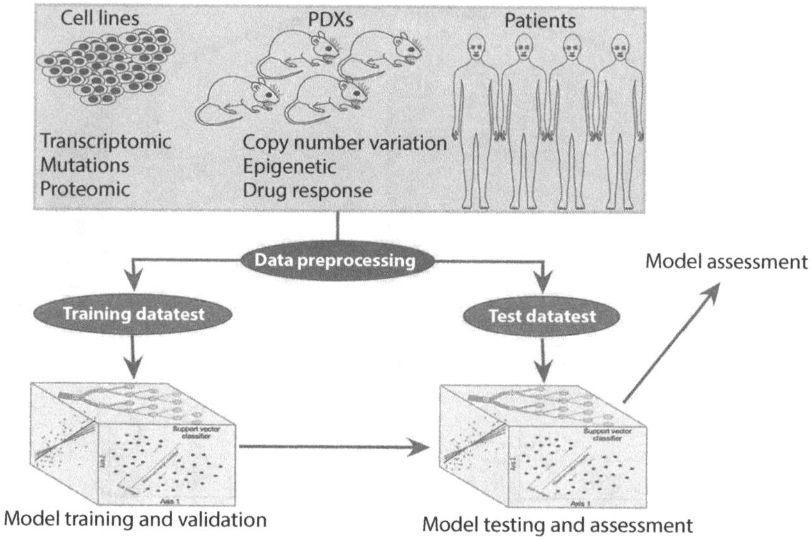

Figure 3.3 Prediction of cancer.

Machine learning algorithms that take into account patient-specific characteristics such as genetic variants, molecular profiles, and comorbidities enable personalized therapy. By recommending personalized remedies based on each person's distinct traits, these algorithms can maximize the effectiveness of treatment [46–53].

3.3 Customized Medical Care

Machine learning algorithms analyze large-scale genomic and molecular datasets to identify genetic variations, mutations, and biomarkers associated with specific cancer types [54–62]. This information is used to stratify patients into subgroups with distinct characteristics, enabling personalized treatment approaches.

Predictive modeling leverages machine learning to develop models that predict treatment outcomes based on patient-specific factors, including genetic information and clinical variables. These models aid in selecting the most appropriate treatment options for individual patients, considering their predicted response and potential side effects.

3.3.1 Overview of Machine Learning in Healthcare

The fields of disease populations, disease status, immune response, and health emergencies have all advanced significantly as a result of significant developments in machine learning (ML) and artificial intelligence (AI) technology. Though there is still doubt about the usefulness of ML-based approaches in practice and how to interpret their findings, their use in healthcare settings is growing quickly [63–70]. Here, we provide a brief overview of machine learning techniques and learning algorithms, including reinforcement learning, unsupervised learning, and supervised learning, along with pertinent examples. The application of machine learning (ML) in a number of healthcare fields, including genetics, neuroimaging, radiology, and electronic health records is covered in our second section. We also present recommendations and quickly go over the dangers and challenges in applying machine learning to the healthcare industry including issues with system privacy and ethics [71–77]. Second, we go over

Figure 3.4 Illustration of heterogeneous sources contributing to healthcare data.

machine learning (ML) applications in numerous healthcare domains, such as genetics, neuroimaging, radiology, and electronic health records. We also offer recommendations for future applications and a brief discussion of the risks and difficulties associated with using machine learning in healthcare, including issues with system privacy and ethics.

3.3.2 Machine Learning Applications in Cancer Therapy

Supervised learning forms the basis of machine learning models, where every data piece has a label assigned to it. Frequently used machine learning (ML) models include support vector machines (SVMs), regression models, random forest models, neural networks, transformers, convolutional neural networks (CNNs), recurrent neural networks (RNNs), and graph neural networks (GNNs). Random forest models estimate by building decision-making trees based on various binary options for the inputs [78–85]. SVM models distinguish different classes of data points, from the largest likely margination across data classes to produce lines or multidimensional hyperplanes for tumor traits. Regression models use a linear combination of inputs to estimate binary labels through logistic regression and continuous labels through linear regression, respectively. To estimate outcomes like the chance of cancer, neural networks, which are made up of multiple neuronal layers, compute input variables iteratively using linear assimilations followed by non-linear functions. RNN models apply comparable methods. In order to examine sequential information, such as genetic sequences and image series, layers of neural networks are applied to all objects contained in the sequences and the seen objects are memorized [86–73]. Neural patches, often known as "filters," are applied by CNN models to scan images and find patterns. While later layers detect traits at a higher level, such as the form of tumor cells, the first layers identify low-level features like edges. Transformers use iterative attention operations to compare sequential data to other components and update internal sequence representations in order to interpret sequential data. The current review focuses on the typical machine learning pipeline for prognostic, therapeutic, and diagnostic image-based cancer estimations using molecular properties of liquid and solid tissue samples, as well as the usage of ML models in oncology.

Machine learning (ML) predictions can assist in selecting the most appropriate course of treatment, stratifying cancer risks, determining the cancer subtype, mutational status, tumor metastasis, microsatellite instability, patient survival, and responsiveness to radiation, chemotherapy, and immunotherapy; evaluating risk factors such as breast density for breast cancer, and identifying tumor cells [74–79].

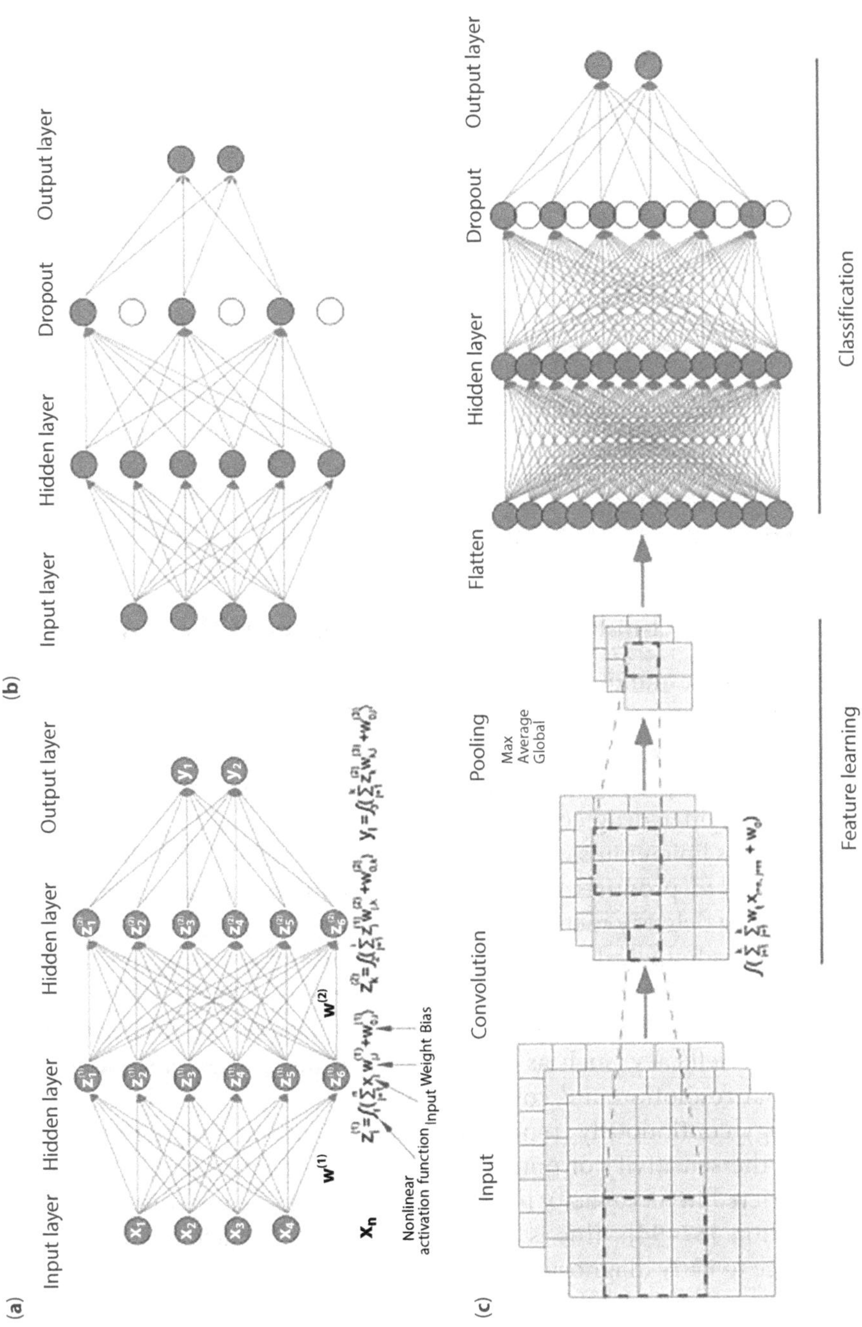

Figure 3.5 An example of a deep learning model.

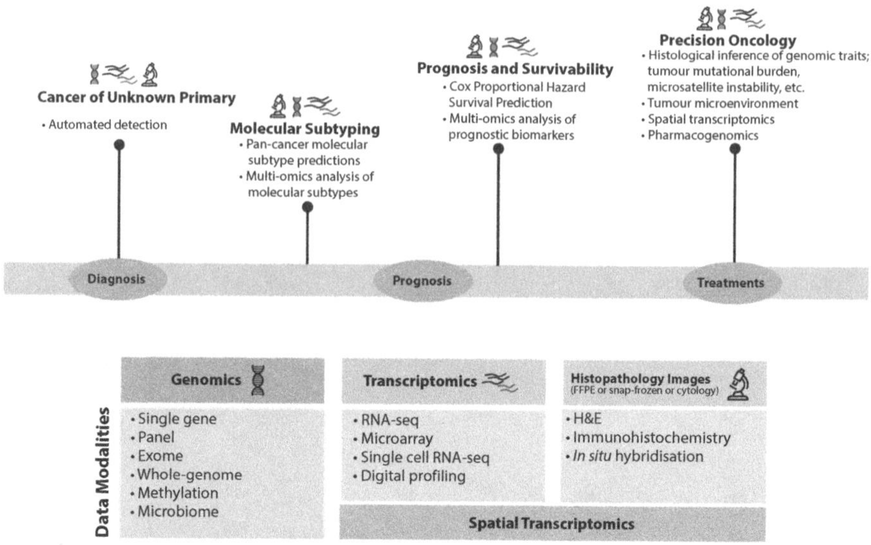

Figure 3.6 Deep learning in cancer diagnosis, prognosis and treatment selection.

3.3.3 Nanotechnology Applications in Cancer Therapy

Metals, ceramics, and polymers are just a few of the materials that can be included into nanoparticles. These particles can take on a variety of sizes and shapes with unique characteristics depending on the materials and production processes employed. Numerous nanoparticles, including micelles, polymer-drug conjugates, liposomes, and other lipid-based carriers (such as lipid emulsions and lipid-drug complexes), as well as various ligand-targeted products (such as immunoconjugates), are being developed as drug delivery methods [80–86].

Because radiological scans can identify solid tumors, assess recurrence, and track the effectiveness of treatment, they are a vital tool in clinical oncology. They determine solid tumors, evaluate recurrence, and monitor therapy efficacy, such as their size, location, and extension, at various spatial resolution and contrast levels. Even while improved imaging technology continuously improves spatial resolution, imaging modalities that use the sensitivity of nontargeted contrast agents, like CT and MRI, it is restricted in its capacity to provide precise and helpful disease-related information [87–94]. This is becoming more widely acknowledged as a hindrance to early diagnosis and treatment response tracking.

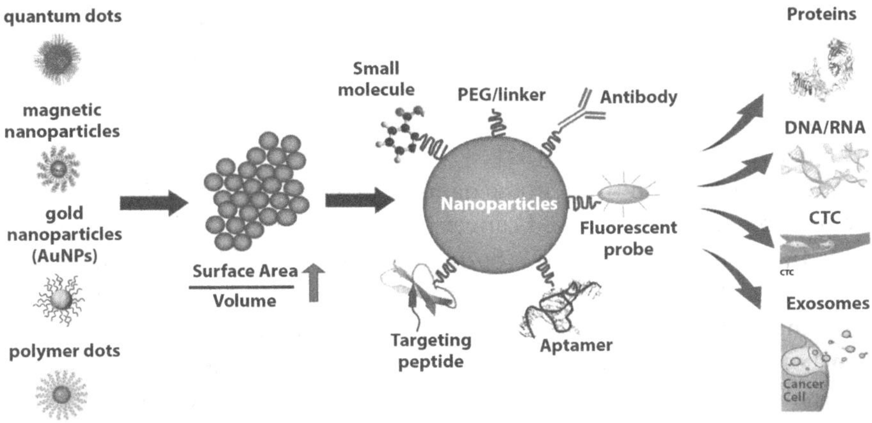

Figure 3.7 Nanotechnology improves cancer detection and diagnosis.

3.4 Result and Future Perspective

Many complex survival mechanisms, such as continuous angiogenesis, tumor invasion, Cancer is known to arise as a result of a number of factors, including self-sufficiency, evasion of apoptosis, limitless replicative capacity, and insensitivity to growth inhibitory signals [95–102]. Currently, clinical and pathologic staging—which is established through the use of morphologic diagnostic instruments including traditional radiographic and histological examinations—forms the basis for cancer therapy decisions. Patients respond differently to the same conventional therapy techniques even though their tumors have the same cellular type and clinical stage, which eventually results in differences in survival rates. This suggests that each patient's experience with cancer-related events is distinct.

Recent advancements in genetic, biochemical, and molecular diagnostic methods have spurred research into cancer-associated biomarkers and how they may affect the disease's onset and progression, revealing that complicated multifactorial pathways rather than a single cause govern cancer formation. "Molecularly targeted therapy" is a more recent innovation that acknowledges our expanding knowledge of these molecular traits in cancer [103–110]. The expression of the targeted molecules determines the efficacy of targeted therapy which can also function as biomarkers unique to cancer. Assays will be able to quickly and accurately measure multiple cancer-related biomarkers on small tumor specimens or single tumor sections at the same time because of improvements in nanotechnology [111–118]. For instance, conjugated QDs may make it possible to identify five cancer-related proteins on the same tissue segment. In addition to *ex vivo* analysis for the identification of molecular biomarkers for early cancer detection, *in vivo* imaging of cancer using different kinds of nanoparticles has also been researched in conjunction with the creation of nanoscale drug delivery systems [119–127].

The creation of multifunctional nanoparticles might have a big impact on the possibility of personalized cancer treatment [128–136]. To create multifunctional nanoparticles, the optimal situation would involve selecting an appropriate mixture of agents (targeting moiety and therapeutic agent) with imaging material affixed to the surface of the nanoparticles, chosen in accordance with exact biological data present in the tumor (patient molecular biomarker profiling) (Figure 3.8). In the future, nanoparticles might be able to identify cancerous cells (active-targeting moiety), locate them in the body and visualize them (real-time *in vivo* imaging), and eradicate the cancerous cells [137–141]. The creation of multifunctional nanoparticles might have a big impact on the possibility of personalized cancer treatment. In a perfect world, to create multifunctional nanoparticles, based on precise biological information within the tumor (patient molecular biomarker profiling), the appropriate combination of agents (therapeutic agent and targeted moiety) with imaging material linked to the nanoparticle surface will be selected [142–148]. A major leap in cancer treatments, the confluence of machine learning and nanotechnology, heralds a new era marked by individualized and precise treatment approaches. Unprecedented opportunities to create tailored and focused treatments that optimize effectiveness while reducing side effects are presented by this integration. Through the utilization of these state-of-the-art technologies' synergistic potential, notable advancements in the efficiency of cancer medicine delivery have been achieved.

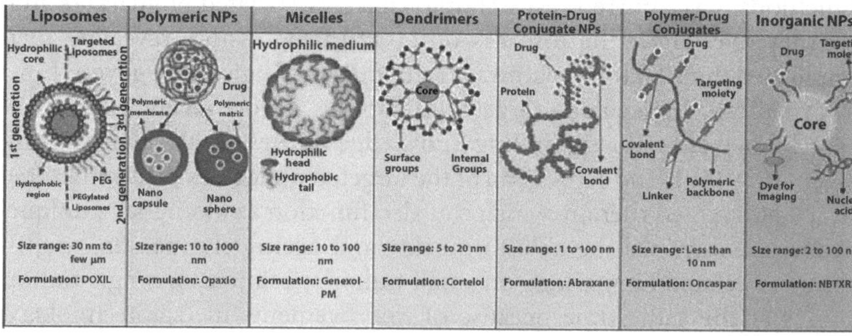

Figure 3.8 Clinical application and future perspective.

References

1. Bhardwaj, R., Nambiar, A.R., Dutta, D., A study of machine learning in healthcare. *2017 IEEE 41st Annual Computer Software and Applications Conference (COMPSAC)*, IEEE, pp. 236–241, 2017.
2. Li, J., Wang, Z., Mao, K., Guo, Y., Zhang, W., Gong, X., Yu, X., AI-Assisted Nanotechnology: Towards Precision Cancer Medicine. *Nano Today*, 35, 100935, 2020.
3. Mura, S., Nicolas, J., Couvreur, P., Stimuli-responsive nanocarriers for drug delivery. *Nat. Mater.*, 12, 11, 991–1003, 2013.
4. Abdar, M., A review of uncertainty quantification in deep learning: Techniques, applications and challenges. *Inf. Fusion*, 76, 243–297, 2021.
5. Li, K.C., Pandit, S.D., Guccione, S., Bednarski, M.D., Molecular imaging applications in nanomedicine. *Biomed. Microdevices*, 6, 113–116, 2004.
6. Siegel, R.L., Wagle, N.S., Cercek, A., *et al.*, Colorectal cancer statistics, 2023. *CA Cancer J. Clin.*, 73, 233–254, 2023.
7. Chen, T.K., Knicely, D.H., Grams, M.E., Chronic kidney disease diagnosis and management: A review. *Jama*, 322, 1294–1304, 2019.
8. Biswas, A.K., Islam, M.R., Choudhury, Z.S., *et al.*, Nanotechnology based approaches in cancer therapeutics. *Adv. Nat. Sci.: Nanosci. Nanotechnol.*, 5, 043001, 2014.
9. Alanazi, A., Using machine learning for healthcare challenges and opportunities. *Inf. Med. Unlocked*, 30, 100924, 2022.
10. Sullivan, E., Understanding from machine learning models. *Br. J. Philos. Sci.*, 2022.
11. Mustafa, A. and Rahimi Azghadi, M., Automated machine learning for healthcare and clinical notes analysis. *Computers*, 10, 24, 2021.
12. Anjum, S., Emerging applications of nanotechnology in healthcare systems: Grand challenges and perspectives. *Pharmaceuticals*, 14, 707, 2021.
13. Maheshwari, P. and Gupta, N.V., Advances of nanotechnology in healthcare. *Int. J. Pharm. Tech. Res.*, 4, 1221–1227, 2012.
14. Liao, J., Artificial intelligence assists precision medicine in cancer treatment. *Front. Oncol.*, 12, 998222, 2023.
15. Siegel, R.L., Giaquinto, A.N., Jemal, A., Cancer statistics, 2024. *CA Cancer J. Clin.*, 2024.
16. García-Domínguez, D.J., *et al.*, Cancer Nano-Immunotherapy: The Novel and Promising Weapon to Fight Cancer. *Int. J. Mol. Sci.*, 25, 2024.
17. Codella, N., *et al.*, *Machine Learning in Medical Imaging*. Zhou, L., Wang, L., Wang, Q., Shi, Y. (eds.), pp. 118–126, Springer, 2015.
18. Cheng, S., Fan, L., Ganta, S., Artificial Intelligence and Nanomedicine in Cancer Treatment. *Adv. Drug Deliv. Rev.*, 170, 113–131, 2020.
19. Esteva, A., Kuprel, B., Novoa, R.A., Ko, J., Swetter, S.M., Blau, H.M., Thrun, S., Dermatologist-level classification of skin cancer with deep neural networks. *Nature*, 542, 7639, 115–118, 2017.

20. Burroni, M., *et al.*, Melanoma computer-aided diagnosis: Reliability and feasibility study. *Clin. Cancer Res.*, 10, 1881–1886, 2004.
21. Sharma, G., Rytting, E., Zhao, F., Nanotechnology-based approaches for siRNA delivery. *J. Drug Deliv. Sci. Technol.*, 29, 123–135, 2015.
22. Tan, P., Chen, X., Zhang, H., Wei, Q., AI-enabled nanomedicines in cancer management, Elsevier, 92, 2023, ISSN 2211-2855.
23. Kour, S., Biswas, I., Sheoran, S., Arora, S., Sheela, P., Duppala, S.K., Murthy, D.K., Pawar, S.C., Singh, H., Kumar, D., Prabhu, D., Vuree, S., Artificial intelligence and nanotechnology for cervical cancer treatment: Current status and future perspectives. *J. Drug Deliv. Sci. Technol.*, 83, 104392, 2023, https://www.sciencedirect.com/science/article/abs/pii/S1773224723002447?via%3Dihub.
24. Skepu, A., Artificial intelligence and nanotechnology in precision medicine. Elsevier, 123–135.
25. Naeem, A., Suhail, M., Basit, A., Yali, L., Xia, Z., Qin, Z., Impact of artificial intelligence on drug design and development in nanotechnology for cancer treatment. Elsevier, 58, 132–138.
26. Adir, O., Poley, M., Chen, G., Froim, S., Krinsky, N., Shklover, J., Shainsky-Roitman, J., Lammers, T., Artificial intelligence and nanotechnology for precision cancer medicine. Elsevier, 51, 138–140.
27. Silver, D., *et al.*, Mastering the game of Go with deep neural networks and tree search. *Nature*, 529, 484–489, 2016.
28. Litjens, G., Kooi, T., Bejnordi, B.E., Setio, A.A.A., Ciompi, F., Ghafoorian, M., Sánchez, C.I., A survey on deep learning in medical image analysis. *Med. Image Anal.*, 42, 60–88, 2017.
29. Gulshan, V., Peng, L., Coram, M., Stumpe, M.C., Wu, D., Narayanaswamy, A., Raman, R., Development and validation of a deep learning algorithm for detection of diabetic retinopathy in retinal fundus photographs. *Jama*, 316, 22, 2402–2410, 2016.
30. Ching, T., Himmelstein, D.S., Beaulieu-Jones, B.K., Kalinin, A.A., Do, B.T., Way, G.P., Xiao, C., Opportunities and obstacles for deep learning in biology and medicine. *J. R. Soc. Interface*, 15, 141, 20170387, 2018.
31. Chartrand, G., Cheng, P.M., Vorontsov, E., Drozdzal, M., Turcotte, S., Pal, C.J., Tang, Deep learning: a primer for radiologists. *Radiographics*, 37, 7, 2113–2131, 2017.
32. Esteva, A., Dermatologist-level classification of skin cancer with deep neural networks. *Nature*, 542, 7639, 115–118, 2019.
33. Nam, J.Y., Real-time prediction of survival outcomes using data mining techniques in cancer patients treated with radiotherapy. *Healthcare Inf. Res.*, 25, 4, 288–294, 2019.
34. Kourou, K., Machine learning applications in cancer prognosis and prediction. *Comput. Struct. Biotechnol. J.*, 13, 8–17, 2015.
35. Liang, H., Personalized cancer treatment selection using molecular landscape topology and genomic alterations. *J. Am. Med. Inf. Assoc.*, 26, 3, 242–250, 2019.

36. Yala, A., Using machine learning to parse breast pathology reports. *Breast Cancer Res. Treat.*, 174, 1, 189–195, 2019.
37. Chen, J.H., Predicting breast cancer metastasis by using serum biomarkers and clinicopathological data with machine learning technologies. *Comput. Biol. Med.*, 109, 197–207, 2019.
38. Su, X., Applications of artificial intelligence in cancer clinical trials. *Nat. Rev. Clin. Oncol.*, 18, 12, 796–808, 2021.
39. McKinney, S.M., International evaluation of an AI system for breast cancer screening. *Nature*, 577, 7788, 89–94, 2020.
40. Clark, W.H., *et al.*, Model predicting survival in stage I melanoma based on tumor progression. *J. Nature Cancer Inst.*, 81, 1893–1904, 1989.
41. De Fauw, J., Clinically applicable deep learning for diagnosis and referral in retinal disease. *Nat. Med.*, 24, 9, 1342–1350, 2018.
42. Lambin, P., Radiomics: extracting more information from medical images using advanced feature analysis. *Eur. J. Cancer*, 48, 4, 44–446, 2013.
43. Cortes, C., Real-world outcomes of immune checkpoint inhibitors in advanced non-small cell lung cancer: results from the Prospective Dutch Molecular Screening Program (MolScreen). *Lancet Oncol.*, 22, 12, 1708–1718, 2021.
44. Hyman, D.M., Precision medicine at Memorial Sloan Kettering Cancer Center: clinical next-generation sequencing enabling next-generation targeted therapy trials. *Drug Discov. Today*, 20, 12, 1422–1428, 2015.
45. Schwaederlé, M., Impact of precision medicine in diverse cancers: a meta-analysis of phase II clinical trials. *J. Clin. Oncol.*, 33, 32, 3817–3825, 2015.
46. Dreaden, E.C., Nanotechnological strategies for cancer treatment therapies. *Trends Mol. Med.*, 18, 7, 385–393, 2012.
47. Peer, D., Nanocarriers as an emerging platform for cancer therapy. *Nat. Nanotechnol.*, 2, 12, 751–760, 2007.
48. Farokhzad, O.C. and Langer, R., Impact of nanotechnology on drug delivery. *ACS Nano*, 3, 1, 16–20, 2009.
49. Hirsch, L.R., Nanoshell-mediated near-infrared thermal therapy of tumors under magnetic resonance guidance. *Proc. Natl. Acad. Sci.*, 103, 40, 14716–14721, 2006.
50. Choi, W.I., Theranostic approaches based on nanoparticles for simultaneous cancer imaging and therapy. *Adv. Drug Deliv. Rev.*, 64, 13, 1390–1406, 2012.
51. Jokerst, J.V., Nanoparticle PEGylation for imaging and therapy. *Nanomedicine*, 6, 4, 715–728, 2011.
52. Chen, H., Emerging nanotechnology and advanced materials for cancer radiation therapy. *Adv. Mater.*, 25, 32, 4564–4580, 2013.
53. Blanco, E., Nanomedicine in cancer therapy: innovative trends and prospects. *Cancer Sci.*, 106, 1, 8–15, 2015.

54. Bhardwaj, A., Kumar, P., Raj, B., Anand, S., Design and Performance Optimization of doping-less Vertical Nanowire TFET using Gate Stack Technique. *J. Electron. Mater. (JEMS)*, Springer, 41, 7, 4005–4013, 2022.
55. Singh, J. and Raj, B., Tunnel Current Model of Asymmetric MIM Structure Levying Various Image Forces to Analyze the Characteristics of Filamentary Memristor. *Appl. Phys. A*, Springer, 125, 3, 203.1–203.11, Feb 2019.
56. Goyal, C., Ubhi, J.S., Raj, B., Low Leakage Zero Ground Noise Nanoscale Full Adder Using Source Biasing Technique. *J. Nanoelectron. Optoelectron.*, American Scientific Publishers, 14, 360–370, March 2019.
57. Singh, G., Sarin, R.K., Raj, B., A Novel Robust Exclusive-OR Function Implementation in QCA Nanotechnology with Energy Dissipation Analysis. *J. Comput. Electron.*, Springer, 15, 2, 455–465, June 2016.
58. Wadhwa, G., Kamboj, P., Raj, B., Design optimisation of junctionless TFET biosensor for high sensitivity. *Adv. Nat. Sci.: Nanosci. Nanotechnol.*, 10, 045001 (7), 2019.
59. Bansal, P. and Raj, B., Memristor Modeling and Analysis for Linear Dopant Drift Kinetics. *J. Nanoeng. Nanomanuf.*, American Scientific Publishers, 6, 1–7, 2016.
60. Ashima, Vaithiyanathan, D., Raj, B., Performance Analysis of Charge Plasma induced Graded Channel Si nanotube. *J. Eng. Res. (JER)*, EMSME Special Issue, 146–154, Aug 2021.
61. Tomar, A.S., Magraiya, V.K., Raj, B., Scaling of Access and Data Transistor for High Performance DRAM Cell Design. *Quantum Matter*, 2, 412–416, Oct. 2013.
62. Jain, N. and Raj, B., Parasitic Capacitance and Resistance Model Development and Optimization of Raised Source/Drain SOI FinFET Structure for Analog Circuit Applications. *J. Nanoelectron. Optoelectron.*, ASP, USA, 13, 531–539, April 2018.
63. Singh, S., Vishvakarma, S.K., Raj, B., Analytical Modeling of Split-Gate Junction-Less Transistor for a Biosensor Application. *Sens. Bio-Sens.*, Elsevier, 18, 31–36, April 2018.
64. Gopal, M. and Raj, B., Low Power 8T SRAM Cell Design for High Stability Video Applications. *ITSI Trans. Electr. Electron. Eng.*, 1, 5, 91–97, 2013.
65. Raj, B., Mitra, J., Bihani, D.K., Rangharajan, V., Saxena, A.K., Dasgupta, S., Analysis of Noise Margin, Power and Process Variation for 32 nm FinFET Based 6T SRAM Cell. *J. Comput. (JCP)*, Academy Publisher, Finland, 5, 6, 1–8, 2010.
66. Sharma, D., Mehra, R., Raj, B., Comparative Analysis of Photovoltaic Technologies for High Efficiency Solar Cell Design. *Superlattices Microstruct.*, Elsevier, 153, 106861, May 2021.
67. Kaur, P., Buttar, A.S., Raj, B., A comprehensive Analysis of Nanoscale Transistor based Biosensor: A Review. *Indian J. Pure Appl. Phys.*, 59, 304–318, April 2021.

68. Yadav, D., Raj, B., Raj, B., Design and Simulation of Low Power Microcontroller for IoT Applications. *J. Sens. Lett.*, ASP, 18, 401–409, May 2020.
69. Singh, S. and Raj, B., A 2-D Analytical Surface Potential and Drain current Modeling of Double-Gate Vertical t-shaped Tunnel FET. *J. Comput. Electron.*, Springer, 19, 1154–1163, April 2020.
70. Singh, J. and Raj, B., An Accurate and Generic Window function for Non-linear Memristor Model. *J. Comput. Electron.*, Springer, 18, 2, 640–647, June 2019.
71. Kaur, M., Gupta, N., Kumar, S., Raj, B., Singh, A.K., Comparative RF and Crosstalk Analysis of Carbon Based Nano Interconnects. *IET Circuits Devices Syst.*, 15, 6, 493–503, Feb 2021.
72. Kandasamy, N., Ahmad, F., Ajitha, D., Raj, B., Telagam, N., Quantum Dot Cellular Automata based Scan Flip Flop and Boundary Scan Register. *IETE J. Res.*, 66, 535–548, 2020.
73. Singh, J. and Raj, B., Design and Investigation of 7T2M NVSARM with Enhanced Stability and Temperature Impact on Store/Restore Energy. *IEEE Trans. Very Large Scale Integr. Syst.*, 27, 6, 1322–1328, June 2019.
74. Bhardwaj, A.K., Gupta, S., Raj, B., Singh, A., Impact of Double Gate Geometry on the Performance of Carbon Nanotube Field Effect Transistor Structures for Low Power Digital Design. *Comput. Theor. Nanosci.*, ASP, 16, 1813–1820, 2019.
75. Jain, N. and Raj, B., Thermal Stability Analysis and Performance Exploration of Asymmetrical Dual-k underlap Spacer (ADKUS) SOI FinFET for Security and Privacy Applications. *Indian J. Pure Appl. Phys. (IJPAP)*, 57, 352–360, May 2019.
76. Jain, N. and Raj, B., Dual-k Spacer Region Variation at the Drain Side of Asymmetric SOI FinFET Structure: Performance Analysis towards the Analog/RF Design Applications. *J. Nanoelectron. Optoelectron.*, American Scientific Publishers, 14, 349–359, March 2019.
77. Singh, J., Sharma, S., Raj, B., Khosla, M., Analysis of barrier layer thickness on performance of In1-xGaxAs based Gate Stack Cylindrical Gate Nanowire MOSFET. *J. Nanoelectron. Optoelectron.*, ASP, 13, 1473–1477, Oct 2018.
78. Jain, N. and Raj, B., Analysis and Performance Exploration of High-k SOI FinFETs Over the Conventional Low-k SOI FinFET toward Analog/RF Design. *J. Semicond. (JoS)*, IOP Science, 39, 12, 124002-1-7, Dec 2018.
79. Goyal, C., Ubhi, J.S., Raj, B., A reliable leakage reduction technique for approximate full adder with reduced ground bounce noise. *J. Math. Probl. Eng.*, Hindawi, 2018, 3501041, 16, 15 Oct 2018.
80. Anuradha, Singh, J., Raj, B., Khosla, M., Design and Performance Analysis of Nano-Scale Memristor-Based Nonvolatile SRAM. *J. Sens. Lett.*, American Scientific Publishers, 16, 798–805, Oct 2018.
81. Wadhwa, G. and Raj, B., Parametric Variation Analysis of Charge-Plasma-Based Dielectric Modulated JLTFET for Biosensor Application. *IEEE Sens. J.*, 18, 15, 6070–6077, August 1, 2018, (SCI).

82. Singh, J. and Raj, B., Comparative Analysis of Memristor Models for Memories Design. *J. Semicond. (JoS)*, IoP, 39, 7, 074006–1-12, July 2018.
83. Yadav, D., Chouhan, S.S., Vishvakarma, S.K., Raj, B., Application Specific Microcontroller Design for IoT based WSN. *Sens. Lett.*, ASP, 16, 374–385, May 2018.
84. Singh, G., Sarin, R.K., Raj, B., Fault-Tolerant Design and Analysis of Quantum-Dot Cellular Automata Based Circuits. *IEEE/IET Circuits Devices Syst.*, 12, 638–64, 2018.
85. Singh, J. and Raj, B., Modeling of Mean Barrier Height Levying Various Image Forces of Metal Insulator Metal Structure to Enhance the Performance of Conductive Filament Based Memristor Model. *IEEE Nanotechnol.*, 17, 2, 268–267, March 2018.
86. Jain, A., Sharma, S., Raj, B., Analysis of Triple Metal Surrounding Gate (TM-SG) III-V Nanowire MOSFET for Photosensing Application. *Opto-Electron. J.*, Elsevier, 26, 2, 141–148, May 2018.
87. Jain, A., Sharma, S., Raj, B., Design and Analysis of High Sensitivity Photosensor Using Cylindrical Surrounding Gate MOSFET for Low Power Sensor Applications. *Eng. Sci. Technol. Int. J.*, Elsevier's, 19, 4, 1864–1870, December 2016.
88. Saiphani Kumar, G., Singh, A., Raj, B., Design and Analysis of Gate All Around CNTFET based SRAM cell Design. *J. Comput. Electron.*, Springer, 17, 1, 138–145, March 2018.
89. pal Singh, G., Sohi, B.S., Raj, B., Material Properties Analysis of Graphene Base Transistor (GBT) for VLSI Analog Circuits. *Indian J. Pure Appl. Phys. (IJPAP)*, 55, 896–902, Dec 2017.
90. Kumar, S. and Raj, B., Estimation of Stability and Performance metric for Inward Access Transistor based 6T SRAM Cell Design Using n-type/p-type DMDG-GDOV TFET. *IEEE VLSI Circuits Syst. Lett.*, 3, 2, 25–39, June 2017.
91. Sharma, S., Kumar, A., Pattanaik, M., Raj, B., Forward Body Biased Multimode Multi-Threshold CMOS Technique for Ground Bounce Noise Reduction in Static CMOS Adders. *Int. J. Inf. Electron. Eng.*, 3, 3, 567–572, 2013.
92. Singh, H., Kumar, P., Raj, B., Performance Analysis of Majority Gate SET Based 1-bit Full Adder. *Int. J. Comput. Commun. Eng. (IJCCE)*, IACSIT Press Singapore, ISSN: 2010-3743, 2, 4, 2013.
93. Bhardwaj, A.K., Gupta, S., Raj, B., Investigation of Parameters for Schottky Barrier (SB) Height for Schottky Barrier Based Carbon Nanotube Field Effect Transistor Device. *J. Nanoelectron. Optoelectron.*, ASP, 15, 783–791, July 2020.
94. Bansal, P. and Raj, B., Memristor: A Versatile Nonlinear Model for Dopant Drift and Boundary Issues. *JCTN*, American Scientific Publishers, 14, 5, 2319–2325, May 2017.
95. Jain, N. and Raj, B., An Analog and Digital Design Perspective Comprehensive Approach on Fin-FET (Fin-Field Effect transistor) Technology - A Review. *Rev. Adv. Sci. Eng. (RASE)*, ASP, 5, 1–14, 2016.

96. Raj, B., Saxena, A.K., Dasgupta, S., Analytical Modeling for the Estimation of Leakage Current and Subthreshold Swing Factor of Nanoscale Double Gate FinFET Device. *Microelectron. Int.*, UK, 26, 53–63, 2009.
97. Soniya, Singh, S., Wadhwa, G., Raj, B., An Analytical Modeling for Dual Source Vertical Tunnel Field Effect Transistor. *Int. J. Recent Technol. Eng. (IJRTE)*, 8, 2, 603–608, July 2019.
98. Singh, S. and Raj, B., Design and analysis of hetrojunction Vertical T-shaped Tunnel Field Effect Transistor. *J. Electron. Mater.*, Springer, 48, 10, 6253–6260, October 2019.
99. Goyal, C., Ubhi, J.S., Raj, B., A Low Leakage CNTFET based Inexact Full Adder for Low Power Image Processing Applications. *Int. J. Circuit Theory Appl.*, Wiley, 47, 9, 1446–1458, September 2019.
100. Raj, B., Saxena, A.K., Dasgupta, S., A Compact Drain Current and Threshold Voltage Quantum Mechanical Analytical Modeling for FinFETs. *J. Nanoelectron. Optoelectron. (JNO)*, USA, 3, 2, 163–170, 2008.
101. Wadhwa, G. and Raj, B., An Analytical Modeling of Charge Plasma based Tunnel Field Effect Transistor with Impacts of Gate underlap Region. *Superlattices Microstruct.*, Elsevier, 142, 106512, June 2020.
102. Singh, S. and Raj, B., Modeling and Simulation analysis of SiGe hetrojunction Double GateVertical t-shaped Tunnel FET. *Superlattices Microstruct.*, Elsevier, 142, 106496, June 2020.
103. Jain, N. and Raj, B., Device and Circuit Co-Design Perspective Comprehensive Approach on FinFET Technology - A Review. *J. Electron Devices*, 23, 1, 1890–1901, 2016.
104. Kumar, S. and Raj, B., Analysis of I_{ON} and Ambipolar Current for Dual-Material Gate-drain Overlapped DG-TFET. *J. Nanoelectron. Optoelectron.*, American Scientific Publishers, USA, 11, 323–333, June 2016.
105. Anjum, N., Bali, T., Raj, B., Design And Simulation Of Handwritten Multiscript Character Recognition. *Int. J. Adv. Res. Comput. Commun. Eng.*, 2, 7, 2544–2549, July 2013.
106. Singh, K. and Raj, B., Performance and analysis of temperature dependent Multi-walled Carbon Nanotubes as Global Interconnects at different technology nodes. *J. Comput. Electron.*, Springer, 14, 2, 469–476, June 2015.
107. Kumar, S. and Raj, B., Compact channel potential analytical Modeling of DG-TFET based on Evanescent-mode Approach. *J. Comput. Electron.*, Springer, 14, 2, 820–827, July 2015.
108. Singh, K. and Raj, B., Temperature Dependent Modeling and Performance Evaluation of Multi-Walled CNT and Single-Walled CNT as Global Interconnects. *J. Electron. Mater.*, Springer, 44, 12, 4825–4835, Dec 2015.
109. Sharma, V.K., Pattanaik, M., Raj, B., INDEP approach for leakage reduction in nanoscale CMOS circuits. *Int. J. Electron.*, Taylor & Francis, 102, 2, 200–215, 2014.

110. Singh, K. and Raj, B., Influence of Temperature on MWCNT Bundle, SWCNT Bundle and Copper Interconnects for Nanoscaled Technology Nodes. *J. Mater. Sci.: Mater. Electron.*, Springer, 26, 8, 6134–6142, 2015.
111. Anjum, N., Bali, T., Raj, B., Design and Simulation of Handwritten Gurumukhi and Devanagri Numerical Recognition. *Int. J. Comput. Appl.*, Foundation of Computer Science, New York, USA, 73, 12, 16–21, 2013.
112. Khandelwal, S., Gupta, V., Raj, B., Gupta, R.D., Process Variability Aware Low Leakage Reliable Nano Scale DG-FinFET SRAM Cell Design Technique. *J. Nanoelectron. Optoelectron.*, 10, 6, 810–817, December 2015.
113. Sharma, V.K., Pattanaik, M., Raj, B., ONOFIC Approach: Low Power High Speed Nanoscale VLSI Circuits Design. *Int. J. Electron.*, Taylor & Francis, 101, 1, 61–73, 2014.
114. Khandelwal, S., Raj, B., Gupta, R.D., FinFET based 6T SRAM Cell Design: Analysis of Performance Metric, Process Variation and Temperature Effect. *J. Comput. Theor. Nanosci.*, ASP, USA, 12, 2500–2506, 2015.
115. Singh, S., Yadav, S., Rahul, J., Srivastava, A., Raj, B., Impact of HfO_2 in Graded Channel Dual Insulator Double Gate MOSFET. *J. Comput. Theor. Nanosci.*, American Scientific Publishers, 12, 6, 950–953, April 2015.
116. Sharma, V.K., Pattanaik, M., Raj, B., PVT variations aware low leakage INDEP approach for nanoscale CMOS Circuits. *Microelectron. Reliab.*, Elsevier, 54, 90–99, 2014.
117. Raj, B., Saxena, A.K., Dasgupta, S., Quantum Mechanical Analytical Modeling of Nanoscale DG FinFET: Evaluation of Potential, Threshold Voltage and Source/Drain Resistance. *Elsevier's J. Mater. Sci. Semicond. Process.*, Elsevier, 16, 4, 1131–1137, 2013.
118. Gopal, M., Prasad, S.S.D., Raj, B., 8T SRAM Cell Design for Dynamic and Leakage Power Reduction. *Int. J. Comput. Appl.*, Foundation of Computer Science, New York, USA, 71, 9, 43–48, June 2013.
119. Pattanaik, M., Raj, B., Sharma, S., Kumar, A., Diode Based Trimode Multi-Threshold CMOS Technique for Ground Bounce Noise Reduction in Static CMOS Adders. *Adv. Mater. Res.*, Trans Tech Publications, Switzerland, 548, 885–889, 2012.
120. Raj, B., Saxena, A.K., Dasgupta, S., Nanoscale FinFET Based SRAM Cell Design: Analysis of Performance Metric, Process Variation, Underlapped FinFET and Temperature Effect. *IEEE Circuits Syst. Mag.*, 11, 2, 38–50, 2011.
121. Sharma, V.K., Pattanaik, M., Raj, B., Leakage Current ONOFIC Approach for Deep Submicron VLSI Circuit Design. *Int. J. Electr. Comput. Electron. Commun. Eng.*, World Academy of Sciences, Engineering and Technology, 7, 4, 239–244, 2013.
122. Kaur, P., Gill, S.S., Raj, B., Comparative Analysis of OFETs Materials and Devices for Sensor Applications. *J. Silicon*, Springer, 14, 4463–4471, 2022.
123. Sharma, S.K., Kumar, P., Raj, B., Raj, B., $In_{1-x}Ga_xAs$ Double Metal Gate-Stacking Cylindrical Nanowire MOSFET for Highly Sensitive Photo Detector. *J. Silicon*, Springer, 14, 3535–3541, 2022.

124. Raj, B., Saxena, A.K., Dasgupta, S., Analytical Modeling of Quasi Planar Nanoscale Double Gate FinFET with Source/Drain Resistance and field dependent carrier mobility: A quantum mechanical study. *J. Comput. (JCP)*, Academy Publisher, Finland, 4, 9, 1–8, 2009.
125. Bhushan, S., Khandelwal, S., Raj, B., Analyzing Different Mode FinFET based Memory Cell at Different Power Supply for Leakage Reduction, Seventh International Conference on Bio-Inspired Computing: Theories and Application, (BIC-TA 2012). *Adv. Intell. Syst. Comput.*, 202, 89–100, 2013.
126. Singh, J. and Raj, B., Temperature Dependent Analytical Modeling and Simulations of Nanoscale Memristor. *Eng. Sci. Technol. Int. J.*, Elsevier's, 21, 862–868, Oct 2018.
127. Singh, S., Bala, S., Raj, B., Raj, B., Improved Sensitivity of Dielectric Modulated Junctionless Transistor for Nanoscale Biosensor Design. *Sens. Lett.*, ASP, 18, 328–333, April 2020.
128. Kumar, V., Vishvakarma, S.K., Raj, B., Design and Performance Analysis of ASIC for IoT Applications. *Sens. Lett.*, ASP, 18, 31–38, Jan 2020.
129. Jaiswal, A., Sarin, R.K., Raj, B., Sukhija, S., A Novel Circular Slotted Microstrip-Fed Patch Antenna with Three Triangle Shape Defected Ground Structure for Multiband Applications. *Adv. Electromagn. (AEM)*, 7, 3, 56–63, Aug 2018.
130. Wadhwa, G. and Raj, B., Label Free Detection of Biomolecules using Charge-Plasma-Based Gate Underlap Dielectric Modulated Junctionless TFET. *J. Electron. Mater. (JEMS)*, Springer, 47, 8, 4683–4693, August 2018.
131. Singh, G., Sarin, R.K., Raj, B., Design and Performance Analysis of a New Efficient Coplanar Quantum-Dot Cellular Automata Adder. *Indian J. Pure Appl. Phys. (IJPAP)*, 55, 97–103, February 2017.
132. Kaur, P., Pandey, V., Raj, B., Comparative Study of Efficient Design, Control and Monitoring of Solar Power using IoT. *Sens. Lett.*, ASP, 18, 419–426, May 2020.
133. Singh, M., Chaudhary, T., Raj, B., Enhancing FeFET Structures for Non-Volatile On-Chip Memories: Design and Comparative Analysis. *Int. J. Numer. Modell. Electron. Netw. Devices Fields*, 38, 1–9, 2024.
134. Singh, M., Chaudhary, T., Raj, B., Drain Current and Transconductance Analysis of GaN GAA Nanowire FET with High K Dielectric. *ECS J. Sci. Technol.*, 12, 6070–6077, 2023.
135. Singh, M., Chaudhary, T., Raj, B., Design of Si and Ge Nanowire FET for Low Power Application. *J. Silicon*, Springer, 15, 1491–1497, 2023.
136. Singh, M., Chaudhary, T., Raj, B., Electrical Characterstics Analysis of FeFET for Low Power Applications. *J. Nano*, 37, 1–8, 2024.
137. Kumar, M., Chaudhary, T., Raj, B., Design and Comparative Analysis of Ferroelectric Nanowire with Dielectric HfO_2 and $Al_2O_3$for Low Power Applications. *J. Electron. Mater.*, Springer, 53, 6785–6791, 2024.

138. Bhardwaj, A.K., Gupta, S., Raj, B., Development & Analysis of Compact Model for Double Gate Schottky Barrier CNTFET. *J. Nanoelectron. Optoelectron.*, ASP, 15, 1199–1208, Aug 2020.
139. Wadhwa, G., Kamboj, P., Singh, J., Raj, B., Design and Investigation of Junctionless DGTFET for Biological Molecule Recognition. *Trans. Electr. Electron. Mater.*, Springer, 22, 282–289, 2021.
140. Verma, S.K., Singh, S., Wadhwa, G., Raj, B., Detection of Biomolecules using Charge-Plasma Based Gate Underlap Dielectric Modulated Dopingless TFET. *Trans. Electr. Electron. Mater. (TEEM)*, Springer, 21, 528–535, June 2020.
141. Jain, N. and Raj, B., Impact of underlap spacer region variation on Electrostatic and analog/RF performance of symmetrical high-k SOI FinFET at 20 nm channel length. *J. Semicond. (JoS)*, IOP Science, 38, 12, 122002, Dec 2017.
142. Singh, S. and Raj, B., Analytical Modeling and Simulation Analysis of T-Shaped III-V Heterojunction Vertical T-FET. *Superlattices Microstruct.*, Elsevier, 147, 106717, Nov 2020.
143. Singh, G., Sarin, R.K., Raj, B., Design and Analysis of Area Efficient QCA Based Reversible Logic Gates. *J. Microprocess. Microsys.*, Elsevier, 52, 59–68, May 2017.
144. Singh, S. and Raj, B., Parametric variation analysis on hetero-junction vertical t-shape TFET for supressing ambipolar conduction. *Indian J. Pure Appl. Phys.*, 58, 478–485, June 2020.
145. Soniya, Singh, S., Wadhwa, G., Raj, B., Design and Analysis of Dual Source Vertical Tunnel Field Effect Transistor for High Performance. *Trans. Electr. Electron. Mater.*, Springer, 21, 74–82, Oct 2019.
146. Kaur, M., Gupta, N., Kumar, S., Raj, B., Singh, A.K., RF Performance Analysis of Intercalated Graphene Nanoribbon Based Global Level Interconnects. *J. Comput. Electron.*, Springer, 19, 1002–1013, June 2020.
147. Wadhwa, G. and Raj, B., Design and Performance Analysis of Junctionless TFET Biosensor for High Sensitivity. *IEEE Nanotechnol.*, 18, 567–574, 2019.
148. Singh, J. and Raj, B., Enhanced Nonlinear Memristor Model Encapsulating Stochastic Dopant Drift. *JNO*, ASP, 14, 958–963, 2019.

4

Multiplexing the Brain Signals for Low Power Robust Electrode Sensing in Medical Diagnosis

Sarin Vijay Mythry[1]*, Dinesh N.[1], Asha V Thalange[2], Chakradhar Adupa[3], Nanditha Krishna[4], Praveen Kumar Reddy[5] and Madhuri Gummineni[6]

[1]*Department of Electronics and Communication Engineering, Vignan Institute of Technology and Science, Hyderabad, India*
[2]*Department of Electronics and Telecommunication Engineering, Walchand Institute of Technology, Solapur, India*
[3]*Department of Electronics and Communication Engineering, SR University, Warangal, India*
[4]*Department of Medical Electronics Engineering, Dayananda Sagar College of Engineering, Bengaluru, India*
[5]*Department of Electronics and Communication Engineering, Guru Nanak Dev Engineering College, Bidar, India*
[6]*Department of Electronics and Instrumentation Engineering, Vignan Institute of Technology and Science, Hyderabad, India*

Abstract

Modern medical diagnostics rely heavily on brain signal monitoring and analysis for the identification and treatment of neurological illnesses including epilepsy, Parkinson's disease, and sleep disturbances. Accurate capture of brain electrical impulses is crucial for technologies like electroencephalography (EEG) and brain-computer interfaces (BCIs). High power consumption, noise sensitivity, and the need for scalable and durable electrode designs are some of the major obstacles that these systems must overcome. A technology that has recently gained popularity in communication systems, multiplexing, offers the potential to address these issues. Improved data handling, lower power consumption, and uncompromised signal integrity are all benefits of multiplexing, which combines several signals for concurrent processing and transmission. The use of dense electrode arrays is

**Corresponding author*: sarinmythry@gmail.com

Ashish Maurya, Mandeep Singh and Balwinder Raj (eds.) Machine Learning in Nanoelectronics: Devices, Circuits and Systems, (89–112) © 2026 Scrivener Publishing LLC

made possible without adding complexity to the system, and multiplexing significantly enhances energy efficiency when applied to the capture of brain signals. Multiplexing brain signals to accomplish low-power, robust electrode sensing in medical diagnostic systems is the topic of this research. Brain signal capture, multiplexing concepts, and their incorporation into new sensing technologies are all covered. Multiplexing has the ability to transform medical diagnostics by tackling these difficulties and making them more efficient, accurate, and accessible. A multiplexer is a device used in electronics that conducts multiplexing; it passes one analogy or digital input signal, chosen from a variety of input signals, into a single line. This study presents the design of a 90nm CMOS 4:1 multiplexer with low power consumption using n-Pass Time Division Techniques. This research compares and simulates a few important multiplexer factors, including area, transistor count, and power dissipation. The measured area is 4.35μm^2 and no DRC violation. We shall specify Vdd as the constant power supply in static CMOS logic. Because energy recovery does not occur as it does in the case of static CMOS logic, the whole amount of energy is wasted across the resistor, resulting in very little energy being held by the capacitor.

***Keywords*:** Multiplexer, wearable medical devices (WMD), CMOS, analog front end (AFE), Cadence Virtuoso

4.1 Introduction

A multiplier is a device that passes many analog or digital input signals into a single output line after selecting one of the signals. A collection of inputs known as selection lines or control lines governs this selection. In many applications, including data routing, signal processing, and communication systems, multiplexers are essential. They are frequently employed in situations when several data sources must share a single transmission line or when data must be processed or examined in order of origin. Electronic switches or logic gates are commonly utilized in the implementation of multiplexers in digital systems. They are essential for simplifying interconnection networks and maximizing the use of available resources in digital circuits. Multiplexers, for example, allow numerous signals to be sent over a single communication channel in telecommunications, increasing efficiency and lowering costs. The design and evaluation of an 8:1 multiplexer and demultiplexer use different adiabatic logic styles like 2N2P, 2N-2N2P, and dual sleep approach in 90nm CMOS technology [1–8].

The brain is made up of oligodendrocytes, microglia, astrocytes, and neurons. The molecular fingerprints of these cells are distinct. Some of these biological signatures, such as Olig2 & Myelin Basic Protein & NeuN (neurons), GFAP (astrocytes), and Iba1 (macrophages/microglia) may be recognizable to you. Compounding RNA probes that identify the transcript using methods like *in situ* hybridization are among the probes that may be used to find these molecular fingerprints. Antibodies have several benefits when it comes to protein identification, even though they may not have the same sensitivity and specificity as RNA-based approaches. For instance, the localization of a certain protein can be revealed by antibody-based protein detection, indicating a specific function. One cytoskeletal protein that displays astrocytic morphologies is the astrocyte protein GFAP. a comparative study of 2:1 multiplexer design using three different logic families, evaluating their power-delay-area performance to guide the selection of an optimal logic style for low power multiplexer implementations [9–14]. The nucleus is where NeuN is found in neurons, which makes sense for a transcription factor. Highly arborized neurons can be shown by labelling dendrites and axons with antibodies such as NFL and MAP2. Further investigation of subcellular proteins, particularly in neurons, can provide more information on the composition and operation of cells [15–21].

A multiplexer's main purpose is to facilitate the effective transfer of data from several sources over a single channel. This is especially helpful in situations when it's necessary to share resources or aggregate data streams for additional processing. A multiplexer consists of $2n$ input lines, n selection lines, and one output line in its most basic configuration n. Presented at the International Conference on Signal Processing and Communication (ICSPC'17) is the design of a high flat gain neural signal amplifier for neuro recording applications. In the neural amplifier design, the main goals are to achieve extremely low power consumption, reject DC offsets, and minimize noise [3]. The maximum number of input lines that may be supported depends on the number of selection lines. A 4-to-1 multiplexer, for example, has one output line, two input lines, and one selection line for selecting between the two inputs [22–29].

Multiplexers are widely used in digital circuit design for functions including memory addressing, signal processing, and data routing as shown in Figure 4.1. Additionally, they are essential parts of communication networks because they allow numerous signals to be sent over a single transmission medium. Multiplexers range from basic analog switches to intricate digital circuits, and they are available in a variety of sizes and configurations. Two new reversible logic gates R-I and R-II provide efficient implementations of multiplexers, demultiplexers and other logic functions adhering to reversible computing principles for potential low-power applications. They are essential to modern electronics because of their efficiency

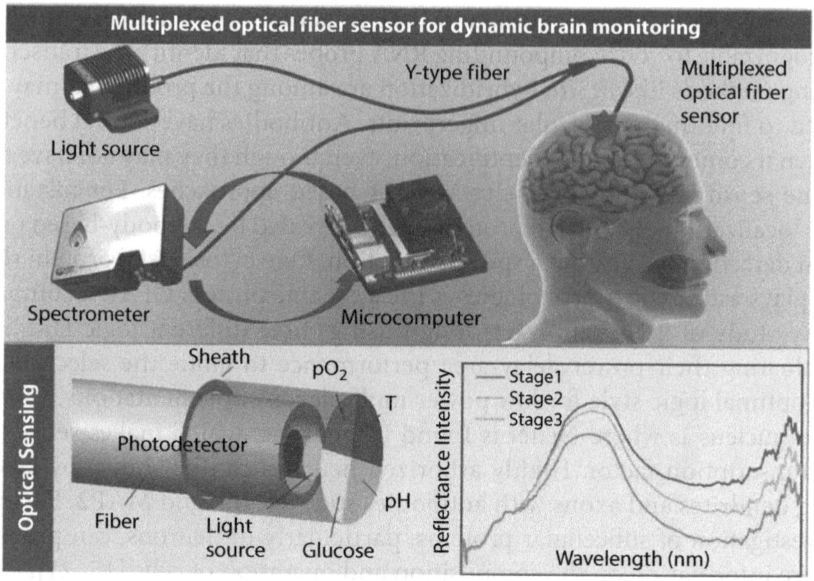

Figure 4.1 Multiplexed sensor for brain signal monitoring.

and adaptability, which allow for the smooth integration and control of many data streams and communication channels [30–37].

There are several varieties of multiplexers, or mux, each designed to meet certain needs and purposes. These are a few typical multiplexer types: Analog Multiplexer, Digital Multiplexer (Data Selector), Time-Division Multiplexer (TDM), Frequency-Division Multiplexer (FDM), Space-Division Multiplexer (SDM), Statistical Multiplexer, Wave Division Multiplexer (WDM), Digital Cross-Connect (DXC) [38–46]. These are a few of the most frequent multiplexer types seen in a range of applications. Each kind meets certain requirements in signal processing, data transfer, and communication with its own special qualities and benefits. Multiplexers, sometimes known as muxes, are adaptable parts having a broad variety of uses in several industries. A new design for a 4:1 multiplexer circuit uses ambipolar double-gate field-effect transistors (DG-FETs) like carbon nanotube FETs (CNTFETs) [5]. Additional information on multiplexers and their uses is provided below: Data Routing and Selection, Analog and Digital Signal Processing, Memory Addressing, Communication Systems, Digital Switching Systems, Test and Measurement Equipment, Control Systems, Digital Logic Design [47–55]. All things considered, multiplexers are essential to contemporary electronics since they make a variety of tasks such as data routing, signal processing, communication, and control possible. Their adaptability, effectiveness, and capacity to manage numerous inputs render them essential elements in both digital and analogy systems. The design and implementation of multiplexers uses schematic diagrams and VHDL (hardware description language) in an EDA (Electronic Design Automation) environment [6].

The typical human brain has more than 100 billion cells—almost as many as there are stars in the Milky Way! Our ability to think, remember, experience emotions, and interact with the outside world is powered by these brain cells working together [56–63]. We are genuinely formed by these cells. The neuron, which is the main kind of cell in the brain, is a highly polarized cell with arbores that are molecularly specialized. The neuron begins and drives information transfer, which in turn drives brain activity. The performance of two different 2:1 multiplexer design based on FinFET technology at the 18nm node [7]. Nevertheless, oligodendrocytes, microglia, and astrocytes are among the numerous non-neuronal cells that contribute to, if not directly affect, the maintenance of normal neuronal function [64–71]. They are also essential for both sickness and development. These brain cell types require staining to be recognized as distinct brain cells as well as to determine the shape of individual brain cells. Neuroscientists may assess numerous molecular targets concurrently in a

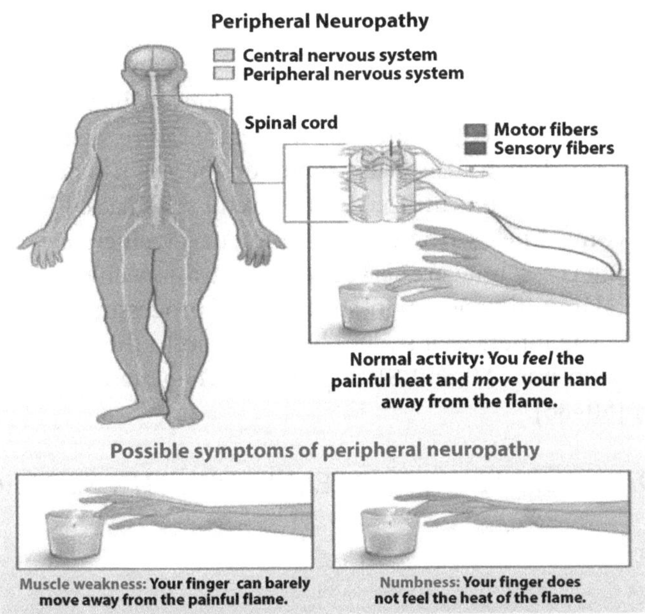

Figure 4.2 ENG signal recording for peripheral neuropathy.

single experiment thanks to multiplex methods and probes. This method makes it easier to molecularly profile individual cells within a network or inside a tissue, giving rise to a snapshot of cellular activity. The performance of the DTMOS 4:1 multiplexer with a conventional NMOS-based 4:1 multiplexer design in terms of power consumption, number of transistors used, and area [8]. Figure 4.2 depicts the ENG signal recording for peripheral neuropathy.

4.2 Methodology

We have designed a 4:1 Multiplexer using n-pass Time Division Techniques. Figure 4.3 shows the suggested 4 × 1 n-pass time division analog multiplexer architecture utilizing 90 nm CMOS technology. Using synchronized switches, the 4 × 1 time division multiplexing (TDM) technology transmits four different signals consecutively across a signal line. Low power pass transistor logic (LPPTL), which employs just six transistors, has been used in the design of the multiplexer. The inputs from electrodes with dimensions of L = 45 nm and W = 120 nm are coupled to the source/drain terminals of n-pass transistors. a reversible logic implementation of a 4:1 multiplexer and 1:4 demultiplexer using a reversible gate called the R gate. The design is analysed and compared against an existing design using Fredkin gates in terms of quantum cost, gate count, garbage outputs, quantum depth, and total cost [9].

The sensors provide the sampled input values, which are 1u V for the EEG, 63 mV for the pH, 100 mV for the temperature, and 10 mV for the ENG. Table 4.1 displays the truth table for the 4:1 n-pass time division analog multiplexer that is utilized in the circuit schematic [72–79]. A wide range of technical fields where combining energy efficiency and fast signal processing is essential are served by the ultra-low energy consumption GDI-based Hamming code high-speed signal processing communication system [10]. The inputs that should be conveyed to the output are chosen by the selection lines S0 and S1. Equation (4.1) generates a potential for each input [80–86].

$$O/P = \bar{S0}\,\bar{S1}\,ENG + \bar{S0}\,S1\,\mathrm{TEMP} + S0\,\bar{S1}\,PH + S0\,S1\,EEG \tag{4.1}$$

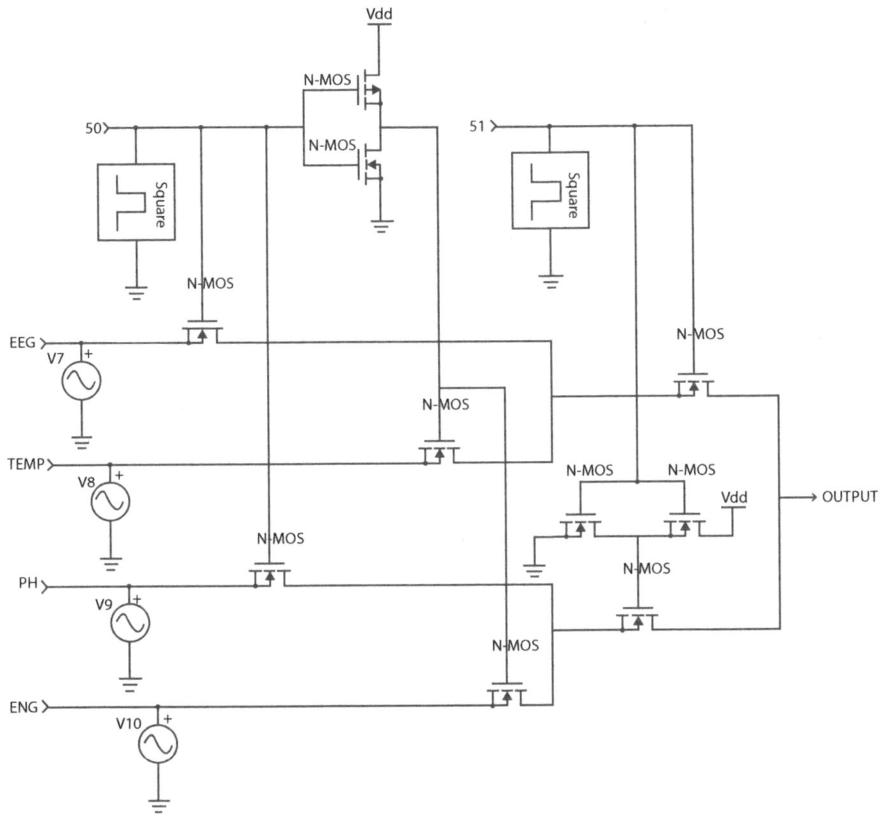

Figure 4.3 Proposed schematic of MULTIPLEXER.

Table 4.1 4X1 MUX truth table.

S0	*S1*	EEG	PH	TEMP	ENG	O/P(V)
0	0	0	0	0	10m	10m
0	1	0	0	100m	0	100m
1	0	0	63m	0	0	63m
1	1	1u	0	0	0	1u

4.3 Simulation Results

Figure 4.4 shows the circuit design of multiplexer designed with 10 transistors which has 4 inputs (EEG, ENG, PH, Tempe). Figures 4.5 to 4.7 describe the transient response, noise, and the power dissipation of the multiplexer [87–92]. Figures 4.8 and 4.9 show the layout of the circuit and area, DRC check of the layout of 4:1 Multiplexer. There is no DRC error, no DRC violation, area of the circuit is 4.3μ*m*2. Tables 4.2–4.5 depict the variation in the noise and power when there is a change in the supply voltage, load capacitance, temperature and EEG, ENG frequencies respectively of the multiplexer [93–99].

Figures 4.10 to 4.12 describe Monte Carlo simulation of transient response and noise with respect to temperature and load capacitance [100–106]. Figure 4.13 describes the variation in noise and power with respect to supply voltage. Table 4.6 depicts the parameters of MUX. And Table 4.7 depicts the comparison of proposed design with various literatures.

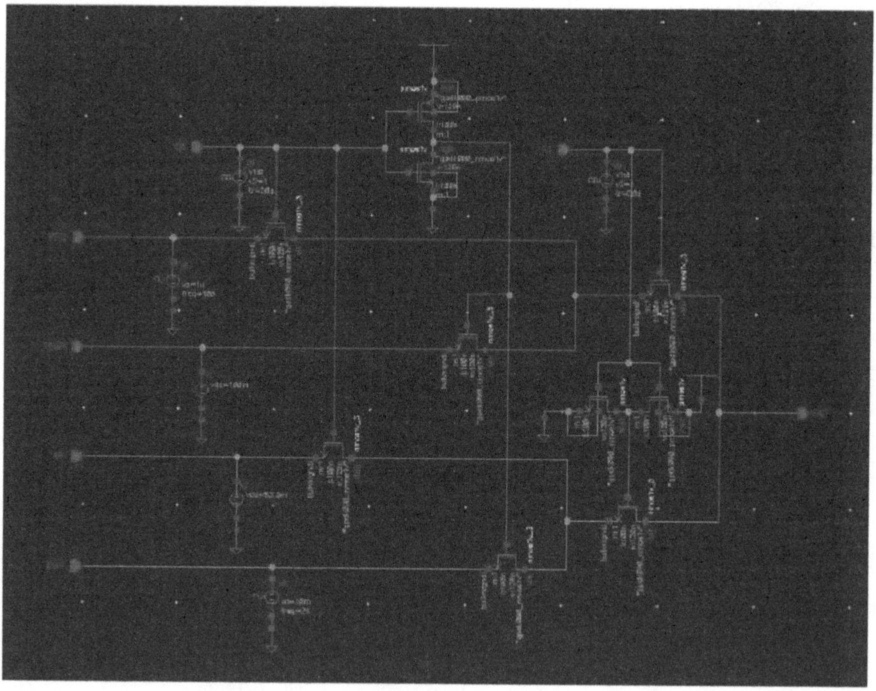

Figure 4.4 Schematic circuit of MULTIPLEXER.

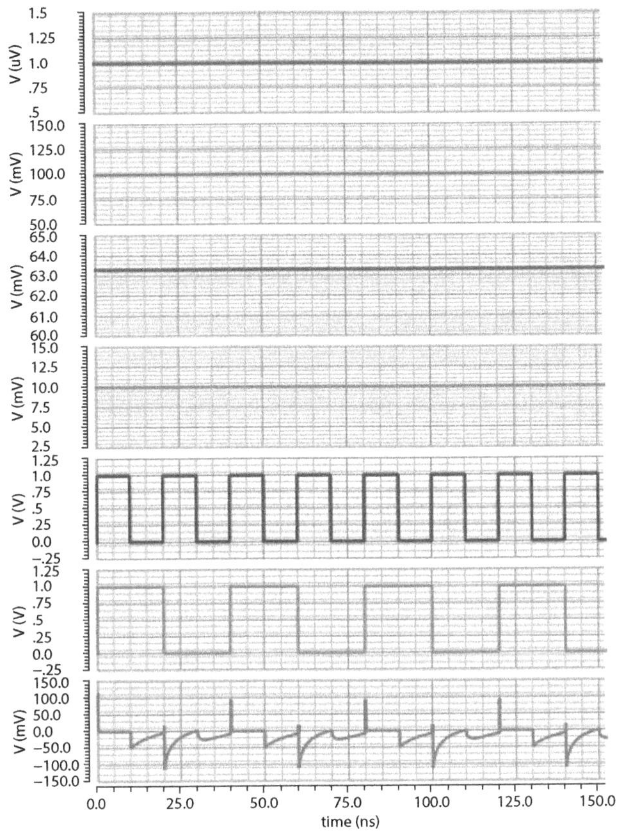

Figure 4.5 Transient response.

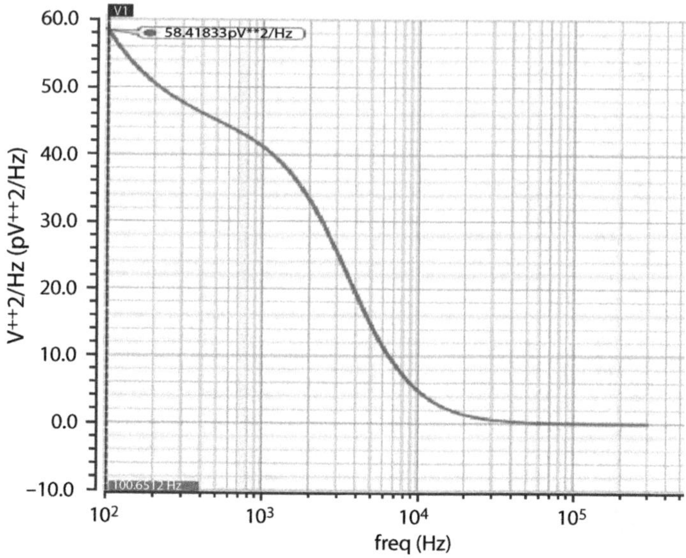

Figure 4.6 Noise analysis.

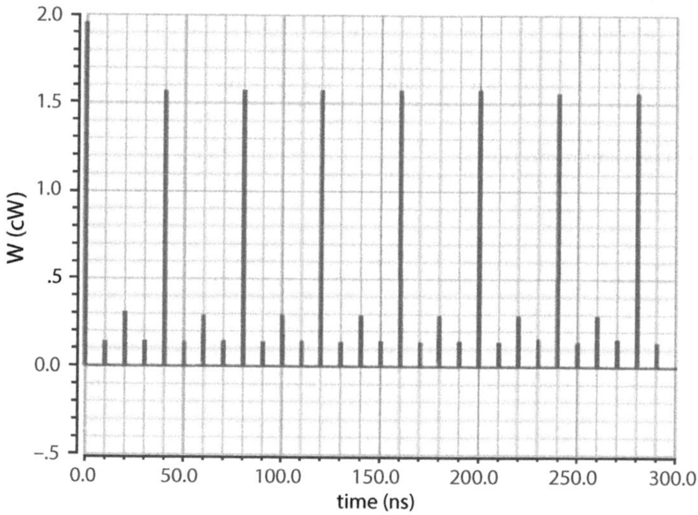

Figure 4.7 Power analysis.

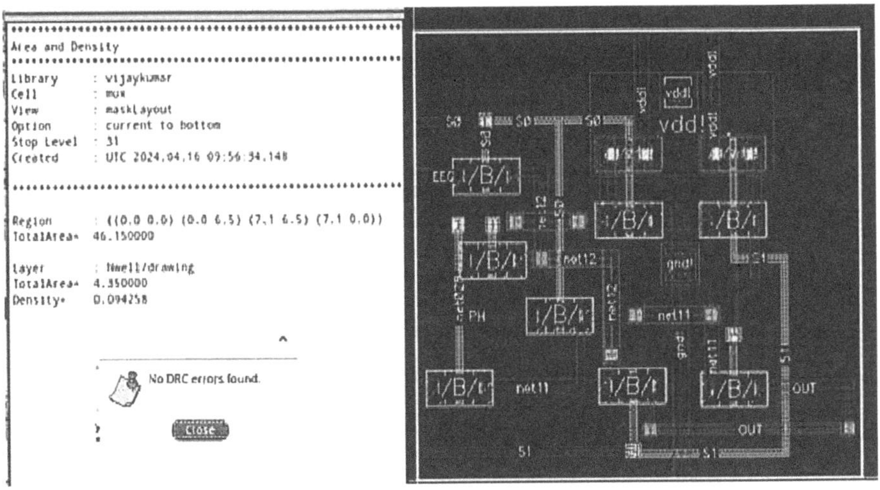

Figure 4.8 Layout and area of MUX with zero DRC errors.

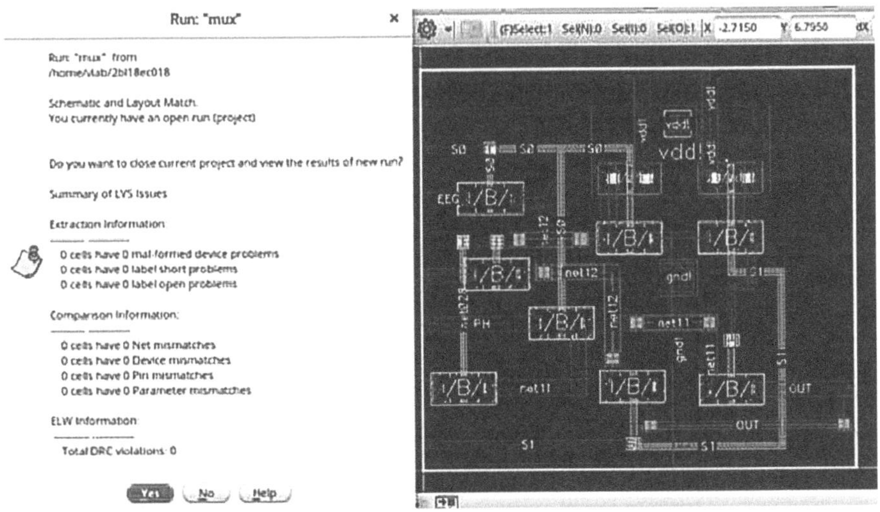

Figure 4.9 Layout vs schematic of MUX.

Table 4.2 Variation in noise, power with respect to voltage.

Vdc (V)	Noise(aV/√*Hz*)	Power (μW)
0.5	447.084	14.5
0.6	290.852	18.6
0.7	222.677	22.03
0.8	184.841	28.25
0.9	160.406	35.01
1	144.026	43.73
1.1	132.431	54.723
1.2	124.09	67.02
1.3	117.819	81.2
-1.4	113.23	97.9

Table 4.3 Variation in noise, power with respect to CL.

CL (pF)	Noise(pV/√*Hz*)	Power (μW)
0.5	58.448	1.56
0.6	58.443	1.56
0.7	58.437	1.56
0.8	58.430	1.56
0.9	58.422	1.56
10	58.414	1.56
1.1	58.404	1.56
1.2	58.394	1.56
1.3	58.383	1.56
1.4	58.370	1.56
1.5	58.357	1.56

Table 4.4 Variation in noise, power with respect to temperature.

Temperature (°C)	Noise($V/\sqrt{Hz}$)	Power (μW)
-75	1.839n	1.76
-58.33	1.054n	1.72
-41.67	500.486p	1.65
-25	251.091p	1.62
-8.33	140.054p	1.57
8.33	87.336p	1.59
25	60.703p	1.55
41.67	46.482p	1.53
58.33	38.54p	1.54
75	33.898p	1.56

Table 4.5 Variation in noise with respect to frequency.

EEG Freq (Hz)	ENG Freq (Hz)	Noise($pV/\sqrt{Hz}$)
10	20Hz	58.506
20	20Hz	58.506
30	20Hz	58.506
40	20Hz	58.506
50	20Hz	58.506
60	2.1k	58.506
70	2.2k	58.506
80	2.3k	58.506
90	2.4k	58.506
100	2.5k	58.506

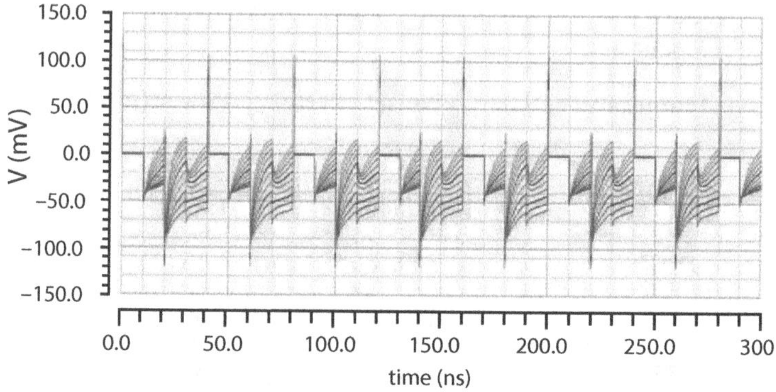

Figure 4.10 Monte Carlo simulation of transient response with respect to temperature.

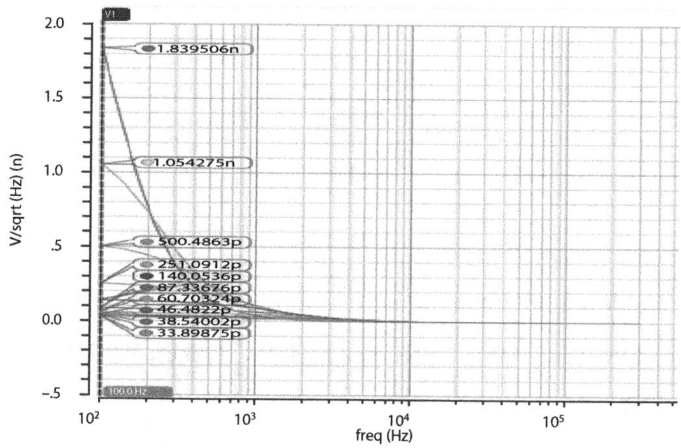

Figure 4.11 Monte Carlo simulation of noise with respect to temperature.

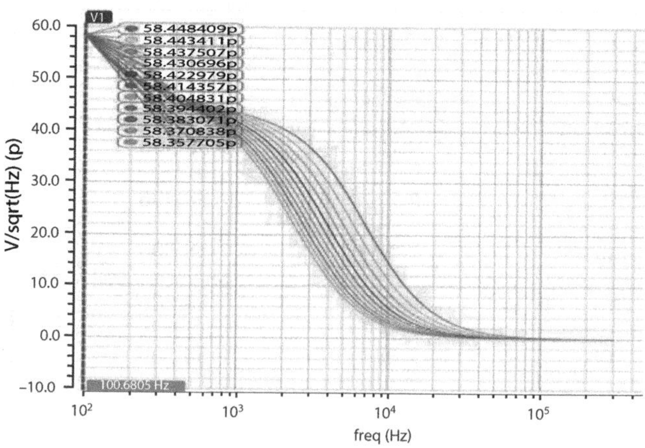

Figure 4.12 Monte Carlo simulation of noise with respect to load capacitance.

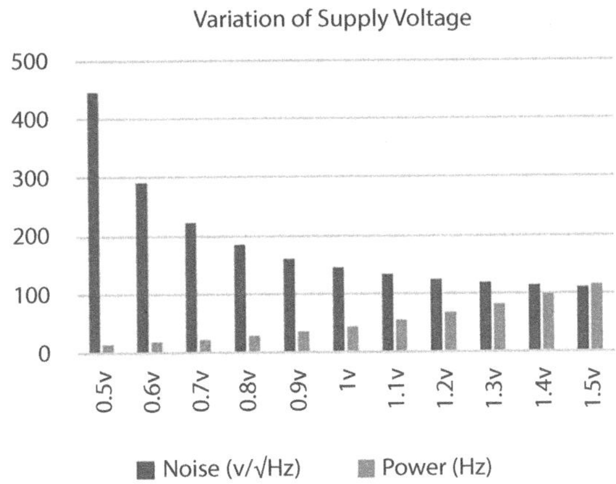

Figure 4.13 Variation in noise and power with respect to supply voltage.

Table 4.6 Parameters of the MUX.

S. no.	Parameter	Outputs
1	VDD	1.5 V
2	Phase Margin	583.66n°
3	Gain Margin	-3.6dB
4	Delay	64.3 pS
5	Power	1.56 μW
6	Load Capacitance	10 pF

Table 4.7 Comparison of MUX with various literatures.

Work	[2]	[11]	[7]	[9]	This work
Year	2020	2019	2020	2017	2024
Technology	90nm	90nm	90nm	90nm	90nm
Noise	55.96a	30.4 μ	20.4n	70.45p	58.44p
Power(W)	219.9p	47.57μ	46.69n	136.5n	1.56μ

4.4 Conclusion

This work effectively used n-Pass Time Division Techniques to examine the 4:1 multiplexer with 90nm technology. Although just four input multiplexers are taken into consideration for specifications in the study, these also apply to larger input multiplexers. Thus, a simpler circuit with reduced power usage was used in the paper's conclusion. Further uses for this performance-enhancing MUX include telephone networks, computer memory, and communication systems. The amount of electricity consumed is 1.95μW.

References

1. Mittal, D. and Niranjan, A., Designing of Multiplexer and De-Multiplexer using different Adiabatic Logic in 90nm Technology, in: *Proceedings of the IEEE - 43488 9th ICCCNT 2018*, Bengaluru, India, July 10-12, 2018, IISC.
2. Kumar, N. and Mittal, P., Performance Investigation of 2:1 Multiplexer using 90nm Technology Node for Low Power Application, in: *Proceedings of 2020 International Conference on Electrical and Electronics Engineering (ICE3-2020)*.
3. Mythry, S.V., Jackuline Moni, D., Meng, W., A bulk-driven, buffer-biased, gain-boosted amplifier for biomedical signal enhancement. *Cogent Eng.*, 6, 1, 2019, DOI: 10.1080/23311916.2019.1658966.
4. Gopal, L., Raj, N., Gopalai, A.A., Singh, A.K., Design of Reversible Multiplexer/De-multiplexer, in: *Proceedings with 2014 IEEE International Conference on Control System, Computing and Engineering*, Penang, Malaysia, 28–30 November 2014.
5. Jabeur, K., O'Connor, I., Yakymets, N., Le Beux, S., High performance 4:1 multiplexer with ambipolar double-gate FETs, in: *Proceedings with 2011 IEEE*.
6. Jiang, L. and Huang, C., Design and Realization of Multiplexer Based on Schematic and VHDL Language, in: *Proceedings with 2010 International Conference on Optics, Photonics and Energy Engineering*, IEEE, 2010.
7. Kumar, N., Mittal, P., Mittal, M., Performance Analysis of FinFET based 2:1 Multiplexers for Low Power Application, in: *Proceedings with 2020 IEEE Students' Conference on Engineering & Systems (SCES)*, Prayag raj, India, July 10–12, 2020.
8. Sheetal, Kumar, A., Kandari, R., Bharti, S., Performance Analysis of 4:1 Multiplexer with DTMOS Technique, in: *Proceedings with 2019 IEEE*.
9. Mann, S. and Jain, R., Designed Analysis of Reversible Multiplexer and Demultiplexer using R-Gates, in: *Proceedings with Proceeding International Conference on (RISE-2017)*, 27–29 October, 2017.

10. Mythry, S.V. and Moni, D.J., High flat gain low noise neural signal recording amplifier. *2017 International Conference on Signal Processing and Communication (ICSPC)*, Coimbatore, India, pp. 12–17, 2017, doi: 10.1109/CSPC.2017.8305837.
11. Sheetal, Kumar, A., Kandari, R., Bharti, S., Performance Analysis of 4:1 Multiplexer with DTMOS Technique, 978-1-7281-1253-4/19/$31.00 © 2019 IEEE.
12. Bhardwaj, A., Kumar, P., Raj, B., Anand, S., Design and Performance Optimization of doping-less Vertical Nanowire TFET Using Gate Stack Technique. *J. Electron. Mater. (JEMS)*, Springer, 41, 7, 4005–4013, 2022.
13. Singh, J. and Raj, B., Tunnel Current Model of Asymmetric MIM Structure Levying Various Image Forces to Analyze the Characteristics of Filamentary Memristor. *Appl. Phys. A*, Springer, 125, 3, 203.1–203.11, Feb 2019.
14. Goyal, C., Ubhi, J.S., Raj, B., Low Leakage Zero Ground Noise Nanoscale Full Adder using Source Biasing Technique. *J. Nanoelectron. Optoelectron.*, American Scientific Publishers, 14, 360–370, March 2019.
15. Singh, G., Sarin, R.K., Raj, B., A Novel Robust Exclusive-OR Function Implementation in QCA Nanotechnology with Energy Dissipation Analysis. *J. Comput. Electron.*, Springer, 15, 2, 455–465, June 2016.
16. Wadhwa, G., Kamboj, P., Raj, B., Design optimisation of junctionless TFET biosensor for high sensitivity. *Adv. Nat. Sci.: Nanosci. Nanotechnol.*, 10, 045001 (7), 2019.
17. Bansal, P. and Raj, B., Memristor Modeling and Analysis for Linear Dopant Drift Kinetics. *J. Nanoeng. Nanomanuf.*, American Scientific Publishers, 6, 1–7, 2016.
18. Ashima, Vaithiyanathan, D., Raj, B., Performance Analysis of Charge Plasma induced Graded Channel Si nanotube. *J. Eng. Res. (JER)*, EMSME Special Issue, 146–154, Aug 2021.
19. Tomar, A.S., Magraiya, V.K., Raj, B., Scaling of Access and Data Transistor for High Performance DRAM Cell Design. *Quantum Matter*, 2, 412–416, Oct. 2013.
20. Jain, N. and Raj, B., Parasitic Capacitance and Resistance Model Development and Optimization of Raised Source/Drain SOI FinFET Structure for Analog Circuit Applications. *J. Nanoelectron. Optoelectron.*, ASP, USA, 13, 531–539, April 2018.
21. Singh, S., Vishvakarma, S.K., Raj, B., Analytical Modeling of Split-Gate Junction-Less Transistor for a Biosensor Application. *Sens. Bio-Sens.*, Elsevier, 18, 31–36, April 2018.
22. Gopal, M. and Raj, B., Low Power 8T SRAM Cell Design for High Stability Video Applications. *ITSI Trans. Electr. Electron. Eng.*, 1, 5, 91–97, 2013.
23. Raj, B., Mitra, J., Bihani, D.K., Rangharajan, V., Saxena, A.K., Dasgupta, S., Analysis of Noise Margin, Power and Process Variation for 32 nm FinFET Based 6T SRAM Cell. *J. Comput. (JCP)*, Academy Publisher, Finland, 5, 6, 1–8, 2010.

24. Sharma, D., Mehra, R., Raj, B., Comparative Analysis of Photovoltaic Technologies for High Efficiency Solar Cell Design. *Superlattices Microstruct.*, Elsevier, 153, 106861, May 2021.
25. Kaur, P., Buttar, A.S., Raj, B., A comprehensive Analysis of Nanoscale Transistor based Biosensor: A Review. *Indian J. Pure Appl. Phys.*, 59, 304–318, April 2021.
26. Yadav, D., Raj, B., Raj, B., Design and Simulation of Low Power Microcontroller for IoT Applications. *J. Sens. Lett.*, ASP, 18, 401–409, May 2020.
27. Singh, S. and Raj, B., A 2-D Analytical Surface Potential and Drain current Modeling of Double-Gate Vertical t-shaped Tunnel FET. *J. Comput. Electron.*, Springer, 19, 1154–1163, April 2020.
28. Singh, J. and Raj, B., An Accurate and Generic Window function for Nonlinear Memristor Model. *J. Comput. Electron.*, Springer, 18, 2, 640–647, June 2019.
29. Kaur, M., Gupta, N., Kumar, S., Raj, B., Singh, A.K., Comparative RF and Crosstalk Analysis of Carbon Based Nano Interconnects. *IET Circuits Devices Syst.*, 15, 6, 493–503, Feb 2021.
30. Kandasamy, N., Ahmad, F., Ajitha, D., Raj, B., Telagam, N., Quantum Dot Cellular Automata based Scan Flip Flop and Boundary Scan Register. *IETE J. Res.*, 66, 535–548, 2020.
31. Singh, J. and Raj, B., Design and Investigation of 7T2M NVSARM with Enhanced Stability and Temperature Impact on Store/Restore Energy. *IEEE Trans. Very Large Scale Integr. Syst.*, 27, 6, 1322–1328, June 2019.
32. Bhardwaj, A.K., Gupta, S., Raj, B., Singh, A., Impact of Double Gate Geometry on the Performance of Carbon Nanotube Field Effect Transistor Structures for Low Power Digital Design. *Comput. Theor. Nanosci.*, ASP, 16, 1813–1820, 2019.
33. Jain, N. and Raj, B., Thermal Stability Analysis and Performance Exploration of Asymmetrical Dual-k underlap Spacer (ADKUS) SOI FinFET for Security and Privacy Applications. *Indian J. Pure Appl. Phys. (IJPAP)*, 57, 352–360, May 2019.
34. Jain, N. and Raj, B., Dual-k Spacer Region Variation at the Drain Side of Asymmetric SOI FinFET Structure: Performance Analysis towards the Analog/RF Design Applications. *J. Nanoelectron. Optoelectron.*, American Scientific Publishers, 14, 349–359, March 2019.
35. Singh, J., Sharma, S., Raj, B., Khosla, M., Analysis of barrier layer thickness on performance of In1-xGaxAs based Gate Stack Cylindrical Gate Nanowire MOSFET. *JNO*, ASP, 13, 1473–1477, Oct 2018.
36. Jain, N. and Raj, B., Analysis and Performance Exploration of High-k SOI FinFETs Over the Conventional Low-k SOI FinFET toward Analog/RF Design. *J. Semicond. (JoS)*, IOP Science, 39, 12, 124002-1–7, Dec 2018.
37. Goyal, C., Ubhi, J.S., Raj, B., A reliable leakage reduction technique for approximate full adder with reduced ground bounce noise. *J. Math. Probl. Eng.*, Hindawi, 2018, 3501041, 16, 15 Oct 2018.

38. Anuradha, Singh, J., Raj, B., Khosla, M., Design and Performance Analysis of Nano-scale Memristor-based Nonvolatile SRAM. *J. Sens. Lett.*, American Scientific Publishers, 6, 798–805, Oct 2018.
39. Wadhwa, G. and Raj, B., Parametric Variation Analysis of Charge-Plasma-based Dielectric Modulated JLTFET for Biosensor Application. *IEEE Sens. J.*, 18, 15, 6070–6077 (SCI), August 1, 2018.
40. Singh, J. and Raj, B., Comparative Analysis of Memristor Models for Memories Design. *JoS*, IoP, 39, 7, 074006-1–12, July 2018.
41. Yadav, D., Chouhan, S.S., Vishvakarma, S.K., Raj, B., Application Specific Microcontroller Design for IoT based WSN. *Sens. Lett.*, ASP, 16, 374–385, May 2018.
42. Singh, G., Sarin, R.K., Raj, B., Fault-Tolerant Design and Analysis of Quantum-Dot Cellular Automata Based Circuits. *IEEE/IET Circuits Devices Syst.*, 12, 638–64, 2018.
43. Singh, J. and Raj, B., Modeling of Mean Barrier Height Levying Various Image Forces of Metal Insulator Metal Structure to Enhance the Performance of Conductive Filament Based Memristor Model. *IEEE Nanotechnol.*, 17, 2, 268–267, March 2018.
44. Jain, A., Sharma, S., Raj, B., Analysis of Triple Metal Surrounding Gate (TM-SG) III-V Nanowire MOSFET for Photosensing Application. *Opto-Electron. J.*, Elsevier, 26, 2, 141–148, May 2018.
45. Jain, A., Sharma, S., Raj, B., Design and Analysis of High Sensitivity Photosensor Using Cylindrical Surrounding Gate MOSFET for Low Power Sensor Applications. *Eng. Sci. Technol. Int. J.*, Elsevier's, 19, 4, 1864–1870, December 2016.
46. Saiphani Kumar, G., Singh, A., Raj, B., Design and Analysis of Gate All Around CNTFET based SRAM cell Design. *J. Comput. Electron.*, Springer, 17, 1, 138–145, March 2018.
47. pal Singh, G., Sohi, B.S., Raj, B., Material Properties Analysis of Graphene Base Transistor (GBT) for VLSI Analog Circuits. *Indian J. Pure Appl. Phys. (IJPAP)*, 55, 896–902, Dec 2017.
48. Kumar, S. and Raj, B., Estimation of Stability and Performance metric for Inward Access Transistor based 6T SRAM Cell Design using n-type/p-type DMDG-GDOV TFET. *IEEE VLSI Circuits Syst. Lett.*, 3, 2, 25–39, June 2017.
49. Sharma, S., Kumar, A., Pattanaik, M., Raj, B., Forward Body Biased Multimode Multi-Threshold CMOS Technique for Ground Bounce Noise Reduction in Static CMOS Adders. *Int. J. Inf. Electron. Eng.*, 3, 3, 567–572, 2013.
50. Singh, H., Kumar, P., Raj, B., Performance Analysis of Majority Gate SET Based 1-bit Full Adder. *Int. J. Comput. Commun. Eng. (IJCCE)*, IACSIT Press Singapore, ISSN: 2010-3743, 2, 4, 2013.
51. Bhardwaj, A.K., Gupta, S., Raj, B., Investigation of Parameters for Schottky Barrier (SB) Height for Schottky Barrier Based Carbon Nanotube Field Effect Transistor Device. *J. Nanoelectron. Optoelectron.*, ASP, 15, 783–791, July 2020.

52. Bansal, P. and Raj, B., Memristor: A Versatile Nonlinear Model for Dopant Drift and Boundary Issues. *JCTN*, American Scientific Publishers, 14, 5, 2319–2325, May 2017.
53. Jain, N. and Raj, B., An Analog and Digital Design Perspective Comprehensive Approach on Fin-FET (Fin-Field Effect transistor) Technology - A Review. *Rev. Adv. Sci. Eng. (RASE)*, ASP, 5, 1–14, 2016.
54. Raj, B., Saxena, A.K., Dasgupta, S., Analytical Modeling for the Estimation of Leakage Current and Subthreshold Swing Factor of Nanoscale Double Gate FinFET Device. *Microelectron. Int.*, UK, 26, 53–63, 2009.
55. Soniya, Singh, S., Wadhwa, G., Raj, B., An Analytical Modeling for Dual Source Vertical Tunnel Field Effect Transistor. *Int. J. Recent Technol. Eng. (IJRTE)*, 8, 2, 603–608, July 2019.
56. Singh, S. and Raj, B., Design and analysis of hetrojunction Vertical T-shaped Tunnel Field Effect Transistor. *J. Electron. Mater.*, Springer, 48, 10, 6253–6260, October 2019.
57. Goyal, C., Ubhi, J.S., Raj, B., A Low Leakage CNTFET based Inexact Full Adder for Low Power Image Processing Applications. *Int. J. Circuit Theory Appl.*, Wiley, 47, 9, 1446–1458, September 2019.
58. Raj, B., Saxena, A.K., Dasgupta, S., A Compact Drain Current and Threshold Voltage Quantum Mechanical Analytical Modeling for FinFETs. *J. Nanoelectron. Optoelectron. (JNO)*, USA, 3, 2, 163–170, 2008.
59. Wadhwa, G. and Raj, B., An Analytical Modeling of Charge Plasma based Tunnel Field Effect Transistor with Impacts of Gate underlap Region. *Superlattices Microstruct.*, Elsevier, 142, 106512, June 2020.
60. Singh, S. and Raj, B., Modeling and Simulation analysis of SiGe hetrojunction Double GateVertical t-shaped Tunnel FET. *Superlattices Microstruct.*, Elsevier, 142, 106496, June 2020.
61. Jain, N. and Raj, B., Device and Circuit Co-Design Perspective Comprehensive Approach on FinFET Technology - A Review. *J. Electron Devices*, 23, 1, 1890–1901, 2016.
62. Kumar, S. and Raj, B., Analysis of I_{ON} and Ambipolar Current for Dual-Material Gate-drain Overlapped DG-TFET. *J. Nanoelectron. Optoelectron.*, American Scientific Publishers, USA, 11, 323–333, June 2016.
63. Anjum, N., Bali, T., Raj, B., Design And Simulation Of Handwritten Multiscript Character Recognition. *Int. J. Adv. Res. Comput. Commun. Eng.*, 2, 7, 2544–2549, July 2013.
64. Singh, K. and Raj, B., Performance and analysis of temperature dependent Multi-walled Carbon Nanotubes as Global Interconnects at different technology nodes. *J. Comput. Electron.*, Springer, 14, 2, 469–476, June 2015.
65. Kumar, S. and Raj, B., Compact channel potential analytical Modeling of DG-TFET based on Evanescent–mode Approach. *J. Comput. Electron.*, Springer, 14, 2, 820–827, July 2015.

66. Singh, K. and Raj, B., Temperature Dependent Modeling and Performance Evaluation of Multi-Walled CNT and Single-Walled CNT as Global Interconnects. *J. Electron. Mater.*, Springer, 44, 12, 4825–4835, Dec 2015.
67. Sharma, V.K., Pattanaik, M., Raj, B., INDEP approach for leakage reduction in nanoscale CMOS circuits. *Int. J. Electron.*, Taylor & Francis, 102, 2, 200–215, 2014.
68. Singh, K. and Raj, B., Influence of Temperature on MWCNT bundle, SWCNT bundle and Copper interconnects for Nanoscaled Technology nodes. *J. Mater. Sci.: Mater. Electron.*, Springer, 26, 8, 6134–6142, 2015.
69. Anjum, N., Bali, T., Raj, B., Design and Simulation of Handwritten Gurumukhi and Devanagri Numerical Recognition. *Int. J. Comput. Appl.*, Foundation of Computer Science, New York, USA, 73, 12, 16–21, 2013.
70. Sharma, S.K., Kumar, P., Raj, B., Raj, B., $In_{1-x}Ga_xAs$ Double Metal Gate-Stacking Cylindrical Nanowire MOSFET for highly sensitive Photo detector. *J. Silicon*, Springer, 14, 3535–3541, 2022.
71. Raj, B., Saxena, A.K., Dasgupta, S., Analytical Modeling of Quasi Planar Nanoscale Double Gate FinFET with Source/Drain Resistance and field dependent carrier mobility: A quantum mechanical study. *J. Comput. (JCP)*, Academy Publisher, Finland, 4, 9, 1–8, 2009.
72. Bhushan, S., Khandelwal, S., Raj, B., Analyzing Different Mode FinFET based Memory Cell at Different Power Supply for Leakage Reduction, Seventh International Conference on Bio-Inspired Computing: Theories and Application, (BIC-TA 2012). *Adv. Intell. Syst. Comput.*, 202, 89–100, 2013.
73. Singh, J. and Raj, B., Temperature Dependent Analytical Modeling and Simulations of Nanoscale Memristor. *Eng. Sci. Technol. Int. J.*, Elsevier's, 21, 862–868, Oct 2018.
74. Singh, S., Bala, S., Raj, B., Raj, B., Improved Sensitivity of Dielectric Modulated Junctionless Transistor for Nanoscale Biosensor Design. *Sens. Lett.*, ASP, 18, 328–333, April 2020.
75. Kumar, V., Vishvakarma, S.K., Raj, B., Design and Performance Analysis of ASIC for IoT Applications. *Sens. Lett.*, ASP, 18, 31–38, Jan 2020.
76. Jaiswal, A., Sarin, R.K., Raj, B., Sukhija, S., A Novel Circular Slotted Microstrip-fed Patch Antenna with Three Triangle Shape Defected Ground Structure for Multiband Applications. *Adv. Electromagn. (AEM)*, 7, 3, 56–63, Aug 2018.
77. Wadhwa, G. and Raj, B., Label Free Detection of Biomolecules using Charge-Plasma-Based Gate Underlap Dielectric Modulated Junctionless TFET. *J. Electron. Mater. (JEMS)*, Springer, 47, 8, 4683–4693, August 2018.
78. Singh, G., Sarin, R.K., Raj, B., Design and Performance Analysis of a New Efficient Coplanar Quantum-Dot Cellular Automata Adder. *Indian J. Pure Appl. Phys. (IJPAP)*, 55, 97–103, February 2017.
79. Kaur, P., Pandey, V., Raj, B., Comparative Study of Efficient Design, Control and Monitoring of Solar Power using IoT. *Sens. Lett.*, ASP, 18, 419–426, May 2020.

80. Bhardwaj, A.K., Gupta, S., Raj, B., Development & Analysis of compact model for Double Gate Schottky Barrier CNTFET. *J. Nanoelectron. Optoelectron.*, ASP, 15, 1199–1208, Aug 2020.
81. Wadhwa, G., Kamboj, P., Singh, J., Raj, B., Design and Investigation of Junctionless DGTFET for Biological Molecule Recognition. *Trans. Electr. Electron. Mater.*, Springer, 22, 282–289, 2021.
82. Verma, S.K., Singh, S., Wadhwa, G., Raj, B., Detection of Biomolecules using Charge-Plasma based Gate Underlap Dielectric Modulated Dopingless TFET. *Trans. Electr. Electron. Mater. (TEEM)*, Springer, 21, 528–535, June 2020.
83. Jain, N. and Raj, B., Impact of underlap spacer region variation on Electrostatic and analog/RF performance of symmetrical high-k SOI FinFET at 20 nm channel length. *J. Semicond. (JoS)*, IOP Science, 38, 12, 122002, Dec 2017.
84. Singh, S. and Raj, B., Analytical Modeling and Simulation analysis of T-shaped III-V heterojunction Vertical T-FET. *Superlattices Microstruct.*, Elsevier, 147, 106717, Nov 2020.
85. Singh, G., Sarin, R.K., Raj, B., Design and Analysis of Area Efficient QCA Based Reversible Logic Gates. *J. Microprocess. Microsys.*, Elsevier, 52, 59–68, May 2017.
86. Singh, S. and Raj, B., Parametric variation analysis on hetero-junction Vertical t-shape TFET for Supressing ambipolar conduction. *Indian J. Pure Appl. Phys.*, 58, 478–485, June 2020.
87. Soniya, Singh, S., Wadhwa, G., Raj, B., Design and Analysis of Dual Source Vertical Tunnel Field Effect Transistor for high performance. *Trans. Electr. Electron. Mater.*, Springer, 21, 74–82, Oct 2019.
88. Kaur, M., Gupta, N., Kumar, S., Raj, B., Singh, A.K., RF Performance Analysis of Intercalated Graphene Nanoribbon Based Global Level Interconnects. *J. Comput. Electron.*, Springer, 19, 1002–1013, June 2020.
89. Wadhwa, G. and Raj, B., Design and Performance Analysis of Junctionless TFET Biosensor for high sensitivity. *IEEE Nanotechnol.*, 18, 567–574, 2019.
90. Singh, J. and Raj, B., Enhanced Nonlinear Memristor Model Encapsulating Stochastic Dopant Drift. *JNO*, ASP, 14, 958–963, 2019.
91. Singh, M., Chaudhary, T., Raj, B., Enhancing FeFET Structures for Non-volatile On-chip Memories: Design and Comparative Analysis. *Int. J. Numer. Modell. Electron. Netw. Devices Fields*, 38, 1–9, 2024.
92. Singh, M., Chaudhary, T., Raj, B., Drain Current and Transconductance Analysis of GaN GAA Nanowire FET with High K Dielectric. *ECS J. Sci. Technol.*, 12, 6070–6077, 2023.
93. Singh, M., Chaudhary, T., Raj, B., Design of Si and Ge Nanowire FET for Low Power Application. *J. Silicon*, Springer, 15, 1491–1497, 2023.
94. Singh, M., Chaudhary, T., Raj, B., Electrical Characteristics Analysis of FeFET for Low Power Applications. *J. Nano*, 37, 1–8, 2024.

95. Kumar, M., Chaudhary, T., Raj, B., Design and Comparative Analysis of Ferroelectric Nanowire with Dielectric HfO_2 and Al_2O_3 for Low Power Applications. *J. Electron. Mater.*, Springer, 53, 6785–6791, 2024.
96. Khandelwal, S., Gupta, V., Raj, B., Gupta, R.D., Process Variability Aware Low Leakage Reliable Nano Scale DG-FinFET SRAM Cell Design Technique. *J. Nanoelectron. Optoelectron.*, 10, 6, 810–817, December 2015.
97. Sharma, V.K., Pattanaik, M., Raj, B., ONOFIC Approach: Low Power High Speed Nanoscale VLSI Circuits Design. *Int. J. Electron.*, Taylor & Francis, 101, 1, 61–73, 2014.
98. Khandelwal, S., Raj, B., Gupta, R.D., FinFET based 6T SRAM Cell Design: Analysis of Performance Metric, Process Variation and Temperature Effect. *J. Comput. Theor. Nanosci.*, ASP, USA, 12, 2500–2506, 2015.
99. Singh, S., Yadav, S., Rahul, J., Srivastava, A., Raj, B., Impact of HfO_2 in Graded Channel Dual Insulator Double Gate MOSFET. *J. Comput. Theor. Nanosci.*, American Scientific Publishers, 12, 6, 950–953, April 2015.
100. Sharma, V.K., Pattanaik, M., Raj, B., PVT variations aware low leakage INDEP approach for nanoscale CMOS Circuits. *Microelectron. Reliab.*, Elsevier, 54, 90–99, 2014.
101. Raj, B., Saxena, A.K., Dasgupta, S., Quantum Mechanical Analytical Modeling of Nanoscale DG FinFET: Evaluation of Potential, Threshold Voltage and Source/Drain Resistance. *Elsevier's J. Mater. Sci. Semicond. Process.*, Elsevier, 16, 4, 1131–1137, 2013.
102. Gopal, M., Prasad, S.S.D., Raj, B., 8T SRAM Cell Design for Dynamic and Leakage Power Reduction. *Int. J. Comput. Appl.*, Foundation of Computer Science, New York, USA, 71, 9, 43–48, June 2013.
103. Pattanaik, M., Raj, B., Sharma, S., Kumar, A., Diode Based Trimode Multi-Threshold CMOS Technique for Ground Bounce Noise Reduction in Static CMOS Adders. *Adv. Mater. Res.*, Trans Tech Publications, Switzerland, 548, 885–889, 2012.
104. Raj, B., Saxena, A.K., Dasgupta, S., Nanoscale FinFET Based SRAM Cell Design: Analysis of Performance metric, Process variation, Underlapped FinFET and Temperature effect. *IEEE Circuits Syst. Mag.*, 11, 2, 38–50, 2011.
105. Sharma, V.K., Pattanaik, M., Raj, B., Leakage Current ONOFIC Approach for Deep Submicron VLSI Circuit Design. *Int. J. Electr. Comput. Electron. Commun. Eng.*, World Academy of Sciences, Engineering and Technology, 7, 4, 239–244, 2013.
106. Kaur, P., Gill, S.S., Raj, B., Comparative Analysis of OFETs Materials and Devices for Sensor Applications. *J. Silicon*, Springer, 14, 4463–4471, 2022.

5

Hardware Architectures and Optimization Techniques for Convolutional Neural Network Accelerators

Hemkant Nehete[1]*, Gaurav Verma, Amit Monga[1], Alok Kumar Shukla[2], Shailendra Yadav[1] and Brajesh Kumar Kaushik[1]

[1]*Department of Electronics and Communication Engineering, Indian Institute of Technology Roorkee, Roorkee, India*
[2]*Department of Electronics and Communication Engineering, Madan Mohan Malaviya University of Technology, Gorakhpur, India*

Abstract
The rapid advancement in artificial intelligence (AI), particularly in convolutional neural networks (CNNs) for machine vision tasks, has been significantly propelled by the increasing availability of large-scale data generated by edge devices that monitor our daily activities. However, CNNs are inherently memory- and compute-intensive, posing significant challenges to their deployment on conventional hardware architectures. This mismatch results in inefficiencies in power consumption, latency, and overall performance, which hinder the scalability and real-time applicability of such systems. While traditional hardware solutions, including application-specific integrated circuits (ASICs), field-programmable gate arrays (FPGAs), and graphic processing units (GPUs), have demonstrated their potential in accelerating CNN-based computations, their adoption is often limited by high development costs, extended design and validation times, elevated power requirements, and constrained throughput. To address these limitations, a variety of deep learning hardware architectures and optimization algorithms have been proposed over recent years. These innovations aim to address critical concerns, including energy efficiency, computational speed, and the adaptability of hardware to evolving AI models. Furthermore, the emergence of techniques such as model compression has significantly contributed to optimizing the deployment of CNNs on resource-constrained devices, enabling them to perform complex

**Corresponding author*: nehete_h@ece.iitr.ac.in

Ashish Maurya, Mandeep Singh and Balwinder Raj (eds.) Machine Learning in Nanoelectronics: Devices, Circuits and Systems, (113–154) © 2026 Scrivener Publishing LLC

computations while minimizing resource utilization. This chapter provides a comprehensive review of the progress made in the design and implementation of CNN accelerators and associated computing hardware. It systematically examines the unique features, benefits, and trade-offs of key hardware platforms, including ASICs, FPGAs, CPUs, and GPUs, in the context of CNN applications. Additionally, the chapter explores recent advancements in architectural and algorithmic optimization techniques, such as model compression and sparsity exploitation, which aim to enhance the efficiency of CNNs. The challenges currently faced in developing scalable, power-efficient, and high-performance AI systems are discussed, along with future directions to address these issues. This holistic analysis serves as a valuable resource for researchers and practitioners striving to bridge the gap between state-of-the-art AI algorithms and their practical implementation.

***Keywords*:** CNN, edge computing, accelerator, FPGA, GPU, ASIC

5.1 Introduction

Massive amounts of data are being generated on a daily basis as a result of the increase in digital computing devices and internet access, creating new opportunities and challenges for researchers. The computation and manipulation of such a large amount of data necessitated the development of deep learning (DL)-based algorithms ranging from simple regression models to complex computer vision tasks, big data analysis, and many more. Various DL architectures, such as the multi-level perceptron (MLP), convolutional neural network (CNN), recurrent neural network (RNN), autoencoders, generative adversarial network (GAN), and fuzzy deep learning networks have been reported for a variety of applications in computer vision tasks related to robotics, surveillance, autonomous driver assistant systems (ADAS), edge-computing, and medical imaging [1–4]. These computer vision tasks can broadly be classified into image classifications [5], object detection [6], and segmentation [7]. CNNs have provided astonishing performance for these computer vision tasks; however, workload of CNN is compute and bandwidth intensive [8].

The rise of big data applications is significantly advancing machine learning (ML) development, but it also presents major challenges in terms of data processing speed and scalability for traditional computer systems. Specifically, conventional von-Neumann architectures, which separate data storage and processing, require constant data transfer between processors and external memory. The frequent movement of data reduces both system performance and energy efficiency, an issue that has worsened with the growing data volumes in AI applications. To address these challenges, AI-dedicated computing platforms have emerged, offering solutions that range from complementing von Neumann systems to serving as independent, specialized stand-alone platforms. These platforms, part of the broader "domain-specific computing" category, focus on tailoring designs to the needs of AI, achieving significant improvements in power consumption and performance by addressing the well-known "memory wall" and "power wall" problems [9].

AI-specific computing systems, i.e., AI accelerators, are often constructed with a large number of highly parallel computing and storage units. GPUs have thousands of cores running in parallel, processing multiple operations simultaneously, making them a suitable choice for CNN implementation. However, one of the main challenges in GPUs is their large power consumption. Field programmable gate arrays (FPGAs) and application specific integrated circuits (ASICs) on the other hand, are more energy efficient while achieving higher throughput. Compared to ASIC, FPGA-based design offers a higher level of reconfigurability, lower cost, and faster deployment, making it an excellent alternative [10]. Architectural modifications such as pruning [10], reduced precision computing [8], loop optimization [12], pipelining, and algorithmic optimizations including Winograd, and fast Fourier transform (FFT) [13] are used to increase the throughput and reduce memory bandwidth for CNN implementation on FPGAs and ASICs.

This chapter provides a thorough analysis of recent advancements in CNN accelerator design from device to architecture level, current issues, and potential future scopes for CNN accelerator architectures in a chronological manner. Both the software and hardware aspects are covered in detail in order of compression, optimization, and implementation. Section 5.2 presents the background and motivation for hardware implementation of CNNs. Trends and technological developments for accelerating CNN operation is described in Section 5.3. Section 5.4 discusses the various model compression algorithms for CNNs. Section 5.5 discusses the hardware optimization techniques. Design space exploration of CNN hardware accelerators are presented in Section 5.6. The recent developments in CNN accelerator designs, challenges, and solutions have been presented in Section 5.7. We extend our discussion to sparse neural networks and its hardware architecture in Section 5.8. Finally, Section 5.9 presents the conclusion and the future prospects.

5.2 Computational Complexities of Convolutional Neural Networks

CNNs extract features in a hierarchical form by integrating various convolution, pooling, and fully connected (FC) layers. Convolution involves a small kernel sliding over an input feature map (IFM) and performing element-wise dot product to get the output feature map (OFM) as shown in Figure 5.1. IFM, OFM, and kernels represented by the matrices I, O, and W, respectively. The dimensions of IFM are $I_X \times I_Y \times C$, while the dimensions of OFM are $O_X \times O_Y \times N_F$, and the dimensions of the kernel are $K_X \times K_Y \times C$ and total of N_F kernels for a given layer. Mathematically the convolution operation is given by the equation:

$$O(f,x,y) = \sum_{c=0}^{C-1} \sum_{i=0}^{Kx-1} \sum_{j=0}^{Ky-1} I(x+i, y+j, c) \times W(f,x,y,c) \quad (5.1)$$

FC layers are typically present towards the end of CNNs and are responsible for classification in accordance with the extracted feature. FC layers are characterized by one-to-one connection between pre- and post-layer neurons. The output of forward propagation through a FC layer is given by Equation 5.2 where O_{fc}, I_{fc}, W and N are output of FC layer, input to FC layer, weights associated between input and output neurons and number of input neurons, respectively.

$$O_{fc}(i) = \sum_{j=0}^{N-1} W(i,j) \times I_{fc}(j) \quad (5.2)$$

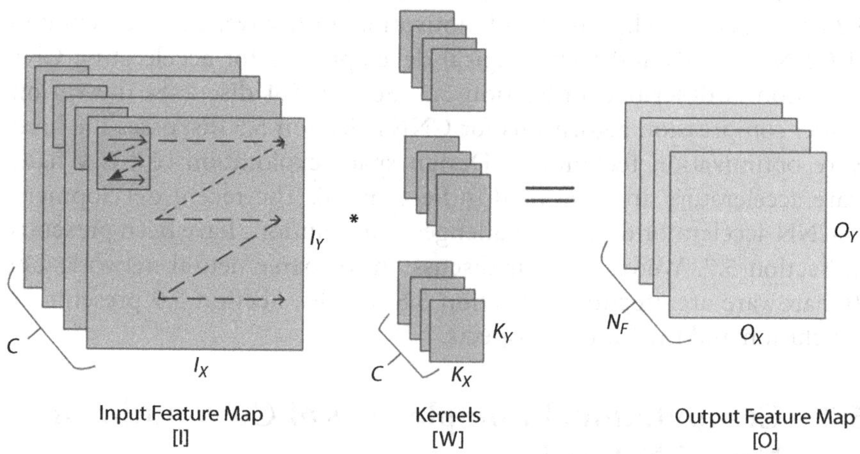

Figure 5.1 Feature maps in convolution operation.

CNN predictions are based on these weights and kernels, also known as parameters. CNNs are trained to optimize these parameters by minimizing the error function and by updating the parameters based on their error gradients using approaches such as stochastic gradient decent. During each iteration of training, forward propagation is executed for evaluating the error, and this error is backpropagated through the layers for updating parameters. It may take a huge number of iterations for multiple inputs to fully optimize the parameters. In the case of convolution layers, during backpropagation, three kinds of gradients are calculated. One for updating weights, calculated as convolution of IFM with gradient received from next layer as per equation:

$$\frac{\partial Error}{\partial W} = \frac{\partial Error}{\partial O} \cdot I \tag{5.3}$$

The second gradient is calculated to update bias by summing up the received gradient for a particular kernel. The third gradient that propagates backward to the previous layer is calculated by convolving dilated gradient with 180^0 rotated kernel (W') by applying Equation 5.4 as:

$$\frac{\partial Error}{\partial I} = \frac{\partial Error}{\partial O} \cdot W' \tag{5.4}$$

While backpropagating through max pooling layer, gradient is propagated to only those locations that contributed during forward propagation, the rest receive zero gradient. Like backpropagation in convolution layer, the FC layer also calculates three gradients for updating parameters, bias, and gradient for the previous layers.

The performance of any CNN model in terms of precision, convergence speed, and accuracy depends on the training data. However, a particular model's training and inference time depends on hardware that implements CNN. Workloads for CNNs are memory and compute-intensive, its performance on a particular processor gets bottlenecked by the number of floating-point computations, memory bandwidth, on-chip memory size, and limited parallel processing. VGG16 is one of the most popular CNN architectures used for image classification, whose architecture has been shown in Figure 5.2. Sizes of each OFM has been represented by notation $A \times B \times C$ where A, B, C are height, width, and number of channels of OFM, respectively. Figure 5.3(a) represents the layer-wise number of parameters

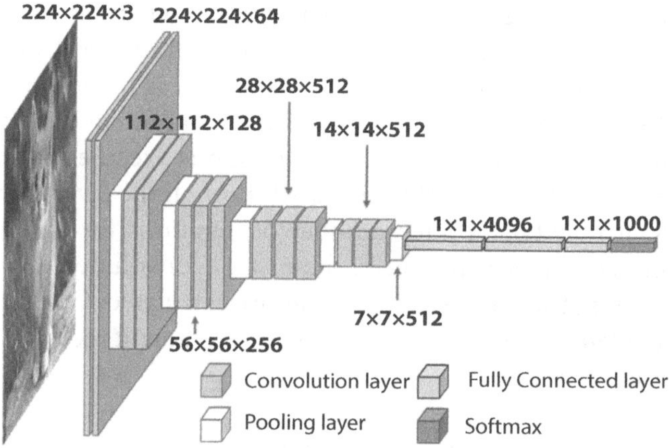

Figure 5.2 Layer-wise architecture of VGG16 network.

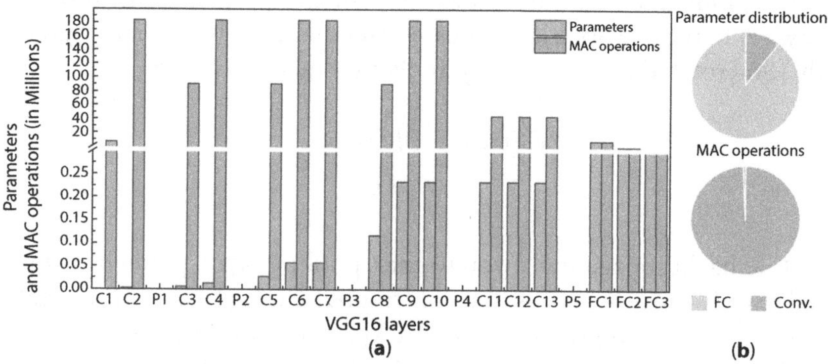

Figure 5.3 Layer-wise (a) computations and (b) parameters for VGG16 architecture.

and multiply and accumulate (MAC) operations required during forward propagation through VGG16 architecture. In the VGG16 architecture, the convolution layer requires nearly 99.2% of total computations while the FC layer has 89.34% of total parameters as shown in Figure 5.3(b). This shows the convolution layer is compute bound, whereas the FC layer is memory bound. New architectural designs must analyse opportunities for model size reduction and optimization techniques along with a suitable hardware platform to implement the CNN model.

5.3 Evolution of CNN Accelerators

There are two distinct working modes for the currently used DL, first, training that learns a set of weights for a CNN designed to solve a specific task, and second, inference that uses trained weights for predicting outputs. Traditionally, CPUs were used for implementing training and inference of CNN models. However, with increasing computational complexity of CNN models due to deeper architectures and large datasets, performance on CPUs is bottlenecked by limited parallelism and memory bandwidth. Complex instruction set and high general-purpose nature of CPUs results in high power consumption making them unsuitable for CNN workloads. GPUs are designed to handle specific tasks with extremely parallelized architecture containing thousands of cores. Training that is a more compute-intensive process compared to inference is suitable for implementing on GPUs. High power consumption is one of the major limitations for avoiding the use of GPUs for the inference stage. ASIC-based CNN architectures are more specialized in performing small sets of operations like matrix-matrix multiplications very efficiently. High performance, low power consumption and area requirements make ASIC CNN accelerators a preferred choice for training and inference. However, lack of reconfigurability and large fabrication time and cost reduced the competitive edge of ASICs. Huge research and frameworks for facilitating design of FPGA-based CNN accelerators were conducted due to its ability of reconfigurability, specialized design, lower design time and cost. It has been observed that generally GPUs and ASIC are used for training the CNN models while ASIC- and FPGA-based architectures are used for inference.

GPUs take up the computationally intensive task of training the CNN architectures. Series of GPU architectures were proposed from 2017 to 2022, innovating in terms of performance, mixed precision support, memory bandwidth and multi-GPU support. Initially GPUs were used for graphics rendering; however, the implementation of tensor cores became a turning point for GPUs path into AI computations. Tensor cores are specialized processing cores capable of performing fused MAC operations. The first-generation tensor cores were introduced in Nvidia Volta series GPU that accepted floating point 16-bit (FP16) precision input and generated output in FP32 format. The second generation of tensor cores was released in Nvidia Turing GPU series that extended the precision formats to integers of 8, 4 and 1 bit accelerating the throughput of the GPU. Nvidia Ampere series introduced the third generation of tensor cores, extending computational capabilities to FP64, TensorFloat

32 and brain floating point 16 bits with an intention of accelerating training operation without any loss in accuracy. Increase in training data size and model depth led to a shift to multi-GPU configuration. DGX-1V is a personal supercomputer with eight Volta series GPUs overcoming the performance and memory constraints. Datacenters also utilize multi-GPU support implemented using NVLink that is a high bandwidth and energy-efficient path between GPUs and CPU [14]. High power consumption, cost, and size are some of the reasons for GPUs to lose their competitive edge in inference operation.

ASIC-based architectures were initially designed for accelerating MLP networks. Neural processing units (NPU) were proposed capable of performing fused MAC operation in parallel [15]. DianNao series was a standalone CNN accelerator having neural functional unit (NFU), input; output; weight buffer along with control processor [16]. NFU performed computational operations by multipliers, adder trees and nonlinear functional units in a pipelined order. An instruction set architecture, Cambricon, was proposed for providing users the freedom of configuring the network architectures [17]. Customizable control, data transfer, vector, matrix, and logical instruction set were introduced. Google proposed its own architecture of CNN inference called Tensor processing unit (TPU), achieving high computational performance using systolic array architecture for matrix-matrix multiplication [18]. Later versions of TPUs were capable of both training and inference operations [19]. Cerebras wafer scale engine (WSE) was another powerful training and inference accelerator proposed with the intention of accelerating AI in datacenters. However, recently the trend has shifted to mobile AI chips where compressed CNN models can be accelerated. Samsung developed an efficient NPU architecture that can accelerate sparse neural networks on mobile devices [20]. We have delved into more details of the ASIC architectures in Section 5.7.iii.

FPGA-based architectures became a popular choice for CNN inference accelerators as they provided a better performance to power ratio, reduced design time, and were cost-effective due to their reconfigurability. Huge research was carried out in the last demi-decade for implementing large-size neural networks with flexible and scalable hardware architectures. DLAU was proposed by Wang *et al.* [21] that presented pipelined architecture for tiled matrix multiplication unit, part sum accumulation unit and activation function acceleration unit. The aim was to accelerate computational operations, but it lacked optimizations for memory transfer operations. Several frameworks were proposed that overcame this drawback such as ALAMO [22] and Angel-Eye [23] that focused on optimizing the computational operations with due concentration given to reduce memory transfers. Furthermore, to reduce computational and memory bandwidth issues even further YodaNN was proposed that implemented binarized CNN [24]. Attempts were made to accelerate CNN operations at data-centers by Microsoft's project Brainwave [25]. CNN operations were split between multiple FPGAs and CPUs with high bandwidth communication links for acceleration of large-scale models. As trends shifted towards edge computing several industrial frameworks like deep neural network development kit (DNNDK) were presented by Xilinx that provided a unified approach for compact DNN inference by applications of pruning, quantization, compilation, efficient hardware architecture and profiler. We have discussed in detail FPGA-based architectures in Section 5.7.ii.

5.4 Model Compression Approaches

The complexity of the CNN architecture should be lowered to reduce its memory requirements and the number of computations for its efficient implementation due to the limited availability of computational resources on edge devices. The focus of this section is to explore methods aimed at minimizing excessive computational loads and redundant parameters.

Depth-wise separable convolution is implemented to reduce the number of parameters and computations by decomposing a higher-dimensional kernel into smaller-dimensional kernels [26]. It applies spatial convolution independently to each IFM channel, followed by 1×1 or pointwise convolution as illustrated in Figure 5.4. The parameters are reduced from $[K_X \times K_Y \times C \times N_F]$ for direct convolution to $[C \times (K_X \times K_Y + N_F)]$ for depth-wise separable convolution, whereas MACs get reduced from $[N_F \times O_X \times O_Y \times K_X \times K_Y \times C]$ to $[C \times O_X \times O_Y \times (K_X \times K_Y + N_F)]$ [27]. Compact CNN architectures like

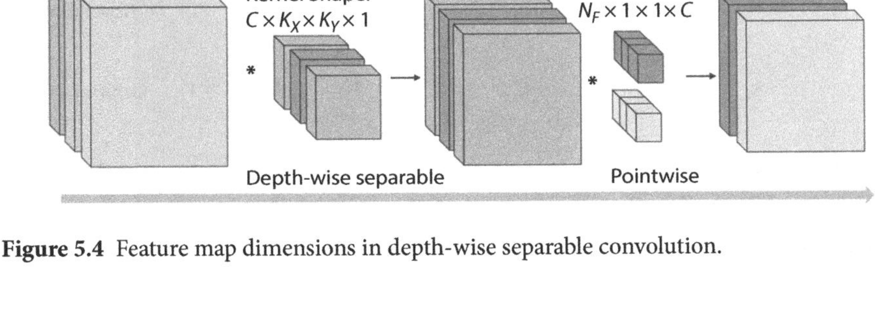

Figure 5.4 Feature map dimensions in depth-wise separable convolution.

MobileNet [28], Xception [29], and ShuffleNet [30] have adopted this approach to reduce the number of MACs and parameters.

Pruning removes insignificant or redundant parameters that don't contribute to generating output and finally fine-tunes the model to recover loss in accuracy [10]. Pruning results in a sparse neural network as shown in Figure 5.5, and reduces overfitting and memory requirements as sparse matrices can be easily compressed by storing them in coordinate format (COO) or compressed sparse row/column (CSR/CSC) format [31]. Sparse matrix storage in CSR format is demonstrated in Figure 5.6. Various pruning methods have been proposed which target weights [32], filters [33, 34] and channels [35, 36]. Pruning was applied to improve energy efficiency of the architectures using energy-aware pruning [37]. Non-uniform sparsity distribution due to pruning leads to an unbalanced load which is quite difficult for hardware processing elements (PE) to handle in parallel. Han *et al.* [38] proposed load-balance-aware pruning that uniformly distributes the load across hardware PEs.

Quantizing the CNN model by lowering the number of bits required to represent each parameter improves computational efficiency, reduces the bandwidth requirements and memory footprint. Researchers have evaluated the performance for weight quantization along with weight and activation quantization [39, 40]. The model size of the architecture gets significantly lowered with just a small decrease in accuracy when weights were quantized to lower fixed point (FxP) formats, for quantize neural network, ternary neural networks and binarized neural networks (BNN), respectively. The model can be compressed by reducing the number of bits needed to describe each weight, achieved through clustering and encoding, as multiple connections may have the same effective weights [10]. Clustering can be performed using the K-means algorithm, grouping weights into k clusters. The dictionary matrix holds the centroids for each cluster in higher precision floating point format, while the weight matrix is

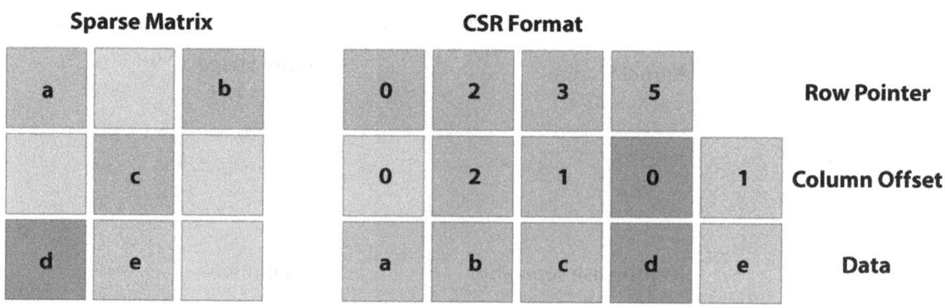

Figure 5.5 Storing of sparse weight matrix in CSR format.

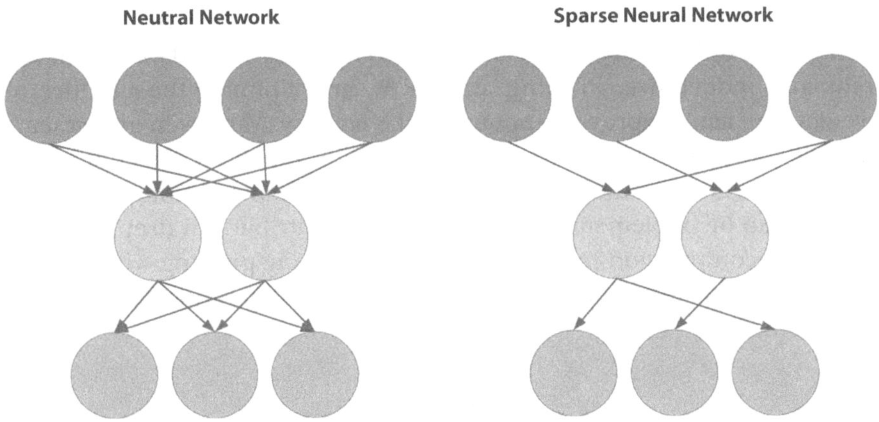

Figure 5.6 Pruning of least significant weights.

replaced with a cluster index matrix encoding the location of the centroid in the dictionary matrix. The clustering and encoding process is illustrated in Figure 5.7.

Employing low-rank approximation (LRA), layer weight matrices can be decomposed into low-order matrices, resulting in a significant reduction in the amount of storage required for parameters and minimizing the number of computations needed. LRA is applied on individual layers that significantly increases the computations during training as updated weights are decomposed after every single iteration. Qiu *et al.* [41] have applied LRA to FC layer weight matrices. Tucker decomposition was used for decomposing the pre-trained weights achieving nearly the same accuracy as VGG-16 with 50% fewer parameters.

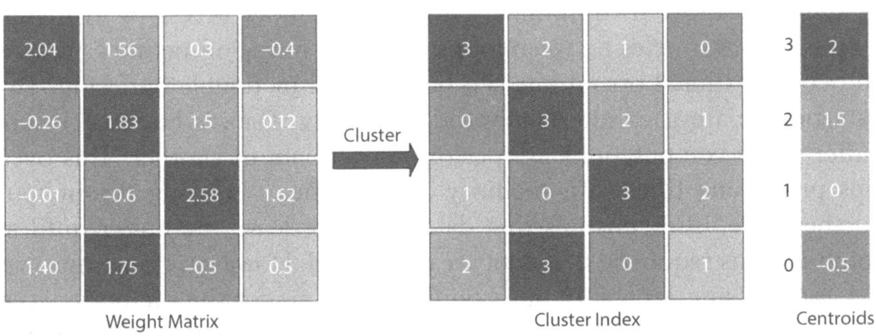

Figure 5.7 Weight matrix generation with clustering and encoding.

These compression algorithms focus on reduction in the number of parameters or lowering the bits required to represent each data, ultimately reducing model size. Pruning and LRA can minimize the number of weights but can't improve computational efficiency. Moreover, implementing LRA additionally requires computationally expensive decomposition of matrices. Quantization and clustering increase computational efficiency as they can be implemented using simpler circuits but can drop accuracy for larger compression ratios. Therefore, combining pruning with quantization can provide a significantly higher compression ratio and computational efficiency [10].

5.5 Hardware Optimization Techniques

This section focuses on recent trends for the effective implementation of CNNs. The implementation of accelerators has been classified on the basis of architectural optimization, algorithmic optimizations. Table 5.1 summarizes the classification of architectures based on design, optimization techniques and approaches for next-generation hardware accelerators focused on CNN. Furthermore, both software and hardware aspects are covered to enhance the understanding of readers.

i. Computational Optimizations

The various optimization techniques to overcome memory bandwidth bottleneck in CNN accelerators include loop control optimizations, batching, double buffering, and tiling. Loop control optimization targets loops with independent operations that can be executed in parallel to increase computational efficiency and reduce latency at the expense of additional hardware resources. Execution of these loops in parallel is known as loop unrolling [11]. Loop reordering is accessing and buffering the inputs in a specific order to minimize redundant memory access by switching loop control variables between loops [57]. Pipelining of memory accesses and computational operations can be achieved by double buffering. Two data buffers are used alternately for processing. Data is buffered in one buffer while computations are performed on data in another. This overlaps processing time with memory access time, increasing throughput. Furthermore, tiling ensures that data does not leave the buffer until all computations requiring that data are completed. However, tiling improves the data reusing capability but significantly degrades the memory access efficiency by fetching fragmented memory blocks. Batching maintains memory access efficiency and processes multiple inputs simultaneously by

Table 5.1 Classification based on optimization and implementation approaches for hardware architectures.

Classification criterion			References	Section
Architectural Optimization	Reducing computation time	Pipelining	[11, 16, 42–56]	5.5.i
		Unrolling	[11, 16, 18, 19, 26, 42, 43, 45, 46, 48–58]	
		Batching	[18, 42, 44, 47, 51, 55, 56, 58]	
		Systolic array architecture	[18, 19, 42, 46, 53]	
	Reducing memory footprint	Pruning	[16, 37, 46–51]	5.4
		Quantization	[18, 39, 41, 45, 46, 54, 58, 59]	
		Clustering and encoding	[10]	
	Reducing access time	Data reuse	[11, 16, 18, 19, 26, 37, 42, 45, 47–50, 52–58]	5.5.i
		Loop reordering	[11, 57, 60]	
		Tiling	[11, 42, 52, 53, 56–59]	
		Double buffering	[43, 56, 58]	
Algorithmic Optimization	Winograd-based convolution		[26, 42, 56, 61, 62]	5.5.ii
	FFT based convolution		[43, 44, 62]	

(Continued)

Table 5.1 Classification based on optimization and implementation approaches for hardware architectures. (*Continued*)

Classification criterion			References	Section
Evaluation Platform	CPU/GPU		[32, 33, 39, 40, 61]	5.7
	FPGA		[11, 18, 26, 38, 42, 43, 45–47, 52, 55–68]	
	ASIC		[16–20, 48–50, 53, 60, 65, 68–81]	
	Hybrid	CPU-FPGA	[43]	
		Multi-FPGA	[51]	
Hardware Design Approach	HLS		[26, 45, 46, 52, 59, 62]	5.7.v
	RTL		[11, 47]	
	HLS-RTL		[58]	

converting a matrix-vector multiplication into matrix-matrix multiplication. Throughput gets enhanced through batching at the cost of increased latency.

Systolic array architecture is one of the most efficient matrix multipliers that reduce memory transfers and perform highly parallelized computations as shown in Figure 5.8. Computational logic of multiplication and accumulation are performed in PEs. These PEs are interconnected to form a two-dimensional array that is optimized for matrix-matrix or matrix-vector multiplications. It exploits massive parallelism, achieving a very high throughput. PEs effectively utilize each data accessed by the array by passing the data along neighboring PEs before moving it out of the array. This simultaneously removes the bottleneck for memory bandwidth and compute bounds. Matrix multiplication operation using a systolic array is shown in Figure 5.8(a) while its output at each time step is shown in Figure 5.8(b).

ii. Algorithmic Optimizations

The convolution process as shown in Figure 5.1 involves multiple loop control instructions for handling corner conditions. Architectures

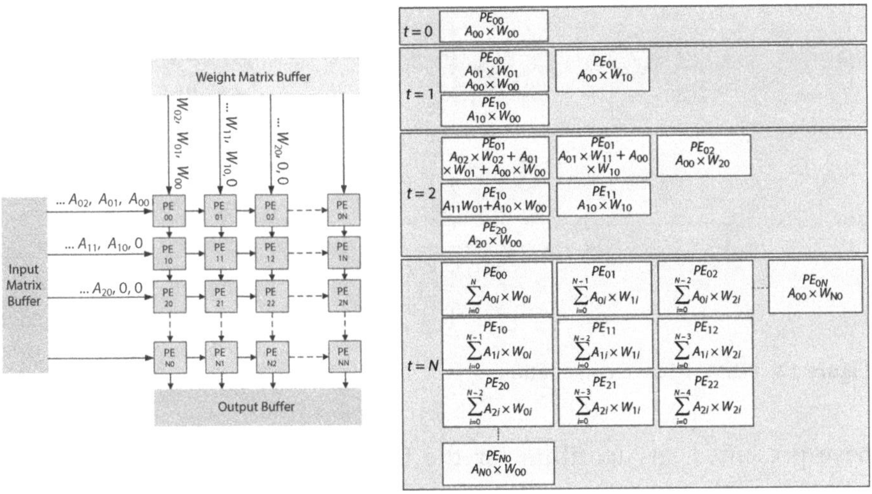

Figure 5.8 (a) Systolic array architecture performing 2D matrix multiplication, (b) timing diagram for execution of operations in PEs.

implementing this approach are optimized for handling specific set configurations like padding and stride but perform poorly when this configuration changes. This subsection discusses the optimizations done at the algorithm level for restructuring the execution of computations to obtain higher computational efficiency and reduce bandwidth requirements than the direct convolution approach while maintaining accuracy. The direct convolution approach is transformed into a matrix-matrix multiplication operation by the general matrix multiplication (GEMM) based convolution approach that reshapes both IFM and the kernels. The resultant gets reshaped back to the proper dimension. The process of GEMM-based convolution is displayed in Figure 5.9. It requires fewer loop control instructions, and high parallelism can get exploited during matrix multiplications resulting in higher arithmetic intensities. However, GEMM-based convolution is effective when large matrices are available, but it also requires higher temporal memory to store reshaped large matrices.

The core principle behind Winograd-based convolution is to perform element-wise multiplications while taking advantage of overlapping computations between adjacent windows to reduce the number of FP multiplication operations at the cost of extra additions and memory bandwidth [61]. For smaller kernels, Winograd is very efficient. However, it requires filter size-dependent specialized processing, making it a less generalized approach. To address issue of increased memory bandwidth Xiao *et al.* [26]

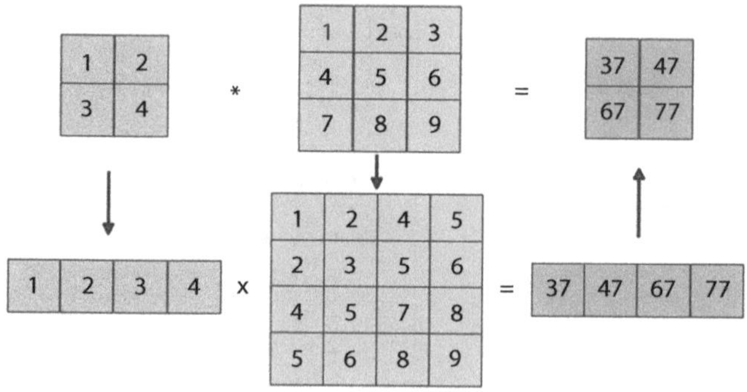

Figure 5.9 GEMM-based convolution.

have presented an algorithm for the fusion of convolution layers. This reuses the intermediate results for computations reducing off-chip memory accesses. Selection of convolution strategy (Direct or Winograd) has been based on minimizing the latency, constrained by resources and memory accesses for each layer. Inter-layer and intra-layer pipelining overlaps the computations for different layers, and load and store are overlapped by computations, respectively, as shown in Figure 5.10. Winograd-GEMM unified algorithm was proposed by Kala *et al.* [42], that accelerated convolution and FC layer by implementing the Winograd approach by GEMM operations on the systolic array. With the negligible increment in resource consumption, a significantly higher gain in performance was observed.

Another approach to implement convolution is by transforming inputs and kernels in the frequency domain to compute element-wise

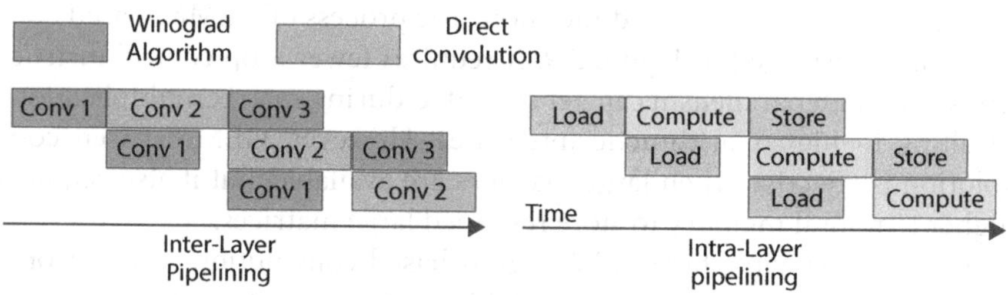

Figure 5.10 Timing diagrams of Winograd and direct convolution-based architectures.

multiplication and get the convolution result back by inverse transform [43, 62]. This FFT-based convolution approach requires fewer multiplications than direct convolution at the cost of additional memory requirements. Kernels are padded with zeros to equalize size in accordance with IFM, making it inefficient in the case of very small kernel sizes. Varying input, kernel sizes, and stride greater than one are tricky for optimization. Performing single multiplication in a complex domain requires four multiplications, increasing the computational overload. However, CNNs using an FF- based approach exploits the property of the Fourier transform of real-valued signals, leading to Hermitian symmetry reducing half of the computations. The 2D overlap-and-add based technique was used by Lin *et al.* [44] to exploit a high level of parallelism in the convolver. However, with the high parallelism and pipelining, the requirement for high memory bandwidth increased. To prevent the convolver from remaining idle, pipelining was controlled by implementing 2D Fourier and inverse Fourier transforms (IFT) by 1D Fourier and IFT, respectively.

5.6 Design Space Exploration

CNN algorithms require substantial data and weights, exceeding the chip's memory capacity, necessitating gigabytes of external memory. A typical CNN accelerator manages this with a three-tier storage hierarchy: external memory, on-chip buffers, and registers connected to processing engines (PEs). Data flows from external memory to on-chip buffers, then to registers and PEs for processing. After processing, results return to buffers and, if needed, to external memory. The core CNN operation, convolution, involves four nested loops for multiply-and-accumulate (MAC) operations as shown in Algorithm 5.1, optimized using loop unrolling, tiling, and interchange to efficiently utilize memory. Y. Ma *et al.* [12] have performed detailed analysis for loop variables and optimization strategies on the performance of CNN accelerators.

Algorithm 5.1 Pseudo code for performing convolution operation.

```
for ( no = 0; no < N_F; no++)                   #loop 4
  for (y = 0; y < O_Y; y++)                     #loop 3
    for (x = 0; x < O_X; x++)
      for (c = 0; c<C; c++)                     #loop 2
        for(ky = 0; ky < K_Y; ky+=S)            #loop 1
          for (kx = 0; kx < K_X; kx+=S)
          {
          O(c;x,y) += I(c; (S × (x+kx)), (S × (y+ky))) × weight(no, c ;kx,ky);
           }
      O(no;x,y) = O(no;x,y) + bias(no);
```

i. Convolutional Loop Optimization Operation

All dimensions and variables in this paper are detailed in Table 5.2. The loop unrolling design variable P^* represents the number of parallel computations, while the loop tiling design variable T^* represents the portion of data from the four loops stored in on-chip buffers. The relationship between input and output variables is governed by Equations (5.5)–(5.7), where S is the stride of the sliding window, and zero padding size is included in I_X, I_Y, T_I_X and T_I_Y.

$$I_X = (O_X - 1)S + K_X, I_Y = (O_Y - 1)S + K_Y \tag{5.5}$$

Table 5.2 Notations for convolution layer parameters, unrolling and tiling variables with respective IFM and OFM dimensions.

	Kernel (width/ height)	**IFM (width/ height)**	**OFM (width/ height)**	**# of IFM**	**# of OFM**
Conv Loop	Loop 1	Loop 3	Loop 3	Loop 2	Loop 4
Conv Dimensions (N^*)	K_X, K_Y	I_X, I_Y	O_X, O_Y	C	N_F
Loop Tilling (T^*)	T_K_X, T_K_Y	T_I_X, T_I_Y	T_O_X, T_O_Y	T_C	T_N_F
Loop Unrolling (P^*)	P_K_X, P_K_Y	P_I_X, P_I_Y	P_O_X, P_O_Y	P_C	P_N_F

$$T\_I_X = (T\_O_X - 1) + K_X, T\_I_Y = (T\_O_Y - 1) + K_Y \tag{5.6}$$

$$P\_I_X = P\_O_X, P\_I_Y = P_{OY} \tag{5.7}$$

Loop unrolling in CNNs enhances parallel computation by influencing the design of PEs based on data reuse and memory access patterns.

a) Loop-1 Unrolling: In each cycle, the inner product of $P\_K_X \times P\_K_Y$ pixels and weights from the same feature and kernel map is computed as shown in Figure 5.11(a). This requires an adder tree with a fan-in of $P\_K_X \times P\_K_Y$ and an accumulator to add these sums to the previous result.
b) Loop-2 Unrolling: During each cycle, P_C pixels and weights from P_C different feature/kernel maps at the same location are used as illustrated in Figure 5.11(b). The structure resembles Loop-1 unrolling but with a fan-in of P_C.
c) Loop-3 Unrolling: In each cycle, $P\_I_X \times P\_I_Y$ pixels from different locations in the same feature map are multiplied by the same weight, reused $P\_I_X \times P\_I_Y$ times as demonstrated in Figure 5.11(c). Separate accumulators are used for each independent output pixel, eliminating the need for an adder tree.

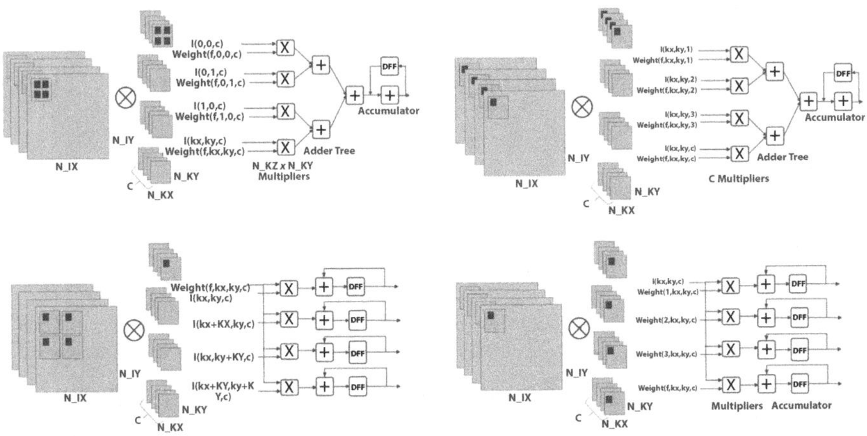

Figure 5.11 Loop unrolling approach across (a) Loop-1, (b) Loop-2, (c) Loop-3 and (d) Loop-4 of convolution layer operation.

d) Loop-4 Unrolling: In each cycle, a single pixel is multiplied by P_N_F weights from different kernel maps at the same location as shown in Figure 5.11(d). This pixel is reused P_N_F times, employing P_N_F multipliers and accumulators without needing an adder tree, similar to Loop-3 unrolling.

On-chip memory is often insufficient for storing all the data required by deep CNNs. To compensate, external DRAMs are used to store weights and intermediate results. Loop tiling divides the dataset into smaller blocks, or tiles, that can fit into on-chip buffers. This enhances data locality, reducing reliance on slow, power-hungry DRAM access. The minimum on-chip buffer size required is determined by the tile size. The minimum on-chip buffer size needed for the input pixel buffer is $T\_I_X \times T\_I_Y \times T\_C \times P_{DW}$. The required buffer size for weights is $T\_K_X \times T\_K_Y \times T\_C \times T\_N_F \times W_{DW}$, and finally, to store the output feature map, the buffer size should be $T\_O_X \times T\_O_Y \times T\_N_F \times P_{DW}$. Here, P_{DW} and W_{DW} represents pixel and weight datawidth, respectively.

ii. Evaluation of CNN Accelerator Architecture

This section presents a quantitative assessment of the influence of loop design variables (P^* and T^*) on the design objectives our CNN accelerator seeks to minimize.

Computational Latency

Computational latency per layer is ideally N_m / P_m, where N_m is the number of multiplications and P_m is the number of multipliers. Actual computing cycles are:

$$\#cycles = \#intertile\_cycle \times \#intratile\_cycles \tag{5.8}$$

Where,

$$\#intertile\_cycles = \left\lceil \frac{C}{T\_C} \right\rceil \left\lceil \frac{K_X}{T\_K_X} \right\rceil \left\lceil \frac{K_Y}{T\_K_Y} \right\rceil \left\lceil \frac{N_F}{T\_N_F} \right\rceil \left\lceil \frac{O_X}{T\_O_X} \right\rceil \left\lceil \frac{O_Y}{T\_O_Y} \right\rceil \tag{5.9}$$

$$\#intratile\_cycles = \left\lceil \frac{T\_C}{P\_C} \right\rceil \left\lceil \frac{T\_K_X}{P\_K_X} \right\rceil \left\lceil \frac{T\_K_Y}{P\_K_Y} \right\rceil \left\lceil \frac{T\_N_F}{P\_N_F} \right\rceil \left\lceil \frac{T\_O_X}{P\_O_X} \right\rceil \left\lceil \frac{T\_O_Y}{P\_O_Y} \right\rceil \tag{5.10}$$

Multiplier and memory utilization may be suboptimal if these ratios are non-integers, impacting overall system latency.

Data Reuse

Data reuse is a technique that significantly reduces on-chip buffer reads, enhancing the efficiency of computations. There are two primary types of data reuse: spatial reuse and temporal reuse.

Spatial Reuse occurs when a pixel or weight is used by multiple multipliers within a single cycle. For instance, the distinct weights per cycle are calculated as: $P_{wt} = P\_N_F \times P\_C \times P\_K_X \times P\_K_Y$. Similarly, the number of distinct pixels per cycle depends on whether a loop is unrolled. If Loop-1 is not unrolled, the distinct pixels per cycle are $P_{px} = P\_C \times P\_I_X \times P\_I_Y$. If Loop-1 is unrolled, the distinct pixels per cycle are $P_{px} = P\_C \times \left((P\_I_X)S + P\_K_X\right) \times \left((P\_I_Y)S + P\_K_Y\right)$.

Temporal Reuse involves using a pixel or weight across multiple cycles. The reuse of weights is given by $W_{reuse} = \frac{P_m}{P_{wt}} = P\_I_X \times P\_I_Y$. Pixel reuse is similarly defined as $P_{reuse} = \frac{P_m}{P_{px}}$. If Loop-1 is not unrolled, the pixel reuse is $P_{reuse} = P\_N_F$. However, if Loop-1 is unrolled, pixel reuse becomes $P_{reuse} = \frac{P\_N_F \times P\_K_X \times P\_K_Y \times P\_I_X \times P\_I_Y}{\left((P\_I_X - 1)S + P\_K_X\right)\left((P\_I_Y - 1)S + P\_K_X\right)}$.

Spatial reuse can be enhanced by unrolling Loop-4 or both Loop-1 and Loop-3. During intra-tile computations, the durations for which data is reused are $\frac{T\_O_X \times T\_O_Y}{P\_O_X \times P\_O_Y}$ for weights and $\frac{T\_N_F}{P\_N_F}$ for pixels. These strategies optimize the use of on-chip resources, reducing the need for frequent buffer reads and improving computational efficiency.

Access of On-Chip Buffer

Data reuse is an effective method for significantly reducing on-chip buffer accesses. In the absence of reuse, the total number of read operations for both pixels and weights is equal to N_m. However, when reuse is applied, the number of read operations is reduced. For weights, the total number of read operations with reuse is calculated as $\#W_{read} = \frac{N_m}{W_{reuse}}$. Similarly, for pixels, the number of read operations becomes $\#P_{read} = \frac{N_m}{P_{reuse}}$. When partial sums are not computed within a single tile, the process involves additional buffer accesses, specifically $2 \times P\_N_F \times P\_O_X \times P\_O_Y$ writes and reads per cycle. Therefore, the total buffer accesses required for partial sums are given by $\#PSum_{read} = \#cycles \times 2 \times P\_N_F \times P\_O_X \times P\_O_Y$. In summary, the total buffer accesses are the sum of all the accesses needed to read and write weights, pixels, and partial sums. This cumulative reduction in buffer accesses, facilitated by data reuse, results in more efficient processing and reduced on-chip resource utilization.

Access of External Memory

For large-scale CNNs on moderate FPGAs, weights and intermediate pixel results are stored in external DRAM due to on-chip memory constraints. DRAM accesses incur higher latency and energy costs compared to on-chip BRAM. To enhance performance and efficiency, it is crucial to minimize DRAM accesses by using large on-chip buffers and optimizing loop computation orders, ensuring that each pixel and weight is transferred from DRAM only once. Repeated DRAM reads for the same pixel or weight for multiple tiles should be avoided.

5.7 Hardware Platforms for Implementing CNNs

The hardware platform for implementing CNNs can vary according to the requirements of applications like performance, power, or cost. The leading platforms for implementing CNN architectures are CPU, GPU, FPGA, or ASIC. The workload during training is even more stringent, requiring a vaster number of computations and storage requirements than inference. Two different types of accelerators with different architectural optimizations are preferred for training and inference. This subsection provides the architectural comparisons for each platform.

i. CPUs and GPUs

Sequential execution of operation poses a huge bottleneck in compute and memory bound for deploying any CNNs. GPUs exploit the highest level of parallelism among all platforms. Since, in both training and inference, computational operations can be highly parallelized, GPUs are considered a prominent choice for implementing CNNs. With a significantly matured software-based framework already developed for GPU-based implementation, the majority of the training of CNNs is performed on GPUs. Performance of GPUs was limited by cuda cores that performed single operation per clock cycle. GPU architectures were revolutionized after the implementation of tensor cores in Nvidia Volta series GPUs. Tensor cores are capable of performing mixed precision fused multiply and add (FMA) operation for 4 x 4 matrix multiplication performing 64 FMA operations in single clock cycle. Subsequent generations of tensor cores were proposed in Turing and Ampere series that enhanced computational performance in range of teraflops with support of multiple precision formats. However, GPUs are not at all power efficient, thus making them inefficient for real-time inferences.

ii. FPGA

FPGAs can achieve an ideal balance of reconfigurability and performance comparable to ASICs. FPGA-based designs for dedicated applications provide an effective solution because they can change their computational structure and are less reliant on software for controlling or scheduling computations as compared to GPUs.

Systolic array-based architecture for mapping CNN on FPGA has been proposed by Wei *et al.* [46]. The algorithm determines the feasible mapping weights and feature maps to PEs to avoid stalling or improper calculations. Layers are effectively mapped with varying input shapes by determining the optimal size of the PE array as per available resources. Systolic array architecture has been shown in Figure 5.7. Significantly high throughput was observed for reduced precision implementation of convolution layers. This architecture had just focused on optimizing the convolution layer whereas optimization strategies for other layers were missing. To overcome this design space exploration for direct convolution for loop unrolling and reordering was conducted by Ma *et al.* [12]. A scalable convolution layer architecture that can handle several kernel sizes was designed, as shown in Figure 5.12. The data path unrolls the loop for sliding the kernel over the feature map and reuses IFM data by shifting it to neighboring buffers to reduce memory access. The element-wise multiplications performed

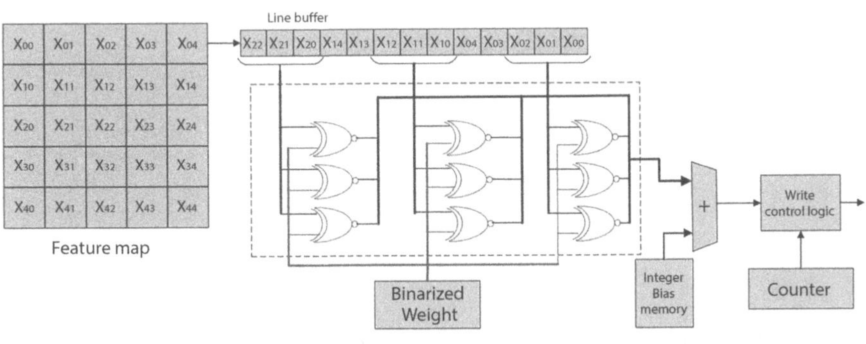

Figure 5.12 XNOR gate-based PE architecture for BNN implementation.

within the kernel are serialized by the scheduling algorithm. The optimal use of hardware resources is ensured by changing the unrolling factor. Additionally, the same architecture was used to implement a FC layer.

Computations and parameters of the CNN model have to be reduced in order to get a compact CNN model efficient for edge computing. Quantization, pruning and depth-wise separable convolutions are some ways of approximating the CNN models. A Binarized CNN network has been implemented by Umuroglu *et al.* [45] that used XNOR gates instead of DSP blocks. Since previous works based on binarized CNNs reported a high error in classification, batch normalization was introduced that significantly increased the accuracy and was implemented using just one adder. Detailed architecture has been shown in Figure 5.13. Since significantly fewer bits of data are transferred from memory and no DSP blocks were used resulted in reduced power consumption of the architecture. However, there is huge drop in accuracy in case of binarized CNNs. Depth-wise separable convolution reduces the number of computations and parameters while maintaining the accuracy. Xuan *et al.* [64] presented an FPGA-based architecture for depth-wise separable convolution (DSC) layer. Primary focus of the work was to reduce off-chip memory accesses for intermediate feature maps with a constraint on size of on-chip buffers. Configurable 16 PE array structure are designed that are capable of handling various sizes of DSC layers. Allocation of PEs were dependent

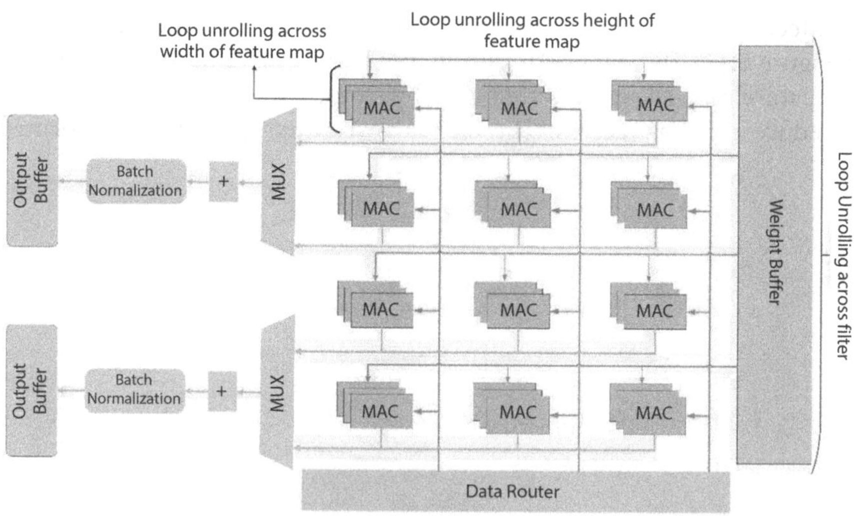

Figure 5.13 Architecture for CNN implementation on FPGA with unrolled MAC units, loop unrolling across height, weight of feature map and filters.

of ratio of computation operations between first and last DSC layer. Four-bit quantization was performed to reduce computational complexity also reconfiguring PE arrays to extend the support for handling 8bit×4bit multiplication in initial DSC layer to retain accuracy. Lookup table-based multiplier has been used to make architecture more energy efficient as compared to DSP-based multiplier architecture. Hemmat *et al.* [63] proposed a feature weight CNN inference architecture called AirNN that performs input dependent approximation. It was based on the observation that a particular input doesn't require predetermined number of computations for correct classification. K-means clustering algorithm was used to divide the weight of pretrained CNN into a fixed number of clusters. Furthermore, minimum 30% of weights were used to maintain accuracy. Hardware architecture reduced the energy consumption by 50%. However, approximation scheme and hardware optimization are limited to the convolution layer itself. FlexCNN has extended the support for optimizations to transpose and dilated convolutions [66]. Optimization strategies like dynamic tiling, layer fusion and layer parallelization with systolic array-based architecture overcame the compute and memory bandwidth bottlenecks for transpose and dilated convolution layers. Support for transpose and dilated convolutions are incorporated by converting them into direct convolution operations with decomposed kernels.

Implementation of a training accelerator is quite complex as it involves a significantly higher number of computations and bigger memory as all intermediate results of each layer must be stored. A training accelerator has been proposed by Xushen *et al.* [47], which combines the convolution, activation, and pooling layer, naming it as super layer. It takes advantage of data reusing within super layer in both forward and backward propagation, reducing memory access because feature maps are nearly identical. Using multiport SRAM banks for caching input data, compute units are prevented from stalling, increasing compute unit utilization ratio.

iii. ASICs

Recent advancements for accelerating CNNs have considered creating a customized ASIC for inference and training as it provides higher performance and power efficiency than FPGA. With rapid developments in CNN architectures, lack of reconfigurability is the major drawback for ASIC apart from large fabrication time and cost required.

DianNao, DaDianNao, ShiDianNao [16, 49, 50], implement neural functional units that pipeline multiplication, adder tree, and activation function. DaDianNao architecture focuses on reducing the latency for memory transfers by combining large eDRAM. ShiDianNao utilizes the weight-sharing approach to reduce the model size so that the entire weight matrix can be stored on-chip, reducing off-chip memory accesses.

Accelerating CNN operations at datacenter levels tensor processing unit (TPU) v1 has been presented by Jouppi *et al.* [18], implementing a huge, reduced precision systolic array-based architecture using weight stationary approach [48]. Systolic arrays reduce the number of memory read writes, making it power efficient. To make hardware design and debugging easier, the CPU sends TPU instructions to execute rather than allowing TPU to fetch instructions on its own like GPUs. TPUs use the complex instruction set computing, which gives them an advantage because they are connected to the host CPU *via* the slow PCIe bus for receiving instructions. TPU v1 was presented as an inference accelerator however later TPU v2 and v3 were proposed that were capable of performing training [19]. Size of systolic arrays was reduced in case of TPU v2 and v3 in order to extend support for sparse matrices and floating-point operations. However, software support for TPUs was restricted to Tensorflow library.

Cerebras WSE overcame the drawback and provided support for multiple software libraries. It has highly optimized architecture with memory distributed along compute data path with high bandwidth inter connections. Floating point operations on tensors are performed in the cores as shown in Figure 5.14. Thousands of these cores are interconnected in 2D mesh topology with local memories ensuring high utilization and efficiency. Compiler places and route to map neural network on entire fabric. This huge fabric requires a tremendous amount of power leading to thermal issues that has been addressed by the liquid cooling technique. Redundant cores are placed on the fabric and interconnected to mesh in

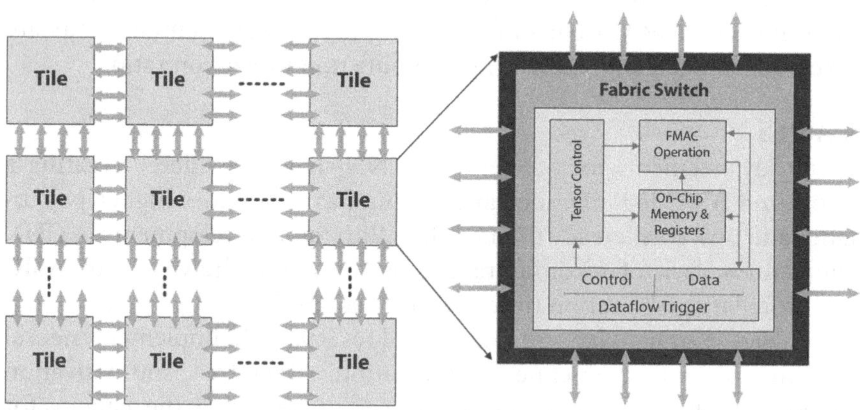

Figure 5.14 Architecture of tensor operation core in Cerebras WSE.

order to increase yield in case of defective cores. Cerebras is well suited for training CNN accelerators in datacenters, but performance to power ratio is quite high for implementation of inference operations at edge.

Development of edge and mobile AI computing Jang *et al.* [20] has proposed a NPU for mobile devices. Architecture consists of two engines that share a common on-chip memory. These engines are equipped with buffers, sparsity unit, and tensor unit. Sparsity units generate dense tensors using zero skipping to eliminate ineffective computations. These dense tensors are provided as input to 16 x 16 MAC arrays for generating partial sums. After accumulation output is passed through activation unit and stored back in buffer. Therefore an energy-efficient, mixed precision and sparsity aware architecture was proposed for high-performance edge computing.

iv. Hybrid Platforms

Collaborative CPU-FPGA architecture [43], mapped compute intensive layers like convolution on FPGA for parallel execution of computations, and mapped layers with low computations like ReLU and pooling onto CPU. Also, data mapping or scheduling for the convolution layer is controlled by the CPU. A shared memory model has been proposed so that FPGA can work with the same set of data as that in CPU. The convolutional layer implemented on FPGA was accelerated by overlap and add-based approach for FFT-based convolution.

Multi-FPGA-based architecture has been proposed by Zhang *et al.* [51] for linearly increasing the throughput with an increase in FPGA boards. In order to maintain the throughput, load balancing between all FPGAs has been ensured using a polynomial time load balancing algorithm which equally divides latency among all FPGAs. Comparisons for various hardware architectures based on FPGA and ASIC are shown in Table 5.3. The tabulation focusses on summarizing the recent advances in optimization techniques for various CNN hardware architectures in addition to significant parameters such as precision, throughput, and power efficiency.

v. Hardware Design Approach

Mapping CNNs onto hardware platforms like FPGA or ASIC requires a huge amount of extra effort to meet the additional needs of hardware efficiency than directly implementing it on well-matured software-based frameworks. High-level synthesis (HLS) tools can speed up the development process by creating finite state machine (FSM) based architectures with a high level of abstraction. Design can be easily optimized by pipelining, unrolling, or buffering algorithms but may not be optimized for hardware efficiency like PE utilization ratio or may have stalling compute units.

Table 5.3 Comparison of various hardware architectures and their optimization techniques.

Architecture	Optimization	Precision	Resource utilization/ area	Throughput	Power efficiency
Optimizing Conv layer to accelerate DNN on FPGA [11] Platform: FPGA	Loop unrolling, loop reordering, design space exploration, scalable and flexible modules for CNNs	16-bit FxP	High	Medium	Medium
A Uniform architecture design for accelerating 2D and 3D CNNs on FPGA [52] Platform: FPGA	GEMM-based convolution, parallelism, double buffering,	8-bit FxP and 16-bit FxP	High	High	Low
Frequency domain acceleration of CNN on CPU-FPGA shared memory system [43] Platform: FPGA	OaA-based FFT convolution, Double buffering, Heterogeneous platform	32-bit FP	High	Medium	Medium
UniWiG [42] Platform: FPGA	Winograd-GEMM–based convolution, Systolic array	32-bit FP	High	Medium	-
FP-BNN [59] Platform: FPGA	Binarized weights, Parallel computing PEs, on-chip buffer	1-bit FxP	Low	High	High
Swan [65] Platform: ASIC	Sparsity aware architecture, systolic array	16-bit FxP	Medium	High	High

(*Continued*)

Table 5.3 Comparison of various hardware architectures and their optimization techniques. (*Continued*)

Architecture	Optimization	Precision	Resource utilization/ area	Throughput	Power efficiency
Eyeriss v2 [53] Platform: ASIC	Sparsity-aware architecture,	8-bit FxP	High	High	High
TPU v2 and v3 [19] Platform: ASIC	Training accelerator, Systolic array, parallel and pipelined computation, data reuse	BF16	Medium	High	-

The HLS-based approach creates the same design for all networks, which are controlled by network parameters.

Register transfer level (RTL) provides more control over the architecture at every clock edge, allowing for higher throughput and energy efficiency at the expense of increased development time and cost. A unique design is made for each network, and therefore, for different hardware or network, a new design has to be prepared based on network parameters and hardware resources. To elevate the advantages of both approaches, Guan *et al.* [58] had used a hybrid HLS-RTL-based approach for implementing CNN architecture. Scheduling or the control path is designed using HLS, whereas data path is designed using RTL.

5.8 Sparse Neural Networks

Sparsity can be explored in activations by reducing the number of computations. Weight reordering-based architecture has been proposed by Akhlaghi *et al.* [60], which terminates the element-wise multiplications for kernel as soon as the accumulator has a negative value, as shown in Figure 5.15. This reduces further computations, which would have resulted in zero finally by the ReLU activation layer. Sparsity in weights gets introduced by reducing the model size by approaches like pruning. Parallelism is quite challenging to implement in case of sparsity. If zeros are substituted in place of eliminated weights and given to PEs, it increases ineffectual computations. Indexing non-zero weights spread non-uniformly causes

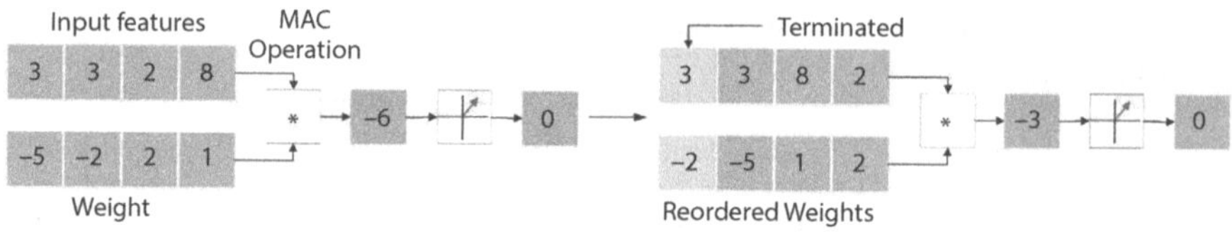

Figure 5.15 Weight reordering for early termination scheme.

indexing overheads and unbalanced PE loads. Thus, sparsity-aware architectures are necessary for maintaining latency and throughput. Efficient inference engine (EIE) architecture [54] stores the sparse matrix in CSC format, making locating the non-zero weights easier. The location of these zero weights is then broadcasted to all PEs to avoid their accessing and performing any computations. This reduced the ineffectual computations maintaining throughput and latency and increased power efficiency.

An innovative approach for accelerating sparse convolutional neural networks (SCNNs) based on systolic array-based architecture for FPGAs was proposed by Nehete *et al.* [67]. The authors employ a combination of software optimizations and hardware design techniques to enhance the efficiency of CNNs on resource-constrained devices. The software optimizations include load-aware pruning, which strategically reduces network weights while maintaining accuracy, and weight quantization to reduce memory footprint. The compressed sparse row (CSR) format is utilized for efficient storage of sparse matrices, significantly reducing memory requirements.

The proposed FPGA architecture leverages a hybrid design, utilizing both the processing system (PS), i.e., processors and programmable logic (PL) of the FPGA. This design allows for efficient task distribution, with the PS handling control flow and system management, while the PL implements parallel processing of computationally intensive CNN layers. The hardware implementation, realized on a PYNQ-Z2 FPGA board, demonstrates superior performance compared to GPU implementations in terms of throughput and power efficiency. At the core of the proposed architecture is the PE design, optimized for handling sparse data in CSR format eliminating the need for sparse matrix reconstruction. The PE extracts the relevant input features based on the column indices stored in the CSR format of the weight matrix. This targeted extraction reduces unnecessary computations on zero values. Each PE is designed to perform efficient vector-vector dot products between non-zero weights and corresponding input features. The architecture of PE is shown in Figure 5.16. The PE architecture incorporates local storage for temporary data holding, reducing

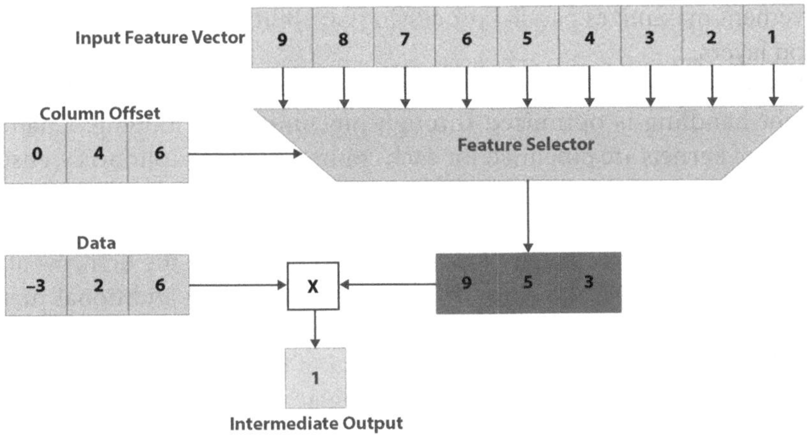

Figure 5.16 Architecture for processing element (PE) of systolic array.

external memory accesses. A key feature is the PE's ability to forward both input data and partial results to neighbouring PE elements, facilitating a streamlined data flow within the systolic array.

The mapping algorithm plays a crucial role in distributing the computational workload across the PE array. It begins by unrolling input feature maps into a 2D matrix, preparing the data for parallel processing. The algorithm implements an intricate data flow mechanism where input vectors traverse horizontally through the PE array, while weight matrices in CSR format propagate vertically as illustrated in Figure 5.17. This data

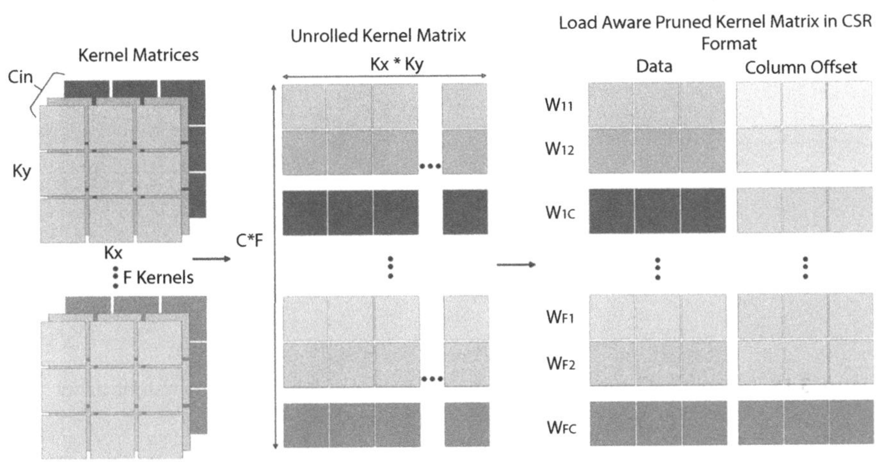

Figure 5.17 Mapping of sparse weight matrices stored in CSR format to systolic array.

movement maximizes parallel processing capabilities within sparse convolution layers.

A notable aspect of the mapping strategy is its emphasis on data reuse. Weight handling is optimized through pipelining and looping. Channel vectors of kernels are pipelined for each column in the systolic array, ensuring a continuous feed of appropriate weights to each PE column. The mapping of kernels in systolic arrays has been shown in Figure 5.18. Similar to input data, weight vectors are looped back to the PEs in the first row after vertical propagation, allowing for weight reuse without additional memory accesses significantly reducing memory bandwidth requirements. The algorithm carefully synchronizes the arrival of inputs and weights at each PE, ensuring optimal computational timing across the systolic array. This synchronization is vital for maintaining processing efficiency and accuracy. The algorithm carefully synchronizes the arrival of input data and weights at each PE, maintaining correct computation timing across the entire systolic array. As computations progress, partial results are accumulated within the PEs, with the final output formed by combining these partial results across the array. The synergy between the PE design and the mapping algorithm results in a highly efficient SCNN accelerator. By maximizing parallel processing, optimizing data reuse, and minimizing memory accesses, this approach achieves significant improvements in both performance and energy efficiency.

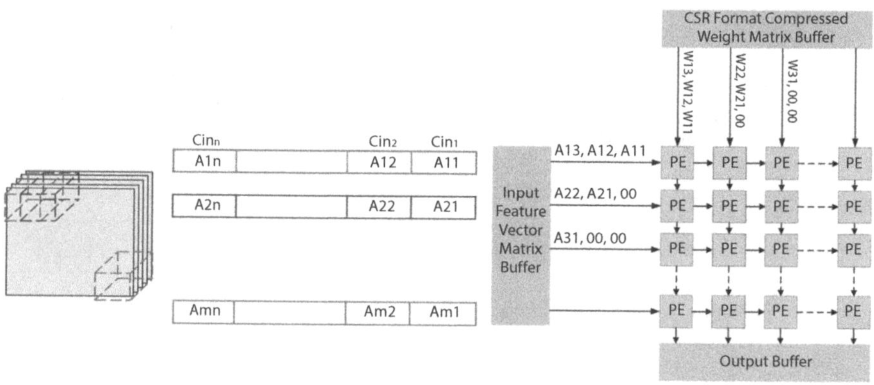

Figure 5.18 Mapping of input feature maps and sparse weight matrix to systolic array.

5.9 Future Scope and Summary

Future Scope

Low power applications, diverse DL tasks, and hardware security are some of the fields that still require significant research. Recently several applications of neural networks are getting explored [82–92]. Therefore, there is a need to explore the architectures tailored for each application. With rise in the number of IoT edge devices monitoring our daily activities, there is a need for accurate results at very low power. Power efficient nano architectures which provide high throughput meeting real-time requirements have to be optimized at software and hardware levels. Apart from these several works have been proposed in making more efficient devices for compute in memory architecture for low power applications [93–109]. However, peripheral circuits are still CMOS based which are the performance bottleneck for these architectures which needs to be addressed in future. Recent trends in developments of generative adversarial networks (GANs) based application for generative modelling have given a remarkable result. There are significant opportunities for the development of an accelerator for the training of GANs. Two different CNN networks have to be implemented to train GANs making it even more challenging. Spiking neural networks implementation can further be researched for noise resilient prediction and power efficient architectures as outputs are not generated at every clock cycle instead, they are evaluated only when accumulator reaches above certain threshold. Growing edge devices and cloud computing-based environments, attacks on the hardware can significantly hamper the CNN classification accuracy. Bit flip attacks and side-channel attacks on CNNs can destroy the output classification accuracy and hamper personal privacy. Techniques for making CNN more reliable must be developed that are resistant to bit flipping that directly impacts the most significant bits.

Summary

The chapter provides a comprehensive understanding of the relevant techniques and applications in the domain of edge computing hardware accelerators focused on deep learning. Edge devices are quickly integrating machine learning-based hardware and require architectures that are both resource and power efficient. The challenges of computational overload and memory bandwidth limitations, which hinder the implementation of computer vision-based applications on conventional von-Neumann architectures, are explored in depth. At the algorithmic level, the chapter discusses convolution strategies that optimize computational efficiency. At the architectural level, techniques such as loop optimizations, pipelining, and parallelism are emphasized as effective methods for addressing computational bottlenecks and enhancing performance. The chapter also tackles fundamental challenges, including the "memory wall" and "power wall," which are significant barriers to achieving high performance and energy efficiency in edge computing systems. Furthermore, the chapter underscores the importance of domain-specific platforms that are tailored to the unique requirements of deep learning workloads. By optimizing both hardware and algorithmic frameworks, these platforms provide effective solutions to meet the growing computational demands of AI applications in edge environments. As edge devices continue to evolve, integrating more advanced AI capabilities, the chapter highlights the need for sustainable design practices that prioritize resource and power efficiency. It provides a forward-looking perspective on how technological innovations in hardware accelerators will play a pivotal role in shaping the future of machine learning-driven edge computing. This comprehensive analysis serves as a guide for researchers and practitioners aiming to design and implement efficient edge computing solutions for the next generation of AI applications.

References

1. Khan, A.S., Zahoora, U., Qureshi, A.S., A survey of the recent architectures of deep convolutional neural networks. *Artif. Intell. Rev.*, 53, 8, 5455–5516, Dec. 2020. doi: 10.1007/s10462-020-09825-6.
2. Liu, W., Wang, Z., Liu, X., Zeng, N., Liu, Y., Alsaadi, F.E., A survey of deep neural network architectures and their applications. *Neurocomputing*, 234, 11–26, Apr. 2017. doi: 10.1016/j.neucom.2016.12.038.
3. Kamthan, S., Singh, H., Meitzler, T., Hierarchical fuzzy deep learning for image classification. *Memories - Mater. Devices Circuits Syst.*, 100016, Oct. 2022, doi: 10.1016/j.memori.2022.100016.
4. Himeur, Y., Video surveillance using deep transfer learning and deep domain adaptation: Towards better generalization. *Engg. Appl. Artif. Intell.*, 119, Mar. 2023. doi: 10.1016/j.engappai.2022.105698.
5. Sharma, N., Jain, V., Mishra, A., An Analysis of Convolutional Neural Networks for Image Classification. *Proc. Comp. Sci.*, 377–384. doi: 10.1016/j.procs.2018.05.198.
6. Liu, L., Deep Learning for Generic Object Detection: A Survey. *Int. J. Comp. Vis.*, 128, 2, 261–318, Feb. 2020, doi: 10.1007/s11263-019-01247-4.

7. Guo, Y., Liu, Y., Georgiou, T., Lew, M.S., A review of semantic segmentation using deep neural networks. *Int. J. Multimed. Inf. Retr.*, 7, 2, 87–93, Jun. 2018. doi: 10.1007/s13735-017-0141-z.
8. Deng, B.L., Li, G., Han, S., Shi, L., Xie, Y., Model Compression and Hardware Acceleration for Neural Networks: A Comprehensive Survey. *Proc. IEEE*, 108, 4, 485–532, Apr. 2020. doi: 10.1109/JPROC.2020.2976475.
9. Chen, Y., Xie, Y., Song, L., Chen, F., Tang, T., A Survey of Accelerator Architectures for Deep Neural Networks. *Engineering*, 6, 3, 264–274, Mar. 2020. doi: 10.1016/j.eng.2020.01.007.
10. Boutros, A., Yazdanshenas, S., Betz, V., You cannot improve what you do not measure: FPGA vs. ASIC efficiency gaps for convolutional neural network inference. *ACM Trans. Recon. Technol. Syst.*, 11, 3, Dec. 2018. doi: 10.1145/3242898.
11. Han, S., Mao, H., Da80lly, W.J., Deep Compression: Compressing Deep Neural Networks with Pruning, Trained Quantization and Huffman Coding, in: *Proc. 4th Inter. Conf. Learn. Rep*, San Juan, Puerto Rico, May 2016, doi: arxiv.1510.00149.
12. Ma, Y., Cao, Y., Vrudhula, S., Seo, J.S., Optimizing the Convolution Operation to Accelerate Deep Neural Networks on FPGA. *IEEE Trans. Very Large Scale Int. Syst.*, 26, 7, 1354–1367, Jul. 2018. doi: 10.1109/TVLSI.2018.2815603.
13. Lavin, A. and Gray, S., Fast Algorithms for Convolutional Neural Networks, in: *Proc. IEEE Comp. Vis. Pat. Recog*, USA, Dec. 2016, pp. 4013–4021, doi: 10.1109/CVPR.2016.435.
14. Foley, D. and Danskin, J., Ultra-Performance Pascal GPU and NVLink Interconnect. *IEEE Micro*, 37, 2, 7–17, Mar. 2017. doi: 10.1109/MM.2017.37.
15. Esmaeilzadeh, H., Sampson, A., Ceze, L., Burger, D., Neural acceleration for general-purpose approximate programs, in: *Proc. IEEE/ACM Inter. Symp. Micro*, Vancouver, Canada, pp. 449–460, 2012, doi: 10.1109/MICRO.2012.48.
16. Chen, T., DianNao: A Small-Footprint High-Throughput Accelerator for Ubiquitous Machine-Learning. *SIGARCH Comp. Archit. News*, 42, 1, 269–284, 2014. doi: 10.1145/http.
17. Liu, S., Cambricon: An Instruction Set Architecture for Neural Networks, in: *Proc. 43rd Inter. Symp. Comp. Arch*, Seoul, South Korea, Aug. 2016, pp. 393–405, doi: 10.1109/ISCA.2016.42.
18. Jouppi, N.P., In-datacenter performance analysis of a tensor processing unit, in: *Proc. Inter. Symp. Comp. Arch*, Canada, Jun. 2017, pp. 1–12, doi: 10.1145/3079856.3080246.
19. Norrie, T., The Design Process for Google's Training Chips: TPUv2 and TPUv3. *IEEE Micro*, 41, 2, 56–63, Mar. 2021. doi: 10.1109/MM.2021.3058217.
20. Jang, J.W., Sparsity-aware and re-configurable NPU architecture for Samsung flagship mobile SoC, in: *Proc. Inter. Symp. Comp. Arch*, Valencia, Spain, Jun. 2021, pp. 15–28, doi: 10.1109/ISCA52012.2021.00011.

21. Wang, C., Gong, L., Yu, Q., Li, X., Xie, Y., Zhou, X., DLAU: A scalable deep learning accelerator unit on FPGA. *IEEE Trans. Comp. Aid. Des. Int. Cir. Sys.*, 36, 3, 513–517, Mar. 2017. doi: 10.1109/TCAD.2016.2587683.
22. Ma, Y., Suda, N., Cao, Y., Vrudhula, S., Sun Seo, J., ALAMO: FPGA acceleration of deep learning algorithms with a modularized RTL compiler. *Integration*, 62, Elsevier B.V, 14–23, Jun. 01, 2018. doi: 10.1016/j.vlsi.2017.12.009.
23. Guo, K., Angel-Eye: A complete design flow for mapping CNN onto embedded FPGA. *IEEE Trans. Comp. Aid. Des. Integ. Cir. Sys*, 37, 1, 35–47, Jan2018. doi: 10.1109/TCAD.2017.2705069.
24. Andri, R., Cavigelli, L., Rossi, D., Benini, L., Yoda NN: An architecture for ultralow power binary-weight CNN acceleration. *IEEE Trans. Comp. Aid. Des. Int. Cir. Sys*, 37, 1, 48–60, 2018. doi: 10.1109/TCAD.2017.2682138.
25. Fowers, J., A configurable cloud-Scale DNN processor for real-Time AI, in: *Proc. Inter. Symp. Comp. Arch*, USA, Jul. 2018, pp. 1–14, doi: 10.1109/ISCA.2018.00012.
26. Xiao, Q., Liang, Y., Lu, L., Yan, S., Tai, Y.W., Exploring Heterogeneous Algorithms for Accelerating Deep Convolutional Neural Networks on FPGAs, in: *Proc. Des. Autom. Conf*, Austin, TX, USA, Jun. 2017, doi: 10.1145/3061639.3062244.
27. Nehete, H., Verma, G., Gupta, A., Kaushik, P., Kaushik, B.K., FPGA based CNN accelerator for high-speed biomedical application, in: *Proc. SPIE High-Speed Biomed. Imag. and Spectr. VIII*, USA, Jan. 2023, p. 56, doi: 10.1117/12.2650101.
28. Sandler, M., Howard, A., Zhu, M., Zhmoginov, A., Chen, L.-C., MobileNetV2: Inverted Residuals and Linear Bottlenecks, in: *Proc. IEEE Comp. Vis. Pat. Recog*, Chicago, pp. 4510–4520, 2018.
29. Chollet, F., Xception: Deep learning with depthwise separable convolutions, in: *Proc. IEEE Comp. Vis. Pat. Recog*, Honolulu, USA, Nov. 2017, pp. 1800–1807, doi: 10.1109/CVPR.2017.195.
30. Zhang, X., Zhou, X., Lin, M., Sun, J., ShuffleNet: An Extremely Efficient Convolutional Neural Network for Mobile Devices, in: *Proc. IEEE Comp. Vis. Pat. Recog*, Salt Lake City, USA, Dec. 2018, pp. 6848–6856, doi: 10.1109/CVPR.2018.00716.
31. Dongarra Xz, J., Lumsdaine, A., Niu, X., Pozo, R., Remington, K., Sparse Matrix Libraries in C++ for High Performance Architectures, in. *Proc. Obj. Orien. Numer.*, 214–218, 1994.
32. Carreira-Perpiñán, M.A. and Idelbayev, Y., 'Learning-Compression' Algorithms for Neural Net Pruning, in: *Proc. IEEE Comp. Vis. Pat. Recog*, Salt Lake City, UT, USA, Dec. 2018, pp. 8532–8541, doi: 10.1109/CVPR.2018.00890.
33. Huang, Q., Zhou, K., You, S., Neumann, U., Learning to prune filters in convolutional neural networks, in: *Proc. IEEE Wint. Conf. Appl. Comp. Vis*, Lake Tahoe, NV, USA, May 2018, pp. 709–718, doi: 10.1109/WACV.2018.00083.

34. Singh, P., Matiyali, M.R.N., Namboodiri, V.P., Multi-layer Pruning Framework for Compressing Single Shot MultiBox Detector, in: *Proc. IEEE Wint. Conf. Appl. Comp. Vis*, Waikoloa, HI, USA, Nov. 2018, pp. 1318–1327, doi: http://arxiv.org/abs/1811.08342.
35. Zhuang, Z., Discrimination-aware Channel Pruning for Deep Neural Networks, in: *Proc. 32nd Intern.Conf. Neur. Inform. Proces. Sys*, Canada, pp. 883–894, 2018.
36. Liu, C. and Wu, H., Channel pruning based on mean gradient for accelerating Convolutional Neural Networks. *Sig. Process.*, 156, 84–91, Mar 2019. doi: 10.1016/j.sigpro.2018.10.019.
37. Yang, T.-J., Chen, Y.-H., Sze, V., Designing Energy-Efficient Convolutional Neural Networks using Energy-Aware Pruning, in: *Proc. IEEE Comp. Vis. Pat. Recog*, Honolulu, HI, USA, Nov. 2017, pp. 5687–5695, doi: 10.1109/CVPR.2017.643.
38. Han, S., ESE: Efficient speech recognition engine with sparse LSTM on FPGA, in: *Proc. ACM/SIGDA Intern. Symp. Field-Programm. Gate Arr*, California, USA, Feb. 2017, pp. 75–84, doi: 10.1145/3020078.3021745.
39. Zhou, S.C., Wang, Y.Z., Wen, H., He, Q.Y., Zou, Y.H., Balanced Quantization: An Effective and Efficient Approach to Quantized Neural Networks. *J. Comput. Sci. Technol.*, 32, 4, 667–682, Jul 2017. doi: 10.1007/s11390-017-1750-y.
40. Hubara, I., Courbariaux, M., Soudry, D., El-Yaniv, R., Bengio, Y., Quantized Neural Networks: Training Neural Networks with Low Precision Weights and Activations. *Journ. Mach. Learn. Res.*, 18, 1, 2018. doi: 10.5555/3122009.3242044.
41. Qiu, J., Going deeper with embedded FPGA platform for convolutional neural network, in: *Proc. ACM/SIGDA Intern. Symp. Field-Programm. Gate Arr*, California, USA, Feb. 2016, pp. 26–35, doi: 10.1145/2847263.2847265.
42. Kala, S., Jose, B.R., Mathew, J., Nalesh, S., High-Performance CNN Accelerator on FPGA Using Unified Winograd-GEMM Architecture. *IEEE Trans Very Large Scale Int. Syst.*, 27, 12, 2816–2828, 2019. doi: 10.1109/TVLSI.2019.2941250.
43. Zhang, C. and Prasanna, V., Frequency domain acceleration of convolutional neural networks on CPU-FPGA shared memory system, in: *Proc. ACM/SIGDA Intern. Symp. Field-Programm. Gate Arr*, California, USA, Feb. 2017, pp. 35–44, doi: 10.1145/3020078.3021727.
44. Lin, J. and Yao, Y., A Fast Algorithm for Convolutional Neural Networks Using Tile-based Fast Fourier Transforms. *Neur. Proc. Lett.*, 50, 2, 1951–1967, Oct 2019. doi: 10.1007/s11063-019-09981-z.
45. Umuroglu, Y., FINN: A framework for fast, scalable binarized neural network inference, in: *Proc. ACM/SIGDA Intern. Symp. Field-Programm. Gate Arr*, California, USA, Feb. 2017, pp. 65–74, doi: 10.1145/3020078.3021744.
46. Wei, X., Automated systolic array architecture synthesis for high throughput CNN inference on FPGAs, in: *Proc. ACM/EDAC/IEEE Des. Auto. Conf*, Austin, TX, USA, pp. 1–6, 2017, doi: 10.1145/3061639.3062207.

47. Xushen, H., Dajiang, Z., Shihao, W., Shinji, K., CNN-MERP: An FPGA-Based Memory-Efficient Reconfigurable Processor for Forward and Backward Propagation of Convolutional Neural Networks, in: *IEEE Inter. Conf. Comp. Des*, Scottsdale, AZ, USA, pp. 320–327, 2016.
48. Wang, B., Ma, S., Zhu, G., Yi, X., Xu, R., A novel systolic array processor with dynamic dataflows. *Integration*, 85, 42–47, 2022. doi: 10.1016/j.vlsi.2022.03.002.
49. Chen, Y., DaDianNao: A Machine-Learning Supercomputer, in: *Proc. Ann. Inter. Symp. Microarch*, Cambridge, UK, Jan. 2015, pp. 609–622, doi: 10.1109/MICRO.2014.58.
50. Du, Z., ShiDianNao: Shifting vision processing closer to the sensor, in: *Proc. Inter. Symp. Comp. Arch*, Portland, USA, Jun. 2015, pp. 92–104, doi: 10.1145/2749469.2750389.
51. Zhang, C., Wu, D., Sun, J., Sun, G., Luo, G., Cong, J., Energy-Efficient CNN Implementation on a Deeply Pipelined FPGA Cluster, in: *Proc. Intern. Symp. Low Pow. Electr. Des*, San Francisco, Aug. 2016, pp. 326–331, doi: 10.1145/2934583.2934644.
52. Liu, Z., Chow, P., Xu, J., Jiang, J., Dou, Y., Zhou, J., A uniform architecture design for accelerating 2D and 3D CNNs on FPGAs. *Electronics*, 8, 1, Jan. 2019. doi: 10.3390/electronics8010065.
53. Chen, Y.H., Yang, T.J., Emer, J.S., Sze, V., Eyeriss v2: A Flexible Accelerator for Emerging Deep Neural Networks on Mobile Devices. *IEEE J. Emerg. Sel. Top Circ. Sys.*, 9, 2, 292–308, Jun 2019. doi: 10.1109/JETCAS.2019.2910232.
54. Han, S., EIE: Efficient Inference Engine on Compressed Deep Neural Network, in: *Proc. Inter. Symp. Comp. Arch*, Seoul, Korea, Aug. 2016, pp. 243–254, doi: 10.1109/ISCA.2016.30.
55. Gong, L., Wang, C., Li, X., Chen, H., Zhou, X., MALOC: A fully pipelined FPGA accelerator for convolutional neural networks with all layers mapped on chip. *IEEE Trans. Comp. Aid. Des. Integ. Cir. Sys.*, 37, 11, 2601–2612, Nov2018. doi: 10.1109/TCAD.2018.2857078.
56. Wang, X., Wang, C., Cao, J., Gong, L., Zhou, X., WinoNN: Optimizing FPGA-Based Convolutional Neural Network Accelerators Using Sparse Winograd Algorithm. *IEEE Trans. Comp. Aid. Des. Integ. Cir. Sys.*, 39, 11, 4290–4302, Nov 2020. doi: 10.1109/TCAD.2020.3012323.
57. Zhang, C., Li, P., Sun, G., Guan, Y., Xiao, B., Cong, J., Optimizing FPGA-based accelerator design for deep convolutional neural networks, in: *Proc. ACM/SIGDA Intern. Symp. Field-Programm. Gate Arr*, California, USA, Feb. 2015, pp. 161–170, doi: 10.1145/2684746.2689060.
58. Guan, Y., FP-DNN: An automated framework for mapping deep neural networks onto FPGAs with RTL-HLS hybrid templates, in: *Proc. IEEE Ann. Intern. Symp. Field-Programm. Cust. Comp. Mach*, Napa, CA, USA, Jun. 2017, pp. 152–159, doi: 10.1109/FCCM.2017.25.

59. Liang, S., Yin, S., Liu, L., Luk, W., Wei, S., FP-BNN: Binarized neural network on FPGA. *Neurocomp.*, 275, 1072–1086, Jan 2018. doi: 10.1016/j.neucom.2017.09.046.
60. Akhlaghi, V., Yazdanbakhsh, A., Samadi, K., Gupta, R.K., Esmaeilzadeh, H., SnaPEA: Predictive early activation for reducing computation in deep convolutional neural networks, in: *Proc. Inter. Symp. Comp. Arch*, Los Angeles, USA, Jul. 2018, pp. 662–673, doi: 10.1109/ISCA.2018.00061.
61. Yepez, J. and Ko, S.B., Stride 2 1-D, 2-D, and 3-D Winograd for Convolutional Neural Networks. *IEEE Trans. Very Large Scale. Int. Sys.*, 28, 4, 853–863, Apr 2020. doi: 10.1109/TVLSI.2019.2961602.
62. Lu, L., Liang, Y., Xiao, Q., Yan, S., Evaluating fast algorithms for convolutional neural networks on FPGAs, in: *Proc. IEEE Ann. Intern. Symp. Field-Programm. Cust. Comp. Mach*, Jun. 2017, pp. 101–108, doi: 10.1109/FCCM.2017.64.
63. Hemmat, M., San Miguel, J., Davoodi, A., AirNN: A Featherweight Framework for Dynamic Input-Dependent Approximation of CNNs. *IEEE Trans. Comp. Aid. Des. Int. Cir. Sys.*, 40, 10, 2090–2103, 2021. doi: 10.1109/TCAD.2020.3033750.
64. Xuan, L., Un, K.F., Lam, C.S., Martins, R.P., An FPGA-Based Energy-Efficient Reconfigurable Depthwise Separable Convolution Accelerator for Image Recognition. *IEEE Trans. Circ. Sys. II Express Briefs*, 69, 10, 4003–4007, Oct 2022. doi: 10.1109/TCSII.2022.3180553.
65. Bosheng, L., *et al.*, Search-free Accelerator for Sparse Convolutional Neural Networks, in: *Proc. Asia South Pacif. Des. Auto. Conf*, Beijing, China, pp. 524–529, 2020.
66. Basalama, S., Sohrabizadeh, A., Wang, J., Guo, L., Cong, J., FlexCNN: An End-to-End Framework for Composing CNN Accelerators on FPGA. *ACM Trans. Reconf. Technol. Syst.*, Dec. 2022. doi: 10.1145/3570928.
67. Nehete, H., Verma, G., Yadav, S., Kaushik, B.K., Accelerating sparse convolutional neural networks with systolic arrays on FPGA, in: *SPIE Proc. Appl. of Mach. Learn. 2023*, vol. 12675, pp. 199–206, 2023.
68. Soni, S., Verma, G., Nehete, H., Kaushik, B.K., Energy Efficient Spin-Based Implementation of Neuromorphic Functions in CNNs. *IEEE Open J. Nanotechnol.*, 4, 102–108, 2023.
69. Soni, S., Raj, R.K., Kaushik, B.K., Antiferromagnetic-Ferromagnetic Heterostructure based Spin Hall Nano-Oscillator. *AIP Appl. Phys. Lett.*, 125, 192401, 2024.
70. Soni, S., Nehete, H., Monga, A., Verma, G., Shukla, A.K., Pramanik, T., Energy Efficient DSHE-MRAM based In-Memory Computing for Image Segmentation. *APL Electron. Devices*, 1, 2, 026121, 2025.
71. Soni, S., Rezaeiyan, Y., Boehnert, T., Farkhani, H., Ferreira, R., Kaushik, B.K., Moradi, F., Shreya, S., Brain-inspired Spintronics-based Hopfield Oscillatory Neural Network for Performing Image Denoising Tasks. *Neuromorph. Comput. Eng.*, 5, 3, 034001, 2025.

72. Soni, S., Verma, G., Kumar Shukla, A., Kaushik, B.K., Energy Efficient DSHE based Analogue Multiply Accumulate Computing Crossbar Architecture, in: *2023 IEEE Asia Pacific Conference on Circuits and Systems (APCCAS)*, Hyderabad, India, pp. 21–25, 2023.
73. Soni, S., *et al.*, A Neuromorphic Computational Model for Spintronics-based Hopfield Oscillatory Neural Network. *IEEE Trans. Magn.*, 2025. early access.
74. Verma, G., Soni, S., Nisar, A., Kaushik, B.K., Multi-bit MRAM based high performance neuromorphic accelerator for image classification. *Neuromorph. Comput. Eng.*, 4, 1, 014008, 2024.
75. Verma, G., Soni, S., Kaushik, B.K., Spin device-based image edge detection architecture for neuromorphic computing. *Nanotechnology*, 35, 5, 055201, 2023.
76. Verma, G., Soni, S., Nisar, A., Dhull, S., Kaushik, B.K., Energy-Efficient CNN Accelerator Using Voltage-Gated DSHE-MRAM. *IEEE Trans. Electron Devices*, 72, 4, 1715–1722, 2025.
77. Nehete, H., Soni, S., Bollu, T.K.R., Raman, B., Kaushik, B.K., Approximation-Aware Training for Efficient Neural Network Inference on MRAM Based CiM Architecture. *IEEE Open J. Nanotechnol.*, 6, 16–26, 2024.
78. Nisar, A., Nehete, H., Verma, G., Kaushik, B.K., Hybrid multilevel STT/DSHE memory for efficient CNN training. *IEEE Trans. Electron Devices*, 70, 3, 1006–1013, 2023.
79. Kaushik, P., Monga, A., Nehete, H., Kaushik, B.K., Enhancing Image Segmentation Performance with MRAM based Processing-in-Memory Architecture, in: *Proceedings of the IEEE Nanotechnology Materials and Devices Conference*, pp. 836–841, 2023.
80. Kaushik, P., Gupta, A., Kaushik, B.K., Nehete, H., MRAM-Based In-Memory Computing for Efficient Acceleration of Generative Adversarial Networks, in: *Proceedings of the IEEE 23rd International Conference on Nanotechnology*, pp. 1–5, 2023.
81. Verma, G., Nisar, A., Dhull, S., Kaushik, B.K., Neuromorphic accelerator for spiking neural network using SOT-MRAM crossbar array. *IEEE Trans. Electron Devices*, 70, 11, 6012–6020, 2023.
82. Nehete, H., Monga, A., Kaushik, P., Kaushik, B.K., Fourier Prior-Based Two-Stage Architecture for Image Restoration, in: *Proceedings of the Computer Vision and Pattern Recognition Conference Workshops*, USA, Jun 2024, pp. 6014–6023.
83. Monga, A., Nehete, H., Kaushik, P., Bollu, T.K.R., Raman, B., Sharma, G., FCTFANet: A Fused CNN-Transformer Feature Aggregator Network for Image Restoration, in: *Proceedings of the Computer Vision and Pattern Recognition Conference Workshops*, Nashville, USA, Jun 2025, pp. 885–894.
84. Ansari, M.S., Nehete, H., Soni, S., Kaushik, B.K., Kaurav, P., Image denoising using simulated bifurcation based Ising machine. *Phys. Scr.*, 100, 7, 076019, 2025.

85. Saini, S., Shukla, A.K., Nehete, H., Bindal, N., Kaushik, B.K., Machine Learning-Based Prediction of Antiferromagnetic Skyrmion Formation. *IEEE Trans. Electron Devices*, 71, 4, 2774–2780, 2024.
86. Sehgal, A., Saini, S., Nehete, H., Das, K.K., Roy, S., Kaushik, B.K., Multitask Learning for Estimation of Magnetic Parameters Using Pattern Recognition. *IEEE Open J. Nanotechnol.*, 5, 149–155, 2024.
87. Shukla, A.K., Nehete, H., Kaushik, P., Soni, S., Kaushik, B.K., Machine Learning Assisted Soft Error Variation Analysis of Radiation Hardened MRAM Circuit, in: *Proceedings of the IEEE 23rd International Conference on Nanotechnology*, pp. 1–6, 2023.
88. Shukla, A.K., Nehete, H., Soni, S., Kaushik, P., Kaushik, B.K., Machine Learning Assisted Statistical Variation Analysis of Voltage Gated Spin Orbit Torque Magnetic Tunnel Junction, in: *Proc. IEEE Nanotechnol. Mater. Devices Conf. (NMDC)*, pp. 53–58, 2023.
89. Yadav, S., Shukla, A.K., Nehete, H., Soni, S., Saini, S., Kaushik, B.K., Variation analysis of spintronic device using machine learning algorithm, in: *Proc. SPIE, Spintronics XVI*, vol. 12656, pp. 261–269, Sep. 2023.
90. Yadav, S., Kaushik, B.K., Giri, A., Energy-Efficient Hybrid STT-MTJ/CMOS Circuit for Machine Learning-Assisted Neuromorphic Computing Applications. *IEEE Can. J. Electr. Comput. Eng.*, 48, 3, 184–191, 2025.
91. Yadav, S., Giri, N., Maurya, A., Kaushik, B.K., Giri, A., Machine learning and explainable-AI based prediction of gate-all-around ferroelectric-FET: how ML models influence XAI. *Phys. Scr.*, 100, 5, 056006, 2025.
92. Kaushik, P., Gupta, A., Nehete, H., Balasubramanian, R., Kaushik, B.K., Design and analysis of high-performance real-time image dehazing using convolutional neural and generative adversarial networks. *Proc. SPIE AI Opt. Data Sci. IV*, 12438, 163–170, Mar. 2023.
93. Verma, R.S., Raj, R.K., Saini, S., Kaushik, B.K., Synthetic antiferromagnetic skyrmion based neuron and synaptic devices under DMI gradient. *Phys. Scr.*, 100, 5, 055002, 2025.
94. Kumar, N., Singh, S., Monga, A., Sharma, A., Gupta, S., A Comprehensive Study on Recognition of Various Indian and Non-Indian Scripts. *J. Adv. Res. Dyn. Control Syst.*, 11, special issue-05, 2220–2228, 2019.
95. Saini, S., Soni, S., Nisar, A., Dhull, S., Bhatti, S., Sbiaa, R., Piramanayagam, S.N., Kaushik, B.K., Meander geometry based skyrmionic synapse for image classification. *J. Magn. Magn. Mater.*, 614, 172700, 2025.
96. Saini, S., Verma, R.S., Kaushik, B.K., Antiferromagnetic skyrmion dynamics in stepped geometry for various applications. *J. Appl. Phys.*, 136, 13, 2024.
97. Saini, S., Bindal, N., Raj, R.K., Kaushik, B.K., A spin wave driven skyrmion-based diode on a T-shaped nanotrack. *Nanoscale*, 16, 18, 9004–9010, 2024.
98. Saini, S., Bindal, N., Kaushik, B.K., Skyrmionium-based leaky integrate and fire neuron, in: *Proc. IEEE International Conference on Nanotechnology (NANO)*, pp. 209–214, 2023.

99. Raj, R.K., Verma, R.S., Saini, S., Kumar, M., Shukla, A.K., Kaushik, B.K., Leaky-integrate-fire neuron based on antiferromagnetic skyrmion under strain gradient, in: *Proc. IEEE International Conference on Nanotechnology (NANO)*, pp. 331–336, 2024.
100. Monga, A. and Vig, R., An Ultra Miniature MEMS Capacitor for Arterial Pressure Measurement. *J. Inst. Eng. India Ser. B*, 93, 271–275, 2012.
101. Monga, A., MEMS Capacitive Sensor for Continuous BP Monitoring, in: *Proceedings of Latest Advancements Science, Engineering and Research Conference*, Punjab, India, 2011.
102. Raj, R.K., Saini, S., Verma, R.S., Kaushik, B.K., Shreya, S., Dzyaloshinskii–Moriya interaction gradient driven skyrmion based energy efficient leaky integrate fire neuron. *J. Magn. Magn. Mater.*, 614, 172694, 2025.
103. Soni, S., Verma, G., Kaushik, B.K., Energy Efficient Ternary Computation Unit Using Differential Spin Hall Effect MRAM. *Semicond. Sci. Technol.*, 38, 025005, 2022.
104. Sharma, V.K., Pattanaik, M., Raj, B., ONOFIC Approach: Low Power High Speed Nanoscale VLSI Circuits Design, in: *Int. J. Electron*, vol. 101, pp. 61–73, Taylor & Francis, 2014.
105. Raj, B., Saxena, A.K., Dasgupta, S., Nanoscale FinFET Based SRAM Cell Design: Analysis of Performance metric, Process variation, Underlapped FinFET and Temperature effect. *IEEE Circuits Syst. Mag.*, 11, 38–50, 2011.
106. Singh, M., Chaudhary, T., Raj, B., Enhancing FeFET structures for non-volatile on-chip memories: Design and comparative analysis. *Int. J. Numer. Modell. Electron. Networks Devices Fields*, 37, 6, e70004, 2024.
107. Singh, J. and Raj, B., Enhanced Nonlinear Memristor Model Encapsulating Stochastic Dopant Drift. *JNO ASP*, 14, 958–963, 2019.
108. Singh, J. and Raj, B., Temperature Dependent Analytical Modeling and Simulations of Nanoscale Memristor. *Eng. Sci. Technol. Int. J.*, 21, 862–868, 2018.
109. Bansal, P. and Raj, B., Memristor Modeling and Analysis for Linear Dopant Drift Kinetics. *J. Nanoeng. Nanomanuf.*, 6, 1–7, 2016.

6

Flexible Energy Storage Devices

Tanya Singh, Akriti Dewangan, Puja Kumari, Balwinder Raj*, Tarun Chaudhary Mandeep Singh and Yogesh Thakur

Department of Electronics and Communication Engineering, Dr. B. R. Ambedkar National Institute of Technology Jalandhar, Punjab, India

Abstract
Flexible energy storage technologies, such as flexible batteries and supercapacitors, have advanced as a result of the growing demand for wearable, flexible, and sustainable electronics. Flexible displays, wearable technology, and next-generation portable electronics all depend on these devices because they can bend, stretch, and fold without losing their functionality. It has been seen how flexible devices have changed over time, how their structures have changed to store energy, and the essential components that give them flexibility and durability—such as carbon-based nanofibers and conductive polymers. Modern applications require mechanical resilience and energy storage capacity, which are optimized by a variety of structures such as fiber, island bridges, and interdigital designs. Issues like low energy density, expensive production, and environmental impact are discussed, highlighting the necessity for more innovation. The development of flexible energy storage devices ensures the improvement of energy efficiency and the facilitating of the shift to a resilient, flexible, and sustainable energy ecosystem.

***Keywords*:** Flexible devices, storage devices, energy storage, materials for energy storage, graphene-based flexible electrodes

6.1 Introduction

Global fossil fuel consumption is increasing day by day, which has resulted in greenhouse gas emissions, damage to the environment, and a lack of energy. It is well acknowledged that employing sustainable clean energy can help mitigate these problems and that it is essential to guaranteeing

**Corresponding author*: rajb@nitj.ac.in

Ashish Maurya, Mandeep Singh and Balwinder Raj (eds.) Machine Learning in Nanoelectronics: Devices, Circuits and Systems, (155–196) © 2026 Scrivener Publishing LLC

sustainable growth on a global scale. The growing need for flexible displays and wearable, portable electronics gave rise to the concept of flexible energy storage devices. The evolution of flexible energy storage technologies, such as supercapacitors and flexible batteries, includes a number of significant turning points. Flexible energy storage systems are power sources that can bend, stretch, fold, or twist while preserving their performance. These devices are meant to be lightweight, thin, and adaptable to diverse forms and surfaces, making them excellent for applications in wearable electronics, flexible displays, and portable gadgets. Energy storage technologies have become increasingly significant in relation to the electric grid in recent decades. The fact that there are now many more applications that need a specific power or voltage level during a brief period of time is one of the primary causes of this [1]. Flexible and wearable energy storage devices (ESDs) with high energy and power densities, as well as exceptional flexibility and durability, are significantly needed for the development of these electronics in order to power a variety of wearable systems. Because of its potential uses in wearable and portable electronics, sensing systems, and medical equipment, flexible energy-storage devices, or FESDs, have garnered a lot of attention. Therefore, a lot of work has gone into creating different kinds of wearable, flexible rechargeable batteries and supercapacitors.

6.1.1 Flexible Devices

Flexible devices are a rapidly advancing field in technology, characterized by their ability to bend, fold, or stretch without losing functionality. They leverage cutting-edge materials and designs, such as flexible displays, sensors, and batteries, to create electronics that are more adaptable, portable, and durable [2]. Examples include foldable smartphones, wearable health trackers, bendable solar cells, and electronic skins (Figure 6.1). These devices hold significant potential across industries, from healthcare to consumer electronics, offering enhanced functionality and innovative applications that traditional rigid electronics cannot achieve.

6.1.2 History and Origins of Flexible Devices

The 20th century saw the beginning of the history of flexible electronics. Dr. Ken Gilleo discovered one of the first descriptions of what may be called a flex circuit, as shown in Figure 6.2 [4], which was revealed in an English patent by Albert Hansen from 1903 that described a device made of paraffin-coated paper with flat metal conductors.

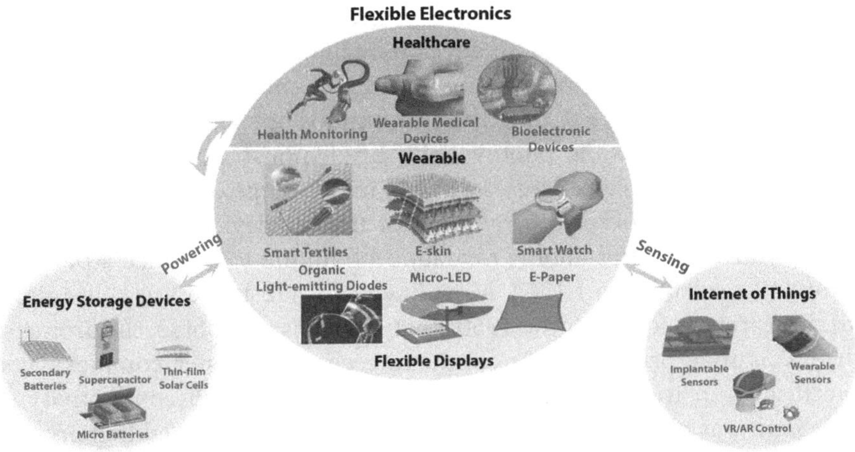

Figure 6.1 The application of flexible electronics in various fields, including wearable devices, flexible displays, healthcare and safety, and the Internet of things [3].

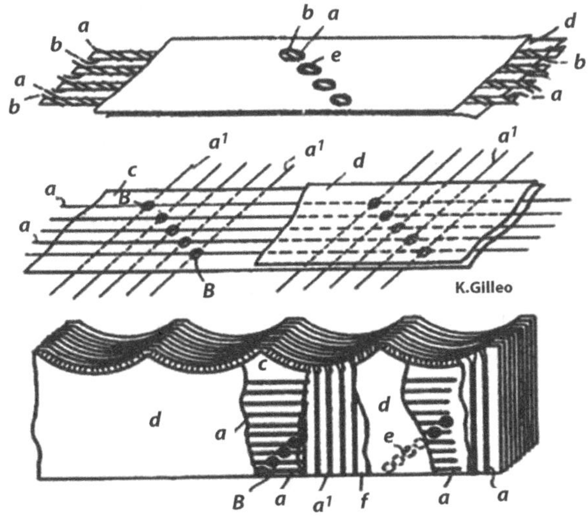

Figure 6.2 First flex circuit patent [4].

Anything that is extremely long or thin can stretch. Although cables and wiring are the best examples of flexibility, silicon wafers used in satellite solar cells were not thinned until the space race in order to increase their power per weight ratio and allow for some warping. In the 1960s, this idea made it possible to create the first flexible solar cells. Researchers A.W. Crabb and

H. Treble made important advances to the field of flexible electronics in 1967 [5]. They concentrated on developing lightweight, flexible solar panels using thin-film technology, namely utilizing cadmium telluride (CdTe) and cadmium sulphide (CdS). Their inventions opened the door for later developments in flexible photovoltaics by demonstrating the possibility for incorporating solar energy solutions into a range of applications. The further research proved to be a boon for flexible devices. Henry Letheby used sulfuric acid and anodic oxidation of aniline to produce a partially conductive substance in 1862. Most likely, the substance was polyaniline [6]. Researchers found in the 1950s that halogens and polycyclic aromatic chemicals may produce semi-conducting charge-transfer complex salts. Specifically, in the perylene-iodine combination, a high conductivity of 0.12 S/cm was observed in 1954 [6]. This discovery suggested that organic materials could conduct electricity. Dr. John McGinness created the first gadget with an organic semiconductor in 1973 [7]. In the decades that followed, significant advancements in flexibility and processability were made possible by organic semiconductors and amorphous silicon. As a result, these materials were used as the foundation for electronic devices in applications that needed characteristics like bending, rolling, folding, and stretching that conventional electronics could not provide. Bernard J. Lechner of RCA Laboratories was the one who first came up with the concept of a TFT-based liquid crystal display (LCD) in 1968. At Westinghouse Electric Corporation, T. Peter Brody, Fang-Chen Luo, and colleagues created the first working AMLCD using thin-film transistors in 1972. Polycrystalline silicon (poly-Si) TFTs with flexibility were constructed on plastic substrates in the late 1990s. Polycrystalline silicon (poly-Si) thin-film transistors (TFTs) are widely used in various applications due to their superior electrical performance compared to amorphous silicon (a-Si) TFTs [8].

6.1.3 The Evolution of Flexible Devices

The goal to get beyond the constraints of rigid electronics produced the rise of flexible devices. Researchers looked to conductive polymers as a novel substitute for traditional materials like silicon, glass, and metal as their shortcomings in satisfying the increasing need for wearable and lightweight technology became evident. These polymers made it possible for electronics to bend and stretch without losing their operation by providing the required electrical conductivity and flexibility [9–16]. Concurrently, the creation of flexible substrates—slim, robust materials like flexible glass and plastic—made it possible to produce bendable displays like OLEDs.

These substrates enabled the integration of electrical components into flexible, foldable, or rollable shapes while preserving their functionality. Thin-film transistors (TFTs) and organic semiconductors further transformed the sector by substituting flexible circuitry for rigid silicon chips, enabling more complex designs and functionality in flexible electronics. As the market for ergonomic, portable, and flexible technology grew, particularly in wearables, smart gadgets, and foldable screens, the sector advanced quickly [17–25]. These developments in materials science transformed flexible technologies from experimental lab concepts into widely used commercial items, such as wearables, folding smartphones, and upcoming breakthroughs like stretchable electronics, all of which changed the face of contemporary technology [9]. Driven by the increasing demand for ergonomic and adaptable technology, flexible devices progressed from laboratory prototypes to commercial products as materials advanced. This technological evolution is just getting started with the continuous integration of flexible batteries, sensors, and displays into consumer electronics and healthcare systems. To sum up, flexible devices have come a long way from the initial discoveries in conductive materials to becoming a significant area of study and industry, with the potential to make electronics more portable, flexible, and a part of everyday life in the future. These days, flexible technologies play a major role in the display business. Numerous firms and research institutions have released cutting-edge flexible technologies, such as wearables, curved-screen smartwatches, and foldable smartphones [26–33].

6.2 Energy Storage

In order to balance supply and demand in different energy systems, energy storage is an essential technology that enables excess energy to be stored and used when needed. Together with other cutting-edge materials, conductive polymers like Polyaniline (PANI) are essential to the advancement of energy storage technologies, especially in batteries and supercapacitors. A vital part of a flexible operating electronic is the power source, or in this case, the energy storage component. Flexible energy storage has gained popularity recently as a means of meeting the needs for portable electronics, flexible displays, healthcare and fitness tracking devices, and other devices that are small, integrated, and self-powered [34–42]. The need to move from all-solid state to flexible energy storage has led to increased interest in carbonaceous materials and nanocarbons to enhance already efficient devices, such as Li-ion batteries and supercapacitors. Some of these issues include low volumetric energy density, high internal resistance, or poor mechanical durability [43–48].

6.2.1 Energy Storage Technologies and Their History

6.2.1.1 Batteries

Figure 6.3 presents the schematic diagram of battery. Battery Storage Systems (BSSs) are still the most affordable technology on the market today, even though they were the first electrical energy storage system to be introduced. Benjamin Franklin first studied the fundamentals of their operation in 1748 when he explained how to connect several Leyden jars, a device for storing static electricity. In 1873, some of the most significant scientific research on batteries was published. The first significant battery applications weren't created until the 20th century [10]. Thus, in 1920, a patent was granted for a battery system for telephone circuits; other uses from that era include flashlights or even batteries that are charged using a generator powered by a gas engine [49–54].

a) **Lead-Acid Battery:** The lead-acid battery, created in 1859 by French physicist Gaston Plante, is the most ancient type of rechargeable battery [10]. A positive electrode and a negative electrode immersed in an electrolyte make up a lead-acid battery (Figure 6.4). The process of electron migration from the positive electrode to the negative electrode charges

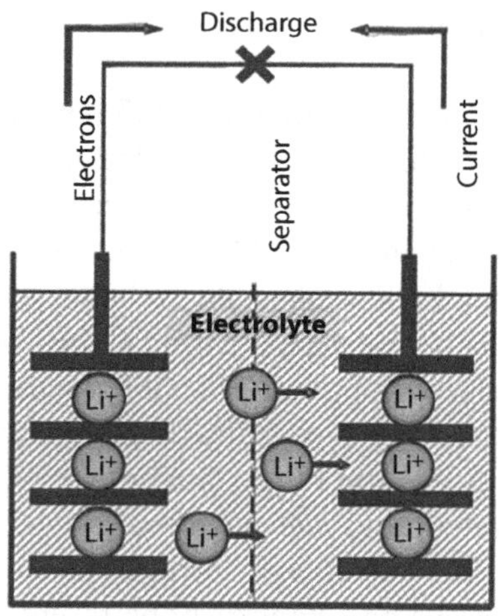

Figure 6.3 Schematic diagram of battery [13].

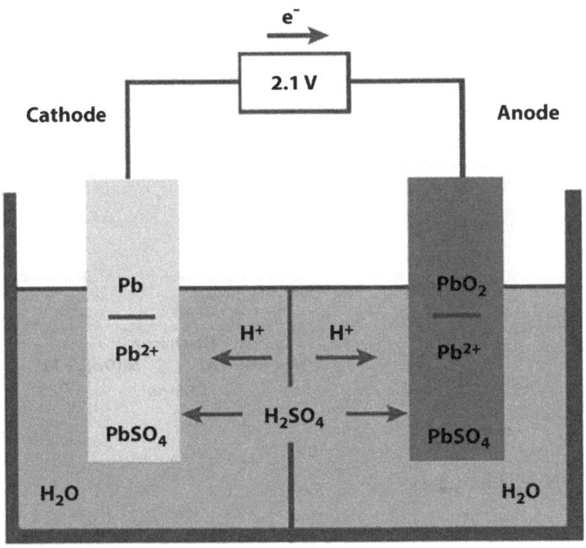

Figure 6.4 Lead-Acid battery.

the battery. Lead dioxide (PbO_2) makes up the positive plate in the charged state, while elemental lead makes up the negative plate. Here, sulfuric acid (H_2SO_4) at a concentration of roughly 33.5% is the electrolyte [55–63]. When electrons move from the negative electrode to the positive electrode, the discharging process occurs. In this instance, both the positive and negative electrodes produce grains of lead sulphate ($PbSO_4$), and the electrolyte starts to lose concentration and turn primarily into water. These grains dissolve during charging. However, if the discharge is too deep, the grains may enlarge and become insoluble, rendering the plates' active material useless. Applications for lead-acid batteries range from 1 kW (uninterruptible power supply, or UPS) to 10 MW (transport and distribution systems). They possess a low energy density, which means they store less energy relative to their size and weight compared to modern battery technologies, making them bulkier and heavier [64–70].

b) **Nickel Cadmium (NiCd)/Nickel–Metal Hydride (NiMH) Batteries:** The second kind of rechargeable batteries was NiCd batteries (Figure 6.5), which were created in 1899 by Swedish engineer Waldemar Jungner. NiMH batteries

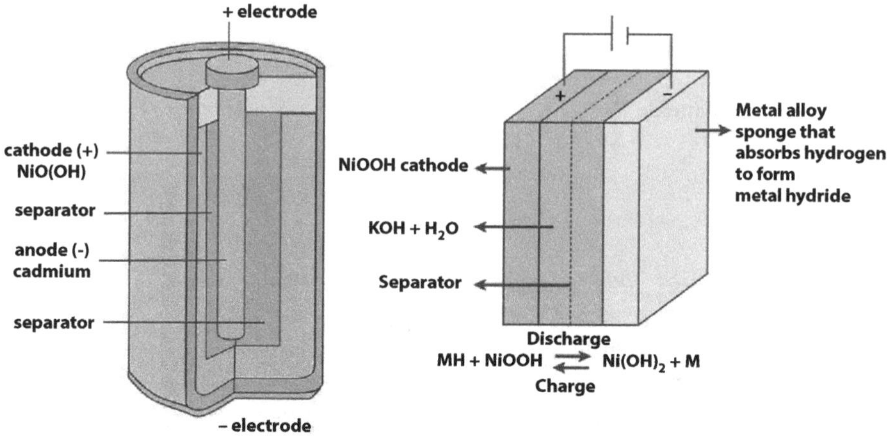

Figure 6.5 NiCd/NiMH batteries.

appeared on the market in 1989 [10]. NiCd batteries use an electrolyte (typically potassium hydroxide), a separator, a positive electrode made of nickel (III) oxide and hydrogen, and a negative electrode made of cadmium when fully charged. In NiMH, the metal M, an intermetallic compound made of a combination of lanthanum, cerium, and other rare earth elements with nickel, aluminium, cobalt, or manganese, makes up the negative electrode [71–78]. Potassium hydroxide serves as the electrolyte, just like in NiCd batteries. NiMH batteries have supplanted NiCd batteries due to their higher energy density, which is suitable for applications ranging from 1 kW to 0.5 MW, as well as the environmental risks associated with them that necessitate elaborate recycling processes. These are utilized for applications ranging from 1 kW to roughly 1 MW and have a higher energy density [10].

$$\textbf{Cell Reaction: } Cd(s) + 2NiO(OH)(s) + 2H_2O \longrightarrow Cd(OH)_2(s) + 2Ni(OH)_2(s) \tag{6.1}$$

c) **Lithium-ion batteries (LIBs):** These were introduced in 1970 by the American chemist Michael Whittingham [10]. The fundamental working principle states that during discharging (Figure 6.6) and charging (Figure 6.7), the positive

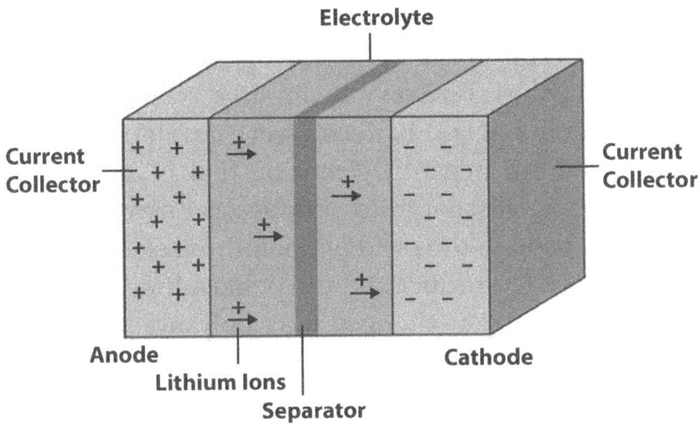

Figure 6.6 Lithium-ion batteries (discharging).

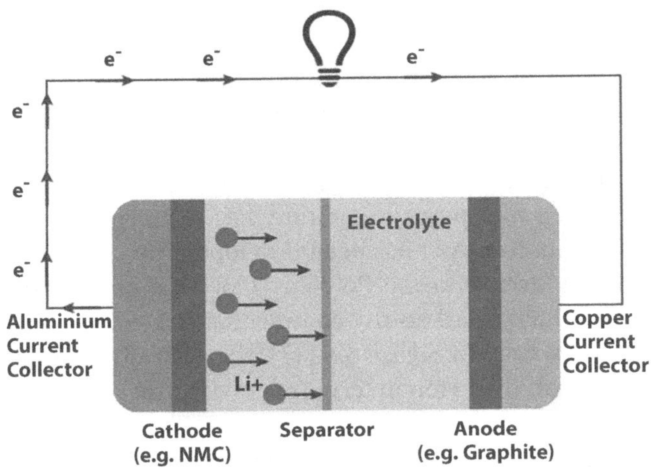

Figure 6.7 Lithium-ion batteries (charging).

Li ions move in the opposite direction from the negative plate—which is often composed of graphite—to the positive plate, which is composed of an alloy containing lithium. Ion circulation is allowed by the electrolyte, but electron conduction is not. Because lithium is highly reactive with water, the electrolyte is either non-aqueous or aprotic (it does not accept or donate hydrogen ions [79–84]. These batteries have a high energy density, no memory effect, and a low discharge rate. The primary drawback is the potential for internal resistance to heat up and lead to battery failure. For this reason, overcurrent and overvoltage protection devices are required to guarantee appropriate functioning [10].

d) **Sodium-Sulphur Battery:** Beginning in the early 1970s, sodium-sulphur (NaS) batteries were developed. They consist of a sodium negative electrode that is oxidized at the surface during discharge to produce positive sodium ions that move through the solid beta-alumina electrolyte before being reduced to produce sodium pentasulfide (Na2S5). This Na2S5 progressively changes into polysulfides with more sulphur. The electrolyte conducts nearly no electrons but conducts sodium ions, which limits the rate of self-discharge (Figure 6.8). Electricity passes through the external load as a result of electrons produced during discharge by the molten elemental sodium-positive electrode [10]. Unfortunately, a number of dangerous substances are present in these batteries, including metallic sodium, which burns when it comes into touch with water. For this reason, NaS cells also include sand, which serves to both fix them and put out any potential fires. The discovery of a high-voltage electrolyte could lead to the possibility of other chemicals [85–92]. One such instance is the pyrotemperature Li/S battery, which Sion Power (Tuscon, AZ) has been developing for over ten years under a license from Polyplus Corporation. Nowadays, some military markets use commercial cells for flight power [11]. As shown in Figure 6.8 [11], they already significantly outperform the Li ion in terms of gravimetric energy storage

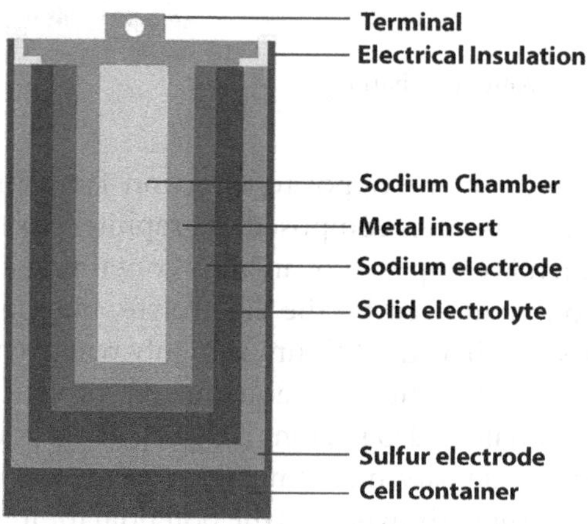

Figure 6.8 Sodium–Sulphur battery.

capacity, but the figure also demonstrates that they have a significantly lower volumetric storage capacity [93–98].

e) **Sodium–Nickel–Chloride ($NaNiCl_2$) Batteries:** The Zeolite Battery Research Africa Project (ZEBRA), first launched this battery in 1985. It operates at high temperatures of approximately 270 C–350 C. Nickel (Ni) and salt (NaCl) are transformed into sodium and nickel chloride ($NiCl_2$) during the charging process. The reactions are reversed during discharge. Sodium serves as the negative electrode, whereas $NiCl_2$ in the charged state and Ni in the discharged state serve as the positive electrodes (Figure 6.9). An electrolyte that separates the two electrodes allows ion conduction but not electron conduction. As a result, the circuit is closed and

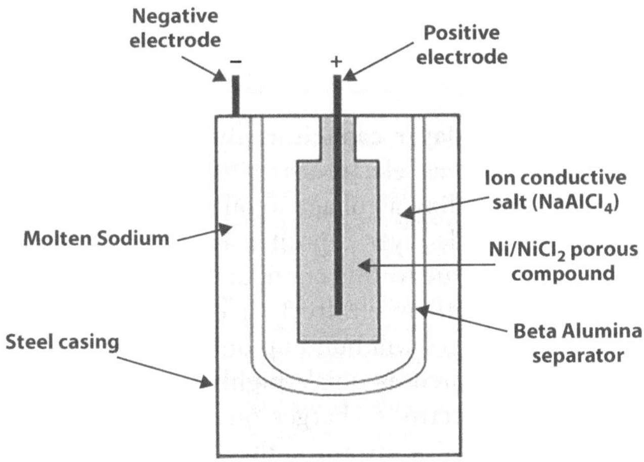

Figure 6.9 Sodium–Nickel–Chloride battery [10].

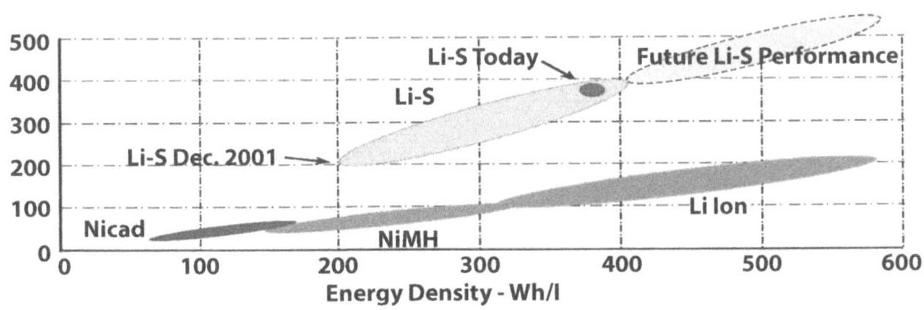

Figure 6.10 Energy storage capability of lithium–sulphur cells compared to other cells [13].

current flows through the battery when an external load is connected to the terminals [10]. Figure 6.10 shows energy storage capability of lithium–sulphur cells compared to other cells.

6.2.1.2 Supercapacitor Storage Systems (SSSs)

Supercapacitors, referred to as ultracapacitors or electrochemical capacitors, are energy-storage devices that, unlike batteries, store and release electrical energy by electrostatic charge separation. They fill the energy storage void between capacitors and batteries with a capacitance that is far higher than that of ordinary capacitors. Compared to batteries, supercapacitors have a lower energy density. They can charge and discharge in seconds, unlike batteries which take more time [99–104]. Three main types of supercapacitors can be distinguished due to their unique structures and internal storing mechanisms: hybrid supercapacitors, electric double-layer capacitors (EDLC), and pseudo capacitors (Figure 6.11).

a) **Electric double-layer capacitor:** By positioning two parallel conductors as electrodes with dielectric interlayers inside and providing a voltage to one, grounding the other, an electric double-layer capacitor is created as shown in Figure 6.12(a). Due to this configuration, charges build up on both sides until an electrostatic equilibrium is reached. Sometimes, charges will build up on both sides of the electrodes and be stored by quick, highly reversible redox processes on the electrode charges on both sides, producing high power densities. However, the energy density is not as great as it is for batteries [12].

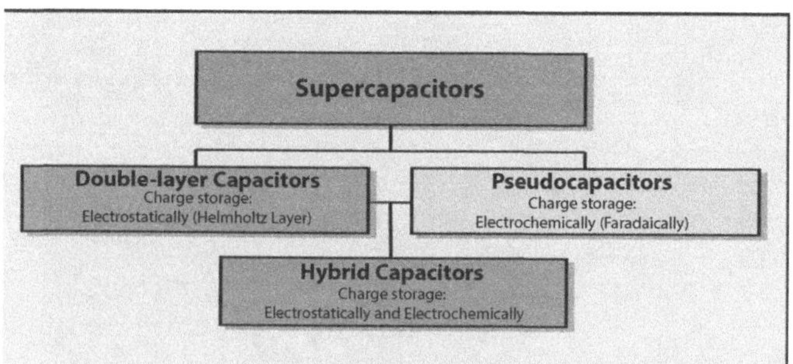

Figure 6.11 Different types of supercapacitors.

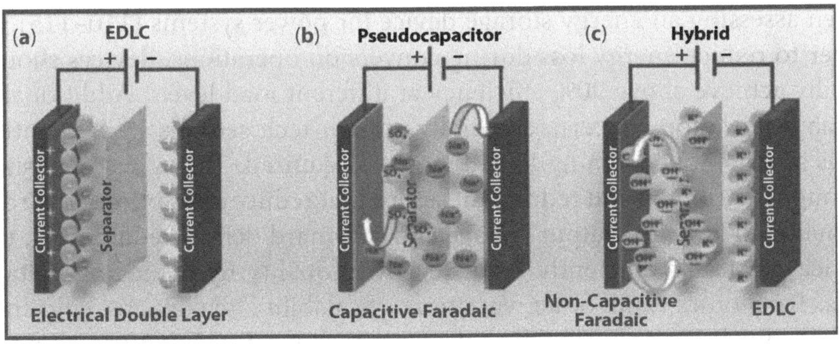

Figure 6.12 Electric double-layer capacitor, pseudocapacitors and hybrid supercapacitors respectively.

b) **Pseudocapacitors:** Pseudocapacitors have a high contact surface, short electron transport channel lengths, short ions diffusion lengths, and even an enhanced cycle life. They store energy by pseudocapacitive or faradaic redox processes [105–109]. Their energy storage mechanism operates in tandem with EDLCs. However, there is a risk of decreased electroactive surface area, adsorption sites, and performance if the electrode film's shape, structure, composition, architecture, and characteristics are not well controlled (Figure 6.12(b)).

c) **Hybrid supercapacitors:** Hybrid supercapacitors are devices that combine an anode or cathode-like capacitive electrode with a battery-type electrode. They combine, on electrodes, the non-Faradaic surface reaction and the Faradaic intercalation. By constructing electrodes based on 3D mesoporous structure materials, hybrid supercapacitors can preserve substantial cycling stability and affordability with both high power and energy densities, despite the poor conductivity of some types of carbon and metal oxide-based electrodes (Figure 6.12) [12].

6.3 Criteria for a Device to Store Energy

High efficiency, dependability, efficient power quality control, scalability, compatibility with distributed energy resources (DER), modular redundancy, and robust thermal management are the main factors considered when assessing an energy storage device for power systems [110–115]. In order to reduce energy loss during conversion operations, devices should ideally achieve above 90% efficiency at different load levels. Additionally, reliability is a top concern, especially in high-tech settings where continuous availability—often up to 99.999%—is required. This is accomplished through distributed and redundant setups that reduce disruptions. In order to maintain a steady output voltage and safeguard delicate equipment, the device must also efficiently regulate power quality by managing voltage sags, harmonics, and other variations. Scalability maximizes efficiency and optimizes costs by enabling the system to modify its power rating in response to changing load demands. The system is further strengthened by compatibility with DER, such as solar or wind, which makes it possible to integrate renewable sources, boost energy resilience, and lessen reliance on the grid. For important loads during outages or voltage disturbances, modular backup and redundancy options—such as distributed configurations and embedded UPS capabilities—offer dependable, temporary power support. Finally, efficient thermal management reduces heat production, particularly in small or high- demand settings, which enhances the system's performance and longevity. When taken as a whole, these standards guarantee that an energy storage system may satisfy the requirements of effectiveness, dependability, and flexibility for a variety of intricate power settings [13].

6.3.1 The Critical Role of Energy Storage in Modern Energy Systems

We need energy storage for several critical reasons, primarily to ensure reliability, efficiency, and sustainability in energy systems. Initially, it aids in balancing supply and demand in the energy grid because energy output, particularly from renewable sources like solar and wind, can vary during the day, while consumption varies. Systems that store excess energy during periods of low demand and release it during periods of high demand guarantee a steady supply of electricity. Storage systems keep the flow of power constant by storing excess energy during times of high output and releasing it when the supply is low [116–119]. By buffering against fluctuations, preventing blackouts, and guaranteeing a continuous power supply—especially during peak demand or unplanned outages—this capacity also improves grid stability and reliability. Energy storage can save money since it allows businesses and households to store energy during periods of low price and use it during periods of high price, which lowers overall energy expenses. Additionally, it aids in the transition to a low-carbon energy system by promoting the use of renewable energy sources and enhancing energy efficiency. By offering vital backup power during natural catastrophes or other disturbances, energy storage improves community resilience. Energy storage will be essential for controlling growing electricity demand and guaranteeing a steady supply as industries like heating and transportation become more electrified. By lowering reliance on fossil fuels and storing extra electricity from sources like solar or wind, storage technologies further maximize the use of renewable energy. They also promote efficiency and cost savings by avoiding expensive infrastructure modifications to handle peak loads and enabling the use of stored energy during times of peak pricing. Energy storage also facilitates a more seamless switch from fossil fuels to renewable energy sources, which lowers carbon emissions and advances climate goals. Storage is valuable for resilience and sustainability in the energy environment because it supplies vital backup power to vital infrastructure in times of crisis, including data centers, hospitals, and communication services [4, 9, 10, 12–14].

6.4 Need of Flexible Energy Storage Devices

The field of flexible electronics is a crucial driver of technological advancement. With its close ties to human life and special applications in flexible electronics, wearable technology and healthcare, flexible electronics is a key force behind technological progress (Figure 6.13). The growing popularity of FESDs can be attributed to their distinct and promising features, including their flexibility, shape diversity, lightweight nature, and so on [15]. As a result, flexible energy storage devices are desperately needed to meet the energy storage requirements of numerous flexible product types. Modern energy systems require flexible energy storage, particularly as we depend more and more on renewable energy sources.

Flexible energy storage is crucial for modern energy systems, especially as we increasingly rely on renewable energy sources like solar and wind.

FESDs can be classified into three categories based on spatial dimension, as follows:

i) **Distributed Energy Storage:** These systems are located close to the point of energy use or generation, such as residential batteries or small-scale storage systems. They provide localized energy management and can help reduce transmission losses.

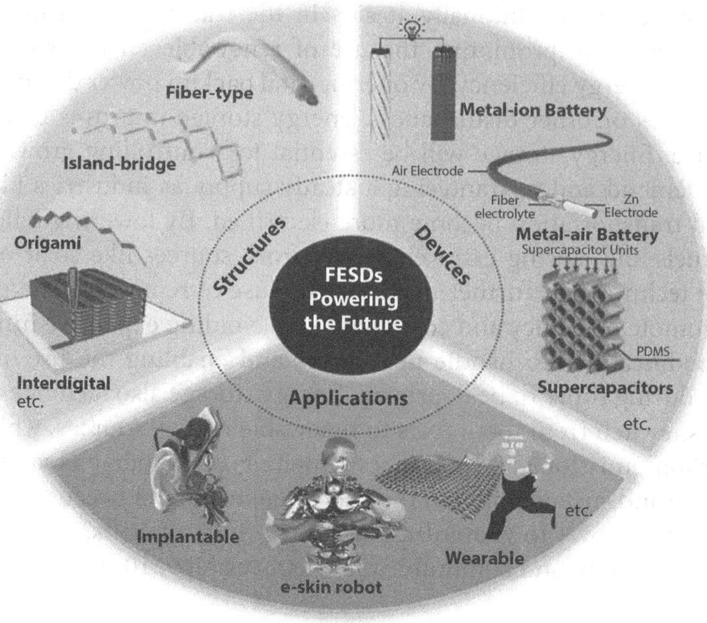

Figure 6.13 FESDs powering the future [3].

ii) **Centralized Energy Storage:** These larger-scale storage facilities are situated away from the point of use and are typically integrated into the grid. Examples include large battery plants or pumped hydro storage facilities that can supply energy to a wider area.

iii) **Utility-Scale Energy Storage:** These systems are designed to provide significant capacity and are often deployed by utilities to support grid stability, peak shaving, and large-scale renewable energy integration. They can include large battery installations, compressed air energy storage, and other technologies.

Each category plays a vital role in enhancing energy flexibility and reliability, catering to different needs and applications within the energy system.

6.4.1 Advantages of Flexible Energy Storage Devices

The growing demand for flexible energy storage devices has led to major innovations that lower costs, making these technologies more affordable.

Researchers at North Carolina State University have developed new manufacturing methods for flexible electronics that improve productivity while reducing prices. Companies are also working hard to make flexible circuits cheaper compared to traditional alternatives. Beyond being affordable, flexible storage solutions improve the reliability of energy supply. They can provide backup power during blackouts or when energy demand is high. These solutions are crucial for supporting renewable energy by storing excess power produced during peak times and releasing it when needed. Advanced energy storage technologies help manage energy use more effectively, reducing waste and improving overall efficiency. Flexible storage is also important for efforts to reduce carbon emissions. By supporting the shift to renewable energy, it helps cut down on greenhouse gases and fight climate change. Additionally, flexible storage provides valuable grid services like frequency control and spinning reserves, helping stabilize the energy grid and making the infrastructure more resilient [16].

6.4.2 Disadvantages of Flexible Energy Storage Devices

Technologies for flexible energy storage have the potential to fundamentally alter how we use and store energy in a variety of situations. However, a number of significant problems must be fixed before their full potential may be realized. One of the primary issues is energy density, or the amount of energy stored per unit volume or weight. Many of the materials used in flexible energy storage solutions, such as organic or polymer-based batteries, typically have lower energy densities than conventional rigid batteries like lithium-ion. This suggests that in order to store the same amount of energy, flexible batteries would require more weight or space, which is a significant disadvantage in applications like wearables, portable electronics, and electric vehicles where size and weight are critical. Cost is still another important obstacle. Advanced materials and specialized manufacturing processes are frequently required for the creation of flexible energy storage devices, which might raise production costs. Adding novel elements, like conductive polymers or novel nanoparticles, might raise costs and reduce the devices' economic viability in comparison to more well-established technology. Price increases may thereby restrict consumer accessibility and impede market penetration, thereby impeding widespread adoption. Although these devices' flexibility presents clear benefits in terms of mechanical stability, it can also pose risks. Compared to their rigid counterparts, flexible batteries' materials might not be as resilient to repetitive bending or stretching. This vulnerability may result in problems. Another important factor to take into account is the flexible battery's cycle life.

The number of charge-discharge cycles a battery can withstand before its capacity visibly degrades is known as cycle life. Many flexible batteries, especially those composed of organic materials, can degrade more quickly due to the mechanical stress caused by bending and stretching. For applications like wearable technology and grid storage, where long-term dependability and durability are crucial for user happiness and functioning, this degradation is particularly worrisome. Scalability is another major obstacle. Although small-scale labs are the source of many innovations in flexible energy storage technologies, it can be difficult to produce these devices in large quantities without compromising quality. Inconsistencies in material quality, performance, and dependability may arise as small-scale invention gives way to mass production, making it more difficult to satisfy rising consumer demand. Furthermore, a major obstacle to broad adoption is the scarcity of adaptable energy storage solutions. The practicality of many of these technologies in real-world applications is limited because they are still in the prototype or experimental stages. Businesses may be reluctant to invest in technologies that have not yet shown to be dependable or acquired a substantial market presence due to this uncertainty. Lastly, there are environmental concerns associated with the manufacture and disposal of flexible energy storage devices. The use of potentially harmful or non-biodegradable materials by these devices throughout their life cycle may result in environmental issues. Furthermore, recycling practices for these newer materials are either experimental or unproven, which complicates waste management and raises questions about the technology's long-term sustainability [16].

Despite their enormous potential to transform energy storage and consumption across a variety of applications, flexible energy storage devices now face a number of problems that need to be fixed. By solving these challenges *via* research, innovation, and strategic development, flexible energy storage can reach its full potential. Wider adoption as well as important technological and long-term advancements will follow from this.

6.5 Different Structures That are Being Used in Flexible Energy Storage

The performance of flexible energy storage devices depends largely on the materials' ability to bend and stretch without failing. This means the material must handle the stress created during use and still remain intact. Research into new materials that are naturally flexible can improve how well these devices work. Materials like conductive polymers, flexible metal oxides, and advanced composites are being studied for their ability to bend and stretch repeatedly without breaking. It's also important to design the device structure in a way that reduces strain. This is where geometric optimization comes in: it helps design devices that spread out stress evenly, which improves both their performance and lifespan. Additionally, using layering techniques where different materials with different properties are stacked can help absorb and spread stress, making the device more durable. Architectural features like folds, corrugations, or other structural designs can also help the device bend and move without losing strength. Early research in Micro-Electro-Mechanical Systems (MEMS) has provided valuable insights, guiding current developments in flexible energy storage by offering a solid reference for designing and analyzing the structure and mechanical aspects of modern devices [3].

6.5.1 Fiber Structures

The creation and functionality of flexible energy storage devices depend on fiber-type architectures. Researchers and engineers can develop high-performance, flexible energy storage solutions by utilizing the distinctive qualities of different fibers, such as conductive polymers, metallic fibers, and carbon nanofibers. In order to increase the applicability and feasibility of flexible energy storage devices across a variety of fields and pave the way for a more connected and energy-efficient future, fiber-type structural integration will be crucial as technology advances [3].

i) Carbon Nanofibers

Carbon Nanofibers are a key element in the creation of flexible energy storage devices. They are perfect for improving the functionality and efficiency of different energy storage technologies, such as batteries and supercapacitors, because of their special qualities, which include excellent electrical conductivity, mechanical strength, and lightweight nature. CNFs are cylindrical fibers with diameters typically ranging from 10 nanometers to several micrometers. There are the different types of CNFs available based on their structure (Figure 6.14). They can possess a graphitic structure, which enhances their electrical conductivity. The high surface area of CNFs facilitates increased electrochemical reactions, which is crucial for energy storage applications. CNFs exhibit exceptional tensile strength and flexibility, allowing them to endure mechanical stress without compromising performance. To create composite electrodes, CNFs are frequently combined with other substances like transition metal oxides or conductive polymers.

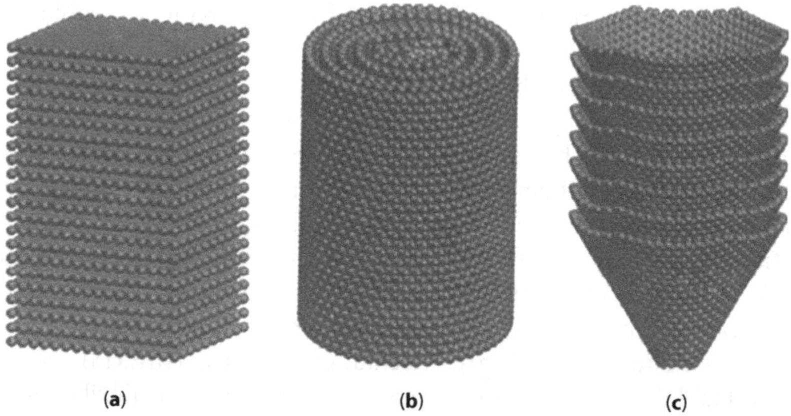

Figure 6.14 Schematic illustration of three different type of CNFs: (a) platelet-type CNF, (b) tubular-type CNF, and (c) fishbone-type CNF [17].

By optimizing the electrode's mechanical and electrical characteristics, this synergy can further improve FESDs' overall performance [17].

ii) Fiber-Based Electrodes: A state-of-the-art advancement in energy conversion and storage technologies are fiber-based electrodes (Figure 6.15). They make use of the special qualities of different fiber materials, including conductive polymers, metallic fibers, and carbon nanofibers, to produce electrodes that are flexible, lightweight, and highly effective. These electrodes are especially well-suited for use in supercapacitors and batteries, two types of flexible energy storage devices (FESDs). Aligned or woven fibers make up the majority of fiber-based electrodes, which can greatly expand the surface area available for electrochemical processes. The electrode's overall performance is improved by the additional active sites made

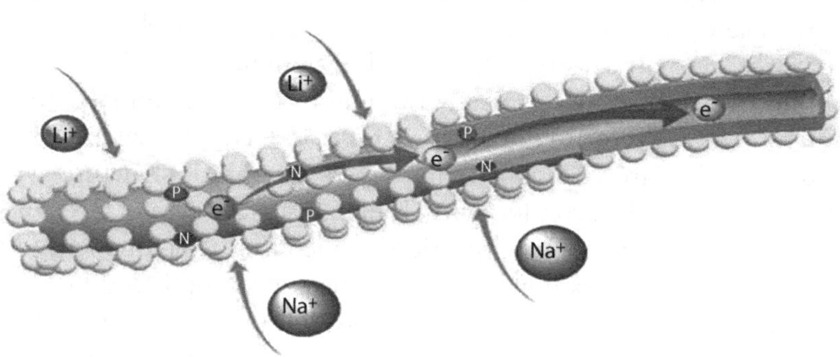

Figure 6.15 Fiber-based electrode [18].

possible by this design. Fiber-based electrodes' intrinsic flexibility makes it possible to integrate them into adaptable energy storage systems without sacrificing their functionality. Applications in portable electronics and wearable technology require this [18].

iii) Parallel-Type Fiber Structure: In order to avoid electrolyte spills or moisture contamination, the anode and cathode are enclosed and positioned side by side on both sides of the separators in parallel construction. Fiber-type flexible energy storage devices (FESDs) are usually made of metal oxides or lightweight, high-energy-density carbon-based materials, which offer a great deal of material selection freedom. Liu *et al.* created Ni-coated cotton yarns using a "polymer-assisted metal deposition (PAMD)" technique and a polyvinyl alcohol (PVA)/LiCl gel wearable solid-state supercapacitor yarn (Figure 6.16(a)). The device was bent at various angles (from 0° to 180°) while the CV property was being measured in order to evaluate the applicability of these supercapacitor yarns for flexible and wearable applications. Figure 6.16(b) shows that the device's performance remained steady regardless of the bending angle. Because wearable electronics may experience parasitic reactions with internal chemicals and changes in liquid electrolytes under specific conditions, like exposure to rain and perspiration, encapsulation is an important consideration when considering practical applications. Guan *et al.* created a rechargeable fiber-shaped Zn/Co3O4 battery using 3D sheet zinc as the anode and improved the insulation of energy storage devices to ensure the quality of its packaging. Although the production process for parallel fiber FESD is rather straightforward, certain restrictions prevent its widespread use. The development of FESDs is hampered by the parallel structure's tiny contact area between the electrode and electrolyte, which leads to poor mass loading of

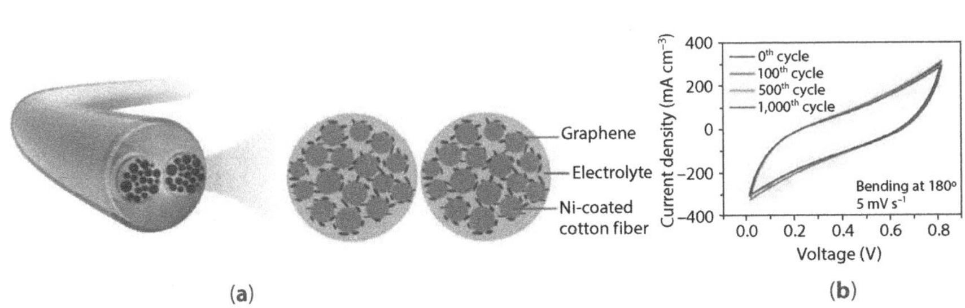

Figure 6.16 Synthesis and performance diagram of parallel fiber type energy storage devices: (a) schematic diagram of supercapacitor yarn; (b) CV curves of the supercapacitor at different bending cycles [3].

active materials and a lengthy ion transport path. In order to get around these limitations, better fiber combinations must be created [3].

iv) Twisted-Type Fiber Structure: An inventive invention, the twisted fiber-type FESD uses a spinning mechanism to twist two electrodes into a double helix shape. An electrolyte must be placed around the electrodes to stop short circuits. Ionic conduction channels between the electrodes are made possible by electrolytes. Solid or gel electrolytes are more frequently utilized in fiber-based FESDs than liquid electrolytes. It is feasible to achieve stability against electrolyte leakage by using gel electrolytes. Ion adsorption and fast redox reactions at the electrode/electrolyte interface are the two types of energy storage mechanisms. According to this idea, Lee *et al.* suggested a flexible fiber-type supercapacitor made up of surface-activated carbon fibers and a gel polymer electrolyte with a redox additive (FFS-SARE), which is produced by twisting the two fibers coated with gel electrode in the S form (Figure 6.17(a)) involving the electrode surface and the redox mediator (Figure 6.17(b)). However, the device's capacitance and ion transfer rate are constrained by the gel electrolyte's greater resistance. Furthermore, the qualities of the material are limited when PVP is directly coated on carbon fibers [3].

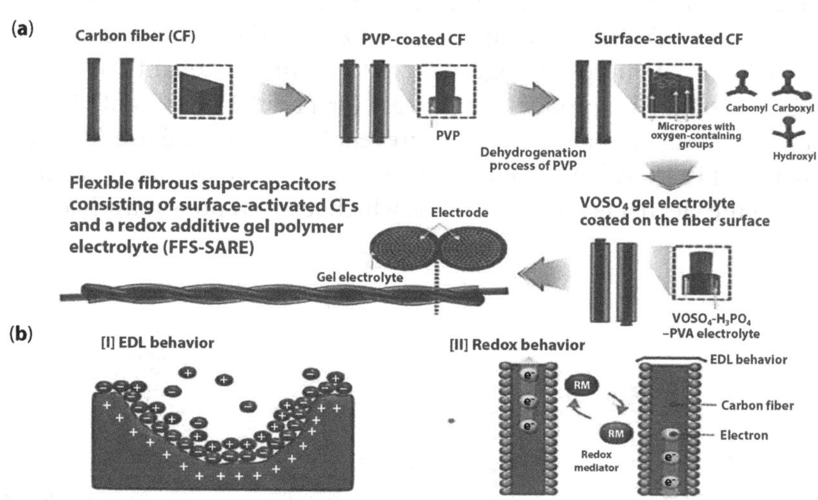

Figure 6.17 Synthesis and performance diagram of twisted fiber-type energy storage devices: (a) schematic of the fabrication of FFS-SARE, (b) schematic illustration of the electrical double layer and redox behavior [3].

6.5.2 Island Bridge Structure

An innovative design technique for flexible energy storage devices (FESDs) that maximizes performance without sacrificing flexibility is the island bridge structure. The structure of electrodes in batteries and supercapacitors is important because it affects how much energy they can store, how quickly they can release it, and how efficient they are overall. One such structure is called the "island bridge" design (Figure 6.18). In this structure, active materials (the parts that store energy) are arranged in small "islands" that are connected by "bridges" made of conductive materials. This design helps maximize the surface area available for chemical reactions, which improves energy storage. The bridges, made from materials like carbon nanofibers or metallic fibers, help electrons move efficiently across the electrode. This arrangement allows for better ion movement between the electrolyte (the material that conducts electricity) and the active materials, improving how quickly the device can charge and discharge. The island and bridge structure also makes the device more flexible, so it can handle mechanical stress without breaking or losing performance. The bridges reduce the distance electrons need to travel, which boosts electrical conductivity and overall efficiency. Because of its unique design, this structure is especially useful for flexible and wearable technologies, such as flexible batteries and supercapacitors. As research continues and challenges are overcome, this innovative design could be key to developing the next generation of energy storage technologies [19].

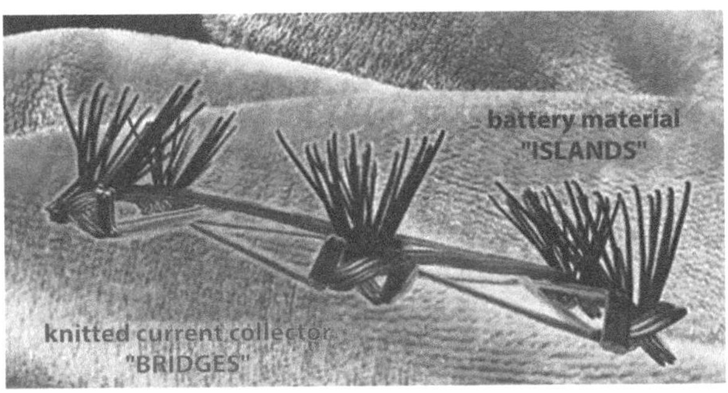

Figure 6.18 Island Bridge structure [19].

6.5.3 Interdigital Structure

Flexible energy storage devices (FESDs) feature interdigital structures, which are a complex design, especially when it comes to battery and supercapacitor electrodes. By arranging conductive and active materials optimally, this structure improves performance and yields better mechanical flexibility and electrochemical qualities. Alternating fingers or prongs of conductive material that stretch outward and interleave with one another make up the basic component of an interdigital structure. By increasing the area of contact between the electrode and the electrolyte, this configuration improves ion transport. These electrodes are typically fabricated on flexible substrates, allowing for integration into various applications, including wearable devices and portable electronics. Flexible substrates are frequently employed, including polyimide, polyethylene terephthalate (PET), and other polymer films. These materials are stable in a variety of environmental circumstances and offer mechanical flexibility. Figure 6.19 shows the optical and SEM images of interdigital electrodes.

The rise of portable electronics has indeed accelerated the demand for miniaturized energy storage solutions, especially in applications where external power sources are impractical. Here is a deeper look at the context, focusing on the advantages and functionalities of microsupercapacitors (MSCs) compared to traditional microbatteries. Microbatteries often struggle to deliver the high power needed for certain applications, leading to performance bottlenecks. Many microbatteries contain toxic materials that pose environmental and safety concerns, limiting their usability in sensitive applications, such as biomedical devices [20].

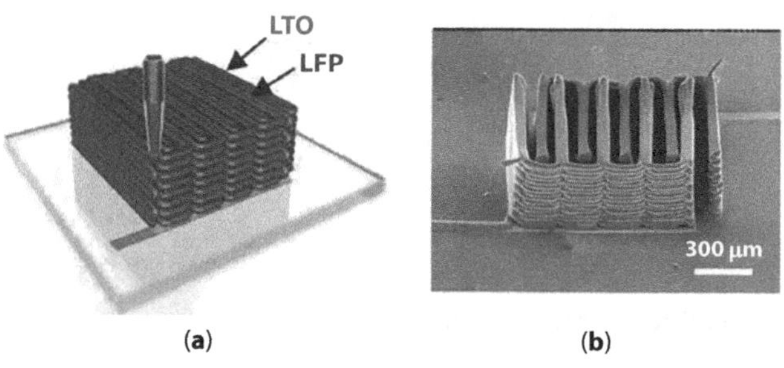

Figure 6.19 (a) Optical and (b) SEM images of interdigitated LTO-LFP electrodes, respectively [3].

6.6 Emergence of Micro-Supercapacitors

Micro-Supercapacitors (MSCs) utilize a two-dimensional layout with interdigitated electrodes, enhancing the surface area available for electrochemical reactions while maintaining a compact design. This configuration not only increases the interface area for ion interaction but also facilitates rapid ion transport, improving both charge and discharge rates.

$$\text{Energy Density } E = 1/2CV^2 \tag{6.2}$$

where C is the Specific capacitance Represents how much charge the MSC can store per unit voltage. Higher capacitance values lead to increased energy density.

A wider voltage window enhances the energy storage capability. This allows the device to operate effectively under varying conditions.

$$\text{Power Density } P = E/t \tag{6.3}$$

where t is the discharge time, this formula highlights how quickly energy can be delivered.

MSCs generally have a footprint in the millimeter to centimeter range, but their electrode thickness is typically less than 10 μm. Having the in-plane electrode structure has technical advantages over the conventional sandwich structure (Figure 6.20). This compact size is ideal for integration into small devices. The planar design allows for more efficient ionic transport. By positioning the electrodes in the same plane, the mean ionic diffusion length is significantly reduced. This arrangement enables easier and quicker movement of electrolyte ions, enhancing performance.

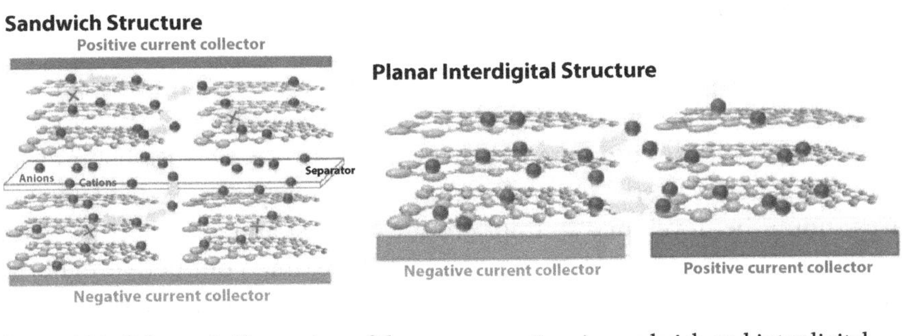

Figure 6.20 Schematic illustration of the supercapacitors in sandwich and interdigital structure [20].

The interdigitated fingers of the electrodes provide numerous open edges for electrolyte ions to diffuse into the electrodes, maximizing surface area utilization. Shortening the width and spacing of these microelectrodes further minimizes the ionic diffusion path, improving power density and response times. In contrast to conventional sandwich structures, where ions must diffuse through the thickness of each electrode and separator, the planar design of MSCs allows for more efficient ionic movement, avoiding bottlenecks that can occur in stacked configurations. The planar design of MSCs facilitates their integration onto various substrates, including silicon wafers for semiconductor applications. This opens up possibilities for on-chip energy storage solutions in conjunction with complementary metal–oxide– semiconductor (CMOS) technology or MEMS. The planar design allows for the vertical arrangement of active materials, enabling the development of 3-D structures. This can further enhance the energy and power density per unit area without compromising ionic diffusion paths [20].

6.7 Materials for Energy Storage Devices

An electrode, electrolyte, separator membrane, and packing material make up flexible energy storage systems. Under a variety of deformation conditions, every part that went into making this energy device works perfectly. Therefore, a number of methods for effectively designing each part for usage in flexible energy systems have been recorded. In the context of the newest component designs for materials used to produce flexible energy, we examine devices with superior mechanical and electrochemical properties.

6.8 Electrode Materials

Active materials, conductive agents, polymeric binders, and current collectors (such Cu, Al, and other metal materials) are frequently found in electrodes. But these components often exhibit stiff properties that prevent them from being used in flexible energy systems [21]. Electrode structures should be developed to improve the loading and adhesion of active materials in order to address this issue. The flexible conductive material should replace the traditional metal materials to achieve the energy storage systems' desired degree of versatility. Rather than utilising conventional materials, gel electrolytes, whether liquid or solid, should be used to stop electrolyte loss when mechanically degraded conditions occur.

This section highlights innovative techniques for creating electrode materials specifically designed for flexible energy devices, with a focus on hybrid electrodes and electrodes made of carbon [3].

6.8.1 Carbon-Based Electrode

Depending on their chemical structures, carbon atoms can be categorised as organic, graphitic, or polymeric. These electrodes use flexible, conductive substrates in conjunction with active components to enhance electrochemical and mechanical performance even when deformed, in addition to the intrinsic advantages of different carbon topologies [21]. Materials for carbon- based substrates, include graphene, carbon cloth, the use of CNFs and CNTs in flexible energy has grown in popularity for storing. Typically, they show strong electrochemical activity and outstanding mechanical qualities that withstand repeated deformations showing their fascinating mechanical, chemical, and physical characteristics [22]. Since redox-active organic molecules are inexpensive and naturally sustainable, they have become one of the most promising alternatives. Guo and colleagues created the organic cathode material pyrene- 4,5,9,10-tetraone (PTO) for flexible, aqueous zinc-ion batteries (ZIBs).

As shown in Figure 6.21, the SEM picture displays the nanorod-like shape of PTO. Figure 6.22 provides the schematic illustration [21].

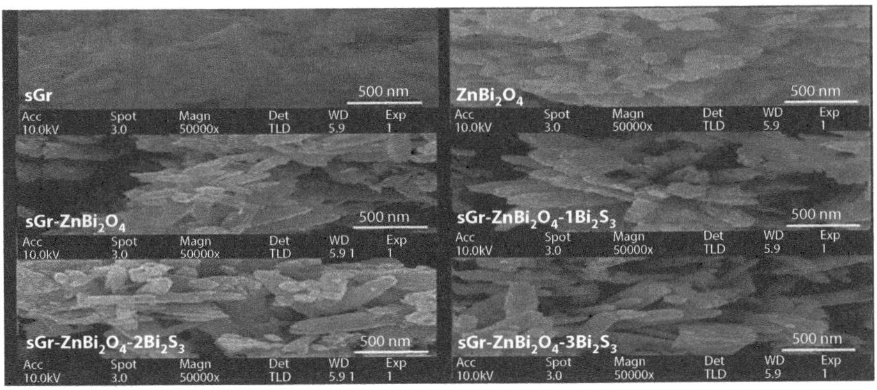

Figure 6.21 The SEM picture displays the nanorod-like shape [21].

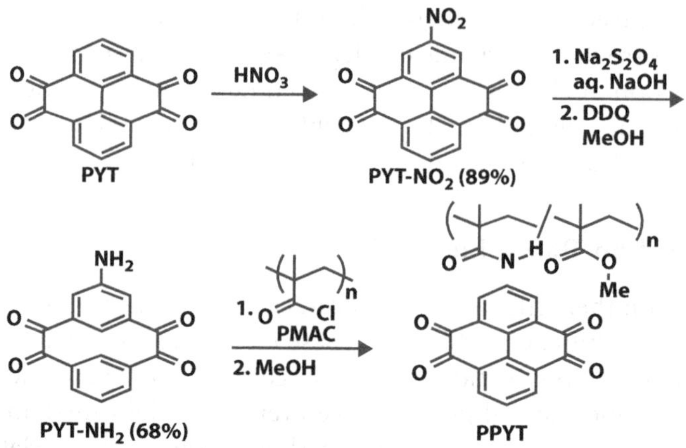

Figure 6.22 The schematic illustration of materials [21].

Jen and colleagues presented an alternative method for creating flexible electrodes using carbon materials. As illustrated in Figure 6.23, they suggested a nano composite electrode composed of 1D and 3D carbon materials [21].

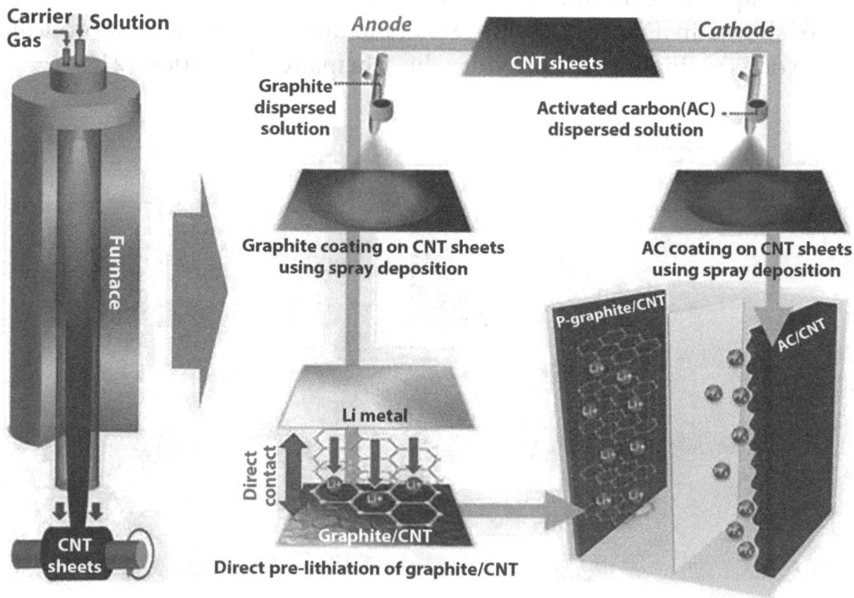

Figure 6.23 Nano composite electrode composed of 1D and 3D carbon materials [21].

As seen in Figure 6.24, the active material in this design is acid-treated activated carbon (a-AC), while carbon nanotubes (CNTs) serve as the flexible substrate [21].

As shown in Figure 6.25, a well-constructed CNT network ensures both exceptional electrochemical performance and mechanical stability during deformation, including folding and twisting. This architecture produces a very porous structure (1459.37 m^2 g^{-1}). The authors created a deformable supercapacitor with exceptional performance under a range of physical deformations using the produced electrode.

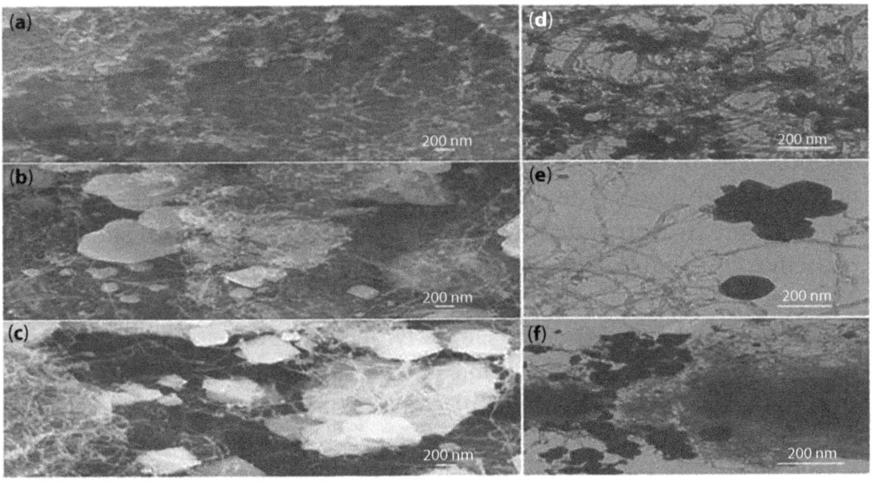

Figure 6.24 The active acid-treated activated carbon [21].

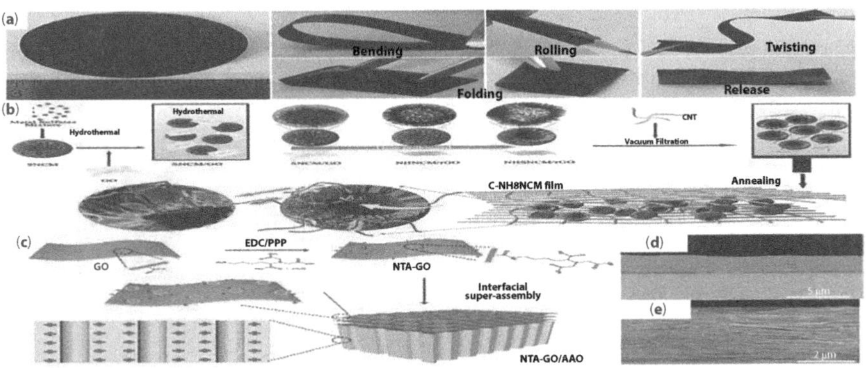

Figure 6.25 A well-constructed CNT [21].

6.8.2 Graphene-Based Flexible Electrodes

Furthermore, another kind of fibre electrode is graphene fibre, which has excellent electrical conductivity and strength [60, 61]. It has the same mechanical pliability as typical textile fibres and can be readily altered in comparison to traditional carbon fibres. Wang *et al.* wrapped two parallel reduced graphene oxide fibre springs to create a stretchy and self-healing supercapacitor using a polymer shell that heals itself at the 7.32mWcm−3 of power density, and a high energy of 0.94 mWhcm−3. The retained capacitance is 82.4% following a lengthy period of 100%, yet it is after the third healing, 54.2%. It offers a necessary approach in the next-generation multipurpose electronic gadget [23]. SEM analysis confirmed a uniform and porous formation of the graphene network with continuous interspaces. This lightweight electrode demonstrated versatile form factors, including bendable and rollable states shown in Figure 6.26.

Using PVA-H_2SO_4 gel as the electrolyte and separator membrane, the produced electrode was utilised to construct a flexible symmetric supercapacitor. High energy density (8.8 Wh kg^{-1}) and power density (178.5 W kg^{-1}) were demonstrated by the supercapacitor, along with stable electrochemical performance even when subjected to mechanical deformation [22].

Finally, a hybrid carbon-based polymer composite that serves as a stretchable substrate for deformable energy storage devices was created by Song and colleagues. The composite consists of carbon black and CNT fillers is shown in Figure 6.27.

The electrode fabrication process was inspired by a breath figure approach, which increased the electrode's surface area nearly fourfold under 100% humidity compared to 60%. SEM images revealed porous and uniform hybrid carbon/polymer (HCP) composites (Figure 6.28).

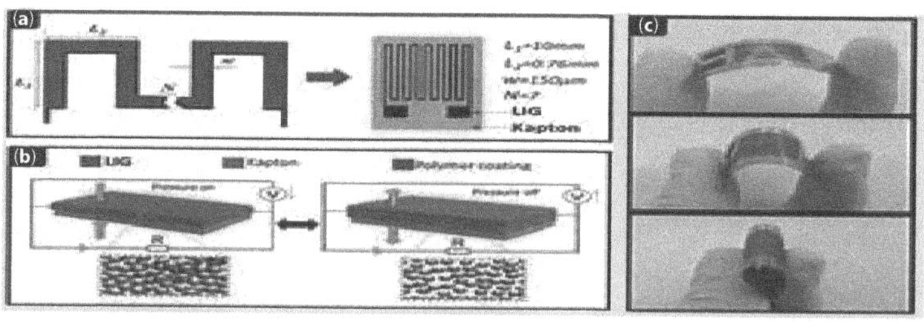

Figure 6.26 Bendable and rollable states [21].

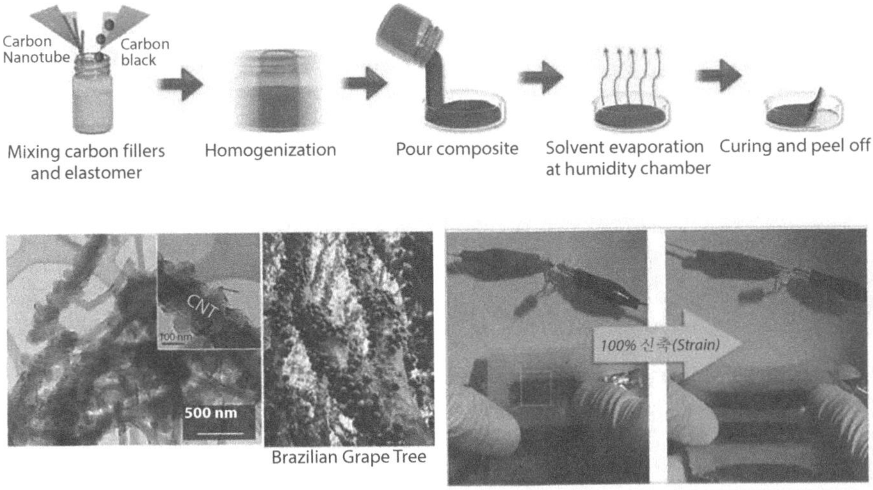

Figure 6.27 The composite of carbon black and CNT [21].

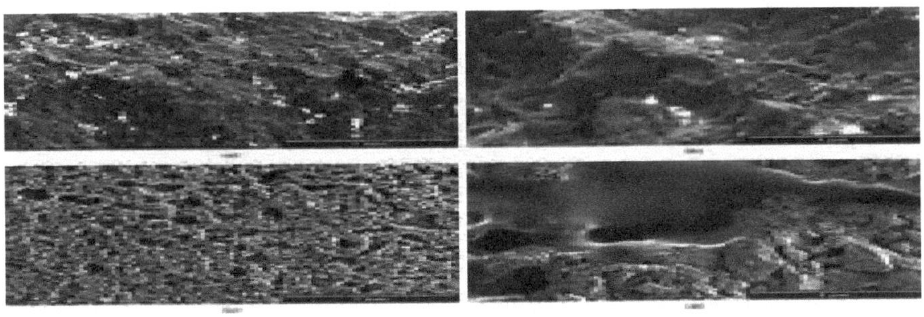

Figure 6.28 Hybrid carbon/polymer (HCP) composites [21].

TEM analysis confirmed that the hybrid carbon fillers self-assembled into a well-connected percolation network, contributing to excellent electrical conductivity as shown in Figure 6.29.

The flexible HCP electrode exhibited significant mechanical endurance under bending and rolling conditions (Figure 6.30).

The authors achieved a breakthrough in deformable energy storage devices by using this design to create aqueous rechargeable lithium-ion batteries (ARLBs) based on the HCP electrode (Figure 6.31).

These studies illustrate the versatility of carbon and graphene materials for flexible electrode applications. Their lightweight nature, high energy density, mechanical durability, and seamless integration of active materials with substrates make carbon-based electrodes ideal candidates for advanced flexible energy storage devices.

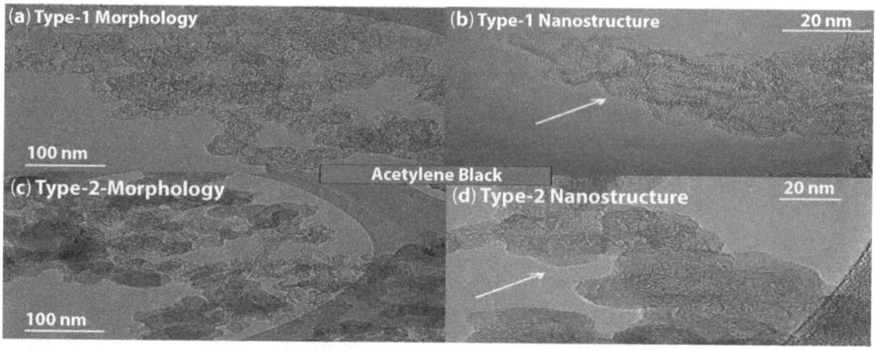

Figure 6.29 TEM image of hybrid carbon fillers [21].

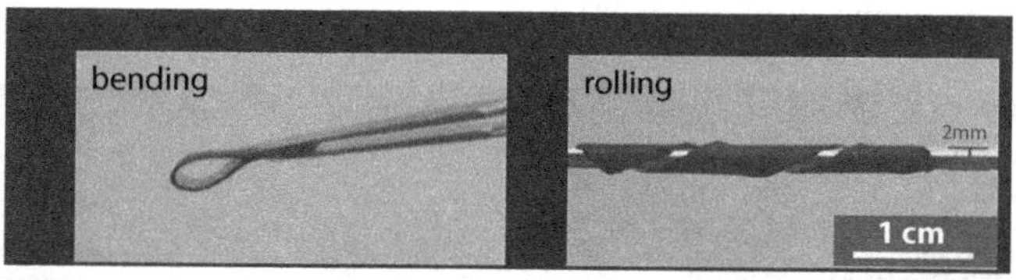

Figure 6.30 Flexible HCP electrode [21].

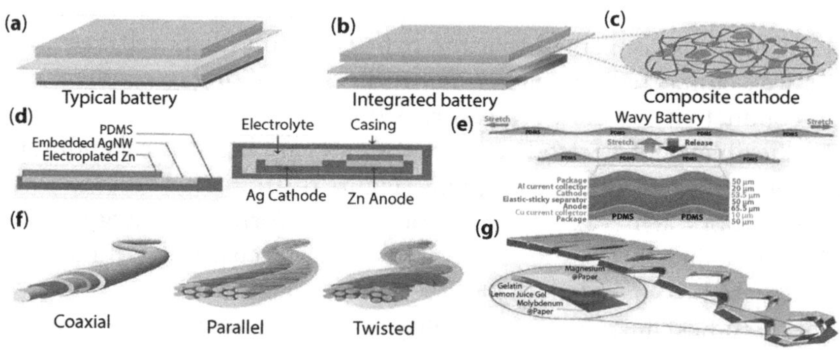

Figure 6.31 Lithium-ion batteries (ARLBs) based on the HCP electrode [21].

6.9 Comparison Sheet of Different Materials

Comparison of different materials in a tabular form:

S. no.	Material	Category	Properties	Application	Advantages	Limitations
1.	Graphene	Electrode	High conductivity, large surface area, flexibility	Flexible supercapacitors, batteries	Excellent charge transport, flexible	Expensive, aggregation issues
2.	Carbon Nanotubes (CNTs)	Electrode	High tensile strength, good conductivity	Supercapacitors, Li-ion batteries	Durable, flexible, lightweight	Complicated processing, aggregation
3	Conductive Polymers	Electrode	Stretchable, lightweight, conductive	Wearable supercapacitors, batteries	Low-cost, flexible	Limited stability, lower conductivity than metals
4.	MXenes (e.g., Ti3_33 C2_22)	Electrode	High conductivity, hydrophilic	Batteries, supercapacitors	High energy density, fast ion transport	Oxidation issues, complex synthesis
5.	Ionic Liquids	Electrolyte	High ionic conductivity, thermally stable	Electrolyte for batteries, supercapacitors	Stable, non- volatile	Expensive, limited compatibility
6.	Polymer Electrolytes	Electrolyte	Flexible, lightweight, conductive	Solid-state batteries	Good flexibility and safety	Lower conductivity than liquid electrolytes
7.	Hydrogels/Gel Electrolytes	Electrolyte	High ionic conductivity, stretchable	Wearable batteries, flexible supercapacitors	Flexible, biocompatible	Limited cycle life, water evaporation
8.	Cellulose Nanofibers	Substrate	Biodegradable, porous, flexible	Paper-based batteries, supercapacitor	Eco-friendly, flexible	Low conductivity, needs hybridization
9.	Reduced Graphene Oxide	Electrode	Moderate conductivity, flexible	Supercapacitors, hybrid batteries	Lower cost than pristine graphene	Lower conductivity, synthesis issues
10.	Composite Materials (e.g., CNT/ Polymer)	Hybrid Material	Synergistic properties of components	Flexible batteries, supercapacitors	Improved performance and flexibility	Complex manufacturin g, costly
11.	Silicon Nanoparticles	Electrode	High capacity, flexible with binders	Flexible Li-ion batteries	Very high energy storage potential	Volume expansion, poor cycling stability
12.	Silicone- Based Elastomers	Substrate	Highly stretchable, durable	Substrates for flexible electronics	Excellent mechanical properties	Insulating, requires conductive fillers

References

1. Buffett, Z., Ummat, P., Datars, W., Properties of solvent-free perylene iodine. *Physica B*, 270, 3–4, 341–349, 1999, https://doi.org/10.1016/S0921-4526(99)00178-7.
2. Evaluating Flexibility and Wearability of Flexible Energy Storage Devices, https://doi.org/10.1016/j.joule.2019.01.013.
3. He, J., Cao, L., Cui, J., Fu, G., Jiang, R., Xu, X., Flexible Energy Storage Devices to Power the Future, https://doi.org/10.1002/adma.202306090.
4. Gilleo, K., The First 105 Years of Flexible Circuitry, ET-Trends LLC, https://www.allflexinc.com//wp-content/uploads/2019/06/IPC-Flex_2007_Gilleo.pdf.
5. Crabb, R.L. and Treble, F.C., Thin silicon solar cells for large flexible arrays. *Nature*, 213, 1223–1224, 1967, https://doi.org/10.1038/2131223a0.
6. Rasmussen, S.C., The Early History of Polyaniline: Discovery and Origins. *Substantia*, *1*, 2, 2017, https://doi.org/10.13128/Substantia-30.
7. McGinness, J., Corry, P., Proctor, P., Amorphous Semiconductor Switching in Melanins. *Science*, 183, 4127, 853–855, March 1, 1974, doi:10.1126/science.183.4127.853.
8. Kawamoto, H., The Inventors of TFT Active-Matrix LCD Receive the 2011 IEEE Nishizawa Medal. *J. Disp. Technol.*, 2012.
9. Cheng, I.-C. and Wagner, S., Overview of Flexible Electronics Technology, in: *Electronic Materials: Science & Technology*, pp. 1–28, 2009, doi: https://doi.org/10.1007/978-0-387-74363-9.
10. Boicea, V.A., Energy Storage Technologies: The Past and the Present. *Proc. IEEE*, 102, 11, 1777–1794, Nov. 2014, doi: https://doi.org/10.1109/JPROC.2014.2359545.
11. SionPower, Lithium Sulfur Batteries, 2012, [Online], http://www.sionpower.Com/.
12. Zhang, J., Gu, M., Chen, X., Supercapacitors for renewable energy applications: A review, Institute of Photonic Chips, University of Shanghai for Science and Technology, Shanghai 200093, China, https://doi.org/10.1016/j.mne.2023.100229.
13. Energy efficiency criteria in uninterruptible power supply selection, https://doi.org/10.1016/j.apenergy.2010.08.017.
14. History, Evolution, and Future Status of Energy Storage.
15. Wang, X., Lu, X., Liu, B., Chen, D., Tong, Y., Shen, G., Flexible Energy-Storage Devices: Design Consideration and Recent Progress, https://doi.org/10.1002/adma.201400910.
16. https://gesrepair.com/future-of-flexible-electronic/.
17. Yadava, D., Aminib, F., Ehrmannc, A., Recent advances in carbon nanofibers and their applications – A review, https://doi.org/10.1016/j.eurpolymj.2020.109963.

18. Qiao, Z., Bian, K., Ding, C., Zhao, Y., Recent progress of carbon-fiber-based electrode materials for energy storage, https://doi.org/10.1016/j.diamond.2023.110208.
19. https://pubs.acs.org/doi/10.1021/acsami.0c16801.
20. Song, B., Moon, K.-S., Wong, C.-P., Recent Developments in Design and Fabrication of Graphene-Based Interdigital Micro-Supercapacitors for Miniaturized Energy Storage Devices, IEEE, https://doi.org/10.1109/TCPMT.2016.2585162.
21. Song, W.-J., Lee, S., Song, G., Son, H.-B., Han, D.-Y., Jeong, I., Bang, Y., Park, S., Recent progress in aqueous based flexible energy storage devices. *Energy Storage Mater.*, 2020, https://doi.org/10.1016/j.ensm.2020.05.006.
22. Li, H., Zhang, X., Zhao, Z., Hua, Z., Liu, X., Yu, G., Flexible sodium-ion based energy storage devices: Recent progress and challenges, https://doi.org/10.1016/j.ensm.2019.12.037.
23. Zhang, Q., Gao, X.-W., Liu, X., Mu, J.-J., Gu, Q., Liu, Z., Luo, W.-B., Flexible wearable energy storage devices: Materials, structures, and applications, https://doi.org/10.1002/bte2.20230061.
24. Faizan, A., Mandeep, S., Tarun, C., Faizan, R.B.S., Comparative Analysis of Nanowire Tunnel Field Effect Transistor for Low Power Application. *J. Silicon*, 14, 12075–12084, 2022.
25. Bhardwaj, A., Kumar, P., Raj, B., Anand, S., Design and Performance Optimization of doping-less Vertical Nanowire TFET using Gate Stack Technique. *J. Electron. Mater. (JEMS)*, Springer, 41, 7, 4005–4013, 2022.
26. Singh, J. and Raj, B., Tunnel Current Model of Asymmetric MIM Structure Levying Various Image Forces to Analyze the Characteristics of Filamentary Memristor. *Appl. Phys. A*, Springer, 125, 3, 203.1–203.11, Feb 2019.
27. Goyal, C., Ubhi, J.S., Raj, B., Low Leakage Zero Ground Noise Nanoscale Full Adder Using Source Biasing Technique. *J. Nanoelectron. Optoelectron.*, American Scientific Publishers, 14, 360–370, March 2019.
28. Singh, G., Sarin, R.K., Raj, B., A Novel Robust Exclusive-OR Function Implementation in QCA Nanotechnology with Energy Dissipation Analysis. *J. Comput. Electron.*, Springer, 15, 2, 455–465, June 2016.
29. Wadhwa, G., Kamboj, P., Raj, B., Design optimisation of junctionless TFET biosensor for high sensitivity. *Adv. Nat. Sci.: Nanosci. Nanotechnol.*, 10, 045001, 7, 2019.
30. Bansal, P. and Raj, B., Memristor Modeling and Analysis for Linear Dopant Drift Kinetics. *J. Nanoeng. Nanomanuf.*, American Scientific Publishers, 6, 1–7, 2016.
31. Ashima, Vaithiyanathan, D., Raj, B., Performance Analysis of Charge Plasma induced Graded Channel Si nanotube. *J. Eng. Res. (JER)*, EMSME Special Issue, 146–154, Aug 2021.
32. Tomar, A.S., Magraiya, V.K., Raj, B., Scaling of Access and Data Transistor for High Performance DRAM Cell Design. *Quantum Matter*, 2, 412–416, Oct. 2013.

33. Jain, N. and Raj, B., Parasitic Capacitance and Resistance Model Development and Optimization of Raised Source/Drain SOI FinFET Structure for Analog Circuit Applications. *J. Nanoelectron. Optoelectron.*, ASP, USA, 13, 531–539, April 2018.
34. Singh, S., Vishvakarma, S.K., Raj, B., Analytical Modeling of Split-Gate Junction-Less Transistor for a Biosensor Application. *Sens. Bio-Sens.*, Elsevier, 18, 31–36, April 2018.
35. Gopal, M. and Raj, B., Low Power 8T SRAM Cell Design for High Stability Video Applications. *ITSI Trans. Electr. Electron. Eng.*, 1, 5, 91–97, 2013.
36. Raj, B., Mitra, J., Bihani, D.K., Rangharajan, V., Saxena, A.K., Dasgupta, S., Analysis of Noise Margin, Power and Process Variation for 32 nm FinFET Based 6T SRAM Cell. *J. Comput. (JCP)*, Academy Publisher, Finland, 5, 6, 1–8, 2010.
37. Sharma, D., Mehra, R., Raj, B., Comparative Analysis of Photovoltaic Technologies for High Efficiency Solar Cell Design. *Superlattices Microstruct.*, Elsevier, 153, 106861, May 2021.
38. Kaur, P., Buttar, A.S., Raj, B., A comprehensive Analysis of Nanoscale Transistor based Biosensor: A Review. *Indian J. Pure Appl. Phys.*, 59, 304–318, April 2021.
39. Yadav, D., Raj, B., Raj, B., Design and Simulation of Low Power Microcontroller for IoT Applications. *J. Sens. Lett.*, ASP, 18, 401–409, May 2020.
40. Singh, S. and Raj, B., A 2-D Analytical Surface Potential and Drain current Modeling of Double-Gate Vertical t-shaped Tunnel FET. *J. Comput. Electron.*, Springer, 19, 1154–1163, April 2020.
41. Singh, J. and Raj, B., An Accurate and Generic Window function for Non-linear Memristor Model. *J. Comput. Electron.*, Springer, 18, 2, 640–647, June 2019.
42. Kaur, M., Gupta, N., Kumar, S., Raj, B., Singh, A.K., Comparative RF and Crosstalk Analysis of Carbon Based Nano Interconnects. *IET Circuits Devices Syst.*, 15, 6, 493–503, Feb 2021.
43. Kandasamy, N., Ahmad, F., Ajitha, D., Raj, B., Telagam, N., Quantum Dot Cellular Automata based Scan Flip Flop and Boundary Scan Register. *IETE J. Res.*, 66, 535–548, 2020.
44. Singh, J. and Raj, B., Design and Investigation of 7T2M NVSARM with Enhanced Stability and Temperature Impact on Store/Restore Energy. *IEEE Trans. Very Large Scale Integr. Syst.*, 27, 6, 1322–1328, June 2019.
45. Bhardwaj, A.K., Gupta, S., Raj, B., Singh, A., Impact of Double Gate Geometry on the Performance of Carbon Nanotube Field Effect Transistor Structures for Low Power Digital Design. *Comput. Theor. Nanosci.*, ASP, 16, 1813–1820, 2019.
46. Jain, N. and Raj, B., Thermal Stability Analysis and Performance Exploration of Asymmetrical Dual-k underlap Spacer (ADKUS) SOI FinFET for Security and Privacy Applications. *Indian J. Pure Appl. Phys. (IJPAP)*, 57, 352–360, May 2019.

47. Jain, N. and Raj, B., Dual-k Spacer Region Variation at the Drain Side of Asymmetric SOI FinFET Structure: Performance Analysis towards the Analog/RF Design Applications. *J. Nanoelectron. Optoelectron.*, American Scientific Publishers, 14, 349–359, March 2019.
48. Singh, J., Sharma, S., Raj, B., Khosla, M., Analysis of barrier layer thickness on performance of In1-xGaxAs based Gate Stack Cylindrical Gate Nanowire MOSFET. *JNO*, ASP, 13, 1473–1477, Oct 2018.
49. Jain, N. and Raj, B., Analysis and Performance Exploration of High-k SOI FinFETs Over the Conventional Low-k SOI FinFET toward Analog/RF Design. *J. Semicond. (JoS)*, IOP Science, 39, 12, 124002-1–7, Dec 2018.
50. Goyal, C., Ubhi, J.S., Raj, B., A reliable leakage reduction technique for approximate full adder with reduced ground bounce noise. *J. Math. Probl. Eng.*, Hindawi, 2018, 3501041, 16, 15 Oct 2018.
51. Anuradha, Singh, J., Raj, B., Khosla, M., Design and Performance Analysis of Nano-scale Memristor-based Nonvolatile SRAM. *J. Sens. Lett.*, American Scientific Publishers, 16, 798–805, Oct 2018.
52. Wadhwa, G. and Raj, B., Parametric Variation Analysis of Charge-Plasma-based Dielectric Modulated JLTFET for Biosensor Application. *IEEE Sens. J.*, 18, 15, 6070–6077 (SCI), August 1, 2018.
53. Singh, J. and Raj, B., Comparative Analysis of Memristor Models for Memories Design. *JoS*, IoP, 39, 7, 074006-1–12, July 2018.
54. Yadav, D., Chouhan, S.S., Vishvakarma, S.K., Raj, B., Application Specific Microcontroller Design for IoT based WSN. *Sens. Lett.*, ASP, 16, 374–385, May 2018.
55. Singh, G., Sarin, R.K., Raj, B., Fault-Tolerant Design and Analysis of Quantum-Dot Cellular Automata Based Circuits. *IEEE/IET Circuits Devices Syst.*, 12, 638–64, 2018.
56. Singh, J. and Raj, B., Modeling of Mean Barrier Height Levying Various Image Forces of Metal Insulator Metal Structure to Enhance the Performance of Conductive Filament Based Memristor Model. *IEEE Nanotechnol.*, 17, 2, 268–267, March 2018.
57. Jain, A., Sharma, S., Raj, B., Analysis of Triple Metal Surrounding Gate (TM-SG) III-V Nanowire MOSFET for Photosensing Application. *Opto-Electron. J.*, Elsevier, 26, 2, 141–148, May 2018.
58. Jain, A., Sharma, S., Raj, B., Design and Analysis of High Sensitivity Photosensor Using Cylindrical Surrounding Gate MOSFET for Low Power Sensor Applications. *Eng. Sci. Technol. Int. J.*, Elsevier's, 19, 4, 1864–1870, December 2016.
59. Saiphani Kumar, G., Singh, A., Raj, B., Design and Analysis of Gate All Around CNTFET based SRAM cell Design. *J. Comput. Electron.*, Springer, 17, 1, 138–145, March 2018.
60. pal Singh, G., Sohi, B.S., Raj, B., Material Properties Analysis of Graphene Base Transistor (GBT) for VLSI Analog Circuits. *Indian J. Pure Appl. Phys. (IJPAP)*, 55, 896–902, Dec-2017.

61. Kumar, S. and Raj, B., Estimation of Stability and Performance metric for Inward Access Transistor based 6T SRAM Cell Design using n-type/p-type DMDG-GDOV TFET. *IEEE VLSI Circuits Syst. Lett.*, 3, 2, 25–39, June 2017.
62. Sharma, S., Kumar, A., Pattanaik, M., Raj, B., Forward Body Biased Multimode Multi-Threshold CMOS Technique for Ground Bounce Noise Reduction in Static CMOS Adders. *Int. J. Inf. Electron. Eng.*, 3, 3, 567–572, 2013.
63. Singh, H., Kumar, P., Raj, B., Performance Analysis of Majority Gate SET Based 1-bit Full Adder. *Int. J. Comput. Commun. Eng. (IJCCE)*, IACSIT Press Singapore, ISSN: 2010-3743, 2, 4, 2013.
64. Anjum, N., Bali, T., Raj, B., Design and Simulation of Handwritten Multiscript Character Recognition. *Int. J. Adv. Res. Comput. Commun. Eng.*, 2, 7, 2544–2549, July 2013.
65. Singh, K. and Raj, B., Performance and analysis of temperature dependent Multi-walled Carbon Nanotubes as Global Interconnects at different technology nodes. *J. Comput. Electron.*, Springer, 14, 2, 469–476, June 2015.
66. Kumar, S. and Raj, B., Compact channel potential analytical Modeling of DG-TFET based on Evanescent-mode Approach. *J. Comput. Electron.*, Springer, 14, 2, 820–827, July 2015.
67. Singh, K. and Raj, B., Temperature Dependent Modeling and Performance Evaluation of Multi-Walled CNT and Single-Walled CNT as Global Interconnects. *J. Electron. Mater.*, Springer, 44, 12, 4825–4835, Dec 2015.
68. Sharma, V.K., Pattanaik, M., Raj, B., INDEP approach for leakage reduction in nanoscale CMOS circuits. *Int. J. Electron.*, Taylor & Francis, 102, 2, 200–215, 2014.
69. Singh, K. and Raj, B., Influence of Temperature on MWCNT bundle, SWCNT bundle and Copper interconnects for Nanoscaled Technology nodes. *J. Mater. Sci.: Mater. Electron.*, Springer, 26, 8, 6134–6142, 2015.
70. Anjum, N., Bali, T., Raj, B., Design and Simulation of Handwritten Gurumukhi and Devanagri Numerical Recognition. *Int. J. Comput. Appl.*, Foundation of Computer Science, New York, USA, 73, 12, 16–21, 2013.
71. Khandelwal, S., Gupta, V., Raj, B., Gupta, R.D., Process Variability Aware Low Leakage Reliable Nano Scale DG-FinFET SRAM Cell Design Technique. *J. Nanoelectron. Optoelectron.*, 10, 6, 810–817, December 2015.
72. Sharma, V.K., Pattanaik, M., Raj, B., ONOFIC Approach: Low Power High Speed Nanoscale VLSI Circuits Design. *Int. J. Electron.*, Taylor & Francis, 101, 1, 61–73, 2014.
73. Khandelwal, S., Raj, B., Gupta, R.D., FinFET based 6T SRAM Cell Design: Analysis of Performance Metric, Process Variation and Temperature Effect. *J. Comput. Theor. Nanosci.*, ASP, USA, 12, 2500–2506, 2015.
74. Singh, S., Yadav, S., Rahul, J., Srivastava, A., Raj, B., Impact of HfO_2 in Graded Channel Dual Insulator Double Gate MOSFET. *J. Comput. Theor. Nanosci.*, American Scientific Publishers, 12, 6, 950–953, April 2015.

75. Sharma, V.K., Pattanaik, M., Raj, B., PVT variations aware low leakage INDEP approach for nanoscale CMOS Circuits. *Microelectron. Reliab.*, Elsevier, 54, 90–99, 2014.
76. Raj, B., Saxena, A.K., Dasgupta, S., Quantum Mechanical Analytical Modeling of Nanoscale DG FinFET: Evaluation of Potential, Threshold Voltage and Source/Drain Resistance. *Elsevier's J. Mater. Sci. Semicond. Process.*, Elsevier, 16, 4, 1131–1137, 2013.
77. Gopal, M., Prasad, S.S.D., Raj, B., 8T SRAM Cell Design for Dynamic and Leakage Power Reduction. *Int. J. Comput. Appl.*, Foundation of Computer Science, New York, USA, 71, 9, 43–48, June 2013.
78. Pattanaik, M., Raj, B., Sharma, S., Kumar, A., Diode Based Trimode Multi-Threshold CMOS Technique for Ground Bounce Noise Reduction in Static CMOS Adders. *Adv. Mater. Res.*, Trans Tech Publications, Switzerland, 548, 885–889, 2012.
79. Raj, B., Saxena, A.K., Dasgupta, S., Nanoscale FinFET Based SRAM Cell Design: Analysis of Performance metric, Process variation, Underlapped FinFET and Temperature effect. *IEEE Circuits Syst. Mag.*, 11, 2, 38–50, 2011.
80. Sharma, V.K., Pattanaik, M., Raj, B., Leakage Current ONOFIC Approach for Deep Submicron VLSI Circuit Design. *Int. J. Electr. Comput. Electron. Commun. Eng.*, World Academy of Sciences, Engineering and Technology, 7, 4, 239–244, 2013.
81. Kaur, P., Gill, S.S., Raj, B., Comparative Analysis of OFETs Materials and Devices for Sensor Applications. *J. Silicon*, Springer, 14, 4463–4471, 2022.
82. Sharma, S.K., Kumar, P., Raj, B., Raj, B., $In_{1-x}Ga_xAs$ Double Metal Gate-Stacking Cylindrical Nanowire MOSFET for highly sensitive Photo detector. *J. Silicon*, Springer, 14, 3535–3541, 2022.
83. Raj, B., Saxena, A.K., Dasgupta, S., Analytical Modeling of Quasi Planar Nanoscale Double Gate FinFET with Source/Drain Resistance and field dependent carrier mobility: A quantum mechanical study. *J. Comput. (JCP)*, Academy Publisher, Finland, 4, 9, 1–8, 2009.
84. Bhushan, S., Khandelwal, S., Raj, B., Analyzing Different Mode FinFET based Memory Cell at Different Power Supply for Leakage Reduction. *Seventh International Conference on Bio-Inspired Computing: Theories and Application, (BIC-TA 2012)*, Advances in Intelligent Systems and Computing, vol. 202, pp. 89–100, 2013.
85. Singh, J. and Raj, B., Temperature Dependent Analytical Modeling and Simulations of Nanoscale Memristor. *Eng. Sci. Technol. Int. J.*, Elsevier's, 21, 862–868, Oct 2018.
86. Singh, S., Bala, S., Raj, B., Raj, B., Improved Sensitivity of Dielectric Modulated Junctionless Transistor for Nanoscale Biosensor Design. *Sens. Lett.*, ASP, 18, 328–333, April 2020.
87. Kumar, V., Vishvakarma, S.K., Raj, B., Design and Performance Analysis of ASIC for IoT Applications. *Sens. Lett.*, ASP, 18, 31–38, Jan 2020.

88. Jaiswal, A., Sarin, R.K., Raj, B., Sukhija, S., A Novel Circular Slotted Microstrip-fed Patch Antenna with Three Triangle Shape Defected Ground Structure for Multiband Applications. *Adv. Electromagn. (AEM)*, 7, 3, 56–63, Aug 2018.
89. Wadhwa, G. and Raj, B., Label Free Detection of Biomolecules using Charge-Plasma-Based Gate Underlap Dielectric Modulated Junctionless TFET. *J. Electron. Mater. (JEMS)*, Springer, 47, 8, 4683–4693, August 2018.
90. Singh, G., Sarin, R.K., Raj, B., Design and Performance Analysis of a New Efficient Coplanar Quantum-Dot Cellular Automata Adder. *Indian J. Pure Appl. Phys. (IJPAP)*, 55, 97–103, February 2017.
91. Kaur, P., Pandey, V., Raj, B., Comparative Study of Efficient Design, Control and Monitoring of Solar Power using IoT. *Sens. Lett.*, ASP, 18, 419–426, May 2020.
92. Bhardwaj, A.K., Gupta, S., Raj, B., Development & Analysis of compact model for Double Gate Schottky Barrier CNTFET. *J. Nanoelectron. Optoelectron.*, ASP, 15, 1199–1208, Aug 2020.
93. Wadhwa, G., Kamboj, P., Singh, J., Raj, B., Design and Investigation of Junctionless DGTFET for Biological Molecule Recognition. *Trans. Electr. Electron. Mater.*, Springer, 22, 282–289, 2021.
94. Verma, S.K., Singh, S., Wadhwa, G., Raj, B., Detection of Biomolecules using Charge-Plasma based Gate Underlap Dielectric Modulated Dopingless TFET. *Trans. Electr. Electron. Mater. (TEEM)*, Springer, 21, 528–535, June 2020.
95. Jain, N. and Raj, B., Impact of underlap spacer region variation on Electrostatic and analog/RF performance of symmetrical high-k SOI FinFET at 20 nm channel length. *J. Semicond. (JoS)*, IOP Science, 38, 12, 122002, Dec 2017.
96. Singh, S. and Raj, B., Analytical Modeling and Simulation analysis of T-shaped III-V heterojunction Vertical T-FET. *Superlattices Microstruct.*, Elsevier, 147, 106717, Nov 2020.
97. Singh, G., Sarin, R.K., Raj, B., Design and Analysis of Area Efficient QCA Based Reversible Logic Gates. *J. Microprocess. Microsys.*, Elsevier, 52, 59–68, May 2017.
98. Singh, S. and Raj, B., Parametric variation analysis on hetero-junction Vertical t-shape TFET for Suppressing ambipolar conduction. *Indian J. Pure Appl. Phys.*, 58, 478–485, June 2020.
99. Soniya, Singh, S., Wadhwa, G., Raj, B., Design and Analysis of Dual Source Vertical Tunnel Field Effect Transistor for high performance. *Trans. Electr. Electron. Mater.*, Springer, 21, 74–82, Oct 2019.
100. Kaur, M., Gupta, N., Kumar, S., Raj, B., Singh, A.K., RF Performance Analysis of Intercalated Graphene Nanoribbon Based Global Level Interconnects. *J. Comput. Electron.*, Springer, 19, 1002–1013, June 2020.
101. Wadhwa, G. and Raj, B., Design and Performance Analysis of Junctionless TFET Biosensor for high sensitivity. *IEEE Nanotechnol.*, 18, 567–574, 2019.

102. Singh, J. and Raj, B., Enhanced Nonlinear Memristor Model Encapsulating Stochastic Dopant Drift. *JNO*, ASP, 14, 958–963, 2019.
103. Singh, M., Chaudhary, T., Raj, B., Enhancing FeFET Structures for Non-volatile On-chip Memories: Design and Comparative Analysis. *Int. J. Numer. Modell. Electron. Netw. Dev. Fields*, 38, 1–9, 2024.
104. Singh, M., Chaudhary, T., Raj, B., Drain Current and Transconductance Analysis of GaN GAA Nanowire FET with High K Dielectric. *ECS J. Sci. Technol.*, 12, 6070–6077, 2023.
105. Singh, M., Chaudhary, T., Raj, B., Design of Si and Ge Nanowire FET for Low Power Application. *J. Silicon*, Springer, 15, 1491–1497, 2023.
106. Singh, M., Chaudhary, T., Raj, B., Electrical Characteristics Analysis of FeFET for Low Power Applications. *J. Nano*, 37, 1–8, 2024.
107. Kumar, M., Chaudhary, T., Raj, B., Design and Comparative Analysis of Ferroelectric Nanowire with Dielectric HfO_2 and $Al_2O_3$for Low Power Applications. *J. Electron. Mater.*, Springer, 53, 6785–6791, 2024.
108. Bhardwaj, A.K., Gupta, S., Raj, B., Investigation of Parameters for Schottky Barrier (SB) Height for Schottky Barrier Based Carbon Nanotube Field Effect Transistor Device. *J. Nanoelectron. Optoelectron.*, ASP, 15, 783–791, July 2020.
109. Bansal, P. and Raj, B., Memristor: A Versatile Nonlinear Model for Dopant Drift and Boundary Issues. *JCTN*, American Scientific Publishers, 14, 5, 2319–2325, May 2017.
110. Jain, N. and Raj, B., An Analog and Digital Design Perspective Comprehensive Approach on Fin-FET (Fin-Field Effect transistor) Technology - A Review. *Rev. Adv. Sci. Eng. (RASE)*, ASP, 5, 1–14, 2016.
111. Raj, B., Saxena, A.K., Dasgupta, S., Analytical Modeling for the Estimation of Leakage Current and Subthreshold Swing Factor of Nanoscale Double Gate FinFET Device. *Microelectron. Int.*, UK, 26, 53–63, 2009.
112. Soniya, Singh, S., Wadhwa, G., Raj, B., An Analytical Modeling for Dual Source Vertical Tunnel Field Effect Transistor. *Int. J. Recent Technol. Eng. (IJRTE)*, 8, 2, 603–608, July 2019.
113. Singh, S. and Raj, B., Design and analysis of hetrojunction Vertical T-shaped Tunnel Field Effect Transistor. *J. Electron. Mater.*, Springer, 48, 10, 6253–6260, October 2019.
114. Goyal, C., Ubhi, J.S., Raj, B., A Low Leakage CNTFET based Inexact Full Adder for Low Power Image Processing Applications. *Int. J. Circuit Theory Appl.*, Wiley, 47, 9, 1446–1458, September 2019.
115. Raj, B., Saxena, A.K., Dasgupta, S., A Compact Drain Current and Threshold Voltage Quantum Mechanical Analytical Modeling for FinFETs. *J. Nanoelectron. Optoelectron. (JNO)*, USA, 3, 2, 163–170, 2008.
116. Wadhwa, G. and Raj, B., An Analytical Modeling of Charge Plasma based Tunnel Field Effect Transistor with Impacts of Gate underlap Region. *Superlattices Microstruct.*, Elsevier, 142, 106512, June 2020.

117. Singh, S. and Raj, B., Modeling and Simulation analysis of SiGe hetrojunction Double GateVertical t-shaped Tunnel FET. *Superlattices Microstruct.*, Elsevier, 142, 106496, June 2020.
118. Jain, N. and Raj, B., Device and Circuit Co-Design Perspective Comprehensive Approach on FinFET Technology - A Review. *J. Electron Devices*, 23, 1, 1890–1901, 2016.
119. Kumar, S. and Raj, B., Analysis of I_{ON} and Ambipolar Current for Dual-Material Gate-drain Overlapped DG-TFET. *J. Nanoelectron. Optoelectron.*, American Scientific Publishers, USA, 11, 323–333, June 2016.

7

VLSI Design for AI Applications

Mandeep Singh*, Tarun Chaudhary, Balwinder Raj, Ravi Teja, Akku Naidu and Sivaram

Department of Electronics and Communication Engineering, Dr. B. R. Ambedkar National Institute of Technology Jalandhar, Punjab, India

Abstract

The rapid growth of Artificial Intelligence (AI) and Machine Learning (ML) has spurred an unprecedented demand for high-performance, energy-efficient hardware platforms. Very-Large-Scale Integration (VLSI) design plays a crucial role in meeting this demand by enabling the development of custom integrated circuits tailored for AI applications. This book chapter provides a detailed exploration of VLSI design methodologies, architectures, and emerging technologies that are shaping the future of AI hardware. The chapter begins by outlining the computational requirements of modern AI workloads, such as deep neural networks (DNNs), convolutional neural networks (CNNs), and transformer-based models. These workloads are characterized by massive parallelism, high data throughput, and stringent latency and power constraints. The discussion then transitions to how VLSI design addresses these challenges through specialized hardware accelerators, including application-specific integrated circuits (ASICs), field-programmable gate arrays (FPGAs), and system-on-chip (SoC) solutions. Key architectural innovations are discussed, including systolic arrays, tensor processing units (TPUs), and in-memory computing architectures. The chapter emphasizes how dataflow optimization, reduced precision arithmetic (e.g., INT8, FP16), and sparsity exploitation contribute to improved energy efficiency and throughput. Low-power design techniques such as voltage scaling, clock gating, and approximate computing are also presented as essential strategies for AI edge devices.

Keywords**:** Modern artificial intelligence, VLSI design, energy efficient, memory wall, IC fabrication, RAM, on-chip memory and multi-core architectures

**Corresponding author*: mandeep.moni.singh@gmail.com

Ashish Maurya, Mandeep Singh and Balwinder Raj (eds.) Machine Learning in Nanoelectronics: Devices, Circuits and Systems, (197–230) © 2026 Scrivener Publishing LLC

7.1 Introduction

Modern artificial intelligence (AI) systems are powered by extremely efficient, specialized hardware that was made possible by the convergence of artificial intelligence (AI) and Very Large-Scale Integration (VLSI) architecture. The necessity for specialized hardware that can satisfy the demanding requirements of AI algorithms has become more and more important as AI continues to expand in complexity and scale. VLSI design for AI applications, where digital systems are customized to maximize computing performance, energy efficiency, and scalability, has seen a rise in attention as a result. At its most basic level, artificial intelligence (AI) is a technology that enables computers to perform tasks that humans would perform, learn from past experiences, and adapt to new inputs [1–5]. AI is being used in many industries, including finance and medical. Artificial intelligence has existed for a while. It was initially theoretically and mathematically investigated, after which it was created and put into software. Since AI is implemented in software and makes use of the current CPU, GPU, and memory system, the AI structure itself does not require hardware architecture. But as the application of AI expanded, it became crucial to implement AI using a neural processing unit as a stand-in for an AI-dedicated process, in addition to CPU and GPU. AI processors have three main problems: on-chip memory capacity, energy efficiency, and memory wall. Computational power has increased by 60% annually since the 1980s as IC fabrication technology has improved according to Moore's Law. But throughout the same time span, memory performance—more especially, Dynamic Random Access Memory, or DRAM—has only increased by 7% annually. The performance difference between CPU and RAM has been widening for even longer than 20 years. As a result, data bandwidth is constrained relative to processing performance [6–11]. This is the location of the well-known RAM memory wall. CPUs have been unable to get through the memory barrier for decades. The memory partition is especially important in AI chip architecture since AI computations require a lot more data than most other purposes. Currently, there are two fundamental methods for resolving the memory wall problem. Increasing the data transfer clock speed is one option. Increasing the breadth of the data transfer is the second option. The first method is applied to memory that is continuously high, such as High Bandwidth Memory (HBM) and Double Data Rate (DDR) memory, which are extraordinarily high memory. The main issue with AI processors is their power consumption. Training an AI model has a carbon footprint that is more than five times greater than training a human.

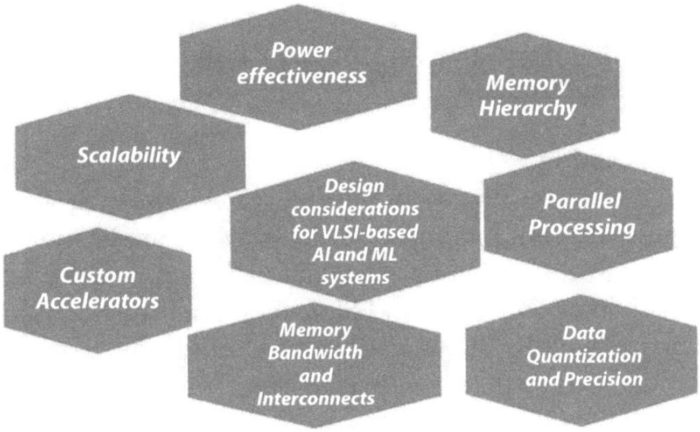

Figure 7.1 Key design considerations for VLSI-based AI and ML considerations.

Data transfer and computing devices are the main sources of power usage. AI circuits need to be capable of handling data transmission tasks in addition to mathematical tasks. Using current IC fabrication technology and minimizing the capacitance burden on data transmission channels are two common methods of cutting power consumption, as opposed to optimizing algorithms. Having fast memory is the third issue with AI processors. Fast memory that incorporates information quickly without slowing down the CPU is called on-chip or near-chip memory. Static Random Access Memory (SRAM) on-chip [12–18]. Figure 7.1 presents key design considerations for VLSI-based AI and ML consideration.

Important design factors for VLSI (Very Large-Scale Integration) systems suited to AI and machine learning applications are highlighted in the diagram [19–25]. The following provides a theoretical analysis of each factor.

1. Power Effectiveness

Due to the high computational needs of AI activities, which can result in excessive power consumption, power efficiency is crucial in VLSI-based AI/ML systems. Using strategies like power gating, clock gating, and dynamic voltage scaling, designers aim to build systems that use less power. In addition to extending the lifespan of battery-operated equipment, efficient power use lowers data center cooling needs [26–32].

2. Memory Hierarchy

Multiple levels of memory organization, including registers, cache, RAM, and secondary storage, are referred to as memory hierarchy. Reducing latency and increasing throughput are the objectives. By placing frequently used data closer to the processor, effective memory hierarchies can significantly increase system performance in AI and ML, fields that require massive datasets and models.

3. Parallel Processing

Massive parallelism is frequently needed for AI and ML algorithms to manage large-scale computations, particularly for applications like deep learning. Through the use of parallel data pathways, multi-core architectures, and GPU-like accelerators, VLSI systems are made to take advantage of parallel processing. By allowing several actions to be executed simultaneously, this parallelism improves performance and cuts down on processing time overall [33–40].

4. Data Quantization and Precision

Without substantially affecting accuracy, data quantization lowers the precision of the numbers used in computation, which can conserve memory and processing power. Cheaper precision (e.g., 8-bit or 16-bit arithmetic instead of 32-bit) is frequently adequate for model inference in VLSI systems for AI, enabling quicker computation and cheaper resource usage. Achieving a balance between model accuracy and performance requires precise adjustment [41–48].

5. Memory Bandwidth and Interconnects

For VLSI systems to facilitate high-speed data flow between various chip components, memory bandwidth and effective interconnects are crucial. Data must move seamlessly between processors, memory, and accelerators in AI/ML applications. To maximize data flow and prevent bottlenecks, strategies including high-speed buses, crossbars, and NoCs (Networks on Chip) are employed.

6. Custom Accelerators

TPUs (Tensor Processing Units) and NPUs (Neural Processing Units) are examples of custom hardware accelerators that are made to perform particular AI/ML tasks more effectively than general-purpose processors. Performance and energy efficiency can be greatly increased by optimizing these accelerators for popular AI activities like convolutions and matrix calculations [49–56].

7. Scalability

The ability of a system to expand and change in response to rising demand is known as scalability. Scalability must be considered in the design of

VLSI-based AI systems in order to support growing models and datasets over time. Scalability is supported by strategies like distributed computing and modular architectures, which allow systems to change without needing to be completely redesigned.

By integrating these design factors into VLSI-based AI and ML systems, effective, high- performing solutions that satisfy the particular requirements of AI applications can be produced [57–64].

7.2 Specialized Neural Networks Accelerators

The development of the internet and multimedia technology has brought with it a number of new challenges for machine learning. In several fields, machine learning has gained popularity as a means of mimicking human brain processes. Researchers from several disciplines work together to exchange ideas and methods, advancing the subject of artificial intelligence (AI). Numerous fields and applications, including speech recognition, image classification, hardware and software fault prediction, text detection, disease detection and prediction, nutrition monitoring, medical treatment, defect inspection, and metrology, use machine learning techniques [1]. The primary obstacles facing existing methods are the provision of a low-cost hardware accelerator and an optimal learning model [65–70].

One essential stage in the development of AI is machine learning. Machine learning is a subfield of artificial intelligence that uses data and algorithms to mimic human learning processes and continuously increase their accuracy. Machine learning uses mathematical models to help computers learn instead of depending on direct instruction. Machine learning algorithms can forecast new output values by using historical data as input. Machine learning, the foundation of artificial intelligence, gives machines the ability to think intelligently. The goal of machine learning research is to create a particular application-based study system that applies knowledge from cognitive science and human physiology to theoretical analysis and algorithmic model advancement through the development of diverse theories and methodologies. Complex human actions in multimedia streams are tracked by machine learning. There are several varieties of machine learning, such as supervised, unsupervised, and reinforcement learning. In supervised learning, a model is trained using labelled data, whereas in unsupervised learning, a model is trained using unlabelled data. In contrast, reinforcement learning necessitates trial and error in order to train a model [1].

Machine learning is significant because it may expedite the development of new goods and provide companies with insights into operational patterns and trends in consumer behavior. Machine learning is used in the operations of many of the top businesses today. Nowadays, machine learning is essential for differentiating companies from their rivals. Every industry is changing as a result of machine learning, including manufacturing, healthcare, education, transportation, food, and entertainment. The domains of material analysis, physics, chemistry, bioinformatics, and other related subjects employ clever techniques that improve their content creation. One of the key technologies used in these techniques is machine learning. It will have a big impact on almost every aspect of people's lives [71–78]. The increased use of machine learning to make devices and objects "smart" on their own is being driven by cloud computing and the Internet of Things (IoT). Convolutional neural networks (CNN), recurrent neural networks (RNN), and artificial neural networks (ANN) are examples of multi-layered architectures commonly used in deep learning to process enormous amounts of unstructured data. Every structure has a unique learning model. The foundation of an ANN is a sequence of interconnected layers. There are several nodes in each layer that carry out the calculation [1]. Until they reach the output layer, the nodes in each layer are connected to the nodes in the one below. Convolutional layers and pooling layers make up a CNN's architecture, with a pooling layer coming after each convolutional layer. The processing of the input data using the stored weights is carried out by a convolutional layer. A pooling layer is used to lower the bulk of the data in order to simplify the following layers. The RNN works well with time series data since it relies on memory for learning.

Accelerator Approaches

A) ANN

Similar to the biological neural network found in the human body, artificial neural networks (ANNs) have layered architectures that allow each network node to process input and send output to other network nodes. We refer to the nodes as neurons. Three or more interconnected layers make up an ANN. Input neurons in the first layer transmit information to the layers that follow. The final output data is generated by the output layer [79–85]. The hidden layers between the input and output layers are composed of units that use a series of transformations to adaptively change the data that was obtained from the preceding layer. Because each layer functions as an input and output layer, the ANN can comprehend increasingly complex objects. These inner layers collectively are referred to as the neural layer. A neural layer's units provide weights according to the ANN's

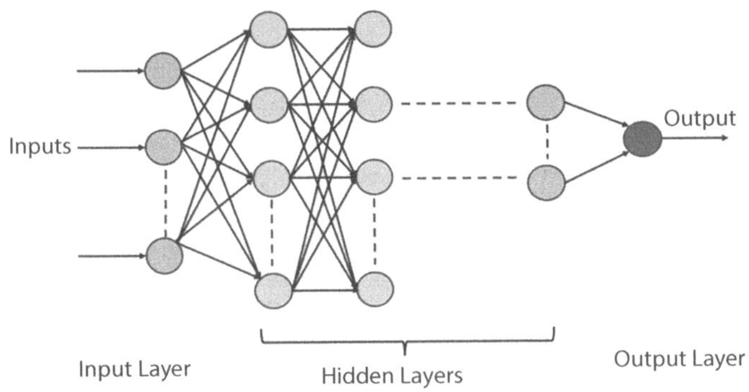

Figure 7.2 Block diagram of ANN [1].

internal design in an effort to learn from the data collected [86–92]. These concepts allow units to produce a modified outcome that is sent to the following layer as an output. The ANN's general block diagram is shown in Figure 7.2. The input from each node is multiplied by a weight and then sent to an adder accumulator. An activation function receives the output from the adder accumulator and returns the outcome. The end result is expressed by **$yk=f(\Sigma l=0nWlk*Xl+bk)$.**

The ultimate output is shown in equation (7.1), where n is the total number of neurons. In this case, Wlk is the synaptic weight between the lth neuron and the kth neuron in the current layer, while Xl is the output of the lth neuron in the preceding layer. Furthermore, b stands for the bias and f for the activation function. Natural language processing (NLP), speech and picture identification, business intelligence predictive analysis, and many other fields are just a few of the many real-world uses for artificial neural networks (ANNs). Accuracy, scalability, and processing speed are just a few benefits of ANNs. High-speed processing, which may be accomplished by parallel implementation, is the main benefit of ANNs.

B) CNN

CNN is a model for deep learning that is used for data processing. Starting with low-level features and working its way up to high-level ones, its architecture is designed to automatically and adaptively learn spatial feature hierarchies [93–98]. A range of building elements make up CNNs, which enable them to extract pertinent information from input data. Convolution layers (CLs), pooling layers, and fully linked layers are the three layers that commonly make up CNN structures, as illustrated in Figure 7.3. For feature extraction from input data, convolution and pooling layers are employed.

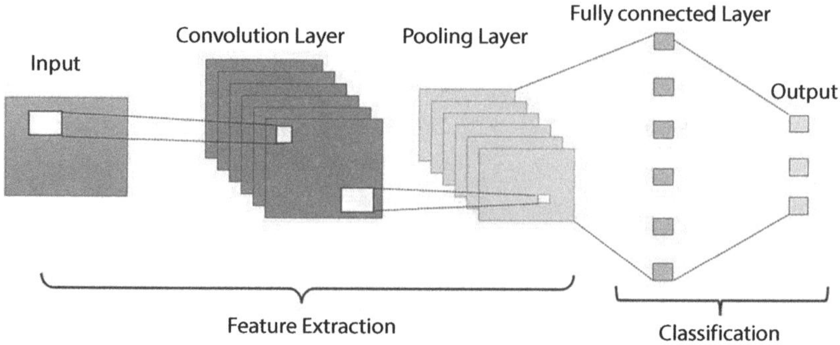

Figure 7.3 Block diagram of CNN [1].

A fully linked layer is then used to translate these features to the final output, which is usually a classification result. The CL, which consists of a stack of mathematical operations, including the convolution linear operation, is an essential part of CNN. Digital images' pixel values are stored in a 2-D grid of numbers. CNNs apply a kernel, a tiny parameter grid, at each location in an image as an optimizable feature extractor. CNNs are therefore especially effective in processing images [93–97]. As the output of one layer is transferred into the next, the retrieved features may become more complex and hierarchical. Training entails enhancing parameters like kernels through an optimization procedure known as backpropagation and gradient descent to lessen the discrepancy between outputs and ground truth labels [1]. Applications such as object detection, facial recognition, semantic segmentation, picture classification, and image captioning have all made extensive use of CNNs. A local receptive field of the same size as the convolution kernel must be located in the input feature map in order to carry out a convolution operation in a CNN.

7.3 Memory Hierarchy Optimization

Artificial intelligence (AI) algorithms based on neural networks have become widely used in many different industries in recent years, which has increased demand for dependable and energy-efficient high-performance computing architectures. Regarding the improvement of reliability for mesh-connected processor arrays, common methods that have been put out in the past include redundancy repair techniques such single-track switches, redundant-core repair, and direct-spare replacement [98–102]. However, in accordance with Moore's Law, the density and capacity of memory devices have been rising due to the constantly developing semiconductor memory technology [2]. It has been observed that embedded memory dominates chip yield and dependability in many sophisticated system chips, taking up over 70% of the chip surface.

Therefore, memory test and repair procedures must be addressed in order to improve overall chip yield and dependability. The majority of contemporary embedded and commodity memories are tested and repaired using memory built-in self-repair (MBISR) systems. Redundancies are used by MBISR to fix memory defects.

For embedded memory repair of the processing cores in the mesh-connected processor array, numerous MBISR techniques have been developed thus far. Nevertheless, the current methods do not yet capitalize on the (a) (b) Figure 7.4. Mesh processor array with (a) MBISR and (b) MBIPR regular topology of the array, meaning that there is potential for additional MBISR scheme development. For embedded memories in the processing cores of the mesh array, we examine the properties of the mesh-connected processor array and suggest a spare sharing memory repair method known as memory built-in peer repair (MBIPR). The spare memories in the four adjacent cores are used by the MBIPR technique in addition to its own spare memories for self-repair. According to experimental data, the mesh-connected processor array can use MBIPR to increase the use of spare memories, extending the array's lifespan; in other words, the suggested MBIPR's repair rate is higher than the regular MBISR's [2]. In particular, MBIPR enhances lifetime by 2.1-7.9× and spare utilization by

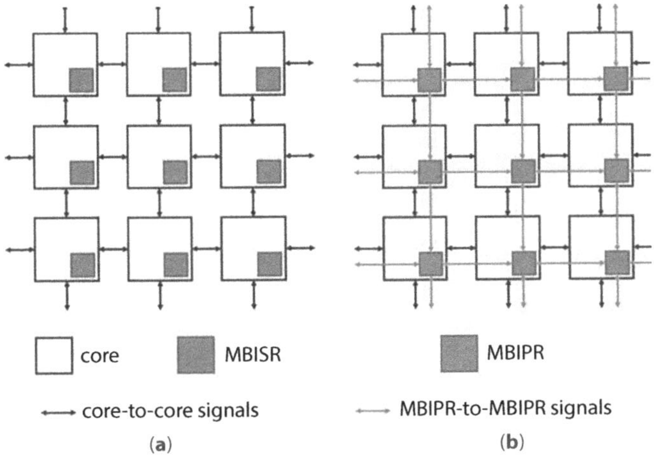

Figure 7.4 Mesh processor array with (a) MBISR and (b) MBIPR [2].

2.1-8.1× when compared to MBISR, with just a 0.2-0.9% increase in area overhead.

A. MBIPR Features

The huge embedded memory of the mesh-connected processor array that need redundancy restoration are the focus of the proposed MBIPR. Figure 7.5 illustrates how the standard and MBISR and the mesh processor array's suggested MBIPR. The MBISRs or MBIPRs for memory testing and repair are located in the processor cores, as seen in the figure. Although the CPU cores use the MBISR architecture, each MBISR in the processor cores solely tests and fixes its own memory. On the other hand, when the processor cores the MBISR scheme, the MBIPRs can not only perform the same functionality as the MBISR, but also be able to repair the memories of the neighbouring processor cores. In other words, the standard MBISR performs only the self-repair, while the proposed MBIPR performs both the self-repair and the peer repair. Although the MBIPR circuit results in a little delay, power, and area overhead, this scheme offers higher repair rate, lifetime, and spare utilization compared to the standard MBISR scheme [2].

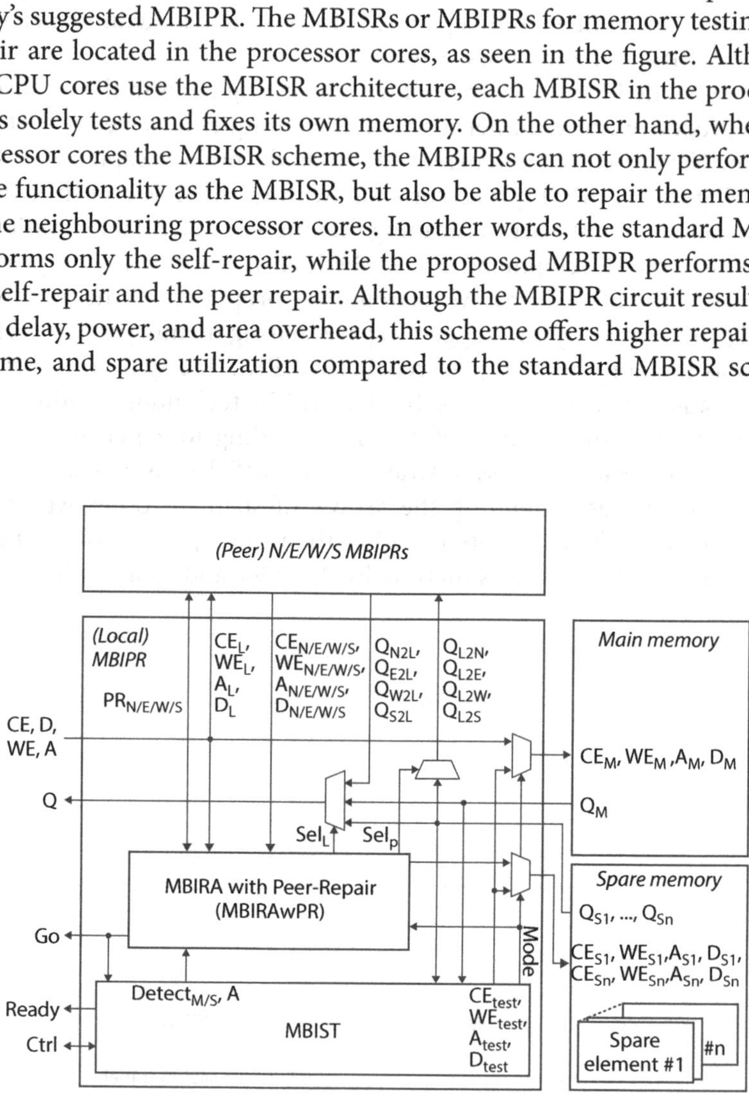

Figure 7.5 The proposed MBIPR architecture [2].

B. MBIPR Architecture

The suggested MBIPR design, depicted in Figure 7.5, consists of a memory built-in self-test (MBIST) and a Peer-repair memory built-in redundancy analyzer (MBIRAWPR). The MBIRAWPR design is adapted from the MBIRA design, which employs a flexible spare mapping scheme and the essential spare pivoting (ESP) algorithm for redundancy analysis. The MBIST manages the entire testing process and runs March-CW on both the spare and main memory. During testing, the MBIST sends the MBIRAWPR the fault information and uses the Mode signal to set the MBIPR to either the test mode or the normal mode. The spare allocation is handled by the MBIRAWPR in the testing mode, while in the normal mode, it acts as the remapping unit address. The MBIRAWPR manages the input and output select multiplexers and interacts with other linked MBIPRs [2]. Based on the address remapping registers, the MBIRAWPR chooses which peer MBIPRs have access to the spare memory. The MBIPR data output to the peer MBIPRs and the local host is likewise determined by the MBIRAWPR.

C. MBIPR Operation Mode

The MBIPR's flow diagram in test mode is displayed in Figure 7.6. The Ctrl signals first launch the MBIST, which then checks the local spare memory to make sure no defective spare is being used. Secondly, the main memory is tested by the MBIST. The MBIRAWPR assigns a local spare for repair if a defect is found and one is available. The local MBIRAWPR uses PRN/E/W/S signals to ask the peer MBIRAWPRs for the spare element in the event that a defect is found and the local spare is unavailable. After receiving the peer spares' availability, the local MBIRAWPR distributes them based on priority, which is east (E), south (S), west (W), and north (N). Nevertheless, the Go signal is de-asserted to stop the MBIST when no local or peer spare is available to fix the issue. Ultimately, following the test, the Ready and Go Signals are asserted [2]. Both the local host and the peer MBIPRs may perform the read and write operations in Normal Mode. Local-operations and peer-operations are the terms used to describe the operations from the local host and peer MBIPRs, respectively. The main memory, MBIRAWPR, and the peer MBIPRs receive the local operations—CE, WE, A, and D—directly. In accordance with the address remapping register, the MBIRAWPR executes the local operation on the local spare memory if the address is self-repaired. According to its address remapping register, one of the peer MBIPRs does the operation on its spare memory if the address is peer-repaired. The MBIRAWPR chooses the data output, or Q, from the main memory, the local spare memory, and the peer spare

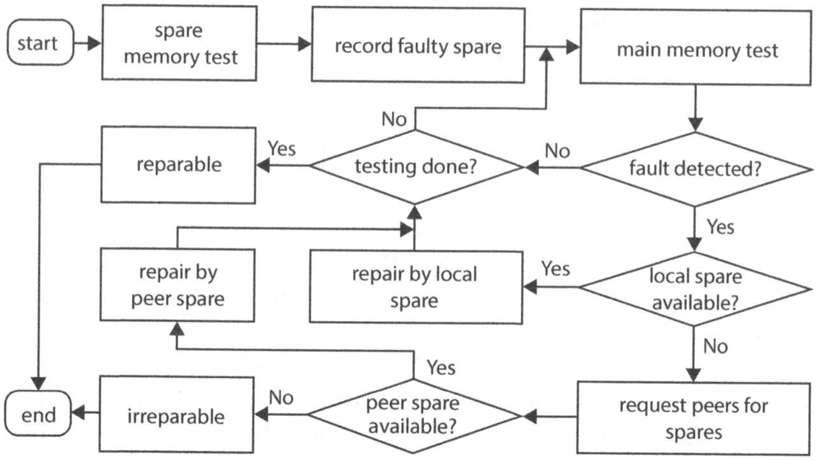

Figure 7.6 Flow diagram of the MBIPR in the test mode [2].

memory if the local operation is a read operation. However, in the case of a peer-operation, the signals—that is, CEN/E/S/W, WEN/E/S/W, AN/E/S/W, and DN/E/S/W—are transmitted straight to the MBIRAWPR. In the event that the local spare memory fixes this peer address, the MBIRAWPR uses the address remapping register to carry out the peer-operation on the local spare memory. If the peer- operation is a read operation, the MBIRAWPR selects the local-to-peer data output, i.e., QL2N/E/W/S, among the spare elements according to the last peer-operation [2]. With this technique, the MBIPR can process up to five operations concurrently, comprising four peer operations and one local operation. In order to divide the spare memory into several concurrent spare elements and execute five operations at once. This allows for the simultaneous execution of each operation on various spare elements. This concurrent spare memory architecture maintains memory speed with negligible area overhead by keeping the process in a single cycle.

7.4 High Speed Interconnects

1. Introduction

VLSI interconnects are now one of the most important considerations in a system's overall design due to the quick rise in operating frequency in today's electronic systems, including computers and digital communication systems. Signal delay and crosstalk are examples of signal integrity degradations caused by poorly constructed interconnects. and ground noise, which restricts the system's overall functionality. Simultaneous optimization of several signal performances can become quite complex for practical circuit boards with a lot of interconnects and different design objectives. The necessity of using the signal integrity criterion directly in the optimization of connection design is growing. Straight use of conventional circuit optimization approaches will not always be suitable due to several difficulties encountered in signal integrity–oriented design, e.g., large-scale optimization by nature, highly repetitive simulation of distributed transmission line models or even EM models. The hierarchical nature of signal integrity at chip, multichip module (MCM), printed circuit board (PCB) levels also possess challenges. In addition, electrical design is now more and more constrained by other design factors such as thermal and Electromagnetic (EM) effects, both of which are becoming important considerations in an overall design. In recent years, research into the interconnect optimization problem has been very active, and several important progresses have been made.

2. Interconnect Models

A signal that can be represented by lumped linear or nonlinear components is delivered from a driver to a receiver *via* a VLSI connection. Various interconnect models have been employed. Chip level interconnects are frequently modelled using the first kind, known as a lumped model, such as a cascaded RC network. The next one is the distributed model [U], which is defined as a lossy coupled multiconductor transmission line with cross-sectional unit length RLCG characteristics and characterized by the Telegrapher equation [U]. This type of approach works well for interconnects at the board or multichip module level [3]. The final kind is the full wave 2D or 3D model, which can handle electromagnetic effects at extremely high frequencies. In the literature, optimization has been done using both lumped and distributed models. Optimization with full wave effects remains a future task.

3. Signal Integrity Oriented Optimization

The performance of transient responses, including delay, rise/fall times, crosstalk, and reflection, can be used to do a direct signal integrity-oriented optimization in the time-domain using error functions. As an alternative, the optimization might be carried out in the frequency domain indirectly. Various goals have been employed. Signal propagation delay information is contained in group delay. By decreasing the group the transient signal delay, crosstalk, and signal distortions are indirectly adjusted by increasing the flatness of the group delay and gain slope responses, as well as the delay and spectrum of cross talks. Using the lumped connection model, Elmore delay is utilized as a rough indicator of delay reduction at the chip level. Higher order moments can be applied generally. The signal behaviour of distributed transmission lines is characterized in moments up to third order so that frequency domain optimization can be developed without the need for time domain simulations [3]. Any network of multiconductor transmission lines that is substituted with a single equivalent impedance undergoes indirect optimization through electrical balancing. Other kinds of goals, such as power dissipation, wiring area, and ground noise, have also been employed. Since all of these characteristics affect interconnect performance, optimization variables include those in the interconnections and/or their terminations. There are two different kinds of variables for connection parameters. One is the interconnects' geometrical and physical parameters, which are frequently employed for optimization. The other category consists of the analogous electrical model parameters, such as the widely used RLCG parameters for simulation. Interconnects' equivalent impedance, which was considered an optimization variable in, is another illustration of an electrical parameter. It may not be an easy task to translate the optimum equivalent electrical parameters into workable physical or geometrical parameters. Design rules must apply to design variables. The design profile should guide the application of simple lower and upper constraints on variables.

Numerous optimization objective formulations, such as optimization and minimax, have been employed. The Quasi-Newton approach for a linearly restricted nonlinear programming issue, Newton-Raphson search, and analytical solution are some of the methods used to tackle the nonlinear minimax interconnect optimization problems. To concurrently handle several error functions for delay, crosstalk, and reflections at different network output ports, a two-stage minimax algorithm was employed. The technique combines the speed of the Quasi-Newton method with the robustness of a Gauss-Newton type first-order method. Techniques for sensitivity analysis have been developed for the use of gradient-based interconnect optimization, such as for linear and nonlinear networks [3].

4. Advanced Optimization Techniques

Several interconnects and design-required specifications/constraints at several connectivity ports are common features of a realistic printed circuit board. The entire computation takes a long time since optimization requires repetitive interconnect simulations using lossy coupled transmission line models consuming. Exploiting parallel processing is one way to speed up simulation for use in either frequency- or time-domain-based interrupt optimization. Signal waveforms are simulated using parallel simulation and a particular simulation method based on the numerical inversion of Laplace transform (NILT). A multilayer strategy was created that makes use of both optimization and network topological breakdown. Parallel processing is used to address a group of independent suboptimization problems that are produced by rephrasing the overall optimization. A model coordinating approach is used to coordinate the suboptimizations. The aforementioned formulation works well with VLSI systems, such as several MCMs on a PCB. A number of MCMs are optimized at the low level, while the PCB interconnect circuitry is improved at the high level. The macro modelling based on the Pade approximation, which is used to simulate the frequency response of a linear subnetwork, such as the transfer function with respect to frequency, is a new advancement in the modelling of massive interconnect networks [3]. Neural network-based connection optimization represents another recent advancement in this field. Within the optimization cycle, neural network models can be applied to the interconnect problem at three different levels: the physical/EM level, where the geometrical parameters of the interconnects are mapped to equivalent electrical parameters; the device level, where neural networks model the device; and the circuit level, where a neural network model replaces the entire circuit. The capacity of computer-aided design tools to capture different elements during the design stage becomes crucial given the industry desire for innovative goods to have shorter time to market. Statistical analysis and interconnect optimization are two examples of how to take into account tolerances in VLSI interconnects and material qualities that cause fluctuations in essential interconnect performances, which can ultimately lead to a lower manufacturing yield. Another example is multidisciplinary optimization which optimizes the physical partitioning and placement of packages on MCM's or PCB's, taking into account the thermal and electrical performance as well as the manufacturability of the design.

7.5 Power Optimization

Power optimization is an essential part of VLSI design since it affects the integrated circuit's performance and efficiency. Power consumption is an important consideration in VLSI design since it affects electronic device operating costs, battery life, and environmental impact. Most recent studies focus on lab experiments or simulations, which may not accurately represent the challenges and constraints of real-world IoT deployments.

Future research may employ extensive field testing of IoT devices utilizing a range of power management strategies to provide a more precise evaluation of their viability and effectiveness. This review of the literature lays the groundwork for future studies on power optimization in VLSI circuits. Because power optimization impacts the integrated circuit's overall performance and efficiency, it is a crucial component of VLSI design. Because power consumption affects electronic devices' running costs, battery life, and environmental effect, it is a crucial factor in VLSI design. In VLSI design, there are several methods for power optimization. Among the methods that are frequently employed are the following:

Voltage scaling: Power consumption can be decreased by lowering the integrated circuit's supply voltage. Nevertheless, lowering the supply voltage also lowers the circuit's performance. Therefore, voltage scaling is utilized to determine the ideal voltage that strikes a balance between performance and power consumption.

Clock gating: This approach turns off the clock signal to circuit segments that are not in use. Power consumption can be decreased by cutting the clock signal to the circuit's inactive components. Power gating: This technique cuts off power to circuit components that are not in use.

Power consumption can be decreased by cutting the power to circuit components that are not in use. There are several low power design strategies that can be applied, including utilizing asynchronous design methodologies, designing the circuit with low-leakage transistors, and reducing the circuit's switching activity [4]. Dynamic voltage and frequency scaling (DVFS) is a method that modifies the integrated circuit's supply voltage and clock frequency in response to workload. Power consumption can be decreased by raising the voltage and frequency when the workload is high and decreasing them when the workload is low. These are but a handful of the power optimization strategies applied in VLSI design.

Innovative approaches to power management in IoT applications: Research papers and industry have suggested a number of creative methods for power management in Internet of Things applications. Here are a few instances [4].

A) Energy Harvesting

Energy harvesting is a technique that turns ambient energy sources like thermal, kinetic, and solar energy into electrical power. This can lessen the need for batteries or mains power, which makes it an affordable and environmentally friendly option for Internet of Things devices.

B) Dynamic Voltage and Frequency Scaling (DVFS)
A technology called DVFS enables a processor's operating voltage and frequency to be dynamically changed in response to workload. During times of low workload, energy consumption can be decreased without sacrificing performance by lowering the operating frequency and voltage.

C) Sleep Modes
It is possible to design Internet of Things devices to switch to low power sleep modes when not in use. This can drastically cut down on power usage when the device is inactive while still enabling fast wake-up and restart times.

D) Duty Cycling
Duty cycling is the process of intermittently shutting off the sensor or radio of the device when it is idle. This can extend the device's battery life and drastically lower energy consumption.

E) Edge Computing
Instead of transferring data to the cloud for processing, edge computing processes it locally on the Internet of Things device or on a nearby edge server. Lowering the volume of data transmitted to the cloud can decrease latency and save energy consumption.

7.6 Scalability

The technique of integrating dozens to millions of transistors on a single chip is known as "very large-scale integration" (VLSI). VLSI technology is essential for scaling AI hardware because it provides a number of benefits that have a direct impact on the computational capacity, power efficiency, and performance of AI models [5].

High Computational Throughput: AI workloads necessitate enormous volumes of concurrent computations, particularly in deep learning. The efficiency of AI training and inference is increased by the construction of specialized AI accelerators made possible by VLSI, such as TPUs (Tensor Processing Units) and GPUs (Graphics Processing Units), which are optimized for matrix multiplications and vector operations.

Power Efficiency: In order to execute billions of operations per second, AI models require more energy as they get larger. Energy consumption can be decreased by integrating power- efficient architectures made possible by VLSI technology [5]. To make sure the system can grow without experiencing exponentially higher power requirements, strategies including dynamic power management, voltage scaling, and low-power design are employed.
Memory Scalability: In order to store and retrieve data for calculations, AI applications frequently require quick and extensive memory access. By facilitating the integration of interfaces between off-chip memory (like DRAM) and on-chip memory (like SRAM), VLSI lowers latency and speeds up data processing. For applications like autonomous driving and real-time image processing, this is essential. Hardware customization for AI applications is made possible by the trend toward Application-Specific Integrated Circuits (ASICs), which are created using VLSI. Compared to general-purpose processors, ASICs are tuned for certain tasks, such neural network processing, allowing for faster and more effective AI solutions.
Heterogeneous Architectures and 3D Integration: VLSI makes it possible for 3D integration, which involves stacking several chip layers vertically to boost the density of transistors and interconnects. As a result, AI hardware operates better and takes up less space. Furthermore, integrating many processor types—such as CPUs, GPUs, and FPGAs—into a single VLSI system offers versatility in handling a range of AI tasks, enabling more adaptable and scalable systems [5].
Thermal Management: As more transistors are packed into a device, controlling heat is crucial to guaranteeing reliable operation. Interconnect bottlenecks, In order to scale up, processing components must be effectively connected; otherwise, data transmission delays may limit performance.
Design Complexity: Chip design and manufacture get more difficult as the VLSI process grows, necessitating the use of increasingly advanced tools and testing and verification methods.

In conclusion, VLSI is crucial to meeting AI's computing requirements. Advances in VLSI technology will be essential to guaranteeing scalable, effective, and potent AI solutions as AI systems continue to develop [5].

7.7 Key Components of VLSI Design for AI

VLSI (Very Large-Scale Integration) design for AI (Artificial Intelligence) involves several key components and considerations to effectively implement AI algorithms and models in hardware [1]. Here are some of the critical components:

Architecture Design:
Custom Architectures: Designing specialized architectures (e.g., ASICs, FPGAs) tailored for specific AI tasks like neural networks, convolutional operations, etc.
Parallel Processing: Utilizing parallel processing capabilities to handle the massive data and computation requirements of AI algorithms.

Data Flow Management:
Memory Hierarchy: Efficient memory management, including on-chip memory, cache, and off-chip memory, to minimize latency and maximize bandwidth.

Power Efficiency:
Low-Power Design Techniques: Implementing techniques such as dynamic voltage and frequency scaling (DVFS), power gating, and clock gating to reduce power consumption.
Energy-Efficient Architectures: Designing architectures that balance performance and power efficiency, crucial for mobile and edge AI applications.

Hardware Acceleration:
Dedicated AI Accelerators: Creating dedicated hardware accelerators (e.g., TPUs, GPUs) that can perform AI computations more efficiently than general-purpose processors.
Neural Network Processors: Designing processors specifically optimized for neural network computations, including support for operations like matrix multiplications and activation functions.

7.7.1 Field Programmable Gate Array (FPGA)

An FPGA is a programmable integrated circuit that may be set up to carry out various circuit operations repeatedly. Unlike processors, which have a set design, Digital signal processors (DSPs), configurable logic blocks (CLBs), I/O pads, on-chip block RAMs (BRAMs), and routing channels are the components that make up an FPGA, as illustrated in Figure 7.7. You can configure your data tracks in FPGA so that pixels move straight between external memory and compute units without the need for any intermediate stages. Additionally, by storing pixels on the chip, distributed BRAMs can be used to leverage data locality in vision kernels. The

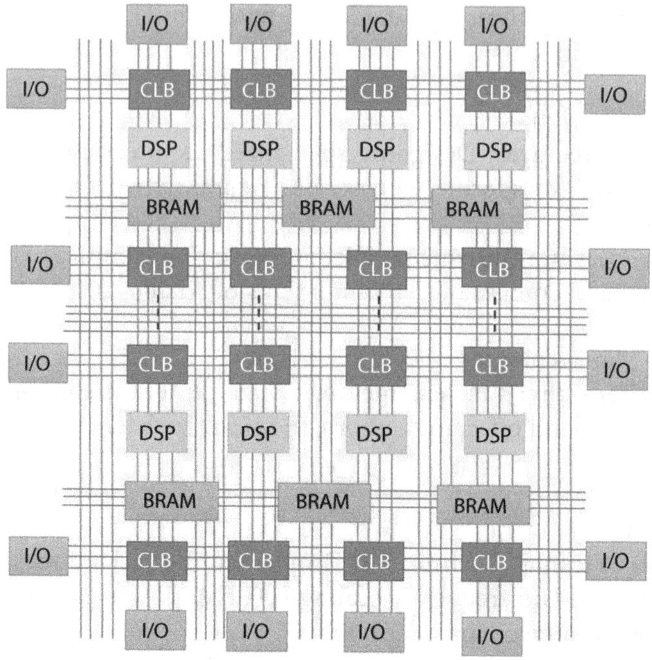

Figure 7.7 FPGA architecture block diagram [1].

hardware of FPGA can be restructured by programmers to take on any desired shape. FPGA is superior to GPU because of its fine-grained parallel architecture [1]. The designer can reduce memory reading delays by optimizing the output mode to limit the requirement for data storage in main memory after the computation clock cycle time has been determined. Programming FPGAs is powerful, and they offer strong reconfigurability and dynamic algorithm reconfiguration. Additionally, FPGA operates better with the same amount of power and consumes far less than GPU, which might greatly aid in the processor's heat removal issue [1].

7.7.2 Application-Specific Integrated Circuit (ASIC)

Whereas a CPU is a general-purpose processor, an ASIC is another kind of integrated circuit that is made to carry out particular functions. While a GPU is still a massively parallel processor with thousands of processing units that can run different algorithms, an ASIC is a processor designed to do a relatively small set of computations, making it more specialized than a GPU [48]. Unlike FPGA, ASIC cannot be reprogrammed to perform a different function once it is needed. Although its logic has been fixed since

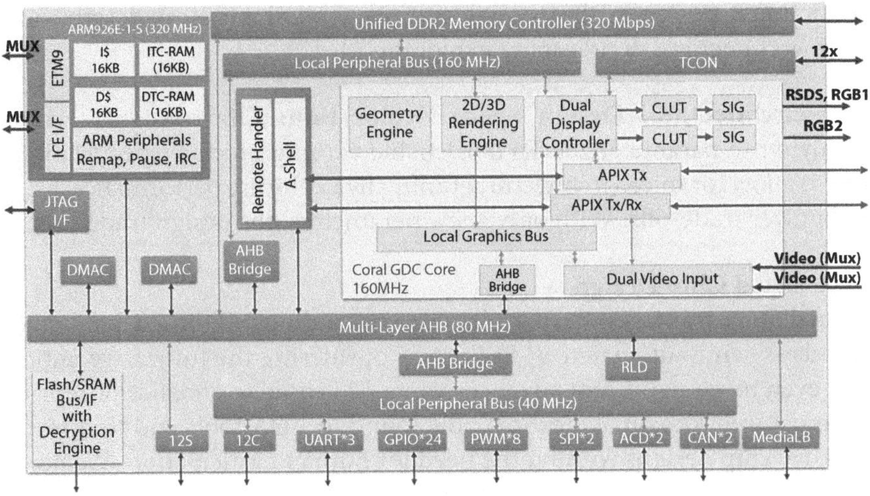

Figure 7.8 ASIC block diagram [1].

it was created, you can create a different design on FPGA that better suits your requirements. Because of this specialization, ASICs are typically far more energy efficient [1]. Figure 7.8 shows ASIC block diagram.

7.8 Accelerating Chip Design Using ML

ML-Based Predictors for Chip Design: The process of designing a semiconductor from specification to layout is usually iterative. Dozens of components make up large, intricate SoCs. Every unit moves through floorplanning, placement, clock tree synthesis (CTS), routing, logic synthesis, timing analysis, power analysis, microarchitecture, RTL design and verification, and final signoff. Typically, design teams work on these flow phases in parallel, running each step in a pipelined fashion on a separate chip revision. Nevertheless, preparing a chip for tapeout requires numerous iterations. Every pipeline stage can often take days of human labour, even with the help of EDA tools. Complete iterations of an RTL-to-layout sequence can take weeks or months for sophisticated semiconductors.

By forecasting downstream outcomes in a chip design cycle, trained machine learning models can assist speed up time to tapeout. This can lower time per iteration or enhance the quality of results (QoR), such as area, power, or performance. Predictions can be given in a matter of seconds as opposed to hours or days. We point up four applications for predictions: power analysis, analog design, VLSI physical design, and microarchitectural design space exploration [6].

Microarchitectural Design Space Exploration: Chip designers commonly write parameterized RTL to enable varying product specifications and to allow for microarchitectural tuning by exploring performance, area, and power trade-offs. With only a few parameters, the design trade-offs.

AI Assisted Chip Design

Immediate advantages can be obtained by adding ML-based predictors to today's semi-automated VLSI flows. Considering the future, we anticipate even more significant advances when AI is used to enhance or replace the most well-known algorithms now found in EDA tools and to directly improve chip designs without the need for human participation. We point up a number of exciting avenues for further study in these fields. In a baseline physical design pipeline, one of the main challenges is that the backend VLSI tools—routing, CTS, and placement—must create final designs with precise timing and design rules using highly advanced current process technologies. They thus function as intricate and sluggish black boxes that process synthesized netlists before routing designs are finalized. Because of time and license limitations, the tools give the designer little control or observability and little room for experimenting. However, the designer's carefully created physical limits to the backend flow also have a significant impact on the likelihood of success with strong QoR [6].

In order to solve this, we foresee a physical design cycle driven by AI (see Figure 7.4) that smartly investigates the design universe of possible physical floorplans, time, and tool placements and limitations.

This flow can avoid expensive iterations using downstream black-box tools by utilizing fast GPU-accelerated placers and DL-based deep QoR predictors, allowing for millions of quick iterations within the AI-driven loop. The AI-driven flow can swiftly and automatically identify standard cell placements, timing constraints, and high-quality floorplans that can produce strong downstream QoR by operating inside a DRL optimization loop [6]. Those candidate placements are then sent to the downstream CTS and routing phases. Three essential technologies make this flow possible: 1) DRL for optimizing physical constraints; 2) quick VLSI placers operating on GPUs and other accelerated computing platforms; and 3) DL-based deep QoR predictors for postplacement outcome classification.

The potential of AI in chip design flows across a range of tools has been demonstrated by preliminary research using ML predictors for VLSI. In the future, we anticipate that ML-based techniques like DRL will be appropriate for a wide range of EDA optimization issues, particularly those where it is challenging to represent the precise objective or constraints. Like simulated annealing, genetic algorithms, and linear/nonlinear programming, DRL may develop into a new general-purpose algorithm for EDA. We anticipate a positive feedback loop whereby the most potent computers in the world are used to design the newest semiconductors, which will enhance the performance of next EDA methods, since DL models are tuned to operate effectively on accelerated computing systems like GPUs [6].

7.9 Future Trends in VLSI Design for AI

We will examine the fascinating upcoming developments in VLSI Design for AI in this section. New possibilities that will influence the field of AI chip design are developing as a result of the rapid advancement of technology. Let us examine a few of these trends and how they might affect semiconductor technology [7].

1. Quantum Computing
AI chip design has a lot of potential thanks to quantum computing. Quantum computers have the potential to transform machine learning algorithms and speed up AI applications because of their unparalleled speed at which they can do complex calculations. VLSI designers are able to achieve unprecedented processing speed and efficiency by utilizing the capabilities of quantum computers.

2. Neuromorphic Engineering
The goal of the developing discipline of neuromorphic engineering is to develop AI processors that are inspired by the workings of the human brain. Neuromorphic devices can improve the performance and energy efficiency of AI applications by simulating the architecture and operation of neural networks. The development of hardware with real-time learning and adaptation capabilities is made possible by this trend in VLSI Design for AI [7].

3. Energy-Efficient Designs
With the increasing prevalence of AI applications, energy-efficient chip architectures are critical. In order to satisfy the increasing need for AI capabilities without sacrificing performance, VLSI designers are concentrating on creating power-efficient architectures and circuits. These designs can extend battery life and lessen the environmental effect of AI gadgets by maximizing power consumption and limiting heat dissipation.

4. Customization and Specialization

It is anticipated that custom chip design would be essential to VLSI design for AI in the future. The need for specialized hardware accelerators will grow as AI applications become more varied and intricate. Improved performance and efficiency can be achieved by using custom-designed chips to deliver customized VLSI Design for AI and Machine Learning solutions for certain AI tasks [7]. This pattern emphasizes how crucial it is for VLSI designers and AI application developers to work together to provide hardware-software systems that are optimal.

5. System-Level Integration

Another significant development in VLSI Design for AI is system-level integration. The need to combine several processors and subsystems into a unified and effective architecture is growing as AI systems become more complicated. VLSI designers can improve the overall performance of AI systems by minimizing latency and maximizing data flow through the optimization of interconnects, communication protocols, and memory hierarchies. Future developments in semiconductor technology and the creation of more potent and effective AI processors are anticipated as a result of these trends in VLSI Design for AI. The cooperation of VLSI designers, AI researchers, and industry professionals will be essential to advancing this subject as research and innovation continue to push the limits of what is feasible in AI [7].

A VLSI design expert states, "The future of VLSI Design for AI holds immense potential, from quantum computing to neuromorphic engineering. These emerging trends will shape the way we design AI chips and pave the way for unprecedented advancements in semiconductor technology."

Trend	Description
Quantum Computing	Utilizing quantum processors for accelerated AI algorithms and computations.
Neuromorphic Engineering	Creating AI chips inspired by structure and functionality of neural networks.
Energy-Efficient Designs	Developing power-efficient architectures and circuits for sustainable AI applications.
Customization and Specialization	Designing custom chips for optimized performance in specific AI tasks.
System-Level Integration	Integrating multiple chips and subsystems for seamless AI system performance.

7.10 Industrial Application of VLSI Design

AI Design for Industrial Uses with VLSI Artificial Intelligence (AI) is a key component of many industries, including manufacturing, healthcare, autonomous vehicles, and consumer electronics, in today's world of rapid digitization. Custom AI chips with high computational throughput, energy efficiency, and real-time data processing capabilities are designed using VLSI (Very Large-Scale Integration) technology to satisfy the particular performance and efficiency requirements of these applications. Millions of transistors can be integrated onto a single chip thanks to VLSI, which makes it easier to create AI accelerators, FPGAs (Field- Programmable Gate Arrays), and Application-Specific Integrated Circuits (ASICs).

1. **Automation and Manufacturing Robotics and Automation Systems:** Smart manufacturing systems are made possible by AI-powered robots, which are essential to contemporary industrial automation. The processing power needed for precise control and real-time decision-making in robotic systems is provided by VLSI-designed AI hardware. Industrial robots with AI accelerators built in enable high-speed image processing, sensor data analysis, and control algorithms that boost productivity and lower operating expenses. For instance, collaborative robots safely work alongside human operators to complete tasks like welding, painting, and assembly on production lines using VLSI-based AI chips. Predictive maintenance is made possible by AI systems built with VLSI technology, which can process machine sensor data in real time to forecast when equipment will break. By guaranteeing that maintenance is carried out only when necessary, downtime is minimized and operations are improved.
2. **Medical Equipment and Healthcare Medical Imaging:** To process high-resolution images and spot patterns suggestive of illnesses, AI-based diagnostic tools like those used for MRIs, CT scans, and X-rays need a lot of processing power. These procedures are sped up by VLSI-based AI chips, which enable physicians to diagnose patients more quickly and precisely. For instance, real-time medical image analysis by AI systems built with VLSI technology can identify early indicators of neurological disorders, cardiovascular diseases, or cancer. Wearable Health Devices: AI algorithms are

used by wearables, like fitness trackers and smartwatches, to track vital signs like blood pressure, heart rate, and activity levels. These devices can process health data in real time and run effectively on battery power for extended periods of time thanks to VLSI-based low-power AI chips. An example is **Apple's S-series processors**, designed using VLSI, which integrate AI capabilities for health monitoring, enabling features like ECG tracking and irregular heartbeat detection [8].

3. **Smart Grids and Energy Smart Grids:** By enabling smart grid systems that can effectively integrate renewable energy sources, optimize distribution, and forecast energy demand, artificial intelligence is revolutionizing the energy sector. Smart meters and energy management systems contain VLSI-based AI chips that process sensor data and make decisions in real time to balance supply and demand. For instance, VLSI- designed AI-powered energy management systems optimize electricity distribution, cut waste, and forecast power consumption trends, all of which increase grid efficiency. Renewable Energy Management: AI systems that use VLSI technology are also used in wind and solar power plants, among other renewable energy sources, to optimize energy storage systems and forecast energy production based on weather conditions. For instance, AI models operating on VLSI-based edge devices forecast solar power production and maximize energy storage system charging and discharging in solar power plants.
4. **Defense and Aerospace:**
   Autonomous Drones and UAVs: Artificial Intelligence (AI) is essential for managing drones and unmanned aerial vehicles (UAVs) for commercial, military, and surveillance uses. These autonomous systems are powered by VLSI-designed AI chips that minimize power consumption to increase flight durations while enabling real-time object detection, navigation, and decision-making. Drones with AI capabilities for surveillance purposes, for instance AI processors based on VLSI, can autonomously navigate complex environments, analyze live video streams, and identify threats. Defense Systems: AI applications for defense VLSI-based processors to support threat detection systems, autonomous weapon systems, and military equipment predictive

maintenance. These systems' high performance and low power consumption in harsh environments are guaranteed by VLSI technology.

5. **Smart Sensors and IoT for Precision Agriculture:**
   Soil Moisture Sensors: To enable real-time soil water level monitoring, VLSI chips can be integrated into soil moisture sensors. This enhances crop yields, minimizes water waste, and optimizes irrigation. Nutrient Monitoring: By analyzing the nutrient level of the soil, integrated circuits can tell farmers when and where to apply fertilizer. Temperature, humidity, and CO2 levels can all affect crop development, and VLSI can be utilized in environmental monitoring devices to measure these variables.

References

1. Mohaidat, T. and Khalil, K., A Survey on Neural Network Hardware Accelerators in. *IEEE Trans. Artif. Intell.*, 5, 8, 3801–3822, Aug. 2024. Doi: 10.1109/TAI.2024.3377147.
2. Tan, P.-Y., Tung, C.-H., Wu, C.-W., Lee, M., Liao, G., A Memory Built-In Peer-Repair Architecture for Mesh-Connected Processor Array, in: *2022 International Symposium on VLSI Design, Automation and Test (VLSI-DAT)*, Hsinchu, Taiwan, pp. 1–4, 2022, Doi: 10.1109/VLSI-DAT54769.2022.9768060.
3. Kumbhare, V.R., High-Speed Interconnects: History, Evolution, and the Road Ahead. *IEEE Microwave Mag.*, 23, 8, 66–82, Aug. 2022. doi: 10.1109/MMM.2021.3136268.
4. Zhao, P., Wang, Z., Hang, G., Power optimization for VLSI circuits and systems, in: *2010 10th IEEE International Conference on Solid-State and Integrated Circuit.*
5. Luke, E.A., Defining and measuring scalability, in: *Proceedings of Scalable Parallel Libraries Conference*, Mississippi State, MS, USA, pp. 183–186, 1993, doi: 10.1109/SPLC.1993.365568.
6. Khailany, B., Accelerating Chip Design with Machine Learning. *IEEE Micro*, 40, 6, 23–32, 1 Nov.-Dec. 2020. doi: 10.1109/MM.2020.3026231.
7. Sasaki, H., The future trend of VLSI technology and business, in: *1998 3rd International Symposium on Plasma Process-Induced Damage (Cat. No.98EX100)*, Honolulu, HI, USA, pp. 1–6, 1998, doi: 10.1109/PPID.1998.725560.
8. Bhardwaj, A., Kumar, P., Raj, B., Anand, S., Design and Performance Optimization of doping-less Vertical Nanowire TFET using Gate Stack Technique. *J. Electron. Mater. (JEMS)*, 41, 7, 4005–4013, Springer, 2022.

9. Singh, J. and Raj, B., Tunnel Current Model of Asymmetric MIM Structure Levying Various Image Forces to Analyze the Characteristics of Filamentary Memristor. *Appl. Phys. A*, 125, 3, 203.1–203.11, Springer, Feb 2019.
10. Goyal, C., Ubhi, J.S., Raj, B., Low Leakage Zero Ground Noise Nanoscale Full Adder using Source Biasing Technique. *J. Nanoelectron. Optoelectron.*, 14, 360–370, American Scientific Publishers, March 2019.
11. Singh, G., Sarin, R.K., Raj, B., A Novel Robust Exclusive-OR Function Implementation in QCA Nanotechnology with Energy Dissipation Analysis. *J. Comput. Electron.*, 15, 2, 455–465, Springer, June 2016.
12. Wadhwa, G., Kamboj, P., Raj, B., Design optimisation of junctionless TFET biosensor for high sensitivity. *Adv. Nat. Sci.: Nanosci. Nanotechnol.*, 10, 045001 (7), 2019.
13. Bansal, P. and Raj, B., Memristor Modeling and Analysis for Linear Dopant Drift Kinetics. *J. Nanoeng. Nanomanuf.*, 6, 1–7, American Scientific Publishers, 2016.
14. Ashima, Vaithiyanathan, D., Raj, B., Performance Analysis of Charge Plasma induced Graded Channel Si nanotube. *J. Eng. Res. (JER)*, EMSME Special Issue, 146–154, Aug 2021.
15. Tomar, A.S., Magraiya, V.K., Raj, B., Scaling of Access and Data Transistor for High Performance DRAM Cell Design. *Quantum Matter*, 2, 412–416, Oct. 2013.
16. Jain, N. and Raj, B., Parasitic Capacitance and Resistance Model Development and Optimization of Raised Source/Drain SOI FinFET Structure for Analog Circuit Applications. *J. Nanoelectron. Optoelectronins*, 13, 531–539, ASP, USA, April 2018.
17. Singh, S., Vishvakarma, S.K., Raj, B., Analytical Modeling of Split-Gate Junction-Less Transistor for a Biosensor Application. *Sens. Bio-sensing*, 18, 31–36, Elsevier, April 2018.
18. Gopal, M. and Raj, B., Low Power 8T SRAM Cell Design for High Stability Video Applications. *ITSI Trans. Electr. Electron. Eng.*, 1, 5, 91–97, 2013.
19. Raj, B., Mitra, J., Bihani, D.K., Rangharajan, V., Saxena, A.K., Dasgupta, S., Analysis of Noise Margin, Power and Process Variation for 32 nm FinFET Based 6T SRAM Cell. *J. Comput. (JCP)*, 5, 6, 1–8, Academy Publisher, Finland, 2010.
20. Jain, N. and Raj, B., Dual-k Spacer Region Variation at the Drain Side of Asymmetric SOI FinFET Structure: Performance Analysis towards the Analog/RF Design Applications. *J. Nanoelectron. Optoelectron.*, 14, 349–359, American Scientific Publishers, March 2019.
21. Singh, J., Sharma, S., Raj, B., Khosla, M., Analysis of barrier layer thickness on performance of In1-xGaxAs based Gate Stack Cylindrical Gate Nanowire MOSFET. *JNO*, 13, 1473–1477, ASP, Oct 2018.
22. Jain, N. and Raj, B., Analysis and Performance Exploration of High-k SOI FinFETs Over the Conventional Low-k SOI FinFET toward Analog/RF Design. *J. Semicond. (JoS)*, 39, 12, 124002-1-7, IOP Science, Dec 2018.

23. Goyal, C., Ubhi, J.S., Raj, B., A reliable leakage reduction technique for approximate full adder with reduced ground bounce noise. *J. Math. Probl. Eng. Hindawi*, 2018, Article ID 3501041, 16, 15, Oct 2018.
24. Anuradha, J.S., Raj, B., Khosla, M., Design and Performance Analysis of Nano-scale Memristor-based Nonvolatile SRAM. *J. Sens. Letter*, 16, 798–805, American Scientific Publishers, Oct 2018.
25. Wadhwa, G. and Raj, B., Parametric Variation Analysis of Charge-Plasma-based Dielectric Modulated JLTFET for Biosensor Application. *IEEE Sens. J.*, 18, 15, 6070–6077, (SCI), August 1, 2018.
26. Singh, J. and Raj, B., Comparative Analysis of Memristor Models for Memories Design. *JoS*, 39, 7, 074006-1-12, IoP, July 2018.
27. Yadav, D., Chouhan, S.S., Vishvakarma, S.K., Raj, B., Application Specific Microcontroller Design for IoT based WSN. *Sens. Letter*, 16, 374–385, ASP, May 2018.
28. Singh, G., Sarin, R.K., Raj, B., Fault-Tolerant Design and Analysis of Quantum-Dot Cellular Automata Based Circuits. *IEEE/IET Circuits Devices Syst.*, 12, 638–64, 2018.
29. Singh, J. and Raj, B., Modeling of Mean Barrier Height Levying Various Image Forces of Metal Insulator Metal Structure to Enhance the Performance of Conductive Filament Based Memristor Model. *IEEE Nanotechnol.*, 17, 2, 268–267, March 2018.
30. Jain, A., Sharma, S., Raj, B., Analysis of Triple Metal Surrounding Gate (TM-SG) III-V Nanowire MOSFET for Photosensing Application. *Opto-electronics J.*, 26, 2, 141–148, Elsevier, May 2018.
31. Jain, A., Sharma, S., Raj, B., Design and Analysis of High Sensitivity Photosensor Using Cylindrical Surrounding Gate MOSFET for Low Power Sensor Applications. *Eng. Sci. Technol. Int. J.*, 19, 4, 1864–1870, Elsevier's, December 2016.
32. Kumar, G.S., Singh, A., Raj, B., Design and Analysis of Gate All Around CNTFET based SRAM cell Design. *J. Comput. Electron.*, 17, 1, 138–145, Springer, March 2018.
33. Singh, G., Sohi, B.S., Raj, B., Material Properties Analysis of Graphene Base Transistor (GBT) for VLSI Analog Circuits. *Indian J. Pure Appl. Phys. (IJPAP)*, 55, 896–902, Dec 2017.
34. Kumar, S. and Raj, B., Estimation of Stability and Performance metric for Inward Access Transistor based 6T SRAM Cell Design using n-type/p-type DMDG-GDOV TFET. *IEEE VLSI Circuits Syst. Letter*, 3, 2, 25–39, June 2017.
35. Sharma, S., Kumar, A., Pattanaik, M., Raj, B., Forward Body Biased Multimode Multi-Threshold CMOS Technique for Ground Bounce Noise Reduction in Static CMOS Adders. *Int. J. Inf. Electron. Eng.*, 3, 3, 567–572, 2013.
36. Singh, H., Kumar, P., Raj, B., Performance Analysis of Majority Gate SET Based 1-bit Full Adder. *Int. J. Comput. Commun. Eng. (IJCCE)*, 2, 4, ISSN: 2010-3743, IACSIT Press Singapore, 2013.

37. Bhardwaj, A.K., Gupta, S., Raj, B., Investigation of Parameters for Schottky Barrier (SB) Height for Schottky Barrier Based Carbon Nanotube Field Effect Transistor Device. *J. Nanoelectron. Optoelectron.*, 15, 783–791, ASP, July 2020.
38. Bansal, P. and Raj, B., Memristor: A Versatile Nonlinear Model for Dopant Drift and Boundary Issues. *JCTN*, 14, 5, 2319–2325, American Scientific Publishers, May 2017.
39. Jain, N. and Raj, B., An Analog and Digital Design Perspective Comprehensive Approach on Fin-FET (Fin-Field Effect transistor) Technology - A Review. *Rev. Adv. Sci. Eng. (RASE)*, 5, 1–14, ASP, 2016.
40. Raj, B., Saxena, A.K., Dasgupta, S., Analytical Modeling for the Estimation of Leakage Current and Subthreshold Swing Factor of Nanoscale Double Gate FinFET Device. *Microelectron. Int. UK*, 26, 53–63, 2009.
41. Soniya, S.S., Wadhwa, G., Raj, B., An Analytical Modeling for Dual Source Vertical Tunnel Field Effect Transistor. *Int. J. Recent Technol. Eng. (IJRTE)*, 8, 2, 603–608, July 2019.
42. Singh, S. and Raj, B., Design and analysis of hetrojunction Vertical T-shaped Tunnel Field Effect Transistor. *J. Electron. Mater.*, 48, 10, 6253–6260, Springer, October 2019.
43. Goyal, C., Ubhi, J.S., Raj, B., A Low Leakage CNTFET based Inexact Full Adder for Low Power Image Processing Applications. *Int. J. Circuit Theory Appl.*, 47, 9, 1446–1458, Wiley, September 2019.
44. Raj, B., Saxena, A.K., Dasgupta, S., A Compact Drain Current and Threshold Voltage Quantum Mechanical Analytical Modeling for FinFETs. *J. Nanoelectron. Optoelectron. (JNO)*, 3, 2, 163–170, USA, 2008.
45. Wadhwa, G. and Raj, B., An Analytical Modeling of Charge Plasma based Tunnel Field Effect Transistor with Impacts of Gate underlap Region. *Superlattices Microstruct.*, 142, 106512, Elsevier, June 2020.
46. Singh, S. and Raj, B., Modeling and Simulation analysis of SiGe hetrojunction Double GateVertical t-shaped Tunnel FET. *Superlattices Microstruct.*, 142, 106496, Elsevier, June 2020.
47. Jain, N. and Raj, B., Device and Circuit Co-Design Perspective Comprehensive Approach on FinFET Technology - A Review. *J. Electron Devices*, 23, 1, 1890–1901, 2016.
48. Kumar, S. and Raj, B., Analysis of I_{ON} and Ambipolar Current for Dual-Material Gate-drain Overlapped DG-TFET. *J. Nanoelectron. Optoelectron.*, 11, 323–333, American Scientific Publishers, USA, June 2016.
49. Anjum, N., Bali, T., Raj, B., Design and Simulation of Handwritten Multiscript Character Recognition. *Int. J. Adv. Res. Comput. Commun. Eng.*, 2, 7, 2544–2549, July 2013.
50. Singh, K. and Raj, B., Performance and analysis of temperature dependent Multi-walled Carbon Nanotubes as Global Interconnects at different technology nodes. *J. Comput. Electron.*, 14, 2, 469–476, Springer, June 2015.

51. Kumar, S. and Raj, B., Compact channel potential analytical Modeling of DG-TFET based on Evanescent-mode Approach. *J. Comput. Electron.*, 14, 2, 820–827, Springer, July 2015.
52. Singh, K. and Raj, B., Temperature Dependent Modeling and Performance Evaluation of Multi-Walled CNT and Single-Walled CNT as Global Interconnects. *J. Electron. Mater.*, 44, 12, 4825–4835, Springer, Dec 2015.
53. Sharma, V.K., Pattanaik, M., Raj, B., INDEP approach for leakage reduction in nanoscale CMOS circuits. *Int. J. Electron.*, 102, 2, 200–215, Taylor & Francis, 2014.
54. Singh, K. and Raj, B., Influence of Temperature on MWCNT bundle, SWCNT bundle and Copper interconnects for Nanoscaled Technology nodes. *J. Mater. Sci.: Mater. Electron.*, 26, 8, 6134–6142, Springer, 2015.
55. Anjum, N., Bali, T., Raj, B., Design and Simulation of Handwritten Gurumukhi and Devanagri Numerical Recognition. *Int. J. Comput. Appl.*, 73, 12, 16–21, Foundation of Computer Science, New York, USA, 2013.
56. Khandelwal, S., Gupta, V., Raj, B., Gupta, R.D., Process Variability Aware Low Leakage Reliable Nano Scale DG-FinFET SRAM Cell Design Technique. *J. Nanoelectron. Optoelectron.*, 10, 6, 810–817, December 2015.
57. Sharma, V.K., Pattanaik, M., Raj, B., ONOFIC Approach: Low Power High Speed Nanoscale VLSI Circuits Design. *Int. J. Electron.*, 101, 1, 61–73, Taylor & Francis, 2014.
58. Khandelwal, S., Raj, B., Gupta, R.D., FinFET based 6T SRAM Cell Design: Analysis of Performance Metric, Process Variation and Temperature Effect. *J. Comput. Theor. Nanosci.*, 12, 2500–2506, ASP, USA, 2015.
59. Singh, S., Yadav, S., Rahul, J., Srivastava, A., Raj, B., Impact of HfO_2 in Graded Channel Dual Insulator Double Gate MOSFET. *J. Comput. Theor. Nanosci.*, 12, 6, 950–953, American Scientific Publishers, April 2015.
60. Sharma, V.K., Pattanaik, M., Raj, B., PVT variations aware low leakage INDEP approach for nanoscale CMOS Circuits. *Microelectron. Reliab.*, 54, 90–99, Elsevier, 2014.
61. Raj, B., Saxena, A.K., Dasgupta, S., Quantum Mechanical Analytical Modeling of Nanoscale DG FinFET: Evaluation of Potential, Threshold Voltage and Source/Drain Resistance. *Elsevier's J. Mater. Sci. Semicond. Process.*, 16, 4, 1131–1137, Elsevier, 2013.
62. Gopal, M., Prasad, S.S.D., Raj, B., 8T SRAM Cell Design for Dynamic and Leakage Power Reduction. *Int. J. Comput. Appl.*, 71, 9, 43–48, Foundation of Computer Science, New York, USA, June 2013.
63. Pattanaik, M., Raj, B., Sharma, S., Kumar, A., Diode Based Trimode Multi-Threshold CMOS Technique for Ground Bounce Noise Reduction in Static CMOS Adders. *Adv. Mater. Res.*, 548, 885–889, Trans Tech Publications, Switzerland, 2012.
64. Raj, B., Saxena, A.K., Dasgupta, S., Nanoscale FinFET Based SRAM Cell Design: Analysis of Performance metric, Process variation, Underlapped FinFET and Temperature effect. *IEEE Circuits Syst. Mag.*, 11, 2, 38–50, 2011.

65. Sharma, V.K., Pattanaik, M., Raj, B., Leakage Current ONOFIC Approach for Deep Submicron VLSI Circuit Design. *Int. J. Electr. Comput. Electron. Commun. Eng. World Acad. Sci. Eng. Technol.*, 7, 4, 239–244, 2013.
66. Kaur, P., Gill, S.S., Raj, B., Comparative Analysis of OFETs Materials and Devices for Sensor Applications. *J. Silicon*, 14, 4463–4471, Springer, 2022.
67. Sharma, S.K., Kumar, P., Raj, B., Raj, B., $In_{1-x}Ga_xAs$ Double Metal Gate-Stacking Cylindrical Nanowire MOSFET for highly sensitive Photo detector. *J. Silicon*, 14, 3535–3541, Springer, 2022.
68. Raj, B., Saxena, A.K., Dasgupta, S., Analytical Modeling of Quasi Planar Nanoscale Double Gate FinFET with Source/Drain Resistance and field dependent carrier mobility: A quantum mechanical study. *J. Comput. (JCP)*, 4, 9, 1–8, Academy Publisher, Finland, 2009.
69. Bhushan, S., Khandelwal, S., Raj, B., Analyzing Different Mode FinFET based Memory Cell at Different Power Supply for Leakage Reduction. *Seventh Int. Conf. Bio-Inspired Computing Theor. Application (BIC-TA 2012) Adv. Intell. Syst. Comput.*, 202, 89–100, 2012.
70. Singh, J. and Raj, B., Temperature Dependent Analytical Modeling and Simulations of Nanoscale Memristor. *Eng. Sci. Technol. Int. J.*, 21, 862–868, Elsevier's, Oct 2018.
71. Singh, S., Bala, S., Raj, B., Raj, B., Improved Sensitivity of Dielectric Modulated Junctionless Transistor for Nanoscale Biosensor Design. *Sens. Letter*, 18, 328–333, ASP, April 2020.
72. Kumar, V., Vishvakarma, S.K., Raj, B., Design and Performance Analysis of ASIC for IoT Applications. *Sens. Letter*, 18, 31–38, ASP, Jan 2020.
73. Jaiswal, A., Sarin, R.K., Raj, B., Sukhija, S., A Novel Circular Slotted Microstrip-fed Patch Antenna with Three Triangle Shape Defected Ground Structure for Multiband Applications. *Adv. Electromagn. (AEM)*, 7, 3, 56–63, Aug 2018.
74. Wadhwa, G. and Raj, B., Label Free Detection of Biomolecules using Charge-Plasma-Based Gate Underlap Dielectric Modulated Junctionless TFET. *J. Electron. Mater. (JEMS)*, 47, 8, 4683–4693, Springer, August 2018.
75. Singh, G., Sarin, R.K., Raj, B., Design and Performance Analysis of a New Efficient Coplanar Quantum-Dot Cellular Automata Adder. *Indian J. Pure Appl. Phys. (IJPAP)*, 55, 97–103, February 2017.
76. Kaur, P., Pandey, V., Raj, B., Comparative Study of Efficient Design, Control and Monitoring of Solar Power using IoT. *Sens. Letter*, 18, 419–426, ASP, May 2020.
77. Bhardwaj, A.K., Gupta, S., Raj, B., Development & Analysis of compact model for Double Gate Schottky Barrier CNTFET. *J. Nanoelectron. Optoelectron.*, 15, 1199–1208, ASP, Aug 2020.
78. Wadhwa, G., Kamboj, P., Singh, J., Raj, B., Design and Investigation of Junctionless DGTFET for Biological Molecule Recognition. *Trans. Electr. Electron. Mater.*, 22, 282–289, Springer, 2021.

79. Verma, S.K., Singh, S., Wadhwa, G., Raj, B., Detection of Biomolecules using Charge-Plasma based Gate Underlap Dielectric Modulated Dopingless TFET. *Trans. Electr. Electron. Mater. (TEEM)*, 21, 528–535, Springer, June 2020.
80. Jain, N. and Raj, B., Impact of underlap spacer region variation on Electrostatic and analog/RF performance of symmetrical high-k SOI FinFET at 20 nm channel length. *J. Semicond. (JoS)*, 38, 12, 122002, IOP Science, Dec 2017.
81. Singh, S. and Raj, B., Analytical Modeling and Simulation analysis of T-shaped III-V heterojunction Vertical T-FET. *Superlattices Microstruct.*, 147, 106717, Elsevier, Nov 2020.
82. Singh, G., Sarin, R.K., Raj, B., Design and Analysis of Area Efficient QCA Based Reversible Logic Gates. *J. Microprocess. Microsys.*, 52, 59–68, Elsevier, May 2017.
83. Singh, S. and Raj, B., Parametric variation analysis on hetero-junction Vertical t-shape TFET for Supressing ambipolar conduction. *Indian J. Pure Appl. Phys.*, 58, 478–485, June 2020.
84. Soniya, S.S., Wadhwa, G., Raj, B., Design and Analysis of Dual Source Vertical Tunnel Field Effect Transistor for high performance. *Trans. Electr. Electron. Mater.*, 21, 74–82, Springer, Oct 2019.
85. Kaur, M., Gupta, N., Kumar, S., Raj, B., Singh, A.K., RF Performance Analysis of Intercalated Graphene Nanoribbon Based Global Level Interconnects. *J. Comput. Electron.*, 19, 1002–1013, Springer, June 2020.
86. Wadhwa, G. and Raj, B., Design and Performance Analysis of Junctionless TFET Biosensor for high sensitivity. *IEEE Nanotechnol.*, 18, 567–574, 2019.
87. Singh, J. and Raj, B., Enhanced Nonlinear Memristor Model Encapsulating Stochastic Dopant Drift. *JNO*, 14, 958–963, ASP, 2019.
88. Singh, M., Chaudhary, T., Raj, B., Enhancing FeFET Structures for Non-volatile On-chip Memories: Design and Comparative Analysis. *Int. J. Numer. Modell. Electron. Netw. Dev. Fields*, 38, 1–9, 2024.
89. Singh, M., Chaudhary, T., Raj, B., Drain Current and Transconductance Analysis of GaN GAA Nanowire FET with High K Dielectric. *ECS J. Sci. Technol.*, 12, 6070–6077, 2023.
90. Singh, M., Chaudhary, T., Raj, B., Design of Si and Ge Nanowire FET for Low Power Application. *J. Silicon*, 15, 1491–1497, Springer, 2023.
91. Singh, M., Chaudhary, T., Raj, B., Electrical Characteristics Analysis of FeFET for Low Power Applications. *J. Nano*, 37, pp. 1–8, 2024.
92. Kumar, M., Chaudhary, T., Raj, B., Design and Comparative Analysis of Ferroelectric Nanowire with Dielectric HfO_2 and Al_2O_3 for Low Power Applications. *J. Electron. Mater.*, 53, 6785–6791, Springer, 2024.
93. Sharma, D., Mehra, R., Raj, B., Comparative Analysis of Photovoltaic Technologies for High Efficiency Solar Cell Design. *Superlattices Microstruct.*, 153, 106861, Elsevier, May 2021.

94. Kaur, P., Buttar, A.S., Raj, B., A comprehensive Analysis of Nanoscale Transistor based Biosensor: A Review. *Indian J. Pure Appl. Phys.*, 59, 304–318, April 2021.
95. Yadav, D., Raj, B., Raj, B., Design and Simulation of Low Power Microcontroller for IoT Applications. *J. Sens. Lett.*, 18, 401–409, ASP, May 2020.
96. Singh, S. and Raj, B., A 2-D Analytical Surface Potential and Drain current Modeling of Double-Gate Vertical t-shaped Tunnel FET. *J. Comput. Electron.*, 19, 1154–1163, Springer, April 2020.
97. Singh, J. and Raj, B., An Accurate and Generic Window function for Non-linear Memristor Model. *J. Comput. Electron.*, 18, 2, 640–647, Springer, June 2019.
98. Kaur, M., Gupta, N., Kumar, S., Raj, B., Singh, A.K., Comparative RF and Crosstalk Analysis of Carbon Based Nano Interconnects. *IET Circuits Devices Syst.*, 15, 6, 493–503, Feb 2021.
99. Kandasamy, N., Ahmad, F., Ajitha, D., Raj, B., Telagam, N., Quantum Dot Cellular Automata based Scan Flip Flop and Boundary Scan Register. *IETE J. Res.*, 66, 535–548, 2020.
100. Singh, J. and Raj, B., Design and Investigation of 7T2M NVSARM with Enhanced Stability and Temperature Impact on Store/Restore Energy. *IEEE Trans. Very Large Scale Integr. Syst.*, 27, 6, 1322–1328, June 2019.
101. Bhardwaj, A.K., Gupta, S., Raj, B., Singh, A., Impact of Double Gate Geometry on the Performance of Carbon Nanotube Field Effect Transistor Structures for Low Power Digital Design. *Comput. Theor. Nanosci.*, 16, 1813–1820, ASP, 2019.
102. Jain, N. and Raj, B., Thermal Stability Analysis and Performance Exploration of Asymmetrical Dual-k underlap Spacer (ADKUS) SOI FinFET for Security and Privacy Applications. *Indian J. Pure Appl. Phys. (IJPAP)*, 57, 352–360, May 2019.

8

Ultra Low Power Adiabatic Logic Circuits at Nanometer Scale

Jitendra Kanungo[1]*, Jitendra Raghuwanshi[1] and Sudeb Dasgupta[2]

[1]Department of Electronics and Communication Engineering, Jaypee University of Engineering and Technology, Guna (M.P.), India
[2]Department of Electronics and Communication Engineering, Indian Institute of Technology, Roorkee, India

Abstract

Energy consumption has been a matter of concern for the implementation of Complementary Metal Oxide Semiconductor (CMOS) based circuits due to the high density of integrated devices. Research work is continuing worldwide to design the energy-efficient circuits for biomedical and space applications that have limited conventional energy. The low-power requirement is becoming a challenge at device, circuit and system architecture level. The conventional CMOS circuit styles are limited by the constant power supply voltage, its significant portion is consumed as thermal energy in resistive circuit elements. Novel device concepts and novel circuit approaches have been investigated for low energy consumption. Adiabatic logic is a circuit level approach that has made it possible to realize the ultra low power computing applications without reducing the supply voltage and node capacitances. A new single phase adiabatic or energy recovery logic and its energy performance with technology scaling have been carried out. Fair comparative study among the proposed logic, existing single phase adiabatic logic and static CMOS logic at different technology nodes has been done. For this purpose, the 4-stage inverter chains of the proposed Single Phase Adiabatic Logic, Source Coupled Adiabatic Logic, Clocked Adiabatic Logic and Static CMOS Logic circuits were simulated at 180 nm, 90 nm and 45 nm technology nodes and results show that the energy recovery or adiabatic logic can be used for nanoscale ultra low power application. In the last few years, multi-phase and single-phase energy recovery logics have been suggested but single-phase energy recovery logic circuits are more attractive for their reasonable speed in ultra low power integrated circuit design. Motivation behind this research

**Corresponding author*: jitendra.kanungo@juet.ac.in

Ashish Maurya, Mandeep Singh and Balwinder Raj (eds.) Machine Learning in Nanoelectronics: Devices, Circuits and Systems, (231–256) © 2026 Scrivener Publishing LLC

work is to explore the energy efficiency and functionality of new single phase energy recovery logic with progressive scaling.

The importance of adiabatic logic for ultra low power applications, and key challenges at 100 nm scale are explained. This work presents the ultra low power CMOS circuits and their applications for arithmetic operations. In this chapter, the work is focused on study of energy efficiency of proposed logic and other single-phase adiabatic logic and their comparison at various nanoscale CMOS technology.

***Keywords*:** Adiabatic logic, nanometer scale, CMOS, clocked adiabatic logic, adiabatic switching

8.1 Introduction

In physics the word "adiabatic" indicates that "all charge transfer is to occur without generating heat" [1]; it is a slow process in which no heat or entropy flows in any part of a system. Adiabatic Switching is the technique of employing adiabatic charging in logical circuits, to enhance the energy efficiency required to perform a digital computation. Switching circuits implemented in CMOS and compatible with adiabatic charging are also called Adiabatic CMOS circuits [2].

Energy efficiency in VLSI circuit design is important as the packaging density is increasing in accordance with Moore's Law. Scaled devices also offer reduced capacitance per transistor. Unfortunately, the increase in the number of integrated transistors exceeds the reduction in capacitance per transistor, so that the dynamic power dissipation is still increasing and has become a major concern of chip design in modern technologies [3]. Adiabatic switching techniques tend to eliminate or reduce one of the main energy consuming processes in CMOS operation, dynamic dissipation, which is intrinsically unavoidable in conventional CMOS circuits [3, 4].

The intention of this chapter is to focus on the adiabatic switching in ultra low power circuit application. Various adiabatic designs have been introduced and compared. This chapter explains the key challenges in context with the scaling, and provides a broad understanding of the scaling trends in adiabatic logic at nanometer scale.

8.2 Adiabatic Charging Principle

Figure 8.1 shows the concept of charging and discharging of adiabatic node. Figure 8.2 (a) shows the voltage waveforms present for conventional CMOS, when the input of the inverter swings from high to low, causing the

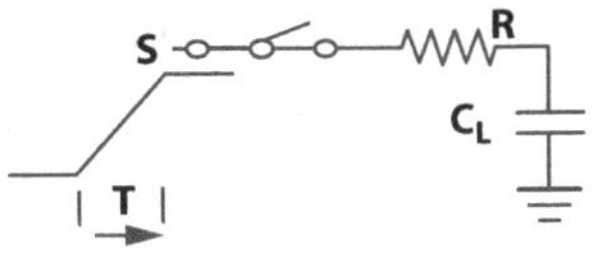

Figure 8.1 Adiabatic charging.

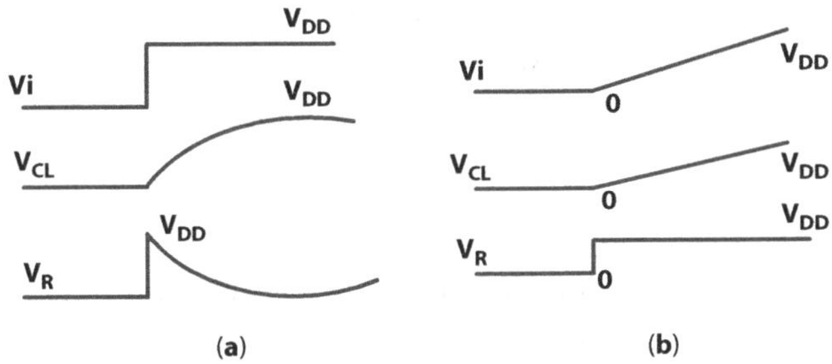

Figure 8.2 Voltage waveforms present in the equivalent circuit when charging the capacitor from 0 V to V_{DD} (a) in a conventional manner and (b) in an adiabatic manner.

capacitor C to begin charging. At the instant of switching, the full supply potential appears across the on-resistance R of the p-type device, the waveform then decays as the capacitor is charged to V_{DD} [5, 6].

Adiabatic switching can be achieved by ensuring that the potential across the switching devices is kept arbitrarily small. In Figure 8.2 (b), it can be seen that the potential V_r, across the switch resistance is high in the conventional case because of the abrupt application of V_{DD} to the RC_L circuit. Adiabatic charging may be achieved by charging the capacitor from a time-varying source, as shown in Figure 8.1. This source has an initial value of $V_i = 0$ V-the ramp increases towards V_{DD} at a slow rate that ensures $V_r = V_i - V_{CL}$ is kept arbitrarily small. This rate is set by ensuring that the period of the ramp $T >> RC_L$. The energy dissipated is [2, 7]:

$$E_{diss} = I^2RT = \left(\frac{C_L V_{DD}}{T}\right)^2 RT = \left(\frac{RC_L}{T}\right) C_L {V^2}_{DD} \tag{8.1}$$

A linear increase in T causes a linear decrease in energy dissipation. Adiabatic discharge can be arranged in a similar manner with a descending ramp.

This energy may be removed from the capacitor and returned to the power supply adiabatically by ramping V_i, back down from V_{DD} to 0 V.

As a result, given a suitable supply, it should be possible then to charge and discharge signal node capacitances with only marginal net losses [5].

8.3 Adiabatic Logic Family

Several semi-reversible or partial adiabatic logic family, based on a bistable circuit structure (flip-flop), like- 2N-2P or ECRL [7, 9, 10], IECRL (Improved ECRL) or 2N-2N2P [8, 10], Positive Feedback Adiabatic Logic (PFAL) [8, 11], and Pass-transistor Adiabatic Logic (PAL) [8, 9] are explained.

(i) ECRL or 2N-2P Circuit:
An ECRL circuit consists of PMOS loads and NMOS pull-down transistors as shown in Figure 8.3. The PMOS transistors are cross-coupled and are used for precharge and evaluation. The Threshold voltage of PMOS causes an initial, non-adiabatic dissipation of approximately $1/2(C_L V^2_{tp})$, where C_L is the load capacitance associated with the output nodes. But subsequently, the charging of C_L, up to V_{DD}, will be adiabatic. During the recovery phase, as the voltage of the power clock $\phi(t)$ approaches V_{tp}, the PMOS transistor MP2 gets turned off and the recovery path to the power clock is disconnected. The charge left on the load capacitance at the end of the recovery phase will either leak away slowly through the turned-off devices, or discharge through MN2, if $\bar{X}$ changes value (from '0' to '1') for the next logic evaluation. Thus, the non-adiabatic dissipation during the recovery phase will either be less than or equal to $1/2(C_L V^2_{tp})$ [12].

This architecture is simple and functional; it exhibits some drawbacks, namely the presence of a floating output, the voltage of which depends on spurious capacitive couplings that can affect the logic levels [3, 4, 13–19].

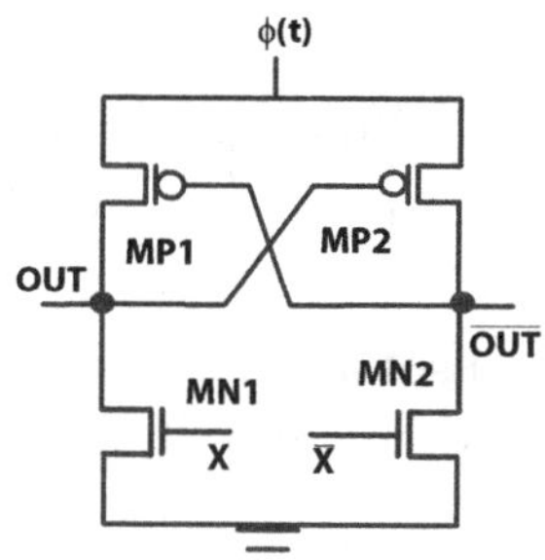

Figure 8.3 ECRL buffer/inverter.

(ii) IECRL or 2N-2N2P:

This architecture (Figure 8.4) is very similar to the ECRL described above, but a PMOS, MP0, is connected between the two outputs, with the substrate connected to the power clock line $\phi(t)$. This device provides a recovery path to the charge stored in the output nodes through the drain- and source-substrate junction diodes. In this case the residual voltage on the nodes is the turn-on voltage of these junction diodes, which is usually lower than the threshold voltage of PMOS [4].

(iii) PAL (Pass Transistor Adiabatic Logic):

In this circuit (Figure 8.5), the NMOS input network, which evaluates the logic function, is applied in parallel to the pull-up PMOS devices [4, 9]. This leads to a full logic swing. Furthermore, the current charging the output capacitor flows into a pass-gate, which has a lower resistance than a simple pass transistor, so the consumed power is reduced [4, 13]. However, PAL logic gates suffer the drawback of spurious capacitive

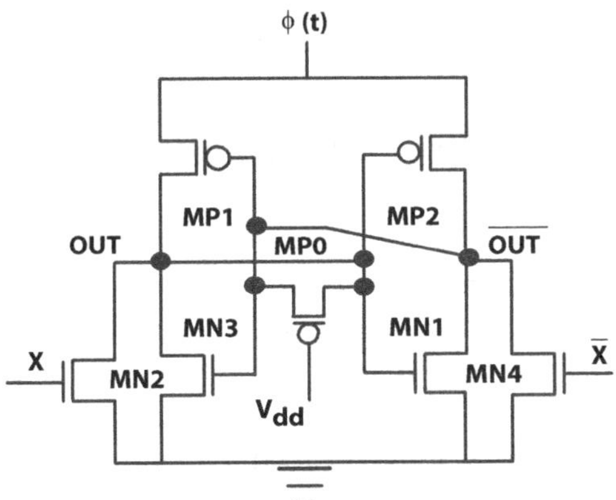

Figure 8.4 IECRL or 2N-2N2P inverter circuit.

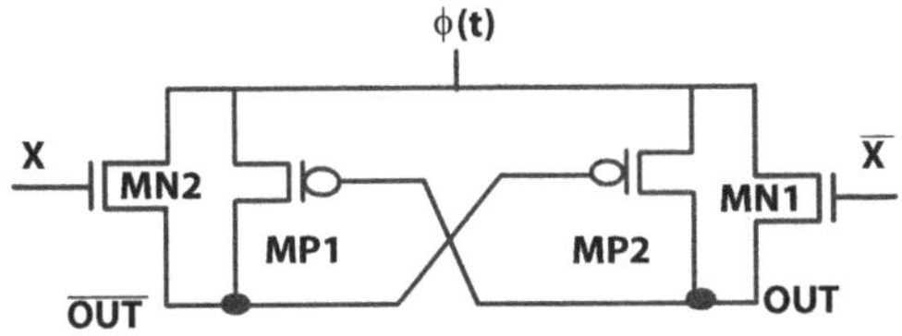

Figure 8.5 PAL inverter circuit.

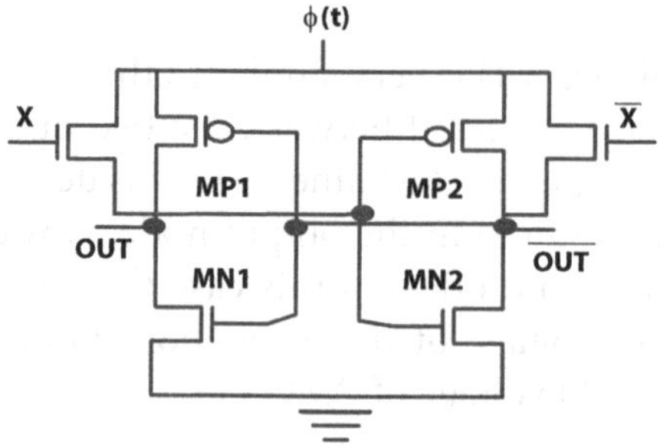

Figure 8.6 PFAL buffer/inverter gate.

couplings, since the output node, which should remain at zero, is kept floating [4].

(iv) PFAL (Positive Feedback Adiabatic Logic):
The basic buffer/inverter PFAL [1] gate is shown in Figure 8.6. The core of all the PFAL gates is an adiabatic amplifier.

In a PFAL gate no output is floating (excluding the idle phase, obviously) and all outputs have full logic swing [4].

8.4 Comparative Simulation Results

The above-mentioned adiabatic architectures are investigated for power dissipation at 90 nm technology node, as a function of the operating frequency by means of Cadence Spectre–based electrical simulations.

From Figure 8.7, it is seen that the energy dissipation does not tend to zero as the frequency does. This is because these architectures are semi-reversible, and a certain amount of charge, and hence energy cannot be recovered and is dissipated in the subsequent cycle; this effect is completely independent of frequency and introduces a constant dissipation term [4].

Similarly, other adiabatic logic architectures like True Single Phase Energy Recovery Logic (TSEL), Clocked Adiabatic Logic (CAL), and Source Coupled Recovery Logic (SCRL) etc. can be used for low power circuit design [20–26].

8.5 Key Challenges

Adiabatic Circuits are distinguished into quasi- and fully adiabatic ones. In quasi-adiabatic circuits not all charge/energy can be recovered because

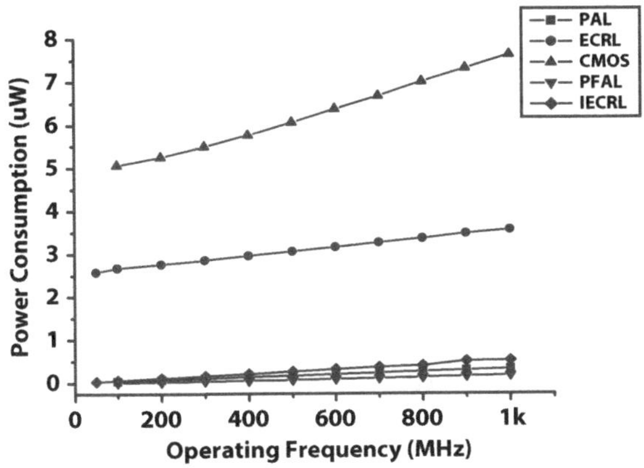

Figure 8.7 Energy dissipation per cycle per cell as a function of operating frequency at constant load.

the recovery path is switched off before the recovery process has ended. The energy of about $E=1/2(C_L V^2_{DD})$ is remains on the capacitance. If the output state switches, this energy will be dissipated. As shown in Figure 8.8 the dissipation due to leakage current is inversely proportional to the frequency, whereas the adiabatic losses increase linearly with the frequency.

When the energy dissipation of the crossing point is higher than $E_{VT}=1/2(CV^2_T)$ the whole losses are only limited by these two mechanisms and they behave like fully adiabatic logic families [14]. The adiabatic logic circuits can be designed more energy efficient if these are able to cope with technology and voltage scaling challenges, as explained below.

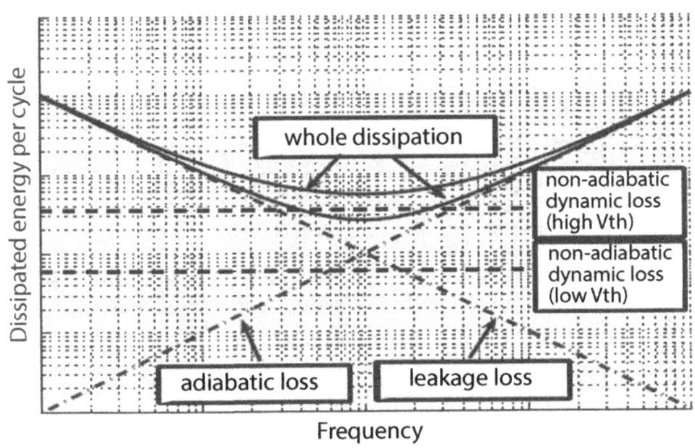

Figure 8.8 Sources of energy dissipation (leakage, adiabatic and non-adiabatic dynamic losses). The non-adiabatic dynamic losses differ with the threshold voltage.

(i) Scaling Technologies

The gate capacitance of a transistor will decrease as the area decreases, this prevails the increase in oxide capacitance per unit area (t_{ox} decreases). According to the following equation, the on-resistance will remain nearly constant if the increase of C_{ox} cancels the decrease of the voltages and the mobility remains constant. The on-resistance R_{on} of a MOSFET with length L and width W amounts to:

$$R_{on} = \left[\mu C_{OX} \frac{W}{L}(V_{GS} - V_T)\right]^{-1} \tag{8.2}$$

Where μ is the mobility, C_{ox} the oxide capacitance per unit area, V_{GS} the gate source voltage and V_T the threshold voltage. Of course, there are additional effects like the decrease of mobility leading to a non-constant switch resistance R_{on}. Additionally, new leakage occurs due to smaller dimensions, for example DIBL, GIDL and gate leakage. Therefore, at low frequencies the energy dissipation will rise for both adiabatic circuits and static CMOS with the same factor [10, 16].

(ii) Scaling Threshold Voltage

In a modern technology it is possible to choose between more than one threshold voltages for a device. The devices with high threshold voltages on the one hand show low leakage currents and on the other hand their on-resistance is high because of the low overdrive voltage V_{GS}-V_T. These effects are summarized in Figure 8.9, at low frequencies the leakage current,

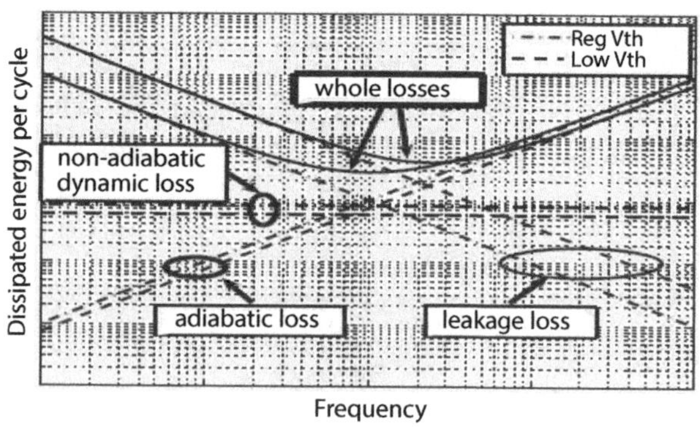

Figure 8.9 Influence of two different threshold voltages on the energy dissipation.

and therefore the leakage loss, will increase exponentially with lower threshold voltage [27–34].

The non-adiabatic dynamic losses are less than the sum of the other sources of dissipation and can be neglected. Leakage currents are exponentially dependent on V_T [14].

In the high frequency regime instead, the on-resistance will be lowered with decreased threshold voltage according to the above equation [35–42]. As long as the non-adiabatic dynamic losses are not noticeable the overall minimum of the energy dissipation is found for high threshold voltage at low frequencies as the exponential dependence of the leakage current is dominating. At a given frequency above the optimum frequency, only the adiabatic losses must be considered, which benefits from the lower on-resistance at a lower V_T [14].

(iii) Scaling Supply Voltage

Voltage scaling represents a proper way for reducing the dynamic power in static CMOS. In adiabatic circuits, the voltage-dependent on-resistance has to be taken into account. According to equation of R_{on}, it is inverse proportional to the overdrive voltage (V_{GS}-V_T). Cadence Spectre simulation results with PFAL inverter chains in the 90 nm CMOS technology parameters using a supply voltage of V_{DD}=1 V are shown in Figure 8.10. Two transistor types with different threshold voltages were used. The regular threshold voltage amounts to approximately 250mV and the low

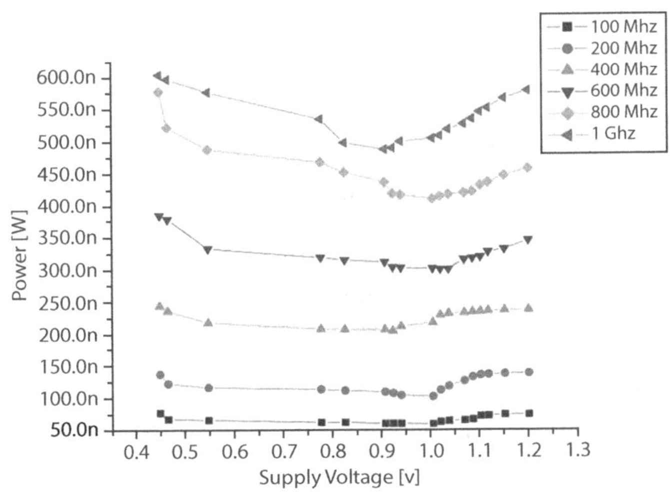

Figure 8.10 Energy dissipation of PFAL inverters with varying supply voltage.

one amount to approximately 200mV. The switching activity was chosen maximum.

In Figure 8.10, the energy dissipation over frequency is shown. The assumed linear dependence of the supply voltage can be observed [14]. Therefore, the above key challenges should be considered in order to design adiabatic circuits to cope with technology scaling and to make robust against threshold voltage, supply voltage and temperature variation [43–50].

8.6 Comparative Analysis of Energy Recovery Logic and Conventional CMOS Logic

Extensive research is going on worldwide to design energy-efficient circuits for such biomedical and space applications which have limited conventional energy. In this chapter a new single-phase adiabatic or energy recovery logic and its energy performance with technology scaling have also been carried out. An extensive comparative study among proposed logic, existing single-phase adiabatic logic and static CMOS logic at different technology nodes have been presented. For this purpose, the 4-stage inverter chains of proposed Single-Phase Adiabatic Logic, Source Coupled Adiabatic Logic, Clocked Adiabatic Logic and Static CMOS Logic circuits were simulated at 180nm, 90nm and 45nm technology nodes and results show that the energy recovery or adiabatic logic can be used for nanoscale ultra low power application.

Figure 8.11 shows the SPAL [13] inverter circuit, which comprises a pair of MOS diodes (P1-P2 and N1-N2), and a functional block (MP and MN). The SPAL uses a single-phase power clock (Φ) that operates SPAL gate for the purpose of charging and discharging. The SPAL circuit works as follows [17]: Charging Process: Let power clock (Φ) ramp up to HIGH, circuit input node "in" and output node "out" are LOW. This makes a conducting path: Φ - MOS diode - MP - out. Hence, circuit output node "out" follows clock supply Φ and swings to HIGH. When "out" reaches Φ_{max} - $|V_{tp}|$, the MOS diode cuts-off and "out" remains at HIGH. The LOW input keeps MN in OFF state that isolates the "out" from supply Φ. In this way, "out" remains unchanged [51–55].

Discharging Process: Let power clock (Φ) ramp down to 0, and both circuit input node "in" and output node "out" are HIGH. This makes a conducting path: out - MN - MOS diode - Φ. Hence, "out" follows Φ as it swings LOW. As a result, a small amount of current flows toward the power

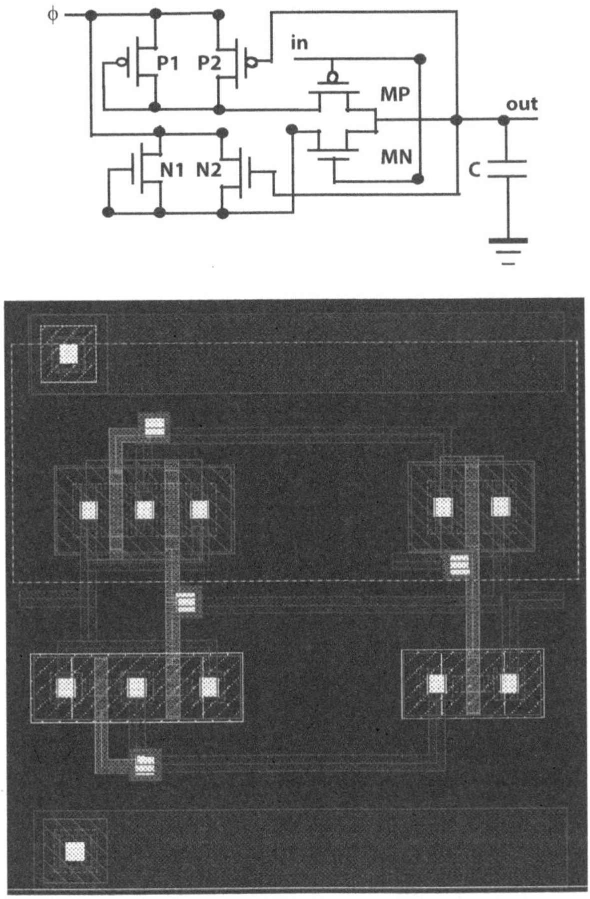

Figure 8.11 SPAL inverter circuit and its layout.

supply Φ, that enables the recycling of energy stored in output capacitance C. When, voltage at "out" node reaches at V_{tn} the transistor MN is turned off and "out" remains at LOW. The output logical state does not change unless the input changes. Hence, charging and discharging of output node depends upon input transition. It is worth mentioning that transistors P2 and N2 provide the conducting path that transit the output "out" fast in accordance with input "in" while P1 and N1 provides the recovery path [56–63].

If a conventional CMOS inverter and the SPAL inverter are compared, then the main differences are: SPAL uses parallel combination of transistors with pull up and pull down networks to charge the output capacitance and it recycles the energy from charge stored in output node capacitance. Threshold voltage drop across pull up network and ON resistance results in the energy dissipation (E_{PUN}) in charging output capacitance [18]; it can be written as:

$$E_{PUN} = \frac{1}{2}C\,|V_{tp}|^2 + R_{P,ON}\frac{C}{T}C\left(V_{\Phi max} - |V_{tp}|\right)^2 \tag{8.3}$$

Where C is the output capacitance, $|V_{tp}|$ is threshold voltage of pull up device, $R_{P,ON}$ is the on-resistance of pull up device MP1, T is charging time of "out" node capacitance, and $V_{\Phi max}$ is maximum supply voltage. Similarly, energy consumption due to parallel combination of PMOS devices P1 and P2 in charging the "out" node capacitance C would be [21, 22]:

$$E_{P1P2} = R_{eq}\frac{C^2}{T}V^2 \tag{8.4}$$

R_{eq} resistance is due to parallel PMOS devices P1 and P2, it can be obtained from the conductance of device in their conducting mode [21, 22]:

$$R_{eq} = \frac{1}{G1 + G2} \tag{8.5}$$

G_1 and G_2 are device conductance of P1 and P2, respectively, and V is the net voltage across MOS diode. Thus, total energy consumption in charging path would be [21, 22]:

$$E = E_{PUN} + E_{P1P2}$$
$$= \frac{1}{2}C\,|V_{tp}|^2 + R_{P,ON}\frac{C}{T}C\left(V_{\Phi max} - |V_{tp}|\right)^2 + R_{eq}\frac{C^2}{T}V^2 \tag{8.6}$$

The discharging process dissipates almost the same amount of energy. Four inverter chains using SPAL (Figure 8.11), CAL (Figure 8.12), SCAL-D (Figure 8.13) and static CMOS logic have been implemented in clock frequency range of 50MHz-500MHz. Load capacitance of 3fF is assumed at the output node of each type of inverter [64–69]. Peak-to-peak sinusoidal voltage supply of 0.8V, 1V and 1.8V are applied at 45nm, 90nm and 180nm

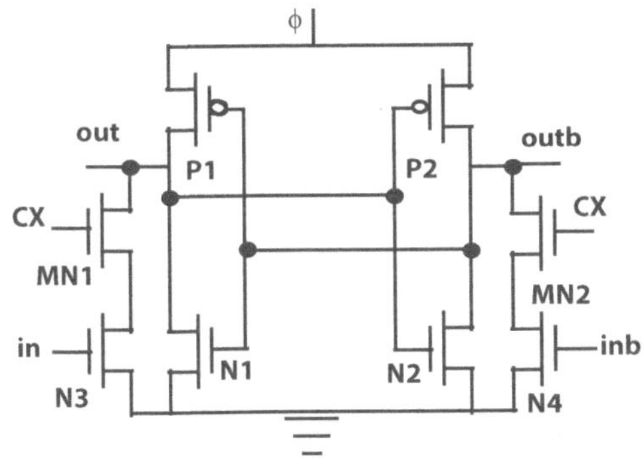

Figure 8.12 CAL inverter/buffer circuit [19].

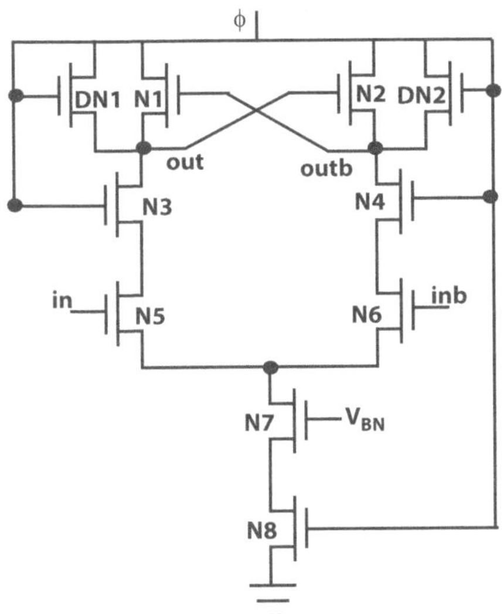

Figure 8.13 SCAL-D NMOS inverter/buffer circuit.

technology nodes [19] respectively. The electrical simulations have been carried out through *Cadence Spectre* simulator. For each type of adiabatic logic, the input signal(s) (in) frequency of 50 MHz (i.e., period of 20ns) is kept fixed and then the energy consumption is measured against various clock frequencies for time period of 20ns. Figure 8.14 (a) shows the energy consumption versus clock frequency for 4 stage inverter chains at 45nm. At 300MHz clock frequency, proposed SPAL gives adiabatic gain (ratio of energy consumption of logically equivalent static CMOS logic and energy

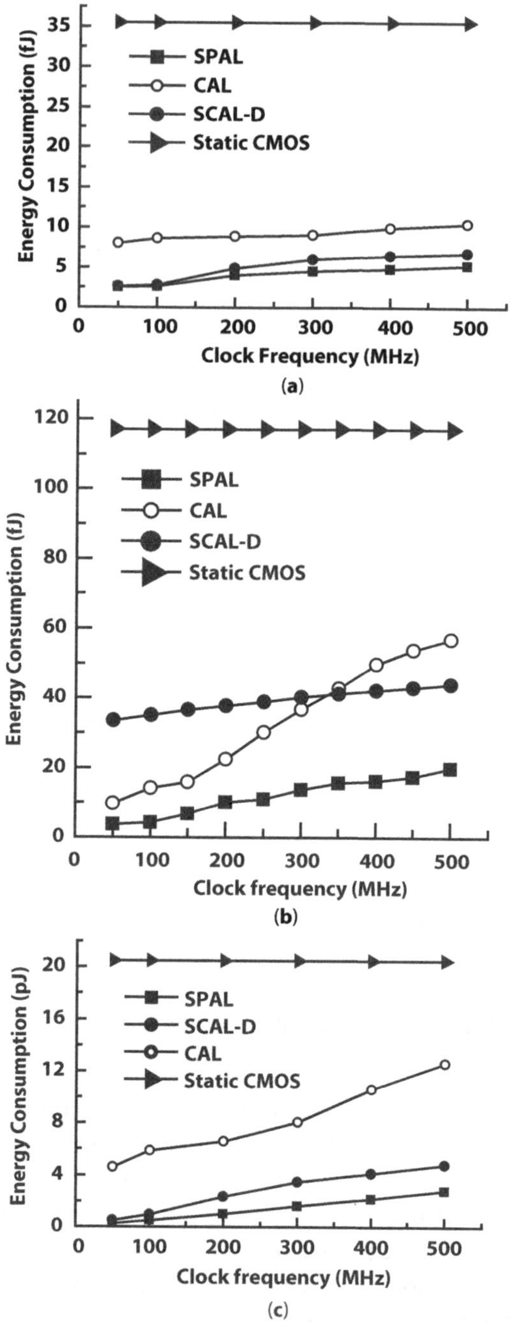

Figure 8.14 Energy consumption versus clock frequency at (a) 45nm (b) 90nm (c) 180nm.

Table 8.1 Adiabatic gain versus clock frequency.

	Adiabatic gain														
	SPAL					**CAL**					**SCAL-D**				
	Clock frequency (MHz)					**Clock frequency (MHz)**					**Clock frequency (MHz)**				
Node	100	200	300	400	500	100	200	300	400	500	100	200	300	400	500
45nm	13.70	8.78	7.87	7.36	6.82	12.76	7.25	5.91	5.53	5.19	4.11	4.01	3.94	3.57	3.41
90nm	20.05	11.58	8.54	7.22	5.88	8.24	5.22	3.17	2.38	2.06	3.33	3.10	2.91	2.78	2.66
180nm	24.18	20.24	12.46	9.29	7.30	21.19	8.58	5.92	4.91	4.25	3.49	3.10	2.53	1.92	1.62

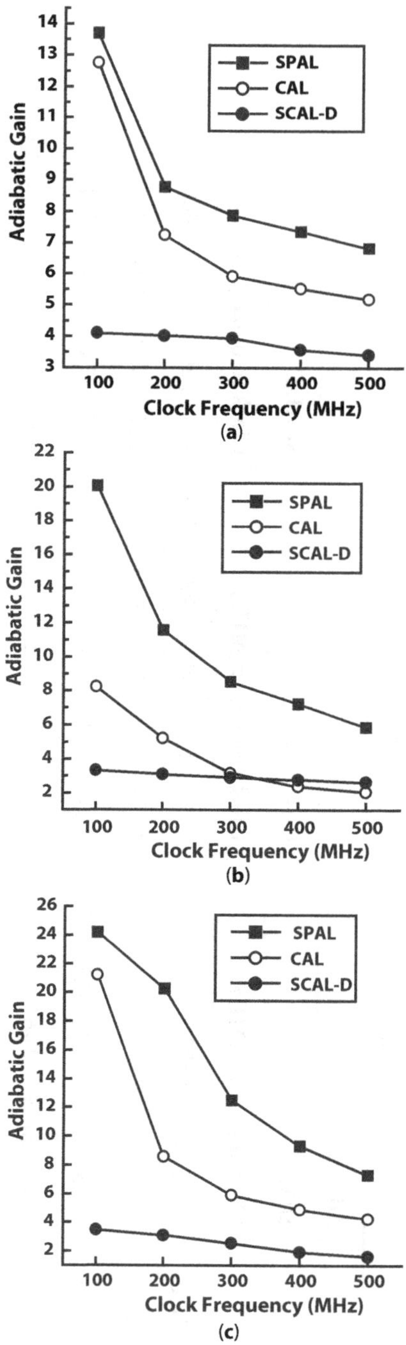

Figure 8.15 Adiabatic gain versus clock frequency at (a) 45nm (b) 90nm (c) 180nm [21].

consumption of adiabatic logic) of 7.87 as compared to 5.91 of SCAL-D and 3.94 of CAL [70–75].

Circuit operation at 500MHz clock frequency the adiabatic gain of 6.82 for SPAL, 5.19 for SCAL-D and 3.41 for CAL have been obtained. In Figure 8.14(b) the energy consumption versus clock frequency is shown for 90nm technology node [21, 22].

The CAL and SCAL-D competes with SPAL at a clock frequency less than 200MHz but at higher frequency SPAL outperforms. Although SPAL circuit shows the output swing dropped by a device threshold voltage and slower speed it enables the better power/energy efficiency [76–81]. Figure 8.14(c) demonstrates the energy consumption of four inverter chains as a function of clock frequency at 180 nm technology node. At 300MHz clock frequency, proposed SPAL shows adiabatic gain of 12.46 while it is 5.92 and 2.53 for SCAL-D and CAL respectively. Similarly, at 500MHz clock frequency adiabatic gain for SPAL is 7.30, 4.25 for SCAL-D and 1.62 for CAL [21].

Thus, SPAL [21, 22] has better energy efficiency than CAL, SCAL-D and static CMOS counterpart. The results are summarized in Table 8.1 and further the energy performance of logic circuits with scaling technology has been drawn in Figure 8.15. The adiabatic gain of each type of single-phase adiabatic logic has been determined [82–88]. It helps us to choose an efficient single-phase adiabatic logic for a clock frequency range. At a clock frequency less than 200MHz the SPAL shows higher adiabatic gain than SCAL-D and CAL.

In fact, with increasing clock frequency associated transit time is decreased that ultimately limits energy saving [89–94].

In clock frequency range of 50MHz-500MHz the SCAL-D logic shows least variation in adiabatic gain, but on the other hand adiabatic gain of SPAL and CAL logics were affected by clock frequency and therefore large variation in their adiabatic gains can be seen [95–104]. Thus, we conclude that SPAL is limited by operating clock frequency and should be taken in to account during design [21, 22].

Summary

Adiabatic switching is a promising approach for circuits that drive large capacitive loads to voltages above four times the threshold voltage. In summary, the adiabatic switching is to be useful for realizing low-power digital systems; it will most likely be in hybrid configurations which include conventional or partially adiabatic latches and logic [105–111]. It is shown that the energy recovery logic is a good candidate for achieving ultra low power nanoscale digital design. The proposed logic is energy efficient at the cost of delay, and related presented work makes it easy for any digital VLSI circuit engineer to adopt energy recovery logic or adiabatic logic among the other low-power CMOS circuit techniques [112–117].

Energy performance has been extensively studied, which helps us in achieving the maximum energy saving from a complete adiabatic system under the variation of supply voltage, process corner and driver transistors' width at sub-100 nm CMOS technology. In recent years, various emerging semiconductor devices have been proposed to reduce the energy loss in VLSI systems. Digital circuits have also been implemented with emerging devices such as carbon nanotubes FET, FinFET and SOI MOSFET. Additional energy advantages can be achieved by applying the adiabatic switching technique to the emerging devices based digital circuits. It would be an interesting and demanding research work to explore the low power strategies in the present scenario.

The adiabatic logic circuits represent an interesting and competitive solution for applications where the frequency of operation can be traded for ultimately low power consumption. Adiabatic circuits are applicable where the conventional energy is limited to use.

References

1. Kim, S. and Papaefthymiou, M.C., True single-phase adiabatic circuitry. *IEEE Trans. VLSI Syst.*, 9, 1, 52–63, February 2001.
2. Athas, W.C., Koller, J.G., Svensson, L.J., An energy-efficient CMOS line driver using adiabatic switching. *Inform. Sci. Inst. CA Tech. Rep. ACMOS-TR-2*, July 1993.
3. Alioto, M. and Palumbo, G., Performance evaluation of adiabatic gates. *IEEE Trans. Circuit System-I*, 47, 9, 1297–1308, 2000.
4. Denker, J.S., A Review of adiabatic Computing, in: *Proc. IEEE Symposium on Low Power Electronics, Digest of Technical Papers*, pp. 94–97, 10-12 October 1994.
5. Dickinson, A.G. and Denker, J.S., Adiabatic dynamic logic. *IEEE J. Solid-State Circuits*, 30, 3, 311–315, March 1995.
6. Kim, S., Ziesler, C.H., Papaefthymiou, M.C., Charge-recovery computing on silicon. *IEEE Trans. Comput.*, 54, 6, 651–659, June 2005.
7. Rabaey, J.M. and Pedram, M., *Low Power Design Methodologies*, Kluwer Academic Publishers, 2002.

8. Arsalan, M. and Shams, M., An investigation into transistor-based adiabatic logic styles, in: *Proc. IEEE 2nd Annual Northeast Workshop on Circuits and Systems (NEWCAS 2004)*, pp. 1–4, 20-23 June 2004.
9. Oklobdzija, V.G., Maksimovic, D., Lin, F., Pass-transistor adiabatic logic using single power-clock supply. *IEEE Trans. Circuits Systems-II Analog Digital Signal Process.*, 44, 10, 842–846, Oct. 1997.
10. Kramer, A., Denker, J.S., Flower, B., Moroney, J., *Proc. Int. Symp. Low Power Des.*, 191–196, 1995.
11. Blotti, A., Castellucci, M., Salctti, R., Designing Carry Look-Ahead Adders with an Adiabatic Logic Standad cell Library, in: *Proc. International Workshop on Power and Timing Modeling, Optimization and Simulation (PATMOS'02)*, pp. 118–127, 2002.
12. Ng, K.W. and Lau, K.T., ECRL based low power flip-flop design. *Microelectron. J.*, 31, 5, 365–370, May 2000.
13. Athas, W.C., Svensson, L.J., Koller, J.G., Tzartzanis, N., Ying-Chin Chou, E., Low-power digital systems based on adiabatic-switching principles. *IEEE Trans. VLSI Syst.*, 2, 4, 398–407, December 1994.
14. Fisher, J., Teichmann, P., Doris Schmit Landsiedel, M., Scaling Trends in Adiabatic logic, in: *Proc. ACM 2nd Conference on Computing Frontiers*, pp. 427–434, May 2005.
15. Lim, J., Kim, D.-G., Chae, S.-I., nMOS reversible energy recovery logic for ultra-low- energy applications. *IEEE J. Solid-State Circuits*, 35, 6, 865–875, June 2000.
16. Wang, B. and Mazumder, P., On optimality of adiabatic switching in MOS energy-recovery circuit, in: *Proc. IEEE International Symposium on Low Power Electronics and Design*, pp. 236–239, August 2004.
17. Kanungo, J. and Dasgupta, S., Study of Energy Efficiency of Single Phase Energy Recovery Logic with Progressive Technology, in: *Proceeding of 15th VLSI Design and Test Symposium*, pp. 1–10, 2011.
18. Kanungo, J. and Dasgupta, S., An Efficient Single-phase Adiabatic Logic and Its Application to Combinational and Sequential Logic. *ASP J. Low Power Electron.*, 7, 381, 2011.
19. Maksimovic, D., Oklobdzija, V.G., Nikolic, B., Current, K.W., Clocked CMOS Adiabatic Logic With Integrated Single Phase Power-clock Supply. *IEEE Transaction Very Large Scale Integr. Syst.*, 8, 460, 2000.
20. Kim, S., Ziesler, C.H., Papaefthymiou, M.C., A true single-phase energy recovery multiplier. *IEEE Transaction Very Large Scale Integr. Syst.*, 11, 194, 2003.
21. Kanungo, J., *Implementation of Adiabatic Logic for Ultra Low Power Applications*, Ph.D. dissertation, Indian Institute of Technology, Roorkee, India, 2013.
22. Kanungo, J. and Dasgupta, S., Single Phase Energy Recovery Logic and Conventional CMOS Logic: A Comparative Analysis. *J. Microelectron. Solid*

State Electron., 2, 2A, 16–21, Scientific & Academic Publishing (SAP), USA, Apr. 2013.
23. Bhardwaj, A., Kumar, P., Raj, B., Anand, S., Design and Performance Optimization of doping-less Vertical Nanowire TFET using Gate Stack Technique. *J. Electron. Mater. (JEMS)*, 41, 7, 4005–4013, Springer, 2022.
24. Singh, J. and Raj, B., Tunnel Current Model of Asymmetric MIM Structure Levying Various Image Forces to Analyze the Characteristics of Filamentary Memristor. *Appl. Phys. A*, 125, 3, 203.1–203.11, Springer, Feb 2019.
25. Goyal, C., Ubhi, J.S., Raj, B., Low Leakage Zero Ground Noise Nanoscale Full Adder using Source Biasing Technique. *J. Nanoelectron. Optoelectron.*, 14, 360–370, American Scientific Publishers, March 2019.
26. Bhardwaj, A.K., Gupta, S., Raj, B., Singh, A., Impact of Double Gate Geometry on the Performance of Carbon Nanotube Field Effect Transistor Structures for Low Power Digital Design. *Comput. Theor. Nanosci.*, 16, 1813–1820, ASP, 2019.
27. Jain, N. and Raj, B., Thermal Stability Analysis and Performance Exploration of Asymmetrical Dual-k underlap Spacer (ADKUS) SOI FinFET for Security and Privacy Applications. *Indian J. Pure Appl. Phys. (IJPAP)*, 57, 352–360, May 2019.
28. Jain, N. and Raj, B., Dual-k Spacer Region Variation at the Drain Side of Asymmetric SOI FinFET Structure: Performance Analysis towards the Analog/RF Design Applications. *J. Nanoelectron. Optoelectron.*, 14, 349–359, American Scientific Publishers, March 2019.
29. Singh, J., Sharma, S., Raj, B., Khosla, M., Analysis of barrier layer thickness on performance of In1-xGaxAs based Gate Stack Cylindrical Gate Nanowire MOSFET. *JNO*, 13, 1473–1477, ASP, Oct 2018.
30. Jain, N. and Raj, B., Analysis and Performance Exploration of High-k SOI FinFETs Over the Conventional Low-k SOI FinFET toward Analog/RF Design. *J. Semicond. (JoS)*, 39, 12, 124002-1-7, IOP Science, Dec 2018.
31. Goyal, C., Ubhi, J.S., Raj, B., A reliable leakage reduction technique for approximate full adder with reduced ground bounce noise. *J. Math. Probl. Eng. Hindawi*, 2018, Article ID 3501041, 16, 15, Oct.
32. Anuradha, J.S., Raj, B., Khosla, M., Design and Performance Analysis of Nano-scale Memristor-based Nonvolatile SRAM. *J. Sens. Letter*, 16, 798–805, American Scientific Publishers, Oct 2018.
33. Wadhwa, G. and Raj, B., Parametric Variation Analysis of Charge-Plasma-based Dielectric Modulated JLTFET for Biosensor Application. *IEEE Sens. J.*, 18, 15, 6070–6077, August 1, 2018. (SCI).
34. Singh, J. and Raj, B., Comparative Analysis of Memristor Models for Memories Design. *JoS*, 39, 7, 074006-1-12, IoP, July 2018.
35. Yadav, D., Chouhan, S.S., Vishvakarma, S.K., Raj, B., Application Specific Microcontroller Design for IoT based WSN. *Sens. Letter*, 16, 374–385, ASP, May 2018.

36. Singh, G., Sarin, R.K., Raj, B., Fault-Tolerant Design and Analysis of Quantum-Dot Cellular Automata Based Circuits. *IEEE/IET Circuits Devices Syst.*, 12, 638–64, 2018.
37. Singh, J. and Raj, B., Modeling of Mean Barrier Height Levying Various Image Forces of Metal Insulator Metal Structure to Enhance the Performance of Conductive Filament Based Memristor Model. *IEEE Nanotechnol.*, 17, 2, 268–267, March 2018.
38. Jain, A., Sharma, S., Raj, B., Analysis of Triple Metal Surrounding Gate (TM-SG) III-V Nanowire MOSFET for Photosensing Application. *Opto-electronics J.*, 26, 2, 141–148, Elsevier, May 2018.
39. Jain, A., Sharma, S., Raj, B., Design and Analysis of High Sensitivity Photosensor Using Cylindrical Surrounding Gate MOSFET for Low Power Sensor Applications. *Eng. Sci. Technol. Int. J.*, 19, 4, 1864–1870, Elsevier's, December 2016.
40. Kumar, G.S., Singh, A., Raj, B., Design and Analysis of Gate All Around CNTFET based SRAM cell Design. *J. Comput. Electron.*, 17, 1, pp 138–145, Springer, March 2018.
41. Singh, G., Sohi, B.S., Raj, B., Material Properties Analysis of Graphene Base Transistor (GBT) for VLSI Analog Circuits. *Indian J. Pure Appl. Phys. (IJPAP)*, 55, 896–902, Dec 2017.
42. Kumar, S. and Raj, B., Estimation of Stability and Performance metric for Inward Access Transistor based 6T SRAM Cell Design using n-type/p-type DMDG-GDOV TFET. *IEEE VLSI Circuits Syst. Letter*, 3, 2, 25–39, June 2017.
43. Sharma, S., Kumar, A., Pattanaik, M., Raj, B., Forward Body Biased Multimode Multi-Threshold CMOS Technique for Ground Bounce Noise Reduction in Static CMOS Adders. *Int. J. Inf. Electron. Eng.*, 3, 3, 567–572, 2013.
44. Singh, H., Kumar, P., Raj, B., Performance Analysis of Majority Gate SET Based 1-bit Full Adder. *Int. J. Comput. Commun. Eng. (IJCCE)*, 2, 4, IACSIT Press Singapore, ISSN: 2010-3743, 2013.
45. Bhardwaj, A.K., Gupta, S., Raj, B., Investigation of Parameters for Schottky Barrier (SB) Height for Schottky Barrier Based Carbon Nanotube Field Effect Transistor Device. *J. Nanoelectron. Optoelectron.*, 15, 783–791, ASP, July 2020.
46. Bansal, P. and Raj, B., Memristor: A Versatile Nonlinear Model for Dopant Drift and Boundary Issues. *JCTN*, 14, 5, 2319–2325, American Scientific Publishers, May 2017.
47. Jain, N. and Raj, B., An Analog and Digital Design Perspective Comprehensive Approach on Fin-FET (Fin-Field Effect transistor) Technology - A Review. *Rev. Adv. Sci. Eng. (RASE)>*, 5, 1–14, ASP, 2016.
48. Raj, B., Saxena, A.K., Dasgupta, S., Analytical Modeling for the Estimation of Leakage Current and Subthreshold Swing Factor of Nanoscale Double Gate FinFET Device. *Microelectron. International UK*, 26, 53–63, 2009.

49. Soniya, S.S., Wadhwa, G., Raj, B., An Analytical Modeling for Dual Source Vertical Tunnel Field Effect Transistor. *Int. J. Recent Technol. Eng. (IJRTE)*, 8, 2, 603–608, July 2019.
50. Singh, S. and Raj, B., Design and analysis of hetrojunction Vertical T-shaped Tunnel Field Effect Transistor. *J. Electron. Mater.*, 48, 10, 6253–6260, Springer, October 2019.
51. Goyal, C., Ubhi, J.S., Raj, B., A Low Leakage CNTFET based Inexact Full Adder for Low Power Image Processing Applications. *Int. J. Circuit Theory Appl.*, 47, 9, 1446–1458, Wiley, September 2019.
52. Raj, B., Saxena, A.K., Dasgupta, S., A Compact Drain Current and Threshold Voltage Quantum Mechanical Analytical Modeling for FinFETs. *J. Nanoelectron. Optoelectron. (JNO)*, 3, 2, 163–170, USA, 2008.
53. Wadhwa, G. and Raj, B., An Analytical Modeling of Charge Plasma based Tunnel Field Effect Transistor with Impacts of Gate underlap Region. *Superlattices Microstruct.*, 142, 106512, Elsevier, June 2020.
54. Singh, S. and Raj, B., Modeling and Simulation analysis of SiGe hetrojunction Double GateVertical t-shaped Tunnel FET. *Superlattices Microstruct.*, 142, 106496, Elsevier, June 2020.
55. Jain, N. and Raj, B., Device and Circuit Co-Design Perspective Comprehensive Approach on FinFET Technology - A Review. *J. Electron Devices*, 23, 1, pp 1890–1901, 2016.
56. Kumar, S. and Raj, B., Analysis of I_{ON} and Ambipolar Current for Dual-Material Gate-drain Overlapped DG-TFET. *J. Nanoelectron. Optoelectron.*, 11, 323–333, American Scientific Publishers, USA, June 2016.
57. Anjum, N., Bali, T., Raj, B., Design and Simulation of Handwritten Multiscript Character Recognition. *Int. J. Adv. Res. Comput. Commun. Eng.*, 2, 7, 2544–2549, July 2013.
58. Singh, K. and Raj, B., Performance and analysis of temperature dependent Multi-walled Carbon Nanotubes as Global Interconnects at different technology nodes. *J. Comput. Electron.*, 14, 2, 469–476, Springer, June 2015.
59. Kumar, S. and Raj, B., Compact channel potential analytical Modeling of DG-TFET based on Evanescent–mode Approach. *J. Comput. Electron.*, 14, 2, 820–827, Springer, July 2015.
60. Singh, K. and Raj, B., Temperature Dependent Modeling and Performance Evaluation of Multi-Walled CNT and Single-Walled CNT as Global Interconnects. *J. Electron. Mater.*, 44, 12, 4825–4835, Springer, Dec 2015.
61. Sharma, V.K., Pattanaik, M., Raj, B., INDEP approach for leakage reduction in nanoscale CMOS circuits. *Int. J. Electron.*, 102, 2, 200–215, Taylor & Francis, 2014.
62. Singh, K. and Raj, B., Influence of Temperature on MWCNT bundle, SWCNT bundle and Copper interconnects for Nanoscaled Technology nodes. *J. Mater. Sci.: Mater. Electron.*, 26, 8, 6134–6142, Springer, 2015.

63. Anjum, N., Bali, T., Raj, B., Design and Simulation of Handwritten Gurumukhi and Devanagri Numerical Recognition. *Int. J. Comput. Appl.*, 73, 12, 16–21, Foundation of Computer Science, New York, USA, 2013.
64. Khandelwal, S., Gupta, V., Raj, B., Gupta, R.D., Process Variability Aware Low Leakage Reliable Nano Scale DG-FinFET SRAM Cell Design Technique. *J. Nanoelectron. Optoelectron.*, 10, 6, 810–817, December 2015.
65. Sharma, V.K., Pattanaik, M., Raj, B., ONOFIC Approach: Low Power High Speed Nanoscale VLSI Circuits Design. *Int. J. Electron.*, 101, 1, 61–73, Taylor & Francis, 2014.
66. Khandelwal, S., Raj, B., Gupta, R.D., FinFET based 6T SRAM Cell Design: Analysis of Performance Metric, Process Variation and Temperature Effect. *J. Comput. Theor. Nanosci.*, 12, 2500–2506, ASP, USA, 2015.
67. Singh, S., Yadav, S., Rahul, J., Srivastava, A., Raj, B., Impact of HfO_2 in Graded Channel Dual Insulator Double Gate MOSFET. *J. Comput. Theor. Nanosci.*, 12, 6, 950–953, American Scientific Publishers, April 2015.
68. Sharma, V.K., Pattanaik, M., Raj, B., PVT variations aware low leakage INDEP approach for nanoscale CMOS Circuits. *Microelectron. Reliab.*, 54, pp 90–99, Elsevier, 2014.
69. Raj, B., Saxena, A.K., Dasgupta, S., Quantum Mechanical Analytical Modeling of Nanoscale DG FinFET: Evaluation of Potential, Threshold Voltage and Source/Drain Resistance. *Elsevier's J. Mater. Sci. Semicond. Process.*, 16, 4, 1131–1137, Elsevier, 2013.
70. Gopal, M., Prasad, S.S.D., Raj, B., 8T SRAM Cell Design for Dynamic and Leakage Power Reduction. *Int. J. Comput. Appl.*, 71, 9, 43–48, Foundation of Computer Science, New York, USA, June 2013.
71. Pattanaik, M., Raj, B., Sharma, S., Kumar, A., Diode Based Trimode Multi-Threshold CMOS Technique for Ground Bounce Noise Reduction in Static CMOS Adders. *Adv. Mater. Res.*, 548, 885–889, Trans Tech Publications, Switzerland, 2012.
72. Raj, B., Saxena, A.K., Dasgupta, S., Nanoscale FinFET Based SRAM Cell Design: Analysis of Performance metric, Process variation, Underlapped FinFET and Temperature effect. *IEEE Circuits Syst. Mag.*, 11, 2, 38–50, 2011.
73. Sharma, V.K., Pattanaik, M., Raj, B., Leakage Current ONOFIC Approach for Deep Submicron VLSI Circuit Design. *Int. J. Electr. Comput. Electron. Commun. Eng.*, 7, 4, 239–244, World Academy of Sciences, Engineering and Technology, 2013.
74. Kaur, P., Gill, S.S., Raj, B., Comparative Analysis of OFETs Materials and Devices for Sensor Applications. *J. Silicon*, 14, 4463–4471, Springer, 2022.
75. Sharma, S.K., Kumar, P., Raj, B., Raj, B., $In_{1-x}Ga_xAs$ Double Metal Gate-Stacking Cylindrical Nanowire MOSFET for highly sensitive Photo detector. *J. Silicon*, 14, 3535–3541, Springer, 2022.
76. Raj, B., Saxena, A.K., Dasgupta, S., Analytical Modeling of Quasi Planar Nanoscale Double Gate FinFET with Source/Drain Resistance and field

dependent carrier mobility: A quantum mechanical study. *J. Comput. (JCP)*, 4, 9, 1–8, Academy Publisher, Finland, 2009.

77. Bhushan, S., Khandelwal, S., Raj, B., Analyzing Different Mode FinFET based Memory Cell at Different Power Supply for Leakage Reduction, in: *Seventh International Conference on Bio-Inspired Computing: Theories and Application, (BIC-TA 2012) Advances in Intelligent Systems and Computing*, vol. 202, pp. 89–100, 20122013.
78. Singh, J. and Raj, B., Temperature Dependent Analytical Modeling and Simulations of Nanoscale Memristor. *Eng. Sci. Technol. Int. J.*, 21, 862–868, Elsevier's, Oct 2018.
79. Singh, S., Bala, S., Raj, B., Raj, B., Improved Sensitivity of Dielectric Modulated Junctionless Transistor for Nanoscale Biosensor Design. *Sens. Letter*, 18, 328–333, ASP, April 2020.
80. Kumar, V., Vishvakarma, S.K., Raj, B., Design and Performance Analysis of ASIC for IoT Applications. *Sens. Letter*, 18, 31–38, ASP, Jan 2020.
81. Jaiswal, A., Sarin, R.K., Raj, B., Sukhija, S., A Novel Circular Slotted Microstrip-fed Patch Antenna with Three Triangle Shape Defected Ground Structure for Multiband Applications. *Adv. Electromagn. (AEM)*, 7, 3, 56–63, Aug 2018.
82. Wadhwa, G. and Raj, B., Label Free Detection of Biomolecules using Charge-Plasma-Based Gate Underlap Dielectric Modulated Junctionless TFET. *J. Electron. Mater. (JEMS)*, 47, 8, 4683–4693, Springer, August 2018.
83. Singh, G., Sarin, R.K., Raj, B., Design and Performance Analysis of a New Efficient Coplanar Quantum-Dot Cellular Automata Adder. *Indian J. Pure Appl. Phys. (IJPAP)*, 55, 97–103, February 2017.
84. Kaur, P., Pandey, V., Raj, B., Comparative Study of Efficient Design, Control and Monitoring of Solar Power using IoT. *Sens. Letter*, 18, 419–426, ASP, May 2020.
85. Bhardwaj, A.K., Gupta, S., Raj, B., Development & Analysis of compact model for Double Gate Schottky Barrier CNTFET. *J. Nanoelectron. Optoelectron.*, 15, 1199–1208, ASP, Aug 2020.
86. Wadhwa, G., Kamboj, P., Singh, J., Raj, B., Design and Investigation of Junctionless DGTFET for Biological Molecule Recognition. *Trans. Electr. Electron. Mater.*, 22, 282–289, Springer, 2021.
87. Verma, S.K., Singh, S., Wadhwa, G., Raj, B., Detection of Biomolecules using Charge-Plasma based Gate Underlap Dielectric Modulated Dopingless TFET. *Trans. Electr. Electron. Mater. (TEEM)*, 21, 528–535, Springer, June 2020.
88. Jain, N. and Raj, B., Impact of underlap spacer region variation on Electrostatic and analog/RF performance of symmetrical high-k SOI FinFET at 20 nm channel length. *J. Semicond. (JoS)*, 38, 12, 122002, IOP Science, Dec 2017.
89. Singh, S. and Raj, B., Analytical Modeling and Simulation analysis of T-shaped III-V heterojunction Vertical T-FET. *Superlattices Microstruct.*, 147, 106717, Elsevier, Nov 2020.

90. Singh, G., Sarin, R.K., Raj, B., Design and Analysis of Area Efficient QCA Based Reversible Logic Gates. *J. Microprocess. Microsys.*, 52, 59–68, Elsevier, May 2017.
91. Singh, S. and Raj, B., Parametric variation analysis on hetero-junction Vertical t-shape TFET for Suppressing ambipolar conduction. *Indian J. Pure Appl. Phys.*, 58, 478–485, June 2020.
92. Soniya, S.S., Wadhwa, G., Raj, B., Design and Analysis of Dual Source Vertical Tunnel Field Effect Transistor for high performance. *Trans. Electr. Electron. Mater.*, 21, 74–82, Springer, Oct 2019.
93. Kaur, M., Gupta, N., Kumar, S., Raj, B., Singh, A.K., RF Performance Analysis of Intercalated Graphene Nanoribbon Based Global Level Interconnects. *J. Comput. Electron.*, 19, 1002–1013, Springer, June 2020.
94. Wadhwa, G. and Raj, B., Design and Performance Analysis of Junctionless TFET Biosensor for high sensitivity. *IEEE Nanotechnol.*, 18, 567–574, 2019.
95. Singh, J. and Raj, B., Enhanced Nonlinear Memristor Model Encapsulating Stochastic Dopant Drift. *JNO*, 14, 958–963, ASP, 2019.
96. Singh, M., Chaudhary, T., Raj, B., Enhancing FeFET Structures for Non-volatile On-chip Memories: Design and Comparative Analysis. *Int. J. Numer. Modell. Electron. Networks Devices Fields*, 38, 1–9, 2024.
97. Singh, M., Chaudhary, T., Raj, B., Drain Current and Transconductance Analysis of GaN GAA Nanowire FET with High K Dielectric. *ECS J. Sci. Technol.*, 12, 6070–6077, 2023.
98. Singh, M., Chaudhary, T., Raj, B., Design of Si and Ge Nanowire FET for Low Power Application. *J. Silicon*, 15, 1491–1497, Springer, 2023.
99. Singh, M., Chaudhary, T., Raj, B., Electrical Characteristics Analysis of FeFET for Low Power Applications. *J. Nano*, 37, 1–8, 2024.
100. Kumar, M., Chaudhary, T., Raj, B., Design and Comparative Analysis of Ferroelectric Nanowire with Dielectric HfO_2 and $Al_2O_3$for Low Power Applications. *J. Electron. Mater.*, 53, 6785–6791, Springer, 2024.
101. Singh, G., Sarin, R.K., Raj, B., A Novel Robust Exclusive-OR Function Implementation in QCA Nanotechnology with Energy Dissipation Analysis. *J. Comput. Electron.*, 15, 2, 455–465, Springer, June 2016.
102. Wadhwa, G., Kamboj, P., Raj, B., Design optimisation of junctionless TFET biosensor for high sensitivity. *Adv. Nat. Sci.: Nanosci. Nanotechnol.*, 10, 045001 (7), 2019.
103. Bansal, P. and Raj, B., Memristor Modeling and Analysis for Linear Dopant Drift Kinetics. *J. Nanoeng. Nanomanuf.*, 6, 1–7, American Scientific Publishers, 2016.
104. Ashima, Vaithiyanathan, D., Raj, B., Performance Analysis of Charge Plasma induced Graded Channel Si nanotube. *J. Eng. Res. (JER)*, EMSME Special Issue, 146–154, Aug 2021.
105. Tomar, A.S., Magraiya, V.K., Raj, B., Scaling of Access and Data Transistor for High Performance DRAM Cell Design. *Quantum Matter*, 2, 412–416, Oct. 2013.

106. Jain, N. and Raj, B., Parasitic Capacitance and Resistance Model Development and Optimization of Raised Source/Drain SOI FinFET Structure for Analog Circuit Applications. *J. Nanoelectron. Optoelectron.*, 13, 531–539, ASP, USA, April 2018.
107. Singh, S., Vishvakarma, S.K., Raj, B., Analytical Modeling of Split-Gate Junction-Less Transistor for a Biosensor Application. *Sens. Bio-sensing*, 18, 31–36, Elsevier, April 2018.
108. Gopal, M. and Raj, B., Low Power 8T SRAM Cell Design for High Stability Video Applications. *ITSI Trans. Electr. Electron. Eng.*, 1, 5, 91–97, 2013.
109. Raj, B., Mitra, J., Bihani, D.K., Rangharajan, V., Saxena, A.K., Dasgupta, S., Analysis of Noise Margin, Power and Process Variation for 32 nm FinFET Based 6T SRAM Cell. *J. Comput. (JCP)*, 5, 6, 1–8, Academy Publisher, Finland, 2010.
110. Sharma, D., Mehra, R., Raj, B., Comparative Analysis of Photovoltaic Technologies for High Efficiency Solar Cell Design. *Superlattices Microstruct.*, 153, 106861, Elsevier, May 2021.
111. Kaur, P., Buttar, A.S., Raj, B., A comprehensive Analysis of Nanoscale Transistor based Biosensor: A Review. *Indian J. Pure Appl. Phys.*, 59, 304–318, April 2021.
112. Yadav, D., Raj, B., Raj, B., Design and Simulation of Low Power Microcontroller for IoT Applications. *J. Sens. Lett.*, 18, 401–409, ASP, May 2020.
113. Singh, S. and Raj, B., A 2-D Analytical Surface Potential and Drain current Modeling of Double-Gate Vertical t-shaped Tunnel FET. *J. Comput. Electron.*, 19, 1154–1163, Springer, April 2020.
114. Singh, J. and Raj, B., An Accurate and Generic Window function for Nonlinear Memristor Model. *J. Comput. Electron.*, 18, 2, 640–647, Springer, June 2019.
115. Kaur, M., Gupta, N., Kumar, S., Raj, B., Singh, A.K., Comparative RF and Crosstalk Analysis of Carbon Based Nano Interconnects. *IET Circuits Devices Syst.*, 15, 6, 493–503, Feb 2021.
116. Kandasamy, N., Ahmad, F., Ajitha, D., Raj, B., Telagam, N., Quantum Dot Cellular Automata based Scan Flip Flop and Boundary Scan Register. *IETE J. Res.*, 66, 535–548, 2020.
117. Singh, J. and Raj, B., Design and Investigation of 7T2M NVSARM with Enhanced Stability and Temperature Impact on Store/Restore Energy. *IEEE Trans. Very Large Scale Integr. Syst.*, 27, 6, 1322–1328, June 2019.

9

High-Frequency Laminate Material-Based Antennas: Deploying Bridge-Coupled Antenna Arrays for mm Wave 5G and IoT V2X Telemetry Systems in Smart Cities

Arun Raj* **and Durbadal Mandal**

ECE-Department, National Institute of Technology, Durgapur, West-Bengal, India

Abstract

This chapter presents a modified bridge-coupled fed fractal array antenna for multiband applications using high-frequency laminate materials. The proposed antennas have a resonance frequency range of 24-40 GHz with ground-defected structure (DGS) design with 36 × 36 mm^2 dimensions with roger substrate, respectively. The central bridge coupled feed feeding technique is integrated with a circular congruent ring pattern ring and a bridge-coupled feed line connected to each element antenna. This integration significantly enhances antenna performance, manifesting in superior radiation properties, increased gain, enhanced directivity, and resonating behavior concerning each element, and exhibits multi-beam patterns for mm-wave 5G: V2X telemetry and IOT applications requirements, respectively.

The suggested design allows for the measurement of radiate power in fractal array antennae with DGS at peak directivities of 4.82 to 8.7 in dBi. With fractal arrays' versatile frequency capabilities and improved performance regarding resonate frequencies like 27.29, 35.14, and 39.1 GHz in the 24–40 GHz range, the proposed array antenna with ground defected structure is essential for telecommunications, military radar, medical imaging, automotive V2X, and consumer electronics like Wi-Fi and broadcasting. Its Phi = 00, Phi = 900, and Theta = 900, respectively. The proposed antenna provides excellent matching IoT applications in the range of 26-32GHz, 34.2-36GHz, and 38.1-39.8GHz with reflection coefficients of -36, -28, -17 dB concerning resonate frequencies such as 27.29, 35.14,

**Corresponding author*: arunraj61299@gmail.com

Ashish Maurya, Mandeep Singh and Balwinder Raj (eds.) Machine Learning in Nanoelectronics: Devices, Circuits and Systems, (257–306)

and 39.1GHz GHz, respectively. It covers span applications in the 'n257', 'n258', 'n259', 'n260', and 'n261' '5G' 'NR bands' as well as the anticipated '6G bands', including 'ground-based radio navigation' and other uses well-suited for 5G and future 6G applications.

Additionally, the suggested array antennae have peak gains between 7.3 and 9.5 dBi; they cover 20.68, 5.12, and 4.36% bandwidths in the 26–32 GHz, 34.2–36 GHz, and 38.1-39.8 GHz ranges, respectively. Computer simulation technology (CST) software was used to design and validate the suggested antenna, guaranteeing its reliable operation and appropriateness for deployment in smart city settings.

***Keywords*:** Fractals, bridge coupled fed antenna, array antenna, IoT, multi-beam patterns, V2X telemetry, laminate materials

9.1 Introduction

The ability of fractal antennas to achieve multiband operation, compact size, and other desirable characteristics for wireless communication systems has drawn much attention [1–30]. The Sierpinski and Hilbert curves and their modified forms are two of the many fractal geometries employed in antenna design and have been the subject of much research [1–12]. To illustrate its potential for wireless applications, Bharti, Bharti, and Sivia [1] proposed a "multiband nested square-shaped ring fractal antenna" with "circular ring elements." Similarly, Kumar and Pharwaha [2] created a multiband-optimized "Hilbert curve" fractal antenna. An "elliptical monopole-based super wideband fractal antenna" was presented by Singhal and Singh [3], demonstrating the adaptability of fractal geometries in attaining wideband operation. Karthikeya *et al.* [4] demonstrated the potential for high-frequency communication systems by presenting "a low-cost", "high-gain triple-band mmWave Sierpinski antenna" loaded with "uniplanar EBG" for "5G applications". Singh and Singh [5] optimized "a modified Sierpinski fractal antenna" for "broadband applications" to improve bandwidth performance. "Miniaturized decagonal Sierpinski UWB fractal antennas" were investigated by Ali *et al.* [6] and [7], proving that small designs are feasible for "ultra-wideband applications". "Wideband frequency reconfigurable Koch snowflake fractal antennas", which provide frequency tuning flexibility for various communication standards, were studied by Choukiker and Behera [8].

Praveena and Ponnapalli [9] offered insights into "array configurations and performance optimization strategies" in their review of fractal antenna array design. "A micro-machined modified Sierpinski gasket fractal antenna" was created by Kumar and Singh [10], especially for "satellite communications", "highlighting the significance of customized designs for particular application needs". The interdisciplinary nature of "fractal antenna research" was demonstrated by Kaur and Sivia [11], who used Minkowski, Giuseppe Peano, and Koch curves to design a "compact hybrid fractal antenna" for "biomedical applications". "A novel compact ultra-wideband planar fractal antenna" with "WLAN band" rejection was proposed by Garg *et al.* [12] to address the interference problems that are frequently present in wireless communication systems. In addition to conventional fractal geometries, scientists have investigated new forms like "wearable hybrid fractal DGS" [18], "snowflake fractals" [13], and "circular shape fractals" [16]. Intending to meet various application needs, from "broadband communication to biomedical sensing", these studies demonstrate the continuous "innovation and exploration" of "fractal antennas."

Nonetheless, scientists have combined fractal components with other "structures, like split ring resonators (SRRs)," in "fractal antennas" [22–27]. In introducing a "fractal microstrip antenna with Minkowski Island SRR" for broadband applications, Ahmad and Nornikman [23] demonstrated the complementary nature of metamaterial-inspired structures and fractal geometries. Fractal antennas are also used in several frequency bands, such as WLAN [20], UHF-RFID [24], and terahertz [15]. These studies highlight how adaptable fractal antennas are to various frequency ranges, making them appropriate for various wireless communication applications. Because of their small size, wideband capabilities, and multi-frequency operation, fractal antennas have become a promising technology in the wireless communication space.

This survey explores the design principles, performance metrics, and applications of fractal antennas in contemporary wireless systems, among other aspects of the technology. Due to their self-similar geometric patterns, fractal antennas have several benefits, including improved radiation characteristics, multiband operation, and miniaturization. In order to create antennas with the desired characteristics, researchers have thoroughly examined fractal geometries such as the Koch curve, Sierpinski carpet, and Sierpinski gasket [31]. Several design approaches and strategies have been proposed to maximize fractal antenna performance. For UHF band applications, Rayno and Sharma (2012) presented a wideband frequency-reconfigurable Spirograph planar monopole antenna [31]. Compact broadband top-loaded planar monopole antennas appropriate for low-frequency operations were the main focus of Indhu and Mohanan (2011) [32]. These studies demonstrate design strategies that accommodate various frequency bands and application needs. Fractal antenna performance is assessed using efficiency, radiation pattern, gain, and bandwidth. The significance of "lowering radar signatures in wireless systems" was highlighted by Rad *et al.* (2019), who proposed a small microstrip antenna based on a fractal metasurface with a wide bandwidth and "low radar cross-section" [34]. "Wideband and dual-frequency CPW-fed monopole antennas" were investigated by Wu (2007) and Shanmuganantham (2008) for particular wireless applications [35, 36]. Thanks to these studies, the trade-offs and optimizations required to achieve the desired antenna performance are better understood. Numerous wireless systems, such as WLAN, WiMAX, RFID, and 5G communication, use fractal antennas. Raj and Mandal (2022) emphasized the necessity of effective designs in next-generation wireless networks by comparing patch antenna arrays and modified fractal antennas for 5G communication [44–47]. Moreover, Abhyuday *et al.* (2022) investigated millimeter-wave wideband Koch fractal antennas, demonstrating their applicability in high-frequency wireless applications [48–50]. Furthermore, cutting-edge designs for new wireless standards like 6G and satellite communication are anticipated to be the main focus of fractal antenna research. In discussing hybrid-fed array antenna design and implementation for Sub-6 GHz and 5G mm-wave communication, Raj and Mandal (2023) emphasized the continuous efforts to improve antenna performance for developing wireless technologies [51–54]. By combining compactness, wideband operation, and frequency band adaptability, fractal antennas are a breakthrough in wireless communication. They use fractal geometries, which enable more effective use of available space, to produce smaller antennas with wider operating bandwidths. Their compact design makes them perfect for contemporary wireless devices with limited space [55–59]. Their versatility for various applications, from military communication systems to mobile phones, is further enhanced by their ability to function efficiently across multiple frequency bands. Furthermore, to increase the potential of fractal antennas, more research and creative antenna design are essential. Performance optimization techniques, such as refining the fractal geometries and materials used, will enhance their efficiency and reliability and fractal antenna technology will play a key role in meeting these needs, supporting the development of next-generation wireless communication systems.

9.2 Antenna Design Equations

In the design of microstrip patch antennas, the width and length of a patch are determined by the following mathematical formulas [55]:

Equation (9.1) determines the "patch's width":

$$'\left((\mathrm{W})=\left(\frac{(C)}{(2f\sqrt{\frac{(\varepsilon\mathrm{r}+1)}{2}})}\right)\right)' \tag{9.1}$$

where, the speed of light in "free space" is $"\mathrm{c}." = 3\times10^{8}\, {}^{m}/_{s}$

'f_r'– 'Resonate freq.', 'ε_r' – 'Relative permittivity'

The effective relative permittivity constant, "εreff," is calculated as follows:

"effective relative permittivity,"'ε_r' can be calculated as [55]:

$$'\left((\mathrm{W})=(\frac{1}{(2\mathrm{fr}\sqrt{(\mu\varepsilon)})})(\sqrt{(\frac{2}{((\epsilon r)+1)})})\right)' \tag{9.2}$$

$$`\left((\varepsilon\mathrm{reff})=(\frac{(\epsilon r+1)}{2})+(\frac{(\varepsilon r-1)}{2})\times\left(1+12(\frac{(h)}{(w)})\right)^{\frac{-1}{2}}\right)' \tag{9.3}$$

Where,

'h' – 'height of dielectric substrate' in 'mm'

'w' –'Patch's width', '$\varepsilon_{\mathrm{reff}}$' – 'Relative permittivity'

The ('Lreff') 'effective' 'length' is accounted as:

$$`\left((\mathrm{Lreff})=(\frac{(c)}{(2f\sqrt{(\varepsilon r)})})-(2.\Delta L)\right)' \tag{9.4}$$

Equation (9.2) is used to compute "W," and the length's extension can be determined as follows:

$$`\left(\Delta L=(h)\times(\frac{((\varepsilon\mathrm{reff})+(0.3))\times\left((\frac{W}{h})+(0.264)\right)}{((\varepsilon\mathrm{reff})-(0.258))\times\left((\frac{W}{h})+(0.8)\right)})\right)' \tag{9.5}$$

"Actual patch length" was determined as follows:

$$`\left(L = \left(\frac{1}{(2fr\sqrt{(\varepsilon)})}\right) \times \left(\frac{1}{(\sqrt{(\mu\varepsilon)})}\right) - (2.\Delta L) \right)' \tag{9.6}$$

'(L1 = (L + 6.h)' as well as "(W1 = (W + 6.h)" as "Effective length & width":

$$`\left(\text{Band width Percentage} = \left(\frac{2(f2 - f1)}{(f1 + f2)}\right) \times 100 \right)' \tag{9.7}$$

For '50 Ohms', the 'feed point Position' can be accounted by,

$$'\left(('\text{Rin}(y = y0)') = ('\text{Rin}(y = 0)') \cos\left(\frac{\pi}{L} y0\right)^2 \right)' \tag{9.8}$$

Where 'R_{in}(y = y0)' as '50 Ohms', Then 'R_{in}(y = 0)' is roughly accounted as,

$$`(`Z_{in}') = (`1/Y_{in}') = (`R_{in}')' = `(`1/2G_1')'$$

$$`\left((G1) = \begin{cases} \left(\frac{1}{90}\left(\frac{W}{\lambda}\right)^2\right) & (W \ll \lambda) \\ \left(\frac{1}{120}\left(\frac{W}{\lambda}\right)\right) & (W \gg \lambda) \end{cases} \right)' \tag{9.9}$$

9.3 Design and Simulation

(i) Simulation and analysis of Simple patch (step 1) to step 2 and final element antenna, respectively

As detailed in Table 9.1, the fractal-inspired array antenna features a compact square design measuring 36 mm by 36 mm on the ground plane, with a substrate height (h) of 1.6 mm and a low loss tangent (Tan δ) of 0.002. It optimally supports its operation across the 24 to 40 GHz frequency range,

Table 9.1 Basic design parameters for fractal inspired array antenna.

Antenna description	**Fractal inspired array antenna (mm)**
Ground as (L Array × W Array)	36 × 36
Height of substrate as (h)	1.6
Loss tangent as (Tan δ)	0.002
Frequency Range as (fr)	24 - 40GHz
Feeding Technique used	Bridge Coupled feeding
Design Shape	Square

crucial for modern high-frequency applications such as 5G and future 6G networks. Utilizing a bridge-coupled feeding technique enhances efficiency in signal transmission and reception. Table 9.2 provides further insight into the antenna's design parameters, delineating specific dimensions and notations that influence its performance. Parameters such as LG, WG, LP, WP, and various slot dimensions are meticulously calibrated to achieve optimal resonance and radiation characteristics [56–62]. The iterative design process, depicted in Figure 9.1, underscores the antenna's evolution through successive optimizations performance metrics.

The optimized antenna design progressed through several iterations, as shown in Figure 9.1. Initially, a primary patch antenna was developed with a feedline coupled through a bridge configuration. Subsequent iterations

Table 9.2 Notation for the design parameters of antennas (in mm) (Figures 9.1, 9.13, and 9.14).

LG	**WG**	**LP**	**WP**	**A**	**B**	**C**	**D**	**E**	**F**
30	30	20	20	5	4	2	3	0.75	1.4
G	H	R1	'R'	I	J	K	L	M	N
0.2	1.2	12.5	11.5	5	0.5	0.5	3	2	3
O	P	Q	R	S	T	U	V	D1	D2 / D3
2.5	1	5	2	7	3	0.2	1.5	9	7 / 5
D4	D5	d1	d2	d3	d4	d5	d6	LGAraay	WGArray
9	3	3	2.5	2	1.5	1	0.5	36	36

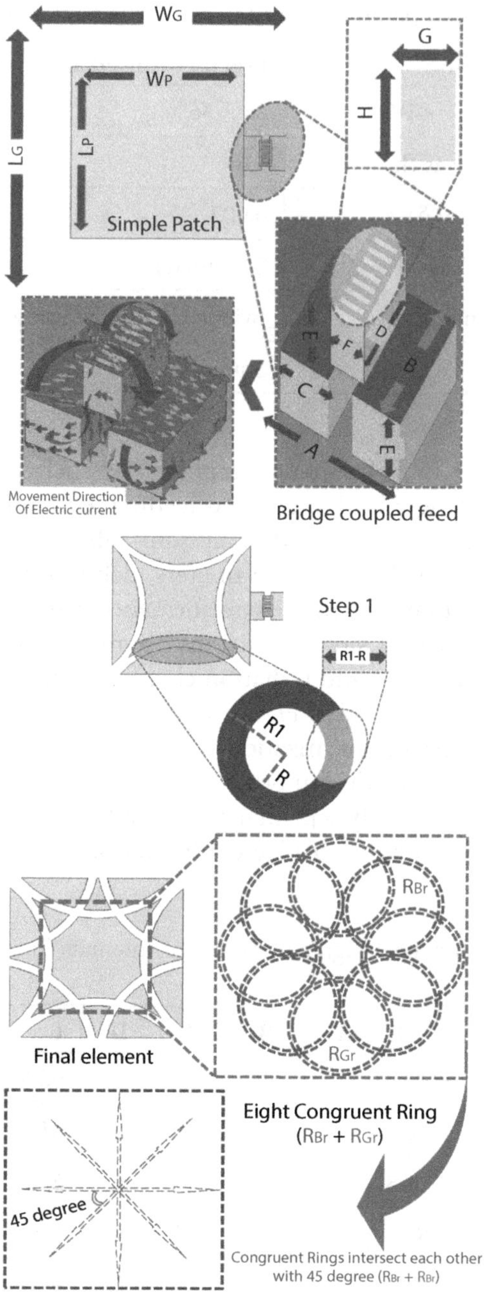

Figure 9.1 Optimized antenna iterations through various iteration as depicted in figure as iteration (simple patch, step 1 to final element antenna).

involved enhancements, such as slotting a congruent ring pattern into the antenna structure [63–70]. The final iteration incorporated four congruent rings, each colored differently, with slots arranged at a 45-degree angle, as detailed in Figure 9.1 and Table 9.2. These modifications aimed to improve antenna performance across multiple frequency bands, including 5G and anticipated 6G applications, by enhancing impedance matching and radiation characteristics through innovative geometrical adjustments and pattern slotting techniques [71–78].

Figure 9.2 illustrates the S11 parameter against frequency for a primary patch antenna. S11, representing the reflection coefficient, indicates how efficiently the antenna transfers power to the transmission line [79–86]. A lower S11 value denotes better impedance matching, minimizing reflections, and optimizing power transfer.

Figure 9.3 shows convergence plots for reflection and radiated power. These plots depict how the antenna's performance stabilizes with increasing frequency, ensuring consistent radiation characteristics across the

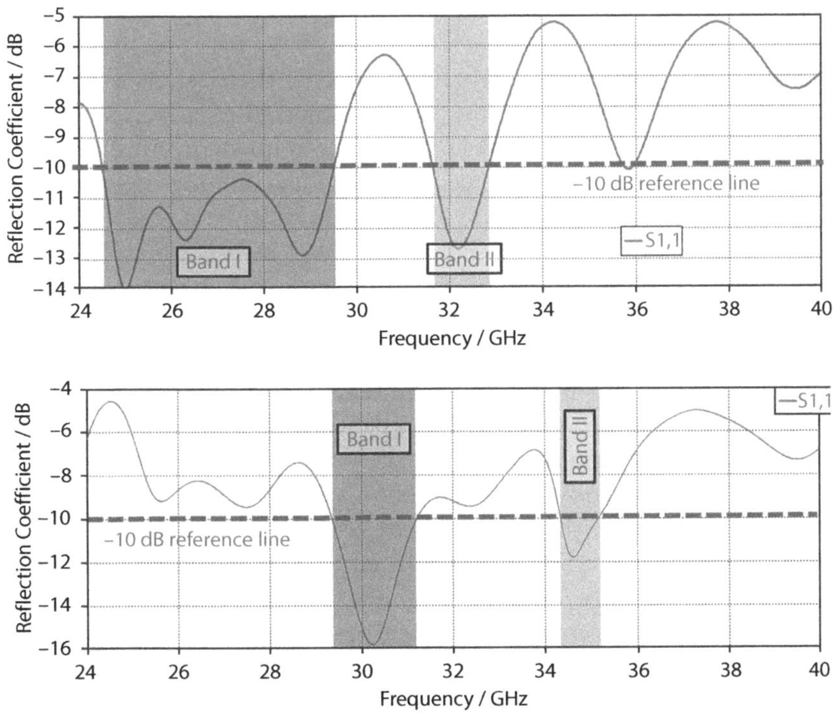

Figure 9.2 S_{11} vs frequency graph concerning simple patch and step 1 through mentioned in Figure 9.1.

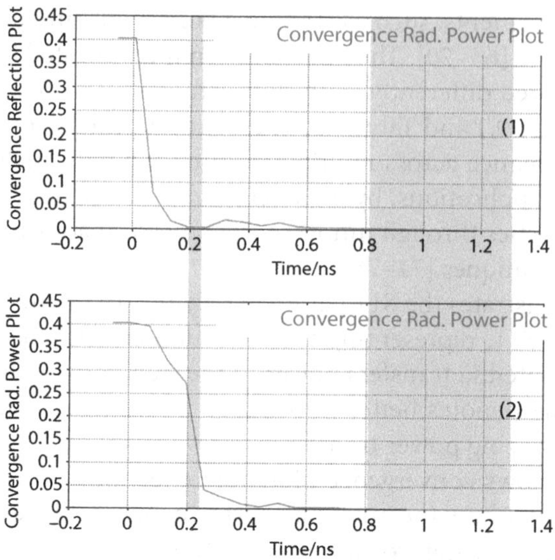

Figure 9.3 Convergence plot concerning frequency for reflection and radiated for simple patch antenna.

operational bandwidth [87–94]. Figure 9.4 further details the current and voltage characteristics of the simple patch antenna across different frequencies. These graphs provide insights into how current distribution influences the antenna's resonance and efficiency. Building upon the simple patch antenna, Step 1 (Figure 9.2) introduces enhancements to refine performance metrics. The S11 plot (Figure 9.2) reveals improvements in impedance matching compared to the primary patch antenna (Figure 9.1), indicating reduced reflections and better overall efficiency. Figure 9.5 delves into current and voltage distribution for the Step 1 antenna. These graphs highlight adjustments in the antenna's electromagnetic behavior, showcasing potential enhancements in bandwidth and efficiency over the simple patch design (Figure 9.4).

Figure 9.6 shows convergence plots for reflection and radiated power for the Step 1 antenna. The convergence over frequency suggests improved stability and consistent radiation performance across the desired operating bands [95–104]. Figure 9.7 presents the proposed element antenna's S11 and 3dB beamwidth versus frequency. These graphs depict the antenna's impedance characteristics and radiation pattern width across frequencies. A broad bandwidth with low S11 values and consistent beamwidth indicates robust performance suitable for diverse communication applications [105–113]. Figure 9.8 details current and voltage distributions across

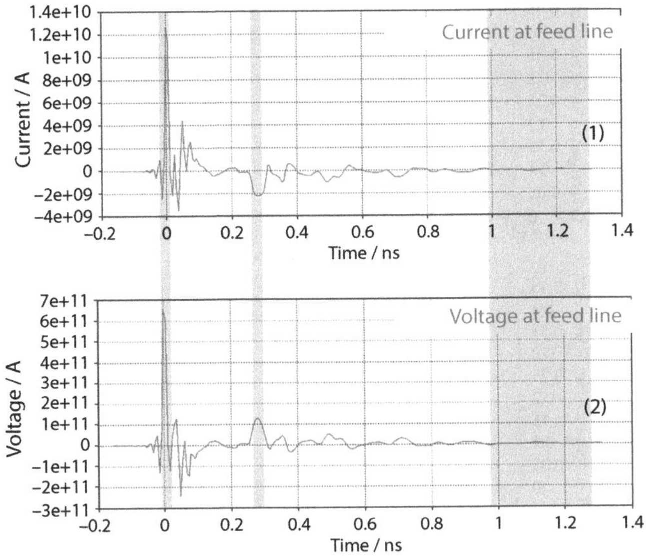

Figure 9.4 Current, voltage concerning frequency for simple patch antenna.

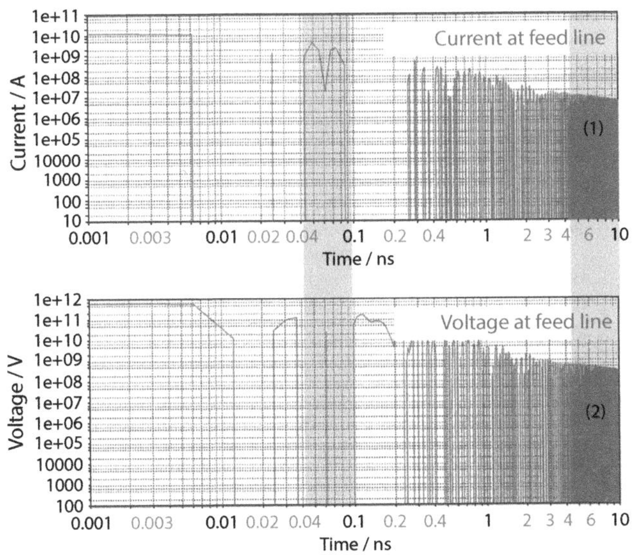

Figure 9.5 Current, voltage concerning frequency for step 1 antenna through mentioned in Figure 9.1.

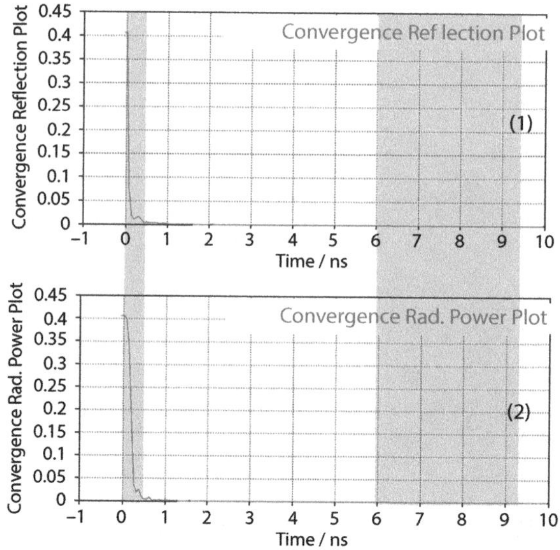

Figure 9.6 Convergence plot concerning frequency for reflection and radiated power step 1 antenna through mentioned in Figure 9.1.

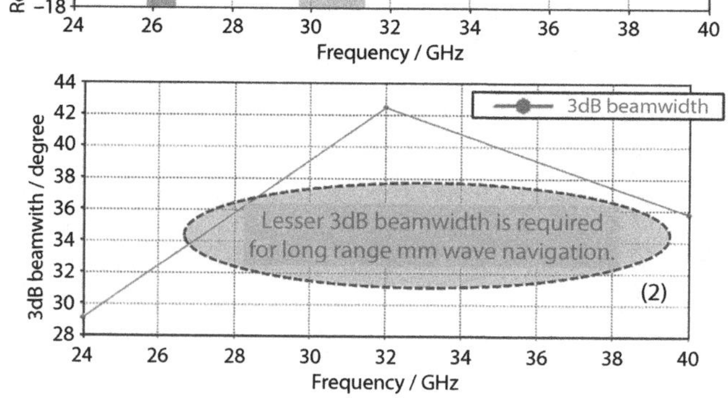

Figure 9.7 S_{11}, 3dB beamwidth vs. frequency graph concerning proposed element antenna, respectively.

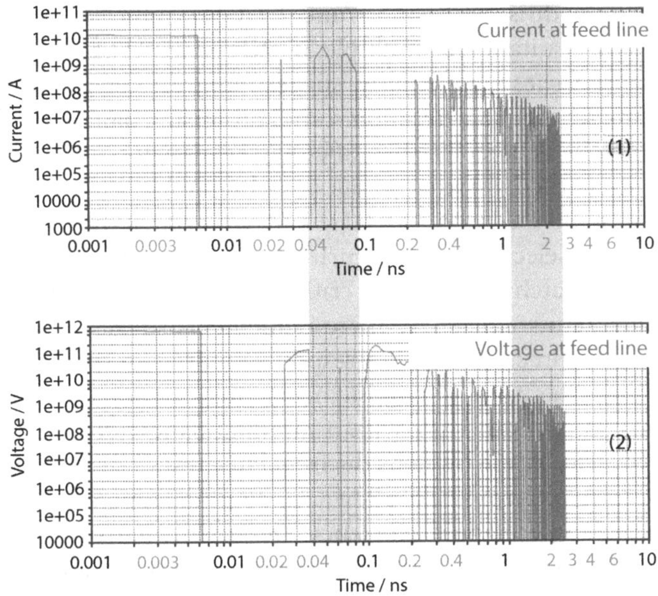

Figure 9.8 Current voltage vs. frequency graph concerning proposed element antenna, respectively.

Table 9.3 Study of different parameters of simple patch, including the different design step between iterations.

Figure 9.1	Res. freq. (fr) (GHz)	f1 (GHz)	f2 (GHz)	Bandwidth (GHz)	Bandwidth (%)	Return loss (dB)
Simple patch	25, 26.7 32.1	24.4 31.6	29.5 32.7	5.1 1.1	18.9 3.4	14 12.5
Step 2	30.1 34.6	29.6 34.3	31.2 35.1	1.6 0.8	5.2 2.3	15.8 11.6
(Final Element)	26.1 30.6	25.8 29.6	26.5 31.5	0.7 1.9	2.6 6.2	12.5 17.6

frequencies for the proposed element antenna. These graphs illustrate optimized electromagnetic characteristics, ensuring efficient power transfer and minimal losses throughout the operational spectrum.

The initial design of the simple patch antenna, as shown in Table 9.3, exhibits resonant frequencies ranging from 25 GHz to 32.1 GHz. It achieves moderate bandwidths between 5.1 and 1.1 GHz, indicating a broad frequency coverage suitable for multiple 5G NR bands [114–121]. However, the return loss varies significantly, suggesting areas for improvement in impedance matching. This iteration shows promising bandwidth but lacks optimal return loss characteristics, affecting efficiency.

In Step 2, marked improvements are observed with a narrower frequency range of 30.1 GHz to 34.6 GHz and reduced bandwidth, indicating better frequency selectivity. The return loss improves marginally, enhancing impedance matching, which is critical for minimizing signal loss and maximizing antenna efficiency. These refinements suggest a step towards achieving a more precise frequency response tailored for specific 5G bands.

By the final iteration (Final Element), frequencies stabilize further within 26.1 GHz to 30.6 GHz with a minimal bandwidth of 0.7 GHz to 1.9 GHz. This refinement tightens the frequency response and significantly improves return loss from 12.5 dB to 17.6 dB, indicating excellent impedance matching and enhanced efficiency. Despite the narrower bandwidth, the antenna demonstrates robust performance characteristics suitable for targeted 5G and future 6G applications [122–127].

Table 9.4 illustrates the impact of these design improvements on radiation efficiency, directivity, and other parameters. The final element antenna achieves a 3dB beamwidth of 33 to 41 degrees, indicating a focused radiation pattern ideal for communication applications. Radiation efficiency exceeds 93%, ensuring minimal power loss during transmission, while directivity and peak gain demonstrate improved directional signal strength and coverage [128–136]. Figure 9.9 displays convergence plots for the proposed element antenna, highlighting stable performance in reflection and radiated power across frequencies. This stability is crucial for maintaining signal integrity and maximizing communication reliability. Figure 9.10 further explores peak gain and efficiency versus frequency for the proposed element antenna [137–145]. These metrics quantify the antenna's ability

Table 9.4 Study of different parameters of final element antenna.

Figure 9.1	**3dB beamwidth (degree)**	**Radiation/total efficiency (Percentage)**	**Front to back ratio (dB)**	**Peak gain (dBi)**	**Directivity (dB)**
Step 5 (Final Element)	33 41	93.22 / 82.22 94.40 / 81.09	19 25	11 9.7	17.6 8.06

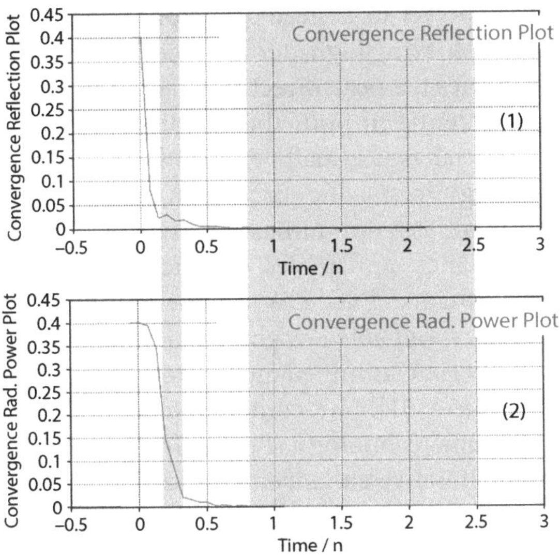

Figure 9.9 Convergence plot vs. frequency graph concerning proposed element antenna, respectively.

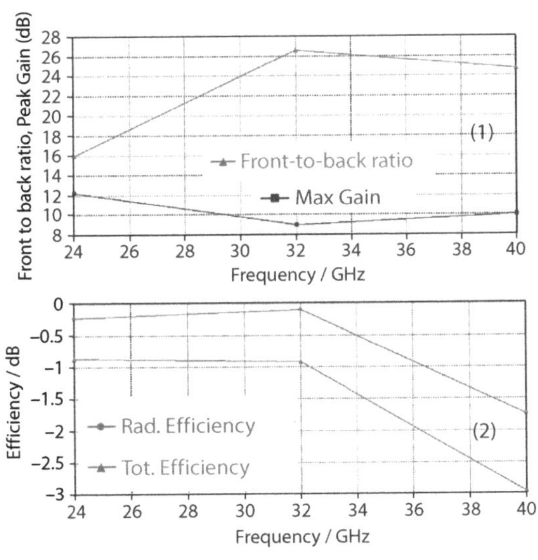

Figure 9.10 Peak gain, efficiency vs. frequency graph concerning proposed element antenna, respectively.

to focus transmitted power in desired directions while minimizing losses, which is crucial for achieving high-performance communication links.

Figure 9.11 illustrates the peak directivity radiation pattern of the newly proposed element antenna in both the "u" and "v" axes. This graphical representation is crucial as it visually depicts how effectively the antenna focuses emitted energy in specific directions. Such directional control is vital for establishing robust communication links reliably transmitting signals over varying distances and angles, enhancing overall communication efficiency and performance. Furthermore, the graphical analysis of these antenna designs offers valuable insights into their overall performance across critical metrics such as impedance matching, radiation characteristics, and efficiency [146–151]. This comprehensive evaluation underscores the evolution of antenna technology, starting from basic patch designs and progressing through iterative enhancements to arrive at the proposed element antenna. These advancements signify significant improvements in optimizing bandwidth utilization, ensuring stability, and achieving precise directional radiation.

The transition from conventional patch antennas to the proposed element antenna marks a notable leap in antenna engineering, highlighting the continuous pursuit of refining and innovating antenna designs.

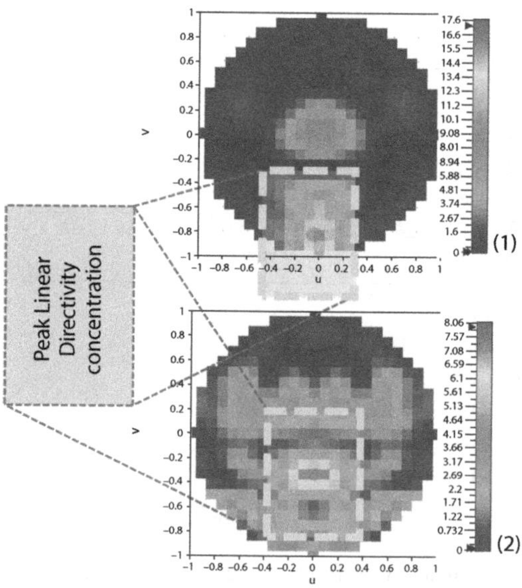

Figure 9.11 Peak Directivity radiation pattern concerning the resolution axis as "u" and "v" concerning proposed element antenna, respectively.

Such advancements are pivotal in meeting the evolving demands of future wireless communication systems, where efficiency and reliability are paramount. The findings underscore the necessity for ongoing research and development efforts to further enhance antenna performance and capabilities, validate the proposed element antenna's effectiveness, and emphasize its potential to contribute significantly to the advancement of wireless communication technologies. This research sets a precedent for future antenna designs, advocating for continual improvement and innovation to meet the growing challenges and opportunities in telecommunications [151–154].

(ii) Simulation and Parametric analysis of Proposed Element antenna

The parametric analysis presented in Figure 9.12 explores the impact of variable R on reflection coefficient, surface impedance, and phase characteristics, as detailed in Figure 9.1. Notably, for R values ranging from 10.5 to 11.5, distinct resonant frequencies and reflection coefficients were observed. At R = 10.5, the antenna resonated at 37 GHz with a reflection coefficient of -9 dB. Increasing R to 10.75 shifted the resonance slightly to 36 GHz, with a slightly increased reflection coefficient of -9.5 dB. Further increasing R to 11 resulted in resonances at 35 GHz with a reflection coefficient of -10 dB, and at R = 11.25, resonances were noted at 31 GHz and near 26 GHz, with reflection coefficients of -12 dB and -10 dB, respectively.

The most significant changes were observed at R = 11.5, where resonances occurred at 26.1 GHz and 30.6 GHz, accompanied by minimum reflection coefficients of -12.5 dB and -17.6 dB, respectively. The impedance and theoretical predictions closely matched across all R values, showing overlapping curves, indicating good agreement between simulated and theoretical models.

Moreover, the phase characteristics exhibited significant changes at R = 11.5, correlating with the resonant points, underscoring the antenna's sensitivity to changes in R. These findings underscore the critical role of parameter R in tuning the antenna's resonance frequencies and optimizing its performance characteristics for specific frequency bands. Such insights are crucial for designing antennas tailored to meet the stringent requirements of modern communication systems, particularly in high-frequency applications like mm-wave 5G and IoT, where precise tuning and performance optimization are paramount.

(iii) Simulation and analysis of Proposed Array antenna through Array 1, respectively

Fractal antennas have emerged as a notable innovation in wireless communication, characterized by their compactness, wideband operation,

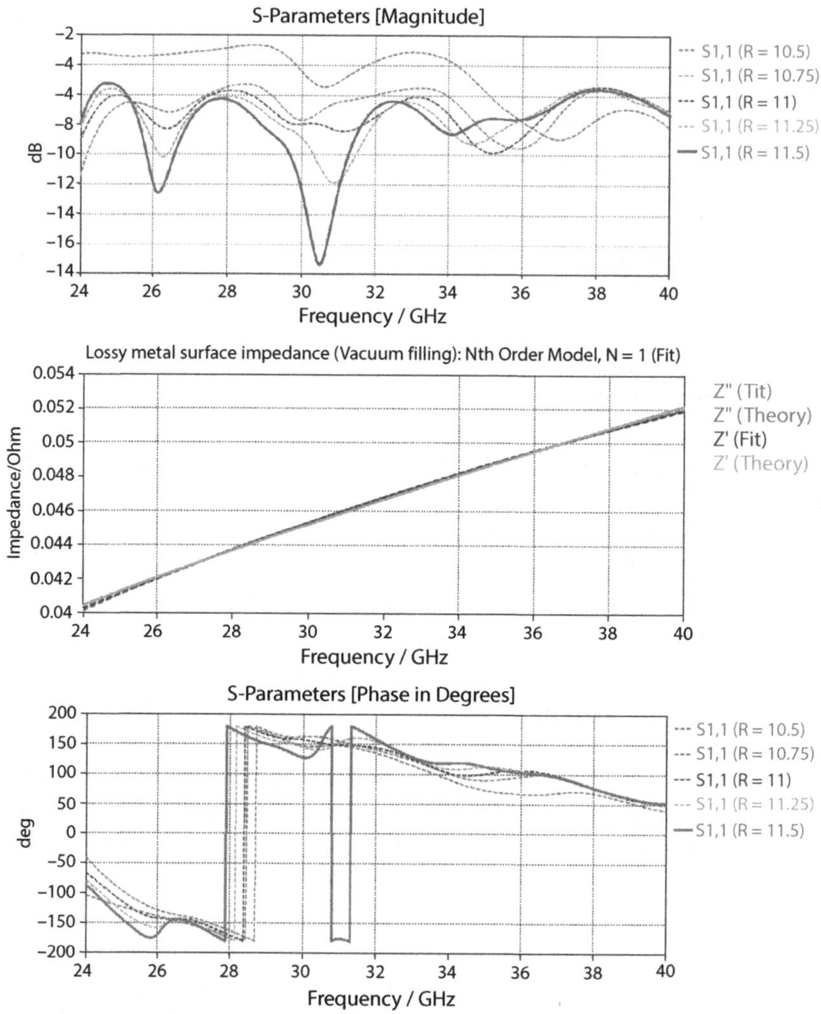

Figure 9.12 Reflection coefficient, surface impedance and phase graphs concerning parametric analysis with variable R as mentioned in Figure 9.1, respectively.

and ability to function across various frequency bands. These antennas utilize a fractal geometry, which involves a regular geometric arrangement of elements, to enhance signal strength and directivity through constructive interference in targeted directions. The proposed fractal array antenna design incorporates several essential parameter and configuration modifications to optimize performance. Tables 9.1 and 9.2 indicate that various structural dimensions and spacing have been adjusted.

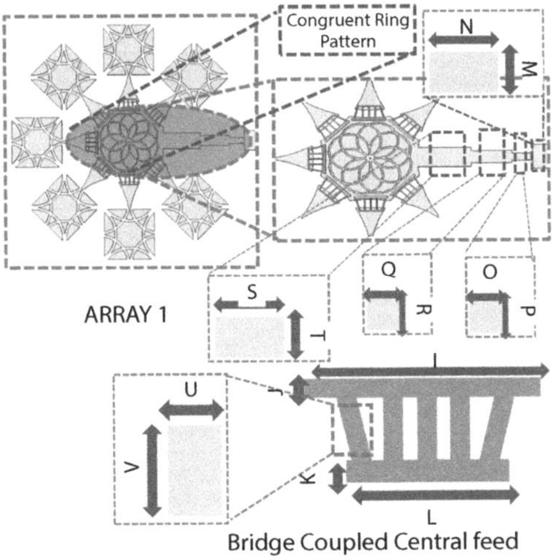

Figure 9.13 Array 1 and proposed fractal array antenna integrated with bridge coupled central feed, respectively.

Figure 9.13 showcases the initial design of ARRAY 1 alongside the proposed fractal array antenna, which integrates a bridge-coupled central feed system and a congruent ring pattern. These elements are crucial for enhancing the antenna's performance. The congruent ring pattern is designed to achieve the desired multi-band resonance characteristics. The design ensures an even signal distribution by symmetrically placing the rings around a central feed. This symmetry is vital for maintaining consistent performance across multiple frequency bands, making the antenna versatile for various applications. The bridge-coupled central feed system connects the central feed to each array element, ensuring efficient signal transmission and reception. This central feed is essential not only for maintaining the structural integrity of the antenna but also for enhancing its radiation properties. The central feed's design ensures that the signals are transmitted and received efficiently, thereby improving the overall performance of the antenna.

Figure 9.14 highlights the proposed fractal array antenna with a multi-concentric ring Defected Ground Structure (DGS). The DGS is a critical component that improves impedance matching, and controls surface current distribution. This structure, illustrated with dimensions d1 through d6 and D1 through D5, helps achieve precise impedance matching near the target of 50 Ohms. The DGS influences both the inductive and capacitive regions, which ensures the antenna's effectiveness in multi-band applications. The Smith Chart, depicted in the bottom right

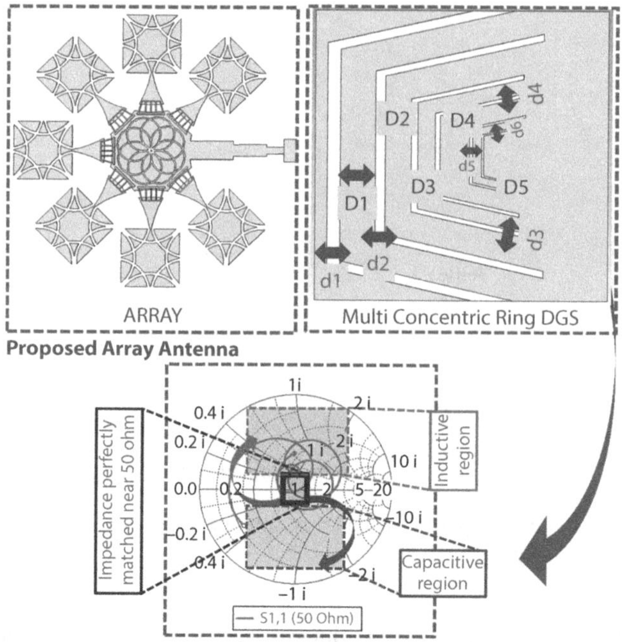

Figure 9.14 Proposed fractal array antenna integrated with half concentric ring pattern ground defected structure that shows extreme impedance matching concerning inductive region and capacitive region, respectively.

of Figure 9.14, provides a visual representation of the impedance-matching performance of the proposed design. It highlights regions where the impedance is perfectly matched to 50 Ohms, indicating that the antenna operates effectively within the desired inductive and capacitive regions. This performance is essential for achieving optimal signal transmission and reception, making the antenna suitable for a wide range of wireless communication applications. Moreover, the proposed fractal array antenna design with its bridge-coupled central feed system, congruent ring pattern, and multi-concentric ring DGS represents a significant advancement in antenna technology. These design elements collectively enhance the antenna's performance, making it a versatile and efficient solution for modern wireless communication needs.

(i) Return loss (S11), Smith Chart, Impedance, Admittance, Efficiency, concerning array 1 and proposed array antenna

Figure 9.15 showcases reflection coefficient graphs that depict various parametric changes made during our antenna design process. The performance

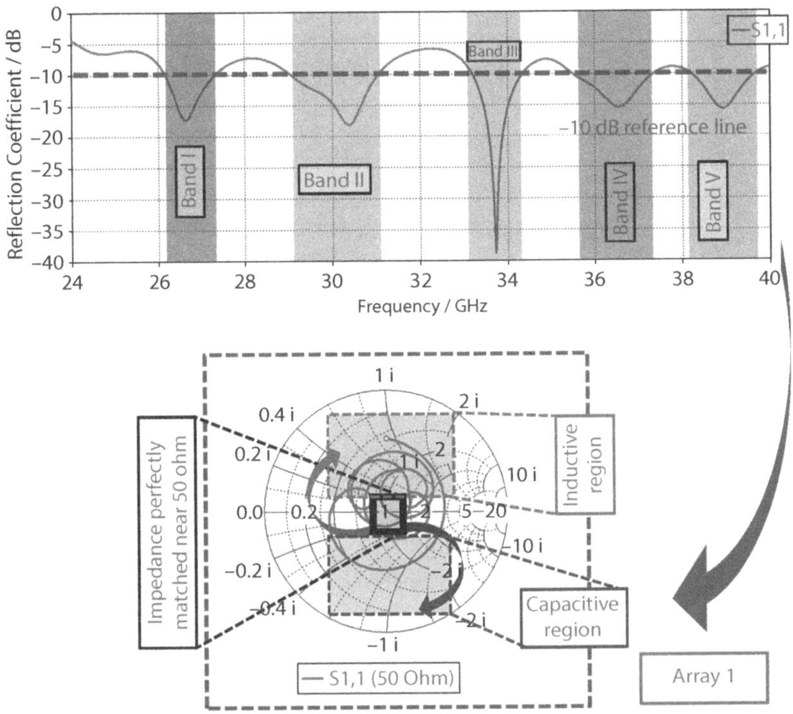

Figure 9.15 S_{11} vs. frequency graph and Smith chart shows extreme impedance matching concerning inductive region and capacitive region concerning array 1, respectively.

analysis of the proposed fractal array antenna integrated with a ground-defected structure is depicted in Figures 9.15 and 9.16.

Figure 9.15 depicts The S11 vs frequency graph, and the Smith chart illustrates the impedance-matching characteristics of Array 1. The Smith chart indicates near-perfect impedance matching at 50 Ohms across inductive and capacitive regions, demonstrating the antenna's effective impedance tuning. Figure 9.16 depicts the S11 and efficiency vs. frequency graph for the proposed array antenna, which shows resonance frequencies at 27.29 GHz, 35.14 GHz, and 39.1 GHz. At 27.29 GHz, the antenna achieves a peak radiation efficiency of 94.8% and a peak total efficiency of 93.5%, indicating its high performance in Band I and Band II.

Figure 9.17 shows the impedance and admittance vs. frequency graph for the proposed fractal array antenna with the integrated ground-defected structure. The graph highlights the antenna's ability to maintain consistent impedance and admittance across the specified frequency bands, ensuring reliable performance and confirming the antenna's capability for excellent

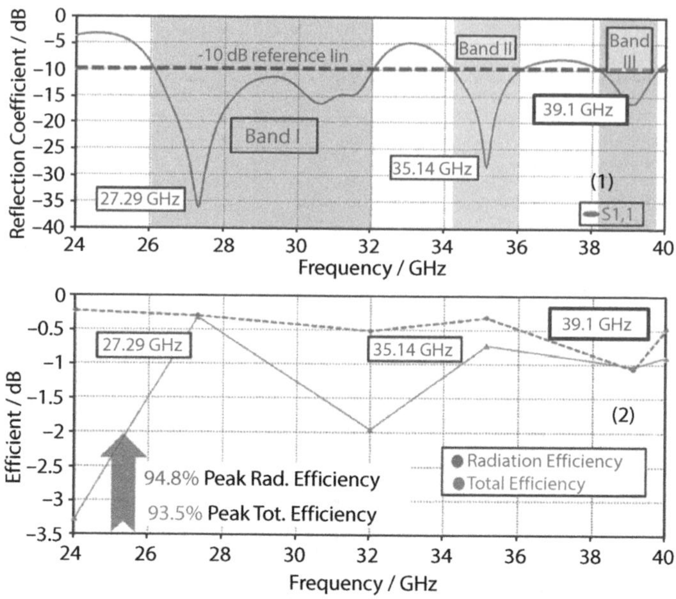

Figure 9.16 S_{11}, efficiency vs. frequency graph concerning proposed array antenna respectively.

Table 9.5 Comparative study with different parameters of concerning array 1 and proposed fractal array antenna design, respectively.

Figure 9.7	Res. freq. (fr) (GHz)	f1 (GHz)	f2 (GHz)	Bandwidth (GHz)	Bandwidth (%)	Return loss (dB)
Array1	26.5 30.4 33.7 36.4 39	26.1 29 33.1 35.5 38.1	27.2 31 34.2 37.4 39.5	1.1 2 1.1 1.9 1.4	4.12 6.66 3.26 5.21 3.60	17.5 18 39 15.5 16
Final Array with DGS	27.29 35.14 39.1	26 34.2 38.1	32 36 39.8	6 1.8 1.7	20.68 5.12 4.36	36 28 17

Table 9.6 Comparative study with different parameters of concerning final array antenna, respectively.

Figure 9.7	Radiation/total efficiency (Percentage)	3dB beamwidth/ noise temperature (degree/K)	Isotropic sensitivity (dB)	Peak gain (dBi)	Front to back ratio, directivity (dB)
Final Array with DGS	94.40/94.40 85.11/93.32 79.43/79.43	15/120 27/121 54/105	-2.7 -2.2 -2	9.5 7.8 7.3	6.2/8.7 13/5.77 7.9/4.82

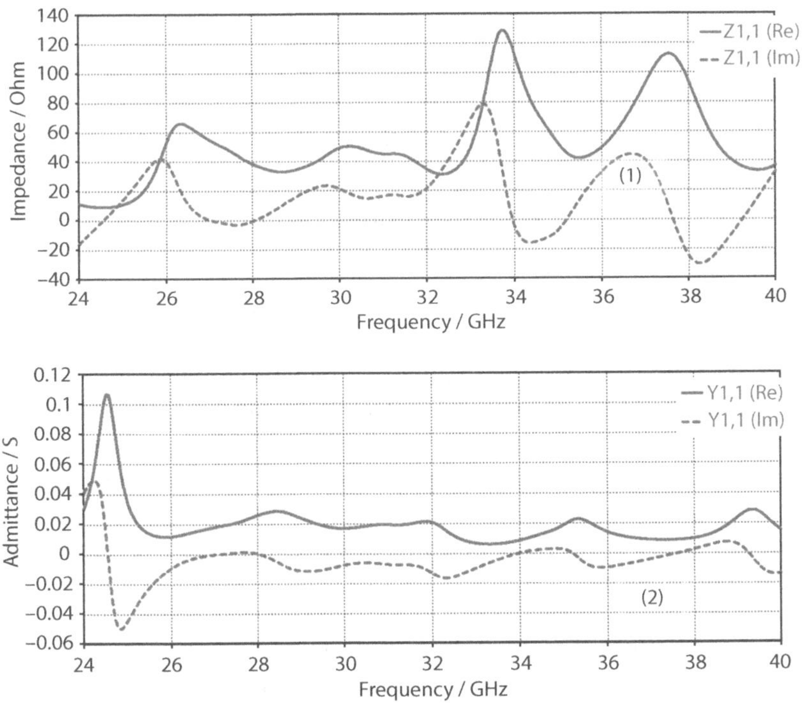

Figure 9.17 Impedance, admittance vs. frequency graph proposed fractal array antenna integrated ground defected structure, respectively.

impedance matching, high efficiency, and effective performance across multiple frequency bands. The comparative analysis between Array1 and the proposed fractal array antenna design reveals significant improvements across several key parameters as depicted in Tables 9.5 and 9.6 respectively. Array1 demonstrates resonant frequencies ranging from 26.5 to 39 GHz, with corresponding bandwidths ranging from 1.1 GHz to 1.9 GHz and return losses between 15.5 to 39 dB. Moreover, the final fractal array with DGS (Defected Ground Structure) exhibits resonant frequencies spanning 27.29 GHz to 39.1 GHz, showcasing wider bandwidths from 1.7 GHz to 6 GHz and improved return losses of 17 to 36 dB. This bandwidth and return loss enhancement suggests improved antenna performance in impedance matching and frequency coverage, which is crucial for modern wireless communication systems.

$$R(c) = \frac{Z(l) - Z(0)}{Z(l) + Z(0)} \tag{9.10}$$

$$R(c) = \frac{VSWR - 1}{VSWR + 1}$$
$$R(L) = -20 * \log_{10}(R(c)) \tag{9.11}$$

where $R(c)$ is reflection coefficient and $R(L)$ is return loss.

Furthermore, the final array with DGS achieves higher radiation efficiency, averaging 94.40%, and maintains competitive figures for 3dB beamwidth and noise temperature. Its isotropic sensitivity and peak gain are notable, demonstrating improvements in directional capability and sensitivity to incoming signals. The front-to-back ratio and directivity measures reflect enhanced signal isolation and focused radiation patterns, essential for reducing interference and optimizing signal reception in complex electromagnetic environments.

(ii) Current Voltage, Power, Refractive Index, Conductance, Inductance, Capacitance Resistance, Concerning Proposed Array Antenna

The integration of a ground-defected structure (DGS) with the fractal array antenna shows significant improvements across multiple parameters; Figures 9.18 and 9.19 indicate that the antenna with DGS exhibits better impedance matching and power handling capabilities compared to traditional designs. This results in enhanced signal transmission efficiency and reduced losses. Figure 9.18 illustrates the current, voltage, and frequency

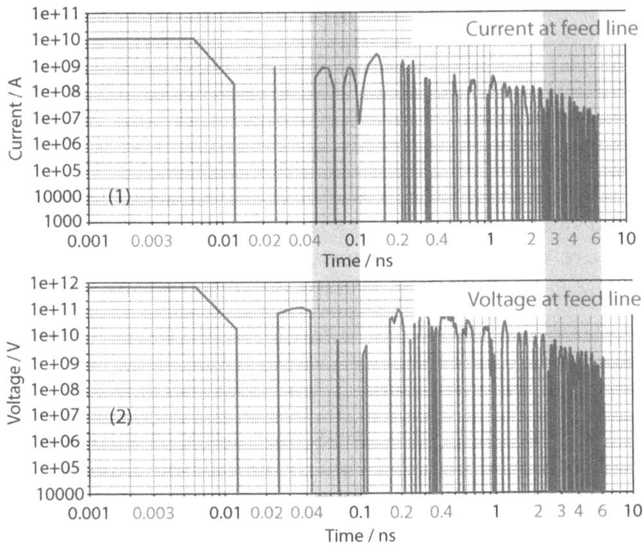

Figure 9.18 Current, voltage vs. frequency graph concerning proposed fractal array antenna integrated ground defected structure, respectively.

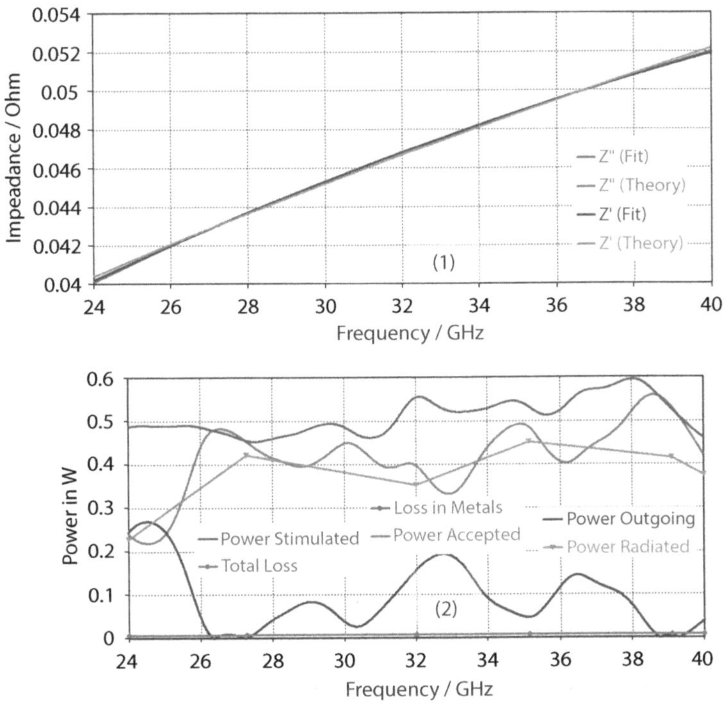

Figure 9.19 Impedance, power vs. frequency graph concerning proposed fractal array antenna integrated ground defected structure, respectively.

relationship for the proposed antenna design. It shows how these parameters vary across the operating frequency range. The trends in current and voltage provide insights into the antenna's electrical behavior and resonance characteristics. Figure 9.19 Impedance and power are critical factors influencing antenna performance, and impedance varies with frequency, affecting power transfer efficiency and signal matching. A stable impedance curve across frequencies is desirable for optimal antenna performance. Figure 9.20 highlights how the refractive index varies with frequency, and the antenna design is optimized for specific frequency bands relevant to current and future wireless communication standards (like 5G and anticipated 6G).

Figure 9.20, the refractive index graph shows how the proposed antenna's materials interact with electromagnetic waves at different frequencies. Understanding this relationship helps in optimizing antenna materials for enhanced performance in terms of propagation and efficiency. Figure 9.21

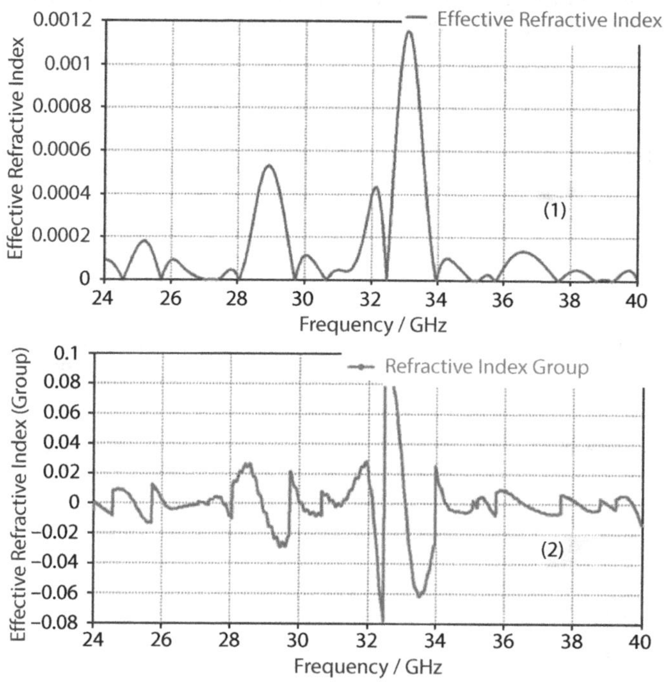

Figure 9.20 Refractive index vs. frequency graph concerning proposed fractal array antenna integrated ground defected structure, respectively.

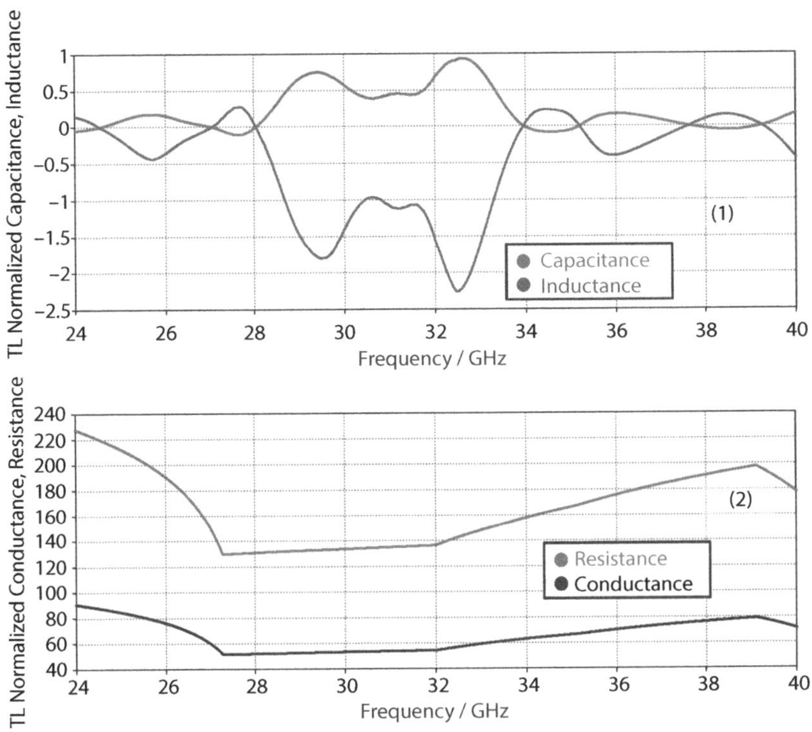

Figure 9.21 Capacitance, inductance, resistance, conductance vs. frequency graph concerning proposed fractal array antenna integrated ground defected structure, respectively.

reveals that the antenna's electrical components (capacitance, inductance, resistance, conductance) are well-balanced across frequencies, ensuring stable performance and minimal signal degradation. Figure 9.21 provides insights into the antenna's electrical components—capacitance, inductance, resistance, and conductance—as frequency functions. These parameters influence antenna efficiency, bandwidth, and radiation characteristics. Variations in these components across frequencies highlight design considerations for impedance matching and overall performance.

Table 9.7 illustrates that the final array antenna with DGS achieves narrower main lobes and more consistent 3dB beamwidths across different angular orientations (Phi and Theta), indicating improved directionality and coverage versatility compared to conventional designs. The table compares vital performance metrics of the final array antenna design with

Table 9.7 Comparative study with different parameters concerning final array antenna design, respectively.

	Phi = 0o		Phi = 90o		Theta = 90o	
Type of designs	**Main lobe**	**3dB beamwidth**	**Main lobe**	**3dB beamwidth**	**Main lobe**	**3dB beamwidth**
Final Array with DGS	11 o 180 o 53 o	13.7 o 28.6 o 41.9 o	24 o 5 o 46 o	18.2 o 11.8 o 14.9 o	184 o 270 o 294 o	16 o 16 o 18.5 o

and without DGS across different angles (Phi = 0°, 90° and Theta = 90°) and includes measurements such as main lobe directionality (in degrees) and 3dB beamwidth, which are crucial for assessing antenna directivity and coverage capabilities in various spatial orientations.

(iii) Convergence reflection and power plot, 3dB beamwidth, Radiometric noise temperature concerning resonance point concerning proposed array antenna

Integrating fractal geometries with ground-defected structures in antenna design collectively underscores the effectiveness, such as integration, enhances bandwidth, reduces reflections, and improves directional properties, making the antenna suitable for diverse applications spanning 5G and future 6G technologies. The findings from these figures validate the practical feasibility and performance enhancements brought by innovative antenna configurations promising advancements in wireless communication, as well as satellite technology. Figure 9.22 and Figure 9.23 depict critical performance metrics of the proposed fractal array antenna integrated with the ground-defected structure. Figure 9.22 illustrates the convergence reflection and power plot, highlighting how the antenna's resonance point affects its efficiency and bandwidth. This plot is crucial for antenna designers as it reveals how well the antenna matches with the transmission line and minimizes signal reflection, thereby maximizing power transfer efficiency.

In Figure 9.23, the 3dB beamwidth and radiometric noise temperature are shown. The 3dB beamwidth indicates the angular coverage within which the antenna radiates most of its power, which is crucial for

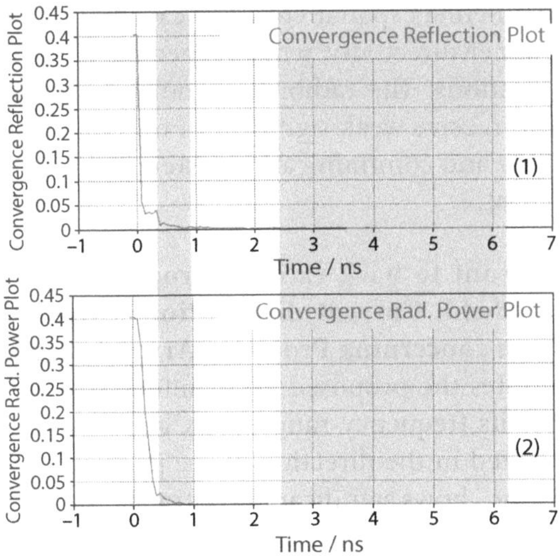

Figure 9.22 Convergence plot concerning proposed fractal array antenna integrated ground defected structure.

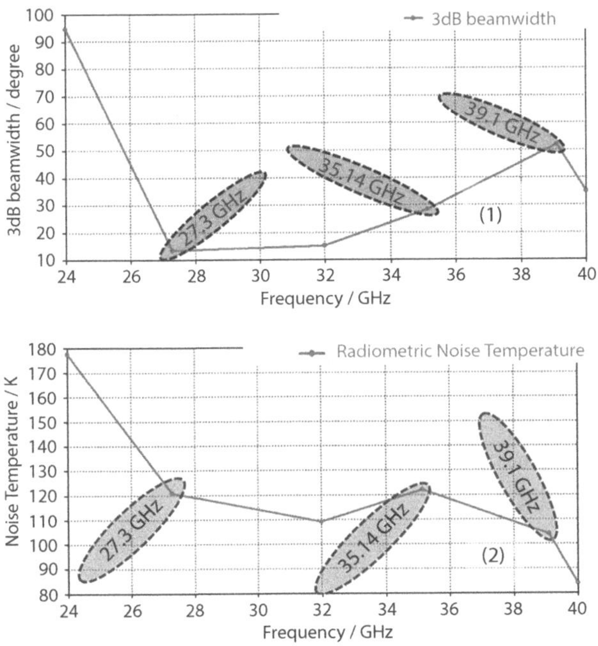

Figure 9.23 3dB beamwidth, noise temperature concerning proposed fractal array antenna integrated ground defected structure.

determining the antenna's spatial coverage capability. A narrower beamwidth suggests higher directivity, which is beneficial for long-range communication applications. The radiometric noise temperature reflects the antenna's ability to receive weak signals with minimal added noise, which is critical in satellite and communication systems where sensitivity to faint signals is paramount.

(iv) Peak Gain, Front to back ratio, Isotropic sensitivity, 3dB beamwidth, E field, H field, Current distribution, Directivity Pattern, 2D power field pattern concerning Proposed Array Antenna

Figure 9.24 illustrates the proposed array antenna's peak gain and front-to-back ratio over its frequency range. Peak gain, a measure of the maximum power radiated in the direction of the peak radiation compared to an isotropic radiator, shows significant variation across different frequency bands. This variability is essential for optimizing signal strength and coverage in specific frequency ranges critical to 5G and beyond.

The front-to-back ratio, depicting the ratio of radiation in the forward direction to that in the backward direction, ensures minimal interference and maximum directional efficiency. The antenna's performance in

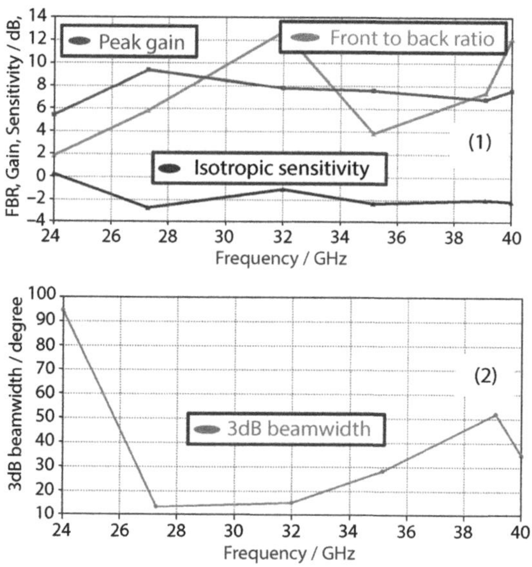

Figure 9.24 Peak gain, front to back ratio, isotropic sensitivity, 3dB beamwidth vs frequency of proposed array antenna.

this regard influences its ability to mitigate unwanted signals from rear directions, enhancing overall signal reception quality in complex urban environments and dense spectrum scenarios. Isotropic sensitivity, another critical parameter depicted in Figure 9.24, measures the antenna's ability to detect signals equally well from all directions. This characteristic is essential for applications requiring omnidirectional coverage, such as satellite communication and mobile network infrastructure. The variation of isotropic sensitivity across frequencies highlights the antenna's adaptability to different operational environments and frequency allocations.

The 3dB beamwidth, representing the angular width of the antenna's main lobe where the radiated power drops to half its maximum value, is crucial for determining coverage area and directivity.

Figure 9.24 demonstrates how the beamwidth changes with frequency, influencing the antenna's spatial coverage and efficiency in transmitting and receiving signals within specific angular ranges. Figures 9.25 and 9.26 delve into the detailed electromagnetic field characteristics of the proposed array antenna. Figure 9.25 shows the transverse electric field (TE mode), highlighting the antenna's mode of operation and polarization characteristics.

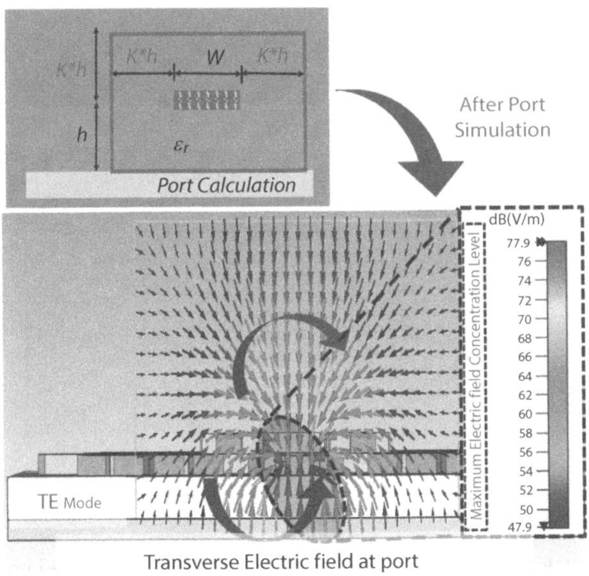

Figure 9.25 Transverse Electric field (TE mode) at proposed array antenna.

This field distribution is essential for understanding how the antenna interacts with electromagnetic waves in practical scenarios, affecting signal propagation and polarization diversity in communication systems.

Figure 9.26 further explores the electric field concerning the integrated ground-defected structure of the antenna. This structure is crucial in enhancing antenna performance by controlling impedance matching, reducing surface wave effects, and improving overall radiation efficiency. The electric field distribution here illustrates the effectiveness of the design modifications in achieving desired operational outcomes across different frequency bands.

$$\boldsymbol{TRP} = \int_{0}^{2\pi}\int_{0}^{\pi} \boldsymbol{R(\theta,\phi)\sin\theta d\theta d\phi} \tag{9.12}$$

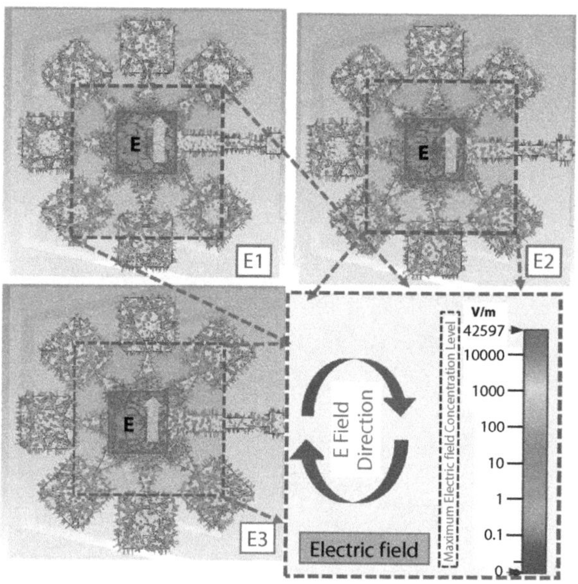

Figure 9.26 Electric field concerning proposed array antenna integrated ground defected structure.

Equation (9.12) defines Total Radiated Power (TRP) in Watts (W). When calculating TRP in an anechoic chamber, the process involves determining the Effective Isotropic Radiated Power (EIRP) at various angles and averaging it over a sphere. This allows us to derive TRP from EIRP:

$$TRP = \frac{1}{4\pi}\int_0^{2\pi}\int_0^{\pi} EIRP(\theta,\phi)\sin\theta d\theta d\phi \tag{9.13}$$

Complementing the electric field analysis, Figure 9.27 depicts the magnetic field concerning the integrated ground-defected structure. Understanding the magnetic field distribution helps optimize antenna efficiency and reduce electromagnetic interference, which is critical for maintaining signal integrity and reducing noise levels in high-density communication environments. Figure 9.28 focuses on the current distribution concerning resonant frequencies of the proposed array antenna. This distribution pattern directly influences the antenna's radiation

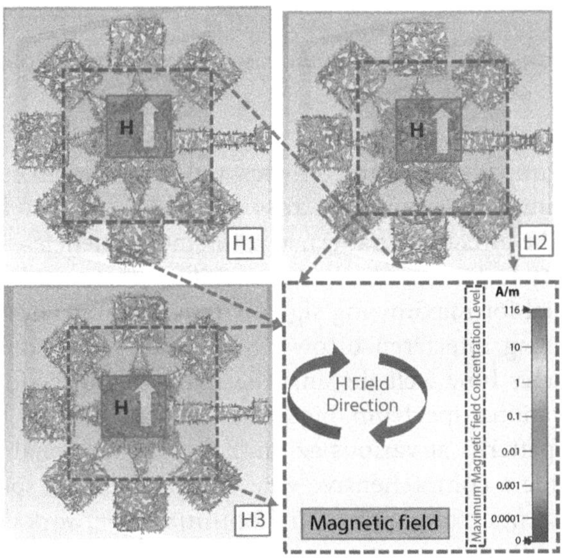

Figure 9.27 Magnetic field concerning proposed array antenna integrated ground defected structure.

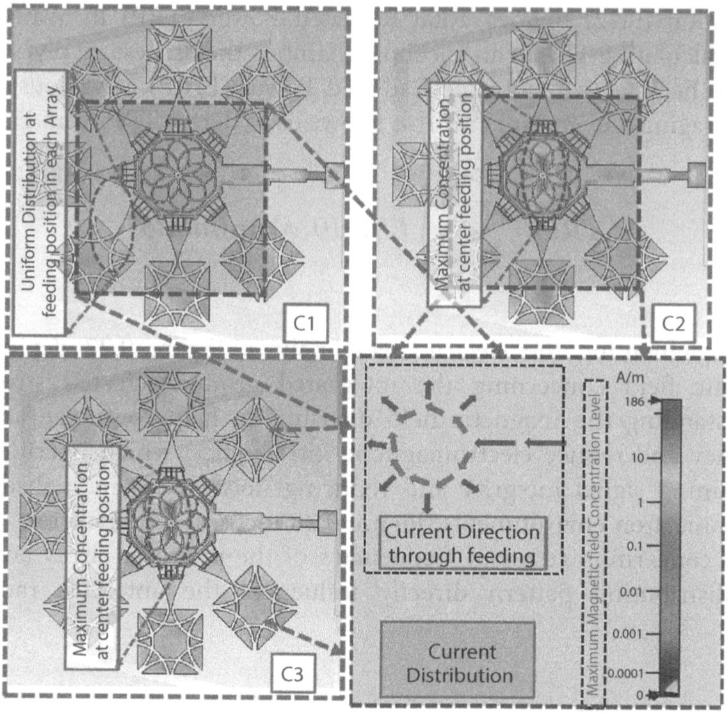

Figure 9.28 Current distribution concerning resonate frequencies concerning proposed array antenna.

efficiency and impedance characteristics, reflecting design effectiveness in achieving optimal performance across targeted frequency bands. Figure 9.29 presents the directivity pattern at resonant frequencies, indicating the antenna's ability to focus radiation in specific directions. Directivity patterns are crucial for maximizing signal strength toward desired locations while minimizing interference toward unwanted directions. The analysis here evaluates how well the antenna maintains directional efficiency across its operational spectrum. Figure 9.30 expands on this by illustrating 2D radiation patterns at various azimuthal and elevational angles. These patterns provide a comprehensive view of the antenna's spatial coverage capabilities, essential for planning and optimizing network deployment in

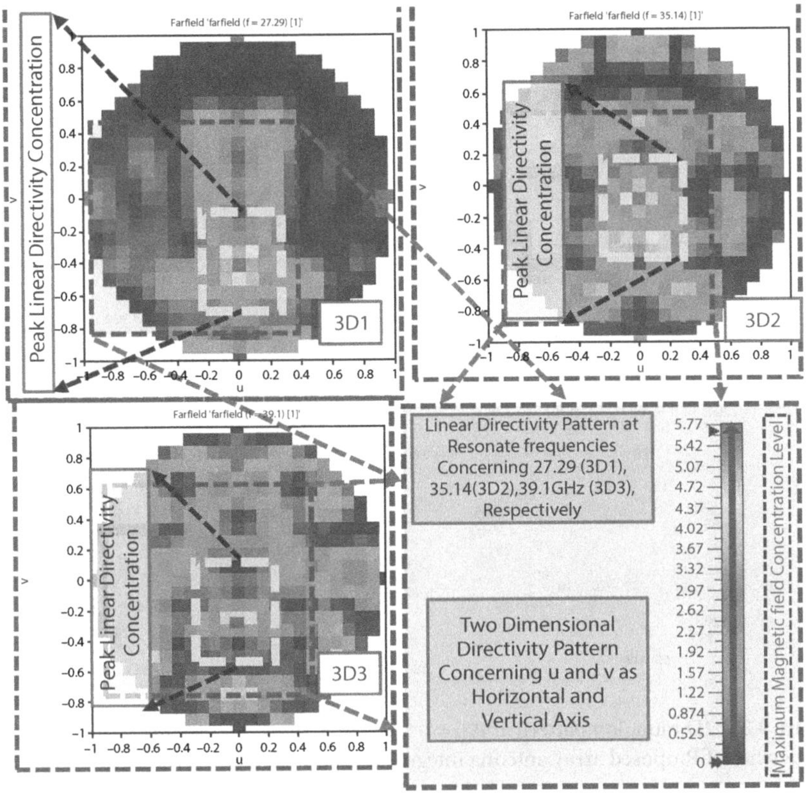

Figure 9.29 Directivity pattern display concerning resonate frequencies concerning proposed array antenna.

diverse environmental and geographical conditions. Moreover, Table 9.8, the proposed antenna, sized at 36 × 36 mm, depicts remarkable performance compared to other published works. It achieves peak gains of 9.5 dBi, 7.8 dBi, and 7.3 dBi across different frequency bands of 6 GHz, 1.8 GHz, and 1.7 GHz, respectively. This performance significantly surpasses existing antennas in both peak gain and bandwidth. The compact size of the antenna further enhances its appeal for diverse applications in upcoming 5G NR and potential 6G bands, demonstrating superior efficiency and versatility compared to larger, less efficient alternatives in the field.

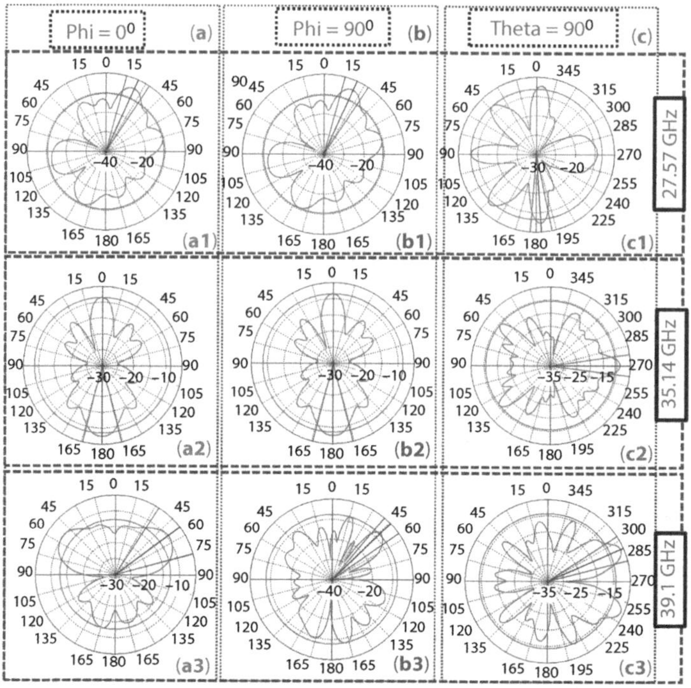

Figure 9.30 2D radiation pattern at Phi = 0 °, 90 ° and Theta = 90 ° concerning resonate frequencies of Proposed array antenna integrated ground defected structure.

9.4 Conclusions

The paper introduces a cutting-edge design and performance analysis of a bridge-coupled compact array antenna specifically engineered for mm-wave 5G applications, including V2X telemetry and IoT. The proposed antenna employs a modified bridge-coupled fed fractal array configuration, targeting multiband applications with a resonance frequency range of 24-40 GHz. Utilizing a ground-defected structure (DGS) design with 36 × 36 mm^2 dimensions, the antenna integrates a central bridge-coupled feeding technique with a circular congruent ring pattern. This innovative integration significantly enhances the antenna's performance, resulting in superior radiation properties, increased gain, enhanced directivity, and multi-beam patterns essential for mm-wave 5G, V2X telemetry, and IoT applications. The antenna design achieves a peak directivity ranging from 4.82 to 8.7 dBi in the fractal array with DGS. It is vital in telecommunications, military radar, medical imaging, automotive V2X, and consumer electronics, including Wi-Fi and broadcasting. The fractal

Table 9.8 Comparative study of proposed antenna's result with other published work concerning different parameter.

References	Size (mm)	Peak gain (dBi)	Bandwidth
[1]	'36 × 32'	'NR'	3.23GHz
[23]	'30 × 38'	'NR'	680 MHz
[24]	'38 × 38'	'NR'	5 MHz
[25]	'45 × 45'	'NR'	200 MHz
[26]	'40 × 46'	'NR'	100 MHz
[29]	'40 × 100'	'3.35'	430 MHz
[30]	'40 × 231'	'1.19'	740 MHz
[31]	'40 × 115'	'3.7'	2.29 GHz
[32]	'55 × 30'	'3'	1.47 GHz
[33]	'86.5 × 86.5'	'4.3'	160 MHz
[34]	'40 × 40'	'3.6'	1.8 GHz
[35]	'30 × 33'	'5.6'	2.19 GHz
[36]	'25× 20.5'	'4'	3.31 GHz
[37]	'32 × 15'	'2.73'	1.93GHz
[38]	'40 × 40'	'5.5'	4.7 GHz
[39]	'40 × 26'	'5'	3.20 GHz
[40]	'50 × 30'	'5'	1.67 GHz
[41]	'52 × 52'	'2.3'	1.04 GHz
[42]	'32 × 12'	'NR'	1.41GHz
[43]	'57.9×57.9' '53.6 × 52'	'6.2','7.1', '7.3', '7.9'	200 MHz,330 MHz, 54 MHz, 80 MHz,250 MHz
Proposed Antenna	'36 × 36'	9.5, 7.8, 7.3	6, 1.8, 1.7 (GHz)

array's versatile frequency capabilities and enhanced performance at resonate frequencies of 27.29, 35.14, and 39.1 GHz within the 24-40 GHz range with Phi = 00, Phi = 900, and Theta = 900, respectively, demonstrate its applicability across various domains. Furthermore, the antenna effectively covers applications in the n257, n258, n259, n260, and n261 5G NR bands and anticipated 6G bands, including ground-based radio navigation. Its matching for IoT applications within the 26-32 GHz, 34.2-36 GHz, and 38.1-39.8 GHz ranges is confirmed by reflection coefficients of -36, -28, and -17 dB at the specified resonate frequencies. The proposed antenna also exhibits a peak gain ranging from 7.3 to 9.5 dBi and covers bandwidths of 20.68%, 5.12%, and 4.36% within the 26-32 GHz, 34.2-36 GHz, and 38.1-39.8 GHz ranges, respectively. These performance metrics highlight the antenna's capability to meet the stringent requirements of modern wireless communication systems. The design and analysis were conducted using computer simulation technology (CST) software, ensuring accuracy and reliability in performance metrics such as signal generation, analysis, and spectrum evaluation. Furthermore, the bridge-coupled compact array antenna with a modified fractal design and DGS represents a significant advancement in antenna technology. Its enhanced performance, including superior radiation properties, increased gain, and multi-beam patterns, underscores its potential for widespread adoption in critical 5G and future 6G applications. This research addresses the growing demand for efficient and compact antennas that support the next generation of wireless technologies, thereby driving innovation and efficiency across the telecommunications, automotive, medical, and consumer electronics industries. As the wireless communication landscape continues to evolve, the proposed antenna offers a robust solution, promising to enhance connectivity and performance in diverse operational environments.

References

1. Bharti, Bharti, G., Sivia, J.S., A design of multiband nested square shaped ring fractal antenna with circular ring elements for wireless applications. *Prog. Electromagn. Res. C*, 108, 115–125, 2021.
2. Kumar, A. and Pharwaha, A.P.S., Development of a modified Hilbert curve fractal antenna for multiband applications. *IETE J. Res.*, 1–10, 2020.
3. Singhal, S. and Singh, A.K., Elliptical monopole based super wideband fractal antenna. *Microwave Opt. Technol. Lett.*, 62, 3, 1324–1328, 2020.
4. Karthikeya, G.S., Abegaonkar, M.P., Koul, S.K., Low cost high gain triple band mmWave Sierpinski antenna loaded with uniplanar EBG for 5G

applications, in: *2017 IEEE International Conference on Antenna Innovations & Modern Technologies for Ground, Aircraft and Satellite Applications (iAIM)*, 2017, November, IEEE, pp. 1–5.

5. Singh, A. and Singh, S., Design and optimization of a modified Sierpinski fractal antenna for broadband applications. *Appl. Soft Comput.*, 38, 843–850, 2016.
6. Ali, T., Subhash, B.K., Biradar, R.C., A miniaturized decagonal Sierpinski UWB fractal antenna. *Prog. Electromagn. Res. C*, 84, 161–174, 2018.
7. Raj, A. and Mandal, D., Design and Simulation of Compact Array Antenna for mm Wave Wireless Biomedical Systems. *Biomed. Mater. Devices*, 2025. https://doi.org/10.1007/s44174-025-00404-3.
8. Choukiker, Y.K. and Behera, S.K., Wideband frequency reconfigurable Koch snowflake fractal antenna. *IET Microwaves Antennas Propag.*, 11, 2, 203–208, 2017.
9. Praveena, A. and Ponnapalli, V.S., A review on "design aspects of fractal antenna arrays", in: *2019 International Conference on Computer Communication and Informatics (ICCCI)*, 2019, January, IEEE, pp. 1–3.
10. Kumar, A. and Singh, A.P., Design of micro-machined modified Sierpinski gasket fractal antenna for satellite communications. *Int. J. RF Microwave Comput. Aided Eng.*, 29, 8, e21786, 2019.
11. Kaur, M. and Sivia, J.S., Minkowski, Giuseppe Peano and Koch curves based design of compact hybrid fractal antenna for biomedical applications using ANN and PSO. *AEU Int. J. Electron. Commun.*, 99, 14–24, 2019.
12. Garg, R.K., Nair, M.V.D., Singhal, S., Tomar, R., A new type of compact ultra-wideband planar fractal antenna with WLAN band rejection. *Microwave Opt. Technol. Lett.*, 62, 7, 2537–2545, 2020.
13. Ullah, H. and Tahir, F.A., A novel snowflake fractal antenna for dual-beam applications in 28 GHz band. *IEEE Access*, 8, 19873–19879, 2020.
14. Kaur, M. and Sivia, J.S., Giuseppe Peano and Cantor set fractals based miniaturized hybrid fractal antenna for biomedical applications using artificial neural network and firefly algorithm. *Int. J. RF Microwave Comput. Aided Eng.*, 30, 1, e22000, 2020.
15. Singhal, S., Four arm windmill shaped superwideband terahertz MIMO fractal antenna. *Optik*, 219, 165093, 2020.
16. Dastranj, A., Ranjbar, F., Bornapour, M., A new compact circular shape fractal antenna for broadband wireless communication applications. *Prog. Electromagn. Res. C*, 93, 19–28, 2019.
17. Bhatia, S.S. and Sivia, J.S., On the design of fractal antenna array for multiband applications. *J. Inst. Eng. India Ser. B*, 100, 5, 471–476, 2019.
18. Sran, S.S. and Sivia, J.S., ANN and IFS based wearable hybrid fractal antenna with DGS for S, C and X band application. *AEU Int. J. Electron. Commun.*, 127, 153425, 2020.

19. Rani, R.B., A compendious review on fractal antenna geometries in wireless communication, in: *2020 International Conference on Inventive Computation Technologies (ICICT)*, 2020, February, IEEE, pp. 888–893.
20. Aravindraj, E., Nagarajan, G., Kumaran, R.S., Design and analysis of recursive square fractal antenna for WLAN applications, in: *2020 International Conference on Emerging Trends in Information Technology and Engineering (ic-ETITE)*, 2020, February, IEEE, pp. 1–5.
21. Sivia, J.S., Singh, A., Kamal, T.S., Design of Sierpinski carpet fractal antenna using artificial neural networks. *Int. J. Comput. Appl.*, 68, 8, 2013.
22. Pandeeswari, R. and Raghavan, S., A CPW-fed triple band OCSRR embedded monopole antenna with modified ground for WLAN and WIMAX applications. *Microwave Opt. Technol. Lett.*, 57, 2413–2418, 2015.
23. Ahmad, B.H. and Nornikman, H., Fractal microstrip antenna with Minkowski Island split ring resonator for broadband application. *IEEE Int. RF and Microwave Conf. (RFM)*, Penang, pp. 214–218, 2013.
24. Dangkham, P. and Phongcharoenpanich, C., A compact split ring resonator antenna of paper based for UHF-RFID passive tag. *IEEE Conf. on Ant. and App. Meas. and App.*, 2016.
25. Sharma, V., Lakwar, N., Kumar, N., Garg, T., A multiband low-cost fractal antenna based on parasitic split ring resonators. *IET Microwaves Antennas Propag.*, 12, 6, 913–919, 2017.
26. Pandeeswari, R. and Raghavan, S., Microstrip antenna with complementary split ring resonator loaded ground plane for gain enhancement. *Microwave Opt. Technol. Lett.*, 57, 292–296, 2015.
27. Rahimi, M., Maleki, M., Soltani, M., Arezomand, A.-S., Zarrabi, F.-B., Wideband SRR-inspired antenna with circular polarization for wireless application. *AEU — Int. J. Electron. Commun.*, 70, 9, 1199–1204, 2016. *Prog. Electromagn. Res. C*, 108, 125, 2021.
28. Rao, M.-V., Madhav, B.-T.-P., Anilkumar, T., Nadh, B.-P., Metamaterial inspired quad band circularly polarized antenna for WLAN/ISM/Bluetooth/WiMAX and satellite communication applications. *AEU — Int. J. Electron. Commun.*, 97, 229–241, 2018.
29. Ji, J.K., Kim, G.H., Seong, W.M., Bandwidth enhancement of metamaterial antennas based on composite right/left-handed transmission line. *IEEE Antennas Wirel. Propag. Lett.*, 9, 36–39, 2010.
30. Zhang, Q. and Gao, Y., Compact low-profile UWB antenna with characteristic mode analysis for UHF TV white space devices. *IET Microw. Antennas Propag.*, 11, 1629–1635, 2017.
31. Rayno, J.T. and Sharma, S.K., Wideband frequency-reconfigurable Spirograph planar monopole antenna (SPMA) operating in the UHF band. *IEEE Antennas Wirel. Propag. Lett.*, 11, 1537–1540, 2012.
32. Indhu, K.K. and Mohanan, P., Compact Broadband Toploaded Planar Monopole Antenna for Low Frequency Applications, in: *Proceedings of the*

2011 Indian Antenna Week (IAW), Kolkata, India, 18–22 December 2011, IEEE, Piscataway, NJ, USA, 2011.

33. Andriamiharivolamena, T., Lemaitre-Auger, P., Tedjini, S., Tirard, F., Compact Planar Monopole Antenna for Wearable Wireless Applications. *C.R. Phys.*, 16, 851–861, 2015.
34. Rad, M.A., Soheilifar, M.R., Zarrabi, F.B., Compact microstrip antenna based on fractal metasurface with low radar cross section and wide bandwidth. *Int. J. Electron. Commun.*, 98, 74–79, 2019.
35. Wu, C.-M., Wideband dual-frequency CPW-fed triangular monopole antenna for DCS/WLAN application. *Int. J. Electron. Commun.*, 61, 563–67, 2007.
36. Shanmuganantham, T., Balamanikandan, K., Raghavan, S., CPW-fed slot antenna for wideband applications. *Hindawi Int. J. Antennas Propag.*, 2008, 1–5, 2008.
37. Cui, Y.-Y., Sun, Y.-Q., Yang, H.-C., Ruan, C.-L., A new triple-band CPW-fed monopole antenna for WLAN and WIMAX applications. *Prog. Electromagn. Res. M*, 2, 141–51, 2008.
38. Ray, K.P., Thakur, S.S., Deshmukh, R.A., Wideband L-shaped printed monopole antenna. *Int. J. Electron. Commun.*, 66, 693–96, 2012.
39. Jothi Chitra, R. and Nagarajan, V., Double L-slot microstrip patch antenna array for WiMAX and WLAN applications. *Elsevier Comput. Electr. Eng.*, 39, 1026–41, 2013.
40. Suma, M.N., Bijumon, P.V., Sebastian, M.T., Mohanan, P., A compact hybrid CPW fed planar monopole/dielectric resonator antenna. *J. Eur. Ceram. Soc.*, 27, 3001–4, 2007.
41. Chen, L., Ren, X., Yin, Y., Wang, Z., Broadband CPW-fed circularly polarized antenna with an irregular slot for 2.45 GHz RFID reader. *Prog. Electromagn. Res. Lett.*, 41, 77–86, 2013.
42. Raj, A. and Mandal, D., Design and implementation of combined array antenna for point to point 5 g mm-wave communication and wireless applications. *Opt. Quant. Electron,* 57, 337, 2025. https://doi.org/10.1007/s11082-025-08248-3.
43. Nhlengethwa, N. and Kumar, P., Fractal Microstrip Patch Antennas for Dual-Band and Triple-Band Wireless Applications. *Int. J. Smart Sens. Intell. Syst.*, 14, 1–9, 2021, 10.21307/ijssis-2021-007.
44. Raj, A. and Mandal, D., Comparative Analysis of the 2×2 Patch Antenna Array with Modified Fractal Antenna for 5G Communication and Wireless Applications. *2022 IEEE Microwaves, Antennas, and Propagation Conference (MAPCON)*, Bangalore, India, pp. 670–675, 2022, doi: 10.1109/MAPCON56011.2022.10046924.
45. Raj, A., Dhubhakarya, D.C., Srivas, D.K., Tiwari, M.K., Design and Analysis of Tri-bands Triangular Shape Fractal Antenna for Wireless Applications, Aug. 2022, doi: 10.21203/rs.3.rs-1926169/v1.

46. Raj, A., Dhubkarya, D.C., Srivastava, D.K., Mandal, D., Design and analysis of square shape slot cut high gain Sierpinski carpet fractal antenna for wireless applications. *Microwave Opt. Technol. Lett.*, 1–7, 2023, doi: 10.1002/mop.33687 RAJET AL.|7.
47. Subramanian, S.N., Nataraj, C., Duraikannan, S., Selvaperumal, S.K., Abdulla, R., Multiband Fractal Antenna for 26/28 GHz Millimeter Wave Band. *2022 International Conference on Edge Computing and Applications (ICECAA)*, Tamilnadu, India, pp. 318–322, 2022, doi: 10.1109/ICECAA55415.2022.9936386.
48. Marasco, I., Quatela, A., Roberto, G., Niro, G., Grande, M., Design of a Compact Reconfigurable Sierpinski Gasket Fractal Antenna for 5G and Satellite Communications. *2022 Int. J. Commun. Antenna Propag. (IRECAP)*, 12, 5.
49. Abhyuday, S.B.T., Reddy, R.R., Darimireddy, N.K., Millimeter-Wave Wideband Koch Fractal Antennas, in: *Machine Learning, Advances in Computing, Renewable Energy and Communication*. Lecture Notes in Electrical Engineering, vol. 768, A. Tomar, H. Malik, P. Kumar, A. Iqbal (Eds.), Springer, Singapore, 2022, https://doi.org/10.1007/978-981-16-2354-7_53.
50. Raj, A. and Mandal, D., A Novel Substrate Cylindrical Cavity 4×4 Fractal inspired MIMO Antenna for 5G - n258 Satellite Communication. *2023 IEEE International Conference on Recent Advances in Systems Science and Engineering (RASSE)*, Kerala, India, pp. 1–7, 2023, doi: 10.1109/RASSE60029.2023.10363453.
51. Raj, A. and Mandal, D., Design and Fabrication of High-Gain Array Antenna for 5G Communication and Wireless Applications, in: *Proceedings of the 4th International Conference on Communication, Devices and Computing. ICCDC 2023*. Lecture Notes in Electrical Engineering, vol. 1046, D.K. Sarkar, P.K. Sadhu, S. Bhunia, J. Samanta, S. Paul (Eds.), Springer, Singapore, 2023, https://doi.org/10.1007/978-981-99-2710-4_31.
52. Raj, A. and Mandal, D., Design of Slot Cut Modified Rectangular Shape and Square Shape Antenna for L band and 5G Applications. *2023 First International Conference on Microwave, Antenna and Communication (MAC)*, Prayagraj, India, pp. 1–4, 2023, doi: 10.1109/MAC58191.2023.10177084.
53. Raj, A. and Mandal, D., Design and experimental analysis of fractal antennae with ground-defected structure for expected 6G and 5G mm-wave communication and wireless applications. *Trans. Emerging Telecommun. Technol.*, 35, 1, e4900, 2024, doi: 10.1002/ett.4900.
54. Raj, A. and Mandal, D., Design and implementation of hybrid fed array antennae for Sub-6 GHz and 5G mm-wave communication and wireless applications. *Int. J. Microwave Wireless Technol.*, 1–20, 2024, doi: 10.1017/S1759078723001496.
55. Raj, A. and Mandal, D., Comparative analysis of fractal antennae for sub-6 GHz and 5G bands for wireless and IoT applications. *Mob. Netw. Appl.*, 2024, https://doi.org/10.1007/s11036-024-02347-3.

56. Raj, A. and Mandal, D., Design and performance analysis of fractal slot array antenna for advanced 5G mm-wave applications. *Int. J. Electron.*, 1–23, 2024, https://doi.org/10.1080/00207217.2024.2408788.
57. Raj, A. and Mandal, D., Design and Analysis of Sierpinski Fractal Antennas for Millimeter-Wave 5G and Ground-Based Radio Navigation Applications. *Trans. Emerging Telecommun. Technol.*, 35, e70001, 2024, https://doi.org/10.1002/ett.70001.
58. Raj, A. and Mandal, D., Design and analysis of graphene-based PBG and EBG array antennas for wideband and multiband mm-wave applications. *Waves Random Complex Medium*, 1–35, 2024, https://doi.org/10.1080/17455030.2024.2415935.
59. Raj, A. and Mandal, D., Design and Performance Analysis of Graphene Integrated CPW Fed Fractal Antennae for 5G mm-Wave and Ground Based Navigation Applications. *MAPAN*, 2024, https://doi.org/10.1007/s12647-024-00777-8.
60. Bhardwaj, A., Kumar, P., Raj, B., Anand, S., Design and Performance Optimization of doping-less Vertical Nanowire TFET using Gate Stack Technique. *J. Electron. Mater. (JEMS)*, Springer, 41, 7, 4005–4013, 2022.
61. Singh, J. and Raj, B., Tunnel Current Model of Asymmetric MIM Structure Levying Various Image Forces to Analyze the Characteristics of Filamentary Memristor. *Appl. Phys. A*, Springer, 125, 3, 203.1–203.11, Feb 2019.
62. Goyal, C., Ubhi, J.S., Raj, B., Low Leakage Zero Ground Noise Nanoscale Full Adder using Source Biasing Technique. *J. Nanoelectron. Optoelectron.*, American Scientific Publishers, 14, 360–370, March 2019.
63. Singh, G., Sarin, R.K., Raj, B., A Novel Robust Exclusive-OR Function Implementation in QCA Nanotechnology with Energy Dissipation Analysis. *J. Comput. Electron.*, Springer, 15, 2, 455–465, June 2016.
64. Wadhwa, G., Kamboj, P., Raj, B., Design optimisation of junctionless TFET biosensor for high sensitivity. *Adv. Nat. Sci.: Nanosci. Nanotechnol.*, 10, 045001 (7), 2019.
65. Bansal, P. and Raj, B., Memristor Modeling and Analysis for Linear Dopant Drift Kinetics. *J. Nanoeng. Nanomanuf.*, American Scientific Publishers, 6, 1–7, 2016.
66. Ashima, Vaithiyanathan, D., Raj, B., Performance Analysis of Charge Plasma induced Graded Channel Si nanotube. *J. Eng. Res. (JER)*, EMSME Special Issue, 146–154, Aug 2021.
67. Tomar, A.S., Magraiya, V.K., Raj, B., Scaling of Access and Data Transistor for High Performance DRAM Cell Design. *Quantum Matter*, 2, 412–416, Oct. 2013.
68. Jain, N. and Raj, B., Parasitic Capacitance and Resistance Model Development and Optimization of Raised Source/Drain SOI FinFET Structure for Analog Circuit Applications. *J. Nanoelectron. Optoelectron.*, ASP, USA, 13, 531–539, April 2018.

69. Singh, S., Vishvakarma, S.K., Raj, B., Analytical Modeling of Split-Gate Junction-Less Transistor for a Biosensor Application. *Sens. Bio-Sens.*, Elsevier, 18, 31–36, April 2018.
70. Gopal, M. and Raj, B., Low Power 8T SRAM Cell Design for High Stability Video Applications. *ITSI Trans. Electr. Electron. Eng.*, 1, 5, 91–97, 2013.
71. Raj, B., Mitra, J., Bihani, D.K., Rangharajan, V., Saxena, A.K., Dasgupta, S., Analysis of Noise Margin, Power and Process Variation for 32 nm FinFET Based 6T SRAM Cell. *J. Comput. (JCP)*, Academy Publisher, Finland, 5, 6, 1–8, 2010.
72. Sharma, D., Mehra, R., Raj, B., Comparative Analysis of Photovoltaic Technologies for High Efficiency Solar Cell Design. *Superlattices Microstruct.*, Elsevier, 153, 106861, May 2021.
73. Kaur, P., Buttar, A.S., Raj, B., A comprehensive Analysis of Nanoscale Transistor based Biosensor: A Review. *Indian J. Pure Appl. Phys.*, 59, 304–318, April 2021.
74. Yadav, D., Raj, B., Raj, B., Design and Simulation of Low Power Microcontroller for IoT Applications. *J. Sens. Lett.*, ASP, 18, 401–409, May 2020.
75. Singh, S. and Raj, B., A 2-D Analytical Surface Potential and Drain current Modeling of Double-Gate Vertical t-shaped Tunnel FET. *J. Comput. Electron.*, Springer, 19, 1154–1163, April 2020.
76. Singh, J. and Raj, B., An Accurate and Generic Window function for Non-linear Memristor Model. *J. Comput. Electron.*, Springer, 18, 2, 640–647, June 2019.
77. Kaur, M., Gupta, N., Kumar, S., Raj, B., Singh, A.K., Comparative RF and Crosstalk Analysis of Carbon Based Nano Interconnects. *IET Circuits Devices Syst.*, 15, 6, 493–503, Feb 2021.
78. Kandasamy, N., Ahmad, F., Ajitha, D., Raj, B., Telagam, N., Quantum Dot Cellular Automata based Scan Flip Flop and Boundary Scan Register. *IETE J. Res.*, 66, 535–548, 2020.
79. Singh, J. and Raj, B., Design and Investigation of 7T2M NVSARM with Enhanced Stability and Temperature Impact on Store/Restore Energy, *IEEE Trans. Very Large Scale Integr. Syst.*, 27, 6, 1322–1328, June 2019.
80. Bhardwaj, A.K., Gupta, S., Raj, B., Singh, A., Impact of Double Gate Geometry on the Performance of Carbon Nanotube Field Effect Transistor Structures for Low Power Digital Design. *Comput. Theor. Nanosci.*, ASP, 16, 1813–1820, 2019.
81. Jain, N. and Raj, B., Thermal Stability Analysis and Performance Exploration of Asymmetrical Dual-k underlap Spacer (ADKUS) SOI FinFET for Security and Privacy Applications. *Indian J. Pure Appl. Phys. (IJPAP)*, 57, 352–360, May 2019.
82. Jain, N. and Raj, B., Dual-k Spacer Region Variation at the Drain Side of Asymmetric SOI FinFET Structure: Performance Analysis towards the Analog/RF Design Applications. *J. Nanoelectron. Optoelectron.*, American Scientific Publishers, 14, 349–359, March 2019.

83. Singh, J., Sharma, S., Raj, B., Khosla, M., Analysis of barrier layer thickness on performance of In1-xGaxAs based Gate Stack Cylindrical Gate Nanowire MOSFET. *JNO*, ASP, 13, 1473–1477, Oct 2018.
84. Jain, N. and Raj, B., Analysis and Performance Exploration of High-k SOI FinFETs Over the Conventional Low-k SOI FinFET toward Analog/RF Design. *J. Semicond. (JoS)*, IOP Science, 39, 12, 124002-1-7, Dec 2018.
85. Goyal, C., Ubhi, J.S., Raj, B., A reliable leakage reduction technique for approximate full adder with reduced ground bounce noise. *J. Math. Probl. Eng.*, Hindawi, 2018, 3501041, 16, 15 Oct 2018.
86. Anuradha, Singh, J., Raj, B., Khosla, M., Design and Performance Analysis of Nano-scale Memristor-based Nonvolatile SRAM. *J. Sens. Lett.*, American Scientific Publishers, 16, 798–805, Oct 2018.
87. Wadhwa, G. and Raj, B., Parametric Variation Analysis of Charge-Plasma-based Dielectric Modulated JLTFET for Biosensor Application. *IEEE Sens. J.*, 18, 15, 6070–6077, August 1, 2018, (SCI).
88. Singh, J. and Raj, B., Comparative Analysis of Memristor Models for Memories Design. *JoS*, IoP, 39, 7, 074006-1-12, July 2018.
89. Yadav, D., Chouhan, S.S., Vishvakarma, S.K., Raj, B., Application Specific Microcontroller Design for IoT based WSN. *Sens. Lett.*, ASP, 16, 374–385, May 2018.
90. Singh, G., Sarin, R.K., Raj, B., Fault-Tolerant Design and Analysis of Quantum-Dot Cellular Automata Based Circuits. *IEEE/IET Circuits Devices Syst.*, 12, 638–64, 2018.
91. Singh, J. and Raj, B., Modeling of Mean Barrier Height Levying Various Image Forces of Metal Insulator Metal Structure to Enhance the Performance of Conductive Filament Based Memristor Model. *IEEE Nanotechnol.*, 17, 2, 268–267, March 2018.
92. Jain, A., Sharma, S., Raj, B., Analysis of Triple Metal Surrounding Gate (TM-SG) III-V Nanowire MOSFET for Photosensing Application. *Opto-Electron. J.*, Elsevier, 26, 2, 141–148, May 2018.
93. Jain, A., Sharma, S., Raj, B., Design and Analysis of High Sensitivity Photosensor Using Cylindrical Surrounding Gate MOSFET For Low Power Sensor Applications. *Eng. Sci. Technol. Int. J.*, Elsevier's, 19, 4, 1864–1870, December 2016.
94. Saiphani Kumar, G., Singh, A., Raj, B., Design and Analysis of Gate All Around CNTFET based SRAM cell Design. *J. Comput. Electron.*, Springer, 17, 1, 138–145, March 2018.
95. pal Singh, G., Sohi, B.S., Raj, B., Material Properties Analysis of Graphene Base Transistor (GBT) for VLSI Analog Circuits. *Indian J. Pure Appl. Phys. (IJPAP)*, 55, 896–902, Dec-2017.
96. Kumar, S. and Raj, B., Estimation of Stability and Performance metric for Inward Access Transistor based 6T SRAM Cell Design using n-type/p-type DMDG-GDOV TFET. *IEEE VLSI Circuits Syst. Lett.*, 3, 2, 25–39, June 2017.

97. Sharma, S., Kumar, A., Pattanaik, M., Raj, B., Forward Body Biased Multimode Multi-Threshold CMOS Technique for Ground Bounce Noise Reduction in Static CMOS Adders. *Int. J. Inf. Electron. Eng.*, 3, 3, 567–572, 2013.
98. Singh, H., Kumar, P., Raj, B., Performance Analysis of Majority Gate SET Based 1-bit Full Adder. *Int. J. Comput. Commun. Eng. (IJCCE)*, IACSIT Press Singapore, ISSN: 2010-3743, 2, 4, 2013.
99. Bhardwaj, A.K., Gupta, S., Raj, B., Investigation of Parameters for Schottky Barrier (SB) Height for Schottky Barrier Based Carbon Nanotube Field Effect Transistor Device. *J. Nanoelectron. Optoelectron.*, ASP, 15, 783–791, July 2020.
100. Bansal, P. and Raj, B., Memristor: A Versatile Nonlinear Model for Dopant Drift and Boundary Issues. *JCTN*, American Scientific Publishers, 14, 5, 2319–2325, May 2017.
101. Jain, N. and Raj, B., An Analog and Digital Design Perspective Comprehensive Approach on Fin-FET (Fin-Field Effect transistor) Technology - A Review. *Rev. Adv. Sci. Eng. (RASE)*, ASP, 5, 1–14, 2016.
102. Raj, B., Saxena, A.K., Dasgupta, S., Analytical Modeling for the Estimation of Leakage Current and Subthreshold Swing Factor of Nanoscale Double Gate FinFET Device. *Microelectron. Int.*, UK, 26, 53–63, 2009.
103. Soniya, Singh, S., Wadhwa, G., Raj, B., An Analytical Modeling for Dual Source Vertical Tunnel Field Effect Transistor. *Int. J. Recent Technol. Eng. (IJRTE)*, 8, 2, 603–608, July 2019.
104. Singh, S. and Raj, B., Design and analysis of hetrojunction Vertical T-shaped Tunnel Field Effect Transistor. *J. Electron. Mater.*, Springer, 48, 10, 6253-6260, October 2019.
105. Goyal, C., Ubhi, J.S., Raj, B., A Low Leakage CNTFET based Inexact Full Adder for Low Power Image Processing Applications. *Int. J. Circuit Theory Appl.*, Wiley, 47, 9, 1446–1458, September 2019.
106. Raj, B., Saxena, A.K., Dasgupta, S., A Compact Drain Current and Threshold Voltage Quantum Mechanical Analytical Modeling for FinFETs. *J. Nanoelectron. Optoelectron. (JNO)*, USA, 3, 2, 163–170, 2008.
107. Wadhwa, G. and Raj, B., An Analytical Modeling of Charge Plasma based Tunnel Field Effect Transistor with Impacts of Gate underlap Region. *Superlattices Microstruct.*, Elsevier, 142, 106512, June 2020.
108. Sharma, V.K., Pattanaik, M., Raj, B., PVT variations aware low leakage INDEP approach for nanoscale CMOS Circuits. *Microelectron. Reliab.*, Elsevier, 54, 90–99, 2014.
109. Raj, B., Saxena, A.K., Dasgupta, S., Quantum Mechanical Analytical Modeling of Nanoscale DG FinFET: Evaluation of Potential, Threshold Voltage and Source/Drain Resistance. *Elsevier's J. Mater. Sci. Semicond. Process.*, Elsevier, 16, 4, 1131–1137, 2013.

110. Gopal, M., Prasad, S.S.D., Raj, B., 8T SRAM Cell Design for Dynamic and Leakage Power Reduction. *Int. J. Comput. Appl.*, Foundation of Computer Science, New York, USA, 71, 9, 43–48, June 2013.
111. Pattanaik, M., Raj, B., Sharma, S., Kumar, A., Diode Based Trimode Multi-Threshold CMOS Technique for Ground Bounce Noise Reduction in Static CMOS Adders. *Adv. Mater. Res.*, Trans Tech Publications, Switzerland, 548, 885–889, 2012.
112. Raj, B., Saxena, A.K., Dasgupta, S., Nanoscale FinFET Based SRAM Cell Design: Analysis of Performance metric, Process variation, Underlapped FinFET and Temperature effect. *IEEE Circuits Syst. Mag.*, 11, 2, 38–50, 2011.
113. Sharma, V.K., Pattanaik, M., Raj, B., Leakage Current ONOFIC Approach for Deep Submicron VLSI Circuit Design. *Int. J. Electr. Comput. Electron. Commun. Eng.*, World Academy of Sciences, Engineering and Technology, 7, 4, 239–244, 2013.
114. Kaur, P., Gill, S.S., Raj, B., Comparative Analysis of OFETs Materials and Devices for Sensor Applications. *J. Silicon*, Springer, 14, 4463–4471, 2022.
115. Sharma, S.K., Kumar, P., Raj, B., Raj, B., $In_{1-x}Ga_xAs$ Double Metal Gate-Stacking Cylindrical Nanowire MOSFET for highly sensitive Photo detector. *J. Silicon*, Springer, 14, 3535–3541, 2022.
116. Raj, B., Saxena, A.K., Dasgupta, S., Analytical Modeling of Quasi Planar Nanoscale Double Gate FinFET with Source/Drain Resistance and field dependent carrier mobility: A quantum mechanical study. *J. Comput. (JCP)*, Academy Publisher, Finland, 4, 9, 1–8, 2009.
117. Bhushan, S., Khandelwal, S., Raj, B., Analyzing Different Mode FinFET based Memory Cell at Different Power Supply for Leakage Reduction. *Seventh International Conference on Bio-Inspired Computing: Theories and Application, (BIC-TA 2012)*, Advances in Intelligent Systems and Computing, vol. 202, pp. 89–100, 2013.
118. Singh, J. and Raj, B., Temperature Dependent Analytical Modeling and Simulations of Nanoscale Memristor. *Eng. Sci. Technol. Int. J.*, Elsevier's, 21, 862–868, Oct 2018.
119. Singh, S., Bala, S., Raj, B., Raj, B., Improved Sensitivity of Dielectric Modulated Junctionless Transistor for Nanoscale Biosensor Design. *Sens. Lett.*, ASP, 18, 328–333, April 2020.
120. Kumar, V., Vishvakarma, S.K., Raj, B., Design and Performance Analysis of ASIC for IoT Applications. *Sens. Lett.*, ASP, 18, 31–38, Jan 2020.
121. Jaiswal, A., Sarin, R.K., Raj, B., Sukhija, S., A Novel Circular Slotted Microstrip-fed Patch Antenna with Three Triangle Shape Defected Ground Structure for Multiband Applications. *Adv. Electromagn. (AEM)*, 7, 3, 56–63, Aug 2018.

122. Wadhwa, G. and Raj, B., Label Free Detection of Biomolecules using Charge-Plasma-Based Gate Underlap Dielectric Modulated Junctionless TFET. *J. Electron. Mater. (JEMS)*, Springer, 47, 8, 4683–4693, August 2018.
123. Singh, G., Sarin, R.K., Raj, B., Design and Performance Analysis of a New Efficient Coplanar Quantum-Dot Cellular Automata Adder. *Indian J. Pure Appl. Phys. (IJPAP)*, 55, 97–103, February 2017.
124. Kaur, P., Pandey, V., Raj, B., Comparative Study of Efficient Design, Control and Monitoring of Solar Power using IoT. *Sens. Lett.*, ASP, 18, 419–426, May 2020.
125. Bhardwaj, A.K., Gupta, S., Raj, B., Development & Analysis of compact model for Double Gate Schottky Barrier CNTFET. *J. Nanoelectron. Optoelectron.*, ASP, 15, 1199–1208, Aug 2020.
126. Wadhwa, G., Kamboj, P., Singh, J., Raj, B., Design and Investigation of Junctionless DGTFET for Biological Molecule Recognition. *Trans. Electr. Electron. Mater.*, Springer, 22, 282–289, 2021.
127. Verma, S.K., Singh, S., Wadhwa, G., Raj, B., Detection of Biomolecules using Charge-Plasma based Gate Underlap Dielectric Modulated Dopingless TFET. *Trans. Electr. Electron. Mater. (TEEM)*, Springer, 21, 528–535, June 2020.
128. Jain, N. and Raj, B., Impact of underlap spacer region variation on Electrostatic and analog/RF performance of symmetrical high-k SOI FinFET at 20 nm channel length. *J. Semicond. (JoS)*, IOP Science, 38, 12, 122002, Dec 2017.
129. Singh, S. and Raj, B., Analytical Modeling and Simulation analysis of T-shaped III-V heterojunction Vertical T-FET. *Superlattices Microstruct.*, Elsevier, 147, 106717, Nov 2020.
130. Singh, G., Sarin, R.K., Raj, B., Design and Analysis of Area Efficient QCA Based Reversible Logic Gates. *J. Microprocess. Microsys.*, Elsevier, 52, 59–68, May 2017.
131. Singh, S. and Raj, B., Parametric variation analysis on hetero-junction Vertical t-shape TFET for Supressing ambipolar conduction. *Indian J. Pure Appl. Phys.*, 58, 478–485, June 2020.
132. Soniya, Singh, S., Wadhwa, G., Raj, B., Design and Analysis of Dual Source Vertical Tunnel Field Effect Transistor for High Performance. *Trans. Electr. Electron. Mater.*, Springer, 21, 74–82, Oct 2019.
133. Kaur, M., Gupta, N., Kumar, S., Raj, B., Singh, A.K., RF Performance Analysis of Intercalated Graphene Nanoribbon Based Global Level Interconnects. *J. Comput. Electron.*, Springer, 19, 1002–1013, June 2020.
134. Wadhwa, G. and Raj, B., Design and Performance Analysis of Junctionless TFET Biosensor for high sensitivity. *IEEE Nanotechnol.*, 18, 567–574, 2019.
135. Singh, J. and Raj, B., Enhanced Nonlinear Memristor Model Encapsulating Stochastic Dopant Drift. *JNO*, ASP, 14, 958–963, 2019.

136. Singh, M., Chaudhary, T., Raj, B., Enhancing FeFET Structures for Non-volatile On-chip Memories: Design and Comparative Analysis. *Int. J. Numer. Modell. Electron. Networks Devices Fields*, 38, 1–9, 2024.
137. Singh, M., Chaudhary, T., Raj, B., Drain Current and Transconductance Analysis of GaN GAA Nanowire FET with High K Dielectric. *ECS J. Sci. Technol.*, 12, 6070–6077, 2023.
138. Singh, M., Chaudhary, T., Raj, B., Design of Si and Ge Nanowire FET for Low Power Application. *J. Silicon*, Springer, 15, 1491–1497, 2023.
139. Singh, M., Chaudhary, T., Raj, B., Electrical Characteristics Analysis of FeFET for Low Power Applications. *J. Nano*, 37, 1–8, 2024.
140. Kumar, M., Chaudhary, T., Raj, B., Design and Comparative Analysis of Ferroelectric Nanowire with Dielectric HfO_2 and $Al_2O_3$for Low Power Applications. *J. Electron. Mater.*, Springer, 53, 6785–6791, 2024.
141. Singh, S. and Raj, B., Modeling and Simulation analysis of SiGe hetrojunction Double GateVertical t-shaped Tunnel FET. *Superlattices Microstruct.*, Elsevier, 142, 106496, June 2020.
142. Jain, N. and Raj, B., Device and Circuit Co-Design Perspective Comprehensive Approach on FinFET Technology - A Review. *J. Electron Devices*, 23, 1, 1890–1901, 2016.
143. Kumar, S. and Raj, B., Analysis of I_{ON} and Ambipolar Current for Dual-Material Gate-drain Overlapped DG-TFET. *J. Nanoelectron. Optoelectron.*, American Scientific Publishers, USA, 11, 323–333, June 2016.
144. Anjum, N., Bali, T., Raj, B., Design and Simulation of Handwritten Multiscript Character Recognition. *Int. J. Adv. Res. Comput. Commun. Eng.*, 2, 7, 2544–2549, July 2013.
145. Singh, K. and Raj, B., Performance and analysis of temperature dependent Multi-walled Carbon Nanotubes as Global Interconnects at different technology nodes. *J. Comput. Electron.*, Springer, 14, 2, 469–476, June 2015.
146. Kumar, S. and Raj, B., Compact channel potential analytical Modeling of DG-TFET based on Evanescent-mode Approach. *J. Comput. Electron.*, Springer, 14, 2, 820–827, July 2015.
147. Singh, K. and Raj, B., Temperature Dependent Modeling and Performance Evaluation of Multi-Walled CNT and Single-Walled CNT as Global Interconnects. *J. Electron. Mater.*, Springer, 44, 12, 4825–4835, Dec 2015.
148. Sharma, V.K., Pattanaik, M., Raj, B., INDEP approach for leakage reduction in nanoscale CMOS circuits. *Int. J. Electron.*, Taylor & Francis, 102, 2, 200–215, 2014.
149. Singh, K. and Raj, B., Influence of Temperature on MWCNT bundle, SWCNT bundle and Copper interconnects for Nanoscaled Technology nodes. *J. Mater. Sci.: Mater. Electron.*, Springer, 26, 8, 6134–6142, 2015.
150. Anjum, N., Bali, T., Raj, B., Design and Simulation of Handwritten Gurumukhi and Devanagri Numerical Recognition. *Int. J. Comput. Appl.*, Foundation of Computer Science, New York, USA, 73, 12, 16–21, 2013.

151. Khandelwal, S., Gupta, V., Raj, B., Gupta, R.D., Process Variability Aware Low Leakage Reliable Nano Scale DG-FinFET SRAM Cell Design Technique. *J. Nanoelectron. Optoelectron.*, 10, 6, 810–817, December 2015.
152. Sharma, V.K., Pattanaik, M., Raj, B., ONOFIC Approach: Low Power High Speed Nanoscale VLSI Circuits Design. *Int. J. Electron.*, Taylor & Francis, 101, 1, 61–73, 2014.
153. Khandelwal, S., Raj, B., Gupta, R.D., FinFET based 6T SRAM Cell Design: Analysis of Performance Metric, Process Variation and Temperature Effect. *J. Comput. Theor. Nanosci.*, ASP, USA, 12, 2500–2506, 2015.
154. Singh, S., Yadav, S., Rahul, J., Srivastava, A., Raj, B., Impact of HfO_2 in Graded Channel Dual Insulator Double Gate MOSFET. *J. Comput. Theor. Nanosci.*, American Scientific Publishers, 12, 6, 950–953, April 2015.

10

Layout Dependent Effects

Kirti* **and Deepti Kakkar**

Department of Electronics and Communication Engineering, Dr. B. R. Ambedkar National Institute of Technology, Jalandhar, Punjab, India

Abstract

The low-speed, low-complexity, small-signal, high-voltage topologies of analog Complementary Metal Oxide Semiconductor (CMOS) circuits have given way to high-speed, high-complexity, low-voltage "mixed-signal" systems with significant amounts of digital circuitry throughout the last forty years. While device scaling has increased transistors' raw speed, non-idealities in architecture and packaging, as well as undesired interaction between various integrated circuit components, are rapidly restricting these systems' speed and precision. Today's layout and packaging have a significant impact on analog circuit design.

While designing analog and mixed-signal circuits, layout-dependent effects (LDEs) invariably result in performance reductions at low technology nodes. The three main LDE sources—the well proximity effect (WPE), length of diffusion (LOD), and oxide-to-oxide spacing effect (OSE)—substantially influence transistor threshold voltage and carrier mobility. Due to LDEs pre- and post-layout simulations are different. There are some layout matching techniques to reduce these effects. To minimize the impact of these effects, techniques like common centroid matching are employed. By symmetrically arranging transistors and other components in the layout, the effects of these non-idealities are balanced, leading to more accurate and reliable circuit performance. Thus, while layout and packaging have become increasingly important in modern analog and mixed-signal design, careful consideration of layout techniques such as common centroid matching is essential to achieving optimal performance.

***Keywords*:** Layout-dependent effects, length of diffusion, deep nanoscale CMOS, design rules multifinger transistors

**Corresponding author*: kirtig.vl.22@nitj.ac.in

Ashish Maurya, Mandeep Singh and Balwinder Raj (eds.) Machine Learning in Nanoelectronics: Devices, Circuits and Systems, (307–342) © 2026 Scrivener Publishing LLC

10.1 Overview of Layout Considerations

The configuration of an IC determines the forms that appear on the masks used during the etching process. The IC's geometries are the n-well, active, poly-silicon, n, and p-type im- plantation, inter-layer contacts, and metal layers [1–11]. Figure 10.1 [12] illustrates the mask shapes required for a (P-channel Metal Oxide Semiconductor) PMOS transistor. It's important to keep the following in mind:

(1) Every "active" location, such as Source/Drain (S/D) regions and the n+ contact with the well, has an appropriate implant shape surrounding it, leaving enough margin.
(2) The n-well surrounds the part with enough room to ensure that the transistor is kept inside the well despite any expected misalignment caused by the fabrication process.
(3) the gate needs its mask during the manufacturing process.
(4) The active and poly areas are connected to the first layer of metal *via* the contact windows mask. Most contemporary layout tools automatically create the implants and even the n-wells from the leftover transistor geometries, simplifying the process.

10.1.1 Design Rules

The circuit design determines each transistor's width and length, while "design rules," or a group of guidelines that ensure correct transistor and interconnect manufacturing despite different processing tolerances,

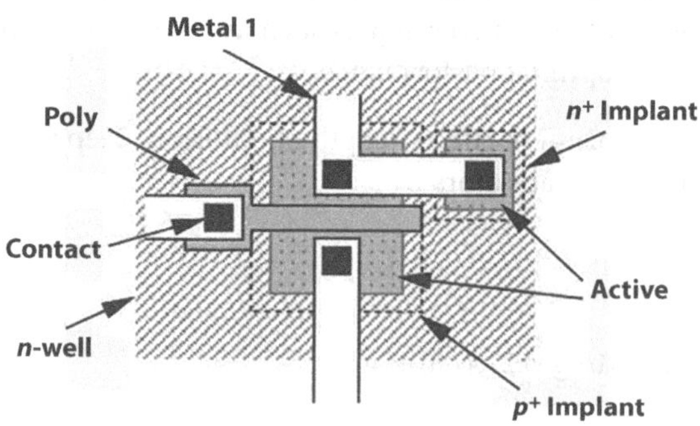

Figure 10.1 Layout of a PMOS transistor.

control most other layout dimensions [13–19]. The majority of design guidelines fall into one of the four classes that are outlined below.

(1) Minimal Width: The widths (and lengths) of the geometries defined on a mask must have a minimum value due to the lithography and technology processing capabilities. For instance, manufacturing tolerances may cause a poly-silicon rectangle that is too thin to shatter or at the very least have a significant local resistance as shown in Figure 10.2 [12]. Generally speaking, a layer's minimum permissible width increases with its thickness, meaning that as technologies advance, the thickness must also shrink proportionately. Examples of minimum widths in a 40-nm technology are shown in Figure 10.3 [12]. Keep in mind that the layout designer does not influence the layer thickness.
(2) Minimal Spacing: There must be a minimum space between the geometries constructed on the same mask or, in some circumstances, distinct masks [20–27]. For instance, as Figure 10.4(a) [12] illustrates, two poly-silicon lines may be shorted if they are positioned too near to one another. Another example would be the scenario depicted in Figure 10.4(b) [12], where a poly-silicon line passes near

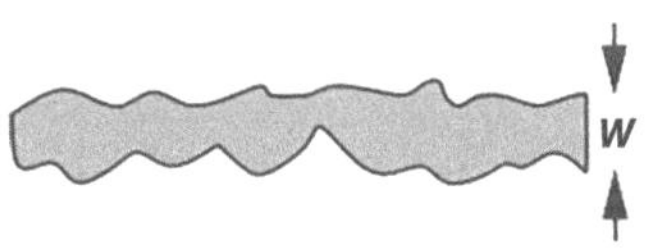

Figure 10.2 A thin poly line with excessive width fluctuation.

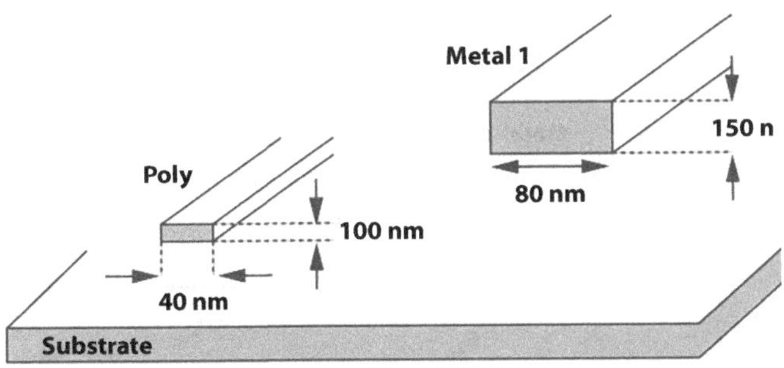

Figure 10.3 Width and height of poly layer and metal.

a transistor's S/D region. To prevent the implant around the transistor from overlapping the poly line, a minimum separation is needed in this location.

(3) Minimal Enclosure: As we previously explained, to guarantee that the device is contained by these geometries regardless of tolerances, the n-well and the p-well implant in the arrangement of Figure 10.1 needs to encircle the transistor with enough space. Another example is shown in Figure 10.5 [12], where a poly-line is connected to a metal 1 line *via* a poly contact window. Both geometries must encircle the contact with sufficient leeway to guarantee that it stays inside the poly and metal 1 square [28–35].

(4) Minimum Extension: Certain geometries must have a minimal amount of overlap with other geometries' edges. For example, as Figure 10.6 [12] illustrates, to guarantee appropriate transistor activity at the edge, the gate poly-silicon needs to extend at least a minimum beyond the active region. Together with the minimum measurements mentioned in the four categories above, there may also be certain maximum acceptable dimensions that are enforced. For instance, to prevent "liftoff" issues, the minimum width for long metal wires is usually greater than that of short wires.

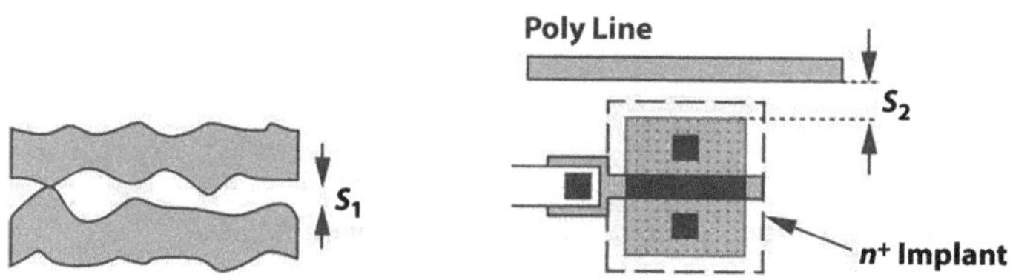

Figure 10.4 (a) Short between poly-lines nearby; (b) minimum spacing between active and poly layer.

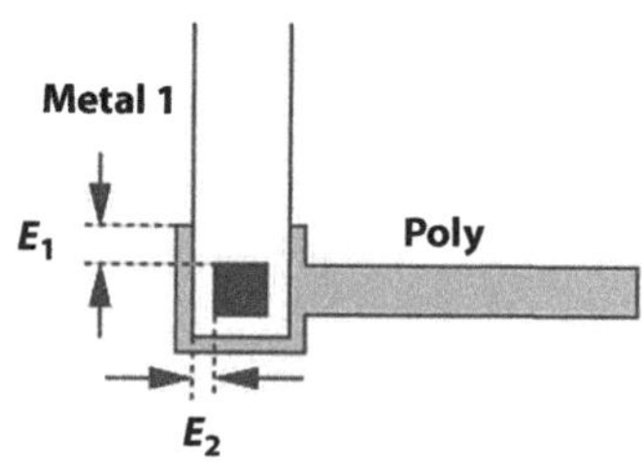

Figure 10.5 Rule of enclosure for metal and poly around a contact.

A subset of the design principles controlling the arrangement of an NMOS differential pair with PMOS current-source loads is summarized in Figure 10.7 [12]. Many hundred layout steps are usually included in modern CMOS technology [36–41].

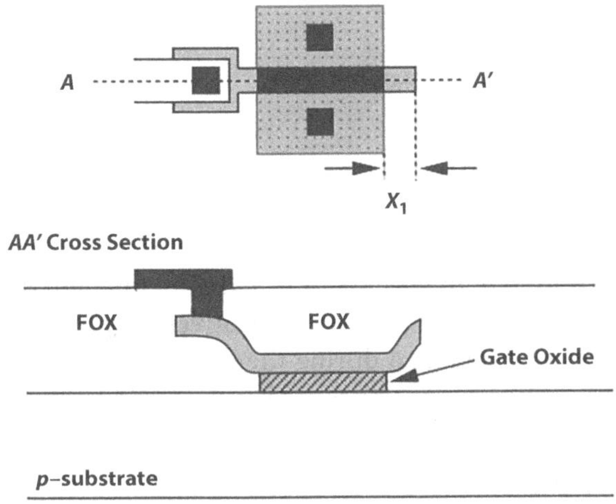

Figure 10.6 Extension of poly beyond the gate area.

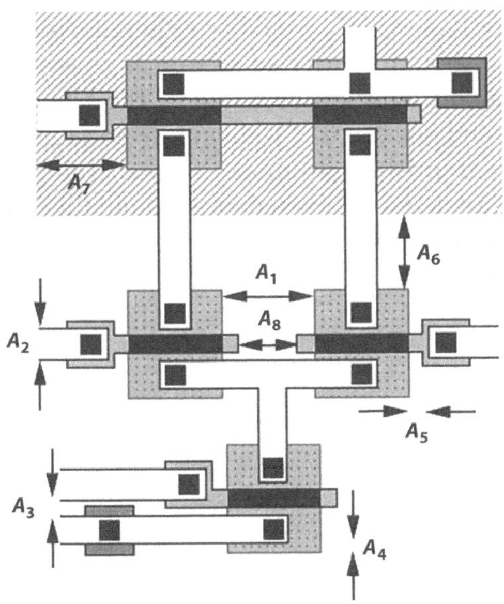

Figure 10.7 A differential pair layout.

where, A1: ActiveActive Spacing

A2: Metal Width
A3: Enclosure of Contact by Active
A4: MetalMetal Spacing
A5: PolyActive Spacing
A6: ActiveWell Spacing
A7: PolyPoly Spacing
A8: Enclosure of Active by Well

10.2 Analog Layout Techniques

Mainstream CMOS techniques enforce vast sets of design constraints that are intended to optimize the production of digital integrated circuits (ICs) while permitting circuit design that is relatively aggressive. Conversely, much more care must be taken during the designing of analog systems to reduce issues like noise, mismatches, and crosstalk [42–49].

10.2.1 Multifinger Transistors

Wide transistors are often "folded" to lower the gate resistance and the S/D junction area. For particularly broad devices, a simple folded construction like that in Figure 10.8 (a) [12] could not be sufficient; numerous "fingers" as shown in Figure 10.8 (b) [12] would be required. As a general guideline, each finger's width should be selected so that its resistance is smaller than the inverse transconductance connected to it. The gate resistance has to be between one-fifth and one-tenth of 1/gm in low-noise applications [50–57].

By splitting the transistor into multiple parallel fingers, the gate resistance can be decreased, but the capacitance around the source/drain region perimeter rises. The entire perimeter of the source or the drain, as demonstrated by the structures in Figure 10.9(a) [12], is equal to [12]

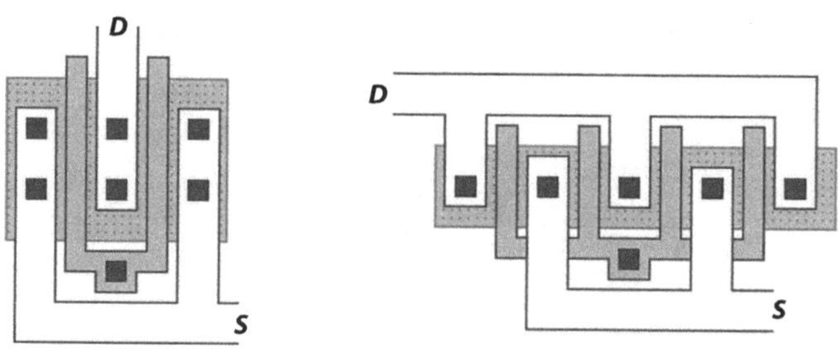

Figure 10.8 (a) Simple folding of a MOSFET; (b) use of multiple fingers.

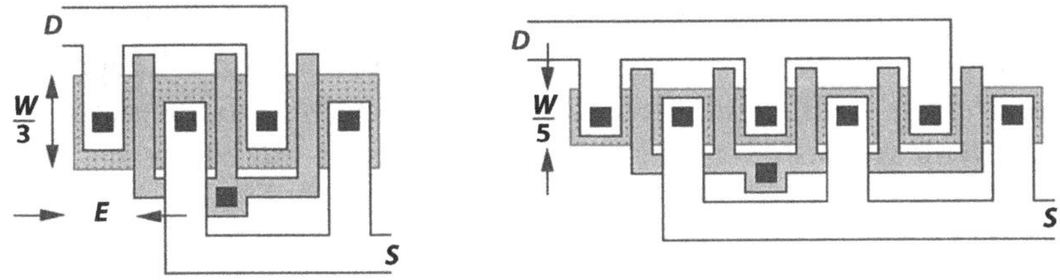

Figure 10.9 MOSFET layout using: (a) 3 fingers; (b) 5 fingers.

$$2\ 2E + \frac{2W}{3} = 4E + \frac{4W}{3} \tag{10.1}$$

when three fingers as shown in Figure 10.9(b) [12] are used, and [12]

$$3\ 2E\ + \frac{2W}{5} = 6E + \frac{6W}{5} \tag{10.2}$$

when five fingers are used. Generally speaking, the S/D perimeter capacitance for an odd number of fingers N is provided by [12]

$$C_p = \frac{N+1}{2}\ \frac{2E+2W}{N}\ C_{jsw} \tag{10.3}$$

$$C_p = (N+1)E + \frac{(N+1)}{N}\ W\ C_{jsw} \tag{10.4}$$

Therefore, to reduce the S/D perimeter capacitance contribution, the number of fingers multiplied by E must be significantly fewer than W. In actuality, these requirements could clash with the one to minimize gate resistance noise, necessitating a trade-off between the two or contacting the gate on both ends to lower the resistance [58–64].

Transistors with a lot of gate fingers can have their structure changed to the one in Figure 10.10 [12], which avoids lengthy geometries and hence disproportionate dimensions in the circuit architecture.

If the widths of the cascade device M_2 and the input device M_1 are equal, the cascade circuit architecture can be made simpler. The drain of M_1 and the source of M_2 may share a junction, as Figure 10.11(a) [12] illustrates. More importantly, this junction may be much smaller since it does not need to accommodate a contact window because it is not linked to any other nodes as shown in Figure 10.11(b) [12]. As a result, M_1's capacitance at the drain is significantly decreased, enhancing high-frequency performance. Wide transistors may require two fingers or more for each transistor [65–71].

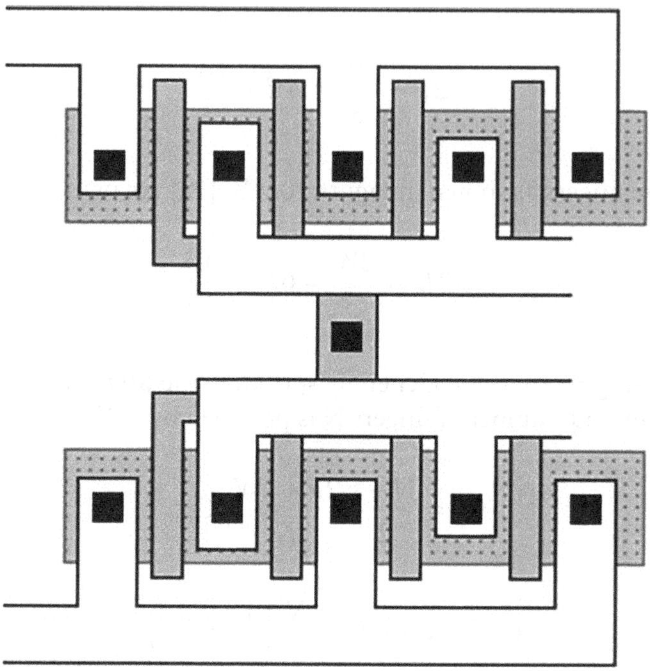

Figure 10.10 Layout of a wide transistor with more than one finger.

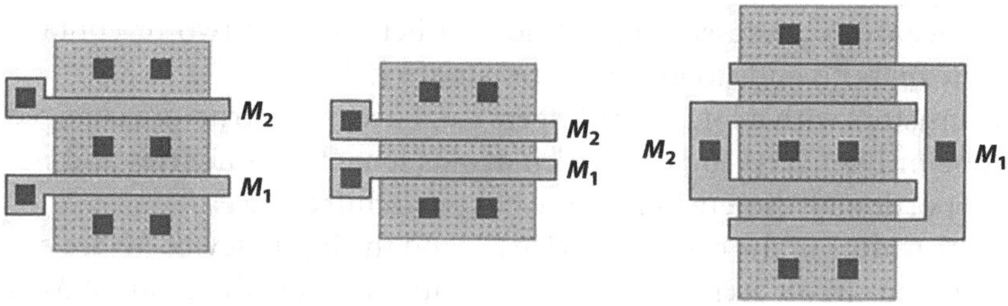

Figure 10.11 Layout of cascode devices with identical width.

10.2.2 Symmetry

Input-referred offsets are introduced by asymmetry in differential circuits, which lowers the lowest signal level that may be detected. While some mismatches are unavoidable, substantial offsets are much larger than the values anticipated and may arise from the layout's lack of attention to symmetry. Additionally, even-order non-linearity and common-mode noise are suppressed by symmetry [72–80]. It is crucial to remember that symmetry needs to be applied to both the important devices and the surroundings in which they are located. Later, we will revisit this subject. First, let us look at the differential pair of Figure 10.12(a) [12]. Because numerous processes in lithography and wafer processing operate differently along various axes, the matching suffers considerably if the two transistors are set out with different orientations, as shown in Figure 10.12(b) [12].

The arrangements shown in Figure 10.12(c) [12] and (d) [12] therefore offer a more likely answer. The decision between these two is based on a minor phenomenon known as "gate shadowing." As seen in Figure 10.13 [12], the implant (or wafer) is slanted by about 7◦ to prevent channeling, which is why the gate poly-silicon causes shadowing during source/drain implantation. When the implanted parts are annealed, this causes a little imbalance between the source and drain side diffusions, with a thin strip in the source or drain region receiving less implantation [81–86].

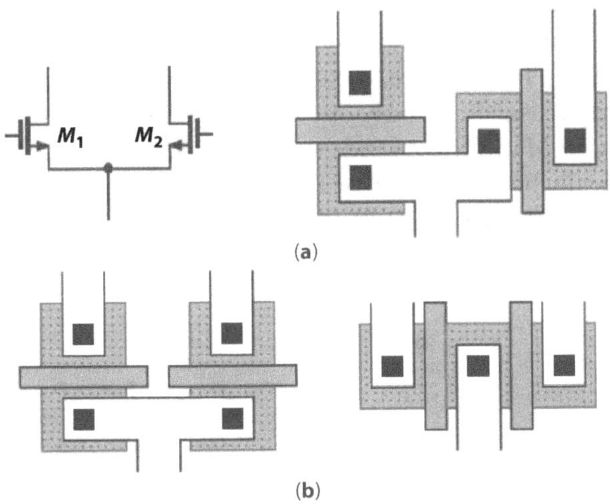

Figure 10.12 (a) Circuit of Differential pair; (b) M_1 and M_2 oriented differently; (c) devices aligned with a gate; (d) devices arranged in a parallel configuration.

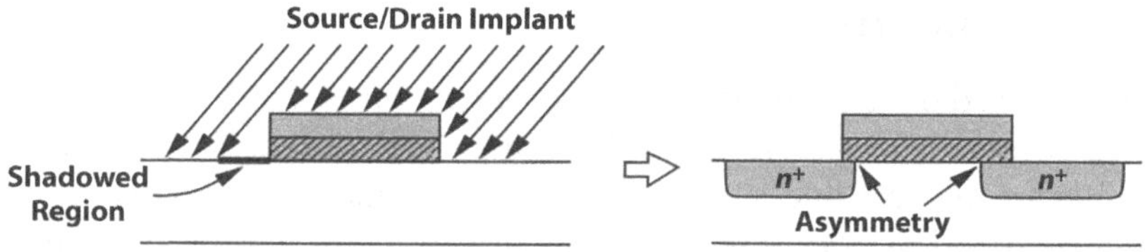

Figure 10.13 Shadowing due to implant tilt.

Now let us examine the configurations shown in Figure 10.12(c) and (d) with gate shadowing (Figure 10.13) present. If the shaded terminal in Figure 10.14(a) [12] can be identified as the drain (or source), then there is no shadowing-related imbalance between the two devices. However, even if the shaded terminals in Figure 10.14(b) [12] may be recognized, the transistors are not the same since the source area of M_1 "sees" M_2 to its right, whereas the source region of M_2 just sees the field oxide [87–92]. Likewise, the M_1 and M_2 drains see distinct buildings to their left. Stated differently, the environment in which M_1 exists is distinct from that of M_2. The topology shown in Figure 10.13(a) is therefore preferred.

By adding "dummy" transistors to both sides, the asymmetry present in Figure 10.15(b) may be lessened, allowing M_1 and M_2 to perceive roughly the same environment (Figure 10.15 [12]). These steps, however, are difficult to implement in more intricate circuits, such as a folded-cascade operational amplifier. Later, we'll see how a more basic form of dummies turns out to be helpful and crucial in today's technological environment [93–97].

The significance of preserving the identical environment on both sides of the axis of symmetry should be emphasized. As seen in the structure of Figure 10.16 [12], for instance, the symmetry is weakened by an unrelated metal line that crosses over only one transistor, in- creasing the mismatch between M_1 and M_2. In these kinds of situations, the cause of the asymmetry should ideally be eliminated, or a dummy must be created on the opposite side (Figure 10.15(b) [12]), even though it can be grounded [98–104].

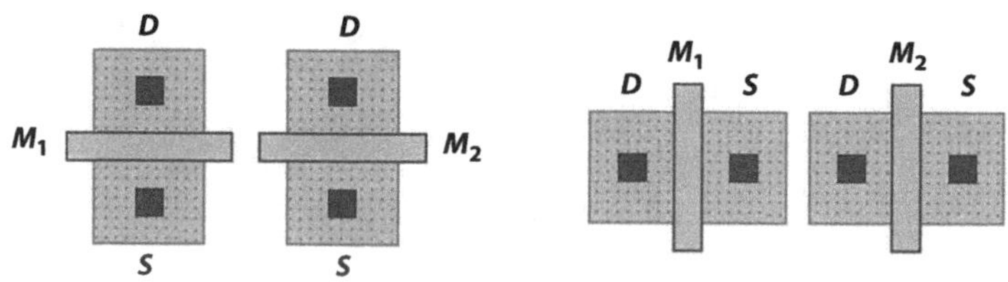

Figure 10.14 Shadowing impact on parallel-gate and gate-aligned transistors.

Large transistors make symmetry more challenging to create. For instance, in the differential pair of Figure 10.17 [12], gradients along the x-axis result in noticeable mismatches despite the two transistors' enormous width allowing for a tiny input offset voltage. A "common-centroid" arrangement that cancels the influence of first-order gradients along both axes can be utilized to lower the inaccuracy.

The concept is to split each transistor into two halves that are positioned diagonally across from one another and linked in parallel, as shown in Figure 10.18 [12]. But because of how challenging it is to route the interconnects in this configuration, systematic asymmetries like the one shown in Figure 10.19(a) [12] or the capacitances between and from the wires to the ground frequently result. The routing for a large circuit, such as

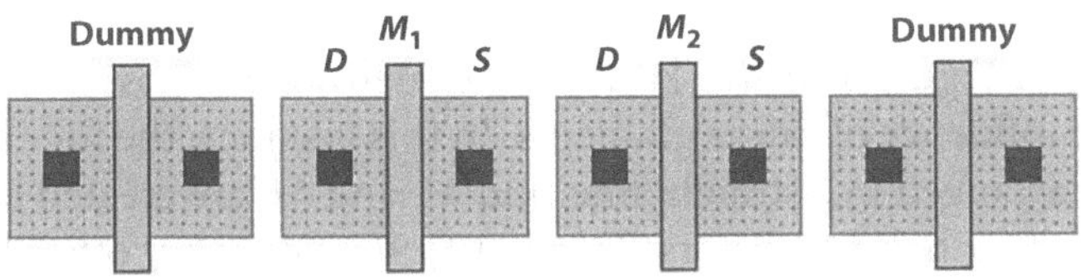

Figure 10.15 Dummy devices are added to enhance symmetry.

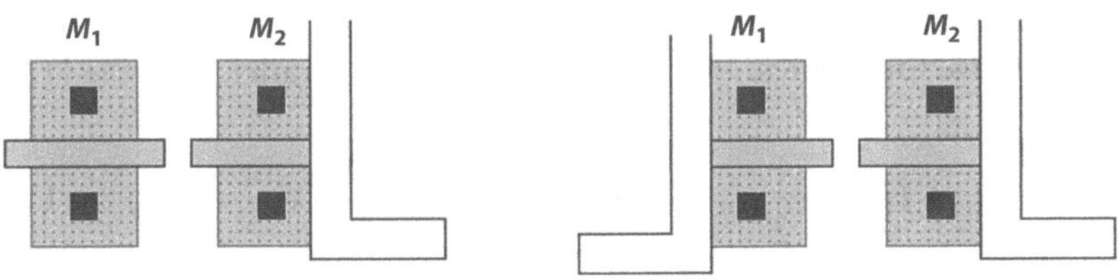

Figure 10.16 (a) An asymmetry resulting from a metal line crossing M_2; (b) the asymmetry being eliminated by duplicating the line above M_1.

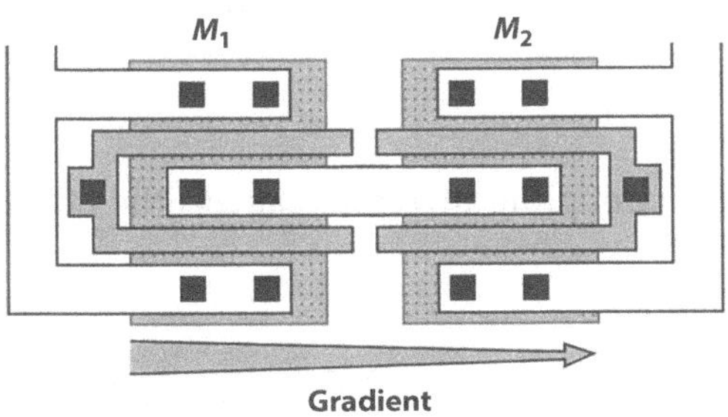

Figure 10.17 Effect of gradient in a differential pair.

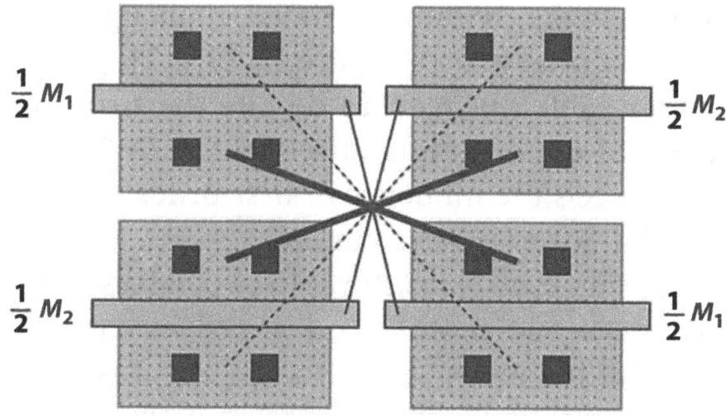

Figure 10.18 Common-centroid layout.

an op-amp, could become unnecessarily complicated. So, we seek easier options.

As seen in Figure 10.19(a) [12], "one-dimensional" cross-coupling can reduce the influence of linear gradients. In this instance, the four half transistors are arranged in a straight line, and M_1 and M_2 are created by joining the near and far half transistors (Figure 10.19(a)) or every other half transistor (Figure 10.19(b)).

The connections between the sources and the drains are not displayed for clarity. Assume for analytical purposes that the gate-oxide capacitance changes by Cox between each half transistor to examine the impact of gradients in these topologies. Placing M_{1a} and M_{4a} in parallel, we have [12]

$$I_{D1a} + I_{D4a} = \frac{1}{2}\mu_n(C_{ox} + C_{ox} + 3\Delta C_{ox})\frac{W}{L}(V_{Gs} - V_{TH})^2 \quad (10.5)$$

and for M_{2a} and M_{3a} [12],

$$I_{D2a} + I_{D3a} = \frac{1}{2}\mu_n(C_{ox} + C_{ox} + C_{ox} + 2\Delta C_{ox})\frac{W}{L}(V_{Gs} - V_{TH})^2 \quad (10.6)$$

This type of cross-coupling therefore cancels the effect of the gradient [12].

$$I_{D1a} + I_{D4a} = \frac{1}{2}\mu_n(C_{ox} + C_{ox} + C_{ox} + 2\Delta C_{ox})\frac{W}{L}(V_{Gs} - V_{TH})^2 \quad (10.7)$$

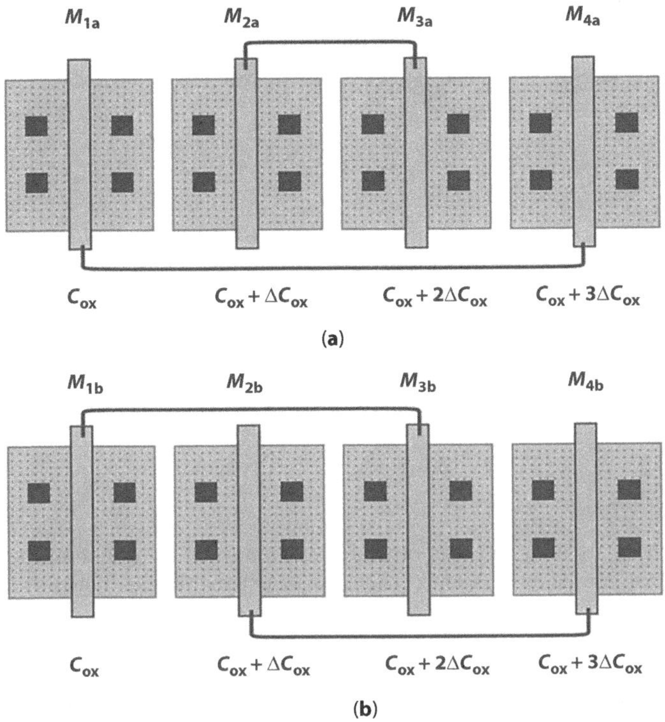

Figure 10.19 One-dimensional cross-coupling.

$$I_{D2a} + I_{D3a} = \frac{1}{2}\mu_n(C_{ox} + C_{ox} + C_{ox} + \Delta C_{ox} + 3\Delta C_{ox})\frac{W}{L}(V_{Gs} - V_{TH})^2 \tag{10.8}$$

According to Equation (10.7), this method only partially eliminates the inaccuracy. The reader may demonstrate that comparable outcomes are achieved for modest gradients in other device parameters, leading to the conclusion that Figure 10.19(a)'s topology has fewer mistakes than Figure 10.19(b). Dummy transistors, however, must be placed to the left of M_{1a} and the right of M_{4a} since the environment viewed by $M_{2a} + M_{3a}$ is different from that seen by $M_{1a} + M_{4a}$.

10.2.3 Shallow Trench Isolation Issues

To prevent a channel from forming between neighboring transistors, modern MOS devices are encircled by a shallow "trench" as shown in

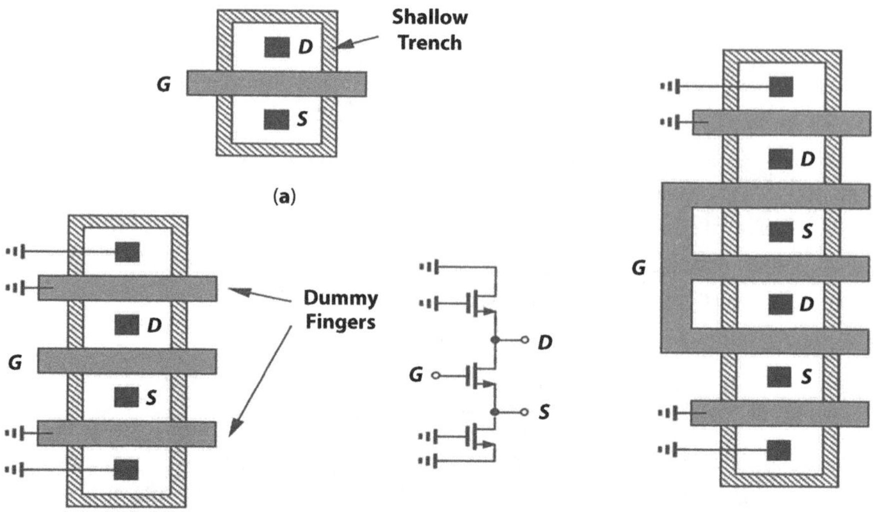

Figure 10.20 (a) Isolating a device with a shallow trench; (b) using dummy fingers to lessen the stress caused by STIs; and (c) an example of a multifinger transistor.

Figure 10.20(a) [12]. This structure, filled with oxide, is known as "shallow trench isolation" (STI) and is formed automatically. Its thermal expansion coefficient differs from silicon's [105–109]. Because of this, the STI and the enclosing silicon region expand and compress in distinct ways during the manufacturing process. The MOS transistor's electrical characteristics are changed by this STI-induced "stress," which significantly affects its I/V characteristics.

We need to reduce the stress propagation toward the gate region to resolve this problem. To do this, we place two fingers on either side of the primary device (Figure 10.20(b)) [12]. Usually, these "dummy" fingers are grounded to prevent interference with the main transistor's operation, as are the S/D junctions connected to them. But take note that the S/D capacitances to earth are increased by the fake gates [110–116]. The dummy gates for transistors with numerous fingers can be added to either end of the array (Figure 10.20(c)) [12].

10.3 Effects of Layout in Deep Nanoscale CMOS

Designers must be mindful that, as CMOS scaling moves into the nanoscale zone, device behavior is dependent not only on conventional geometric factors like channel length and breadth but also on specifics related to the

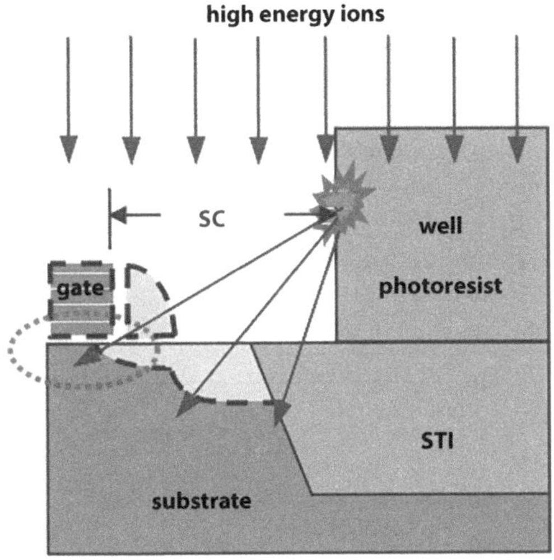

Figure 10.21 The alteration in the doping profile due to the scattering of ions by the photoresist from the edge of the well.

device's implementation and the neighborhood around it. New geometric dependencies have also been introduced by the emergence of stress engineering, which applies mechanical stress on purpose to enhance device performance. The device's behavior was mostly independent of its surroundings in the sub-micron region due to sufficiently large dimensions. The necessity of simulating both the device and its environment became evident as device scaling proceeded into the nanoscale zone. Figure 10.21 presents the alteration in the doping profile due to the scattering of ions by the photoresist from the edge of the well.

10.3.1 Types of LDEs

(1) Well-implant Proximity Effect (WPE)
Figure 10.22 [17] illustrates, from a cross-sectional perspective, the cause of the WPE on MOSFET devices. The scattering of high-energy ions at the edge of the well photoresist results in the introduction of additional dopant atoms into the silicon adjacent to the well edge. As the gate of the MOSFET gets closer to the well edge, there is an increase in the dopant concentration within the core area of the MOSFET, which consequently leads to a relative rise in the threshold voltage, as demonstrated in Figure 10.22 [7].

The distance between the well edge and the gate is represented by SC. A reduction in SC leads to a rise in the threshold voltage, which in turn results

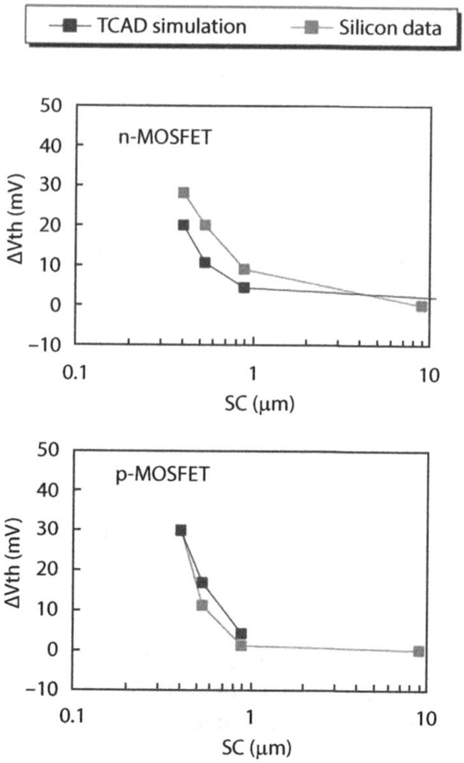

Figure 10.22 Variation in the MOSFET threshold voltage relative to the distance between the well edge and the gate in silicon, as observed from experimental data and results simulated using TCAD.

in a lower drive current. The primary cause of this phenomenon is the alteration in the dopant profile of the MOSFET. To account for the variations induced by this effect, three related MOSFET parameters—threshold voltage, body effect coefficient, and carrier mobility—are adjusted accordingly [20].

The Compact Modeling Council (CMC) has defined a WPE model for use with Metal Oxide Semiconductor (MOS) compact models in circuit modeling. Figure 10.23 [17] shows the layout measurements required for the WPE model. To take into consideration the uneven shape of the well, the model employs a weighted average of the individual measurements in each direction.

In this WPE model, the three MOSFET instance parameters (SCA, SCB, and SCC) reflect the first, second, and third distribution function integrals for distributed dopants.

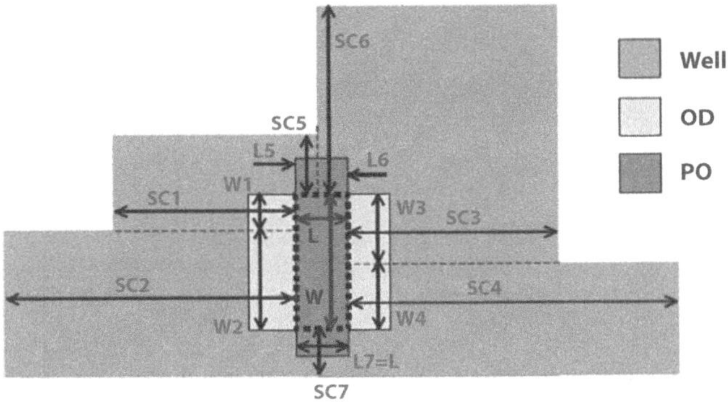

Figure 10.23 Measurements of the WPE model arrangement for the CMC model. The oxide definition, or active area, is OD. Gate is polysilicon (PO).

(2) Shallow Trench Isolation (STI) Effect

Silicon exhibits piezoelectric properties, meaning that any disturbance to its atoms can alter the silicon's band structure. This may result in band splitting, modifications to the effective mass and shape of the bands, and a redistribution of carriers among different sub-bands. These changes to the band structure can have an impact on carrier transport characteristics including mobility at the device level, which in turn affects the device current [21]. Stress can also alter the band structure or dopant diffusivity, which can affect the device threshold voltage. Due to its piezoelectric qualities, silicon can have its band structure changed by any perturbation to the atoms' balanced state locations. These band structure changes may have an impact on the mobility of charge carriers, which alters the device current at the device level. Stress can also alter the band structure or dopant diffusivity, which can both have an impact on the device threshold voltage. NMOS and PMOS transistors react to stress in different ways. While PMOS devices function better under compressive stress in the same direction, NMOS devices usually benefit from tensile stress along the channel length. Nonetheless, tensile stress over the channel width is typically preferred by both NMOS and PMOS transistors.

The process of Shallow Trench Isolation (STI) formation generates compressive stress in the active regions of the device, which are defined by the oxide. The level of stress experienced by the device is influenced by how far the device channel is from the STI edges as shown in Figure 10.24 [17]. When the edges are nearer, the stresses combine. These stress profiles are usually estimated to have a dependence on 1/LOD (length of diffusion).

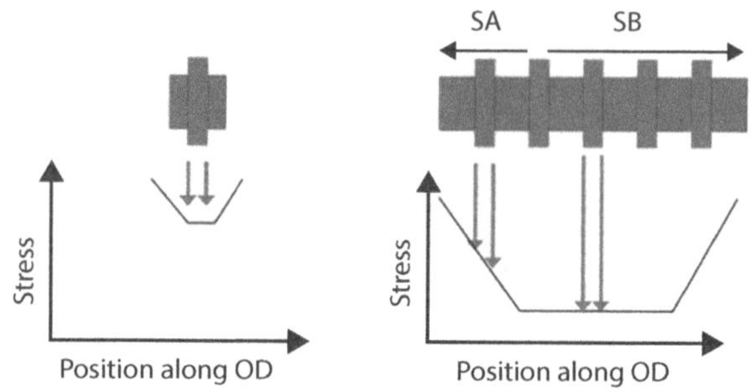

Figure 10.24 Stress against location for two distinct OD lengths.

Since STI leads to compressive stress, being close to the STI edge can worsen NMOS efficiency but improve PMOS efficiency. To minimize differences between gate fingers that are supposed to be identical, it is recommended to utilize the middle fingers of an extended OD stripe or to lengthen the OD stripe and incorporate dummy devices at both extremities.

(3) Length of Diffusion (LOD)

Preliminary research and evaluation of stress-related effects included the impact of Shallow Trench Isolation (STI) proximity on device performance. Compressive stress is produced on the active device surface (Oxide Diffusion, or OD, as shown in Figure 10.25 [6]) as a result of STI production. An idealized stress curve for two distinct lengths of OD (LOD) is shown in Figure 10.25. The distance between the device channel and both

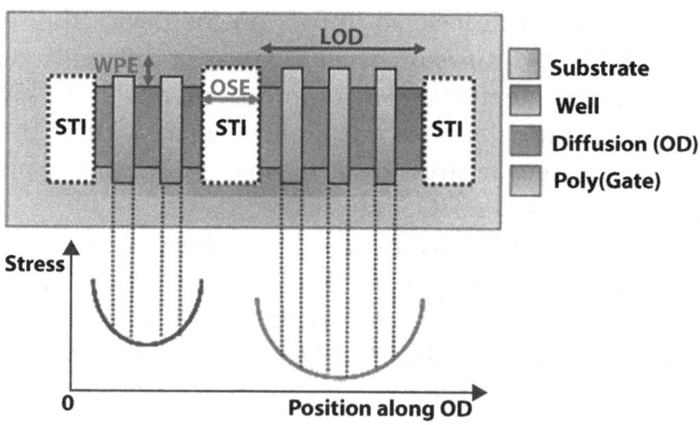

Figure 10.25 LOD and OSE: Dispersion of stress across different devices as a result of STI.

STI edges determines the strain that the device undergoes. The tension increases when two edges are near to one another.

A 1/LOD dependency is frequently used to approximate the stress profiles. The SA and SB parameters, which measure the distances from the gate to the left and right STI edges, respectively, are commonly used to execute this in the compact model. Being at the edge of STI reduces NMOS performance while enhancing PMOS performance because it creates compressive stress. The middle fingers of a lengthy OD stripe should be used, or the OD stripe should be extended, and dummy devices added to the left and right, to reduce variation among "identical" gate fingers.

(4) Oxide to oxide Spacing (OSE)

The compressive or tensile stress produced by the structures, such as shallow trench isolation (STI), is the cause of both LOD and OSE. Theoretically, as seen in Figure 10.23, LOD relates to the channel distance from the stress source, and changes in this distance might affect carrier mobility. OSE, on the other hand, stands for the stress source scale. Its rise could also cause carrier mobility to change. While an increase in oxide-to-oxide spacing causes big STI wells and, thus, substantial stress to arise from the STI, an increase in channel and stress source spacing appears to lessen the effect of stress on the device channel.

(4) Antenna Effect

Assume that a tiny MOSFET gate is connected to a large-area metal 1 connection [Figure 10.26(a) [12]. The metal portion functions as an "antenna" during the etching of metal 1, gathering ions and increasing in potential. Therefore, it's feasible that during manufacture, the MOS device's gate voltage rises to a point where the gate oxide breaks down (irreversibly). Any substantial piece of conductive material connected to the gate, even polysilicon itself, may produce the antenna effect. Because of this, the overall area of such designs is usually limited to sub-micron CMOS technologies,

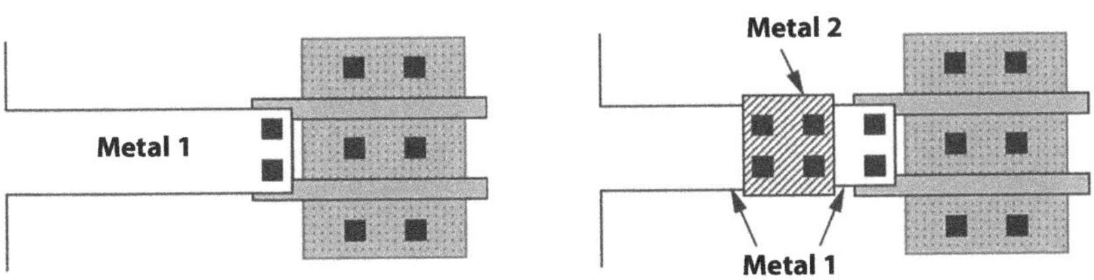

Figure 10.26 (a) Antenna effect-prone layout; (b) metal 1 layer discontinuity to prevent antenna effect.

reducing the likelihood of gate-oxide damage. If large portions are unavoidable, a discontinuity can be made, as shown in Figure 10.26(b) [12], so that the big area is not linked to the gate during the etching of metal 1.

10.4 Mismatch of Devices

For calculations of differential amplifiers, we often assume that the circuits were symmetric, meaning that the bias currents and other characteristics were the same on both sides. In practice, however, there is a finite gap between supposedly identical devices because of uncertainties in every stage of the manufacturing process. For instance, as Figure 10.27 [12] shows, MOSFET gate dimensions are subject to random, microscopic fluctuations that result in mismatches between two identically laid-out transistors' equivalent lengths and widths. Additionally, MOS devices have threshold voltage mismatches because, according to an equation of threshold voltage [12],

$$V_{TH} = \phi_{MS} + 2_{\phi F} + \frac{Qdep}{C_{ox}} \tag{10.9}$$

It depends on the doping levels in the gate and the channel, which differ randomly throughout the devices.

The two processes in the study of mismatch are:

(1) Identifying and formulating the mechanisms that result in device mismatches
(2) Analyzing the impact of device mismatches on circuit performance.

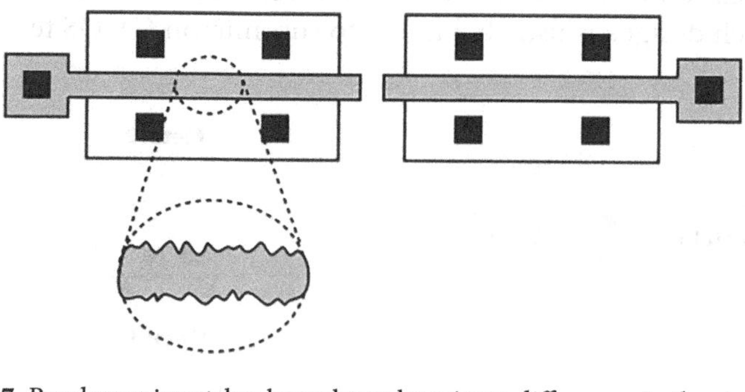

Figure 10.27 Random mismatches brought on by minute differences in the size of the device.

Figure 10.28 shows decrease in the mismatch in length due to an increase in width. Regretfully, the initial stage is rather intricate and highly reliant on the plan and production technologies, frequently necessitating precise measurements of mismatches. For instance, it is common knowledge that the possible misfit between capacitors is 0.1%; nevertheless, this figure is not based on any basic facts. We discover that discrepancies in *mu*, Cox, W, L, and V_{TH} lead to discrepancies in drain currents (for a specific V_{GS}) or gate-source voltages (for a specific drain current) between two ostensibly similar transistors. The properties of a MOSFET in saturation may be expressed as [12]

$$I_D = \frac{1}{2}\mu C_{ox}\frac{W}{L}(V_{GS} - V_{TH})^2 \tag{10.10}$$

It seems sense that as W and L rise, their relative mismatches $\frac{\Delta W}{W}$ and $\frac{\Delta L}{L}$, respectively should fall; that is, larger devices should have fewer mismatches. A further significant finding is that all of the mismatches get smaller as the transistor's area, W L, grows. For instance, raising W lowers $\frac{\Delta W}{W}$ and $\frac{\Delta L}{L}$. This is because random fluctuations undergo more "averaging" and hence decrease in size as W L grows. This scenario is illustrated in Figure 10.29 [12], $\Delta L_1 < \Delta L_2$.

When the MOSFET is perceived as several tiny parallel transistors (Figure 10.30 [12]), every one possessing a width of W0, the corresponding length may be expressed as [12]

$$L_{eq} \approx \frac{L_1 + L_2 + \cdots + L_n}{n} \tag{10.11}$$

The overall variation is therefore given by [12]

$$L_{eq} \approx \frac{(\Delta L_1^2 + \Delta L_2^2 + \cdots \Delta L_n^2)^{1/2}}{n} \tag{10.12}$$

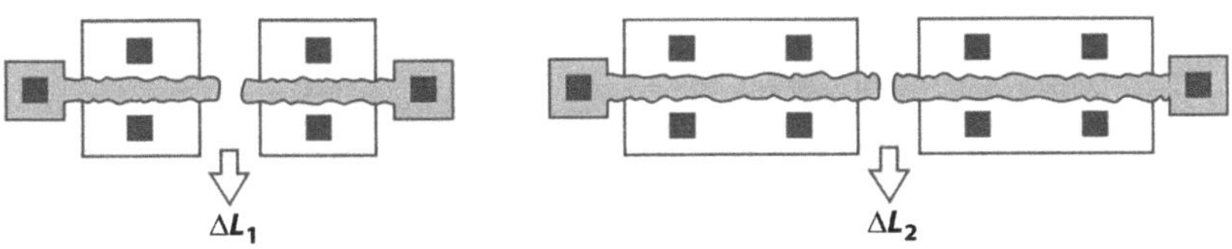

Figure 10.28 Decrease in the mismatch in length due to an increase in width.

$$L_{eq} + \frac{(n\Delta L_0^2)^{1/2}}{n} \tag{10.13}$$

$$L_{eq} = \frac{\Delta L}{\sqrt{\frac{o}{n}}} \tag{10.14}$$

It is possible to apply the aforementioned outcome to other device parameters. For instance, we hypothesize that as the device area rises, μC_{OX} and V_{TH} experience less mismatch. The reason is that a big transistor may be broken down into a series and parallel combination of tiny unit transistors with dimensions of W0 and L0, each of which exhibits $\mu C_{OX})_j$ and $V_{TH}j$ This is shown in Figure 10.29. When the quantity of unit transistors rises for a given W0 and L0, μC_{OX} and V_{TH} undergo increased averaging, which results in a reduced misfit between two big transistors. Mathematical and experimental verification has been provided for the previously mentioned qualitative findings. Here, we assert without evidence that [12]

$$\Delta V_{TH} = \frac{A_{VTH}}{\sqrt{WL}} \tag{10.15}$$

$$\Delta(\mu C_{ox}\frac{W}{L}) = \frac{A_K}{\sqrt{WL}} \tag{10.16}$$

where the proportionality factors, A_K and AV_{TH}, are derived from measurements. We observe that there is a trade-off between threshold voltage and the channel capacitance since the channel capacitance is proportional to WLC_{OX}.

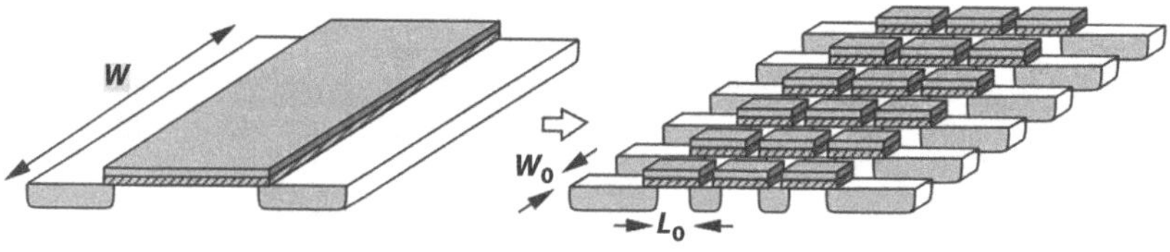

Figure 10.29 Large MOSFET shown as a collection of tiny components.

10.4.1 Impact of Mismatch

When constructing analog integrated circuits (ICs), a thorough grasp of the matching behavior of the components available in a certain integrated circuit technology is essential. The importance of device mismatch issues is growing as technological advancements result in smaller feature sizes and stricter design limits. After obtaining the layout, we carry out post-layout parasitic extraction and examine the connections between the extracted parasitic, layout, and circuit. Unwanted parasites have the potential to alter design performance by up to 90% [13]. For this reason, structures including both passive (such as resistor or capacitor arrays) and active (such as differential pairs and current mirrors) devices are matched. There are many layout-matching techniques like inter-digitization, half symmetry, and common centroid.

Mismatches cause three important phenomena: decreased common-mode rejection, limited even-order distortion, and DC offsets. To avoid or reduce mismatching, we place devices in two types of arrangement.

10.4.2 Types of Matching

(1) Interdigitate Interdigitated (ID) layouts, such as the 1-D "ABAB" layout in Figure 10.30 [16], alternate where each device's unit cells are placed. The centroid for the A cells in the picture is located to the left of the centroid for the B cells, indicating that interdigitated schemes lack a common centroid for the devices.

Figure 10.31 shows the abstract view inter-digitize configuration of the current mirror circuit respectively in BCD technology.

(2) Common Centroid
In analog design, common centroid (CC) layouts (Figure 10.18) are commonlyemployedtomatchdevicepropertiesandmakecircuitsresistanttofluctuations. Compared to other alternative layout techniques, CC layout may,

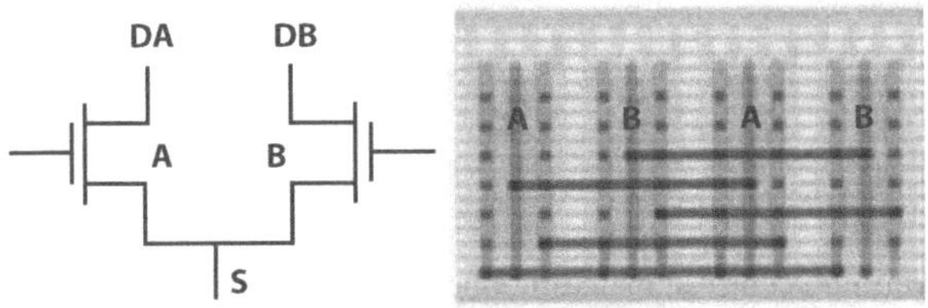

Figure 10.30 ID MOSFET layout of a 2× differential pair.

Figure 10.31 Inter-digitize matching of current mirror circuit.

however, include greater parasitic and increased routing complexity. The basic presumptions underlying the use of common-centroid layouts are examined critically in this work, which also considers the effects of common-centroid layout on performance as well as systematic and random changes. To make designs more sensitive to differential variability, which is simpler to limit, and less sensitive to absolute variability which is difficult to control analog designers have over time created a set of widely accepted best practices. Using layout strategies to lessen the process-induced differential mismatch between parts in a layout is a crucial component of these practices. For this reason, structures including both passive (such as resistor or capacitor arrays) and active (such as differential pairs and current mirrors) devices are matched. We will discuss the common centroid (CC) layout method for transistor arrays, concentrating on MOSFET technology. CC works to counteract process variability in transistor arrays and look at the trade-offs associated with its application. By shortening the distance between the centroids of the matched devices, gradient-induced mismatches can be reduced. There are layout configurations that can make the separation between the centroids zero. When long-range variations are linear functions of distance, common-centroid layouts can eliminate their impacts. Over short distances, the variations stay approximately linear even if they include a nonlinear component. The common- centroid architecture is less vulnerable to nonlinear gradients the more compact it can be made. The most effective MOS transistor layouts combine compactness and precise centroidal alignment.

Figure 10.32 shows the abstract view of the current mirror circuit in common centroid configuration respectively in BCD technology.

Figure 10.32 Common centroid matching of current mirror circuit.

10.4.3 Advantages and Limitations of CC

In analog design, common-centroid (CC) layouts are frequently employed to match device properties and create circuits that are resistant to fluctuations. Compared to other alternative layout techniques, CC layout may, however, entail increased routing complexity. The Common Centroid (CC) and various other layout configurations also influence layout-dependent effects (LDEs). Compared to smaller designs, larger layouts might gain advantages from implementing the CC layout strategy. While some designs might not necessitate the use of a CC layout, there are cases where CC could enhance performance more effectively than alternative layout styles. The common-centroid (CC) technique designs a layout for a group of i elements, where each device a consisting of s_a units. The CC layout is designed to align the central points of all the units within each device. Given that the location of unit a of device b is (x^a,y^a), for a 1D layout the CC criterion is [5]

$$\frac{1}{S_M}\sum_{a=1}^{S_M} X_1^M = \frac{1}{S_N}\sum_{a=1}^{S_N} X_2^N \tag{10.17}$$

where S_M and $S_N = 2$ unit cells. Using CC layouts makes sense since they eliminate linear systematic fluctuations brought on by first-order processes. A tiny disturbance, ΔP, in the circuit performance parameter P, is caused by a fluctuation ΔP in the process parameter p. A Taylor series expansion in linear form can be used to simulate this [5]

$$\Delta P = S_p \Delta p \tag{10.18}$$

where the responsiveness at the standard condition is determined by [5]

$$\S_p = \frac{\partial P}{\partial p} \tag{10.19}$$

The changes are determined by a plane [5]

$$\Delta p = \alpha \cdot x \tag{10.20}$$

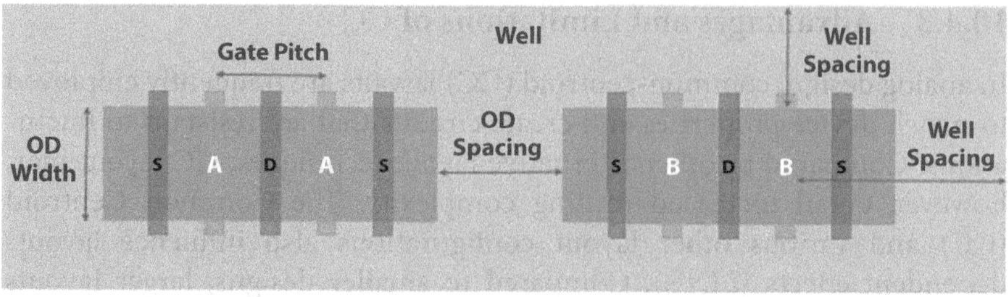

Figure 10.33 OD width and spacing, gate pitch is shown for devices.

where α is the gradient of the variation, with the centroid serving as the origin. In dimension x, which is horizontal, the spacing and width of the Oxide Definition (OD), also referred to as the Oxide Spacing Effect (OSE), are depicted in Figure 10.33. This phenomenon affects the stress levels within a transistor as a result of changes in the distance between the OD regions, which are the active areas, consequently modifying the threshold voltage. Furthermore, a transistor's produced stress changes with its OD width, or active area width. By keeping the OD width and spacing the same, mismatch may be prevented.

As seen in Figure 10.33 [16] for device A, adjusting the gate pitch leads to variations in the stress experienced by a transistor. The volume of the stressor material near the poly rises with gate pitch, which causes an increase in stress in the transistor channel and a perturbation in threshold voltage. Using the same poly-pitch minimizes mismatch in analog cells.

All LDEs, except LOD and WPE, may be eliminated by using matching unit cells for matched devices.

Smaller layouts—where the size is much less than the correlation distance—are dominated by random variations and do not require CC for matching, whereas larger layouts need CC to process gradients and cancel spatial variations. Deterministic shifts and parasitics are also important: whereas ID layouts have better parasitics, clustered and ID layouts have lower LDE. Even for small buildings, CC design for differential structures may be advantageous because of their capacity to reduce the effects of parasitics.

References

1. Liao, T., Analog Integrated Circuit Sizing and Layout Dependent Effects: A Review. *Microelectron. Solid State Electron.*, 2014.

2. Scott, G., Lutze, J., Rubin, M., Nouri, F., Manley, M., NMOS drive current reduction caused by transistor layout and trench isolation induced stress, in: *International Electron Devices Meeting 1999. Technical Digest (Cat. No.99CH36318)*, pp. 827–830, 1999, doi: 10.1109/IEDM.1999.824277. keywords: MOS de[2] vices; Stress; Degradation; Testing; Foundries; Isolation technology; MOSFETs; Photonic band gap.
3. Bianchi, R.A., Bouche, G., Roux-dit-Buisson, O., Accurate modeling of trench isolation induced mechanical stress effects on MOSFET electrical performance. *Digest. Int. Electron Devices Meeting San Francisco CA USA*, 117–120, 2002, doi: 10.1109/IEDM.2002.1175792. keywords: MOSFET circuits; Semiconductor device modeling; Shape; Compressive stress; Geometry; MOS devices; Testing; CMOS technology; Thermal stresses; Research and development.
4. Liao, T. and Zhang, L., An LDE-Aware gm/ID-Based Hybrid Sizing Method for Analog Integrated Circuits. in. *IEEE Trans. Comput. Aided Des. Integr. Circuits Syst.*, 40, 8, 1511–1524, Aug. 2021, doi: 10.1109/TCAD.2020.3025068. keywords: Optimization; MOSFET; Layout; Mathematical model; Analog circuits; Integrated circuit modeling; Evolutionary computation; Analog IC; circuit sizing; device and circuit modeling; floorplan optimization; g/ID;layout-dependent effects (LDEs); many-objective evolutionary algorithm (many-OEA).
5. Karmokar, N., Madhusudan, M., Sharma, A.K., Harjani, R., Lin, M.P.H., Sapatnekar, S.S., Common-Centroid Layout for Active and Passive Devices: A Review and the Road Ahead. *2022 27th Asia and South Pacific Design Automation Conference (ASP-DAC)*, Taipei, Taiwan, pp. 114–121, 2022, 6. keywords: Performance evaluation; Systematics; Design automation; Roads; Layout; Asia; Routing, doi: 10.1109/ASP-DAC524010.2022.971257.
6. Thasreefa, A.K., Patyal, A., H. -Y. Chi, M.P., Lin, H., Chen, XXXH. M., On Reducing LDE Variations in Modern Analog Placement. in. *IEEE Trans. Comput. Aided Des. Integr. Circuits Syst.*, 42, 4, 1268–1279, April 2023, doi: 10.1109/TCAD.2022.3199307. keywords: Lay-out; Stress; Optimization; Minimization; Simulated annealing; Random access memory; Linear programming; Analog layout; analog placement; hierarchical B*-tree (HB*-tree); layout-dependent effect (LDE); length of oxide diffusion (LOD); oxide-to-oxide spacing effect (OSE); well proximity effect (WPE).
7. Sheu, Y., Modeling well edge proximity effect on highly-scaled MOS- FETs. *Proceedings of the IEEE 2005 Custom Integrated Circuits Conference, 2005*, San Jose, CA, pp. 831–834, 2005, . keywords: Proximity effect; MOSFETs; Semiconductor device modeling; CMOS technology; Circuit simulation; Scattering; CMOS process; Physics; Visualization; SPICE, doi: 10.1109/CICC.2005.1568798.
8. Dong, X. and Zhang, L., EA-Based LDE-Aware Fast Analog Layout Retargeting with Device Abstraction. *IEEE Trans. Very Large Scale Integr. VLSI Syst.*, 27, 4, 854–863, April 2019, doi: 10.1109/TVLSI.2018.2883710.

keywords: Layout; Circuit optimization; Transistors; Analog circuits; Performance evaluation; Integrated circuit modeling; Analog layout retargeting; device abstraction; evolutionary algorithm (EA); layout-dependent effects (LDE).

9. Tolić, I.P., Mikulić, J., Schatzberger, G., Barić, X.X.X.A., Design of Sense Amplifiers for Non-Volatile Memory. *2019 42nd International Convention on Information and Communication Technology, Electronics and Microelectronics (MIPRO)*, Opatija, Croatia, pp. 59–64, 2019, keywords: Computer architecture; Transistors; Sensors; Microprocessors; Switches; Voltage control; Timing; non-volatile memory; sense amplifiers; integrated circuit design; layout design; chip measurements; 180 nm CMOS technology, doi: 10.23919/MIPRO.2019.8757026.
10. Martins, R.L., Nuno, H., Nuno, LAYGEN II: Automatic analog ICs layout generator based on a template approach. *GECCO'12 - Proceedings of the 14th International Conference on Genetic and Evolutionary Computation*, 2012, 10.1145/23301610.2330319.
11. Hastings, A., *The Art of Analog Layout*, Prentice-Hall, 2001.
12. Razavi, B., *Design of Analog CMOS Integrated Circuits*, 2001.
13. Lin, M.P.-H., He, Y.-T., Hsiao, V.W.-H., Chang, R.-G., Lee, XXXS.-Y., Common-Centroid Capacitor Layout Generation Considering Device Matching and Parasitic Minimization. *IEEE Transactions on Computer-Aided Design of Integrated Circuits and Systems*, vol. 32, pp. 991–1002, July 2013, keywords: Ca[13] pacitors; Routing; Arrays; Layout; Wires; Systematics; Minimization; Analog layout; capacitor matching; common-centroid constraint; parasitic minimization; placement; routing, doi: 10.1109/TCAD.2012.2226457.
14. Golla, C. and Ghezzi, S., Flash memory architecture. *Microelectron. Reliab.*, 38, 2, 179–184, 1998. ISSN 0026-2714.
15. Martin, A., Berger, J., Kamp, A., Nielen, H., Plasma induced charging damage (PID) from well charging in a BCD technology with deep trenches causing MOS device reliability lifetime degradation. *2022 IEEE International Integrated Reliability Workshop (IIRW)*, South Lake Tahoe, CA, USA, 20221-7, doi: 10.1109/IIRW56459.2022.10032749. keywords: Degradation; Negative bias temperature instability; MOSFET; Thermal variables control; Logic gates; Plasmas; Leakage currents; plasma damage; PID; MOS; transistor; reliability; gate oxide; lifetimes; well charging; deep trench; antenna; AR;NBTI; charge trapping; hot carrier; DNW; triple well.
16. Sharma, A.K., Common-Centroid Layouts for Analog Circuits: Advantages and Limitations. *2021 Design, Automation Test in Europe Conference Exhibition (DATE), Grenoble*, France, pp. 1224–1229, 2021, doi: 10.23919/DATE51398.2021.9474244. key[16] words: Performance evaluation; Systematics; Layout; Routing; Complexity theory.
17. Faricelli, J.V., Layout-dependent proximity effects in deep nanoscale CMOS. *IEEE Custom Integrated Circuits Conference 2010*, San Jose, CA, USA, pp. 1–8,

2010, doi: 10.1109/CICC.2010.5617407. keywords: Stress; MOS devices; Layout; Logic gates; Integrated circuit modeling; Silicon; Performance evaluation.

18. Niranjana, M., II, Dhanasekar, J., Blesson, N., Immansingh, G.D., Boopathi, M., Raman, S.M., A Framework for Block-Level Physical Design using ICC2 in 14nm Technology. *2023 7th International Conference on Electronics, Communication and Aerospace Technology (ICECA)*, Coimbatore, India, pp. 413–417, 2023, doi: 10.1109/ICECA58529.20210.10394906. keywords: Layout; Metals; Routing; Planning; Transistors; Physical design; Clocks; Physical Design[18] - VLSI; Floorplan; Power Planning; Placement; Routing; Static Timing Analysis (STA); Physical Verification (DRC;LVS).
19. Rana, V. and Raj Ganesh, R., Non-Volatile memory with reduced sub-threshold leakage during read and erase operation. *Int. Symp. Circuits Syst.*, pp. 601–604, 2015.
20. Sheu, Y.-M., Modeling the Well-Edge Proximity Effect in Highly Scaled MOS- FETs. *IEEE Trans. Electron Devices*, 53, 11, 2792–2798, Nov. 2006. doi: 10.1109/TED.2006.884070. keywords: CMOS wells; high-energy ion implantation; ion scattering; MOSFETs; SPICE model; technology computer-aided design (TCAD) simulation.
21. Su, K.-W., A scaleable model for STI mechanical stress effect on layout dependence of MOS electrical characteristics. *Proceedings of the IEEE 2003 Custom Integrated Circuits Conference*, San Jose, CA, USA, 20032003245-248, doi: 10.1109/CICC.20010.1249396. keywords: Stress; Electric variables; Semiconductor device modeling; CMOS technology; MOS devices; Threshold voltage; Circuit simulation; Circuit synthesis; Semiconductor process modeling; Analytical models.
22. Bhardwaj, A., Kumar, P., Raj, B., Sunny Anand, Design and Performance Optimization of doping-less Vertical Nanowire TFET using Gate Stack Technique. *J. Electron. Mater. (JEMS)*, Springer, 41, 7, 4005–4013, 2022.
23. Singh, J. and Raj, B., Tunnel Current Model of Asymmetric MIM Structure Levying Various Image Forces to Analyze the Characteristics of Filamentary Memristor. *Appl. Phys. A*, Springer, 125, 3, 203.1– 203.11, Feb 2019.
24. Goyal, C., Ubhi, J.S., Raj, B., Low Leakage Zero Ground Noise Nanoscale Full Adder using Source Biasing Technique. *J. Nanoelectron. Optoelectron.*, American Scientific Publishers, 14, 360–370, March 2019.
25. Singh, G., Sarin, R.K., Raj, B., A Novel Robust Exclusive-OR Function Implementation in QCA Nanotechnology with Energy Dissipation Analysis. *J. Comput. Electron.*, Springer, 15, 2, 455–465, June 2016.
26. Wadhwa, G., Kamboj, P., Raj, B., Design optimisation of junctionless TFET biosensor for high sensitivity. *Adv. Nat. Sci.: Nanosci. Nanotechnol.*, 10, 7, 045001, 2019.
27. Bansal, P. and Raj, B., Memristor Modeling and Analysis for Linear Dopant Drift Kinetics. *J. Nanoeng. Nanomanuf.*, American Scientific Publishers, 6, 1–7, 2016.

28. Ashima, Vaithiyanathan, D., Raj, B., Performance Analysis of Charge Plasma induced Graded Channel Si nanotube. *J. Eng. Res. (JER)*, EMSME Special Issue, 146–154, Aug 2021.
29. Tomar, A.S., Magraiya, V.K., Raj, B., Scaling of Access and Data Transistor for High Performance DRAM Cell Design. *Quantum Matter*, 2, 412–416, Oct. 2013.
30. Jain, N. and Raj, B., Parasitic Capacitance and Resistance Model Development and Optimization of Raised Source/Drain SOI FinFET Structure for Analog Circuit Applications. *J. Nanoelectron. Optoelectron.*, ASP, USA, 13, 531–539, April 2018.
31. SinghVishvakarma, S.S.K. and Raj, B., Analytical Modeling of Split-Gate Junction-Less Transistor for a Biosensor Application. *Sens. Bio-sensing*, Elsevier, 18, 31–36, April 2018.
32. Gopal, M. and Raj, B., Low Power 8T SRAM Cell Design for High Stability Video Applications. *ITSI Transact. Electr. Electron. Eng.*, 1, 5, 91–97, 2013.
33. Raj, B., Mitra, J., Bihani, D.K., Rangharajan, V., Saxena, A.K., Dasgupta, S., Analysis of Noise Margin, Power and Process Variation for 32 nm FinFET Based 6T SRAM Cell. *J. Comput. (JCP)*, Academy Publisher, Finland, 5, 6, 1–8, 2010.
34. Sharma, D., Mehra, R., Raj, B., Comparative Analysis of Photovoltaic Technologies for High Efficiency Solar Cell Design. *Superlattices Microstruct.*, Elsevier, 153, 106861, May 2021.
35. Kaur, P., Buttar, A.S., Raj, B., A comprehensive Analysis of Nanoscale Transistor based Biosensor: A Review. *Indian J. Pure Appl. Phys.*, 59, 304–318, April 2021.
36. Yadav, D., Raj, B., Raj, B., Design and Simulation of Low Power Microcontroller for IoT Applications. *J. Sens. Lett.*, ASP, 18, 401–409, May 2020.
37. Singh, S. and Raj, B., A 2-D Analytical Surface Potential and Drain current Modeling of Double-Gate Vertical t-shaped Tunnel FET. *J. Comput. Electron.*, Springer, 19, 1154–1163, April 2020.
38. Singh, J. and Raj, B., An Accurate and Generic Window function for Non-linear Memristor Model. *J. Comput. Electron.*, Springer, 18, 2, 640–647, June 2019.
39. Kaur, M., Gupta, N., Kumar, S., Raj, B., Singh, A.K., Comparative RF and Crosstalk Analysis of Carbon Based Nano Interconnects. *IET Circuits Devices Syst.*, 15, 6, 493–503, Feb 2021.
40. Kandasamy, N., Ahmad, F., Ajitha, D., Raj, B., Telagam, N., Quantum Dot Cellular Automata based Scan Flip Flop and Boundary Scan Register. *IETE J. Res.*, 66, 535–548, 2020.
41. Singh, J. and Raj, B., Design and Investigation of 7T2M NVSARM with Enhanced Stability and Temperature Impact on Store/Restore Energy. *IEEE Trans. Very Large Scale Integr. Syst.*, 27, 6, 1322–1328, June 2019.
42. Bhardwaj, A.K., Gupta, S., Raj, B., Singh, A., Impact of Double Gate Geometry on the Performance of Carbon Nanotube Field Effect Transistor Structures

for Low Power Digital Design. *Comput. Theor. Nanosci.*, ASP, 16, 1813–1820, 2019.
43. Jain, N. and Raj, B., Thermal Stability Analysis and Performance Exploration of Asymmetrical Dual-k underlap Spacer (ADKUS) SOI FinFET for Security and Privacy Applications. *Indian J. Pure Appl. Phys. (IJPAP)*, 57, 352–360, May 2019.
44. Jain, N. and Raj, B., Dual-k Spacer Region Variation at the Drain Side of Asymmetric SOI FinFET Structure: Performance Analysis towards the Analog/RF Design Applications. *J. Nanoelectron. Optoelectron.*, American Scientific Publishers, Vol. 14, 349–359, March 2019.
45. Singh, J., Sharma, S., Raj, B., Khosla, M., Analysis of barrier layer thickness on performance of In1-xGaxAs based Gate Stack Cylindrical Gate Nanowire MOSFET. *JNO*, ASP, 13, 1473–1477, Oct 2018.
46. Jain, N. and Raj, B., Analysis and Performance Exploration of High-k SOI FinFETs Over the Conventional Low-k SOI FinFET toward Analog/RF Design. *J. Semicond. (JoS)*, IOP Science, 39, 12, 124002–1-7, Dec 2018.
47. Goyal, C., Ubhi, J.S., Raj, B., A reliable leakage reduction technique for approximate full adder with reduced ground bounce noise. *J. Math. Probl. Eng., Hindawi, 2018*, Article ID 3501041, 16, 15 Oct 2018.
48. Anuradha, Singh, J., Raj, B., Khosla, M., Design and Performance Analysis of Nano-scale Memristor-based Nonvolatile SRAM. *J. Sens. Letter*, American Scientific Publishers, 16, 798–805, Oct 2018.
49. Raj, B., Parametric Variation Analysis of Charge-Plasma-based Dielectric Modulated JLTFET for Biosensor Application. *IEEE Sens. J.*, 18, 15, 6070–6077 (SCI), August 1, 2018.
50. Singh, J. and Raj, B., Comparative Analysis of Memristor Models for Memories Design. *JoS*, IoP, 39, 7, 074006–1-12, July 2018.
51. Yadav, D., Chouhan, S.S., Vishvakarma, S.K., Raj, B., Application Specific Microcontroller Design for IoT based WSN. *Sens. Letter*, ASP, 16, 374–385, May 2018.
52. Singh, G., Sarin, R.K., Raj, B., Fault-Tolerant Design and Analysis of Quantum-Dot Cellular Automata Based Circuits. *IEEE/IET Circuits Devices Syst.*, 12, 638–64, 2018.
53. Singh, J. and Raj, B., Modeling of Mean Barrier Height Levying Various Image Forces of Metal Insulator Metal Structure to Enhance the Performance of Conductive Filament Based Memristor Model. *IEEE Nanotechnol.*, 17, 2, 268–267, March 2018.
54. Jain, A., Sharma, S., Raj, B., Analysis of Triple Metal Surrounding Gate (TM-SG) III-V Nanowire MOSFET for Photosensing Application. *Opto-electronics J.*, Elsevier, 26, 2, 141–148, May 2018.
55. Jain, A., Sharma, S., Raj, B., Design and Analysis of High Sensitivity Photosensor Using Cylindrical Surrounding Gate MOSFET for Low Power Sensor Applications. *Eng. Sci. Technol. Int. J.*, Elsevier's, 19, 4, 1864–1870, December 2016.

56. Kumar, G.S., Singh, A., Raj, B., Design and Analysis of Gate All Around CNTFET based SRAM cell Design. *J. Comput. Electron.*, Springer, 17, 1, 138–145, March 2018.
57. Singh, G.P., Sohi, B.S., Raj, B., Material Properties Analysis of Graphene Base Transistor (GBT) for VLSI Analog Circuits. *Indian J. Pure Appl. Phys. (IJPAP)*, 55, 896–902, Dec 2017.
58. Kumar, S. and Raj, B., Estimation of Stability and Performance metric for Inward Access Transistor based 6T SRAM Cell Design using n-type/p-type DMDG-GDOV TFET. *IEEE VLSI Circuits Syst. Letter*, 3, 2, 25–39, June 2017.
59. Sharma, S., Kumar, A., Pattanaik, M., Raj, B., Forward Body Biased Multimode Multi-Threshold CMOS Technique for Ground Bounce Noise Reduction in Static CMOS Adders. *Int. J. Inf. Electron. Eng.*, 3, 3, 567–572, 2013.
60. Singh, H., Kumar, P., Raj, B., Performance Analysis of Majority Gate SET Based 1-bit Full Adder. *Int. J. Comput. Commun. Eng. (IJCCE)*, IACSIT Press Singapore, ISSN: 2010-3743, 2, 4, 2013.
61. Bhardwaj, A.K., Gupta, S., Raj, B., Investigation of Parameters for Schottky Barrier (SB) Height for Schottky Barrier Based Carbon Nanotube Field Effect Transistor Device. *J. Nanoelectron. Optoelectron.*, ASP, 15, 783–791, July 2020.
62. Bansal, P. and Raj, B., Memristor: A Versatile Nonlinear Model for Dopant Drift and Boundary Issues. *JCTN*, American Scientific Publishers, 14, 5, 2319–2325, May 2017.
63. Jain, N. and Raj, B., An Analog and Digital Design Perspective Comprehensive Approach on Fin-FET (Fin-Field Effect transistor) Technology - A Review. *Rev. Adv. Sci. Eng. (RASE)*, ASP, 5, 1–14, 2016.
64. Raj, B., Saxena, A.K., Dasgupta, S., Analytical Modeling for the Estimation of Leakage Current and Subthreshold Swing Factor of Nanoscale Double Gate FinFET Device. *Microelectron. Int.*, UK, 26, 53–63, 2009.
65. Soniya, S.S., Wadhwa, G., Raj, B., An Analytical Modeling for Dual Source Vertical Tunnel Field Effect Transistor. *Int. J. Recent Technol. Eng. (IJRTE)*, 8, 2, 603–608, July 2019.
66. Singh, S. and Raj, B., Design and analysis of hetrojunction Vertical T-shaped Tunnel Field Effect Transistor. *J. Electron. Mater.*, Springer, 48, 10, 6253–6260, October 2019.
67. Goyal, C., Ubhi, J.S., Raj, B., A Low Leakage CNTFET based Inexact Full Adder for Low Power Image Processing Applications. *Int. J. Circuit Theory Appl.*, Wiley, 47, 9, 1446–1458, September 2019.
68. Raj, B., Saxena, A.K., Dasgupta, S., A Compact Drain Current and Threshold Voltage Quantum Mechanical Analytical Modeling for FinFETs. *J. Nanoelectron. Optoelectron. (JNO)*, USA, 3, 2, 163–170, 2008.
69. Wadhwa, G. and Raj, B., An Analytical Modeling of Charge Plasma based Tunnel Field Effect Transistor with Impacts of Gate underlap Region. *Superlattices Microstruct.*, Elsevier, 142, 106512, June 2020.

70. Singh, S. and Raj, B., Modeling and Simulation analysis of SiGe hetrojunction Double GateVertical t-shaped Tunnel FET. *Superlattices Microstruct.*, Elsevier 142, 106496, June 2020.
71. Jain, N. and Raj, B., Device and Circuit Co-Design Perspective Comprehensive Approach on FinFET Technology - A Review. *J. Electron Devices*, 23, 1, 1890–1901, 2016.
72. Kumar, S. and Raj, B., Analysis of I_{ON} and Ambipolar Current for Dual-Material Gate-drain Overlapped DG-TFET. *J. Nanoelectron. Optoelectron.*, American Scientific Publishers, USA, 11, 323–333, June 2016.
73. Anjum, N., Bali, T., Raj, B., Design and Simulation of Handwritten Multiscript Character Recognition. *Int. J. Adv. Res. Comput. Commun. Eng.*, 2, 7, 2544–2549, July 2013.
74. Singh, K. and Raj, B., Performance and analysis of temperature dependent Multi-walled Carbon Nanotubes as Global Interconnects at different technology nodes. *J. Comput. Electron.*, Springer, 14, 2, 469–476, June 2015.
75. Kumar, S. and Raj, B., Compact channel potential analytical Modeling of DG-TFET based on Evanescent–mode Approach. *J. Comput. Electron.*, Springer, 14, 2, 820–827, July 2015.
76. Singh, K. and Raj, B., Temperature Dependent Modeling and Performance Evaluation of Multi-Walled CNT and Single-Walled CNT as Global Interconnects. *J. Electron. Mater.*, Springer, 44, 12, 4825–4835, Dec 2015.
77. Sharma, V.K., Pattanaik, M., Raj, B., INDEP approach for leakage reduction in nanoscale CMOS circuits. *Int. J. Electron.*, Taylor & Francis, 102, 2, 200–215, 2014.
78. Singh, K. and Raj, B., Influence of Temperature on MWCNT bundle, SWCNT bundle and Copper interconnects for Nanoscaled Technology nodes. *J. Mater. Sci.: Mater. Electron.*, Springer, 26, 8, 6134–6142, 2015.
79. Anjum, N., Bali, T., Raj, B., Design and Simulation of Handwritten Gurumukhi and Devanagri Numerical Recognition. *Int. J. Comput. Appl.*, Foundation of Computer Science, New York, USA, 73, 12, 16–21, 2013.
80. Khandelwal, S., Gupta, V., Raj, B., Gupta, R.D., Process Variability Aware Low Leakage Reliable Nano Scale DG-FinFET SRAM Cell Design Technique. *J. Nanoelectron. Optoelectron.*, 10, 6, 810–817, December 2015.
81. Sharma, V.K., Pattanaik, M., Raj, B., ONOFIC Approach: Low Power High Speed Nanoscale VLSI Circuits Design. *Int. J. Electron.*, Taylor & Francis, 101, 1, 61–73, 2014.
82. Khandelwal, S., Raj, B., Gupta, R.D., FinFET based 6T SRAM Cell Design: Analysis of Performance Metric, Process Variation and Temperature Effect. *J. Comput. Theor. Nanosci.*, ASP, USA, 12, 2500–2506, 2015.
83. Singh, S., Yadav, S., Rahul, J., Srivastava, A., Raj, B., Impact of HfO_2 in Graded Channel Dual Insulator Double Gate MOSFET. *J. Comput. Theor. Nanosci.*, American Scientific Publishers, 12, 6, 950–953, April 2015.

84. Sharma, V.K., Pattanaik, M., Raj, B., PVT variations aware low leakage INDEP approach for nanoscale CMOS Circuits. *Microelectron. Reliab.*, Elsevier, 54, 90–99, 2014.
85. Raj, B., Saxena, A.K., Dasgupta, S., Quantum Mechanical Analytical Modeling of Nanoscale DG FinFET: Evaluation of Potential, Threshold Voltage and Source/Drain Resistance. *Elsevier's J. Mater. Sci. Semicond. Process.*, Elsevier, 16, 4, 1131–1137, 2013.
86. Kaur, P., Pandey, V., Raj, B., Comparative Study of Efficient Design, Control and Monitoring of Solar Power using IoT. *Sens. Letter*, ASP 18, 419–426, May 2020.
87. Bhardwaj, A.K., Gupta, S., Raj, B., Development & Analysis of compact model for Double Gate Schottky Barrier CNTFET. *J. Nanoelectron. Optoelectron.*, ASP, 15, 1199–1208, Aug 2020.
88. Wadhwa, G., Kamboj, P., Singh, J., Raj, B., Design and Investigation of Junctionless DGTFET for Biological Molecule Recognition. *Trans. Electr. Electron. Mater.*, Springer, 22, 282–289, 2021.
89. Verma, S.K., Singh, S., Wadhwa, G., Raj, B., Detection of Biomolecules using Charge-Plasma based Gate Underlap Dielectric Modulated Dopingless TFET. *Trans. Electr. Electron. Mater. (TEEM)*, Springer, 21, 528–535, June 2020.
90. Jain, N. and Raj, B., Impact of underlap spacer region variation on Electrostatic and analog/RF performance of symmetrical high-k SOI FinFET at 20 nm channel length. *J. Semicond. (JoS)*, IOP Science, 38, 12, 122002, Dec 2017.
91. Singh, S. and Raj, B., Analytical Modeling and Simulation analysis of T-shaped III-V heterojunction Vertical T-FET. *Superlattices Microstruct.*, Elsevier, 147, 106717, Nov 2020.
92. Singh, G., Sarin, R.K., Raj, B., Design and Analysis of Area Efficient QCA Based Reversible Logic Gates. *J. Microprocess. Microsys.*, Elsevier, 52, 59–68, May 2017.
93. Singh, S. and Raj, B., Parametric variation analysis on hetero-junction Vertical t-shape TFET for Suppressing ambipolar conduction. *Indian J. Pure Appl. Phys.*, 58, 478–485, June 2020.
94. Soniya, Singh, S., Wadhwa, G., Raj, B., Design and Analysis of Dual Source Vertical Tunnel Field Effect Transistor for high performance. *Trans. Electr. Electron. Mater.*, Springer, 21, 74–82, Oct 2019.
95. Kaur, M., Gupta, N., Kumar, S., Raj, B., Singh, A.K., RF Performance Analysis of Intercalated Graphene Nanoribbon Based Global Level Interconnects. *J. Comput. Electron.*, Springer, 19, 1002–1013, June 2020.
96. Wadhwa, G. and Raj, B., Design and Performance Analysis of Junctionless TFET Biosensor for high sensitivity. *IEEE Nanotechnol.*, 18, 567–574, 2019.
97. Singh, J. and Raj, B., Enhanced Nonlinear Memristor Model Encapsulating Stochastic Dopant Drift. *JNO*, ASP 14, 958–963, 2019.

98. Singh, M., Chaudhary, T., Raj, B., Enhancing FeFET Structures for Non-volatile On-chip Memories: Design and Comparative Analysis. *Int. J. Numer. Modell. Electron. Networks Devices Fields*, 38, 1–9, 2024.
99. Singh, M., Chaudhary, T., Raj, B., Drain Current and Transconductance Analysis of GaN GAA Nanowire FET with High K Dielectric. *ECS J. Sci. Technol.*, 12, 6070–6077, 2023.
100. Singh, M., Chaudhary, T., Raj, B., Design of Si and Ge Nanowire FET for Low Power Application. *J. Silicon*, Springer, 15, 1491–1497, 2023.
101. Singh, M., Chaudhary, T., Raj, B., Electrical Characteristics Analysis of FeFET for Low Power Applications. *J. Nano*, 37, 1–8, 2024.
102. Kumar, M., Chaudhary, T., Raj, B., Design and Comparative Analysis of Ferroelectric Nanowire with Dielectric HfO_2 and $Al_2O_3$for Low Power Applications. *J. Electron. Mater.*, Springer, 53, 6785–6791, 2024.
103. Gopal, M., Sankar, S., Prasad, D., Raj, B., 8T SRAM Cell Design for Dynamic and Leakage Power Reduction. *Int. J. Comput. Appl.*, Foundation of Computer Science, New York, USA, 71, 9, 43–48, June 2013.
104. Pattanaik, M., Raj, B., Sharma, S., Kumar, A., Diode Based Trimode Multi-Threshold CMOS Technique for Ground Bounce Noise Reduction in Static CMOS Adders. *Adv. Mater. Res.*, Trans Tech Publications, Switzerland, 548, 885–889, 2012.
105. Balwinder Raj, A.K. and Dasgupta, S., Nanoscale FinFET Based SRAM Cell Design: Analysis of Performance metric, Process variation, Underlapped FinFET and Temperature effect. *IEEE Circuits Syst. Mag.*, 11, 2, 38–50, 2011.
106. Sharma, V.K., Pattanaik, M., Raj, B., Leakage Current ONOFIC Approach for Deep Submicron VLSI Circuit Design. *Int. J. Electrical Computer Electron. Commun. Eng.*, World Academy of Sciences, Engineering and Technology, 7, 4, 239–244, 2013.
107. Kaur, P., Gill, S.S., Raj, B., Comparative Analysis of OFETs Materials and Devices for Sensor Applications. *J. Silicon*, Springer, 14, 4463–4471, 2022.
108. Sharma, S.K., Kumar, P., Raj, B., Raj, B., $In_{1-x}Ga_xAs$ Double Metal Gate-Stacking Cylindrical Nanowire MOSFET for highly sensitive Photo detector. *J. Silicon*, Springer 14, 3535–3541, 2022.
109. Raj, B., Saxena, A.K., Dasgupta, S., Analytical Modeling of Quasi Planar Nanoscale Double Gate FinFET with Source/Drain Resistance and field dependent carrier mobility: A quantum mechanical study. *J. Comput. (JCP)*, Academy Publisher, Finland, 4, 9, 1–8, 2009.
110. Bhushan, S., Khandelwal, S., Raj, B., Analyzing Different Mode FinFET based Memory Cell at Different Power Supply for Leakage Reduction. *Seventh Int. Conf. Bio-Inspired Computing Theor. Application (BIC-TA 2012) Adv. Intell. Syst. Comput.*, 202, 89–100 (2013), 2012.
111. Singh, J. and Raj, B., Temperature Dependent Analytical Modeling and Simulations of Nanoscale Memristor. *Eng. Sci. Technol. Int. J.*, Elsevier's, 21, 862–868, Oct 2018.

112. Singh, S., Bala, S., Raj, B., Raj, B., Improved Sensitivity of Dielectric Modulated Junctionless Transistor for Nanoscale Biosensor Design. *Sensor Letter*, ASP, 18, 328-333, April 2020.
113. Kumar, V., Vishvakarma, S.K., Raj, B., Design and Performance Analysis of ASIC for IoT Applications. *Sens. Letter*, ASP, 18, 31–38, Jan 2020.
114. JaiswalSarin, A.R.K. and RajSukhija, B.S., A Novel Circular Slotted Microstrip-fed Patch Antenna with Three Triangle Shape Defected Ground Structure for Multiband Applications. *Adv. Electromagn. (AEM)*, 7, 3, 56–63, Aug 2018.
115. Wadhwa, G. and Raj, B., Label Free Detection of Biomolecules using Charge-Plasma-Based Gate Underlap Dielectric Modulated Junctionless TFET. *J. Electron. Mater. (JEMS)*, Springer, 47, 8, 4683–4693, August 2018.
116. SinghSarin, G.R.K. and Raj, B., Design and Performance Analysis of a New Efficient Coplanar Quantum-Dot Cellular Automata Adder. *Indian J. Pure Appl. Phys. (IJPAP)*, 55, 97–103, February 2017.

11

Study of FIR Filter Hardware Architecture for Real-Time Multimedia Applications

Anuraj V.* and Dhandapani Vaithiyanathan

Department of Electronics and Communication Engineering, National Institute of Technology Delhi, Delhi, India

Abstract

Digital signal processing is everywhere in the world of communication. COVID-19 hit the world in a storm, so our technology helps us communicate and reduces the distance between us and the world. We are trying to improvise communication with signal processing. Digital signal processing is a ubiquitous module used in a communication system. In today's digital era, digital processing is a necessary part. The performance of digital signal processing Integrated Circuits (ICs) are driving the world now. All signals present in the universe are in analog format. The complexity of processing the analog signal is challenging, so we change the analog signal into digital format as ones and zeros and do all the processing. The analysis and study of FIR (Finite Impulse Response) filtering play a crucial role in the development of efficient DSP (Digital Signal Processing) processors, as it directly impacts their performance and optimization. A well-designed and thoroughly documented manuscript on FIR filters, covering both theoretical and practical aspects, is readily available. This chapter provides an in-depth explanation of FIR filters, detailing the design methodologies and offering a comprehensive comparison of various hardware architectures. This chapter also examines and reports on various multiplier and adder circuits that enhance the performance of an MAC-based FIR filter. Such comparisons highlight the trade-offs between performance, resource utilization, and efficiency in different FIR filter implementations, making it an essential resource for understanding and improving DSP systems. ADSP-21062 (Analog Devices), TMS320C6000 (Texas Instruments), XC2000/XE166 (Infineon), etc., are some of the available DSP ICs in the market. Xilinx and Altera (now part of Intel) give the FPGA DSP IC.

**Corresponding author*: anuraj@nitdelhi.ac.in
Dhandapani Vaithiyanathan: ORCID: 0000–0001–5235–2620

Ashish Maurya, Mandeep Singh and Balwinder Raj (eds.) Machine Learning in Nanoelectronics: Devices, Circuits and Systems, (343–362) © 2026 Scrivener Publishing LLC

Keywords: FIR, DSP, MAC, FPGA, signal processing

11.1 Introduction

Digital processing is a necessary part of today's digital era. The performance of digital signal processing integrated circuits (DSP ICs) is driving the world now. All signals in the universe exist in analog format, but processing analog signals is highly complex. To simplify this, we convert the analog signals into digital format—represented as ones and zeros—and perform all the necessary processing digitally. Some of the DSP ICs available in the market include ADSP-21062 from Analog Devices, TMS320C6000 from Texas Instruments, and XC2000/XE166 from Infineon. Additionally, companies like Xilinx and Altera (now part of Intel) offer Field-Programmable Gate Array (FPGA) DSP ICs, which are widely used for digital signal processing applications. Filters, particularly Finite Impulse Response (FIR) filters, are essential components in real-time digital signal processing (DSP) systems, designed using multipliers and adders to determine the output. As the filter order increases, constructing higher-order filters becomes increasingly complex due to the linear rise in the number of multiple and accumulated operations required per filter. Applications that require high throughput and energy-efficient designs face difficulties because of this complexity. FIR filters are frequently used in feed-forward control systems to provide inverse response filtering, which enhances performance and control. Various design techniques, such as pipelining and parallel processing, have gained traction to address the need for enhanced computing speed. These techniques leverage the inherent parallelism in computing algorithms, allowing for significant improvements in both data processing rates and overall computing time. By utilizing such strategies, engineers can optimize the performance of FIR filters, achieving the necessary efficiency and speed for demanding real-time applications, ultimately leading to more effective signal-processing solutions in various industries [1].

DSP processors are used for a variety of communication applications, including software-defined radio, echo cancellation, adaptive noise cancellation, loudspeaker equalization, and speech processing. The hearing loss system model utilizes a variable bandwidth Finite Impulse Response (FIR) Filter (VBF) and adaptive algorithms to enhance listening experiences. The adjustable band filter is specifically designed to deliver optimal sound levels [2].

In this chapter, we will begin by exploring the advantages of digital filtering, laying the groundwork for a deeper understanding of its significance in signal processing. Following this introduction, we will then delve into the hardware architecture of FIR filters. We will examine the relationship between the direct form and transposed form of FIR filters, then provide a comprehensive study that includes the design of adder logic and multiplier techniques, then some words about the Multiplier-Accumulator (MAC) unit. Additionally, we will explore FIR filter designs that do not rely on traditional multipliers, showcasing alternative approaches. To illustrate the practical implications of these concepts, we will present simulation results that demonstrate the performance of the various implementations. The chapter will conclude with a summary of key findings and insights, reinforcing the importance of efficient FIR filter design in digital signal processing applications.

11.2 Digital Filtering Techniques

There are two important types of digital filters: FIR (Finite Impulse Response) and IIR (Infinite Impulse Response) filters. The IIR filter has a faster computational speed compared to the FIR filter, making it more efficient in terms of processing time. However, the phase or delay of an FIR filter remains constant, which is not the case for the IIR filter, where the phase can vary. One key advantage of the FIR filter is its inherent stability, meaning it does not oscillate or produce unintended behavior, while the IIR filter requires careful design to ensure stability. These distinctions make each filter suitable for different applications depending on the requirements for speed, stability, and phase characteristics.

The FIR (Finite Impulse Response) filter design process often involves the use of different spectral windows when transforming from the frequency domain to the time domain. Each window method has unique characteristics that affect the performance of the filter. For instance, the Chebyshev window is known for having the lowest amount of ripple in the stop band, which helps in attenuating unwanted frequencies, but it also results in the widest transition band, meaning it takes longer to move from passband to stopband. The Hamming window offers a narrower transition zone than the Chebyshev, with smaller ripple in the stop band compared to the Hanning window, making it a balanced option for various applications. The Kaiser window has the benefit of producing a small amplitude ripple in the stop zone, and while its transition width is wide, it has a lower amplitude ripple than the Chebyshev window, making it a popular choice in certain scenarios. The Hanning window, while providing the narrowest transition band, unfortunately suffers from a larger ripple in the stop band, which can impact its performance in rejecting unwanted frequencies. Lastly, the Rectangular window has the largest amount of ripple and lobes, which not only affects the stop band but also impacts the pass band, leading to less precise frequency response. Each of these window methods offers trade-offs between ripple, transition width, and overall performance, making the choice of window crucial in designing an effective FIR filter for specific digital signal processing tasks.

The various IIR filter methods each have distinct attributes that make them suitable for different signal processing applications. The Butterworth filter is known for its flat frequency response in both the pass band and stop band, which ensures minimal signal distortion. However, it has a relatively wide transition zone, meaning it takes longer for the filter to move from the pass band to the stop band, which can be a drawback in certain applications requiring sharp cutoffs. The Inverse Chebyshev filter provides a flat response in the pass band, similar to the Butterworth filter, but with a narrower transition width, making it more effective at separating signals. However, it introduces ripple in the stop band, which might not be an issue in applications where the stop band ripple can be tolerated. In such cases, the Inverse Chebyshev filter may be preferred over the Butterworth filter due to its steeper roll-off.

The Chebyshev filter, on the other hand, has a steeper roll-off than the Inverse Chebyshev, making it more efficient at filtering out unwanted frequencies. However, this comes at the cost of ripple in the pass band, which could cause some distortion in the desired signal. The Cauer filter, also known as the Elliptic filter, has the narrowest transition zone of all, providing the sharpest separation between the pass and stop bands. However, this design introduces ripple in both the pass and stop bands, which can be a limitation in precision-sensitive applications. Finally, the Bessel filter stands out for its sloping amplitude response in both the pass and stop bands, accompanied by a very wide transition zone. Its unique feature is its delay versus frequency response, which is the flattest among all the listed filters, making it ideal for applications where maintaining the phase integrity of the signal is critical, such as in audio processing or communications systems. Each of these IIR filter designs offers trade-offs between transition zone width, ripple, and overall performance, allowing engineers to choose the best-suited filter depending on the specific requirements of their digital signal processing task.

Depending on the application we select the suit for the filter method. This chapter discusses more about the FIR filter and its design using the MAC unit. Apart from analog filtering digital filters have some advantages. They are highly accurate and perform well. They are easy to design [3] and they are linear (preserve the signal integrity in the time domain). The dependency on component variation is less in the digital filters. They are more flexible than analog filters. In the real-world application we cannot design a system with a digital filter [4]. The presence of the analog filter is required for antialiasing. The lack of a high-speed Analog-to-Digital Converter (ADC) design negatively affects the performance of a digital filter.

11.3 Hardware Architecture

Block diagram Figure 11.1 shows the filtering process. The core component of a DSP's hardware architecture is the finite impulse response filter. In the digital hardware implementation using the logic gate, we create an adder circuit, and in the adder, we build a multiplier logic. Identifying the best-performing multiplier and adder, we create a MAC unit. Using that MAC unite we create an FIR filter [5]. Figure 11.2 shows the inside view of one of the FIR filter hardware architectures. That module filters the input signal or in other words, it processes the input digital data and gives the filtered output. The fundamental method by which digital filters manipulate frequency is through the introduction of time delay, which alters the phase relationship of the input signal components. By strategically applying this delay, filters can enhance or attenuate specific frequency ranges, allowing for precise control over the signal's frequency response.

$$y(n) = h(n) * x(n) = \sum_{i=0}^{N-1} h(i)x(n-i) \tag{11.1}$$

The mathematical expression of an FIR filter is in the Eq. 11.1. The convolution in the time domain is the same as the multiplication in the frequency domain. The transfer function in the frequency domain is translated to the time domain by the Fourier transform. This transformation produces an impulse response in the time domain. Convolution with the impulse response can filter the signal.

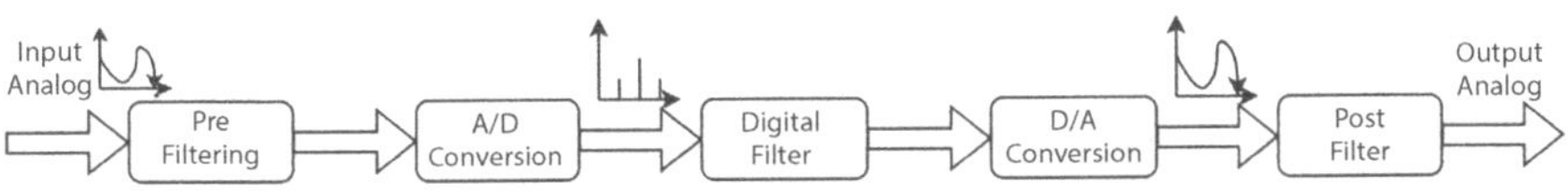

Figure 11.1 Flow chart for digital filtering process.

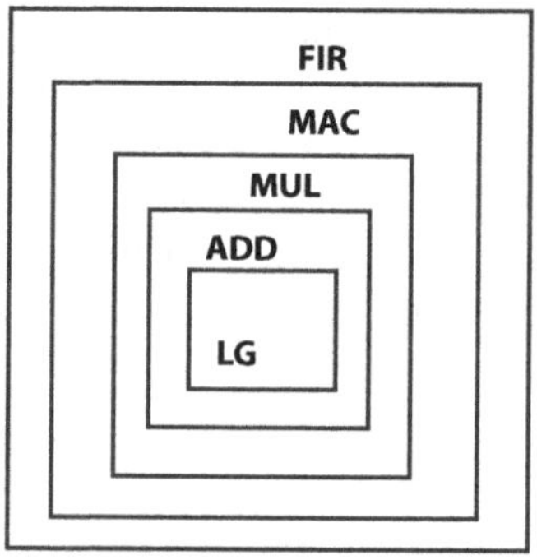

Figure 11.2 The functional blocks for building an FIR filter in digital design.

The FIR filter is exactly this process. A nonmathematical approach to designing an FIR filter would be to create the response in the frequency domain and then perform inverse Fast Fourier Transform (FFT). This converts the signal from the frequency domain to the time domain. The results would be an impulse response whose sample value can be mapped to a filter coefficient.

The hardware implementation of the direct form FIR filter [6] is in Figure 11.3. The block diagram shows the FIR filter contains a delay element, a Multiplier, and an adder. The input signal is multiplied by the coefficient and the product is added with the other delayed multiplied signal. In the direct form the FIR filter structures the number of delay elements that give the tap number. If the number of taps is increased it provides a smooth filtered output. Figure 11.3 has tap structures, but in the real-life scenario, we use 256, 1024, etc., more tap FIR filters. The averaging FIR

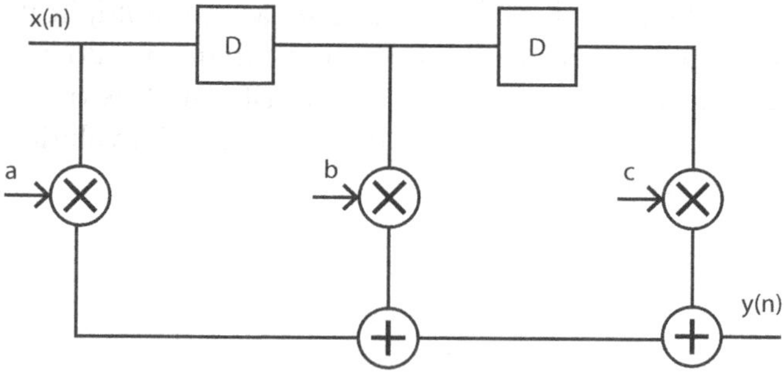

Figure 11.3 Direct form of an FIR filter implementation.

filter is one of the simplest and most straightforward designs in digital signal processing. In this architecture, the coefficient is the same. However, it does not provide a response of good magnitude. The coefficient selection is the main part of the FIR filter design. Today algorithms are available to choose the best coefficient for the application. Depending on the coefficient selection the FIR filter will act as the Low pass, High pass, Band pass, etc. The impulse signal is a test signal for the filter. The Impulse signal contains a sinusoid of all possible frequencies. All the filter's purely feedforward topology is always an FIR filter. Feedforward filter non-zero values of impulse response are identical to the filter coefficient. The impulse response is the time domain of the filter. The coefficient of each of the taps represents the filter's impulse response.

In this chapter on filter architecture design, we explore both direct form and pipelined implementations [7]. The direct form architecture of an FIR filter is depicted in Figure 11.3. If in a setup, multiplication operations apply the coefficients h(0)-h(5) to the signal from the delay elements. The products of these multiplications are then summed to produce the filter's output. A key component of this design is the MAC unit, which efficiently handles these operations. For example, in a direct form FIR filter, the sampling frequency is determined by Eq. 11.2, which reflects how the system processes and outputs filtered data according to the filter's tap count and operational frequency.

$$f_{Sampling-Dir} = \frac{1}{(T_{mul} + 2T_{add})} \tag{11.2}$$

Pipelining and retiming techniques are utilized to achieve optimal performance. By shortening the critical path, pipelining enhances speed and reduces power consumption through minimized delays. The pipelined design illustrated in Figure 11.4 is optimized for both speed and space efficiency. For a pipelined filter, the sampling rate, as indicated by Eq. 11.3, increases by approximately 75% when considering the delays of 2 units for multipliers and 1 unit for adders.

$$f_{Sampling-Pip} = \frac{1}{(T_{mul} + T_{add})} \tag{11.3}$$

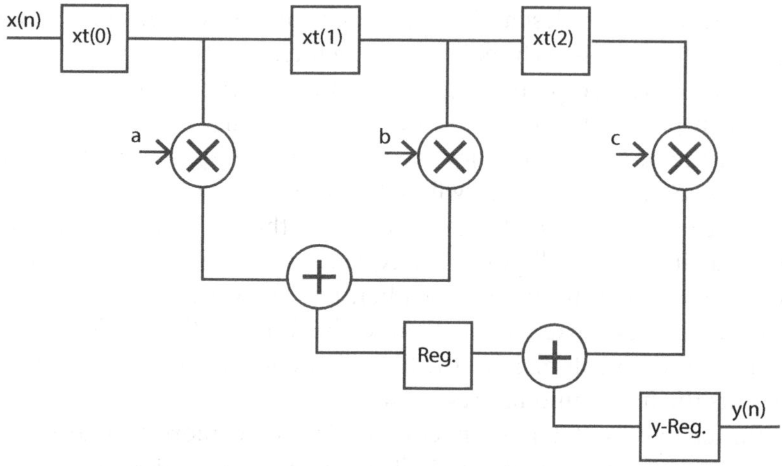

Figure 11.4 Design implementation of 3-tap FIR filter in pipelined architecture.

11.3.1 Direct Form and Transposed Form

The direct form and transposed form of a Finite Impulse Response (FIR) filter are two widely used implementations in digital signal processing, each designed to process input signals and generate filtered output in distinct ways. The direct form FIR filter employs a tapped delay line structure, consisting of multiple delay elements and multipliers, where each input sample is delayed and multiplied by the corresponding filter tap coefficients. This structure facilitates a clear visualization of how each component contributes to the overall output, often referred to as a transversal filter or tapped delay line. In this setup, the outputs of the multipliers are summed to produce the final filtered output. By contrast, the transposed form rearranges the processing elements, emphasizing the feedback nature of the filter's design. Both forms have their advantages and applications, making them fundamental in the development of efficient FIR filter implementations tailored for various signal processing tasks.

Looking into Figure 11.5 we can write the Eq. 11.4,

$$y_n = x_n + a_1 y_{n-1} + a_2 y_{n-2} \tag{11.4}$$

Rearrange the Eq. 11.4, we get Eq. 11.5,

$$y_n - a_1 y_{n-1} - a_2 y_{n-2} = x_n \tag{11.5}$$

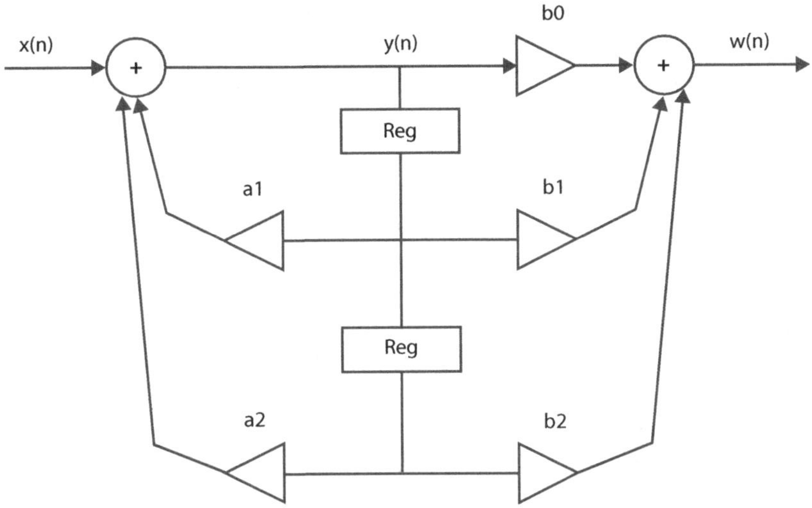

Figure 11.5 Architectural view of design of direct form implementation of an FIR filter.

$$y_z[1 - a_1 z^{-1} - a_2 z^{-2}] = x_z \tag{11.6}$$

$$\frac{y_z}{x_z} = \frac{1}{1 - a_1 z^{-1} - a_2 z^{-2}} \tag{11.7}$$

$$w_n = b_0 y_n + b_1 y_{n-1} + b_2 y_{n-2} \tag{11.8}$$

$$\frac{w_z}{y_z} = b_0 + b_1 z^{-1} + b_2 z^{-2} \tag{11.9}$$

If we multiply the Eq. 11.7 and Eq. 11.9 the result in Eq. 11.10,

$$\frac{w_z}{x_z} = \frac{b_0 + b_1 z^{-1} + b_2 z^{-2}}{1 - a_1 z^{-1} - a_2 z^{-2}} \tag{11.10}$$

The transposed form of an FIR filter is derived by applying the transposition theorem, which involves reversing the signal flow graph of the direct form while maintaining the overall functionality. In this structure, the filter coefficients are fed into the multipliers simultaneously, creating a broadcast effect where the input signal is applied to all multipliers at once. This approach contrasts with the direct form, where input samples are processed sequentially over multiple clock cycles. The transposed structure inherently supports pipelined operations, allowing it to update output values and accept new input samples with minimal delays. Additionally, it generally requires fewer registers compared to the direct form, making it a more hardware-efficient solution for implementation. However, special attention must be given to the fan out of the input signal, as the simultaneous feeding of input to all multipliers can complicate circuit design. Overall, the transposed form offers advantages in speed and resource utilization, making it a valuable choice in many digital signal processing applications [8].

The transposed form of an FIR filter is illustrated in Figure 11.6. From this figure, we can derive Eq. 11.11. We can then rearrange this equation up to Eq. 11.13.

$$w_n = b_2\, x_{n-2} + b_1\, x_{n-1} + b_0\, x_n + a_1\, w_{n-1} + a_2\, w_{n-2} \tag{11.11}$$

$$w_n - a_1\, w_{n-1} - a_2\, w_{n-2} = b_2\, x_{n-2} + b_1\, x_{n-1} + b_0\, x_n \tag{11.12}$$

$$w_z[1 - a_1 z^{-1} - a_2 z^{-2}] = [b_0 + b_1 z^{-1} + b_2 z^{-2}]x_z \tag{11.13}$$

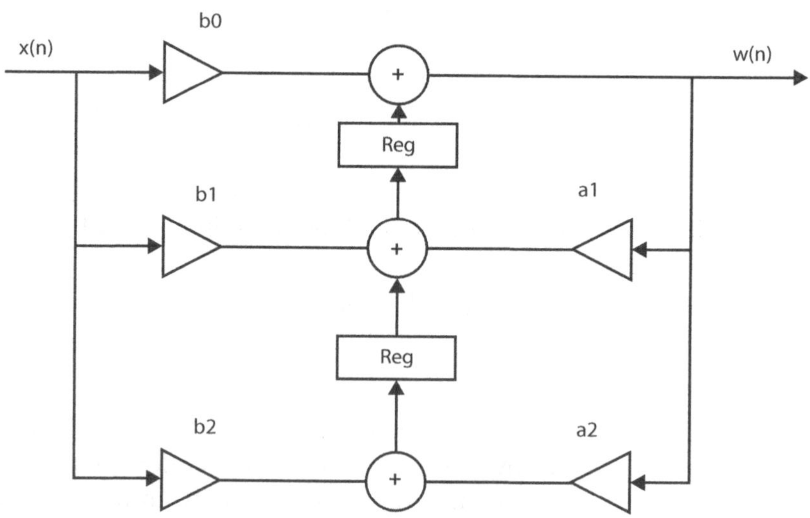

Figure 11.6 Top-level schematic of Transposed form implementation of a FIR filter.

The Eq. 11.10 and Eq. 11.13 has the same, which proves that there is no functional change in these two types (direct and transposed form) of configuration.

11.3.2 Hardware Analysis of an FIR Filter

The direct implementation of an N-tap FIR filter involves N-MAC operations, which are often too complex and area-intensive for practical hardware implementation. To address these constraints, an architecture must be designed to reduce complexity. One effective approach is to use Time Division Multiplexing (TDM) to implement a multichannel FIR filter [4, 9], which, independent of the quantity of taps or channels, makes use of a single multiplier and adder. This method relies on resource sharing and increased filter operating frequency. Two strategies—Output Product Coding (OPC) and Dual Port Schematic Architectures—are used to further optimize the multiplier's complexity. These schemes reduce design complexity by manipulating odd multiples of fixed coefficients in the Look-Up Table (LUT). The performance of these schemes is evaluated based on area and speed, with variations in the number of taps.

In fine-grain pipelining, a filter coefficient is divided into two parts (e.g., h0 into h01 and h02), with a delay inserted between these coefficients. This approach reduces the critical path delay. The critical path of the structure is assessed by evaluating input-to-delay, delay-to-delay, and delay-to-output paths. By decreasing the coefficient multiplier and introducing delays, the critical path delay is significantly reduced, leading to improved operational speed compared to a non-pipelined structure [10, 11].

11.3.3 Adder Logic

An adder is a digital circuit designed for the addition of numbers, with the half-adder handling single binary digits by using an XOR gate to generate the sum and an AND gate to produce the carry [12]. To create an n-bit adder, n Full Adder (FA) units are connected in series, forming a ripple-carry adder (RCA) where each FA's carry-out (Cout) feeds into the next FA's carry-in (Ci). The RCA's performance is limited by the propagation delay of the carry signal across all stages, making it proportional to the number of bits. The Carry Save Adder (CSA) improves on this by saving carry outputs for subsequent stages rather than combining them immediately, with a final RCA stage producing the overall sum and carry-out. The Carry Look-Ahead (CLA) adder enhances speed by pre-calculating carry bits to reduce delay, making it ideal for high-performance processors and Arithmetic Logic Units (ALUs). The Conventional Carry Skip Adder (CSkA) further optimizes delay by incorporating carry skip logic to bypass unnecessary wait times, integrating RCA blocks with skip logic based on propagation signals. The Kogge-Stone Adder (KSA), a parallel prefix form of CLA developed in 1973, generates carries in logarithmic time and is renowned for its speed, although it may require more area due to its simultaneous carry calculations. KSA is favored in high-performance circuits due to its efficient structure and minimal logic depth [13].

11.3.4 Multiplier Technique

The conventional multiplier or array multiplier follows a regular structure, so its layout is tightly packed. In the case of Vedic Multiplier, its implementation is easy, because the logic requires a 4 $n/2$ Vedic Multiplier and a 3 n-bit adder unit in this particular design. Regarding the Wallace multiplier, it provides an optimized performance (Area, Power, and Delay (APD)) design than the conventional algorithm. The adder unit is an important module for any multiplier. Increasing the adder performance or efficient usage of the adder logic will directly provide high performance in the multiplier unit [14]. The Wallace multiplier algorithm [15, 16] also provides comparatively better Area, Power, and Delay results while calculating in higher bits, without compromising the accuracy of results. So the System on Chip (SoC) design which contains the DSP processors is good for using the Wallace multiplier algorithm. Compared to Conventional algorithms Vedic Multiplier and Wallace multiplier give appreciable performance results. All three key parameters APD show much improvement in the Wallace multiplier technique [17].

11.3.5 Multiplier-Accumulator (MAC) Unit

The Multiplier-Accumulator (MAC) unit is a specialized digital circuit designed to perform multiplication and accumulation operations with exceptional efficiency. It excels at swiftly executing multiply-and-add instructions, which are essential for various algorithms used in tasks such as filtering, convolution, and real-time data processing. A novel approach involves an approximate MAC unit that computes the expression $Y=A\times B+C$ using static segmentation. In a typical MAC implementation, the unit adds the row corresponding to the input C to the partial product matrix (PPM) generated from the multiplication of A and B. This process employs a unique carry-propagate adder to effectively compute the final result Y. By optimizing these operations, the MAC unit significantly enhances computational efficiency in digital signal processing applications [18–20].

11.3.6 FIR Filter Design without Using Multiplier

In FIR filter design, the multiplier unit is often a significant contributor to area, power consumption, and delay. To enhance performance, we can replace traditional multiplier logic with more efficient methods, such as using a MAC design in conjunction with distributive algorithms (DA) [21]. In FPGAs, if the FIR filter coefficients are predetermined, they can be stored in Read-Only Memory (ROM), effectively allowing the ROM to function as a multiplier. By employing a shift-and-add approach, we can eliminate the need for dedicated multipliers, leading to a more optimized FIR filter design. This method capitalizes on the flexibility of Lookup Tables (LUTs) within the Configurable Logic Blocks (CLBs) of FPGAs, which can precompute and store all possible coefficient multiplications with the input. Consequently, this approach results in significantly lower utilization of registers and flip-flops, making it a highly efficient solution in terms of area and performance within the FPGA environment.

We can transform Eq. 11.1 into Eq. 11.14, and finally rearrange it to obtain the form presented in Eq. 11.15.

$$y_n = -\Sigma_{k=1}^{K}(b_{k0} \cdot A_k) + \Sigma_{k=1}^{K}[\Sigma_{n=1}^{N-1}(b_{kn} \cdot A_k)\, 2^{-n}] \tag{11.14}$$

$$y_n = -\Sigma_{k=1}^{K}(b_{k0} \cdot A_k) + \sum_{k=1}^{K}[(A_k \cdot B_{k1})\, 2^{-1} + (A_k \cdot B_{k2})\, 2^{-2}] + \cdots + (A_k \cdot B_{k(N-1)})^{2^{-(N-1)}} \tag{11.15}$$

The implementation design of Eq. 11.15 is shown in Figure 11.7. An effective look-up table (LUT)-based method for computing inner products that eliminates the requirement for conventional multiplication is called distributed arithmetic (DA). Because it enables computations to be finished in a number of execution cycles proportional to the bit-length of the input rather than the number of coefficients in the equation, this technique is very beneficial in digital signal processing. The throughput of DA implementations is primarily limited by the size of the LUT, which can be a critical factor in design. Numerous FIR filter architectures both reconfigurable and non-reconfigurable can be developed using DA. Among these,

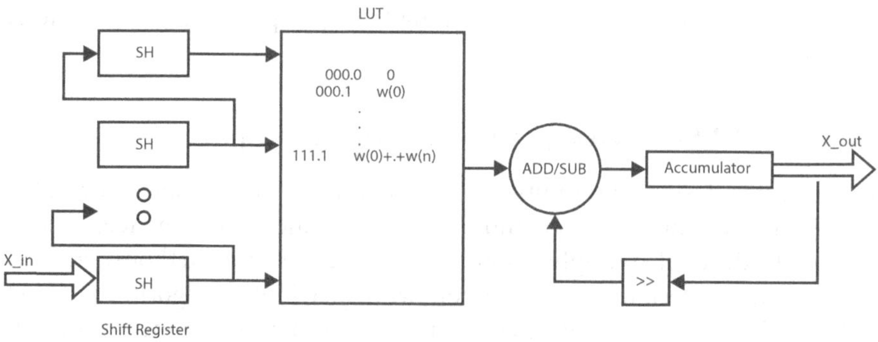

Figure 11.7 Realization of FIR filter using DA algorithm.

LUT-based DA and LUT-less DA are significant methods for implementing non-reconfigurable filters, offering designers flexibility in balancing performance and resource utilization [22, 23]. Despite its advantages, DA also has limitations, particularly its bit-serial nature, which can lead to slower processing speeds. Nevertheless, the time needed to input K words serially equals the time needed to input all K words in parallel over several wires when the number of input words K is proportionate to the number of bits in each input word N. This characteristic positions DA as a versatile architecture in FIR filter design, gaining popularity for its high throughput processing capability and efficiency. This brief illustrates the continued applicability of DA in contemporary digital signal processing applications by highlighting the area and power reports of non-reconfigurable FIR filter designs based on both LUT-based and LUT-less DA [24].

11.4 Simulation Setup and Results Analysis

The ASIC design flow typically follows a well-defined sequence of steps, beginning with the Specification phase, where performance, power, and area requirements for the design are outlined. In the Design Entry phase, the design is implemented using hardware description languages (HDLs) such as Verilog or VHDL. Functional Verification ensures that the design behaves as expected through simulation. During Synthesis, the HDL code is transformed into a gate- level netlist, optimized for performance, power, and area constraints. The Place and Route stage determines the physical layout of logic gates and establishes connections between them. Physical Verification checks the design against the foundry's manufacturing rules to ensure it can be fabricated without errors. After these steps, Tapeout prepares the final design for manufacturing, and Testing validates that the fabricated ASIC functions as intended in real-world conditions.

In the case of the FPGA design flow which is very much suitable for prototyping, the process begins similarly with the Functional Specification phase, followed by design implementation using Verilog or VHDL. The design is then checked for functional correctness through simulation. Next, during synthesis, the tool optimizes the design based on the specifications of the FPGA board selected during design time, generating performance parameters such as area, power, and timing. The design is then implemented on the hardware. The FPGA design flow is faster and less expensive compared to ASIC, as FPGA hardware does not require custom fabrication. However, ASIC designs offer superior performance in terms of power, speed, and area efficiency due to their custom hardware implementation. In this context, performance reports are typically generated using the Cadence tool for ASIC designs and the Xilinx tool for FPGA implementations.

In this experiment, we utilized the Xilinx Artix-7 FPGA (The Artix-7 AC701 Evaluation board, which is part of Xilinx's Artix-7 family of FPGAs, is built using 28nm (nanometer) CMOS technology) in conjunction with the AC701 evaluation platform to investigate signal processing capabilities. To perform accurate power calculations, we employed the Cadence tool alongside the Generic Process Design Kit (GPDK) in a CMOS 90nm technology. The experimental setup began with generating a noisy sine wave (Figure 11.8) using MATLAB, which served as the input signal for our

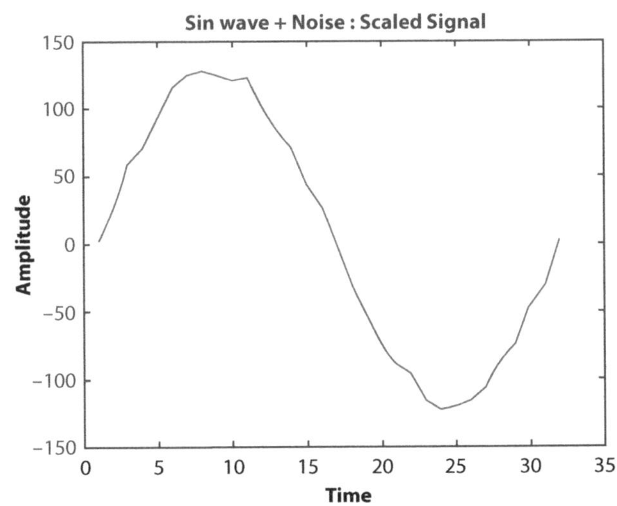

Figure 11.8 Noisy sin wave from the Matlab.

processing system. (This is most of the time the signal available in the universe and may be in audio or video signal.) This generated data was then sampled and saved in a data format (Figure 11.9 and it in **.data** for- mat), ensuring that it could be easily integrated into our subsequent processing steps. The binary data file has 16-bit input data, which is the representation of an analog noisy sin wave signal. The sampled data was fed into a Finite Impulse Response (FIR) filter, which we designed using Verilog HDL. The design was simulated using Xilinx tools, allowing us to verify the functionality and performance of the FIR filter before implementing it on the FPGA.

In FPGA designs, area utilization is commonly measured by slice usage, with a focus on designs that rely solely on look-up tables (LUTs) for implementing adders and multipliers. However, more complex FIR filter designs often incorporate both LUTs and flip-flops (FFs), which significantly impacts area and power consumption. Table 11.1 illustrates that the direct architecture exhibits higher slice and power utilization compared to its pipelined counterpart. Pipelined FIR filter designs, as previously noted, achieve a remarkable 63% reduction in delay compared to direct-form FIR filters, highlighting their efficiency and effectiveness in optimizing both performance and resource utilization in FPGA implementations. This efficiency makes pipelined architectures a preferred choice for applications requiring high-speed processing while managing area and power constraints.

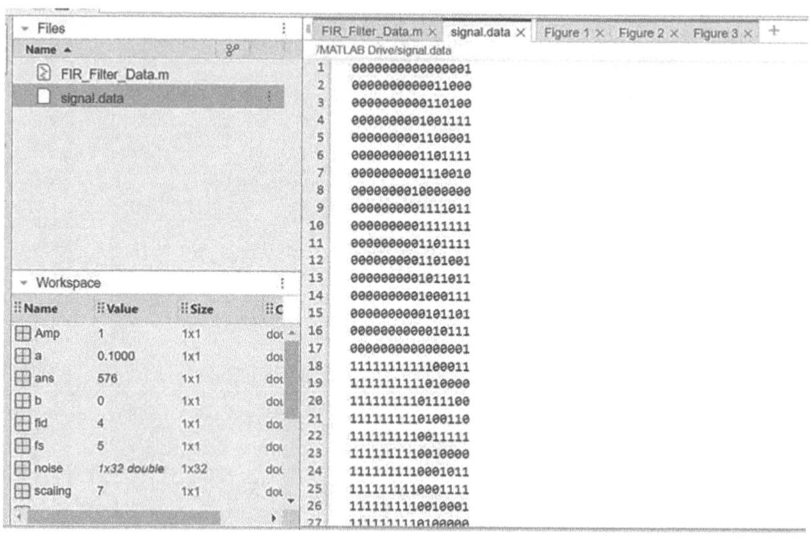

Figure 11.9 Sampled data from the Matlab.

Table 11.1 16-bit 3-tap FIR filter with parameter.

FIR filter type	Slice (LUT,FF) [a]	Power(nW) 90nm GPDK[b]	Delay(nS)[a]
DIRECT	155,50	51556.692	5.567
PIPELINE	23,18	22628.889	3.521

a Results from Xilinx tool
b Results from Cadence tool

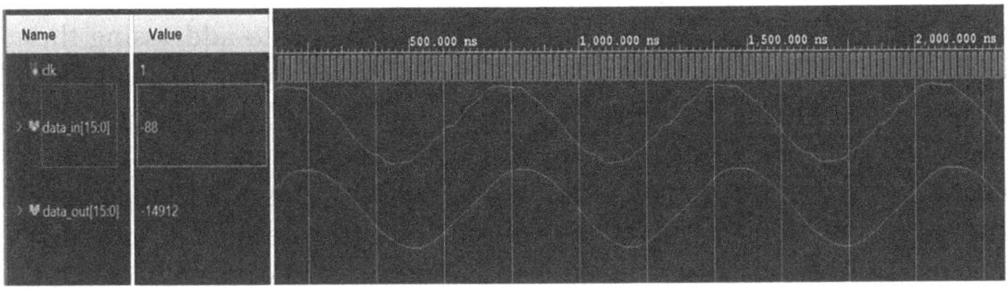

Figure 11.10 Smooth simulation waveform from moving average filter designed using FIR filter.

The simulated output waveform of the 5-tap signal processing FIR moving average filter is shown in Figure 11.10. The moving average filter is the simplest type of FIR filter, characterized by its uniform coefficients. After synthesis, it uses 38 LUT and 44 Flip flops in the area side and 8.099nS as the delay in Xilinx toolkit, Artix-7 AC701Evaluation Platform and 1016381nW power and 7223$um2$ as the area in Generic Process Design Kit (GPDK) 90nm slow library technology using the Cadence tool.

11.5 Summary

Filters play a crucial role in digital signal processing, serving as fundamental components in a variety of applications, including speech and image processing. Within the Very-Large-Scale Integration (VLSI) industry, designing high-performance hardware for filters is an ongoing challenge that demands continuous innovation. Among these filters, the Finite Impulse Response (FIR) filter is particularly significant due to its inherent stability and linear phase characteristics, making it a preferred choice in many digital signal processing tasks. The Design focus is on creating a hardware design that excels in these areas to achieve superior performance and efficiency in multimedia tasks.

However, designing FIR filters presents its own set of complexities, especially when it comes to hardware implementation. The core of this complexity often lies in the multiplier techniques used, which are essential for the filter's performance. As these multipliers are integral to the FIR filter's operation, their design and optimization are critical areas of focus for engineers. The challenge is to balance performance, power consumption, and area constraints while achieving the desired filter specifications. Advances in hardware design, including specialized multiplier architectures and efficient implementation strategies, are key to addressing these challenges. The ever-evolving nature of digital design means that engineers must stay abreast of the latest techniques and technologies to create efficient and effective FIR filter hardware. This continuous development is vital for meeting the demands of modern applications where high-speed and high-accuracy processing is required. Thus, the design and optimization of FIR filters remain a vibrant and important field within digital signal processing and VLSI hardware design.

References

1. Balaji, M. and Padmaja, N., High-Speed DSP Pipelining and Retiming Techniques for Distributed-Arithmetic RNS-based FIR Filter Design. *WSEAS Trans. Syst. Control*, 17, 2022, 549–556.
2. Mariammal, K., Sherin Mary, R., Brittopari, J., Vaithiyanathan, D., Multiple Bandwidth FIR Filter Design with Adaptive Algorithms for Hearing Aid Systems. *Indian J. Pure Appl. Phys. (IJPAP)*, 58, 605–623, 2000, [Accessed: August 2016].
3. Zahoor, S., Naseem, S., Meng, W., Design and implementation of an efficient FIR digital filter. *Cogent Eng.*, 4, 1, 2017, doi: doi.org/10.1080/23311916.2017.1323373.
4. Britto Pari, J. and Vaithiyanathan, D., An Efficient Multichannel FIR Filter Architecture for FPGA and ASIC Realizations. *Int. J. Appl. Eng. Res.*, 12, 10, 2209–2220, 2017, ISSN 0973-4562.
5. Nikolaidis, S., Karaolis, E., Kyriakis-Bitzaros, E.D., Estimation of signal transition activity in FIR filters implemented by a MAC architecture. *IEEE Trans. Comput. Aided Des. Integr. Circuits Syst.*, 19, 1, 164–169, Jan. 2000, doi: 10.1109/43.822629.
6. Mohanty, B.K. and Meher, P.K., A High-Performance FIR Filter Architecture for Fixed and Reconfigurable Applications. *IEEE Trans. Very Large Scale Integr. VLSI Syst.*, 24, 2, 444–452, Feb. 2016, doi: 10.1109/TVLSI.2015.2412556.

7. Vaithiyanathan, D., James, B.P., Mariamm, K., Mariammal, K., A High-Speed Computational Pipeline Single MAC-Based VLSI Architecture for Real-Time Signal and Image Processing. *2024 Fourth International Conference on Advances in Electrical, Computing, Communication and Sustainable Technologies (ICAECT)*, Bhilai, India, pp. 1–6, 2024, doi: 10.1109/ICAECT60202.2024.10469571.
8. Arar, S., Pipelined Direct Form FIR Versus the Transposed Structure. All about circuit. [Accessed:21 May 2018].
9. K., M., M., H.B., J., B.P., Dhandapani, V., Decisive structures for multirate FIR filter incorporating retiming and pipelining schemes. *Circuit World*, 47, 4, 427–444, 2021, doi: doi.org/10.1108/CW-05-2020-0094.
10. Sarma, R.K., Khan, M.T., Shaik, R.A., Hazarika, J., A Novel Time-Shared and LUT-Less Pipelined Architecture for LMS Adaptive Filter. *IEEE Trans. Very Large Scale Integr. VLSI Syst.*, 28, 1, 188–197, Jan. 2020, doi: 10.1109/TVLSI.2019.2935399.
11. Cho, S.M., Meher, P.K., Nhat Trung, L.T., Cho, H.J., Park, S.Y., Design of Very High-Speed Pipeline FIR Filter Through Precise Critical Path Analysis. *IEEE Access*, 9, 34722–34735, 2021, doi: 10.1109/ACCESS.2021.3061759.
12. Vaithiyanathan, D., Sonar, S.M., Parri, J.B., Mariammal, K., Kunaraj, K., Performance Analysis of Full Adder Circuit using Conventional and Hybrid Techniques. *2021 IEEE Madras Section Conference (MASCON), Chennai, India*, pp. 1–7, 2021, doi: 10.1109/MASCON51689.2021.9563407.
13. Dhandapani, V., An efficient architecture for carry select adder. *World J. Eng.*, 14, 3, 249–254, 2017, https://doi.org/10.1108/WJE-08-2016- 0043.
14. Vaithiyanathan, D., James, B.P., Mariammal, K., Comparative Study of Single MAC FIR Filter Architectures with Different Multiplication Techniques. *2023 Second International Conference on Electrical, Electronics, Information and Communication Technologies (ICEEICT)*, Tiruchirappalli, India, pp. 01–10, 2023, doi: 10.1109/ICEEICT56924.2023.10157620.
15. Wallace, C.S., A Suggestion for a Fast Multiplier. *IEEE Trans. Electron. Comput.*, EC-13, 1, 14–17, Feb. 1964, doi: 10.1109/PGEC.1964.263830.
16. Waters, R.S. and Swartzlander, E.E., A Reduced Complexity Wallace Multiplier Reduction. *IEEE Trans. Comput.*, 59, 8, 1134–1137, Aug. 2010, doi: 10.1109/TC.2010.103.
17. A. V, and D. Vaithiyanathan, Performance Analysis of Multiplier with Different Bits Size for MAC Unit. *2024 International Conference on Advances in Modern Age Technologies for Health and Engineering Science (AMATHE)*, Shivamogga, India, pp. 1–6, 2024, doi: 10.1109/AMATHE61652.2024.10582134.
18. Meo, G.D., Saggese, G., Strollo, A.G.M., De Caro, D., Approximate MAC unit using Static Segmentation. *IEEE Trans. Emerg. Top. Comput.*, doi: 10.1109/TETC.2023.3315301.
19. Xiao, H., Xu, H., Chen, X., Wang, Y., Han, Y., Fast and High-Accuracy Approximate MAC Unit Design for CNN Computing. *IEEE Embedded Sys. Lett.*, 14, 3, 155–158, Sept. 2022, doi: 10.1109/LES.2021.3137335.

20. Britto Pari, J., Mariammal, K., Vaithiyanathan, D., A Reconfigurable High-Speed and Low Complexity Residue Number System based Multiply-Accumulate Channel Filter for Software Radio Receivers. *World J. Eng.*, 21, 1, 16–30, January 2024, doi: https://doi.org/10.1108/WJE-11-2021- 0644.
21. Rai, A., Qamar, S., *et al.*, Modeling and simulation of FIR filter using distributed arithmetic algorithm on FPGA. *Multimed. Tools Appl.*, 83, 75855–75868, 2024, https://doi.org/10.1007/s11042-024- 18637-7.
22. Khan, M.T., Alhartomi, M.A., Alzahrani, S., Shaik, R.A., Alsulami, R., Two Distributed Arithmetic Based High Throughput Architectures of Non-Pipelined LMS Adaptive Filters. *IEEE Access*, 10, 76693–76706, 2022, doi: 10.1109/ACCESS.2022.3192619.
23. Vun, C.H., Premkumar, A.B., Zhang, W., A New RNS based DA Approach for Inner Product Computation. *IEEE Trans. Circuits Syst. I Regul. Pap.*, 60, 8, 2139–2152, Aug. 2013, doi: 10.1109/TCSI.2013.2239164.
24. NagaJyothi, G. and SriDevi, S., Distributed arithmetic architectures for FIR filters-A comparative review. *2017 International Conference on Wireless Communications, Signal Processing and Networking (WiSPNET)*, Chennai, India, pp. 2684–2690, 2017, doi: 10.1109/WiSPNET.2017.8300250.

12

Recent Trends in Deep Neural Networks and Their Hardware Implementation for Biomedical Applications

Amit Monga*, Hemkant Nehete, Seema Dhull, Arshid Nisar, Shailendra Yadav and Brajesh Kumar Kaushik

Department of Electronics and Communication Engineering, Indian Institute of Technology Roorkee, Roorkee, Uttarakhand, India

Abstract

The development of dedicated deep learning (DL) accelerators and neuromorphic processors has opened up new possibilities for implementing neural network algorithms in healthcare and biomedical applications. These specialized hardware systems present unmatched opportunities to improve the effectiveness and usefulness of DL algorithms in medical contexts, including image enhancement, disease diagnosis, and treatment monitoring. Although DL has progressed rapidly in terms of network complexity, effectiveness, and training efficiency, the evolution of specialized hardware tailored for DL algorithms lags behind. Innovative advancements in algorithms and architectures are essential to fulfill the demanding standards of efficient and affordable healthcare devices. Implementing these algorithms at the edge level is imperative to safeguard data privacy, particularly in critical medical applications. By processing data locally on specialized devices, edge computing reduces the risk of sensitive medical information being exposed to external servers, ensuring compliance with privacy regulations and enhancing patient trust. Edge computing not only minimizes the risks of data breaches but also supports applications where low-latency responses are essential, such as in wearable health monitors or portable diagnostic tools. In this study, we evaluate the numerous technological advances in DL approaches used on medical images for classification, recognition, and enhancement, both at the algorithmic and hardware levels that have been reported to address a variety of healthcare problems. Finally, we present our analysis and discuss our views on the benefits, drawbacks,

**Corresponding author*: amit_m@ece.iitr.ac.in

Ashish Maurya, Mandeep Singh and Balwinder Raj (eds.) Machine Learning in Nanoelectronics: Devices, Circuits and Systems, (363–408) © 2026 Scrivener Publishing LLC

and opportunities that different algorithms and neuromorphic processors bring to the biomedical and healthcare domains. This analysis signifies the importance of a synergistic evolution of algorithms and hardware to revolutionize modern healthcare.

***Keywords*:** Deep learning, biomedical, hardware, classification, recognition, enhancement

12.1 Introduction

Deep learning (DL) is becoming popular in a variety of fields, ranging from cutting-edge technology to healthcare and biomedical applications [1]. As the reliability of DL grows, it has encompassed many aspects of healthcare, including monitoring [2, 3], prediction [4], diagnosis [5], treatment [6], and prognosis [7]. Artificial intelligence (AI) in the healthcare industry is expected to exceed $102.7 billion by 2028, with the associated workload on medical practitioners increasing concurrently [8]. The ability of AI to perform well in medical data analysis can be linked to ongoing improvements in DL algorithms, high-end computing boards as graphics processing units (GPU) [9], and customized DL hardware [10]. These algorithms and hardware are capable of processing and learning from huge amounts of medical data and predicting outcomes with high accuracy. Performance of DL algorithms is enhanced by availability of large medical data. However, healthcare datasets are massive, unorganized, noisy, and sparse, making it difficult to effectively extract the useful information hidden within them [11]. As a result, an efficient algorithm is required to process these massive biomedical datasets and obtain accurate information. Convolutional neural networks (CNN), recurrent neural networks (RNN), long short-term memory networks (LSTMs), and generative adversarial networks (GANs) are the most popular DL algorithms. While the field of DL has been rapidly expanding, the realization of dedicated hardware to handle these advanced algorithms has lagged in terms of energy consumption, throughput/latency, and cost [12]. While significant progress has been made in tailoring deep network models and algorithms for various healthcare and biomedical applications [13], the majority of high-computation deep networks are trained in data centers or on GPUs [9]. The former typically necessitates performing the computation on a cloud server, which is not only energy-intensive, and costly, but also reduces data privacy. On the other hand, edge computing allows for offline processing while also providing data security, low area consumption, high energy efficiency, and high speed at a low cost [14].

The market for CMOS-based application specific integrated circuits (ASIC) for facilitating deep neural networks (DNN) has grown rapidly in recent years. Several of these chips have been tested to run large and deep CNNs and RNNs, allowing them to perform high computation tasks within power budget limits for biomedical applications [15]. The reconfigurable hardware, field programmable gate array (FPGAs), is relatively inexpensive and has been used to accelerate DNNs. FPGA-based DNN accelerators developed particularly for biomedical applications have significantly lower power consumption than CPUs and GPUs [16, 17]. FPGA design, on the other hand, is more difficult and necessitates high-level designs and tools that are more powerful. Many studies have used emerging memory technology in DNN architectures to achieve massive parallelism and reduced memory access. The use of any accelerator for complex healthcare applications requires a robust hardware- software co-design that can be easily programmed and operated for healthcare tasks [18].

This chapter discusses various DL techniques used on medical images for classification, recognition, and enhancement from both algorithms as well as hardware realization standpoints. The rest of the chapter is organized as follows: Section 12.2 presents various architectures of neural networks along with fundamental concepts such as transfer learning and convolution and deconvolution operations. In Section 12.3, the advancements in DL algorithms for medical image classification, recognition, and enhancement approaches are discussed in detail. Section 12.4 presents the recent trends in hardware architectures and optimization techniques for dedicated ASIC/FPGA applications. Section 12.5 discusses the challenges and opportunities of applying DL techniques in the medical and healthcare sectors. Section 12.6 concludes the review and discusses our views on the benefits, drawbacks, problems, and opportunities from both algorithm and hardware viewpoint.

12.2 Neural Network Architectures

Over the last two decades, several neural network architectures have been presented, and for a particular application in the medical domain, analyzing each architecture is essential in deciding the most efficient architecture. This section presents the most prominent types of neural network architectures including artificial neural networks (ANN), CNN, RNN, autoencoder, and GAN.

i. Artificial Neural Network

ANN resembles the brain of a human being where different neurons are connected with each other and signal flows from one neuron to another through the synapse. Multiple hidden layers are present between input and output layers as shown in Figure 12.1(a) that are responsible for learning hidden features and patterns [19]. During training, the input signal is propagated from the input layer to the output layer, and the error is propagated back to the input layer updating the weights, thus, these networks are known as feed-forward and feed-backward neural networks, respectively. ANN serves as the foundational building block of neural networks. When combined with other neural networks, it becomes a flexible tool for integrating high- level features and generating accurate prediction results.

ii. Convolutional Neural Network

CNN is made up of convolution, max-pooling, and fully connected layers that are arranged in a specific order with or without repetition as shown in Figure 12.1(b) [20]. Different features are extracted through the convolution layer by applying different kernels of varying size on input feature maps followed by rectified linear unit (ReLU) activation function. For improving the effectiveness of network, max-pooling layer aggregates information from the previous layer and reduces the size of feature maps. To mitigate overfitting and enrich the learning capability of CNN, dropout layers are incorporated within both convolutional and fully connected layers. These layers randomly omit forward and backward connections of certain neurons. The extracted feature map serves as the input to a fully connected layer, flattened to create a one- dimensional array feature vector.

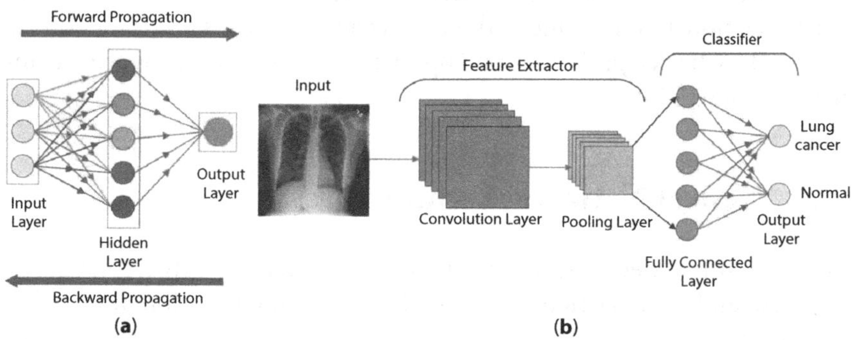

Figure 12.1 Generalized architecture of (a) artificial neural network, (b) convolutional neural network.

Fully connected layers are responsible for generating probabilities corresponding to each class. Batch normalization layers can be added after the input or activation layers to facilitate learning at large learning rates resulting in fast convergence and saving training time. Training of CNN involves forward and back propagation stages to evaluate loss and update weights respectively. Depending on the arrangements of these layers in the appropriate order and the types of kernels used for each layer, many variants of CNNs like AlexNet [21], VGGNet [22], GoogleNet [23], and ResNet [24] have been proposed.

iii. Recurrent Neural Network

Processing of time series and sequential data is possible with RNNs due to its capability of memorizing output that is further used as feedback for generating output at the next time step [25]. Figure 12.2 illustrates how different layers in NN are overlapped on each other to make vertical layers. RNNs possess the capability to handle sequential data of varying lengths, operating either in a unidirectional or bidirectional manner. Bidirectional RNNs leverage information from future timestamps to improve model performance, while their unidirectional counterparts rely solely on present and past timestamp data. The primary issue with RNN techniques is the vanishing gradient problem which prevents the weights of initial layers from being updated, resulting in the untrained network. For learning the long- and short-term dependencies of the data, LSTM was proposed to overcome this problem by preserving information through cell and memory manipulation with gates like forget gate that prevent information loss [26]. In the literature, these networks are utilized to sequentially diagnose liver diseases from various phases of CT images.

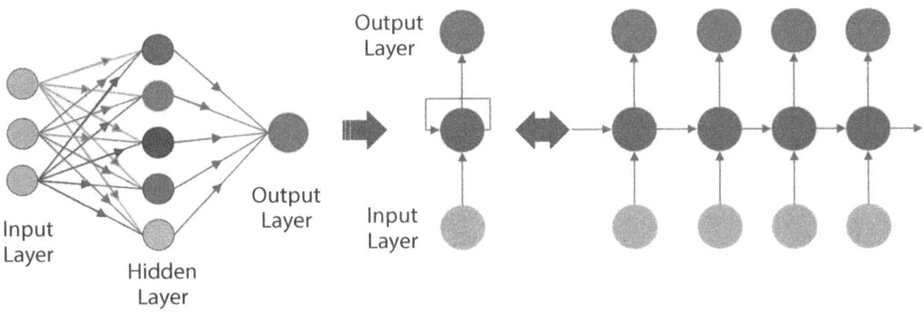

Figure 12.2 Rolling and unrolling of recurrent neural network.

iv. Autoencoder

Autoencoder learns a lower dimensional representation of the input and recreates a higher dimensional representation. Autoencoder comprises encoder, decoder, and bottleneck blocks as shown in Figure 12.3. The encoder block contains multiple convolution and pooling layers that encode the image information by compressing the feature maps. The bottleneck block stores the compressed representation of encoded data. The decoder block consists of several up- sampling and convolution layers that decompress the encoded data to generate a feature map in the form of a reconstructed image. Over the years, several variants have been proposed like convolutional, de-noising, variational, and deep autoencoder [27]. Convolutional autoencoder uses the convolution layer as encoder and deconvolution layer as a decoder. De-noising autoencoder learns to remove noise added to the input image. The encoder retrieves the most important features of the input image and thus learns to remove the noise itself.

v. Generative Adversarial Network

GANs are essentially a system of two competing neural network models that assess, capture, and duplicate the variation within a dataset. It has two parts: generator and discriminator as shown in Figure 12.4. Fake images are created by the generator and the discriminator's mission is to distinguish between real and fake images. Both the generator and discriminator are trained with random vector and ground truth images, respectively, in an

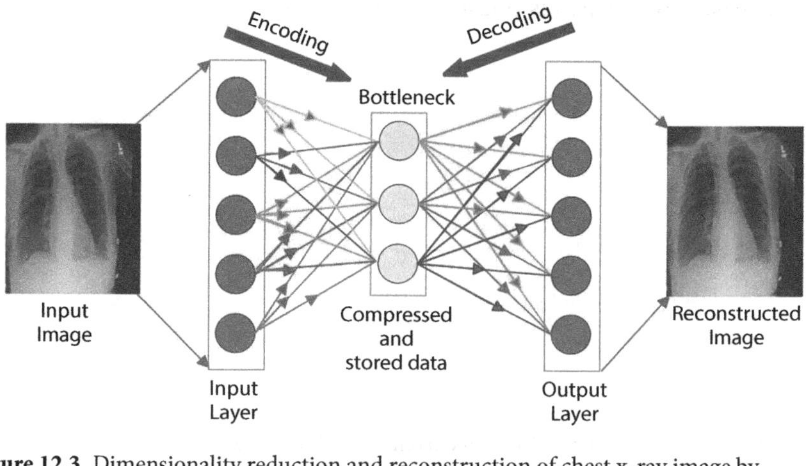

Figure 12.3 Dimensionality reduction and reconstruction of chest x-ray image by autoencoder.

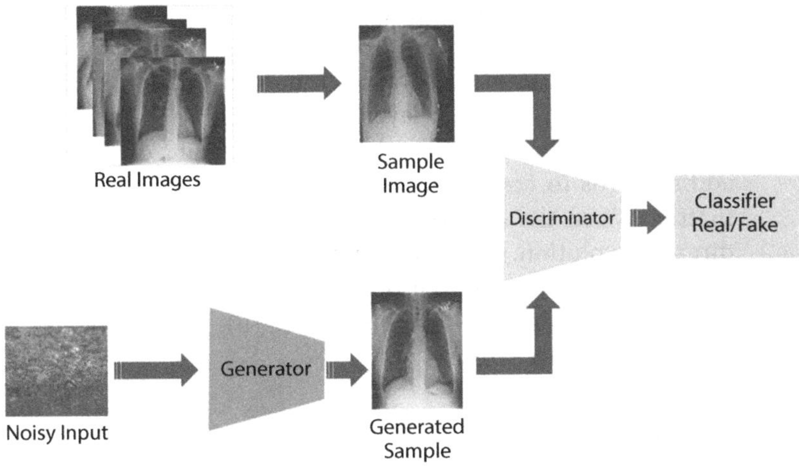

Figure 12.4 Structure of generative adversarial network.

adversarial manner where both the architectures compete with each other to get their predictions [28]. The generator tries to reduce the loss function by learning to generate images that are more realistic while the discriminator increases the loss by learning to classify real and fake images. GAN is available in varieties such as deep convolutional GAN (DCGAN), conditional GAN (CGAN), and super-resolution GAN (SRGAN). DCGAN uses CNN with ReLU and tanh activations for finding relevant features for generating new images. Input data class labels are provided along with random noise vector to both generator and discriminator in CGAN for faster model convergence and generating qualitatively enhanced images. SRGAN utilizes CNN in both generator and discriminator for the conversion of a low-quality image into a high-quality image.

vi. Convolution Operation

For optimization of DL algorithms in terms of hardware perspective, this section discusses and distinguishes the diverse types of convolution operations used in neural network architectures.

- Direct and strided convolution: A parameter stride, s is added to standard convolution which tells about the shifting of kernel or filter in the x and y direction on the input feature map to get the output feature map. For direct convolution, the stride value is taken as unity. A typical example of strided convolution with stride 2 with kernel size 5 × 5 applied on 9

× 9 input image is shown in Figure 12.5(a), which gives the output feature size as 3 × 3.

- Dilated convolution: A parameter named dilation rate is added to the convolution layer, for controlling the spacing among values inside a kernel [29]. Kernels are diluted by adding zeros to cover a larger receptive field on the input matrix. When the dilation rate becomes one it behaves as direct convolution. A typical example of dilated convolution with dilation rate 2 and kernel size 3 × 3 applied on 8 × 8 input image is shown in the Figure 12.5(b), which provides the output feature size as 4 × 4.

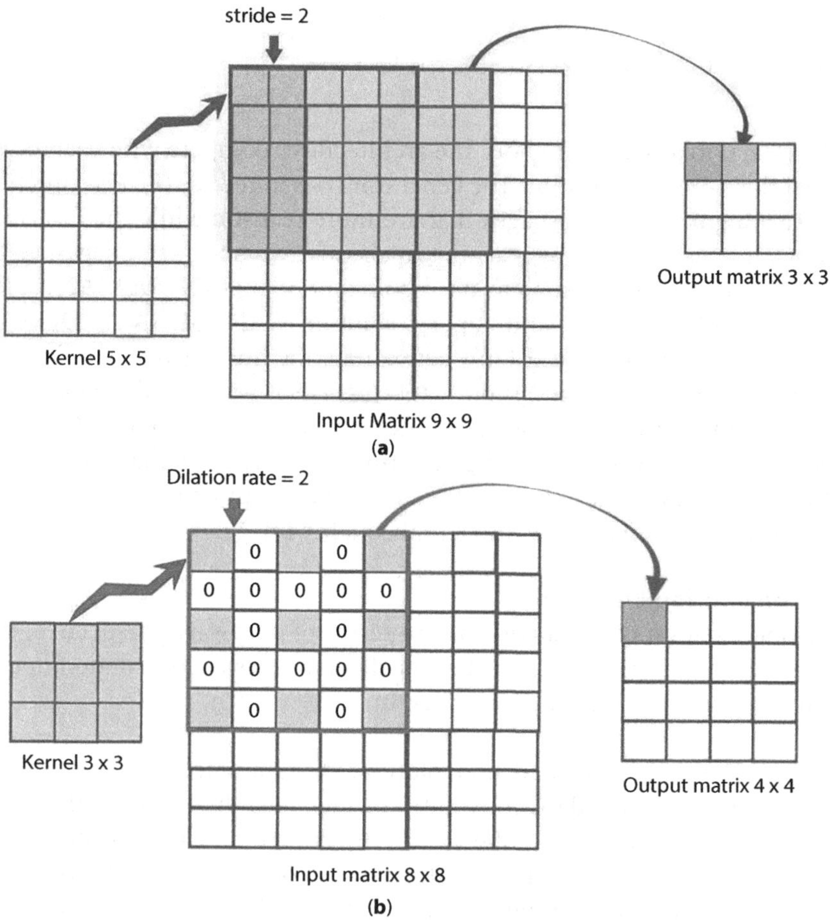

Figure 12.5 Depiction of (a) strided convolution, (b) dilated convolution.

- Transposed convolution: Up sampling enlarges any given input dimensions to match the output dimensions similar to the standard convolution but reverses spatial transformation. The input matrix is padded appropriately with zero before the convolution operation. When the input matrix is of size N × N and kernel size m x m, then the output matrix from transposed convolution for stride 1 is of size (N + m – 1) × (N + m – 1) and gets initialized with zeros. However, the output matrix will be different for different stride values. To get the output feature map, the kernel is applied to the padded feature map by sliding it over the input and then performing element-wise multiplication as shown in Figure 12.6(a). The output feature map size becomes (2 + 2 – 1) × (2 + 2 -1) i.e., 3 × 3 for a 2 × 2 kernel applied on 2 × 2 input feature map.
- Pointwise convolution: Kernel size of 1 × 1 is used for reducing the dimensionality of input matrix, i.e., reducing the number of the input matrix channels. For dimensionality increase after the pooling layer prior to another convolution, pointwise convolution can be used also. The major advantage of pointwise convolution is the reduction of multiply accumulation operations. Figure 12.6(b) illustrates how the 1 × 1 filter will convolve over the whole input matrix pixel by pixel.
- Spatial separable convolution: Separable kernels are created by dividing higher-dimensional kernels into the

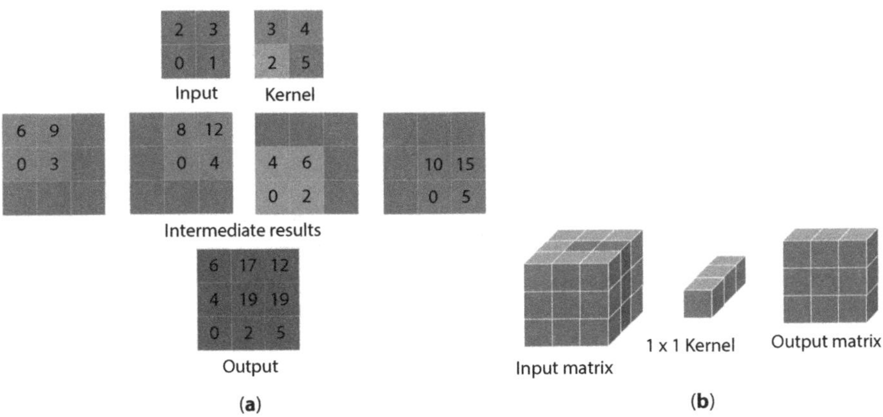

Figure 12.6 Method of (a) transpose convolution, (b) pointwise convolution.

lower-dimensional kernels. Performing convolution by these low dimensional kernels significantly increases the computational efficiency. Some commonly used separable kernels are Sobel, Averaging, and Gaussian kernels. All these 3 × 3 kernels can be divided into 3 × 1 and 1 × 3 kernels, respectively, and then applied to the input matrix to get the resultant output as shown in Figure 12.7(a). Separable kernels reduce the number of multiplication, which helps in the reduction of computational complexity and enhancing the training speed of the network.

- Depthwise separable convolution: Kernels that cannot be spatially separated into lower dimensions kernels can be trained using a depthwise separable convolution layer that performs depthwise and pointwise convolution operation together [30]. In depthwise convolution, shown in Figure 12.7(b), for getting the intermediate feature maps, the input

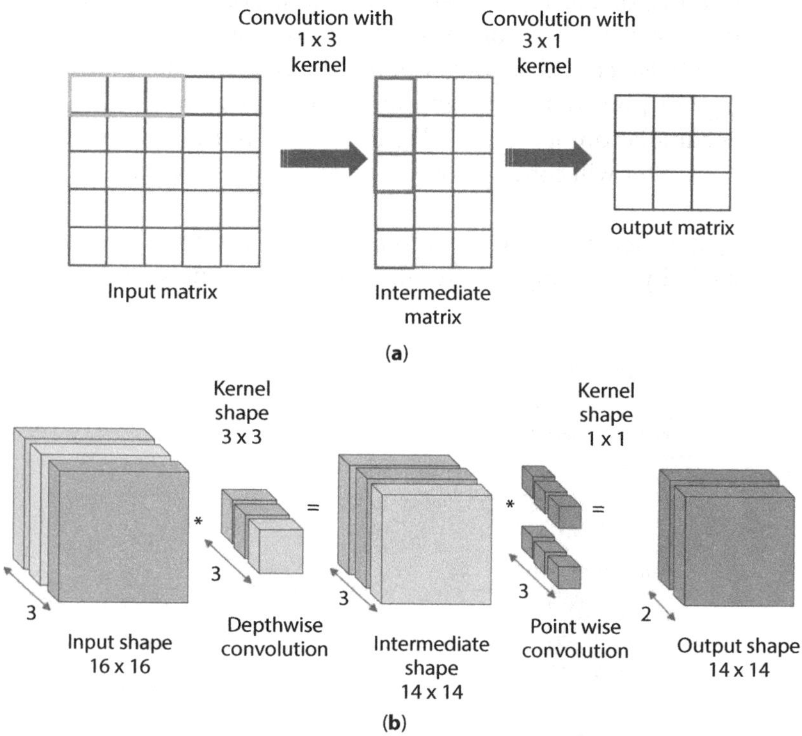

Figure 12.7 Illustration of (a) spatial separable convolution, (b) depthwise separable convolution.

matrix is first convolved with number of varying-size kernels of the same depth as the number of channels in the input matrix. Now for varying the number of channels in the intermediate matrix, pointwise convolution is further applied. Depthwise separable layers have the added advantage of reducing layer parameters but are slower in computation than normal convolution.

12.3 Deep Learning Algorithms for Medical Images

DL techniques help to identify important information in medical and healthcare source data that can further utilized for disease diagnosis and treatment. This section discusses various DL techniques used on medical images for classification, recognition, and enhancement.

i. Image Classification

One of the most important jobs in computer vision (CV) tasks is the assignment of a label to an image. For medical images, the task of getting high-quality labelled data is expensive and laborious, due to the need for medical professionals/experts to annotate images. Traditional image classification uses a trainable classifier to assign labels after extracting low or mid-level features to represent an image [31]. This section presents various DNNs that have been explored for image classification in the medical domain, for example, breast cancer, wound, chest X-ray (CXR), thorax disease, skin lesion, and brain tumor.

Alzubaidi *et al.* [32] proposed a hybrid deep CNN model for classifying biopsy images of hematoxylin and eosin-stained into four categories as benign, normal tissue, *in situ* carcinoma, and invasive carcinoma. The classification was applied to medical images of varying sizes, colours, and complex shapes. The model had multiple parallel convolutional layers with different kernel sizes, residual linkages, and global average pooling for generating multiscale feature maps. The developed model was also used for classifying foot images and wound types by considering knowledge gained from one dataset transferred to another dataset by using the transfer-learning technique. Guan *et al.* [33] introduced attention guided-convolutional neural network (AG-CNN) to classify thorax disease from CXR. AG-CNN had three branches; the global branch that considered the global image as input, the local branch that cropped a local disease-specific lesion region, and the fusion branch that fused the previous two branches' output to fine-tune and make decisions. The recognition performance in the proposed model was enhanced by adjusting image alignment and minimizing the effects of noise outside the lesion region.

Frid-Adar *et al.* [34] presented GAN-produced synthetic liver lesion images to increase small datasets by data augmentation. Overfitting of the network occurred due to limited numbers of training images and with data augmentation, the problem of overfitting can be reduced. The proposed architecture utilized strided convolution for the reduction of spatial dimensionality instead of pooling layers in the discriminator for the classification of liver lesions. Mahbod *et al.* [35] proposed melanoma, benign nevi, and seborrheic keratosis classification using fine-tuned CNNs that were already trained on ImageNet with dermoscopic lesion images. In the proposed work, fine-tuning of different CNN networks was performed by removing FC layers, and the extracted deep features were further fused and used to train different support vector machines for classifying the lesion types as malignant melanoma, seborrheic keratosis, and benign nevi. Liu *et al.* [36] recommended a relation-driven semi-supervised system for classifying medical images instead of consistency-centered methods, which performed well across single-label and multi-label classification problems. The author suggested unlabeled data could be used to extract additional semantic information for greater performance gains in a similar way as doctors consider previous cases for accurate disease diagnosis. The proposed model with backbone DenseNet was used for skin lesion and thorax disease classification.

Kaldera *et al.* [37] proposed an architecture based on a CNN model for feature extraction and classification as a meningioma or glioma types brain tumor on pre-processed dimensionally reduced tumor images. An intelligence medical imaging recognition (IMR-FSL) system was developed by Abbas [38], which utilized few labeled examples for training the model with few shot learning (FSL). The model comprised a prototypical network-based (PNB) FSL model, a pre-trained ResNet-34, and a Siamese network. PNB model and k-means clustering divided the input images into clusters, and a few images from each class were passed through ResNet-34 for training and classifying the unseen images.

Some literature related to DNN utilization in the classification of various diseases such as brain cancer, cervical, gastrointestinal disease, breast cancer, diabetic retinopathy, eye disease, pneumonia, lung cancer, dermatology, and chest disease are provided in Table 12.1.

ii. Object Detection

This is a process through which any object like a retina lesion or brain tumor is detected and classified. Region-based convolutional neural

Table 12.1 Deep learning architectures in various medical image classification applications.

References	Application	Architecture	Technique	Datasets
[106]	Brain cancer, cervical	CNN, RNN	Big data analytics with cat swarm optimization based deep learning (BDA- CSODL) technique having bilateral filtering-based noise removal, Inception v3 as feature extractor and LSTM based classification	CT brain, chest, and cervical images dataset
[107]	Gastrointestinal disease from endoscopic images	CNN	Explainable artificial intelligence (XAI) method based on ResNet-152	KVASIR dataset
[108]	Benign and malignant breast cancer	Hybrid CNN LSTM	Pre-trained InceptionResNetv2 CNN model with LSTM output merged using element-wise multiplication and passed to dense layer for classification	The breast cancer histopathological image classification (BreakHis) dataset
[109]	Eye	CNN	Pre-trained AlexNet and ResNet-18 on ImageNet dataset used for dry and wet AMD classification	JPEG OCT
[110]	Skin lesion, COVID-19	CNN, GAN	Modular group attention block for channel and space with ResNet model	ISIC2017 ISIC2018 COVID19-CT
[111]	Glioma, meningioma, and pituitary type brain tumor	CNN	Hierarchical deep learning- based brain tumor classifier with data acquisition training and validation phases	Kaggle brain dataset

(*Continued*)

Table 12.1 Deep learning architectures in various medical image classification applications. (*Continued*)

References	Application	Architecture	Technique	Datasets
[112]	Diabetic retinopathy	CNN	Ensemble deep learning model with Ada boost algorithm and class activation map	Beijing Tongren eye center dataset
[113]	Pneumonia	CNN	SVM classifier with oriented fast and rotated binary (ORB) robust features and transfer learning of VGG16 and InceptionV3 with training capsule network	OCT and chest X-ray 2017 Mendeley dataset
[114]	Skin lesion Ulcer Pneumonia retinal disease	CNN	Tri-Net with cross-balanced pseudo supervision (TNCB) with a student-teacher network to handle class imbalance and scarcity in medical data	ISIC 2018 Kvasir-Capsule OCT Chest X-ray
[115]	Lung cancer	CNN, RNN	ResNet trained on the ImageNet merged with RNN with softmax layer for classification	CT images of non-small cell lung cancer
[116]	Dermatology and chest disease	CNN	Multi-Instance Contrastive Learning (MICLe) with ResNet pretrained on ImageNet	Derm and CheXpert dataset
[117]	Skin lesion	CNN	Double decker convolution neural network (DDCNN) features fusion automated framework	ISIC 2019 ISIC 2020

network (R-CNN), fast R-CNN, faster R-CNN, mask R-CNN, and YOLO techniques are used for it. In R-CNN [39], first using selective search algorithm same size region proposal in an image is pulled out and passed to the CNN network for finding the features and finally these features are classified with support vector machine (SVM) as shown in Figure 12.8(a).

In faster R-CNN, the region proposal network (RPN) is used as a substitute for selective search in R-CNN for getting the region proposals of the input image depicted in Figure 12.8(b). R-CNN and faster R-CNN have one major difference: R-CNN utilizes input pixel-level region proposals, whereas faster R-CNN uses feature-level region proposals extracted from a fully convolutional network as input [40]. For labelling pixel-level positions of the detected objects, region of interest (RoI) pooling splits the received input feature map into equal regions, and for getting the same-size feature maps max pooling is applied on every region [41]. YOLO works as a single-stage object detector, which finds the position and class of objects without utilizing region proposal as in R-CNN and faster R-CNN. It uses an end-to-end regression method for target detection [42]. The input

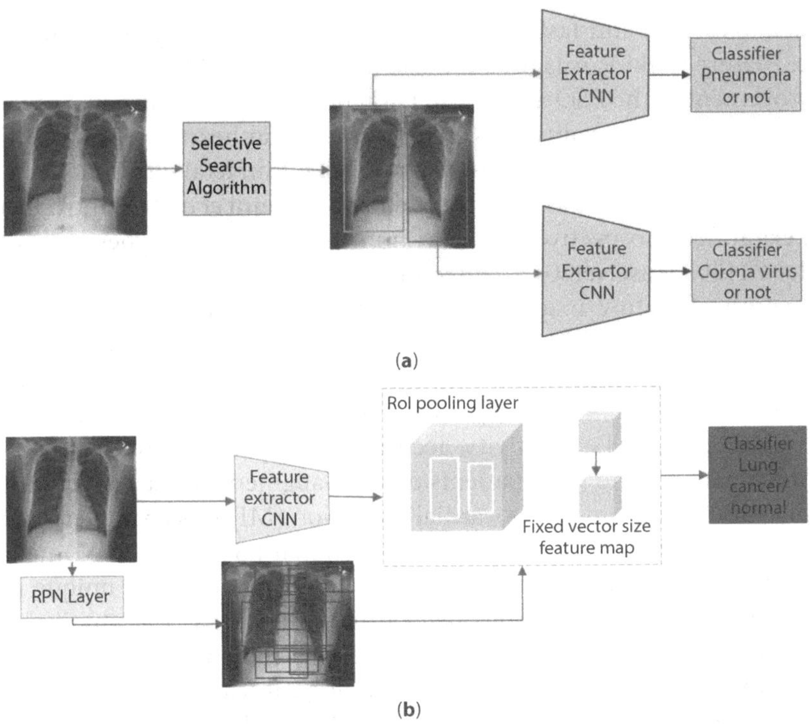

Figure 12.8 Structure of (a) R-CNN (b) faster R-CNN.

image is divided into a grid of cells, with each cell assigned the task of predicting a bounding box if the center of the bounding box lies within that cell. Class predictions are also made on a per-cell basis. Each grid cell predicts a bounding box by determining the x and y coordinates, width, height, and a confidence score.

iii. Image Recognition

Effective early disease diagnosis is a significant unmet need on a global scale. The development of a tool for early diagnosis and an efficient course of treatment is extremely difficult due to the complex mechanisms of the various diseases and basic symptoms of the patients. DL has been extensively used to solve these problems. This section presents various DNNs that have been explored for disease diagnosis of various critical diseases for example heart disease, diabetes, breast cancer, kidney disease, epilepsy, Parkinson's, and Alzheimer's.

Several researchers have utilized DL techniques for the identification of cardiac disease. Feshki *et al.* [43], used feed-forward backpropagation neural network (FFBP) along with particle swarm optimization (PSO) algorithm for optimization of selected features such as age, sex, chest pain type, cholesterol, and fast blood sugar considered to diagnose heart disease. Feature ranking was used for cost calculation and FFBP for accuracy improvement in the PSO algorithm. Early prenatal screening is required to reduce newborn mortality triggered by congenital heart diseases (CHD). Researchers have explored DL to diagnose CHDs in fetal ultrasounds [44]. Using fetal ultrasounds as a source of data, Nurmaini *et al.* [45] introduced and examined prospective DL algorithms to classify eight types of defects under CHD. DenseNet201 architecture having skip connections and concatenation of feature maps at later layers was used for CHD diagnosis. For getting fine-grained information from the abnormal images, localization and visualization of features based on gradient-weighted class activation map (Grad-CAM) and guided backpropagation were utilized. The DenseNet201 model's sensitivity, accuracy, and specificity were predicted for intra-patients and inter-patients on data-augmented images. A kind of cardiac disease known as myocardial infarction (MI) was characterized by quick growth and major mortality. Bidirectional LSTM (BiLSTM) neural network classification was used by Xu *et al.* [46] to develop a unique recognition strategy for numerous myocardial infarctions. The physikalisch technische bundesanstalt (PTB) database was the source of their algorithm, through which twelve lead morphological features, including beat segmentation and noise reduction, from ECG signals were extracted. From the pre-processed ECG signal, waveform amplitude and distance features were extracted and then passed to the BiLSTM network for identification and detection of myocardial infarction disease.

Kidney disease is a life-threatening disorder that requires early detection and treatment to avoid kidney failure, which necessitates dialysis or a kidney transplant to maintain life. Chronic kidney disease (CKD) has impacted 10% of people worldwide, as per the national kidney foundation report. To improve survivability and early diagnosis, DL can provide a possible solution to diagnose kidney disease [47]. Researchers have explored various DL techniques to diagnose CKD. Ma *et al.* [48] suggested a heterogeneous modified ANN (HMANN) model for segmentation, early detection, and diagnosis of CKD. For getting a segmented image of the kidney, noise was first removed from the raw image by wavelet technique in this work. Extracted Haralick, Histogram, and adaptive features were utilized for the classification process using SVM, Multilayer Perceptron, and Back Propagation techniques. Bhaskar *et al.* [49] presented a DL model utilizing a BiLSTM network and one-directional correlational NN for CKD diagnosis from human saliva samples. The proposed model extracted the optimal features from the input signal through correlation and sub-sampling layers and passed these features to bidirectional LSTM for time series analysis and finally dense classification was carried out to predict and classify CKD.

DL-based breast cancer analysis has been explored by many research scholars in the medical field. Alshayeji *et al.* [50], developed an ANN model and breast cancer dataset for classifying breast cancer. A shallow ANN with one hidden layer was proposed to diagnose and classify breast cancer as malignant or benign. Sultana *et al.* [51] employed various neural networks such as MLP NN, Jordan/Elman NN, probabilistic NN (PNN), modular NN (MNN), self- organizing feature map (SOFM), generalized feed-forward NN (GFFNN), SVM NN, and recurrent NN (RNN) to detect breast cancer. Real valued features from each cell nucleus were used as input to different networks. PNN performed the best among all these networks as a breast cancer detector.

Diabetes is a very common disease worldwide that can lead to the damage of blood vessels and nerves. The international diabetes federation (IDF) predicted the number of individuals having diabetes is over 382 million and this number is expected to reach 629 million by 2045 [52]. Various studies based on DL have been explored to detect diabetes. Naz *et al.* [52] demonstrated ANN, decision tree (DT), naive bayes (NB), and DL models for diabetes diagnosis. Yahyaoui *et al.* [53] demonstrated a clinical decision support system (CDSS) to detect diabetes by utilizing SVM and random forest (RF) machine learning and CNN DL techniques.

Table 12.2 Deep learning architectures in various medical image recognition applications.

References	Architecture	Application	Technique	Dataset
[81]	CNN, LSTM	Brain tumor detection	Pseudo data generation approach that enhances the model's capacity for migration learning by replacing crucial information globally at random	CCKS2019
[82]	Linear support vector machine and CNN	ECG Arrhythmia for Heart Disease	Principle component analysis network (PCNET) has been used to classify and recognize noisy and non-noisy heart beats	MIT-BIH
[83]	CNN	Diagnosis of fractures	Fracture detection using SABL, RetinaNet, RegNet, PAA, Libra R-CNN, Dynamic R- CNN, faster RCNN, FSAF, and DCN	Wrist X-rays datasets from Gazi University Hospital
[84]	Mask R-CNN	Lesion detection	Lesion detection, segmentation and tagging using multitask universal lesion analysis network	DeepLesion
[85]	CNN	Giga-pixel histopathology image analysis	CNN-based neural image compression	TUPAC16, Camelyon16 Histopathology
[86]	CNN	Lung and breast lesion detection	Object detection and segmentation using Retina U-Net architecture	LIDC-IDRI and DWI
[87]	ANN and kernel KMC	Kidney stone detection and Segmentation	Combination of cluster and classification for detection and segmentation of kidney disease	Ultrasound images of 100 patients
[88]	CNN-SVM	Chronic kidney disease	A CNN learning network and a sensing module has been used to detect CKD non- invasively from saliva samples	Saliva samples
[89]	CNN	Kidney stone diagnosis	CNN with data augmentation and context specific optimization algorithm	CT Kidney Dataset

(Continued)

Table 12.2 Deep learning architectures in various medical image recognition applications. (*Continued*)

References	Architecture	Application	Technique	Dataset
[90]	KNN and ANN	Parkinson's disease identification	ANN and KNN algorithms have been utilized for distinguishing between Parkinson's patient and healthy individual by voice disorder	Parkinson's UI machine learning dataset
[91]	ANN, KMC	Diagnosis system for Parkinson's disease	k-means clustering based feature weighting and complex valued ANN	Parkinson's dataset
[92]	CNN, LSTM	COVID-19 disease detection	An ensemble model composed of Xception, NasNetMobile, and MobileNetV2	Mixed dataset
[93]	CNN+SVM	Automatic diagnosis of Alzheimer's disease and mild cognitive impairment	3D CNN for feature extraction and SVM for classification	F-FDG PET:PET
[94]	SVM, DT, ANN, and LR	Predict diabetic retinopathy and identify interpretable	Decision trees, logistic regression, ANNs, and SVM have been incorporated to predict diabetic retinopathy	Privately owned
[95]	LR and ANN	Hypertension	Integration of LR and ANNs has been presented to predict chronic disease	BRFSS
[96]	Skin disease, lesion, gastrointestinal image	CNN	Multi-Dimensional U-Convolutional Neural Network (MDU-CNN) with encoder- decoder convolutional path	BraTS2020 ISIC2020 EndoSLAM

Epilepsy, a nervous disorder, affects millions of lives annually due to the occurrence of recurrent seizures that can lead to violent behaviour, strange ambiances, contraction of muscles, and unconsciousness. DL-based techniques proved a boon for the automatic prediction of epileptic seizures. Singh *et al.* [54] presented CNN-based technique with spectral-band features for predicting epileptic seizures. In the proposed method, the first

23-channel EEG signal was pre-processed and filtered for de-noising and then using fast Fourier transform (FFT) this short duration segmented EEG signal was converted to frequency domain for describing different seizure states based on the interpretation of EEG patterns. Mean amplitude features and spectral power are extracted from the spectral bands used in this study, which are further used by the CNN architecture for the prediction of seizures. Zhou *et al.* [55] proposed an architecture based on the inception network that integrates a data pre-processing method with a residual-based inception and hybrid-attention network (RIHANet). This approach combines empirical mode decomposition (EMD) and short-time Fourier transform (STFT) techniques to effectively extract and characterize features for detecting epileptic seizures in both the time and frequency domains. First the EEG signal at various scales is extracted and then transformed to create image spectrum with Fourier transform and finally multidimensional relationships is extracted through hybrid attention network.

Some literature related to DNN utilization in detection of various diseases such as heart disease, skin lesion, diabetes, breast cancer, kidney stone, hypertension, Parkinson's, brain tumor, COVID-19, and Alzheimer's are provided in Table 12.2.

iv. Image Enhancement

High-quality images are sought to provide more details for accurate and useful information or references for medical diagnoses. Image enhancement is the technique of improving digital photographs using features such as noise reduction, super-resolution, contrast enhancement, and deblurring to make them more suited to display or further analyze the images [56].

Super-resolution (SR) image reconstruction is a potential approach that utilizes signal processing methods to produce images with high resolution (HR) from images having low resolution (LR) as illustrated in Figure 12.9. To create an HR image from LR versions, it integrates de-noising, de-blurring, and scaling-up techniques [57]. SR is classified into two types based on the input images: multi-frame image SR (MISR) and single image SR (SISR) [58]. The traditional MISR requires a collection of LR images captured from the same scene with their displacement information. This strategy, however, is restricted to a minor enhancement in resolution. DL-based SISR approaches have been demonstrated to be more exact and quicker than traditional multi-frame SR techniques, therefore attracting the attention of researchers.

CNN for 2D-SR reconstruction was first proposed and improved by Dong *et al.* [59–61]. However, the technique was limited to small image

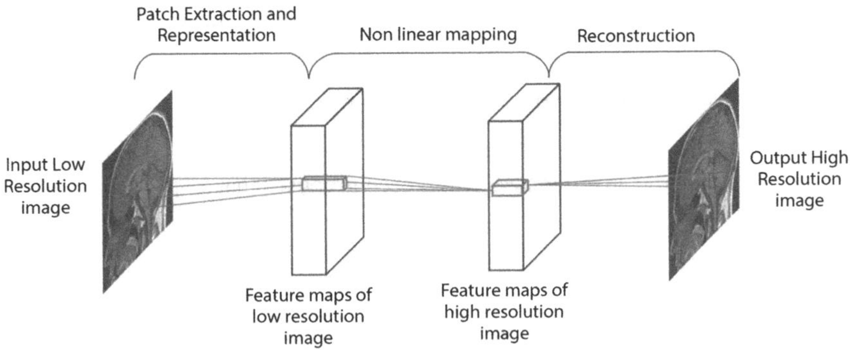

Figure 12.9 Image super resolution.

regions, converged too slowly due to low learning rate requirements, and only worked on a single scale. To address these concerns, a new CNN-based very deep SR (VDSR) network has been proposed by Kim *et al.* [62], which employed a very deep CNN based on Simonyan and Zisserman architecture [22]. Similar to SRCNN, this network predicted image features from an input that is an interpolated LR image. Shi *et al.* [63] presented efficient sub-pixel CNN (ESPCN) to upscale LR images by just raising the resolution from LR to HR at the last layer of the network and to recover HR data from LR feature maps [60, 64, 65]. Because of the reduced input resolution, smaller filters can carry the same amount of information while retaining a certain required area. Furthermore, resolution and filter size reduction decrease the memory requirements and computational complexity that allows real-time SR processing of high-definition images.

Deeper networks perform well in SR due to utilization of a larger receptive field; capturing additional information from low-quality images allows them to anticipate information in HR space. Tong *et al.* [131] developed Dense Skip Connections–based CNN for SR that employs dense connected CNNs. It provided benefits such as elimination of gradient vanishing, the ability to reuse feature maps from prior layers, the integration of low-level and high-level features to offer richer information for SR reconstruction, and the addition of deconvolution layers to recover the image details and accelerate the reconstruction process. Previous SR experiments, however, have failed to adequately leverage the information of each convolutional layer because the local convolutional layers lack direct connection to the succeeding layers.

Zhang *et al.* presented the dense ResNet, which utilized all of the hierarchical attributes from the low-quality image to produce global dense

Table 12.3 Deep learning architectures in various medical image enhancement applications.

References	Architecture	Application	Technique	Dataset
[97]	CNN	CT-Chest images	SRCNN architecture has been proposed that enhanced CT-chest images from low resolution image	The Cancer Imaging Archive
[98]	CNN	CT-Brain images	UNet-based architecture for solving super resolution and denoising problem has been presented	PET/CT dataset
[99]	GAN	CT and MRI images	SRGAN to create DL-based approach to obtain HR volumetric scans from LR data	Privately owned dataset
[100]	GAN	CT images	To solve CT SR problem, GAN- CIRCLE has been created using two GAN networks having deep CNN, residual learning, and network in network method for feature extraction and restoration	Tibia dataset Abdominal dataset
[101]	CNN	2D MRI	SRCNN has been extended utilizing multi-scale global and local residual learning network to get high-frequency details	Brainweb database, ALVIN dataset, BRATS dataset

(Continued)

Table 12.3 Deep learning architectures in various medical image enhancement applications. (*Continued*)

References	Architecture	Application	Technique	Dataset
[102]	CNN	2D/3D MRI	Channel splitting network with SRCNN extended to take advantage of DenseNet and residual learning for enhancing the reuse of features and network stabilization	IXI dataset
[103]	GAN	Retinal vascular images	Salient map for quantifying pixel's perceptual relevance has been integrated with GAN to minimize weighted mean square error between predicted and ground truth images, MSE-based ResNet utilized in generator	Retinal fundus images
[104]	CNN	Cardiac images	3D residual network has been used while replacing the interpolation operation by deconvolution layer in initial layers	Cine cardiac MR images
[105]	CNN, LSTM	CT-Chest images	Multiscale guided-learning dense residual block (MGLDB) with dilated convolution, CNN and LSTM based attention mechanism, fuzzy uncertainty measurement rule to characterize the fuzzy uncertainty of the pixels and recursive sub-pixel reconstruction module for image reconstruction	COVID-CT

features [66]. SRCNN was originally created for 2D image processing; these networks operate slice-by-slice rather than using continuous structures in 3D, which is more suitable for biomedical applications. Chen *et al.* introduced 3D densely connected SR networks (DCSRN) and demonstrated that advanced network topologies with skip connections and layer recycling improve the performance, speed, and training time [67]. He *et al.* [68] presented HQG-Net in which high-quality cues are extracted from ground truth images and utilized to guide lowquality images for image enhancement. To improve the visual fidelity of the enhanced results and effective downstream performance a bi-level optimization (BLO) cooperative training strategy was utilized. The application of various DL-based image enhancement techniques in medical images is provided in Table 12.3.

12.4 Recent Trends in Hardware Architectures of DNN

This section discusses various emerging memory technologies to be utilized in the crossbar of processing in memory (PIM) architecture for the reduction of data latency, movements, and energy consumption. Different convolution and optimization strategies for hardware architectures for CNN and GAN will also be discussed. Conventional von Neumann architecture suffers from memory-bound bottlenecks for advanced applications like CNNs. This high latency data transfer utilizing off-chip memory is also termed as memory or speed wall problem. The possible way to overcome this problem is through keeping memory near to processing unit. Therefore, performing computations near or inside memory can avoid the von Neumann bottleneck.

In the modern memory hierarchy of processors, static random access memory (SRAM) is widely employed as on-chip cache and register file volatile storage device. SRAM technology can achieve limited endurance, high energy efficiency, and low latency; therefore, conventional SRAM-PIM can be used to design and implement a wide variety of neural networks at the hardware level through hardware implementation. Low integration density, high leakage power dissipation, and noticeably large area consumption are problems faced by the different approaches of analogue as well as digital CMOS-based neural network implementation. Therefore, there is a need to explore PIM architectures with emerging memory technologies.

i. Emerging Memory Technologies for Crossbar Design of PIM Architecture

The growth in emerging memory technologies offers the potential to store larger amounts of data at a reduced cost compared to the costly silicon chips utilized in edge devices. These cutting-edge technologies such as resistive RAM (ReRAM), phase change RAM (PCRAM), and magnetic RAM (MRAMs) have the potential to serve as viable alternatives to traditional memories in upcoming computing systems.

- ReRAM, a two-terminal device implemented by creating both conducting and non- conducting paths between two metal electrodes using oxide molecules to store bits [69]. A metal/insulator/metal (MIM) stack that functions as a resistive switch with top and bottom electrodes is the base of ReRAM as shown in Figure 12.10(a). ReRAM device suffers low write endurance and suboptimal read/write performance for the applications based on low-power.
- PCRAM operates by transitioning between crystalline and amorphous phases for storing binary bits but this process demands a substantial quantity of drive current during the change of phase. The material of PCRAM provides high resistance in the amorphous phase and low in the crystalline phase. PCRAM gives higher performance when fast write operation is required but it has a limited lifetime due to thermal expansion during programming, and metal migration.
- MRAM operates on the principle of spin and stores the information in the form of a magnetic moment. MRAM possesses various advantages, including non-volatility, excellent writing endurance, small form factor, very low leakage current,

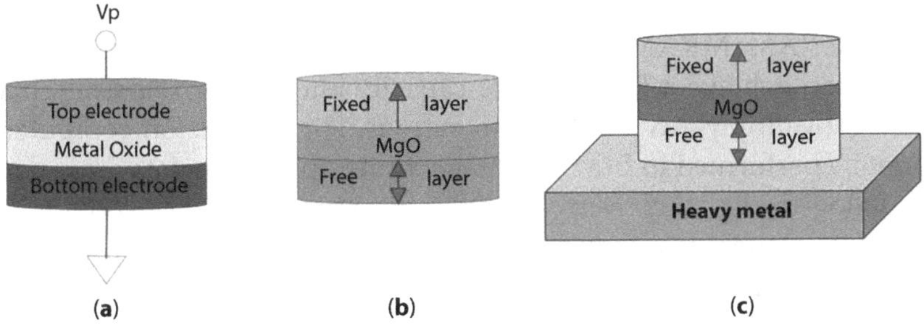

Figure 12.10 Structure of (a) ReRAM, (b) STT-MRAM, and (c) SOT-MRAM.

> and providing compatibility with CMOS technology, but it faces limitations in terms of speed compared to its conventional counterpart, SRAM. To address these challenges, researchers and industries have proposed novel switching mechanisms like spin transfer torque (STT), and spin-orbit torque (SOT). In STT-MRAM, current passed through a thin magnetic layer creates the spin-polarized current, flips the spin of the electrons as shown in Figure 12.10(b). STT-MRAM has the same read and write path and needs a large electrical current for high-speed write operation that creates high-stress conditions on tunnel junctions [70]. SOT-MRAM is a three-terminal non-volatile storage device with a free layer placed on top of the heavy metal strip, as shown in Figure 12.10(c) with an ability of ultrafast magnetization switching that leads to higher spin-torque efficiency. SOT-MRAM provides better durability due to isolated read and write operations [71].

PIM-based architectures combine memory arrays with arithmetic units for performing in- location data storage and processing to reduce data latency, movements, and energy consumption. PIM architecture comprises an interconnect network, input and output buffers, local and global memory, processing elements (PEs) containing emerging devices crossbars, control logic, and a memory hierarchy as shown in Figure 12.11. PE operations and dataflow are controlled by the control logic, weight mapping is handled by the CPU [72]. Crossbar array is a cutting-edge architecture for high-density, low-power memory and computation systems.

Crossbar arrays that incorporate various emerging non-volatile memory technologies, including PCRAM, ReRAM, and MRAM devices, have been shown to have a great deal of potential for enabling advanced functionalities and enhancing performance. Potential candidates for the processing in memory (PIM) implementation are emerging memory devices such as ReRAM, MRAM, and PCRAM. Due to their compact nature, these devices can achieve a high storage capacity and enable massively parallel MAC (Multiply-Accumulate) operations. High-precision computation cannot be performed in PIM due to the limited precision data array device and analog-to-digital converter (ADC)/digital-to-analog converter (DAC) used. Hence, there is a requirement for low-precision model of DNN for PIM before implementation.

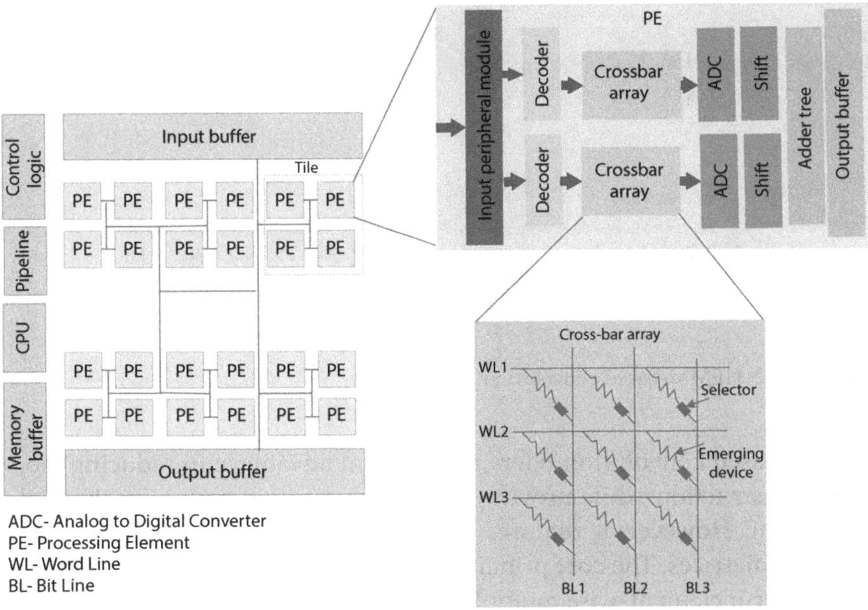

Figure 12.11 PIM-based architecture with emerging devices in crossbar array of processing element.

ii. Architectures for Convolutional Neural Networks

Implementation of DL algorithms on CPUs is executed by sequential operations that make them unsuitable for high-performance applications. GPUs on the other hand, have thousands of cores running in parallel, processing multiple operations simultaneously, making them a suitable choice for CNN implementation. However, one of the main challenges in GPUs is their high power dissipation. FPGAs and ASICs on the other hand, are more energy efficient while achieving high throughput. Compared to ASIC, FPGA-based design offers a higher level of re-configurability, lower cost, and faster deployment, making it an excellent alternative.

Architectural modifications such as pruning [73], reduced precision computing [74], loop optimization [75], pipelining, and algorithmic optimizations including winograd, and FFT [76] are used to increase the throughput and simultaneously reduce memory bandwidth for CNN implementation on FPGAs and ASICs.

One of the earliest ways of optimizing the convolution layer is by transforming direct convolution into a matrix-matrix multiplication operation that is known as general matrix multiplication (GEMM) based convolution. GEMM-based convolution is illustrated in Figure 12.12.

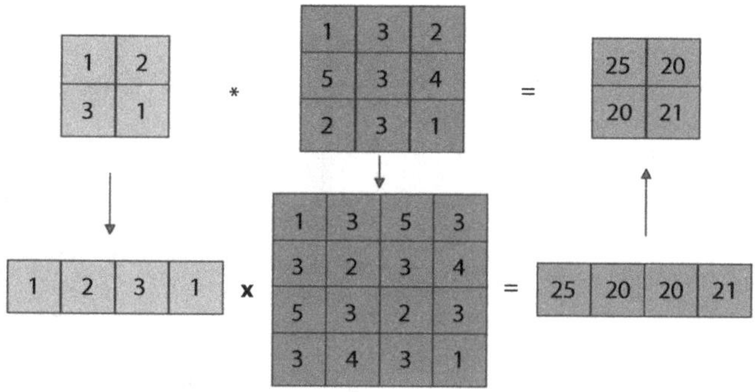

Figure 12.12 GEMM-based convolution.

GEMM-based convolution offers a significant advantage in reducing loop control instruction while proving an opportunity for exploiting the high parallelism. However, it requires large temporal memory to store large, reshaped matrices. The core principle behind winograd-based convolution is to perform element-wise multiplications while taking advantage of overlapping computations between adjacent windows to reduce the number of FP multiplication operations at the cost of extra additions and memory bandwidth [74]. For smaller kernels, winograd is very efficient. However, it requires filter size-dependent specialized processing, making it a less generalized approach.

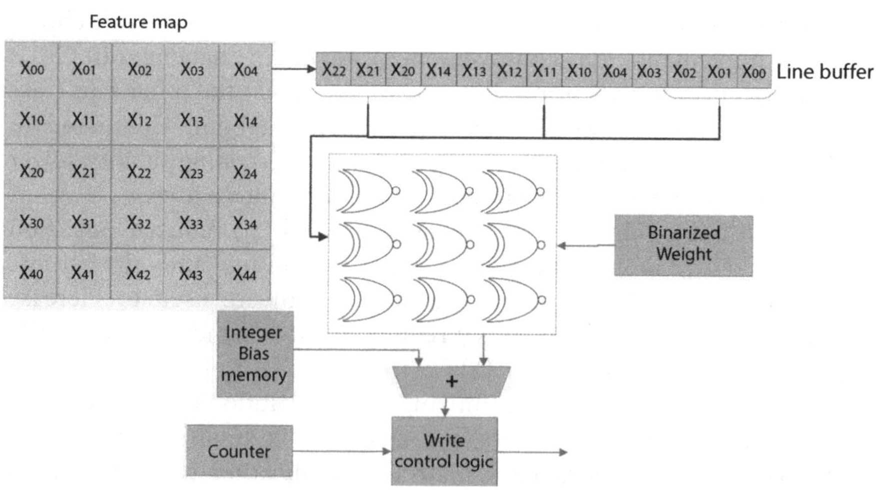

Figure 12.13 Binarized CNN architecture performing XNOR operation.

PIM-based architecture for binarized CNNs (BCNNs) has been proposed by Pham *et al.* [77] that used a low-bit level memristive device along with lower precision of ADC/DAC resulting in faster and energy-efficient operations. Compute-intensive multiplications were replaced by XNOR operations as shown in Figure 12.13. Table 12.4 provides different hardware architectures with potential applications that have been explored in the literature for CNNs.

Table 12.4 Hardware architectures for convolutional neural networks.

Platform	References	Convolution strategy	Optimization techniques	Potential applications
FPGA	[75]	Direct convolution	Pipelining, Unrolling, Data reuse, Loop reordering, Tiling	Brain tumor classification and detection using faster RCNN [37]
	[118]	Winograd	Systolic array architecture, Pipelining, Unrolling, Data reuse, Batching	Two-layer convolution network with fully connected layer as classifier [37]
	[119]	GEMM, Depthwise separable convolution	Unrolling, multi-layer Pipelining, Data reusing	CNN centered neural image compression [85]
ASIC	[10]	GEMM	Systolic array architecture, Pipelining, Unrolling, Data reuse	Lesion detection, segmentation, and tagging using multitask universal lesion analysis network [84]
	[120]	Direct convolution	Unrolling, Data reuse, pipelining	Chest X-Ray classification by ResNet networks [121]

(*Continued*)

Table 12.4 Hardware architectures for convolutional neural networks. (*Continued*)

Platform	References	Convolution strategy	Optimization techniques	Potential applications
	[77]	Direct convolution	Sparsity aware mesh network for weights, Unrolling, Data reuse, pipelining	Malignant melanoma skin Cancer detection using pre-trained Alexnet [35]
PIM	[122]	GEMM	Quantization, Unrolling, Data reuse, pipelining	Diagnosis of X-Rays for detection of factures using several object detection networks [83]
	[121]	GEMM	Sparsity aware PEs, Quantization, Unrolling, Data reuse, pipelining	Lightweight networks such as Xception, MobileNetV2 for COVID-19 detection [92]

iii. Architectures for GANs

Accelerating GANs presents additional constraints in hardware architecture for bandwidth requirements as compared to traditional CNN accelerators. Previously presented CNN accelerators can be utilized for accelerating discriminators however, the generator network uses upscaling or deconvolution layers that have significantly different operations. Furthermore, irregular data dependency involved in GANs results in the requirement of higher bandwidth. DeConv operation performs upscaling of input feature maps by addition of zeros or nearest neighbor (NN) based approach that requires a huge number of redundant operations or repetitive multiplications. Zero insertion and NN-based upscaling approach have been shown in Figure 12.14. Accelerators for GANs should be generic that can accelerate both the discriminator as well as generator network.

Optimization schemes like Zero skipping/removal, transforming DeConv into Conv (TDC), reverse looping, Fermat number transform

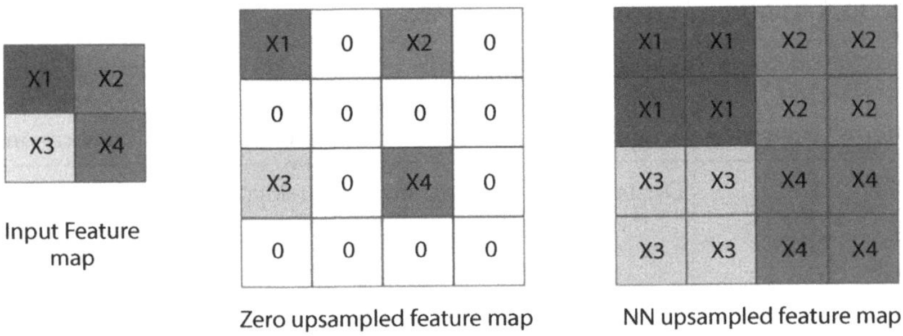

Figure 12.14 Zero insertion and NN based upscaling approaches.

(FNT), kernel-based operations like decomposition and conversion are implemented to accelerate DeConv operations. Zero skipping or removal focuses on dividing the DeConv operation into several computational modes that feed respective inputs to PEs skipping zero entries [78]. This can increase data reuse and facilitate parallel execution. Another method to avoid this overlapping summation issue was proposed by Chang *et al.* [79] by transforming deconvolution operation into sparse convolution known as TDC. Dimensions of IFM are determined to generate output blocks in parallel that do not overlap.

NN-based approaches have been alternatively studied as a replacement for zero insertion-based upscaling by Yu *et al.* [80]. As the up-sampled feature map is dense, avoiding the zero-related computation is not feasible. However, by leveraging repeated patterns among inputs, we can combine computations and reduce the overall number of operations. Kernel conversion pre-adds the weights for generating dilated kernel to eliminate the up-sampling process to reduce computational requirements. Table 12.5 give an overview of different hardware architecture for GANs and their potential applications.

12.5 Challenges and Opportunities

The deployment of DL algorithms in the healthcare and medical field shows potential for improving and predicting a patient's prognosis based on available data. Despite DL advantages in the biomedical and healthcare domains, there are still certain difficulties and issues to be addressed. This section outlines a few of the difficulties that come with putting DL approaches into the biomedical domain.

Table 12.5 Hardware architectures for GANs.

Platform	References	Algorithm for upscaling	Proposed architectures for layers	Optimization techniques	Potential applications
FPGA	[78]	DeConv	Conv-DeConv	Zero skipping	Enhancing CT Brain images by UNet architectures [98]
	[79]	DeConv	Conv-DeConv	TDC, Kernel decomposition	Implementing SRGAN for obtaining high resolution images of CT and MRI [99]
	[80]	NN-TConv	Conv-NN-DeConv	Kernel Conversion	GAN-based SR architecture using NN interpolation for 3D MRI images [123]
	[124]	Dilated Conv	DeConv-Dilated Conv	TDC, Kernel decomposition	SR in retinal vascular images by GANs [103]
	[125]	DeConv	Conv-DeConv	TDC, Kernel decomposition	Enhancing CT Chest images by SRCNN [97]
ASIC	[126]	DeConv	Conv-Deconv	FNT	Liver lesion detection by enhancing the images for classification [34]
	[127]	DeConv	Conv-Deconv	Kernel conversion	CT image enhancement by GAN-Circle [99]

(Continued)

Table 12.5 Hardware architectures for GANs. (*Continued*)

Platform	References	Algorithm for upscaling	Proposed architectures for layers	Optimization techniques	Potential applications
	[128]	DeConv	DeConv	Zero skipping	Breast cancer detection by realistic lesions in a multi-scale class-conditional GAN [129]
PIM	[130]	DeConv	Conv-DeConv	Zero skipping	Enhancing CT Brain images by UNet architectures. [73]

- Data privacy of patients: DL datasets contain sensitive information of patients that can be misused and are vulnerable to attack. Techniques that allow for training of architectures without disclosing the raw data are required and it may be necessary to train models using a differential privacy framework frequently. A challenge that must be taken into account in the implementation of DL in biomedical is finding ways to make full use of the benefits of big data to boost the growth of DL while protecting patients' private data.
- Data heterogeneity: The data available in the medical field are extremely diverse having both structured and unstructured data. Patients' height, weight, blood pressure, glucose level, lab test results, and, demographic information come under the category of structured data while discharge summary, medical images, and, clinical notes are unstructured data. The data in the healthcare industry are also unreliable, multidimensional, low quality, and noisy. Implementing and training a DL model that works well is challenging due to the existence of this heterogeneous data.
- Choice of model and hardware: Due to the significant impact of data types on algorithm performance, discovering an optimal algorithm for a specific type of medical image analysis

is a challenging task. Similarly, the hardware requirements vary based on the particular problem being addressed.
- Requirement of expert opinion: The task of manual inspection and comprehension of the features generated by algorithms must be undertaken by physicians, which can be both costly and time-consuming. Consequently, many research studies avoid expert review due to the associated expenses.
- Need for Associations: Effective collaboration among physicians, radiologists, medical image analysts, and computational data analysts plays an important role in enhancing the efficiency of the healthcare system. It also enables the system to address challenges such as chronic diseases, data scarcity, and knowledge gaps.
- Acceptability among health professionals: DL algorithms have proven to be a valuable solution for previously unsolved problems, but their acceptance and recognition among medical professionals remain a topic of ongoing debate due to the challenge of comprehending how the DL model generates its output.

In summary, DL is a wide-open area where researchers can contribute by creating a novel DL training approach. Wearable and edge devices capture multiple vital signals continuously and simultaneously. For accurate classification and analysis of these vital signals, future studies should require a single universal DL approach that might meet many vital signal categories. Employing this approach can save the amount of time and work that would otherwise be needed to develop methods for individual signal classification and analysis. Furthermore, it is imperative for each country to formulate strategies for governing the utilization of AI.

12.6 Summary

DL-based algorithms have improved the quality of the life cycle for individuals and medical practitioners due to its ability to handle large amounts of sensitive data for giving immediate prognosis. This chapter initially discusses applications of DL algorithm for disease classification, localization or segmentation of biomedical images. Furthermore, dedicated FPGA, ASIC, and PIM-based hardware architectures have been discussed for accelerating the workload that provides higher power and area efficiency than traditional CPU or GPU-based architectures. Designing efficient hardware can have a huge impact on the healthcare industry not just by delivering effective prognosis to end users but also by improving the performance of algorithms with additional data acquired from users.

The growing number of interconnected wearable edge devices are generating huge amounts of data that can be used for specific tuning of algorithms. However, current edge device hardware is not capable of performing on-device training. Designing power, area, and computationally efficient architectures for training is one of the major research gaps that has been observed. PIM-based training architectures can provide a balance between performance and power by overcoming memory bottlenecks. Secondly, GANs have evolved in recent years by improvised learning algorithms and loss functions. Cooperating with these rapid changes in GAN learning algorithms on hardware would require shifting the focus on designing tools, frameworks, and reconfigurable hardware to reduce time to market. Thirdly, the privacy of the user is of extreme importance when dealing with their sensitive medical data. The DL algorithms can be susceptible to adversarial attacks causing failure of diagnosis and prognosis adversely affecting users' health. Detailed analysis of the attacks with their preventive strategies must be done beforehand. Finally, using DL algorithms to tune the algorithms as well as architecture can reduce a significant amount of manual intervention and also reduce time to market. The exploration of AI for the development of efficient hardware will become a leading focus of research in the upcoming years.

Acknowledgements

One of the authors, Amit Monga, acknowledges iHUB DivyaSampark, Indian Institute of Technology Roorkee, India, for providing the necessary support to complete this chapter.

References

1. Bolhasani, H., Mohseni, M., Rahmani, A.M., Deep learning applications for IoT in health care: A systematic review. *Inf. Med. Unlocked*, 23, 100550, 2021, doi: 10.1016/j.imu.2021.100550.
2. Jindal, V., Integrating mobile and cloud for PPG signal selection to monitor heart rate during intensive physical exercise, in: *Proceedings of the International Conference on Mobile Software Engineering and Systems*, Austin, USA, May 2016, pp. 36–37, doi: 10.1145/2897073.2897132.

3. Sundaravadivel, P., Kesavan, K., Kesavan, L., Mohanty, S.P., Kougianos, E., Smart-Log: A deep-learning based automated nutrition monitoring system in the IoT. *IEEE Trans. Consum. Electron.*, 64, 3, 390–398, 2018, doi: 10.1109/tce.2018.2867802.
4. Shi, B., Grimm, L.J., Mazurowski, M.A., Baker, J.A., Marks, J.R., King, L.M., Maley, C.C., Hwang, E.S., Lo, J.Y., Prediction of occult invasive disease in ductal carcinoma *in situ* using deep learning features. *J. Am. Coll. Radiol.*, 15, 527–534, 2018, doi: 10.1016/j.jacr.2017.11.036.
5. Liu, X., *et al.*, A comparison of deep learning performance against health-care professionals in detecting diseases from medical imaging: A systematic review and meta-analysis. *Lancet Digit. Health*, 1, e271–e297, 2019, doi: 10.1016/s2589-7500(19)30123-2.
6. Liu, F., Yadav, P., Baschnagel, A.M., McMillan, A.B., MR-based treatment planning in radiation therapy using a deep learning approach. *J. Appl. Clin. Med. Phys.*, 20, 3, 105–114, 2019, doi: 10.1002/acm2.12554.
7. Zhu, W., Xie, L., Han, J., Guo, X., The application of deep learning in cancer prognosis prediction. *Cancers*, 12, 603, 2020, doi: 10.3390/cancers12030603.
8. Artificial intelligence in healthcare market, Jan. 2023, Accessed: Aug. 16, 2023. [Online]. Available: https://www.marketsandmarkets.com/Market-Reports/artificial-intelligence-healthcare-market- 54679303.html.
9. Kalaiselvi, T., Sriramakrishnan, P., Somasundaram, K., Survey of using GPU CUDA programming model in medical image analysis. *Inf. Med. Unlocked*, 9, 133–144, 2017, doi: 10.1016/j.imu.2017.08.001.
10. Jouppi, N.P., *et al.*, In-datacenter performance analysis of a tensor processing unit, in: *Proceedings of the International Symposium on Computer Architecture*, Toronto, Canada, Jun. 2017, pp. 1–12, doi: 10.1145/3079856.3080246.
11. Yang, S., Zhu, F., Ling, X., Liu, Q., Zhao, P., Intelligent health care: applications of deep learning in computational medicine. *Front. Genet.*, 12, 607471, 2021, doi: 10.3389/fgene.2021.607471.
12. Christensen, D.V., *et al.*, 2022 roadmap on neuromorphic computing and engineering. *Neuromorph. Comput. Eng.*, 2, 022501, 2022, doi: 10.1088/2634-4386/ac4a83.
13. Zemouri, R., Zerhouni, N., Racoceanu, D., Deep learning in the biomedical applications: recent and future status. *Appl. Sci.*, 9, 1526, 2019, doi: 10.3390/app9081526.
14. Hartmann, M., Hashmi, U.S., Imran, A., Edge computing in smart health care systems: review, challenges, and research directions. *Trans. Emerging Telecommun. Technol.*, 33, e3710, 2019, doi: 10.1002/ett.3710.
15. Reuther, A., Michaleas, P., Jones, M., Gadepally, V., Samsi, S., Kepner, J., Survey of machine learning accelerators, in: *Proceedings of the 2020 IEEE High Performance Extreme Computing Conference*, Boston, USA, Sep. 2020, pp. 1–9, doi: 10.1109/hpec43674.2020.9286149.
16. Wess, M., Manoj, P.D.S., Jantsch, A., Neural network based ECG anomaly detection on FPGA and trade-off analysis, in: *Proceedings of IEEE*

International Symposium on Circuits and Systems, Baltimore, MD, USA, May 2017, pp. 1–4, doi: 10.1109/iscas.2017.8050805.
17. Shrivastwa, R.R., Pudi, V., Chattopadhyay, A., An FPGA-based brain computer interfacing using compressive sensing and machine learning, in: *Proceedings of the IEEE Computer Society Annual Symposium on VLSI*, IEEE, Hong Kong, China, pp. 726–731, 2018, doi: 10.1109/isvlsi.2018.00137.
18. Bolhasani, H., Jassbi, S.J., Sharifi, A., DLA-E: A deep learning accelerator for endoscopic images classification. *J. Big Data*, 10, 1, 2023, doi: 10.1186/s40537-023-00775-8.
19. Agatonovic-Kustrin, S. and Beresford, R., Basic concepts of artificial neural network (ANN) modeling and its application in pharmaceutical research. *J. Pharm. Biomed. Anal.*, 22, 717–727, 2000, doi: 10.1016/s0731-7085(99)00272-1.
20. Yamashita, R., Nishio, M., Do, R.K.G., Togashi, K., Convolutional neural networks: an overview and application in radiology. *Insights into Imaging*, 9, 611–629, 2018, doi: https://doi.org/10.1007/s13244-018-0639-9.
21. Krizhevsky, A., Sutskever, I., Hinton, G.E., ImageNet classification with deep convolutional neural networks, in: *Proceedings of the Neural Information Processing Systems*, pp. 1106–14, 2012, doi: https://doi.org/10.1145/3065386.
22. Simonyan, K. and Zisserman, A., Very deep convolutional networks for large-scale image recognition, in: *Proceedings of 3rd International Conference on Learning Representations*, pp. 1–14, 2015.
23. Szegedy, C., Liu, W., Jia, Y., Sermanet, P., Reed, S., Anguelov, D., Erhan, D., Vanhoucke, V., Rabinovich, A., Going deeper with convolutions, in: *Proceedings of IEEE Computer Society Conference on Computer Vision and Pattern Recognition*, Jun. 2015, pp. 1–9, doi: 10.1109/cvpr.2015.7298594.
24. He, K., Zhang, X., Ren, S., Sun, J., Deep residual learning for image recognition, in: *Proceedings of IEEE Computer Society Conference on Computer Vision and Pattern Recognition*, Dec. 2016, pp. 770–778, doi: 10.1109/cvpr.2016.90.
25. Schuster, M. and Paliwal, K.K., Bidirectional recurrent neural networks. *IEEE Trans. Signal Process.*, 45, 11, 2673–2681, 1997, doi: 10.1109/78.650093.
26. Gers, F.A., Schraudolph, N.N., Schmidhuber, J., Learning precise timing with LSTM recurrent networks. *J. Mach. Learn. Res.*, 3, 115–143, 2003, doi: 10.1162/153244303768966139.
27. Zhai, J., Zhang, S., Chen, J., He, Q., Autoencoder and its various variants, in: *Proceedings of IEEE International Conference on Systems, Man, and Cybernetics, SMC 2018*, Miyazaki, Japan, Oct. 2019, pp. 415–419, doi: 10.1109/smc.2018.00080.
28. Li, C., Xu, K., Zhu, J., Zhang, B., Generative adversarial nets, in: *Proceedings of the Advances in Neural Information Processing Systems*, Montreal, Canada, Dec. 2017, pp. 4089–4099.
29. Zhang, X., Zou, Y., Shi, W., Dilated convolution neural network with leaky relu for environmental sound classification, in: *Proceedings of the International*

Conference on Digital Signal Processing, London, UK, Aug. 2017, pp. 1–5, doi: 10.1109/icdsp.2017.8096153.
30. Chollet, F., Xception: Deep learning with depthwise separable convolutions, in: *Proceedings of the IEEE Conference on Computer Vision and Pattern Recognition*, pp. 1251–1258, 2017, doi: 10.1109/cvpr.2017.195.
31. Xu, Y., Lin, L., Hu, H., Wang, D., Zhu, W., Wang, J., Han, X.H., Chen, Y.W., Texture-specific bag of visual words model and spatial cone matching-based method for the retrieval of focal liver lesions using multiphase contrast-enhanced CT images. *Int. J. Comput. Assisted Radiol. Surg.*, 13, 151–164, 2018, doi: 10.1007/s11548-017-1671-9.
32. Alzubaidi, L., Fadhel, M.A., Al-Shamma, O., Zhang, J., Santamaría, J., Duan, Y., Robust application of new deep learning tools: an experimental study in medical imaging. *Multimedia Tools Appl.*, 81, 13289–13317, 2022, doi: 10.1007/s11042-021-10942-9.
33. Guan, Q., Huang, Y., Zhong, Z., Zheng, Z., Zheng, L., Yang, Y., Thorax disease classification with attention guided convolutional neural network. *Pattern Recognit. Lett.*, 131, 38–45, 2020, doi: 10.1016/j.patrec.2019.11.040.
34. Frid-Adar, M., Klang, E., Amitai, M., Goldberger, J., Greenspan, H., Synthetic data augmentation using GAN for improved liver lesion classification, in: *Proceedings of the International Symposium on Biomedical Imaging*, pp. 289–293, 2018, doi: 10.1109/isbi.2018.8363576.
35. Mahbod, A., Schaefer, G., Ellinger, I., Ecker, R., Pitiot, A., Wang, C., Fusing fine-tuned deep features for skin lesion classification. *Comput. Med. Imaging Graphics*, 71, 19–29, 2019, doi: 10.1016/j.compmedimag.2018.10.007.
36. Liu, Q., Yu, L., Luo, L., Dou, Q., Heng, P.A., Semi-supervised medical image classification with relation-driven self-ensembling model. *IEEE Trans. Med. Imaging*, 39, 3429–3440, 2020, doi: 10.1109/tmi.2020.2995518.
37. Kaldera, H.N.T.K., Gunasekara, S.R., DIssanayake, M.B., Brain tumor classification and segmentation using faster R-CNN, in: *Proceedings of 2019 Advances in Science and Engineering Technology International Conferences*, Dubai, United Arab Emirates, Apr. 2019, doi: 10.1109/icaset.2019.8714263.
38. Abbas, Q., An intelligent medical image classification system using few-shot learning. *Concurrency Comput. Pract. Exper.*, 35, 2, 1–24, 2023, doi: 10.1002/cpe.7451.
39. Bharati, P. and Pramanik, A., Deep learning techniques- R-CNN to mask R-CNN: a survey, in: *Advances in Intelligent Systems and Computing*, pp. 657–668, 2020, doi: 10.1007/978-981-13-9042-5_56.
40. Ren, S., He, K., Girshick, R., Sun, J., Faster R-CNN: Towards real-time object detection with region proposal networks, in: *Proceedings of the Advances in Neural Information Processing Systems*, pp. 91–99, 2015, doi: 10.4324/9780080519340-12.
41. He, K., Gkioxari, G., Dollár, P., Girshick, R., Mask R-CNN. *IEEE Trans. Pattern Anal. Mach. Intell.*, 42, 2, 386–397, 2020, doi: 10.1109/TPAMI.2018.2844175.

42. Redmon, J., Divvala, S., Girshick, R., Farhadi, A., You only look once: unified, real-time object detection, in: *Proceedings of the IEEE Computer Society Conference on Computer Vision and Pattern Recognition*, Las Vegas, USA, Jun. 2016, pp. 779–788, doi: 10.1109/cvpr.2016.91.
43. Feshki, M.G. and Shijani, O.S., Improving the heart disease diagnosis by evolutionary algorithm of PSO and feed forward neural network, in: *Proceedings of 2016 Artificial Intelligence and Robotics*, Qazvin, Iran, Apr. 2016, pp. 48–53, doi: 10.1109/rios.2016.7529489.
44. Saikumar, K., Rajesh, V., Srivastava, G., Lin, J.C.W., Heart disease detection based on internet of things data using linear quadratic discriminant analysis and a deep graph convolutional neural network. *Front. Comput. Neurosci.*, 16, 1–15, 2022, doi: 10.3389/fncom.2022.964686.
45. Nurmaini, S., Rachmatullah, M.N., Sapitri, A.I., Darmawahyuni, A., Jovandy, A., Firdaus, F., Tutuko, B., Passarella, R., Accurate detection of septal defects with fetal ultrasonography images using deep learning-based multiclass instance segmentation. *IEEE Access*, 8, 196160–196174, 2020, doi: 10.1109/access.2020.3034367.
46. Xu, W., Wang, L., Wang, B., Cheng, W., Intelligent recognition algorithm of multiple myocardial infarction based on morphological feature extraction. *Processes*, 10, 11, 1–15, 2022, doi: 10.3390/pr10112348.
47. Khamparia, A., Saini, G., Pandey, B., Tiwari, S., Gupta, D., Khanna, A., KDSAE: chronic kidney disease classification with multimedia data learning using deep stacked autoencoder network. *Multimed. Tools Appl.*, 79, 35425–35440, 2020, doi: 10.1007/s11042-019-07839-z.
48. Ma, F., Sun, T., Liu, L., Jing, H., Detection and diagnosis of chronic kidney disease using deep learning-based heterogeneous modified artificial neural network. *Future Gener. Comput. Syst.*, 111, 17–26, 2020, doi: 10.1016/j.future.2020.04.036.
49. Bhaskar, N., Suchetha, M., Philip, N.Y., Time series classification-based correlational neural network with bidirectional LSTM for automated detection of kidney disease. *IEEE Sens. J.*, 21, 4811–4818, 2020, doi: 10.1109/jsen.2020.3028738.
50. Alshayeji, M.H., Ellethy, H., Abed, S., Gupta, R., Computer-aided detection of breast cancer on the Wisconsin dataset: an artificial neural networks approach. *Biomed. Signal Process. Control*, 71, 103141, 2022, doi: 10.1016/j.bspc.2021.103141.
51. Sultana, Z., Rahman Khan, M.A., Jahan, N., Early breast cancer detection utilizing artificial neural network. *WSEAS Trans. Biol. Biomed.*, 18, 32–42, 2021, doi: 10.37394/23208.2021.18.4.
52. Naz, H. and Ahuja, S., Deep learning approach for diabetes prediction using PIMA Indian dataset. *J. Diabetes Metab. Disord.*, 19, 391–403, 2020, doi: 10.1007/s40200-020-00520-5.
53. Yahyaoui, A., Jamil, A., Rasheed, J., Yesiltepe, M., A decision support system for diabetes prediction using machine learning and deep learning

techniques, in: *Proceedings of the International Informatics and Software Engineering Conference*, Ankara, Turkey, Nov. 2019, pp. 1–4, doi: 10.1109/ubmyk48245.2019.8965556.
54. Singh, K. and Malhotra, J., Predicting epileptic seizures from EEG spectral band features using convolutional neural network. *Wirel. Pers. Commun.*, 125, 3, 2667–2684, 2022, doi: 10.1007/s11277-022-09678-y.
55. Zhou, Q., Zhang, S., Du, Q., Ke, L., RIHANet: A residual-based inception with hybrid-attention network for seizure detection using EEG signals. *Comput. Biol. Med.*, 171, 2024, doi: 10.1016/j.compbiomed.2024.108086.
56. Elad, M. and Feuer, A., Restoration of a single super resolution image from several blurred, noisy, and under sampled measured images. *IEEE Trans. Image Process.*, 6, 12, 1646–1658, 1997, doi: 10.1109/83.650118.
57. Park, S.C., Park, M.K., Kang, M.G., Super-resolution image reconstruction: a technical overview. *IEEE Signal Process Mag.*, 20, 3, 21–36, 2003, doi: 10.1109/msp.2003.1203207.
58. Zhou, L. and Feng, S., A review of deep learning for single image super-resolution, in: *Proceedings of 4th International Conference on Intelligent Informatics and Biomedical Sciences*, Shanghai, China, Nov. 2019, pp. 139–142, doi: 10.1109/iciibmsS46890.2019.8991477.
59. Dong, C., Loy, C.C., He, K., Tang, X., Learning a deep convolutional network for image super-resolution, in: *Proceedings of the European Conference on Computer Vision*, Zurich, Switzerland, Sep. 2014, pp. 184–199, doi: 10.1007/978-3-319-10593-2_13.
60. Dong, C., Loy, C.C., He, K., Tang, X., Image super-resolution using deep convolutional networks. *IEEE Trans. Pattern Anal. Mach. Intell.*, 38, 2, 295–307, 2016, doi: 10.1109/tpami.2015.2439281.
61. Dong, C., Loy, C.C., Tang, X., Accelerating the super-resolution convolutional neural network, in: *Proceedings of the European Conference on Computer Vision*, Amsterdam, The Netherlands, Oct. 2016, pp. 391–407, doi: 10.1007/978-3-319-46475-6_25.
62. Kim, J., Lee, J.K., Lee, K.M., Accurate image super-resolution using very deep convolutional networks, in: *Proceedings of IEEE Computer Society Conference on Computer Vision and Pattern Recognition*, Las Vegas, USA, Jun. 2016, pp. 1646–1654, doi: 10.1109/cvpr.2016.182.
63. Shi, W., Caballero, J., Huszar, F., Totz, J., Aitken, A.P., Bishop, R., Rueckert, D., Wang, Z., Real-time single image and video super-resolution using an efficient sub-Pixel convolutional neural network, in: *Proceedings of the IEEE Computer Society Conference on Computer Vision and Pattern Recognition*, pp. 1874–1883, 2016, doi: 10.1109/cvpr.2016.207.
64. Wang, Z., Liu, D., Yang, J., Han, W., Huang, T., Deep networks for image super-resolution with sparse prior, in: *Proceedings of IEEE International Conference on Computer Vision*, Santiago, Chile, Dec. 2015, pp. 370–378, doi: 10.1109/iccv.2015.50.

65. Chen, Y. and Pock, T., Trainable nonlinear reaction diffusion: a flexible framework for fast and effective image restoration. *IEEE Trans. Pattern Anal. Mach. Intell.*, 39, 6, 1256–1272, 2017, doi: 10.1109/tpami.2016.2596743.
66. Zhang, Y., Tian, Y., Kong, Y., Zhong, B., Fu, Y., Residual dense network for image super-resolution, in: *Proceedings of IEEE Conference on Computer Vision and Pattern Recognition*, Salt Lake City, USA, Jun. 2018, pp. 2472–2481, doi: 10.1109/cvpr.2018.00262.
67. Chen, Y., Xie, Y., Zhou, Z., Shi, F., Christodoulou, A.G., Li, D., Brain MRI super resolution using 3D deep densely connected neural networks, in: *Proceedings of IEEE 15th International Symposium on Biomedical Imaging*, Washington DC, USA, Apr. 2018, pp. 1–4.
68. He, C., Li, K., Xu, G., Yan, J., Tang, L., Zhang, Y., Wang, Y., Li, X., HQG-Net: Unpaired medical image enhancement with high-quality guidance. *IEEE Trans. Neural Netw. Learn. Syst.*, 1–15, 2023, doi: 10.1109/tnnls.2023.3315307.
69. Kim, J., Kim, B., Kim, T.T.-H., *Processing-in-Memory for AI From Circuits to Systems*, 1st ed., Springer Cham, Switzerland, 2023, doi: 10.1007/978-3-030-98781-7.
70. Soni, S., Verma, G., Kaushik, B.K., Energy efficient ternary computation unit using differential spin Hall effect MRAM. *Semicond. Sci. Technol.*, 38, 025005, 2023, doi: 10.1088/1361-6641/acad95.
71. Shukla, A.K., Dhull, S., Nisar, A., Soni, S., Bindal, N., Kaushik, B.K., Novel Radiation Hardened SOT-MRAM Read Circuit for Multi-Node Upset Tolerance. *IEEE Open J. Nanotechnol.*, 3, 78–84, 2022, doi: 10.1109/ojnano.2022.3181040.
72. Wabnitz, M. and Gemmeke, T., Toolflow for the Algorithm-Hardware Co-Design of Memristive ANN Accelerators. *Mem. - Mater. Devices Circuits Syst.*, 5, 100066, 2023, doi: 10.1016/j.memori.2023.100066.
73. Zhou, S.C., Wang, Y.Z., Wen, H., He, Q.Y., Zou, Y.H., Balanced quantization: an effective and efficient approach to quantized neural networks. *J. Comput. Sci. Technol.*, 32, 4, 667–682, 2017, doi: 10.1007/s11390-017-1750-y.
74. Zhang, C. and Prasanna, V., Frequency domain acceleration of convolutional neural networks on CPU-FPGA shared memory system, in: *Proceedings of 2017 ACM/SIGDA International Symposium on Field-Programmable Gate Arrays*, California, USA, Feb. 2017, pp. 35–44, doi: 10.1145/3020078.3021727.
75. Ma, Y., Cao, Y., Vrudhula, S., Seo, J.S., Optimizing the convolution operation to accelerate deep neural networks on FPGA. *IEEE Trans. Very Large Scale Integr. VLSI Syst.*, 26, 7, 1354–1367, 2018, doi: 10.1109/tvlsi.2018.2815603.
76. Yepez, J. and Ko, S.B., Stride 2 1-D, 2-D, and 3-D Winograd for convolutional neural networks. *IEEE Trans. Very Large Scale Integr. VLSI Syst.*, 28, 4, 853–863, 2020, doi: 10.1109/tvlsi.2019.2961602.
77. Pham, T.N., Trinh, Q.K., Chang, I.J., Alioto, M., STT-BNN: a novel STT-MRAM in-memory computing macro for binary neural networks. *IEEE J. Emerging Sel. Top. Circuits Syst.*, 12, 2, 569–579, 2022, doi: 10.1109/jetcas.2022.3169759.

78. Song, M., Zhang, J., Chen, H., Li, T., Towards efficient microarchitectural design for accelerating unsupervised GAN-based deep learning, in: *Proceedings of the International Symposium on High-Performance Computer Architecture*, Vienna, Austria, Feb. 2018, pp. 66–77, doi: 10.1109/hpca.2018.00016.
79. Chang, J.W., Kang, K.W., Kang, S.J., An energy-efficient FPGA-based deconvolutional neural networks accelerator for single image super-resolution. *IEEE Trans. Circuits Syst. Video Technol.*, 30, 281–295, 2020, doi: 10.1109/tcsvt.2018.2888898.
80. Yu, Y., Zhao, T., Wang, M., Wang, K., He, L., Uni-OPU: an FPGA-based uniform accelerator for convolutional and transposed convolutional networks. *IEEE Trans. Very Large Scale Integr. VLSI Syst.*, 28, 7, 1545–1556, 2020, doi: 10.1109/tvlsi.2020.2995741.
81. Dhiman, G., Juneja, S., Viriyasitavat, W., Mohafez, H., Hadizadeh, M., Islam, M.A., El Bayoumy, I., Gulati, K., A novel machine-learning-based hybrid CNN model for tumor identification in medical image processing. *Sustainability*, 14, 1447, 1–13, 2022, doi: 10.3390/su14031447.
82. Yang, W., Si, Y., Wang, D., Guo, B., Automatic recognition of arrhythmia based on principal component analysis network and linear support vector machine. *Comput. Biol. Med.*, 101, 22–32, 2018, doi: 10.1016/j.compbiomed.2018.08.003.
83. Hardalaç, F., Uysal, F., Peker, O., Çiçeklidağ, M., Tolunay, T., Tokgöz, N., Kutbay, U., Demirciler, B., Mert, F., Fracture detection in wrist X-ray images using deep learning-based object detection models. *Sensors*, 22, 3, 1–30, 2022, doi: 10.3390/s22031285.
84. Yan, K., Tang, Y., Peng, Y., Sandfort, V., Bagheri, M., Lu, Z., Summers, R.M., MULAN: multitask universal lesion analysis network for joint lesion detection, tagging, and segmentation, in: *Proceedings of the International Conference on Medical Image Computing and Computer-Assisted Intervention 2019*, Shenzhen, China, Oct. 2019, pp. 194–202, doi: 10.1007/978-3-030-32226-7_22.
85. Tellez, D., Litjens, G., Van Der Laak, J., Ciompi, F., Neural image compression for gigapixel histopathology image analysis. *IEEE Trans. Pattern Anal. Mach. Intell.*, 43, 2, 567–578, 2021, doi: 10.1109/tpami.2019.2936841.
86. Jaeger, P.F., Kohl, S.A.A., Bickelhaupt, S., Isensee, F., Kuder, T.A., Schlemmer, H.-P., Maier-Hein, K.H., Retina U-Net: embarrassingly simple exploitation of segmentation supervision for medical object detection, in: *Proceedings of the Machine Learning Research Machine Learning for Health ML4H NeurIPS Workshop*, Vancouver, British Columbia, Canada, Apr. 2020, pp. 171–183.
87. Nithya, A., Appathurai, A., Venkatadri, N., Ramji, D.R., Anna Palagan, C., Kidney disease detection and segmentation using artificial neural network and multi-kernel k-means clustering for ultrasound images. *Measurement*, 149, 106952, 2020, doi: 10.1016/j.measurement.2019.106952.

88. Navaneeth, B. and Suchetha, M., A dynamic pooling based convolutional neural network approach to detect chronic kidney disease. *Biomed. Signal Process. Control*, 62, 102068, 2020, doi: 10.1016/j.bspc.2020.102068.
89. Liu, H. and Ghadimi, N., Hybrid convolutional neural network and flexible dwarf mongoose optimization algorithm for strong kidney stone diagnosis. *Biomed. Signal Process. Control*, 91, 106024, 2024, doi: 10.1016/j.bspc.2024.106024.
90. Asmae, O., Abdelhadi, R., Bouchaib, C., Sara, S., Tajeddine, K., Parkinson's disease identification using KNN and ANN algorithms based on voice disorder, in: *Proceedings of 2020 International Conference on Innovative Research in Applied Science, Engineering and Technology*, Meknes, Morocco, Apr. 2020, pp. 1–6, doi: 10.1109/iraset48871.2020.9092228.
91. Gürüler, H., A novel diagnosis system for Parkinson's disease using complex-valued artificial neural network with k-means clustering feature weighting method. *Neural Comput. Appl.*, 28, 1657–1666, 2017, doi: 10.1007/s00521-015-2142-2.
92. Wang, W., Liu, S., Xu, H., Deng, L., COVIDX-LwNet: a lightweight network ensemble model for the detection of COVID-19 based on chest X-ray images. *Sensors*, 22, 21, 8578, 2022, doi: 10.3390/s22218578.
93. Sun, M., Huang, Z., Guo, C., Automatic diagnosis of Alzheimer's disease and mild cognitive impairment based on CNN + SVM networks with end-to-end training, in: *Proceedings of 13th International Conference on Advanced Computational Intelligence*, Wanzhou, China, May 2021, doi: 10.1155/2021/9121770.
94. Tsao, H.Y., Chan, P.Y., Su, E.C.Y., Predicting diabetic retinopathy and identifying interpretable biomedical features using machine learning algorithms. *BMC Bioinf.*, 19, 111–121, 2018, doi: 10.1186/s12859-018-2277-0.
95. Wang, A., An, N., Xia, Y., Li, L., Chen, G., A logistic regression and artificial neural network-based approach for chronic disease prediction: a case study of hypertension, in: *Proceedings of 2014 IEEE International Conference on Internet of Things*, Taipei, Taiwan, Sep. 2014, pp. 45–52, doi: 10.1109/ithings.2014.16.
96. Srinivasan, S., Durairaju, K., Deeba, K., Mathivanan, S.K., Karthikeyan, P., Shah, M.A., Multimodal biomedical image segmentation using multi-dimensional U-convolutional neural network. *BMC Med. Imaging*, 24, 1, 1–20, 2024, doi: 10.1186/s12880-024-01197-5.
97. Umehara, K., Ota, J., Ishida, T., Application of super-resolution convolutional neural network for enhancing image resolution in chest CT. *J. Digit. Imaging*, 31, 441–450, 2018, doi: 10.1007/s10278-017-0033-z.
98. Park, J., Hwang, D., Kim, K.Y., Kang, S.K., Kim, Y.K., Lee, J.S., Computed tomography super- resolution using deep convolutional neural network. *Phys. Med. Biol.*, 63, 145011, 2018, doi: 10.1088/1361-6560/aacdd4.
99. Mansoor, A., Vongkovit, T., Linguraru, M.G., Adversarial approach to diagnostic quality volumetric image enhancement, in: *Proceedings of the*

International Symposium on Biomedical Imaging, Washington DC, USA, Apr. 2018, pp. 353–356, doi: 10.1109/isbi.2018.8363591.

100. You, C., Cong, W., Vannier, M.W., Saha, P.K., Hoffman, E.A., Wang, G., Li, G., Zhang, Y., Zhang, X., Shan, H., Li, M., Ju, S., Zhao, Z., Zhang, Z., CT super-resolution GAN constrained by the identical, residual, and cycle learning ensemble (GAN-CIRCLE). *IEEE Trans. Med. Imaging*, 39, 1, 188–203, 2020, doi: 10.1109/tmi.2019.2922960.
101. Shi, J., Liu, Q., Wang, C., Zhang, Q., Ying, S., Xu, H., Super-resolution reconstruction of MR image with a novel residual learning network algorithm. *Phys. Med. Biol.*, 63, 085011, 2018, doi: 10.1088/1361-6560/aab9e9.
102. Zhao, X., Zhang, Y., Zhang, T., Zou, X., Channel splitting network for single MR image super-resolution. *IEEE Trans. Image Process.*, 28, 11, 5649–5662, 2019, doi: 10.1109/tip.2019.2921882.
103. Mahapatra, D., Bozorgtabar, B., Hewavitharanage, S., Garnavi, R., Image super resolution using generative adversarial networks and local saliency maps for retinal image analysis, in: *Proceedings of the 20th International Conference on Medical Image Computing and Computer Assisted Intervention*, Quebec City, Quebec, Canada, 2017, doi: https://doi.org/10.1007/978-3-319-66179-7_4.
104. Oktay, O., Bai, W., Lee, M., Guerrero, R., Kamnitsas, K., Caballero, J., De Marvao, A., Cook, S., O'Regan, D., Rueckert, D., Multi-input cardiac image super-resolution using convolutional neural networks, in: *Proceedings of the International Conference on Medical Image Computing and Computer-Assisted Intervention*, Athens, Greece, Oct. 2016, pp. 246–254, doi: 10.1007/978-3-319-46726-9_29.
105. Wang, C., Lv, X., Shao, M., Qian, Y., Zhang, Y., A novel fuzzy hierarchical fusion attention convolution neural network for medical image super-resolution reconstruction. *Inf. Sci.*, 622, 424–436, 2023, doi: 10.1016/j.ins.2022.11.140.
106. Alqahtani, T.M., Big data analytics with optimal deep learning model for medical image classification. *Comput. Syst. Sci. Eng.*, 44, 2, 1433–1449, 2023, doi: 10.32604/csse.2023.025594.
107. Mukhtorov, D., Rakhmonova, M., Muksimova, S., Cho, Y.I., Endoscopic image classification based on explainable deep learning. *Sensors*, 23, 3176, 2023, doi: 10.3390/s23063176.
108. Srikantamurthy, M.M., Rallabandi, V.P.S., Dudekula, D.B., Natarajan, S., Park, J., Classification of benign and malignant subtypes of breast cancer histopathology imaging using hybrid CNN-LSTM based transfer learning. *BMC Med. Imaging*, 23, 19, 1–15, 2023, doi: 10.1186/s12880-023-00964-0.
109. Serener, A. and Serte, S., Dry and wet age-related macular degeneration classification using OCT images and deep learning, in: *2019 Scientific Meeting on Electrical-Electronics and Biomedical Engineering and Computer Science*, Apr. 2019, IEEE, Istanbul, Turkey, pp. 1–4, doi: 10.1109/EBBT.2019.8741768.

110. Cheng, J., Tian, S., Yu, L., Gao, C., Kang, X., Ma, X., ResGANet: residual group attention network for medical image classification and segmentation. *Med. Image Anal.*, 76, 102313, 2022, doi: 10.1016/j.media.2021.102313.
111. Khan, A.H., Abbas, S., Khan, M.A., Farooq, U., Khan, W.A., Siddiqui, S.Y., Ahmad, A., Intelligent model for brain tumor identification using deep learning. *Appl. Comput. Intell. Soft Comput.*, 2022, 8104054, 2022, doi: 10.1155/2022/8104054.
112. Jiang, H., Yang, K., Gao, M., Zhang, D., Ma, H., Qian, W., An interpretable ensemble deep learning model for diabetic retinopathy disease classification, in: *Proceedings of the Annual International Conference of the IEEE Engineering in Medicine and Biology Society*, Berlin, Germany, Jul. 2019, pp. 2045–2048, doi: 10.1109/embc.2019.8857160.
113. Yadav, S.S. and Jadhav, S.M., Deep convolutional neural network based medical image classification for disease diagnosis. *J. Big Data*, 6, 113, 2019, doi: 10.1186/s40537-019-0276-2.
114. Qu, A., Wu, Q., Wang, J., Yu, L., Li, J., Liu, J., TNCB: Tri-net with cross-balanced pseudo supervision for class imbalanced medical image classification. *IEEE J. Biomed. Health. Inf.*, 28, 4, 2187–2198, 2024, doi: 10.1109/jbhi.2024.3362243.
115. Xu, Y., Hosny, A., Zeleznik, R., Parmar, C., Coroller, T., Franco, I., Mak, R.H., Aerts, H.J.W.L., Deep learning predicts lung cancer treatment response from serial medical imaging. *Clin. Cancer Res.*, 25, 11, 3266–3275, 2019, doi: 10.1158/1078-0432.ccr-18-2495.
116. Azizi, S., Mustafa, B., Ryan, F., Beaver, Z., Freyberg, J., Deaton, J., Loh, A., Karthikesalingam, A., Kornblith, S., Chen, T., Natarajan, V., Norouzi, M., Big self-supervised models advance medical image classification, in: *Proceedings of IEEE International Conference on Computer Vision*, Montreal, Canada, Oct. 2021, pp. 3458–3468, doi: 10.1109/iccv48922.2021.00346.
117. Veeramani, N., Jayaraman, P., Krishankumar, R., Ravichandran, K.S., Gandomi, A.H., DDCNN-F: double decker convolutional neural network 'F' feature fusion as a medical image classification framework. *Sci. Rep.*, 14, 1, 1–24, 2024, doi: 10.1038/s41598-023-49721-x.
118. Wang, X., Wang, C., Cao, J., Gong, L., Zhou, X., WinoNN: Optimizing FPGA-based convolutional neural network accelerators using sparse Winograd algorithm. *IEEE Trans. Comput. Aided Des. Integr. Circuits Syst.*, 39, 11, 4290–4302, 2020, doi: 10.1109/tcad.2020.3012323.
119. Park, S.S. and Chung, K.S., CONNA: Configurable matrix multiplication engine for neural network acceleration. *Electronics*, 11, 15, 2373, 2022, doi: 10.3390/electronics11152373.
120. Chen, T., Du, Z., Sun, N., Wang, J., Wu, C., Chen, Y., Temam, O., DianNao: A small-footprint high-throughput accelerator for ubiquitous machine-learning. *ACM Sigarch Comput. Archit. News*, 42, 1, 269–284, 2014, doi: 10.1145/2654822.2541967.

121. Baltruschat, I.M., Nickisch, H., Grass, M., Knopp, T., Saalbach, A., Comparison of deep learning approaches for multi-label chest X-ray classification. *Sci. Rep.*, 9, 1–10, 2019, doi: 10.1038/s41598-019-42294-8.
122. Zhang, Y., Wang, X., Jiang, X., Yang, Y., Shen, Z., Jia, Z., PQ-PIM: a pruning–quantization joint optimization framework for ReRAM-based processing-in-memory DNN accelerator. *J. Syst. Archit.*, 127, 102531, 2022, doi: 10.1016/j.sysarc.2022.102531.
123. Sanchez, I. and Vilaplana, V., Brain MRI super-resolution using 3D generative adversarial networks, in: *Proceedings of the Conference on Medical Imaging with Deep Learning*, Amsterdam, TheNetherlands, pp. 1–8, 2018.
124. Im, D., Han, D., Choi, S., Kang, S., Yoo, H.J., DT-CNN: an energy-efficient dilated and transposed convolutional neural network processor for region of interest based image segmentation. *IEEE Trans. Circuits Syst. I*, 67, 10, 3471–3483, 2020, doi: 10.1109/tcsi.2020.2991189.
125. Mao, W., Lin, J., Wang, Z., F-DNA: fast convolution architecture for deconvolutional network acceleration. *IEEE Trans. Very Large Scale Integr. VLSI Syst.*, 28, 8, 1867–1880, 2020, doi: 10.1109/tvlsi.2020.3000519.
126. Xu, W., Zhang, Z., You, X., Zhang, C., Reconfigurable and low-complexity accelerator for convolutional and generative networks over finite fields. *IEEE Trans. Comput. Aided Des. Integr. Circuits Syst.*, 39, 12, 4894–4907, 2020, doi: 10.1109/tcad.2020.2973355.
127. Hsiao, S.F., Chen, K.C., Lin, C.C., Chang, H.J., Tsai, B.C., Design of a sparsity-aware reconfigurable deep learning accelerator supporting various types of operations. *IEEE J. Emerging Sel. Top. Circuits Syst.*, 10, 3, 376–387, 2020, doi: 10.1109/jetcas.2020.3015238.
128. Chen, Q., Huang, Y., Sun, R., Song, W., Lu, Z., Fu, Y., Li, L., An efficient accelerator for multiple convolutions from the sparsity perspective. *IEEE Trans. Very Large Scale Integr. VLSI Syst.*, 28, 6, 1540–1544, 2020, doi: 10.1109/tvlsi.2020.2976454.
129. Wu, E., Wu, K., Cox, D., Lotter, W., Conditional infilling GANs for data augmentation in mammogram classification. *Image Analysis for Moving Organ Breast, and Thoracic Images*, pp. 98–106, 2018, doi: 10.1007/978-3-030-00946-5_11.
130. Mao, H., Shu, J., Song, M., Li, T., LrGAN: a compact and energy efficient PIM-based architecture for GAN training. *IEEE Trans. Comput.*, 70, 9, 1427–1442, 2021, doi: 10.1109/tc.2020.3011122.
131. Tong, T., Li, G., Liu, X., Gao, Q., Image super-resolution using dense skip connections, in: *Proceedings of the IEEE international conference on computer vision*, Venice, Italy, pp. 4799–4807, Oct. 2017, doi: 10.1109/iccv.2017.514.

13

Integration with IoT for Smart Homes

Akash Kumar Prajapati, Shubham Patel, Suramya Kumar Rawat, Mandeep Singh, Tarun Chaudhary and Balwinder Raj*

Department of Electronics and Communication Engineering, Dr. B.R. Ambedkar National Institute of Technology, Jalandhar, India

Abstract

The Internet of Things (IoT) has drastically changed the idea of smart homes by connecting various devices, gadgets and systems to improve convenience, efficiency, and security of the house. In smart homes, IoT consists of a network of devices like sensors, appliances, and controllers that communicate *via* the internet. This connectivity allows homeowners to remotely monitor, control, and automate several aspects of their living space, ultimately enhancing their quality of life and managing the energy use more effectively. The key uses of IoT in smart homes include smart lighting, thermostats, security systems, and appliances. Smart lighting and thermostats adjust to user preferences and environmental factors, helping to optimize energy consumption and lower the expenses. IoT-enabled security systems—like smart cameras, motion sensors, and smart locks—offers real-time monitoring and notifications for improving safety and providing peace of mind.

Advanced IoT solutions utilize machine learning and artificial intelligence to meet the users' needs and offer customized automation. For example, a smart home can also adapt to a resident's habits, adjusting lighting, temperatures, and entertainment options accordingly. Integration with voice-activated virtual assistants like Amazon Alexa or Google Assistant has made these IoT systems even more user-friendly and accessible. However, along with its benefits, IoT for smart homes presents challenges, particularly in terms of data privacy and security. The gathering and transmission of sensitive information between devices and cloud platforms can create vulnerabilities that cybercriminals might exploit. To address these risks, it is crucial to ensure strong encryption, secure communication protocols, and timely updating the software by giving updates.

**Corresponding author*: rajb@nitj.ac.in

Ashish Maurya, Mandeep Singh and Balwinder Raj (eds.) Machine Learning in Nanoelectronics: Devices, Circuits and Systems, (409–448) © 2026 Scrivener Publishing LLC

In summary, IoT for smart homes marks a significant shift in how people engage with their living spaces. By providing automation, improved efficiency, and enhanced security, IoT technologies hold the potential to transform modern living for the better.

Keywords: Smart homes, Internet of Things, security systems, sensors, smart sound devices

13.1 Introduction

A huge network of connected gadgets which can exchange information and also communicate with each other over the internet is called Internet of Things (IoT) [1–14]. These gadgets or devices can gather data and also can transmit data. Since they are typically equipped with software and hardware sensors, in this context they can improve features like monitoring, automation and controlling [15–19].

This is an important technological development that is altering our interactions with the surroundings and the devices in them. It is made up of a several types of physical objects that may collect data and also can share it data online. We can enable communication, data processing, and the capacity to carry out tasks independently or with minimal assistance of manpower; this connectedness turns ordinary things into smart gadgets and devices [1].

Key Components of IoT

1. **Devices and Sensors:** There are very common items such as home appliances, wearable devices, and industrial machines, which now feature sensors for data collection.
2. **Connectivity:** The devices can transmit data to the cloud or other devices employing several protocols such as Wi-Fi, Bluetooth, and cellular.
3. **Data Processing:** Insights are derived from data processed and analysed, frequently in the cloud, by devices.
4. **User Interface:** Users interact with IoT systems through dashboards, apps, and voice commands for control and monitoring.

Benefits of IoT

- IoT offers new business opportunities by enabling the collection of data from the network and leveraging advanced analytics to discover business insights and potential opportunities.
- Predictive and proactive abilities.
- Quick reaction time.
- Fresh sources of income.
- Enhanced management of operational procedures.
- Boost in productivity.
- Anticipatory analysis.
- Reducing human errors.
- Enhancing monitoring using IoT sensors and smart home devices offers the ability to control a network of physical objects.

One of the Internet of Things initiatives that needs more study is "smart homes," which is the installation of sensors to make household life easier. It is difficult to renovate ancient homes or to improve the features of more contemporary ones. Home sensors are being incorporated into the design of structures of intelligent houses [2]. A smart house verifies the installed framework in order to automate some tasks and aggregate others. In home automation, we may incorporate smart lighting, air conditioning systems, and HVAC and CCTV systems. In this manner, the homeowner can enjoy total local control and oversight of a house *via* wall switches, remote controls or online from a distance [20–27].

Various sensors and actuators; a home area network (wireless, low power, star or mesh topology); a central gateway for home control; smart sockets for energy management; and so, on are all included in home automation architecture.

Smart Homes

A smart home refers to a residence equipped with a network of interconnected devices and systems that enhance automation, convenience, and security through technology. By leveraging the Internet of Things (IoT), smart homes allow homeowners to control various aspects of their living environment remotely, improving energy efficiency, comfort, and overall quality of life [28–34].

Furthermore, a plethora of integrated, "batteries included" home automation solutions are available on the market from different vendors, including Apple's Home Kit [5], Google's Home Assistant [6], Samsung's Smart Things [3], and Amazon's Alexa Cloud [4]. Some of these systems allow users to connect with them *via* voice commands, a web page or smart phone app (Google Home, Apple Home, Mi Home), or even natural language (Amazon Alexa, Apple Siri, Circe).

Applications for residential sensors and the most popular sensory devices used to configure smart home automation systems are briefly discussed in this article. The analysis is divided into four main sections: It discusses the essential sensor devices for smart automation and presents examples of well-executed sensor-enabled home applications. These recommendations can be used to create smart houses with low-cost microcontrollers and minicomputers like the Raspberry Pi and Arduino [35–39].

Application for Residential Sensors

Moore [7] correctly anticipated that as processing power in computer systems rises annually, component costs fall. This means that homes may now be outfitted with a multitude of networked sensors, which hit the market just after 2000. For these sensors to be readily installed, maintained, and updated on a large scale, they should be inexpensive and low power.

- **Smart lighting:** identifying the current flowing into light bulbs.
- **Smart sound devices:** these employ noises, like clapping and voice, to activate and deactivate various processes.
- **Smart thermostats:** also known as boiler and refrigerator monitors.
- **Smart meters:** can track how much electricity and gas are used.
- **Smart security cameras:** these act as a catalyst for applications that control everything from kitchen appliances to ventilation systems.
- **Smart windows:** also known as switchable glasses are able to adjust the lighting of their windows by changing it from translucent to transparent or vice versa in response to changes in lighting or the opening or closing of the windows.

It should go without saying that building connected wireless sensor networks (WSNs) with the right low-power communication technologies is essential to making these applications possible [40–47].

13.2 Sensors for Smart Homes

Even though residential sensors are widely available, not all of them qualify as "smart." In particular, a sensor is considered smart if it has the ability to use a processing unit to process signals. There are several methods for doing this, including noise cancellation, accuracy-sensitivity error reduction, automatic calibration, and memory-feedback. Many smart home sensors are described below.

13.2.1 Motion Detection

Motion sensors are often used in smart home devices to detect movement in a specified region. These sensors detect changes in infrared energy, such as body temperature, in their surroundings [48–56]. Motion sensors are frequently used in smart lighting systems, security cameras, and automatic door locks to improve home security and energy efficiency.

13.2.2 Flame-Gas Detection Sensor

Smart sensor applications for fire alarm systems are becoming more and more in demand. A flame detector is a type of sensor that is intended to identify and react to flames or fires [11]. Detecting radiation (UV, IR, Visible, and combinations) released at the moment of ignition is how optical flame detectors operate. Ionization and photoelectric detectors are used to identify high-burning and slow-burning flames [57–64].

Figure 13.1 present passive infrared (PIR). In particular, the first makes use of a light-sensing chamber that, when smoke enters, disrupts the laser

Figure 13.1 Passive infrared (PIR) [10].

Figure 13.2 Different types of gas sensors [12].

beams pattern and sounds an alarm. In order to confirm flame presence and quality, the second method uses two electrically charged (ionized) plates that cause the current (ions) to flow improperly.

Since ionization sensors can be activated by steam or even dust and are extremely sensitive, it is best to utilize photoelectric detecting devices [13]. Furthermore, thermocouples are widely utilized in gas cookers and combustion heating systems to detect the presence of flames. A carbon dioxide sensor can identify high carbon dioxide (CO2) levels, which may be a sign of a fire [65–72].

A fire suppression system can be activated, a fuel line (such as a propane or natural gas line) can be turned off, and an alarm can be sounded in reaction to a detected flame, depending on the installation (Figure 13.2).

13.2.3 Toxic Gas Detection

Gas leaks are one of the primary home hazards for occupants, next to fire smoke. They pose a risk to health, particularly if they are odorless and poisonous. Many gases, including propane, hydrogen, methane, alcohol, smoke, and carbon monoxide, can be detected using toxic gas sensors. The way they work is that when a sensor's outer layer gets heated in hot air, it takes in oxygen from its surroundings. In addition to detecting current flow, these sensors can identify the kind of gas based on the density of oxygen [15]. But the great majority of inexpensive poisonous gas sensors are not trustworthy. Moreover, they only offer a general approximation based on a reference gas and are unable to differentiate between other gases (Figure 13.2).

13.2.4 Moisture Leak Detection

Moisture sensors, which are primarily utilized in applications for the agricultural business, are another fascinating area. These sensors can also be used in residences to keep an eye on moisture levels and any leaks [73–78]. Figure 13.3 gives details of toxic gas monitoring.

Thermal conductivity, capacitive, and resistive are the three types of humidity sensors [16]. These sensors work as follows: resistive sensors employ two electrodes that make contact with a sensor surface, and an intermediate layer (substrate) is positioned between them. The middle layer collects moisture, or water vapor, and as a result, a change in resistance, or an alteration in the electric flow, is detected.

Instead of measuring resistance, recent attempts use capacitive sensors to detect the charging and discharging times of capacitors [17]. By measuring the difference between the thermal conductivity of moist and dry air, thermal conductivity sensors determine humidity. These sensors are capable of measuring relative or absolute humidity. Because of rust and grime, resistive sensors are prone to errors [17].

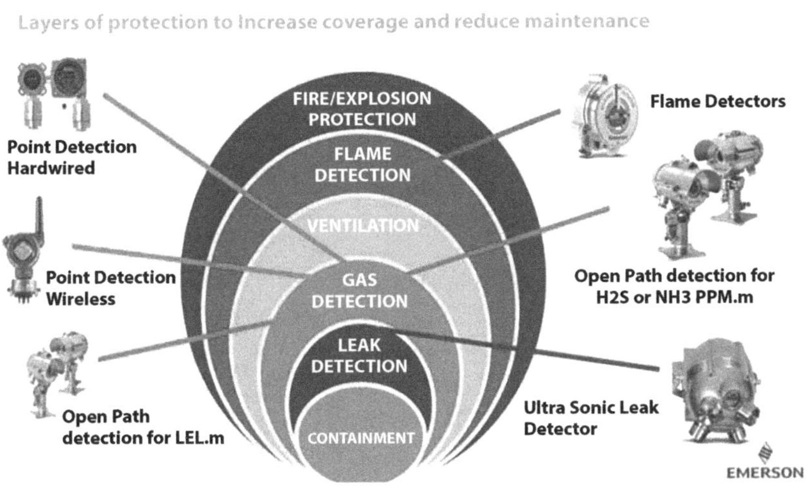

Figure 13.3 Toxic gas monitoring [14].

13.2.5 Proximity Sensors

Proximity sensors detect adjacent items without requiring physical contact, making them perfect for smart home applications like touchless faucets, automatic doors, and smart security systems. Smart devices that use proximity sensors can provide hands-free interaction and increased convenience for users. These sensors improve the performance and accessibility of smart home devices [21]. Figure 13.4 provides the different proximity sensors.

Incorporating a variety of sensors into smart home devices is essential for creating a completely automated and adaptable living space. By familiarizing themselves with the different types of sensors and their roles, homeowners can make better choices when choosing and enhancing their smart home technology. It's important to position sensors strategically in key areas of the home to guarantee optimal performance and seamless compatibility with other smart devices [21].

13.2.6 Temperature Sensors

Because they monitor and control the interior temperature, temperature sensors are crucial to smart home systems. By giving smart thermostats and heating systems access to real-time temperature data, they enable the creation of a cozy living environment. Households can save money on electricity bills while maintaining a comfortable level by using temperature sensors [22]. Figure 13.5 gives temperature sensor.

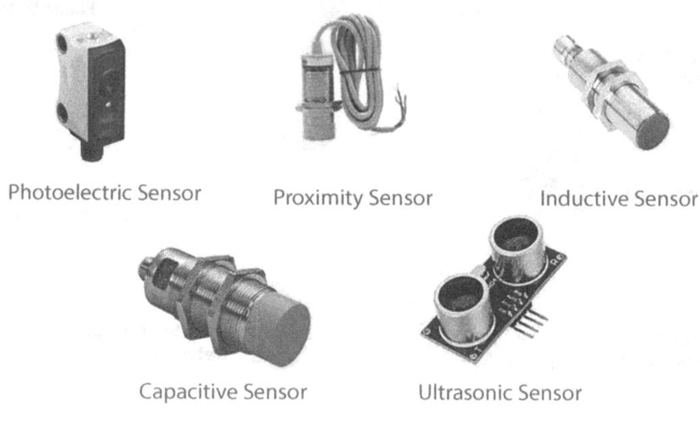

Figure 13.4 Different proximity sensors [60].

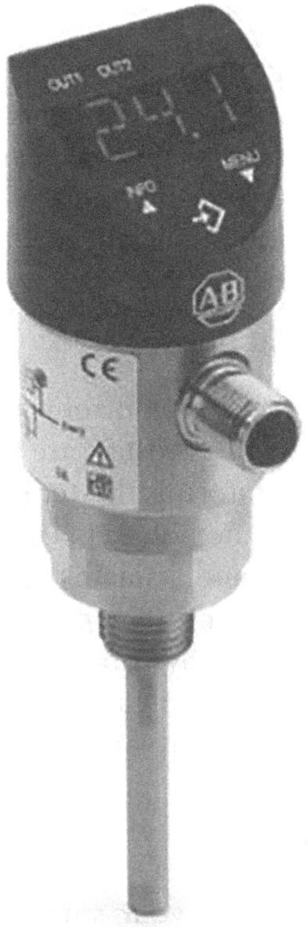

Figure 13.5 Temperature sensor [61].

13.2.7 Humidity Sensors

Smart devices can successfully control indoor humidity thanks to humidity sensors, which measure the amount of moisture in the air. To prevent mold growth, improve air quality, and increase overall comfort at home, they are frequently found in smart HVAC systems, air purifiers, and weather monitors. These sensors are especially useful in areas where seasonal variations in humidity levels are substantial [24].

13.2.8 Light Sensors

Light sensors, or ambient light sensors, are designed to measure the light levels in a particular space. They identify variations in brightness, enabling smart devices to modify screen brightness, control lighting systems, and conserve energy. These sensors are commonly found in smart thermostats, outdoor lighting solutions, and intelligent window curtains [25].

13.2.9 Smart Thermostat Sensor

The smart thermostat allows you to control your home's heating and cooling from any location. Smart thermostats are not only cool, but they also help you save money by monitoring the temperature and humidity levels inside and outside your home [79–83]. The temperature in your home changes as you enter and exit, and a smart thermostat can adjust the temperature based on your behavior and room usage. The best thermostats adjust the temperature on a room-by-room basis, allowing you to maintain your preferred temperature when you are present while also defaulting to an energy-saving mode when you are not [23].

13.2.10 Intercom/Hub

You've installed sensors to create your smart home, and now you need to manage everything from a single location. The smart home hub and intercom system gives you access to all of your smart home sensors, a communication system throughout the house, and the ability to call for services (emergency or repair) with the touch of a button. An intercom system allows you to see through walls and communicate *via* video and voice between rooms in your home. You can also use your smartphone to call a room in the house while you are away at work; this could be useful for checking in on an elderly parent while you are away.

As you can see, there are several sensors on the market that can assist you in creating a safe, smart home that is secure even when you are not present. The adoption of this type of technology is quickly gaining traction, and it is even becoming an insurance incentive. Insurance companies want you and your home to be safe, and many are starting to offer services to assist you in making your home smarter, more proactive in protecting you and your wallet [26].

13.3 Connectivity Protocols for IoT Smart Homes

The performance and efficiency of smart devices are impacted by smart home protocols, which manage communication, authentication, and error detection between them. For a seamless smart home experience, selecting the appropriate protocol helps prevent problems with connectivity and battery life. Additionally, maximizing these interactions requires an understanding of smart home communication standards [84–89].

It's critical to comprehend the differences between these methods because each has advantages and disadvantages. Although Ethernet is an option for devices that require reliable connectivity, wireless protocols are currently the most popular in smart homes due to their ease. Wi-Fi, Z-Wave, Zigbee, Bluetooth Low Energy and NFC are common protocols used in smart homes [55]. Some important connectivity protocols are listed below.

13.3.1 Zigbee

- Zigbee is a low-power, wireless mesh networking protocol that follows the IEEE 802.15.4 standard. It uses the same frequency band as Wi-Fi and Bluetooth, which is 2.4 GHz [24].
- Mesh networking allows devices to communicate with one another and relay messages, extending network range without requiring additional infrastructure.
- Low Power Consumption: Ideal for battery-powered devices such as sensors and smart bulbs.
- Interoperability: Supports a wide variety of devices and brands.
- Use cases include smart lighting, home security systems, and environmental sensors.

13.3.2 Z-Wave

- Z-Wave is another mesh networking protocol that uses a lower frequency (900 MHz) to reduce interference with Wi-Fi networks [56].
- Low latency means faster response times for device interactions.
- Robustness: Designed to provide dependable communications in home automation applications.

- Wide Ecosystem: A wide range of certified devices are available from various manufacturers.
- Use cases include smart locks, HVAC controls, and smart plugs.

13.3.3 Wi-Fi

- Wi-Fi uses the IEEE 802.11 standards to provide wireless internet connectivity.
- **Technical specifications:** Supports both 2.4 GHz and 5 GHz bands, with rates ranging from Mbps to several GBPS with newer standards (such as Wi-Fi 6).
- **Typical applications:** include smart speakers, cameras, thermostats, and any other device that requires high bandwidth for streaming or big data transfers.
- **Best use cases:** There are some examples like living rooms and home offices environments that can have a steady power resource which requires high-speed internet access [90–96].

13.3.4 Bluetooth and Bluetooth Low Energy (BLE)

- **Overview:** Bluetooth allows the devices to link up over short ranges but it takes more power, whereas Bluetooth Low Energy (BLE) is designed specifically for minimal power usage.
- **Technical Details:** BLE generally transmits data in small bursts, making it well- suited for infrequent data exchanges. It can be operated in the range of approximately 10 to 30 meters.
- **Technical Applications:** Common uses of BLE include wearable, smart home devices, and location-based services like key finders.
- **Best Use Cases:** Ideal for personal devices that need to connect with smartphones or tablets, as well as scenarios that involve sporadic communication between devices.

13.3.5 MQTT (Message Queuing Telemetry Transport)

- **Overview:** A lightweight messaging protocol tailored for networks with limited capacity and significant latency.

- **Technical Details:** Uses TCP/IP and implements a publish/subscribe model to facilitate effective message distribution.
- **Use Cases:** Ideal for monitoring systems, remote sensor networks, and applications needing real-time information.
- **Optimal Scenarios:** Particularly useful when devices need to frequently send small data packets, such as temperature readings from multiple sensors.

13.3.6 CoAP (Constrained Application Protocol)

- **Overview:** A web transfer protocol designed specifically for networks and devices with constraints.
- **Technical Specifics:** CoAP uses UDP and is optimized for low overhead, enabling quick and light communication.
- **Common Uses:** Applied to smart home appliances and lighting that require minimal data packets and low energy consumption.
- **Ideal Use Cases:** Especially useful in settings with severe network limitations when quick reaction is crucial [97–102].

13.3.7 LoRa WAN (Long Range Wide Area Network)

- **Overview:** For Internet of Things devices spread across large regions, this energy-efficient, long-range communication protocol is perfect.
- **Technical details:** It operates in unlicensed sub-GHz frequency bands, has data speeds appropriate for sporadic transmissions, and can travel up to 15 kilometres in rural areas.
- Typical applications include ecological monitoring, intelligent urban infrastructure, and smart farming.
- **Ideal scenarios:** This protocol is very helpful for devices that need to communicate over great distances while preserving battery life, like distant agricultural sensors.

13.3.8 NFC (Near Field Communication)

- **Overview:** A collection of protocols for short-range communication between devices that are interoperable. usually has a range of roughly 4 cm and works at a frequency of

13.56 MHz. Both active and passive communication modes are supported [102–108].
- Common uses include device synchronization, access control, and mobile payments.
- **Best Uses:** Circumstances where close proximity is necessary, including when completing transactions or connecting devices.

13.3.9 Cellular(4G/5G)

- **Overview:** Leverages mobile telecom networks to provide internet access.
- **Technical Specifics:** 5G greatly increases speed, capacity, and latency, whilst 4G LTE provides rapid data rates.
- **Common Uses:** Facilitates high-bandwidth applications, remote monitoring systems, and smart cars.
- **Best Uses:** Perfect for gadgets that require dependable connectivity over large regions, such as health monitoring systems or remote security cameras in places lacking Wi-Fi.

13.4 Smart Appliances for Smart Homes

The goal of smart appliances is to improve home connectivity, efficiency, and convenience. A closer look at a few popular kinds of smart appliances and their features is provided below.

13.4.1 Smart Kitchen Appliances

- **Smart Refrigerators:** They can track inventories, recommend recipes, and provide remote temperature control.
- **Smart Ovens:** Pre-heat remotely, monitor cooking progress, and receive notifications when food is ready.
- **Smart Coffee Makers:** Set brewing times, alter brew strength, and control with a smartphone.

13.4.2 Smart Laundry Appliances

- Smart washers include remote start, cycle notifications, and troubleshooting assistance.

- Smart dryers provide similar characteristics as washers, but also allow for fabric- specific drying cycles.

13.4.3 Smart Cleaning Devices

- Robotic vacuums: They clean floors automatically, negotiate obstacles, and may be scheduled *via* an app.
- Smart mop: Some models can mop floors automatically and be controlled remotely.

13.4.4 Smart Security Devices

- Smart cameras offer live views, motion warnings, and two-way communication.
- Smart doorbells allow you to observe and communicate with visitors from a distance.

13.4.5 Smart Lighting

- **Smart lights:** Enable remote control, scheduling, and custom lighting scenes.
- **Smart light switches:** Allow control of standard lighting fixtures *via* app or voice commands.

13.4.6 Smart Speaker and Hubs

- **Smart speakers:** Act as a central control point for other devices and respond to voice commands.
- **Smart hub:** Connects multiple devices, allowing automation and control through a single interface.

13.4.7 Smart Energy Monitors

- **Smart Plugs:** Monitor energy consumption and allow remote control of devices.
- **Smart Power Strips:** Manage multiple devices and monitor energy consumption.

13.4.8 Integration and Automation

- **Interconnectivity:** Many smart devices work together. For example, a smart thermostat can communicate with smart blinds to optimize heating and cooling based on sunlight.
- **Routines and scenes:** Set up routines like "Good morning" that adjust lighting, make coffee, and start the dishwasher with a single command.
- **Voice control:** Most smart devices can be integrated with voice assistants (such as Alexa or Google Assistant), allowing for hands-free operation.

13.4.9 Benefits of Smart Devices

- **Convenience:** Control devices from anywhere, set schedules, and receive notifications.
- **Energy Efficiency:** Optimize use, maintain consumption and reduce accounts.
- **Safety:** Check your home remotely and receive notices for unusual activities.
- **Time-Saving:** Automate repetitive activities, giving you more time for other activities.
- **Adjustment:** Settings of size and routine that correspond to your lifestyle and preferences.
- The integration of intelligent devices in your home can efficiently facilitate daily activities and contribute to a more sustainable lifestyle.

13.5 Voice Assistants

Voice assistants for smart homes are becoming increasingly popular, as they provide ease and control over a variety of devices [58]. Here are some important aspects and considerations:

- **Device Control:** Voice commands can control lights, thermostats, security systems, and appliances.
- **Routine Automation:** Create routines for specified times or events, such as "Good Morning" to activate the lights and start the coffee maker.

- **Intercom Functionality:** Use the assistant to communicate with other rooms or devices.
- **Integration:** Works with a variety of brands and devices, including Amazon Alexa, Google Assistant, and Apple HomeKit.
- **Customization:** Users can develop personalized instructions and settings for their specific needs.

Some popular voice assistants are described below [59].

13.5.1 Amazon Alexa

- **Overview:** Alexa is Amazon's voice assistant, available on Echo devices and many third-party products.
- **Features:**
- Controls a wide range of smart home devices (lights, thermostats, cameras, etc.).
- Supports routines to automate multiple actions (e.g., turning off lights, adjusting thermostat).
- Offers a large library of skills for additional functionality (e.g., ordering groceries, playing games).
- Integrates with music services like Spotify and Apple Music.
- **Compatibility:** Works with many brands including Philips Hue, Ring, Nest and more.

13.5.2 Google Assistant

- **Compatibility:** Supports a wide range of smart devices and connects with Google services.
- Features include natural language processing, contextual awareness, routines, and smart home control.
- **Ecosystem:** Integrates smoothly with Android devices and Google services such as Calendar and Maps.

13.5.3 Apple Siri

- **Compatibility:** Best with Apple ecosystem devices (iPhone, iPad, and Home Pod).
- Features include voice control for smart devices, messaging, phone calls, and app integration.

- **Ecosystem:** Emphasizes privacy and security, with extensive integration with iOS and macOS.

13.5.4 Microsoft Cortana

- **Compatibility:** Designed primarily for Windows devices, but also works with some smart home systems.
- Features include task management, reminders, and rudimentary smart home control.
- **Ecosystem:** Performs better within the Microsoft environment and has switched its attention towards enterprise solutions.

13.5.5 Samsung Bixby

- **Compatibility:** Integrated with Samsung smartphones and smart appliances.
- Features include device control, contextual commands, and connection with Samsung services.
- **Ecosystem:** Best for Samsung product owners, particularly those who own smart appliances and televisions.

13.5.6 Raspberry Pi and Custom Assistants

- **Compatibility:** Can be adjusted in such a way that you work with various smart devices.
- Features include highly flexible and programmable that allows tailored solutions.
- **Ecosystem:** Ideal for technically experienced users who wish to create their own voice assistant.

13.6 Security and Surveillance

Digital technologies have revolutionized the way that information is sent and received by connecting various objects and people. With the aid of online services, it hopes to help individuals. In the Internet of Things (IoT), sensors and other devices are connected to the internet in order to share and gather data. It makes it possible for different gadgets to work together, communicate, and gain knowledge from one another's experiences in the same way that people do. In a multitude of applications, billions of items are intelligently connected through the Internet of Things. IoT is widely used in a number of fields, including smart cities, healthcare, and agriculture. With the help of underlying communication and monitoring infrastructure made up of smart devices like actuators, cameras, sensors, meters, and RFIDs, smart buildings and smart security are becoming a reality [109–115].

Because embedded systems and security awareness are developing at a rapid pace, societies today have a strong demand for security and monitoring. To increase the security and monitoring capabilities of remote locations, a lot of research is still being done to improve the design of intelligent surveillance and security systems. This paper's primary goal is to put wireless home automation and security features into practice. If an intruder attempts to enter the house without authorization, the current system model uses the Internet of Things to send the owner an alert message. The system will identify the user and take a picture using the security camera before sending the message and picture to the owner's email [116–121].

A number of building surveillance concepts have already been put forth. These models used wireless sensor networks [29], solar arrays [28], and ultrasonic sensors [32] to optimize the surveillance system. The surveillance system was enhanced with the introduction of telemonitoring and intelligent fish eye camera systems. However, these methods were unable to manage the surveillance operation while seated in a faraway location at the time of the incident. The author of [30] proposed a sensor network-based intelligent and automated smart home system. The author developed an energy-efficient smart home system utilizing IEEE 802.15.4 and ZigBee, which uses occupancy, photo, and passive infrared (PIR) sensors to gather data. The author of [31] suggested a Raspberry Pi and Internet of Things-based smart home automation system. The internet is used to link and monitor household equipment. The Raspberry Pi is able to operate in both sensing and surveillance. To detect movements and intruders at the door, a motion sensor and camera were employed [122–128].

13.7 Home Healthcare System

Healthcare plays a significant role in modern life, and as technology advances, so do the opportunities for providing care. The strain on the current healthcare system, caused by an aging population and related chronic conditions, has been well documented. There is a consensus that the high demand on the system negatively affects both patients and healthcare providers [33, 34]. Integrating the medical Internet of Things (IoT) with traditional healthcare practices has the potential to reduce some of this stress. By shifting non-critical monitoring and data collection to a system that can record and analyze patient data, it becomes possible to identify anomalies that may require professional intervention. Research focusing on the IoT in healthcare has largely centred on monitoring patients with specific chronic conditions that significantly impact their quality of life as they age, such as Parkinson's disease and diabetes [35, 36]. These conditions become integral to a person's life and necessitate ongoing attention. For instance, while Parkinson's disease currently has no cure, symptoms can be managed, and patient conditions can be monitored as the disease progresses. In the case of diabetes, the use of implanted devices for continuous glucose monitoring has become common and is highly recommended; these devices provide real-time information on blood glucose levels [36].

13.7.1 Features for Healthcare in Smart Home

Smart buildings, which encompass smart homes, are advanced structures that utilize the Internet of Things (IoT) and integrated wired devices to improve resident comfort while lowering operational costs through efficient resource management. These buildings are equipped with local controllers that gather and analyse data, enabling them to operate actuators and modify the environment based on predefined or user-defined settings. When considering a smart home that incorporates a medical IoT system with Wireless Body Area Networks (WBANs), there are many parallels to smart buildings. Nevertheless, the foremost priority in this setting is ensuring user safety, with comfort coming in second. Important features of a medical IoT system within a smart home include those described below.

13.7.2 User Safety

In a medical Internet of things (IoT) architecture, patient safety is the first priority. Having a trustworthy way to get in touch with emergency services or careers is essential because of the possible risk of serious health issues. To minimize false alarms, the system will initially try to acquire a response from the patient when it notices odd events or measurements. A carer will be notified if the patient doesn't respond. Emergency services may potentially be notified, depending on how serious the situation is. Informing a carer to evaluate the patient's condition and the sensor's positioning can assist prevent needless emergency service calls because sensors can occasionally get misaligned and offer erroneous but non-critical data [129–134].

For individuals living with dementia, integrating common household appliances into the IoT network can help mitigate injury risks. For instance, if an oven or stovetop has been left on longer than usual, the smart home system should notify a resident or caregiver. A context-aware controller can utilize the same passive infrared (PIR) sensors used for security monitoring to detect such incidents. Additionally, incorporating medical technology within a smart home offers various benefits compared to short-term care facilities for personalized care. The network can be designed to accommodate patient routines by integrating monitoring into fixed utilities and furniture. For example, as noted in [37], sensors can be embedded in a bathtub to detect if someone becomes submerged or incapacitated while bathing. A chair equipped with electrocardiogram (ECG) sensors is described in [38] for monitoring patients with limited mobility who may remain in one spot for extended periods. Moreover, if patients with dementia are known to wander outside, caretakers can be alerted if the individual leaves the building at odd hours or lingers outside for too long [135–139].

13.7.3 Patient Health

Medical IoT networks represent a revolutionary enhancement to traditional healthcare, offering a powerful tool to complement—not replace—professional medical advice and care. Patients can receive more individualized care than they would from traditional consultations by combining these networks with the knowledge of medical specialists. Medical IoT technology can be tailored to make patients and carers feel at ease when engaging with the system, especially in a home setting. Traditionally, a medical facility remains a reliable choice for people who might find these technologies difficult to utilize. But for individuals who choose to use this technology, it provides a great deal of autonomy and control over their health care. Wearable body area networks (WBAN) are essential for collecting vitals data, in cases where insurance coverage may be restricted for extended hospital monitoring. This allows medical practitioners to make well-informed judgments from a distance. Additionally, applying machine learning can increase the accuracy of diagnoses and act as a predictor of future health issues. Studies have shown that advanced wearable sensors can effectively identify and monitor the conditions like Parkinson's disease [39], diabetes [40], and Friedreich's ataxia [41], ultimately enhancing patient health and the quality of life.

13.7.4 Design Flexibility

Smart buildings have flexible architecture that allows for a wide range of modification options. There are certain areas, such as floors or rooms which can be temporarily taken offline for improvements without affecting the operation of other units in the building by using a distributed control system, which is made up of multiple independent control units cooperating under the direction of a main controller. This configuration ensures coherence among several subsystems while permitting customizing alterations in specific spaces or areas. For example, a controller device in a garage might regulate security and lighting systems, while a controller device in a kitchen might be able to control heating, cooling, lighting, and gas leak detection [140–146]. Because of their different functions and applications, these systems don't have to work together, but they also don't have to work in the same way in every room or areas. In a smart home, it's possible that only the living space of a medical IoT user needs to respond to specific indication from their health data. In homes where medical IoT users live with a caretaker, if mobility issues prevent users from accessing certain parts of the building, like elderly individuals with difficulty navigating stairs, those less accessible areas can be customized for the caregiver's needs or left unchanged.

13.7.5 Information and User Engagement

Many devices come with user interfaces in the form of applications that enable users to access their data. Given the numerous apps and gateways required for traditional IoT networks, various solutions have been proposed to effectively manage device connections [44]. The resulting dashboards or interfaces often resemble those used commercially in smart buildings for monitoring environmental conditions. By allowing users to access their own data, it fosters greater engagement and reduces the likelihood of technology abandonment [42, 43]. This capability also empowers patients to stay updated on their care by viewing relevant data whenever they wish.

13.8 User Interfaces and Experiences

When it comes to smart homes, user interfaces (UI) and user experience (UX) are essential in determining how users engage with the extensive network of systems and gadgets that make a house "smart." The way we interact with our home technology is being shaped by the growing sophistication of UI and UX in the connected device ecosystem [45]. In addition to being practical, the environment should be easy to use, customizable, and pleasurable. The following are some ways that the development of UI/UX is impacting the smart home experience.

13.8.1 Mobile Apps and Dashboards

- **Centralized Control through Apps:** Most smart home ecosystems provide users with a centralized mobile app or web dashboard, where they can monitor and control connected devices.
- These apps allow users to:
  - Turn appliances on/off
  - Set schedules for devices
  - Receive real-time alerts (e.g., security breaches, appliances left on)
  - Monitor energy usage
  - Track sensor data (like temperature or air quality)

- **Real-Time Status Monitoring:** Apps often provide real-time status updates, such as whether doors are locked or if a smart camera has detected movement.
- **Multi-Device Support:** A well-designed app will support multiple smart devices and brands, allowing users to control everything from lights to security cameras in a unified interface [46].

13.8.2 Wearable and Voice Interaction

- **Wearable Devices:** Smart watches and fitness trackers are becoming more integrated into smart home ecosystems. Users can manage their home environments through these devices by issuing voice commands, receiving notifications (such as alerts for home security or tips on conserving energy), monitoring health data that syncs with home health management systems [147–153].
- **Voice Interfaces:** Voice assistants like Amazon Alexa, Google Assistant, and Apple Siri offer an intuitive method for interacting with smart homes. Key features include:

- **Hands-Free Control:** Users can control lights, adjust thermostat settings, lock doors, or play music simply by speaking.
- **Natural Language Processing (NLP):** Sophisticated NLP technology allows these systems to comprehend a broad array of voice commands, enhancing the user experience.
- **Customizable Routines:** Voice assistants enable users to set up routines (for instance, a "Good morning" routine that adjusts lighting, plays music, and brews coffee).

13.8.3 Intuitive Design for Usability

- **Simplicity:** Smart home user interfaces (UIs) should prioritize a straightforward design to catering for both tech-savvy users and those who are less familiar with technology.
- **User-Friendly Navigation:** Interfaces should incorporate easy-to-use manuals or menus with clearly visible buttons for frequently accessed functions, such as turning lights on and off or adjusting the thermostat.
- **Customization Options:** There are some users who enjoy having advanced customization features to modify device behaviors; other people might prefer normal settings that require little adjustment in the system or devices.
- **Accessibility:** The design should consider inclusivity by including features like voice control for individuals with mobility challenges and visual aids, such as screen readers.
- **User Feedback and Error Prevention:** The interface should offer prompt user feedback (like confirmation that a command was successfully carried out) and implement strategies to minimize mistakes, such as verifying important commands like unlocking doors.

13.8.4 Remote and In-Home Control Panels

- **Touchscreens:** Certain smart homes feature touchscreens installed on walls that enable local management of devices, security systems, and climate settings.
- **Custom Profiles:** In homes with several users, interfaces can support distinct profiles, allowing for personalized adjustments such as lighting preferences or temperature settings for individual rooms [48].

13.9 Sustainability and Smart Homes

In recent years, there has been increased interest in the development of energy technologies, alongside a growing awareness of simple and cost-effective methods to decrease energy consumption in households through smart energy management. Many of these changes primarily require residents to modify their behaviour. In one research project, scientists implemented a monitoring system using Wi-Fi-enabled smart switches aimed at reducing energy usage in typical homes [49]. The researchers recommended enhancing this technology by incorporating various types of sensors to facilitate autonomous monitoring and environmental regulation tailored to individual user preferences. In a separate study, researchers investigated a multi-agent system aimed at promoting energy conservation in residential buildings. In order to address the present issues and guarantee that smart homes may realize their full potential in the future, they are concentrating to create a full comprehensive system design. The foundation of this system is a vast body of knowledge that includes all the details we needed to maximize energy efficiency while putting users comfort first. The system intelligence is structured as a multi-agent framework that permits communication with outside variables. A global thing agent, a control agent, a user agent, a data agent, and an interface agent are among the agents that make up the suggested framework. Every agent has a different area of expertise, including control setting, data management, and user preferences. These illustrations show the different approaches that can be used to reduce the energy amount in our houses.

13.9.1 Energy Management

- **Smart Thermostats:** Devices like the Nest and Ecobee automatically adjust the temperature to save energy when the house is empty based on the user's preferences.
- **Geofencing:** These devices use GPS data from smartphones to detect when a homeowner is not home, modifying climate controls to reduce waste.
- **Smart Lights:** By allowing customers to adjust lights to fit their daily schedules, smart bulbs and systems like Philips Hue help consumers use less electricity.
- **Motion Sensors:** To further reduce energy consumption, lights in unoccupied rooms are made to switch off automatically.

- **Energy Consumption Analytics:** A lot of smart home systems give homeowners historical and real-time information about how much energy is being used, which helps them identify areas that could use improvement.
- **Recommendations:** Some platforms may also offer suggestions on how to reduce energy consumption based on the data collected [51].

13.9.2 Sustainable Appliances

- **Water Conservation:** By adjusting their water usage according to the load volume or the time of day, intelligent dishwashers and washing machines enable consumers to take advantage of cheaper electricity prices during off-peak hours.
- **Solar-Operated Smart Devices:** To reduce reliance on the electrical grid, devices like solar-powered outdoor lights or cameras are being used more and more.
- **Reducing Waste:** By keeping track of expiration dates and reminding users to eat products before they spoil, smart refrigerators with built-in cameras and food management tools can help reduce food waste.

13.9.3 Smart Grids and Renewable Integration

- **Smart Grids:** When connected to smart grids, smart homes can adjust their energy use in real time in response to demand from the grid and the availability of renewable energy sources.
- **Demand Response:** By reducing energy consumption during periods of high demand, intelligent devices can relieve grid strain and save consumers money.
- **Renewable Electricity Integration:** IoT solutions can manage how electricity from wind turbines or solar panels installed at homes is distributed, enabling excess energy to be stored in batteries or fed back into the grid.

13.9.4 Automated Water and Climate Control

- **Smart Irrigation Systems:** To ensure outdoor sustainability, smart irrigation systems keep an eye on soil moisture levels and weather patterns to establish the best time to irrigate lawns and gardens.

- **Smart Windows and Blinds:** The automated windows and blinds can change according to the sun or the time of day, which lessens the need for artificial cooling and lighting in the house.

13.10 Future Trends in Smart Home IoT

The future of smart homes with the Internet of Things (IoT) ecosystem is extremely bright as technology keeps developing and becomes increasingly integrated into our daily lives. Our living spaces could undergo a significant transformation as a result of this continuous progress, becoming more connected, effective, and user-friendly. The smart home of the future will be driven by intricate networks of connected devices that leverage data, artificial intelligence (AI), and real-time communication to enhance sustainability, comfort, security, and overall quality of life of the people. We can explore how these innovations are likely to impact our homes in the coming years.

13.10.1 AI and Machine Learning

- **Smart Home Automation:** By using AI and machine learning, homes will be able to adjust to the preferences of their occupants, improving comfort and energy efficiency.
- **Insights into User Behaviour:** For example, an AI-powered system would be able to identify when a person typically wakes up and make proactive changes to the home environment, such as turning on lights, drawing the curtains, and modifying the temperature.
- **Better Voice Assistants:** AI developments will improve voice assistants, making them more responsive and able to carry on natural conversations. They will also be able to send user's customized reminders, such as reminding them to switch off forgotten equipment.
- **Self-Regulating Systems:** In the future, there may be a chance of a home that is able to function independently, with features like lighting, heating, and cooling modifying themselves in response to patterns that are identified without the need for human input.

13.10.2 Edge Computing

- **Local Data Processing:** By keeping data inside the house, there may be an increasing number of smart home gadgets that will use edge computing to handle the data locally, reducing latency and enhancing privacy of the smart home.
- **Real-Time Control:** Edge computing can make it possible for critical smart home features like energy management, security, and health monitoring to operate faster and more responsively according to the user's input.
- **Improved Privacy:** Edge computing helps to reduce worry about privacy violations in IoT ecosystems. It accomplishes this by reducing the quantity of data sent to external servers by depending less on cloud services.

13.10.3 5G and the Future of Connectivity

- **Enhanced Speed and Dependable Connections:** The advent of 5G networks can facilitate quicker and more dependable communication among IoT devices, particularly in regions that have a high concentration of devices.
- **Reduced Latency:** Thanks to diminished latency, users will enjoy almost immediate responses when engaging with smart home devices, like security cameras or remote locks.
- **Growth of IoT:** 5G will support the expansion of IoT networks, allowing for the connection of thousands of devices within single household devices, including smart appliances and wearables, while maintaining optimal performance of the system.

13.10.4 Interoperability and Universal Standards

- **Matter Protocol:** Matter is a new Internet of Things (IoT) standard created by the Connectivity Standards Alliance (CSA) that seeks to improve device compatibility across various manufacturers.
- **Cross-Brand Integration:** The goal of Matter is to ensure seamless interaction between leading brands such as Amazon, Google, Apple, and Samsung, thereby removing the necessity for multiple control applications.

- **Simplified Setup:** Matter will facilitate easier device installation for users by eliminating concerns about compatibility.
- **Self-Healing Networks:** Future smart home systems may possess the ability to identify and autonomously resolve issues, minimizing downtime and the need for manual troubleshooting.

13.10.5 Sustainability and Green Energy Solutions

- **AI in Energy Efficiency:** Artificial intelligence will automate and enhance energy management, enabling the prediction of energy requirements and the efficient regulation of consumption across various devices in ways that were previously unattainable.
- **Connection with Electric Vehicles (EVs):** Smart homes will evolve into key centers for managing EVs, automatically adjusting vehicle charging in response to electricity prices, grid requirements, and the availability of renewable energy sources.

13.11 Conclusions

The utilization of IoT and smart home technology applications has seen a recent disruptive trend. Though relevant descriptions and restrictions are still unclear, research on this topic is still ongoing. Gaining knowledge about this new trend is crucial. This article surveys and categorizes relevant works in an effort to provide such insights. From the numerous smart home app projects, several trends may be identified. For the most part, these works fall into four categories: evaluations or surveys, app research studies, development attempts, and general design schemes. A thorough examination of the articles aids in identifying and outlining the difficulties, advantages, and suggestions pertaining to IoT and smart home applications [1].

The findings show the kinds of apps that are now on the market as well as the gaps in their adoption in IoT smart homes. Researchers have pointed out problems and offered solutions, such as using gadgets correctly. Additionally, we advise users to adhere to the specified runtime. Many smart home system applications offer advice to users, such as lowering energy use, alerting users to malfunctioning devices, choosing trustworthy devices and software, diagnosing issues, giving accurate instructions (e.g., proper exercises for senior citizens *via* TV tutorials), medical advice, diagnosing and helping patients, offering guidance on how to use and maintain electrical and fire systems, and offering security systems and device connectivity [2].

These suggestions can address the difficulties that IoT applications in smart homes face and create new avenues for study in this field. These issues pertain to marketing, security systems, safety, energy usage, and device communication. The current analysis identifies the findings and provides an overview of earlier research on the Internet of Things and its applications in smart homes. Researchers may find the review of these books useful as a reference. Researchers must become knowledgeable about new trends and technology since people will continue to accept them. IoT-enabled wearable technology could be the next big thing in smart homes. These devices are powered by new-generation integrated sensors and controlled by applications. Research on IoT-based smart home applications that manage wearable technology or embedded sensors in real-world scenarios is still in its infancy [30]. Adopting interdisciplinary approaches with other scientific and technological domains is another factor to be taken into account for research.

References

1. Kumar, V. and Chawda, R.K., A research paper on smart home. *Int. J. Eng. Appl. Sci. Technol.*, 5, 3, 2020.
2. Gunge, V.S. and Yalagi, P.S., Smart home automation: a literature review. *Int. J. Comput. Appl.*, 975, 8887, 2016.
3. https://smartthings.developer.samsung.com.
4. https://github.com/alexa/avs-device-sdk.
5. https://developer.apple.com/homekit.
6. https://nest.com.
7. Moore, G.E., Cramming more components onto integrated circuits, reprinted from Electronics, Vol. 38, no. 8, April 19, 1965, pp. 114 ff. *IEEE Solid-State Circuits Soc. Newsl.*, 11, 3, 33–35, 2006.
8. Insurance Information Institute, Facts and Statistics: Homeowners and renters insurance. https://www.iii.org/fact-statistic/facts-statisticshomeowners-and-renters-insurance.
9. Gazis, A., Ioannou, E., Katsiri, E., Examining the sensors that enable self-driving vehicles. *IEEE Potentials*, 39, 1, 46–51, 2020.
10. https://www.safewise.com/resources/motion-sensor-guide.
11. http://www.microtech.co.th/pdf/flame-detector.pdf

12. https://www.renkeer.com/gas-sensors-types-working-principles/.
13. Hoefer, U. and Gutmachera, D., Fire gas detection. *Procedia Eng.*, 47, 1446–1459, 2012.
14. Firouzi, F., Farahani, B., Weinberger, M., DePace, G., Aliee, F.S., IoT Fundamentals: Definitions, Architectures, Challenges, and Promises, in: *Intelligent Internet of Things*, pp. 3–50, Springer International Publishing, Cham, 2020.
15. Durán A, C.M., Monsalve, P.A., Mosquera, C.J., Multisensor system for toxic gases detection generated on indoor environments. *IOP Conf. Ser.: Mater. Sci. Eng.*, 157, 1, 012029, 2016, Nov 1, IOP Publishing.
16. Yamazoe, N. and Shimizu, Y., Humidity sensors: principles and applications. *Sens. Actuators*, 10, 3–4, 379–398, 1986.
17. Sehrawat, D. and Gill, N.S., Smart sensors: Analysis of different types of IoT sensors. *3rd International Conference on Trends in Electronics and Informatics (ICOEI)*, pp. 523–528, 2019.
18. Faizan, A., Mandeep, S., Tarun, C., SankariaFaizan, R.B., Comparative Analysis of Nanowire Tunnel Field Effect Transistor for Low Power Application. *J. Silicon*, 14, 12075–12084, 2022.
19. Mandeep, S., Tarun, C., Balwinder, R., Drain Current and Transconductance Analysis of GaN GAA Nanowire FET with High K Dielectric. *ECS J. Solid State Sci. Technol.*, 12, 113007, 2023.
20. Mandeep, S., Tarun, C., Balwinder, R., Design and Simulation Analysis of Silicon Germanium Nanowire FET for Low Power Applications. *J. Silicon*, 15, 1491–1497, 2023.
21. Chen, Z. and Luo, R., Design and implementation of capacitive proximity sensor using microelectromechanical systems technology. *IEEE Trans. Ind. Electron.*, 45, 6, 886–894, 1998.
22. Meijer, G.C.M., Smart temperature sensors and temperature-sensor systems, in: *Smart Sensor Systems*, G.C.M. Meijer, (Ed.), p. 151e183, Wiley, Chichester, 2008a.
23. Qu, W., Wlodarski, Q., Meyer, J.U., *Sens. Actuators, B*, 64, 76, 2000.
24. Ying, J., Wan, C., He, P., *Sens. Actuators, B*, 62, 165, 2000.
25. Yuk, J. and Troczynski, T., *Sens. Actuators, B*, 94, 290, 2003.
26. Viani, F., Robol, F., Alessandro, P., Wireless Architectures for Heterogeneous Sensing in Smart Home Applications: Concepts and Real Implementation. *Proc. IEEE*, 101, 11, Nov. 2013.
27. Rowe, Internet of Things Requirements and protocols. *Embedded Computing*, 2015.
28. Sulc, V., Home Automation with IQRF Wireless Communication Platform: A Case Study, pp. 212–217, 2011.
29. Wibowo, S.B., Putra, G.D., Hantono, B.S., Development of embedded gateway for Wireless Sensor Network and Internet Protocol interoperabilit0079, in: *2014 6th International Conferenceon Information Technology and Electrical Engineering (ICITEE)*, 7-8 October, pp. 1–4, 2014.

30. Han, D.-M. and Lim, J.-H., Smart Home Energy Management System using IEEE 802.15.4 and ZigBee. *IEEE Trans. Consum. Electron.*, 56, 3, 1403–1410, August 2010.
31. Patchava, V., Kandala, H.B., Babu, P.R., A smart home automation technique with raspberry pi using IOT. *International Conference on Smart Sensors and Systems (IC-SSS)*, Dec 2015, pp. 1–4.
32. Bai, Y.-W., Xie, Z.-L., Li, Z.-H., Design and implementation of an embedded home surveillance system with zero alert power using a photovoltaic array, in: *2011 IEEE 15th International Symposium on Consumer Electronics (ISCE)*, 14-17 June, pp. 373–378, 2011.
33. Howdon, D. and Rice, N., Health care expenditures, age, proximity to death and morbidity: Implications for an ageing population. *J. Health Econ.*, 57, 60–74, Jan. 2018.
34. McHugh, M.D., Kutney-Lee, A., Cimiotti, J.P., Sloane, D.M., Aiken, L.H., Nurses' widespread job dissatisfaction, burnout, and frustration with health benefits signal problems for patient care. *Health Aff.*, 30, 2, 202–210, Feb. 2011.
35. Pasluosta, C., Gabner, H., Winkler, J., Klucken, J., Eskofier, B., An emerging era in the management of Parkinson's disease: Wearable technologies and the internet of things. *IEEE J. Biomed. Health. Inf.*, 19, Jul. 2015.
36. Gomez, A.M. and Umpierrez, G.E., Continuous glucose monitoring in insulin-treated patients in non-ICU settings. *J. Diabetes Sci. Technol.*, 8, 5, 930–936, Sep. 2014.
37. Bujnowski, A., Palinski, A., Koscinski, P., Skalski, L., Skurczynska, A., Wtorek, J., Detection of person presence and its activity in the bathtub. *J. Phys. Conf. Ser.*, 434, 20–35, Apr. 2013.
38. Bujnowski, A., Kaczmarek, M., Osiski, K., Goka, M., Wtorek, J., Capacitively coupled ECG measurements - a CMRR circuit improvement. *EMBEC and NBC 2017*, pp. 1109–1112, 2018.
39. Saini, M.K., Khosla, M., Raj, B., Exploring Emerging Materials for Memristor Fabrication: A Review of Recent Progress. *ECS J. Solid State Sci. Technol.*, 13, 115004, Dec 2024.
40. Thakur, Y., Khosla, M., Raj, B., Performance-Driven OFET Design for Advanced Hydrogen Gas Sensing Applications. *Analog Integrated Circuits and Signal Processing*, Springer, 123, 58, April 2025.
41. LeMoyne, R., Heerinckx, F., Aranca, T., Jager, R.D., Zesiewicz, T., Saal, H.J., Wearable body and wireless inertial sensors for machine learning classification of gait for people with Friedreich's ataxia. *IEEE 13th International Conference on Wearable and Implantable Body Sensor Networks (BSN)*, pp. 147–151, 2016.
42. Federici, S., Meloni, F., Borsci, S., The abandonment of assistive technology in Italy: A survey of users of the national health service. *Eur. J. Phys. Rehabil. Med.*, 52, 516–526, 2016.

43. Sun, N. and Rau, P.-L.P., The acceptance of personal health devices among patients with chronic conditions. *Int. J. Med. Inf.*, 84, 4, 288–297, Apr. 2015.
44. McEwen, A. and Cassimally, H., *Designing the Internet of Things*, John Wiley & Sons, 2014.
45. Vermesan, O. and Friess, P., *Internet of Things Applications - From Research and Innovation to Market Deployment*, River Publishers, 2014.
46. Islam, R. and Kwak, D., The Internet of Things for Health Care: A Comprehensive Survey. *IEEE Access*, 3, 678–708, 2015.
47. Asplund, M., Usability of smart home technology: Towards a user-centered and technology-accepted framework. *J. Ambient Intell. Hum. Comput.*, 11, 5, 1823–1833, 2020.
48. Yang, R. and Lam, K.-H., Energy efficiency in smart homes. *Energy Rep.*, 6, 1515–1534, 2020.
49. Khosrow-Pour, M., *Smart Home Systems and Renewable Energy Integration*, IGI Global, 2019, ISBN: 9781522562585.
50. Tushar, W., Internet of Things for green building management: Disruptive innovations through low-cost sensor technology and wearable IoT. *IEEE Internet Things J.*, 5, 5, 4058–4066, 2018.
51. Liu, Y., Smart home energy management system using IoT. *J. Energy Storage*, 21, 857–868, 2019.
52. Farooq, M.U., A review on Internet of Things (IoT) for smart homes and green building management: Opportunities and challenges. *Sustain. Cities Soc.*, 61, 101650, 2020.
53. Feng, S., Edge computing for the internet of things: A survey. *IEEE Internet Things J.*, 5, 2, 530–544, 2018.
54. Alliance, Z., zigbeespecification [white paper]. Tech. Rep., 2017, [Online]. Available: https://csa-iot.org/wp-content/uploads/2022/ 01/docs-05-3474-22-0csg-zigbee-specification-1.pdf.
55. Fouladi, B. and Ghanoun, S., Security evaluation of the z-wave wireless protocol. *Black Hat USA*, vol. 24, pp. 1–2, 2013.
56. Gladence, M.V., Anu, M.V., Rathna, R., Brumancia, E., Recommender system for home automation using IoT and artificial intelligence. *J. Ambient Intell. Hum. Comput.*, 1–9, 2020.
57. Chung, H., Iorga, M., Voas, J., Lee, S., Alexa, can I trust you? *Computer*, 50, 9, 100–104, 2017.
58. Hoy, M.B., Alexa, Siri, Cortana, and more: an introduction to voice assistants. *Med. Ref. Serv. Q.*, 37, 1, 81–88, 2018.
59. Bhardwaj, A., Kumar, P., Raj, B., Anand, S., Design and Performance Optimization of doping-less Vertical Nanowire TFET using Gate Stack Technique. *J. Electron. Mater. (JEMS)* Springer, 41, 7, 4005–4013, 2022.

60. Singh, J. and Raj, B., Tunnel Current Model of Asymmetric MIM Structure Levying Various Image Forces to Analyze the Characteristics of Filamentary Memristor. *Appl. Phys. A*, Springer, 125, 3, 203.1–203.11, Feb 2019.
61. Goyal, C., Ubhi, J.S., Raj, B., Low Leakage Zero Ground Noise Nanoscale Full Adder using Source Biasing Technique. *J. Nanoelectron. Optoelectron.*, American Scientific Publishers, 14, 360–370, March 2019.
62. Singh, G., Sarin, R.K., Raj, B., A Novel Robust Exclusive-OR Function Implementation in QCA Nanotechnology with Energy Dissipation Analysis. *J. Comput. Electron.*, Springer, 15, 2, 455–465, June 2016.
63. Wadhwa, G., Kamboj, P., Raj, B., Design optimisation of junctionless TFET biosensor for high sensitivity. *Adv. Nat. Sci.: Nanosci. Nanotechnol.*, 10, 7, 045001, 2019.
64. Bansal, P. and Raj, B., Memristor Modeling and Analysis for Linear Dopant Drift Kinetics. *J. Nanoeng. Nanomanuf.*, American Scientific Publishers, 6, 1–7, 2016.
65. Ashima, Vaithiyanathan, D., Raj, B., Performance Analysis of Charge Plasma induced Graded Channel Si nanotube. *J. Eng. Res. (JER)*, EMSME Special Issue, 146–154, Aug 2021.
66. Tomar, A.S., Magraiya, V.K., Raj, B., Scaling of Access and Data Transistor for High Performance DRAM Cell Design. *Quantum Matter*, 2, 412–416, Oct. 2013.
67. Jain, N. and Raj, B., Parasitic Capacitance and Resistance Model Development and Optimization of Raised Source/Drain SOI FinFET Structure for Analog Circuit Applications. *J. Nanoelectron. Optoelectron.*, ASP, USA, 13, 531–539, April 2018.
68. Singh, S., Vishvakarma, S.K., Raj, B., Analytical Modeling of Split-Gate Junction-Less Transistor for a Biosensor Application. *Sens. Bio-Sens.*, Elsevier, 18, 31–36, April 2018.
69. Gopal, M. and Raj, B., Low Power 8T SRAM Cell Design for High Stability Video Applications. *ITSI Trans. Electr. Electron. Eng.*, 1, 5, 91–97, 2013.
70. Raj, B., Mitra, J., Bihani, D.K., Rangharajan, V., Saxena, A.K., Dasgupta, S., Analysis of Noise Margin, Power and Process Variation for 32 nm FinFET Based 6T SRAM Cell. *J. Comput. (JCP)*, Academy Publisher, Finland, 5, 6, 1–8, 2010.
71. Sharma, D., Mehra, R., Raj, B., Comparative Analysis of Photovoltaic Technologies for High Efficiency Solar Cell Design. *Superlattices Microstruct.*, Elsevier, 153, 106861, May 2021.
72. Kaur, P., Buttar, A.S., Raj, B., A Comprehensive Analysis of Nanoscale Transistor Based Biosensor: A Review. *Indian J. Pure Appl. Phys.*, 59, 304–318, April 2021.
73. Yadav, D., Raj, B., Raj, B., Design and Simulation of Low Power Microcontroller for IoT Applications. *J. Sens. Lett.*, ASP, 18, 401–409, May 2020.

74. Singh, S. and Raj, B., A 2-D Analytical Surface Potential and Drain current Modeling of Double-Gate Vertical t-shaped Tunnel FET. *J. Comput. Electron.*, Springer, 19, 1154–1163, April 2020.
75. Singh, J. and Raj, B., An Accurate and Generic Window function for Non-linear Memristor Model. *J. Comput. Electron.*, Springer, 18, 2, 640–64, June 2019.
76. Kaur, M., Gupta, N., Kumar, S., Raj, B., Singh, A.K., Comparative RF and Crosstalk Analysis of Carbon Based Nano Interconnects. *IET Circuits Devices Syst.*, 15, 6, 493–503, Feb 2021.
77. Kandasamy, N., Ahmad, F., Ajitha, D., Raj, B., Telagam, N., Quantum Dot Cellular Automata based Scan Flip Flop and Boundary Scan Register. *IETE J. Res.*, 66, 535–548, 2020.
78. Singh, J. and Raj, B., Design and Investigation of 7T2M NVSARM with Enhanced Stability and Temperature Impact on Store/Restore Energy. *IEEE Trans. Very Large Scale Integr. Syst.*, 27, 6, 1322–1328, June 2019.
79. Bhardwaj, A.K., Gupta, S., Raj, B., Singh, A., Impact of Double Gate Geometry on the Performance of Carbon Nanotube Field Effect Transistor Structures for Low Power Digital Design. *Comput. Theor. Nanosci.*, ASP, 16, 1813–1820, 2019.
80. Jain, N. and Raj, B., Thermal Stability Analysis and Performance Exploration of Asymmetrical Dual-k underlap Spacer (ADKUS) SOI FinFET for Security and Privacy Applications. *Indian J. Pure Appl. Phys. (IJPAP)*, 57, 352–360, May 2019.
81. Jain, N. and Raj, B., Dual-k Spacer Region Variation at the Drain Side of Asymmetric SOI FinFET Structure: Performance Analysis towards the Analog/RF Design Applications. *J. Nanoelectron. Optoelectron.*, American Scientific Publishers, 14, 349–359, March 2019.
82. Singh, J., Sharma, S., Raj, B., Khosla, M., Analysis of barrier layer thickness on performance of In1-xGaxAs based Gate Stack Cylindrical Gate Nanowire MOSFET. *J. Nanoelectron. Optoelectron.*, ASP, 13, 1473–1477, Oct 2018.
83. Jain, N. and Raj, B., Analysis and Performance Exploration of High-k SOI FinFETs Over the Conventional Low-k SOI FinFET toward Analog/RF Design. *J. Semicond. (JoS)*, IOP Science, 39, 12, 124002-1-7, Dec 2018.
84. Goyal, C., Ubhi, J.S., Raj, B., A reliable leakage reduction technique for approximate full adder with reduced ground bounce noise. *J. Math. Probl. Eng.*, Hindawi, 2018, Article ID 3501041, 16p., 15 Oct 2018.
85. Anuradha, Singh, J., Raj, B., Khosla, M., Design and Performance Analysis of Nano-scale Memristor-based Nonvolatile SRAM. *J. Sens. Lett.*, American Scientific Publishers, 16, 798–805, Oct 2018.
86. Wadhwa, G. and Raj, B., Parametric Variation Analysis of Charge-Plasma-based Dielectric Modulated JLTFET for Biosensor Application. *IEEE Sens. J.*, 18, 15, 6070–6077, August 1, 2018, (SCI).

87. Singh, J. and Raj, B., Comparative Analysis of Memristor Models for Memories Design. *JoS*, IoP, 39, 7, 074006-1-12, July 2018.
88. Yadav, D., Chouhan, S.S., Vishvakarma, S.K., Raj, B., Application Specific Microcontroller Design for IoT based WSN. *Sens. Lett.*, ASP, 16, 374–385, May 2018.
89. Singh, G., Sarin, R.K., Raj, B., Fault-Tolerant Design and Analysis of Quantum-Dot Cellular Automata Based Circuits. *IEEE/IET Circuits Devices Syst.*, 12, 638–64, 2018.
90. Singh, J. and Raj, B., Modeling of Mean Barrier Height Levying Various Image Forces of Metal Insulator Metal Structure to Enhance the Performance of Conductive Filament Based Memristor Model. *IEEE Nanotechnol.*, 17, 2, 268–267, March 2018.
91. Jain, A., Sharma, S., Raj, B., Analysis of Triple Metal Surrounding Gate (TM-SG) III-V Nanowire MOSFET for Photosensing Application. *Opto-electron. J.*, Elsevier, 26, 2, 141–148, May 2018.
92. Jain, A., Sharma, S., Raj, B., Design and Analysis of High Sensitivity Photosensor Using Cylindrical Surrounding Gate MOSFET for Low Power Sensor Applications. *Eng. Sci. Technol., Int. J.*, Elsevier's, 19, 4, 1864–1870, December 2016.
93. Saiphani Kumar, G., Singh, A., Raj, B., Design and Analysis of Gate All Around CNTFET based SRAM cell Design. *J. Comput. Electron.*, Springer, 17, 1, 138–145, March 2018.
94. Singh, G.P., Sohi, B.S., Raj, B., Material Properties Analysis of Graphene Base Transistor (GBT) for VLSI Analog Circuits. *Indian J. Pure Appl. Phys. (IJPAP)*, 55, 896–902, Dec 2017.
95. Kumar, S. and Raj, B., Estimation of Stability and Performance Metric for Inward Access Transistor based 6T SRAM Cell Design using n-type/p-type DMDG-GDOV TFET. *IEEE VLSI Circuits Syst. Lett.*, 3, 2, 25–39, June 2017.
96. Sharma, S., Kumar, A., Pattanaik, M., Raj, B., Forward Body Biased Multimode Multi-Threshold CMOS Technique for Ground Bounce Noise Reduction in Static CMOS Adders. *Int. J. Inf. Electron. Eng.*, 3, 3, 567–572, 2013.
97. Singh, H., Kumar, P., Raj, B., Performance Analysis of Majority Gate SET Based 1-bit Full Adder. *Int. J. Comput. Commun. Eng. (IJCCE)*, IACSIT Press Singapore, 2, 4, 2013, ISSN: 2010-3743.
98. Bhardwaj, A.K., Gupta, S., Raj, B., Investigation of Parameters for Schottky Barrier (SB) Height for Schottky Barrier Based Carbon Nanotube Field Effect Transistor Device. *J. Nanoelectron. Optoelectron.*, ASP, 15, 783–791, July 2020.
99. Bansal, P. and Raj, B., Memristor: A Versatile Nonlinear Model for Dopant Drift and Boundary Issues. *JCTN*, American Scientific Publishers, 14, 5, 2319–2325, May 2017.

100. Jain, N. and Raj, B., An Analog and Digital Design Perspective Comprehensive Approach on Fin-FET (Fin-Field Effect transistor) Technology - A Review. *Rev. Adv. Sci. Eng. (RASE)*, ASP, 5, 1–14, 2016.
101. Raj, B., Saxena, A.K., Dasgupta, S., Analytical Modeling for the Estimation of Leakage Current and Subthreshold Swing Factor of Nanoscale Double Gate FinFET Device. *Microelectron. Int.*, UK, 26, 53–63, 2009.
102. Soniya, Singh, S., Wadhwa, G., Raj, B., An Analytical Modeling for Dual Source Vertical Tunnel Field Effect Transistor. *Int. J. Recent Technol. Eng. (IJRTE)*, 8, 2, 603–608, July 2019.
103. Singh, S. and Raj, B., Design and analysis of hetrojunction Vertical T-shaped Tunnel Field Effect Transistor. *J. Electron. Mater.*, Springer, 48, 10, 6253–6260, October 2019.
104. Goyal, C., Ubhi, J.S., Raj, B., A Low Leakage CNTFET based Inexact Full Adder for Low Power Image Processing Applications. *Int. J. Circuit Theory Appl.*, Wiley, 47, 9, 1446–1458, September 2019.
105. Raj, B., Saxena, A.K., Dasgupta, S., A Compact Drain Current and Threshold Voltage Quantum Mechanical Analytical Modeling for FinFETs. *J. Nanoelectron. Optoelectron. (JNO)*, USA, 3, 2, 163–170, 2008.
106. Wadhwa, G. and Raj, B., An Analytical Modeling of Charge Plasma based Tunnel Field Effect Transistor with Impacts of Gate Underlap Region. *Superlattices Microstruct.*, Elsevier, 142, 106512, June 2020.
107. Singh, S. and Raj, B., Modeling and Simulation analysis of SiGe hetrojunction Double GateVertical t-shaped Tunnel FET. *Superlattices Microstruct.*, Elsevier, 142, 106496, June 2020.
108. Jain, N. and Raj, B., Device and Circuit Co-Design Perspective Comprehensive Approach on FinFET Technology - A Review. *J. Electron Devices*, 23, 1, 1890–1901, 2016.
109. Kumar, S. and Raj, B., Analysis of I_{ON} and Ambipolar Current for Dual-Material Gate-drain Overlapped DG-TFET. *J. Nanoelectron. Optoelectron.*, American Scientific Publishers, USA, 11, 323–333, June 2016.
110. Anjum, N., Bali, T., Raj, B., Design and Simulation Of Handwritten Multiscript Character Recognition. *Int. J. Adv. Res. Comput. Commun. Eng.*, 2, 7, 2544–2549, July 2013.
111. Singh, K. and Raj, B., Performance and analysis of temperature dependent Multi-walled Carbon Nanotubes as Global Interconnects at different technology nodes. *J. Comput. Electron.*, Springer, 14, 2, 469–476, June 2015.
112. Kumar, S. and Raj, B., Compact channel potential analytical Modeling of DG-TFET based on Evanescent–mode Approach. *J. Comput. Electron.*, Springer, 14, 2, 820–827, July 2015.

113. Singh, K. and Raj, B., Temperature Dependent Modeling and Performance Evaluation of Multi-Walled CNT and Single-Walled CNT as Global Interconnects. *J. Electron. Mater.*, Springer, 44, 12, 4825–4835, Dec 2015.
114. Sharma, V.K., Pattanaik, M., Raj, B., INDEP approach for leakage reduction in nanoscale CMOS circuits. *Int. J. Electron.*, Taylor & Francis, 102, 2, 200–215, 2014.
115. Singh, K. and Raj, B., Influence of Temperature on MWCNT bundle, SWCNT bundle and Copper interconnects for Nanoscaled Technology nodes. *J. Mater. Sci. Mater. Electron.*, Springer, 26, 8, 6134–6142, 2015.
116. Anjum, N., Bali, T., Raj, B., Design and Simulation of Handwritten Gurumukhi and Devanagri Numerical Recognition. *Int. J. Comput. Appl.*, Foundation of Computer Science, New York USA, 73, 12, 16–21, 2013.
117. Khandelwal, S., Gupta, V., Raj, B., Gupta, R.D., Process Variability Aware Low Leakage Reliable Nano Scale DG-FinFET SRAM Cell Design Technique. *J. Nanoelectron. Optoelectron.*, 10, 6, 810–817, December 2015.
118. Sharma, V.K., Pattanaik, M., Raj, B., ONOFIC Approach: Low Power High Speed Nanoscale VLSI Circuits Design. *Int. J. Electron.*, Taylor Francis, 101, 1, 61–73, 2014.
119. Khandelwal, S., Raj, B., Gupta, R.D., FinFET based 6T SRAM Cell Design: Analysis of Performance Metric, Process Variation and Temperature Effect. *J. Comput. Theor. Nanosci.*, ASP USA, 12, 2500–2506, 2015.
120. Singh, S., Yadav, S., Rahul, J., Srivastava, A., Raj, B., Impact of HfO_2 in Graded Channel Dual Insulator Double Gate MOSFET. *J. Comput. Theor. Nanosci.*, American Scientific Publishers, 12, 6, 950–953, April 2015.
121. Sharma, V.K., Pattanaik, M., Raj, B., PVT variations aware low leakage INDEP approach for nanoscale CMOS Circuits. *Microelectron. Reliab.*, Elsevier, 54, 90–99, 2014.
122. Raj, B., Saxena, A.K., Dasgupta, S., Quantum Mechanical Analytical Modeling of Nanoscale DG FinFET: Evaluation of Potential, Threshold Voltage and Source/Drain Resistance. *Elsevier's J. Mater. Sci. Semicond. Process.*, Elsevier, 16, 4, 1131–1137, 2013.
123. Gopal, M., Sankar, S., Prasad, D., Raj, B., 8T SRAM Cell Design for Dynamic and Leakage Power Reduction. *Int. J. Comput. Appl.*, Foundation of Computer Science, New York, USA, 71, 9, 43–48, June 2013.
124. Wadhwa, G., Kamboj, P., Singh, J., Raj, B., Design and Investigation of Junctionless DGTFET for Biological Molecule Recognition. *Trans. Electr. Electron. Mater.*, Springer, 22, 282–289, 2021.
125. Verma, S.K., Singh, S., Wadhwa, G., Raj, B., Detection of Biomolecules using Charge-Plasma based Gate Underlap Dielectric Modulated Dopingless TFET. *Trans. Electr. Electron. Mater. (TEEM)*, Springer, 21, 528–535, June 2020.
126. Jain, N. and Raj, B., Impact of underlap spacer region variation on Electrostatic and analog/RF performance of symmetrical high-k SOI FinFET

at 20 nm channel length. *J. Semicond. (JoS)*, IOP Science, 38, 12, 122002, Dec 2017.

127. Singh, S. and Raj, B., Analytical Modeling and Simulation analysis of T-shaped III-V heterojunction Vertical T-FET. *Superlattices Microstruct.*, Elsevier, 147, 106717, Nov 2020.
128. Singh, G., Sarin, R.K., Raj, B., Design and Analysis of Area Efficient QCA Based Reversible Logic Gates. *J. Microprocess. Microsyst.*, Elsevier, 52, 59–68, May 2017.
129. Singh, S. and Raj, B., Parametric variation analysis on hetero-junction Vertical t-shape TFET for Supressing ambipolar conduction. *Indian J. Pure Appl. Phys.*, 58, 478–485, June 2020.
130. Soniya, Singh, S., Wadhwa, G., Raj, B., Design and Analysis of Dual Source Vertical Tunnel Field Effect Transistor for high performance. *Trans. Electr. Electron. Mater.*, Springer, 21, 74–82, Oct 2019.
131. Kaur, M., Gupta, N., Kumar, S., Raj, B., Singh, A.K., RF Performance Analysis of Intercalated Graphene Nanoribbon Based Global Level Interconnects. *J. Comput. Electron.*, Springer, 19, 1002–1013, June 2020.
132. Wadhwa, G. and Raj, B., Design and Performance Analysis of Junctionless TFET Biosensor for high sensitivity. *IEEE Nanotechnol.*, 18, 567–574, 2019.
133. Singh, J. and Raj, B., Enhanced Nonlinear Memristor Model Encapsulating Stochastic Dopant Drift. *JNO*, ASP, 14, 958–963, 2019.
134. Singh, M., Chaudhary, T., Raj, B., Enhancing FeFET Structures for Non-volatile On-chip Memories: Design and Comparative Analysis. *Int. J. Numer. Modell. Electron. Netw. Dev. Fields*, 38, 1–9, 2024.
135. Singh, M., Chaudhary, T., Raj, B., Drain Current and Transconductance Analysis of GaN GAA Nanowire FET with High K Dielectric. *ECS J. Sci. Technol.*, 12, 6070–6077, 2023.
136. Singh, M., Chaudhary, T., Raj, B., Design of Si and Ge Nanowire FET for Low Power Application. *J. Silicon*, Springer, 15, 1491–1497, 2023.
137. Singh, M., Chaudhary, T., Raj, B., Electrical Characterstics Analysis of FeFET for Low Power Applications. *J. Nano*, 37, 1–8, 2024.
138. Kumar, M., Chaudhary, T., Raj, B., Design and Comparative Analysis of Ferroelectric Nanowire with Dielectric HfO_2 and $Al_2O_3$for Low Power Applications. *J. Electron. Mater.*, Springer, 53, 6785–6791, 2024.
139. Pattanaik, M., Raj, B., Sharma, S., Kumar, A., Diode Based Trimode Multi-Threshold CMOS Technique for Ground Bounce Noise Reduction in Static CMOS Adders. *Adv. Mater. Res.*, Trans Tech Publications, Switzerland, 548, 885–889, 2012.
140. Raj, B., Saxena, A.K., Dasgupta, S., Nanoscale FinFET Based SRAM Cell Design: Analysis of Performance metric, Process variation, Underlapped FinFET and Temperature effect. *IEEE Circuits Syst. Mag.*, 11, 2, 38–50, 2011.
141. Sharma, V.K., Pattanaik, M., Raj, B., Leakage Current ONOFIC Approach for Deep Submicron VLSI Circuit Design. *Int. J. Electr. Comput. Electron.*

Commun. Eng., World Academy of Sciences, Engineering and Technology, 7, 4, 239–244, 2013.

142. Kaur, P., Gill, S.S., Raj, B., Comparative Analysis of OFETs Materials and Devices for Sensor Applications. *J. Silicon*, Springer, 14, 4463–4471, 2022.
143. Sharma, S.K., Kumar, P., Raj, B., Raj, B., $In_{1-x}Ga_xAs$ Double Metal Gate-Stacking Cylindrical Nanowire MOSFET for highly sensitive Photo detector. *J. Silicon*, Springer, 14, 3535–3541, 2022.
144. Raj, B., Saxena, A.K., Dasgupta, S., Analytical Modeling of Quasi Planar Nanoscale Double Gate FinFET with Source/Drain Resistance and field dependent carrier mobility: A quantum mechanical study. *J. Comput. (JCP)*, Academy Publisher, Finland, 4, 9, 1–8, 2009.
145. Bhushan, S., Khandelwal, S., Raj, B., Analyzing Different Mode FinFET based Memory Cell at Different Power Supply for Leakage Reduction. *Seventh International Conference on Bio-Inspired Computing: Theories and Application, (BIC-TA 2012), Advances in Intelligent Systems and Computing*, vol. 202, pp. 89–100, 20122013.
146. Singh, J. and Raj, B., Temperature Dependent Analytical Modeling and Simulations of Nanoscale Memristor. *Eng. Sci. Technol., Int. J.*, Elsevier's, 21, 862–868, Oct 2018.
147. Singh, S., Bala, S., Raj, B., Raj, B., Improved Sensitivity of Dielectric Modulated Junctionless Transistor for Nanoscale Biosensor Design. *Sens. Lett.*, ASP, 18, 328–333, April 2020.
148. Kumar, V., Vishvakarma, S.K., Raj, B., Design and Performance Analysis of ASIC for IoT Applications. *Sens. Lett.*, ASP, 18, 31–38, Jan 2020.
149. Jaiswal, A., Sarin, R.K., Raj, B., Sukhija, S., A Novel Circular Slotted Microstrip-fed Patch Antenna with Three Triangle Shape Defected Ground Structure for Multiband Applications. *Adv. Electromagn. (AEM)*, 7, 3, 56–63, Aug 2018.
150. Wadhwa, G. and Raj, B., Label Free Detection of Biomolecules using Charge-Plasma-Based Gate Underlap Dielectric Modulated Junctionless TFET. *J. Electron. Mater. (JEMS)*, Springer, 47, 8, 4683–4693, August 2018.
151. Singh, G., Sarin, R.K., Raj, B., Design and Performance Analysis of a New Efficient Coplanar Quantum-Dot Cellular Automata Adder. *Indian J. Pure Appl. Phys. (IJPAP)*, 55, 97–103, February 2017.
152. Kaur, P., Pandey, V., Raj, B., Comparative Study of Efficient Design, Control and Monitoring of Solar Power using IoT. *Sens. Lett.*, ASP, 18, 419–426, May 2020.
153. Bhardwaj, A.K., Gupta, S., Raj, B., Development & Analysis of compact model for Double Gate Schottky Barrier CNTFET. *J. Nanoelectron. Optoelectron.*, ASP, 15, 1199–1208, Aug 2020.

About the Editors

Dr. Ashish Maurya is currently working as an Assistant Professor in the department of Electronics and Communication Engineering Department at Bennett University. He has also served as Faculty at Indian Institute of Information Technology (IIIT), Una, Himachal Pradesh and Kanpur Institute of Technology (KIT) (an Autonomous Institution) Kanpur, as an Assistant Professor in the Electronics and Communication Engineering Department. At KIT, Kanpur, he also handled the Research and Development (R&D) of the Institute as Assistant Dean. He received a master's degree from the Indian Institute of Information Technology and Management (IIITM) Gwalior, India, in 2017. His M-Tech thesis was sponsored by SMDP project of Govt. of India, in collaboration with CEERI Pilani. He did his Ph.D. degree with the Department of Electronics Engineering, IIT (ISM) Dhanbad, Dhanbad, India, in 2023. He has published ten SCI journals/Transactions, eight international conference papers and a book chapter in international publication as author and co-author. His current research interests include Machine Learning in semiconductor physics, nanoelectronics, and emerging semiconductor materials and their applications in various Analog/Digital circuits.

Dr. Mandeep Singh did his B.Tech in Electronics & Communication Eng., earned his M.Tech ECE (VLSI DESIGN) from Punjabi University Patiala, and his Ph.D. from NIT Jalandhar. He has five years' teaching experience of undergraduate, and master's level students in Punjab Technical University, National Institute of Technology Uttarakhand, and Indian Institute of Information Technology (IIIT) Surat. Currently he is working in the Indian Institute of Technology Kanpur as a Postdoc Fellow. He has published three books, 10 book chapters and various research papers in the domain of VLSI Design & Circuit. A versatile individual, he has participated in multiple workshops and conferences worldwide, underscoring his commitment to cutting-edge research. His areas of research are semiconductor device modelling, memory design, CNT & Nanowire, FeFET, and low power VLSI design.

Dr. Balwinder Raj (MIEEE'2006) is currently working as Associate Professor at National Institute of Technology Jalandhar, India. Earlier, he worked at NITTTR Chandigarh and at ABV-IIITM Gwalior. He did his B. Tech, Electronics Engineering (PTU Jalandhar), M. Tech-Microelectronics (PU Chandigarh) and Ph.D-VLSI Design (IIT Roorkee), India, in 2004, 2006, and 2010, respectively. For further research work, the European Commission awarded him "Erasmus Mundus" Mobility of life research fellowship for postdoc research work at University of Rome, Tor Vergata, Italy, in 2010-2011. Dr. Raj received India4EU (India for European Commission) Fellowship and worked as visiting researcher at KTH University, Stockholm, Sweden, Oct-Nov 2013. He also visited Aalto University Finland as visiting researcher during June 2017. He received Best Teacher Award from Indian Society for Technical Education (ISTE) New Delhi on 26 July, 2013. Dr. Raj received Young Scientist Award from Punjab Academy of Sciences during the 18th Punjab Science Congress held on 9 February, 2015. He has also received a research paper award at the International Conference on Electrical and Electronics Engineering held at Pattaya, Thailand, from 11-12 July 2015. Dr. Raj has authored/co-authored ten books, fifteen book chapters and more than 150 research papers in peer-reviewed international/national journals and conferences. His areas of interest in research are Classical/Non-Classical Nanoscale Semiconductor Device Modeling; Nanoelectronic and their applications in hardware security, sensors and circuit design, FinFET-based Memory design, Low Power VLSI Design, Digital/Analog VLSI Design and FPGA implementation.

Index

Also of Interest

Check out these other related titles from Scrivener Publishing

Nanoelectronics: Fundamentals, Advances, and Applications, Edited by Vijay Kumar Sharma, ISBN: 9781394275168. *Nanoelectronics: Fundamentals, Advances, and Applications* is an essential resource for anyone looking to stay at the forefront of innovation, as it thoroughly explores cutting-edge methodologies and design principles for ultra-nanoscale technology.

Nanotechnology in Modern Aquaculture, Edited by Jyothis Mathew, Midhun Sebastian Jose, Radhakrishnan E.K. and Riya Alex, ISBN: 9781119857242.

Electrical and Electronic Devices, Circuits, and Materials: Technical Challenges and Solutions, Edited by Suman Lata Tripathi, Parvej Ahmad Alvi and Umashankar Subramaniam, ISBN: 9781119750369. Covering every aspect of the design and improvement needed for solid-state electronic devices and circuit and their reliability issues, this new volume also includes overall system design for all kinds of analog and digital applications and developments in power systems.

Risk, Safety, and Ethical Concerns in Nanotechnology, Edited by Madhuri Sharon, ISBN: 9781119640387.

Functionalized Nanomaterials for Electronic and Optoelectronic Devices: Design, Fabrications and Applications, Edited by Gopal Rawat, Gautam Patel, Kalim Deshmukh and Chaudhery Mustansar Hussain, ISBN: 9781394214075. The book gives invaluable insights and expertise from leading researchers on the latest advancements, challenges, and applications of functionalized nanomaterials.

Two-Dimensional Nanomaterials for Biosensing and Imaging Applications, Edited by Ram Sevak Singh, Kalim Deshmukh and Chaudhery Mustansar Hussain, ISBN: 9781394199921. The book is essential for anyone eager to understand the transformative potential of 2D nanomaterials in biotechnology and medical science, offering in-depth insights into their unique properties, synthesis methods, and practical applications in an ever-evolving field.

Nanoformulations for Agricultural Applications, Edited by Radhakrishnan E.K, Aswani R., and Visakh. P. M., ISBN: 9781119819097. This book is a comprehensive guide to nanoformulations revolutionizing agriculture, enhancing sustainability, and advancing agrochemical applications.

Nanochitosan Applications for Enhanced Crop Production and Food Security, Edited by Charles Oluwaseun Adetunji, Maulin P. Shah, Yerima Mohammed Bello, Daniel Hefft, Jay Singh, Shyam S. Pandey, Ravindra Pratap Singh, ISBN: 9781394212576. This unique, important, and timely book provides detailed information about the application of nanochitosan to increase agricultural productivity to enhance food security and nutrition.

Sustainable Nanomaterials for Treatment and Diagnosis of Infectious Diseases, Edited by Rajasekhar Chokkareddy, Suvardhan Kanchi and Gan G. Redhi, ISBN: 9781394200016. The book focuses on the design and novel synthetic routes of sustainable nanomaterials in diagnosing and treating infectious diseases offering potential benefits in terms of efficiency, biocompatibility, and environmental impact.

Bioactive-Based Nanotherapeutics, Edited by Rakesh K. Sindhu, Sumitra Singh and Evren Algin Yapar, ISBN: 9781394287314. The book provides essential insights into the revolutionary potential of nanotechnology in medicine, exploring innovative approaches that harness natural materials for targeted and effective disease management.

Nanoengineered Materials for Medical and Healthcare Applications, Edited by Radhakrishnan E.K., Ashitha Jose and Visakh. P. M., ISBN: 9781119791645. This book is a comprehensive guide on the new-generation nanoengineered materials' contribution to the ongoing development of medical devices and other healthcare applications.

Printed in the USA/Agawam, MA
September 16, 2026

910661.148